12th International Conference on Strategic Management and Its Support by Information Systems 2017

Ostrava, Czech Republic
25 – 26 May 2017

Editors:

Radek Nemec
Lucie Chytilova

ISBN: 978-1-5108-4091-1

Printed from e-media with permission by:

Curran Associates, Inc.
57 Morehouse Lane
Red Hook, NY 12571

Some format issues inherent in the e-media version may also appear in this print version.

Printed by Curran Associates, Inc. (2017)

For permission requests, please contact VŠB - Technical University of Ostrava
at the address below.

VŠB - Technical University of Ostrava
17. Listopadu 15/2172
708 33 Ostrava - Poruba
Czech Republic

Phone: +420 597 325 278
Fax: +420 596 918 507

university@vsb.cz

Additional copies of this publication are available from:

Curran Associates, Inc.
57 Morehouse Lane
Red Hook, NY 12571 USA
Phone: 845-758-0400
Fax: 845-758-2633
Email: curran@proceedings.com
Web: www.proceedings.com

VŠB - Technical University of Ostrava, Faculty of Economics

SMSIS

Proceedings of the 12th International Conference

on

Strategic Management and its Support by Information Systems

2017

Radek Němec
Lucie Chytilová
(Eds.)

May 25th-26th
Ostrava
Czech Republic

EDITORS	Radek Němec, Lucie Chytilová
COVER DESIGN	Radek Němec *(background graphic is a free vector art downloaded from the URL: http://4vector.com/)*
PUBLISHER	VŠB – Technical University of Ostrava Faculty of Economics Department of Systems Engineering
PUBLICATION YEAR	2017
NUMBER OF PAGES	496
@ COPYRIGHT	the author/authors of each paper

ISSN 2570-5776

PAPER CITATION EXAMPLE:

AUTHOR, A. (2017). Title of the paper. In: NEMEC, R. and CHYTILOVA, L. (eds.) *Proceedings of the 12th International Conference on Strategic Management and its Support by Information Systems 2017*. May 25.-26., 2017, Ostrava, Czech Republic. Ostrava: VŠB – Technical University of Ostrava, Faculty of Economics, pp. x-y.

All papers published in the proceedings have been peer-reviewed by 2 independent reviewers. Editors are not responsible for the grammar and language used in papers.

MEMBERS OF THE PROGRAMME COMMITTEE

MEMBERS OF THE ORGANIZING COMMITTEE

CHAIR

Lucie Chytilová, Mgr. Ing.
VŠB – Technical University of Ostrava, Czech Republic

MEMBERS

Jitka Baňařová, Ing. Ph.D.
VŠB – Technical University of Ostrava, Czech Republic

Blanka Bazsová, Ing. Ph.D.
VŠB – Technical University of Ostrava, Czech Republic

Kamila Friedrichová, Ing.
VŠB – Technical University of Ostrava, Czech Republic

Jan Manďák, Ing.
VŠB – Technical University of Ostrava, Czech Republic

Radek Němec, Ing. Ph.D.
VŠB – Technical University of Ostrava, Czech Republic

František Zapletal, Mgr. Ing. Ph.D.
VŠB – Technical University of Ostrava, Czech Republic

Jana Závacká, Mgr.
VŠB – Technical University of Ostrava, Czech Republic

CONFERENCE WEBSITE

http://www.ekf.vsb.cz/smsis/en/

PREFACE

Two years have passed and, once again, we are here with our international meeting of academics and professionals – the conference on Strategic Management and its Support by Information Systems (SMSIS). This year, the conference is held for the 12th consecutive year and, again, we are glad for the support from the dean of the Faculty of Economics, VŠB – Technical University of Ostrava, prof. Zdeněk Zmeškal.

The first SMSIS conference has been held in 1995 and, to this day, it continues as a traditionally bi-annual platform for professional discussions and exchange of experiences between research teams from various countries and institutions around the world, namely Germany, Poland, Slovakia, Spain, Slovenia, Hungary, Italy and Russian Federation. The conference focuses on a relatively broad scale of topics that are associated with:

- strategic management,
- project management,
- quantitative methods and their applications in management issues,
- and advances in information systems design and implementation methods.

This year's event venue was temporarily moved to Ostrava, the home of the VŠB – Technical University of Ostrava and the Faculty of Economics. The programme and organizing committees made such a decision because we would like to celebrate symbolically the founding of the Faculty of Economics 40 years ago as well as the 50th anniversary of the establishment of the Systems Engineering and Informatics as a study program on the VŠB – Technical University of Ostrava.

The SMSIS 2017 conference is organized in cooperation with the Czech Society for Systems Integration (CSSI) and three Czech universities: VŠB – Technical University of Ostrava (Faculty of Economics), University of Economics in Prague (Faculty of Informatics and Statistics) and Masaryk University in Brno (Faculty of Informatics).

The SMSIS conference proceedings usually contains about 50 to 70 carefully selected scholarly and professional papers which are double-blind reviewed by members of the programme committee who certainly deserve thanks for their devoted work. I would like to thank the members of the organizing committee as well, for their dedication and hard-work during the preparation and organization of the SMSIS 2017 conference event.

I wish all of us to be successful in the presentation of our work, our contributions to be beneficial to conference participants and that the event will meet everyone's expectations.

To a successful conference!

Jana Hančlová

May 2017

TABLE OF CONTENTS

SECTION A

Strategic management

SECTION B

Project management

SECTION C

Quantitative methods and their applications in management issues

SECTION D

Advances in information systems design and implementation methods

Section
A

Strategic management

Possible bottlenecks in the strategic management of environmentally engaged companies – Transition to the world of circular businesses

Balint Horvath[1], Robert Magda [2]

Abstract. The recognition of the market-driven economy's harmful impact on society and environment has led to the concept of sustainable development. In the world of business, sustainability has been interpreted in different ways. Several researches aimed at developing an expression for initiatives, which truly extend their value proposition to ecological and social horizons. This aspect has been referred as 'businesses for sustainability' in the past couple of years. However, despite the initial positive intentions, the expected outcomes seem to come undone in some cases. This paper presents a historic overview of principles developed by environmental economists. Furthermore, it introduces a case study for a novel environmental-based economic approach – the circular economy. The idea of circular economy has been neglected for a long time. Although, it is in governmental and corporate strategic plans by now, the case study proves the lack of appropriate practical background. The present study argues how the application of 'Transition management' appears to be essential in order to realize such a new economic paradigm.

Keywords: Environmental economics, externalities, circular economy, circular rebound effect, transition management.

JEL Classification: Q50, Q57

1 Introduction

"It is never enough only to wound a lion"
-Unknown

The rapid development of knowledge and technology has brought fundamental changes to western societies in the 20th. century. The growth of economy and population appeared as evidences for the increasing quality of life. Meanwhile, the side-effects of these phenomena have hardly been considered. Throughout the 'economic triumph' of humanity, the modus operandi of capitalism caused several damages to social welfare and natural ecosystems (Schaltegger, Lüdeke-Freund and Hansen, 2012). The recognition of the market-driven economy's harmful impact on society and environment has led to the concept of sustainable development. The report of the Brundtland Commission, 'Our Common Future' marks a milestone in sustainable economics by defining sustainable development as a process where the needs of the present generation is satisfied without preventing future generations to satisfy theirs (World Commission on Environment and Development, 1987). In the world of business, sustainability has been interpreted in different ways. Based on the regular recognition, the term implies to the economic viability of companies (Fogarassy, Szabó and Poór, 2017). Thus, a 'sustainable company' means a financially profitable organization. The strength of environmental and social orientation comes

[1] Szent István University, Climate Change Economics Research Centre, Hungary, 2100 Gödöllő, Páter Károly Street 1., horvath@carbonmanagement.hu
[2] Szent István University, Institute of Economics, Law and Methodology, Hungary, 2100 Gödöllő, Páter Károly Street 1., magda.robert@gtk.szie.hu

on different levels at firms. Some companies only fulfil the regulatory CSR obligations and mostly focus on marketing possibilities. Several researches aimed at developing an expression for initiatives which truly extend their value proposition to ecological and social horizons. This aspect has been referred as 'businesses for sustainability' in the past couple of years (Schaltegger, Hansen and Lüdeke-Freund, 2016).

However, despite the initial positive intentions, the expected outcomes seem to come undone in some cases. According to previous studies, the implementation of extended corporate sustainability requires a holistic perspective to avoid unintended consequences (Genovese et al., 2017). This paper presents a historic overview of theories developed by environmental economists. The elaborated ontology shows how malfunctions of capitalism have been highlighted by visionary researchers, yet their advices remained neglected. Eventually, the current work introduces a case study for a novel environmental-based economic approach – the circular economy. The adaptation to circular economy is a major challenge to governments and businesses as well but the transition must be achieved through bottom-up approaches (Loorbach and Rotmans, 2010). Since the theoretical and practical background of the concept is still under development, the early circular initiatives might mislead themselves by following misinterpreted principles. The aim of the present study is to analyze the evolution of environmental economics and to sort out the most relevant bottlenecks which caused the failure of previous environmental initiatives. Therefore, the main question of the research is that which factors are the most influential regarding the success of corporate sustainability? The present study equips decision makers and entrepreneurs to set truly circular enterprises.

2 Literature review

2.1 The basics of environmental economics

Although, the second half of 20th. century has been associated as the doorstep of emerging environmental problems, the roots of related scientific theories originate far back in time. A part of current researches – conducted under the aegis of ecological economics – are focused on the treatment of externalities (Fogarassy and Neubauer, 2016). The concept of externalities is mostly credited to economist Arthur C. Pigou (1987-1959) from the early 1910's. However, its true origins have been defined by Henry Sidgwick (1838-1900) in the 1880's. As welfare economists, they both examined how economic mechanisms influence social well-being. During their work, they realized that in some cases the profit-and self-oriented business mentality induces unintended social consequences. Sidgwick defined these effects as spillover costs and benefits (Sidgwick, 1885), while the narrow application of the term 'externality' comes from Pigou (Pigou, 1912). The latter theorist used the example of sparks from railway engines to illustrate the negative results of externalities. In his elaboration, railway transportation could be responsible for destroying timber or corps through sparks which ignite woodlands or farmlands near the rail line. Obviously, the act from the railway company is utterly unintended since their purpose is to provide people with a transport opportunity. Still, the owners of the land are not compensated for their losses so the true costs of the company are not fully accurate. They lack the costs of the damage caused by their activity (Pigou, 1912). For the better understanding of negative externalities, this example can be extended even to the passengers of the train. The moment they bought themselves tickets, they paid a price not including the financial consequences of the activity they took part of. If the railway company would be forced to compensate the harmed parties, their tickets would be much more expensive. For the demonstration of positive externalities, Pigou presented the case of an individual person planting a forest. This reforestation surely benefits the surrounding land owners as well by providing natural seeding for their vacant land. Nevertheless, if this benefit is not compensated either, that person will lose interest in planting more trees. As a result of being neglected, the number of trees planted will not reach the level which would be optimal for the society (Pigou, 1912). Therefore, both negative and positive externalities occur as social deadweight losses eventually (Fogarassy and Bakosné Böröcz, 2014).

According to Pigou's description of externalities, two major characteristics of the notion could be highlighted: 1. they always come unintended (meaning that their appearance does not fall under the primary aim of the business), 2. they do not make part of market processes (since the one causing spillover costs cannot be forced to pay the victim and the beneficiary of spillover benefits cannot be obliged to pay compensation either). Based on the second aspect, welfare and ecological economists focused on the so-called 'internalization' of externalities. The internalization in this context means their involvement into the market. Pigou himself offered the application of taxes which must be paid by the producer of negative externalities (Pigou, 1912). Many years later, another economist, Ronald Coase (1910-2013) argued that governmental interventions are not necessary to overcome the problem of externalities. He suggested well-defined property rights as key to the solution. The concerned parties (the source of the externality and the affected one) would be able to negotiate the terms of compensation with each other (Coase, 1960). Several criticisms have emerged for both perspectives but one remained as a true bottleneck in the field of market internalization. Since spillover costs and benefits cannot be accurately defined in monetary terms, none of the presented methods would treat them properly. A relatively high amount of compensation – for negative externalities – would punish the producer to an extent which is not equal to the caused effects. On the other hand, an underestimated price would allow the responsible party to do more harm than it is socially acceptable (Kremenc and Miles, 2012).

Despite the deficiency of both theories, the Coase theorem stresses an interesting question. While he assumed that well-defined property rights would answer the question of externalities, the real problem is that they do not always occur at private properties. Only a few years after Coase, ecologist Garrett Hardin (1915-2003) published his well-known work, 'The Tragedy of The Commons'. His scientific contribution describes an environmental application for the 'Law of Diminishing Returns', caused by the overexploitation of resources. The theory describes a situation where individual actors – led by their own self-interest – overutilize a shared-resource system. Their behavior violates the common good of all users and collectively depletes that resource (Hardin, 1968). Like in the case of externalities, the roots of this observation originate in the work of another economist. More than a century before Hardin, a Victorian economist William Forster Lloyd (1794-1852) has created the fundamentals of this theory. In the year of 1833, his work called 'Two Lectures on the Checks to Population' already introduced a concept based on the overuse of a common. The interesting part of his researches is that he was an early representative of scientists stressing the negative aspects of population growth (Lloyd, 1833).

The growth of population is not only a side-effect but also an engine to capitalism. The continuous consumption – which is essential to its mechanism – can be achieved the most efficiently through the increasing number of consumers (Szaky, 2014). Over a century after Lloyd's observation – and a few years after its renewal through Hardin's work – the Club of Rome published their widely-anticipated book, 'The Limits to Growth'. In 1972, this publication was a milestone in the world of ecological economics since it highlighted the negative impacts of uncontrolled population growth. It stressed that the activity of human population already surpassed the carrying capacity of the earth. Furthermore, the book stated that the environmental degradation of the planet is significantly related to economic processes (Meadows et al., 1972). Only a few years later, ecological economist Herman Daly (1938-) manifested this perspective into an economic framework. His theory, the 'Steady-state economy' used the classical economic concept of 'Stationary states' in terms of stabilizing constant stocks of capital and population. However, it highly differs from it by introducing the importance of the flow of natural resources. Daly urged governments and policy makers to set birth control systems in accordance with this new ecological feature (Daly, 1977). Surprisingly, not only the representatives of the capitalist system but also theorists with similar perspectives criticized Daly's statements. Although, the proposed concept of Daly was a bit too radical from a traditional point of view, it was still not enough to achieve significant changes. Economist Nicholas Georgescu-Roegen (1906-1994), the most influential figure behind the idea of 'Degrowth' criticized both the Club of Rome and Daly. He argued that the zero-growth state of economy – which they offered – is as unsustainable in long-term as the current one. According to his perception "…not only growth, but also a zero-growth state, even a declining state which does not converge toward annihilation, cannot exist in a finite environment" (Georgescu-Roegen, 1975).

2.2 The idea of Degrowth

The statement of Georgescu-Roegen might seem too radical for the first sight, but all he did was going back to the basics of environmental economics. As in case of the other presented theories (e. g. externalities, tragedy of commons), the roots of Georgescu-Roegen's thoughts on Degrowth originates in the 19th. century. William Stanley Jevons (1835-1882) published his book called 'The Coal Question' in 1865 which is considered as the birth of environmental economics. In his fundamental work, Jevons examined the continuous exhaustion of the UK's coal assets. He realized that the efficiency improvement of coal based factories only increased total energy consumptions in long-term. The reason was the innovative Watt steam engine which made coal a more cost-effective resource (Jevons, 1865). Later on, this observation has become popular as 'Jevons paradox' and has been applied to the use of any other resources (Sorrell, 2009). Even though there is a different purpose between the theory of Jevons and Georgescu-Roegen, they both imply to the same conclusion. The developments aiming to improve the efficiency of current systems will not move the course of the system further at all. Moreover, they will only strengthen its function in a long run perspective.

Following the logic of these arguments, economists Daniel Khazzoom (1932-) and Leonard Brookes (1919-2016) examined oil market trends after the OPEC oil crises of 1973 and 1979. According to their publications from the 1980's, the mechanism of the Jevons paradox seemed to apply to those cases as well. The OPEC oil shock has led to rising demand for more fuel-efficient cars. While the new automobiles functioned on a higher level of fuel efficiency, the oil consumption began to increase (Khazzoom, 1989). Since Khazzoom and Brookes' work extended the resource-based thinking of Jevons to a broader field of energy economics, other economists also utilized their practical findings to strengthen economic growth theories. It was Harry Saunders in 1992, who employed their findings (which he labeled as the 'Khazzoom-Brookes postulate') to prove a wide range of assumptions regarding neo-classical growth. He found that without energy efficiency improvements, energy use would only grow with the same speed as the economy – when energy prices are fixed. Whenever energy efficiency gains occur, the consumption increases either by economic growth (which induces higher energy use) or by making energy look cheaper than other resources (Saunders, 1992). This context by now is mostly referred as the 'rebound effect' (Grubb, 1990).

The rebound effect (RE) – in energy economics – means the loss of benefits from new technologies that improve the efficiency of a resource use. The utilization of these technological innovations is initially expected to result in gains but the beneficial effects usually come undone due to behavioral or other systemic reactions (Brockway et al, 2017). The rebound effect is mostly calculated based on the ratio of the lost and expected benefits (Equation 1).

$$RE = \frac{Lost\ benefit}{Expected\ benefit} \tag{1}$$

In a practical example, it is assumed that the improved efficiency of an energy system equals 10%. Meanwhile, the total energy consumption only decreases by 4%. In this case, the energy use was expected to drop by 10% as the innovation offered the same level of improvement. However, the increased efficiency encouraged users to raise their consumption which resulted in a 60% rebound effect *(0,6 = (10-4)/10)*. Even though the calculation of exact values remained questionable (Sorrell, 2007), experts agree that the effect itself is uncontroversial. There are five forms of the phenomenon which can be distinguished according to its magnitude (Saunders, 2008):

1) *Super conservation (RE<0):* the achieved resource savings come at a higher volume than expected (which means the rebound effect is negative). This appears in cases when the efficiency improvement reduces costs.
2) *Zero rebound (RE=0):* the rebound effect results in zero as the resource savings are equal to the initial expectations.
3) *Partial rebound (0<RE<1):* this is the most common observation of the rebound effect in practice. The effect is between the value of 0% and 100% which is also known as 'take-back'. It occurs when the resource savings happen to be less than the expected gains.
4) *Full rebound (RE=1):* the increase in usage equals the level of resource savings.
5) *Backfire (RE>1):* this situation applies to the Jevons paradox when the efficiency improvement eventually induces an even higher level of total energy consumption.

Based on the technological changes causing the rebound effect, there are three related economic reactions. The first is the increasing consumption of a good due to its lower costs. Economic theories define this case as the 'substitution effect', but in terms of RE it is referred as 'Direct rebound effect'. The 'Indirect rebound effect' occurs as the result of the 'income effect', when the lower cost of a service causes the increasing consumption of other services. Eventually, there is also an 'Economy wide effect' because the decreasing service costs will be followed by the shrinking prices of other goods. This phenomenon further encourages growth in production and therefore in economy as well (Sorrell and Dimitropoulos, 2008).

2.3 The hidden paradoxes of consumer society

The thorough analysis on the Jevons paradox and its historic applications serves the better understanding of Georgescu-Roegen's arguments on the necessity of Degrowth. The example of fallacious energy efficiency improvements showed that not only 'business-as-usual' (BAU) processes lead to unintended consequences. Even in case of innovations, there is a major chance to strengthen the current system and cause significant damages in long-term. As it was stressed before, the growing population is not only an effect but also an engine to economic growth. The circle of capitalism goes through the increasing supply of goods which answers and also induces higher levels of demand. Throughout the 20th. century, the system established its own tools to artificially increase the demand side. The original purpose of loans was to raise the willingness of society towards investments. Thereby, to enable people to earn more income and boost the economy. Nowadays, loans for simple consumption activities are more widespread. This might also contribute to economic growth but surely leaves the members of society in debt. Another application of capitalism is marketing, which aims to convince consumers about the obsolescence of their owned goods. This leads to the disposal of products before the end of their useful life (EoL). In the latter half of the 1900's, producers developed an even more effective approach, the production of shortened life cycle goods. It meant that they artificially shortened the effective lifetime of goods during the production process (Agrawal et al., 2015). The idea of 'planned obsolescence' was conceptualised in the early 1930's. An American economist, Bernard London suggested its usage to negate the effects of the economic depression. Though it was not put into practice that time, it has become a routine part of production 20 years later (Bulow, 1986). This perspective still helps sustaining the consumer economy which is based on over-production.

The intentionally shortened lifespan in some cases meant a drop in product quality and therefore in prices as well. The easily affordable goods appeared to be more alluring to consumers and their mass production and consumption has developed into a regular practice. Nowadays, a serious bottleneck of returning to old production systems is that wage levels continuously followed this trend. Thus, conscious consumers do not always have the opportunity to buy their desired products. Currently, the growth of consumption intensity has become an essential feature of capitalism. Regarding the introduced environmental economics principles, the following questions rightfully emerges: does economic growth truly represents an increase in human well-being? Furthermore, is this progress a real growth for the economy? The former question has already been answered by many welfare and ecological economists in the past decades. There were several attempts to substitute economy's main progress indicator, the GDP (Gross Domestic Product). The alternatives aimed at considering environmental and social losses. Even if these endeavors turned to be fruitless (due to the lack of accurate and available data), the estimated values indicated surprising differences to the GDP. Concerning the purpose of the current study, the latter question is more interesting and its answer leads back to externalities.

In 1993 Paul Hawken (1946-) environmentalist phrased that the real reason behind the cheap price of the short life cycle products lies in a 'hidden subsidy'. It means that consumers do not pay the real price of goods due to the lack of non-monetized environmental and social costs (as in Pigou's example of railway transport) (Hawken, 1993). As a result, modern economy is about to experience an inevitable pattern. In the 20th. century, only ecological and welfare economists warned policy makers about the costs of negative externalities. By the 21st. century, these spill-overs seem to reach sustainability's economic pillar as well – besides the environmental and social one. Meaning that the costs induced by externalities do not only emerge in hidden features anymore, but the economy has to face them in tangible values. Ecological economist, Clive Spash recalled early externality theories and their major malfunctions to highlight the controversy of the current economic system. He stated that the recognition of externalities appears to be misleading by considering these effects external to economy. The concept presents externalities as minor aberrations in a fundamentally efficient scheme. Despite previous theories, they must be treated as part of the economy. Their 'internalization' (monetized compensation) does not resolve the elementary structural deficiencies of economy (Spash, 2010). Spash's interpretation of externalities apparently resembles with the perception of the Jevonsian logic. They both tend to solve occurring problems at their roots instead of superficial treatments. Spash even raises the level of intervening by promoting the pervasive nature of externalities. He certainly suggests a radical change in the current flow of economy to prevent serious deadweight losses in future.

3 Case study for a circular economy bottleneck

The currently developing, novel economic concept, circular economy aims to target the issues stressed above. The first mention of the notion originates in the late 1980's by environmental economists David Pearce (1941-2005) and Kelly R. Turner (1948-). They appointed the disadvantages of the current linear (or open-ended) economy which generates tremendous amount of waste by its 'take-make-use-dispose' approach (Pearce and Turner, 1989). Nowadays, the idea of circular economy has rather become an umbrella which covers many environmental-oriented perspectives. One of its important pillar is the 'Natural Capitalism' concept of Paul Hawken, who also argued for the hidden subsidies regarding short life cycle products. His perception transforms economy into a system based upon environmental principles. In nature, the term 'waste' simply does not exist, since nature does not employ the linear flow of materials (Hawken, Lovins and Lovins, 1999). The output of a certain organism would always be utilized as another's input. A similar approach is 'Industrial Ecology' by Robert A. Frosch (1928-) and Nicholas E. Galoppoulus who proposed a new industrial mechanism based on natural ecosystems (Frosch and Galoppoulus, 1989). However, nature does not only function without the generation of waste but its creatures do not even consume unnecessary resources in the first place. Meaning that the overconsuming behavior of humanity does not apply to ecological structures at all.

This pattern helps to develop a better understanding of the frequently misinterpreted circular economy. The name itself might be misleading, since – for some people – it implies to continuous circulation of material flows. That is the reason why most people interpret circular economy as a novel waste management approach based on more efficient recycling systems. As a bottleneck example of truly circular systems, the case of a Dutch manure management initiative can be applied. The province of Friesland produces over 9 million tons of manure (mostly from cows) each year. They mainly store it in liquid form and spread it out on the land. The composition and amount of the manure indirectly influences the local soil and water quality. Due to the increasing production of milk, local stakeholders investigated the possibilities of turning the harmful end product into valuable assets. As a result, they started to utilize manure in a power plant which recovers its nutrients and produces biogas through fermentation. Their case is usually considered as a "circular success story". Nevertheless, based on the scientific findings of environmental economics from the last 200 years, Friesland's long-term recognition might differ from the current form.

The utilization of the otherwise worthless manure may appear useful, but does not solve the real problem. The true bottleneck is the major environmental effect of cattle breeding, as the animal has serious greenhouse gas emissions and water consumption (Fogarassy et al, 2014). The seemingly more efficient system would easily lead to higher amount of total production. The fundamental problem with the presented example is that it takes place at the end of the process. In the world of environmental economics, similar treatments are identified as 'end-of-pipe' solutions. The goal of circular economy is to find solutions in the beginning. The truly efficient movement would be the decoupling of cattle breeding from the growing population trends. However, as long as the developments aim to improve the efficiency of waste treatment (e. g. recycling, waste-to-energy), it will encourage decision makers to maintain or even increase the application of 'business-as-usual' processes. Therefore, an important outcome of this research is that the Jevons paradox cannot only be extended to any resources – as it was done by the mechanism of rebound effect – but it is valid to businesses which only focus on closing the loop of their material flow. The 'circular rebound effect' can only be avoided by not even creating or reducing the material flow.

4 Conclusion

The case study of Friesland's manure management proved the disciplines of Jevons and Georgescu-Roegen regarding deceptive efficiency improvements and Degrowth. That leads to the perception that humanity functions in a historic economic cycle facing the same issues – only in different magnitudes. The fact that circular economy is built upon principles discovered long ago, implies to the strength of current systems which hinders transition processes. It means that the world of business does not need new perspectives, but room for implementing the ones which already exist. The concept of 'Transition management' was created for the very same purpose. The creators of that notion realized the pressure of current systems (regimes) on novel approaches. In the initial phase, innovations are always inferior to regnant regimes but their decent application could lead to quick acceleration. Thus, a bottom-up approach is required for the establishment of a new economic paradigm. The idea of circular economy has been neglected for a long time. Although, it is in governmental and corporate strategic plans by now, it still lacks the appropriate practical background. The transition thinking is expected to steer businesses towards good directions and to prevent them from strengthening the current regime in long-term.

References

Agrawal, V. V., Kavadias, S. and Toktay, L. B. (2015). 'The limits of planned obsolescence for conspicuous durable goods'. *Manufacturing & Service Operations Management,* 18 (2), pp. 216-226.

Brockway, P. E., Saunders, H., Heun, M. K., Foxon, T. J., Steinberger, J. K., Barrett, J. R. and Sorrell, S. (2017). 'Energy rebound as a potential threat to a low-carbon future: Findings from a new exergy-based national-level rebound approach'. *Energies*, 10 (1), 51.

Bulow, J. (1986). 'An economic theory of planned obsolescence'. *The Quarterly Journal of Economics,* 101 (4), pp. 729-749

Coase, R. H. (1960) 'The Problem of Social Cost'. *Journal of Law and Economics,* 3, pp. 1-44.

Daly, Herman E. (1977). *Steady-state economics.* Washington, D.C.: Island Press.

Fogarassy, Cs. and BakosnéBöröcz, M. (2014). 'Externality analysis of sustainable cattle breeding systems'. Hungarian Agricultural Engineering, 26, pp. 5-10.

Fogarassy, Cs., Neubauer, E, Borocz Bakosné, M., Zsarnóczai, J. S. and Molnár, S. (2014). 'Water footprint based water allowance coefficient'. *Water Resources and Industry*, 7-8, pp. 1-8.

Fogarassy, Cs. and Neubauer, E. (2016). 'Evaluation of the regional water usage in Hungary with Water Allowance Coefficient (WAC)'. *Applied Ecology and Environmental Research,* 14 (1), pp. 161-173.

Fogarassy, Cs., Szabó, K. and Poor, J. (2017). 'Critical issues of human resource planning, performance evaluation and long-term development on the central region and non-central areas: Hungarian case study for investors'. *International Journal of Engineering Business Management,* 9 (1), pp. 1-9.

Frosch, R. A. and Gallopoulos, N. E. (1989). 'Strategies for Manufacturing'. *Scientific American,* 261 (3), pp. 144–152.

Genovese, A., Acquaye, A. A., Figueroa, A. and Koh, S. C. L., (2017). 'Sustainable supply chain management and the transition towards a circular economy: Evidence and some applications'. *Omega,* 66 (B) pp. 344-357.

Georgescu-Roegen, N. (1975). 'Energy and Economic Myths'. *Southern Economic Journal,* 41 (3), pp. 347-381.

Grubb, M. J. (1990). 'Energy efficiency and economic fallacies'. *Energy Policy,* 18, pp. 783–785.

Hardin, G. (1968). 'The Tragedy of the Commons'. *Science*, 168 (3859), pp. 1243-1248.

Hawken, P. (1994). *The Ecology of Commerce.* New York: Harper Business

Hawken, P., Lovins, A. and Lovins H. L. (1999). *Natural Capitalism: Creating the Next Industrial Revolution*. Boston: Little, Brown and Company.

Jevons, W. S. (1865). *The coal question*. London: Macmillan & Co.

Khazzoom, J. D. (1989). 'Energy Savings from More Efficient Appliances: A Rejoinder'. *The Energy Journal,* 10 (1): 157–166.

Kremenc, C. and Miles, A. (2012). 'Ecosystem Services in Biologically Diversified versus Conventional Farming Systems: Benefits, Externalities, and Trade-Offs'. *Ecology and Society,* 17 (4), pp. 40.

Lloyd, W. F. (1833). *Two Lectures on the Checks to Population.* Unknown Publisher.

Loorbach, D. and Rotmans, J. (2010): 'The practice of transition management: Examples and lessons from four distinct cases'. *Futures*, 42, pp. 237-246.

Meadows, D. H., Meadows, D. L., Randers, J. and Behrens, W. W. (1972). *The Limits to Growth.* New York: Universe Books.

Pearce, D. W. and Turner, R. K. (1989). *Economics of Natural Resources and the Environment*. Baltimore: Johns Hopkins University Press.

Pigou, A. C. (1912) *Wealth and Welfare.* London: Macmillan.

Saunders, H. D. (1992). 'The Khazzoom-Brookes postulate and neoclassical growth'. *The Energy Journal*, 13 (4), pp. 131–148

Saunders, H. D. (2008). 'Fuel conserving (and using) production functions'. *Energy Economics*, 30 (5), pp. 2184–2235.

Schaltegger, S., Lüdeke-Freund, F. and Hansen, E. (2012): 'Business cases for sustainability: the role of business model innovation for corporate sustainability'. *International Journal of Innovation and Sustainable Development*, 6 (2), pp. 95-119.

Schaltegger, S., Hansen, E. and Lüdeke-Freund, F. (2016): 'Business Models for Sustainability: Origins, Present Research, and Future Avenues'. *Organization & Environment*, 29 (1), pp. 3-10.

Sidgwick, H. (1885). *The Scope and Method of Economic Science. In Miscellaneous Essays and Addresses,* London: Macmillan, 1904, pp. 170-99.

Sorrell, S. (2007). *The rebound effect: An assessment of the evidence for economy-wide energy savings from improved energy efficiency.* London: Energy Research Centre

Sorrell, S. and Dimitropoulos, J. (2008). 'The rebound effect: Microeconomic definitions, limitations and extensions'. *Ecological* Economics, 65 (3), pp. 636–649.

Sorrell, S. (2009). 'Jevons' Paradox revisited: The evidence for backfire from improved energy efficiency'. *Energy Policy,* 37 (4), pp. 1456-1469.

Spash, C. L. (2010). 'The brave new world of carbon trading'. *New Political Economy*, 15 (2), pp. 169–95.

Szaky, T. (2014). *Outsmart waste: the modern idea of garbage and how to think our way out of it.* California: Berrett-Koehler Publishers.

World Commission on Environment and Development (1987). *Our Common Future*. Oxford: Oxford University Press

Implementation of multidimensional analytical methods to compare performance between corporations

Sylvia Jenčová[1], Eva Litavcová[2], Petra Vašaničová[3], Martina Košíková[4]

Abstract. Financial-economic analyzes often use multidimensional analytical methods to compare performance between enterprises. This comparison between companies requires a tool for assessment of financial stability and performance, as well for interpreting values calculated by other methods. This paper discusses the implementation of multivariate methods which allow for the comparison of businesses in the electro-technical industry in the Slovak Republic. Data for this paper were obtained from the Register of the Slovak Republic, and includes accounts and financial statements for individual companies. The paper deals with the sixty largest companies (by sales volume in a given year) in the Slovak Republic. Rating sixty companies in the electrical engineering industry is the contribution realized by defined criteria that represent proportional Financial indicators, basic production enterprise strength, return on sales, financial performance and financial one employee productivity. Financial and economic position of the company in the space is realized on the basis of order method, the scoring method, a normalized variable method and method of distance from a fictitious object. Set the order of the objects in the electrical engineering industry market space.

Keywords: business entity, the electronic industry, multivariate methods, criteria.

JEL Classification: C29, G39

1 Introduction

Electro-technical industries have significantly enhanced the rate of industrial globalization. The electronics industry, as a specific carrier of the latest in technology, provides a synergistic effect that significantly improves the quality of production in other industries. The driving force behind the development of the electrical engineering industry is mainly the automotive industry, Jenčová and Litavcová (2015). Overall industrial performance of both the automotive and electronics industries separately are relatively stable, maintaining an added value and profitability in both industries. The electro-technical industry has a stable position in the structure of the economy, and is still a main contributor to the three key sectors of exports, production and employment. When undertaking comparisons, one should have available data for businesses in the same industry. Zalai et al (2013) describes the terms of comparability which include the materials produced, format of operations, time period and size of businesses being compared.

[1] University of Presov, Faculty of Management, Department of Finance, sylvia.jencova@unipo.sk.
[2] University of Presov, Faculty of Management, Department of Matematical Methods and Managerial Informatics, eva.litavcova@unipo.sk.
[3] University of Presov, Faculty of Management, Department of Matematical Methods and Managerial Informatics, petra.vasanicova@smail.unipo.sk.
[4] University of Presov, Faculty of Management, Department of Matematical Methods and Managerial Informatics, martina.kosikova@smail.unipo.sk.

Under conditions comparable to the same: design parameters; balance sheet policy; time period; business activity; and macroeconomic framework.

Dluhošová (2008) points out that important roles of financial management include: ensuring sufficient financial resources are available; ensuring they are used effectively; and aligning solvency (liquidity), capital structure (debt) and financial performance (profitability) in order to achieve financial balance.

1.1 Multi-criteria evaluation

The aim of all methods of multi-criteria evaluation is the transformation and synthesis of values for different variables into one integral indicator that comprehensively expresses the activity level of individual companies in the surveyed sample. The methods differ both, first of all, in sub-points, and the method of aggregation of these sub-points in the overall evaluation (Zalai et al, 2013).

The financial analysis of companies requires comparison between a range of monitored corporate indicators, such as the intensity of use of tangible fixed assets, which is reflected in the acquisition of new equipment. Depreciated assets might signal the need for additional funds for recovery or restitution of investments, etc., per Jenčová (2016).

Business evaluation is, in practice, often implemented on the proportional financial metrics of the company. This paper identifies four criteria: Return on Assets (ROA), which is the basis of production value (Basic Earning Power); earning power of the enterprise quantifying the amount generating an operating profits before interest and taxes (EBIT) from one monetary unit average balance of assets at the period's end; stocks, which represent how the assets change during the period in size, usually growing; and, EBIT as a flow variable accumulating throughout the year.

The second criterion is the operating profit margin, or Return on Sales (ROS), which quantifies how many monetary units of profit fall on one unit of sales. When comparing different companies in the design of this indicator, we refer to earnings before interest and taxes (EBIT) before Net profit (Earnings After Taxes, EAT). This indicator is also referred to as the profit margin or rate of return on sales. This indicator is particularly interesting in the fields of marketing and pricing policy. The third criterion is the evaluation of financial performance of one employee expressed as a multiplicative proportionate bond, with personnel costs attributable to one employee. The fourth criterion is productivity characterized as the amount of added value that is generated by employees.

1.2 Multivariate Methods

Multivariate methods of comparison between companies pursue a goal to gain a comprehensive picture of the status of enterprises based on multiple financial indicators, i.e. criteria, which apply the principle of multi-criteria decision making, Bondareva (2014).

Zmeškal et al (2013), in his scientific paper, points out problems with multi-criteria decision making in finances and economics. In the area of financial decision-making, it is necessary to take into account more than one criterion.

Multivariate methods are based on fundamental characteristics, such as arithmetic means, variances, standard deviations, coefficients of variation and variation margins. Multivariate methods allow the assessment of phenomena by applying different methods. When scoring, the method for each i-th company is on each monitored variable xi,j. The analysis seeks the best value, which is selected for the item being analyzed. When productivity indicators achieve maximum level, as is given by equation (1), the variable's intensity minimum value is determined according to equation (2). The values of this indicator are based on points (nearby) under the above relationships, as determined by linear interpolation. In this method, normalized variables are the original values of selected indicators converted into a normalized form. When normalized methods are calculated, first by xpj arithmetic means, the standard deviation and variance are calculated for each indicator separately. From the original value, the arithmetic mean is subtracted and the difference is divided by the standard deviation. Normalized value of the j-th indicator of the i-th company with a positive higher value is given by equation (3), and with a positive lower value is given by equation (4). Companies according to this method are listed in order from the smallest deviation from the normalized shape of standard deviation to the largest.

To obtain the most accurate results, the multi-criteria method utilizes a fictitious distance from the object, which indicates the distance of the company from the ideal, with regards to all indicators, i.e. their criteria; it being understood that the lower the value the enterprise reaches, the better the score. All variables are expressed in normalized shape. Subsequently distance calculations, from each object to the fictitious object, are Euclidean. Electro-technical industry enterprises are compared on the basis of equation (6), (Štefko and Sojka, 2015), (Kubíčková and Jindřichovská, 2015).

$$b_{ij} = \frac{x_{ij}}{x_{i\,max}} \cdot 100 \tag{1}$$

$$b_{ij} = \frac{x_{i\,min}}{x_{ij}} \cdot 100 \tag{2}$$

$$u_{ij} = \frac{x_{ij} - x_{pj}}{\delta_j^2} \tag{3}$$

$$u_{ij} = \frac{x_{pj} - x_{ij}}{\delta_j^2} \tag{4}$$

$$\delta^2 = \frac{1}{n}\sum_{i=1}^{n}\left(x_{ij} - x_{pj}\right)^2 \tag{5}$$

$$k_{ij} = \sqrt{\sum_{j=1}^{m}\left(u_{ij} - u_{oj}\right)^2} \tag{6}$$

$$R = 1 - \frac{6\sum\left(i_x - i_y\right)^2}{n(n^2 - 1)} \tag{7}$$

2 Results and discussion

The selection of companies is given a serial number by 1, ..,n, as shown in Table 1. Table 1 quantifies the ranking of non-financial corporations in the Electro-technical Industry of the Slovak Republic, which was ranked by amount of sales and number of employees in 2013. The figures in brackets in the second column reflect the positions of the companies in terms of volume of sales achieved in 2014. The following new companies were among the first 35 places in terms of size of sales in 2014: in 5th place, Topaz LGP, Ltd., Piestany; in 19th place, Samsung Display Slovakia, Ltd., Voderady; 22nd place Unomedical, Ltd., Michalovce; in 29th place, KraussMaffei Technologies, Ltd., Sucany; in 30th place Alcatel-Lucent Slovakia, Inc., Bratislava; and in 35th place Elster Water Metering, Ltd., Stara Tura.

The analysis of assessment methods by multi-critiques entered by 60 companies, where precise values pertaining to workforce were known. The second column in Table 2 indicates the serial number of companies according to the amount of the revenues earned in thousands. Total Euros earned by the 66 non-financial corporations in Slovakia. Financial ratios ex-post amount to a selected criterion ($m = 4$). Table 2 provides the results of four methods. The fourth column is to compare companies according to the summation of their order: in the fifth column by scoring method; in the sixth column by the method of normalized variables; and in the seventh column by the rank of the companies according to the method of fictitious distance. Under this method, the least distant was Samsung Electronics Slovakia, Ltd., Galanta, and the furthest is ICS Industrial Cables Slovakia, Ltd. Nitra, which is in terms of sales and number of employees is at the 45th place in the ranking of electro-technical companies.

id	Company	SK NACE	Sales (EUR '000)	Empl.
1.	Samsung Electronics Slovakia, Ltd., Galanta (1)	26400	3 144 279	1 392
2.	Foxconn Slovakia, Ltd.,Nitra (2)	26400	919 777	924
3.	Whirlpool Slovakia, Ltd.,Bratislava (3)	27510	276 922	1 083
4.	Emerson, Inc., Nove Mesto nad Vahom (6)	27110	246 199	1 390
5.	Hella Slovakia Front-Lighting, Ltd., Kocovce (8)	27400	201 395	863
6.	BSH Drives and Pumps, Ltd., Michalovce (7)	27110	200 787	761
7.	Universal Media Corporation, Ltd., BA (4)	26400	200 355	523
8.	TRW Automotive, Ltd., Nove Mesto nad Vahom (9)	27110	172 803	543
9.	Hella Slovakia Signal-Lighting, Ltd., Banovce/B (10)	27400	148 768	1 208
10.	Seong Ji Slovakia, Ltd., Bratislava (15)	26110	139 596	224
11.	Panasonic Industrial Devices Slovakia, Ltd., Trstena (11)	26400	139 301	1 456
12.	Delta Electronics /Slovakia/, Ltd., Dubnica nad Vahom (17)	27900	129 782	667
13.	Elster, Ltd., Stara Tura (16)	26510	129 569	424
14.	ZKW Slovakia, Ltd., Krusovce (12)	27400	128 956	1 043
15.	Osram, Inc., Nove Zamky (13)	27400	123 430	1 234
16.	Semikron, Ltd., Vrbove (18)	26110	98 425	645
17.	Panasonic AVC Networks Slovakia, Ltd., Krompachy (25)	26400	87 996	610
18.	OMS, Ltd., Dojc (27)	27400	66 799	995
19.	Askoll Slovakia, Ltd., Nove Mesto nad Vahom (26)	27110	65 217	446
20.	Datalogic Slovakia, Ltd., Zavar (20)	26200	64 079	171
21.	PPA Energo, Ltd., Bratislava	33200	61 360	500

22.	Enics Slovakia, Ltd., Nova Dubnica (23)	27900	59 222	405
23.	Eltek, Ltd., Liptovsky Hradok (24)	27900	57 243	490
24.	Nuritech SK, Ltd., Hurbanovo	26120	54 836	129
25.	Vicente Torns Slovakia, Inc., Velke Kosihy (28)	27320	51 274	90
26.	PPA Controll, Inc., Bratislava (14)	33200	49 878	718
27.	Hansol Technics Europe, Ltd., Voderady	26110	48 994	3
28.	Power - One, Ltd., Dubnica nad Vahom	27110	44 613	559
29.	Shin Heung Precision Slovakia, Ltd., Sala (21)	26110	43 143	264
30.	Draka Comteq Slovakia, Ltd., Presov (31)	27320	40 529	123
31.	ABB, Ltd., Bratislava (34)	33200	36 277	180
32.	Dometic Slovakia, Ltd., Filakovo (33)	27510	33 029	238
33.	Schneider Electric Slovakia, Ltd., Bratislava	27330	29 942	
34.	Honeywell, Ltd., Bratislava	33200	29 484	54
35.	Elteco, Inc., Zilina	27110	25 634	333
36.	Sensus Slovensko, Inc., Stara Tura (43)	26510	24 670	229
37.	Danfoss, Ltd., Zlate Moravce	26510	24 319	223
38.	BEZ Transformatory, Inc., Bratislava (39)	27110	23 733	258
39.	Air Liquide Welding Central Europe, Ltd., Luzianky	27900	22 832	104
40.	Elektronika Slovensko, Inc., Trnava	26110	21 766	151
41.	Vacuumschmelze, Ltd., Horna Streda	27110	19 977	850
42.	EVPU, Inc., Nova Dubnica	27110	19 709	252
43.	Tesla Stropkov, Inc., Stropkov (46)	26309	19 677	776
44.	ZTS-Kabel, Ltd., Dubnica nad Vahom	27320	19 388	101
45.	Klauke Slovakia, Ltd., Dolny Kubin	27900	18 048	296
46.	Enpay Transformer Components, Ltd., Krskany	27110	17 894	241
47.	Hydac Electronic, Ltd., Tvrdosin	27900	17 743	183
48.	Elba, Inc., Kremnica	27120	17 561	308
49.	Tatramat - ohrievace vody, Ltd., Poprad	27510	17 551	250
50.	Linak Slovakia, Ltd., Zupcany	27900	17 360	126
51.	ICS Industrial Cables Slovakia, Ltd., Nitra	27320	15 940	65
52.	Thorma Vyroba, k.s., Filakovo	27520	13 168	319
53.	Delipro, Ltd., Piestany	26110	12 424	243
54.	Hengstler, Ltd., Kezmarok	27120	12 358	296
55.	Elcom, Ltd., Presov	28230	9 755	162
56.	VUKI, Inc., Bratislava	27310	8 772	69
57.	Avex electronics, Ltd., Dolny Kubin	27400	8 088	132
58.	ProCS, Ltd., Sala	33200	7 922	91
59.	Telegrafia, Inc., Kosice	33200	5 950	62
60.	Elmax Zilina, Inc., Zilina	27120	5 679	98
61.	Datamars Slovakia, Ltd., Luzianky	85590	5 252	46
62.	CRT - Electronic, Ltd., Oravska Lesna	26110	4 011	109
63.	TTS Martin, Ltd., Pribovce	27120	3 637	33
64.	Krizik GBI, Inc., Presov	26510	3 608	125
65.	VEM Slovakia, Ltd., Piestany	27110	3 166	141
66.	Cab Tech, Ltd., Prievidza	27320	2 774	61

Table 1 Ranks enterprises of electro-technical industry by size of revenues [own processing on the basis of the accounts of companies]

1 Companies of Electro-Technical Industry SR	2 id	3 n	4 MO	5 SM	6 MNV	7 DFO
Samsung Electronics Slovakia, Ltd., Galanta	1	1	21	7	1	1
Hella Slovakia Front-Lighting, Ltd., Kocovce	5	2	12	8	7	5
BSH Drives and Pumps, Ltd., Michalovce	6	3	18	18	13	6
Universal Media Corporation /Slovakia/, Ltd., Bratislava	7	4	54	51	50	51
TRW Automotive (Slovakia), Ltd., Nove Mesto nad Vahom	8	5	59	57	57	57
Hella Slovakia Signal-Lighting, Ltd., Banovce nad Bebravou	9	6	33	40	33	29
Seong Ji Slovakia, Ltd., Bratislava	10	7	46	49	47	45
Panasonic Industrial Devices Slovakia, Ltd., Trstena	11	8	7	14	12	13
Delta Electronics /Slovakia/, Ltd., Dubnica nad Vahom	12	9	34	34	31	28
Elster, Ltd., Stara Tura	13	10	39	48	24	14
ZKW Slovakia, Ltd., Krusovce	14	11	1	2	3	2
Osram, Inc., Nove Zamky	15	12	50	44	43	42
Semikron, Ltd., Vrbove	16	13	5	6	6	7
Panasonic AVC Networks Slovakia, Ltd., Krompachy	17	14	3	10	5	3
OMS, Ltd., Dojc	18	15	35	41	39	39
Askoll Slovakia, Ltd., Nove Mesto nad Vahom	19	16	13	21	17	10
Datalogic Slovakia, Ltd., Zavar	20	17	14	13	9	4
PPA Energo, Ltd., Bratislava	21	18	19	4	10	19
Enics Slovakia, Ltd., Nova Dubnica	22	19	38	39	35	36
Nuritech SK, Ltd., Hurbanovo	24	20	16	24	20	17
Vicente Torns Slovakia, Inc., Velke Kosihy	25	21	31	42	32	26
PPA Controll, Inc., Bratislava	26	22	24	20	56	56
Power - One, Ltd., Dubnica nad Vahom	28	23	40	37	37	37
Shin Heung Precision Slovakia, Ltd., Sala	29	24	51	50	49	46
Draka Comteq Slovakia, Ltd., Presov	30	25	37	29	27	32
ABB, Ltd., Bratislava	31	26	32	28	46	41
Dometic Slovakia, Ltd., Filakovo	32	27	20	26	23	21
Honeywell, Ltd., Bratislava	34	28	26	27	55	54
Elteco, Inc., Zilina	35	29	36	36	34	34
Sensus Slovensko, Inc., Stara Tura	36	30	28	22	22	24
Danfoss, Ltd., Zlate Moravce	37	31	15	11	14	18
BEZ Transformatory, Inc., Bratislava	38	32	52	54	51	49
Air Liquide Welding Central Europe, Ltd., Luzianky	39	33	55	56	54	50
Elektronika Slovensko, Inc., Trnava	40	34	58	58	58	58
Vacuumschmelze, Ltd., Horna Streda	41	35	25	23	25	30
EVPU, Inc., Nova Dubnica	42	36	44	33	36	35
Tesla Stropkov, Inc., Stropkov	43	37	11	16	19	22
ZTS-Kabel, Ltd., Dubnica nad Vahom	44	38	60	59	59	59
Klauke Slovakia, Ltd., Dolny Kubin	45	39	6	15	15	16
Enpay Transformer Components, Ltd., Krskany	46	40	8	17	16	15
Hydac Electronic, Ltd., Tvrdosin	47	41	10	5	8	8
Elba, Inc., Kremnica	48	42	9	3	4	11
Tatramat, Ltd., Poprad	49	43	30	35	30	31
Linak Slovakia, Ltd., Zupcany	50	44	4	12	11	12

ICS Industrial Cables Slovakia, Ltd., Nitra	51	45	42	46	38	25
Thorma Vyroba, k.s., Filakovo	52	46	29	30	29	43
Delipro, Ltd., Piestany	53	47	2	1	2	9
Hengstler, Ltd., Kezmarok	54	48	43	38	40	44
Elcom, Ltd., Presov	55	49	27	32	28	33
VUKI, Inc., Bratislava	56	50	48	47	45	38
Avex electronics, Ltd., Oravska Lesna	57	51	56	60	60	60
ProCS, Ltd., Sala	58	52	41	31	41	40
Telegrafia, Inc., Kosice	59	53	22	19	21	20
Elmax Zilina, Inc., Zilina	60	54	45	45	42	47
Datamars Slovakia, Ltd., Luzianky	61	55	49	52	48	52
CRT - Electronic, Ltd., Oravska Lesna	62	56	47	43	44	48
TTS Martin, Ltd., Pribovce	63	57	57	53	52	53
Krizik GBI, Inc., Presov	64	58	17	9	18	23
VEM Slovakia, Ltd., Piestany	65	59	53	55	53	55
Cab Tech, Ltd., Prievidza	66	60	23	25	26	27

Table 2 Ranks electro-technical companies using the methods of comparison between companies [own processing]

Method	**order**	**scoring**	**normalized variable**	**distance from the fictitious object**
Order (MO)	1	0,9485	0,8990	0,8671
Scoring method (SM)		1	0,8959	0,8342
Method of normalized variable (MNV)			1	0,9673
Method of distance from the fictitious object (DFO)				1

Table 3 Conformity assessment methods [own processing]

Evaluation of the order of the methods was subject to peer testing to check for the conformity of their results. I utilized design methods with comparisons between businesses, and calculated the results of different methods for individual companies. According to that order for businesses in Table 2, it is possible by means of Spearman's rank correlation coefficient R to determine the degree of correlation between the methods. To limit the size of the contribution is not in the paper, but is referred to in the corresponding table. Matrix coefficients speak volumes about the strength of the correlation between the two methods. The calculated value of the coefficient R according to (7) are significant at the significance level $\alpha = 0.001$, suggesting a proven high conformity between the order of selection of the electrical engineering companies with all the methods implemented (Table 3).

3 Conclusion

The aim at this paper was to outline the implementation of multivariate methods in the field of financial-economic analysis, to allow the comparison of non-financial corporations in the electro-technical industry in the Slovak Republic. It went into the analysis of the first 60 companies active in the Slovak Republic, ranked by the amount of revenue they generated during a 12-

month period, which was compared with data on the number of employees within each company. The number of employees in six of the companies was not available, so data from these companies did not enter into the analysis of that company's rating among Slovakia's electro-technical companies. On the basis of precise data from the Register of the financial statements of the accounts and financial management statements from these companies, I have calculated financial ratios, all of which were in the analysis of the multi-criteria evaluation of selected indicators of productivity and performance. The defined four criteria specifically represented: the basic production enterprise strength, return on sales, financial performance and financial productivity by employee, were used for analysis of the four methods. Business evaluations of the electrical engineering companies was carried out by implementing advice in the scoring method, order method, a normalized variable method and method of distance from a fictitious object. The expected result being the order of the companies in the electrical engineering market space in Slovakia. Based on the above analysis, we can say that of all of the businesses already in operation for many years in Slovakia, Samsung Electronics Slovakia, Ltd., Foxconn Galanta and Slovakia, Ltd., Nitra, are dominant. These businesses should probably not be included in further analyzes as they are significant in several respects that are very different from other companies in the electro-technical industry, which are (in Slovakia as elsewhere) broken down by SK NACE Standards 26 - Manufacture of Computers, Electronics and Optical Products and 27 - Manufacture of electrical equipment. Given that this is a larger set of enterprises and the limited extent of the contributions available for this analysis, this paper does not include sub-analysis of individual methods. This does not affect the defined objectives, which is the evaluation of businesses using statistical methods to guide the financial management of these companies, to allow the assessment of the individual company's market position.

Acknowledgements

VEGA1/0945/17 "Economic research on quantif. of marketing processes improving values for patients, multidimen. analysis of the mark. mix of HCF and quantif. of their importance in the process of establis. a system to measure the quality and efficiency of the Slovak HHC."

References

Bondareva, I. (2014). 'Benchmarking as a Management Tool Competitiveness of SMEs'. *Journal of MANagement and ECOnomics MANEKO,* 6 (1), pp. 16-25.

Dluhošová, D. (2008). *Finanční řízení a rozhodování podniku,* 2nd ed. Prague:Ekopress.

Jenčová, S. (2016). *Finančno-ekonomicka analýza podnikateľskych subjektov,* 3rd ed. Presov: Book-Man.

Jenčová, S. and Litavcová, E. (2015). 'Status of electrical engineering industry in the structure of the Slovak economy'. *Reviewed scientific online Journal, Economic Spectrum,* 10 (3), pp. 35-45.

Kubičková, D. and Jindřichovská, I. (2015). *Finanční analýza a hodnocení vykonnosti firmy.* Prague: C.H. Beck.

Štefko, R. and Sojka, L. (2015). 'Analysis of the impact of globalisation on selected indicators of firm's activities'. *European scientific Journal,* 1 (special), pp. 149-162.

Zalai, K. et al. (2013). *Finančno-ekonomicka analýza podniku,* 8th ed. Bratislava: Sprint 2.

Zmeškal, Z., Dluhošová, D. and Tichý, T. (2013). *Finanční modely. Koncepty, metody, aplikace*, 3rd ed. Prague: Ekopress.

All-inclusive system in Dominican Republic. An analysis of satisfaction and loyalty

Juan Antonio Jimber Del Río[1], Petr Seda[2], Francisco Orgaz Agüera[3], Jesús Claudio Pérez Galvez[4]

Abstract. The "all inclusive" is defined as a planned in advance trip with prepaid covering transportation, lodging, meals and sightseeing, and enjoyed in a complex offering lodging, meals and recreational activities at a single price. The aim of this paper is to analyze satisfaction and loyalty in the All-Inclusive in Puerto Plata, Dominican Republic. The methodology used was based on surveys to tourists. The data from this research have been analyzed with SPSS 23 and AMOS IBM SPSS 23. The results of this research have shown that the role of agents and responsible destination for tourist loyalty is truly important, what they owe, through its various actions, attracting tourist visitors with appropriate socio-demographic profile, improving knowledge and attitude of the visitor about the various tourist attractions in the all-inclusive system. The value perceived impact on satisfaction tourists would help reinforce loyalty to the destination.

Keywords: all-inclusive system, loyalty, satisfaction, structural equations, Dominican Republic.

JEL Classification: Z3, C3

1 Introduction

Travel in the all-inclusive regime (AIS) typology refers to a way of travel, organized by tour operators, in which the trip includes a set of tourist goods and services that are marketed as a single product and is sold at a global price. For Heung and Chu (2000), an "all-inclusive" package is defined as a pre-planned and prepaid trip that covers transportation, accommodation, meals and sightseeing, and is enjoyed in a complex that offers accommodation, meals and recreational activities at a single price. The AIS has been studied in different tourist destinations (Anderson, 2009, Anderson, 2012).

The aim of this paper is to analyze the satisfaction and loyalty of tourists who use the all-inclusive modality during their stay in the Dominican Republic, through a structural equations model. The paper is structured as follows: after Introduction, the second section deliver the review of the literature, the third section presents the methodology used, and the fourth section shows empirical results of our research. The paper ends with the Conclusions and used bibliographical references.

[1] University of Córdoba, Faculty of Law and Business and Economic Sciences, Department of Statistics, Econometrics, Operations Research, Business Organization and Applied Economics, Plaza Nueva S/N, 14001 Córdoba, Spain, jjimber@uco.es.
[2] VSB-Technical University of Ostrava, Faculty of Economics, Department of Mathematical Methods in Economics, Sokolská třída 33, 701 21 Ostrava 1, Czech Republic, petr.seda@vsb.cz.
[3] Technological University of Santiago (UTESA), Vice-Rector of Research, Santiago, Dominican Republic, franorgaz@hotmail.com.
[4] University of Córdoba, Faculty of Law and Business and Economic Sciences, Department of Statistics, Econometrics, Operations Research, Business Organization and Applied Economics, Plaza Nueva S/N, 14001 Córdoba, Spain, dt1pegaj@uco.es.

2 Review of the literature

According to Anderson et al. (2009), we can note that there are five different packages in this holidays typology (basic package, bed and breakfast, half board, full board and all-inclusive), and that each package would include different services. On the other hand, Wong and Kwong (2004) identifies only two types of packages: the basic and the "all-inclusive".

However, what does reveal the appearance of AIS is that it has generated changes in the organization of hosting companies. However, according to Çizel et al. (2013), the concept of an all-inclusive package was, in principle, an initial trend that has been adopted to adapt to the tourist market conditions, even this type of accommodation is becoming increasingly frequent in a growing number of destinations. The "all-inclusive" modality has a number of strengths and weaknesses (Anderson, 2009). Among the first ones, it should be noted that tourists could plan the holiday better and know in advance what the total cost will be, tourists feel safer about the travel expense, and being it an easier pack to sell for travel agencies. Among the weaknesses, we can highlight that this system eliminates the monetary incentives for hotel workers, does not generate many expenses outside the hotel and limits the interaction with local residents. For their part, Issa and Jayawardena (2003) also point out, and specifically referring to the Caribbean, that with this system tourist may feel "imprisoned" in the hotel. In this sense, some authors (Wickens, 2002; Wong and Kwong, 2004) speak of the safety of this modality as one of the motivations that generate the trip for tourists.

Wong and Kwong (2004) show that another motivation is the possibility of knowing other people who do the same trip, an aspect that these authors call "social contact". On the other hand, through the "all-inclusive" modality, tourists receive a large number of services at attractive prices (Wickens, 2002; Wong and Kwong, 2004), which means that they choose this form of travel instead to request each service separately (Enoch, 1996). In addition, this implies that tourists are not surprised at unexpected costs with the hiring of the "all-inclusive" modality (Issa and Jayawardena, 2003).

2.1 Hypothesis to be tested

- **H1.** There is a significant relation of the expected quality on the perceived quality by the tourist.
- **H2.** There is a significant relation of expected quality to the value perceived by the tourist.
- **H3.** There is a significant relation of perceived quality to the value perceived by the tourist.
- **H4.** There is a significant relation of perceived quality to customer satisfaction.
- **H5.** There is a significant relation of expected quality to customer satisfaction.
- **H6.** There is a significant relation of perceived value to customer satisfaction.
- **H7.** There is a significant relation of customer satisfaction and customer loyalty.

3 Methodology

The chosen methodology has consisted in the collection of the data through a structured questionnaire. In this phase, a useful tool was developed in order to gather the necessary information to achieve the objectives of this research. Among the available options to collect information, the design of a closed questionnaire to be self-administered was chosen. In order to guarantee the validity of the questionnaire, the formulation of the items is based on selected items from previous research (Anderson, 2012; Özdemir et al., 2012). From this initial set of items, a debugging process was followed in two phases: first, a researcher specialized in tourism analyzed the proposed items; second, the resulting questionnaire was reviewed by a person responsible for the country's tourism activity. In this way, the validity of the items that form the constructs of the model proposed in this research was verified twice (Figure 1).

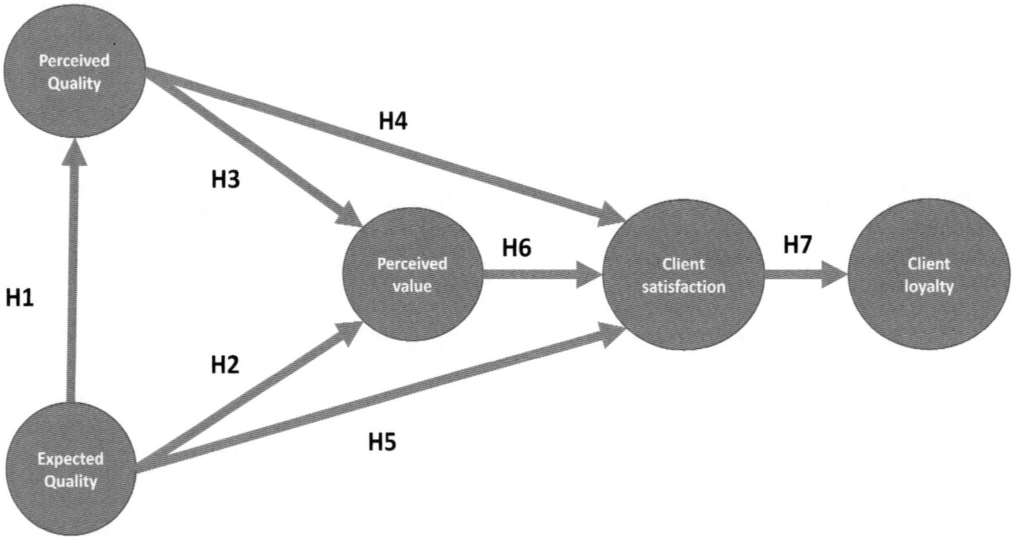

Figure 1 Research model. [Own elaboration]

Surveys were personally conducted to tourists visiting some of the most tourist sites in the Dominican Republic. The questionnaire responds to four clearly differentiated parts: details of the tourist trip; valuation and opinions of the visitor on the modality of all-inclusive and the hotel in which he/she is housed; assessment and opinions of the visitor on the destination in the Dominican Republic; and socio-demographic profile of tourists.

This way, the total number of items was 21, after the purification process by calculating the Cronbach's alpha coefficient for each construct. The field work was carried out from March to May 2014, by means of a convenience sampling.

It was carried out a pretest of 20 surveys. In total, the number of valid questionnaires was 652, out of a total of 677, obtaining a confidence level of 95%, by means of convenience sampling, at a confidence level of 95%.

Data from this research was tabulated and analyzed using the IBM SPSS 23 statistical system, and the estimators and structural equations with IBM SPSS AMOS 23.

4 Results of research and discussion

The aim of this section is to construct indicators of perceived quality in tourist destinations and the loyalty of tourists through a methodology based on structural equation models. These models allow estimating multiple dependency ratios and represent unobserved or dormant variables in these relationships, taking into account the measurement error in the estimation process (Reisinger and Turner, 1999). Table 1 presents the variables used in the proposed model.

Latent variables	Perceived Quality, Expected Quality, Perceived Value, Customer Satisfaction and Customer Loyalty
Observed variables	Rooms, food, drink, sports, entertainment, customer service, sports activities, cleaning, shopping area, beaches, shows, excursions, touring the island, hotel syst. Tourist, quality of services, price, tourist alternatives, method of payment, satisfaction, repeat.
Measurement errors	e4, e5, e6, e7, e8, e9, e10, e11, e12, e13, e14, e15, e16,e17, e18, e19, e20, e21, e22, e23, e24, e25, e26, e27, e28 y e29.

Table 1 Variables used in the proposed model. [Own elaboration]

The model has been estimated by the Asymptotically Distribution Free (ADF) method. In order to optimize the proposed initial model, we proceed to eliminate the following non-significant observed variables and make a new estimation of the structural coefficients by presenting the causal diagram or "Path diagram" in Figure 2. Table 2 shows the structural coefficients standardized. In order to confirm the degree of adjustment of the proposed model (Table 3), the absolute adjustment measures, the incremental adjustment measures and the parsimony adjustment measures were calculated.

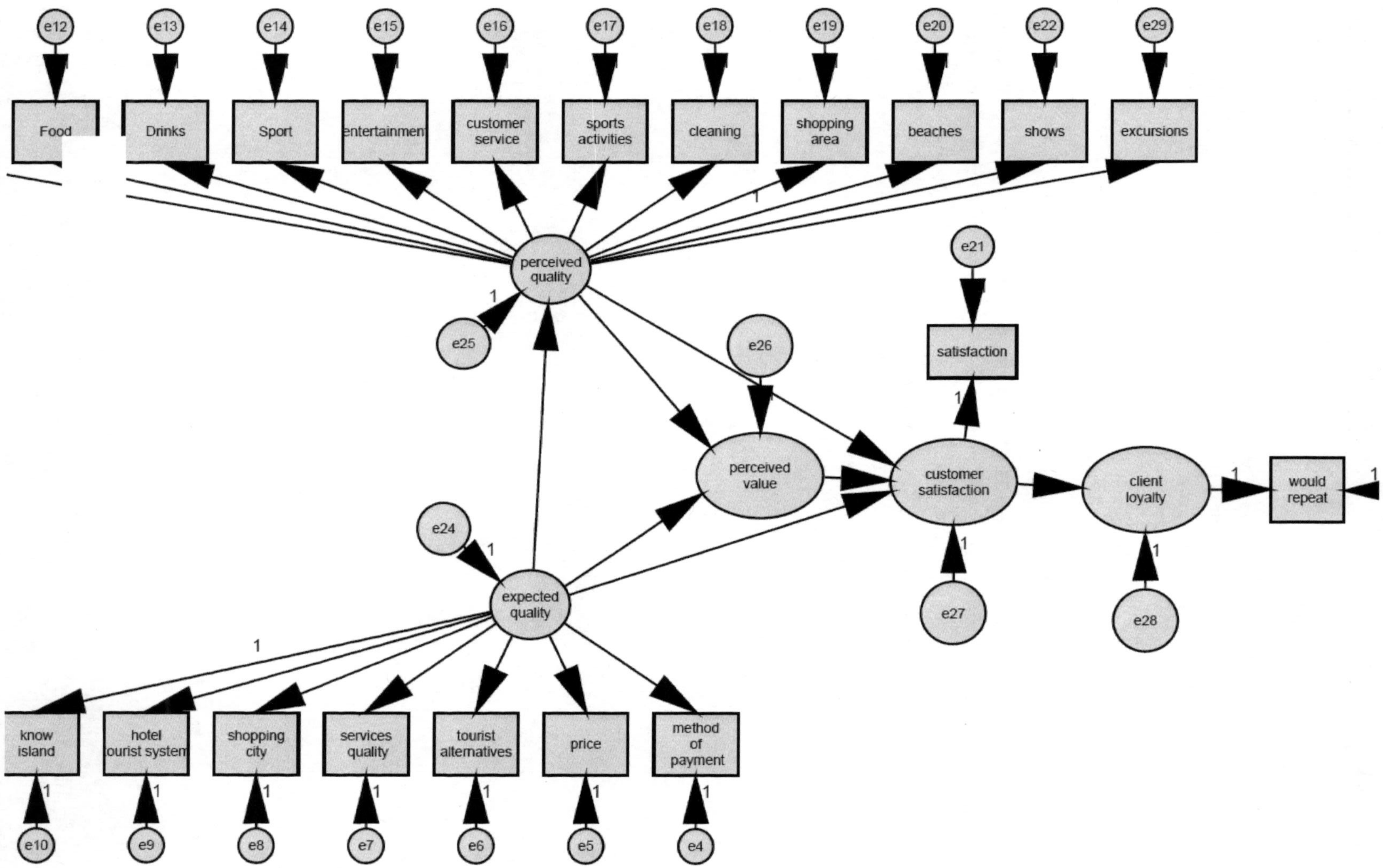

Figure 2 Path diagram of the proposed model. [Own elaboration]

			Estimations
Perceived quality	←	Quality Expected	0.222
Perceived value	←	Quality Expected	0.077
Perceived value	←	Perceived quality	0.082
Customer Satisfaction	←	Quality Expected	-0.061
Customer Satisfaction	←	Perceived value	0.166
Customer Satisfaction	←	Perceived quality	0.602
Customer loyalty	←	Customer Satisfaction	-0.536
To know island	←	Quality Expected	0.806
Hotel Tourist Syst.	←	Quality Expected	0.734
Shopping city	←	Quality Expected	0.722
Quality Services	←	Quality Expected	0.777
Price	←	Quality Expected	0.421
Tourist Attractions	←	Quality Expected	0.869
Method to pay	←	Quality Expected	0.671
Beaches	←	Perceived quality	0.738
Shopping area	←	Perceived quality	0.679
Cleaning	←	Perceived quality	0.71
Sport activities	←	Perceived quality	0.844
Customer service	←	Perceived quality	0.82
Entertainment	←	Perceived quality	0.864
Sport	←	Perceived quality	0.786
Drinks	←	Perceived quality	0.864
Food	←	Perceived quality	0.853
Rooms	←	Perceived quality	0.728
Satisfaction	←	Customer Satisfaction	0.618
Would repeat	←	Customer loyalty	0.764
Shows	←	Perceived quality	0.865
Tours	←	Perceived quality	0.71

Table 2 Standardized Structural Coefficients of the Model. [Own elaboration]

The model evaluation was carried out using several indexes: first, the Normed Fit Index (NFI), which is a measure of discrepancy between the adjusted model and the base model; second, the Goodness of Fit Index (GFI), similar to the previous one, and which compares the discrepancies between the adjusted model and the pre-adjustment one; third, the Adjusted Goodness of Fit Index (AGFI), which is the same indicator as the previous one but weighted by a ratio of the degrees of freedom of the base model and adjusted; fourth, the Parsimony Normed Fit Index (PNFI), obtained from the NFI index and weighted by the ratio of the degrees of freedom of the adjusted model and the base model; and fifth, the Root Mean Square Error Approximation (RMSEA), which is obtained as the square root of the ratio of the non-central parameter adjusted by the degrees of freedom (Sucháček et al, 2015).

Absolute adjustment measures	
χ^2	426.448
Df	160.000
χ^2 / Df	2.665
RMSEA	0.062
RMR	0.146
GFI	0.969
Incremental adjustment measures	
AGFI	0.955
NFI	0.890
Measures of adjustment of parsimony	
PNFI	0.678
PGFI	0.671

Table 3 Adjustment of the proposed model. [Own elaboration]

As for the absolute adjustment measures, the Chi-square test reaches a value of 426,448 by the asymptotic distribution method with a p-value of 0.000, which implies that there are discrepancies between the correlation matrix and the observed one. The GFI adjustment measure exceeds 0.9 being an optimum value. In addition, the RMSEA measure, with a value of 0.062, is optimal. On the other hand, some incremental measures of adjustment, like the AGFI, are sensitive to the number of indicators and are close to GFI. With respect to the parsimony adjustment measures, PNFI and PGFI are significant from values higher than 0.06, as is the case. Therefore, and based on the above, the model is considered to have adequate adjustment indices.

The results of this research highlight the relationship, influence and positive and direct impact of the visitor's knowledge, attitude, perceived value, satisfaction and loyalty to the Dominican Republic destination in the all-inclusive modality. Consequently, the structural coefficients estimated in the model allow us to contrast the starting hypotheses:

H1. The hypothesis is confirmed; a higher quality expected have significant positive effects on the quality perceived by the tourist.

H2. The hypothesis is confirmed; a higher quality expected have significant positive effects on the value perceived by the tourist.

H3. The hypothesis is confirmed; a higher perceived quality have significant positive effects on the value perceived by the tourist.

H4. The hypothesis is confirmed; a higher perceived quality have significant positive effects on the value perceived by the tourist.

H5. The hypothesis is confirmed; higher expected quality have significant positive effects on customer satisfaction.

H6. The hypothesis is confirmed; a higher perceived value have significant positive effects on customer satisfaction.

H7. The hypothesis is confirmed; greater customer satisfaction have significant positive effects on customer loyalty.

5 Conclusions

The results obtained in the present study emphasize that the opinion that the visitors have about the all-inclusive modality exerts a direct and positive influence on the attitude of the tourist toward the all-inclusive modality. It is also evidenced a direct and positive relationship between the attitude towards the all-inclusive modality, the motivation and the satisfaction perceived by the tourist in different used services.

The result of Chi-square test indicates that presented model is relatively adequate (especially due to high values of fit indices, for example GFI or NFI), but most likely there will be an even better model with a lower $\chi 2$ and RMSEA values. The optimal values are RMSEA < 0,05 and p-value of Chi-square test > 0,05. It would be interesting to try to find such a model and compare it with original one, which would be is an interesting topic for another paper. The variables satisfaction and loyalty are closely related and satisfaction is a variable that precedes loyalty (Dick and Basu, 1994). Our research confirms the direct and positive relationship between satisfaction perceived by the client in the all-inclusive modality, the intention of behavior and the loyalty of using this modality again. Likewise, it is also concluded that surveyed tourists recommend the tourist destination.

Academic literature also shows the existence of a positive relationship between consumer satisfaction and loyalty, being the first predecessor of the latter, which is usually measured as the intention of post-purchase behavior (Henard and Szymanski, 2001).

Given that a tourist's image of the destination will significantly influence his/her intention to visit it/return, recommend it and even how he values the experience there, his/ her management becomes a vital issue for the success of destiny. This importance is reinforced by the fact that destinations basically compete with their image given that, before being visited, tourists will have an image about them that will attract them to the place. Likewise, the experience lived in the destination may lead to a modification of the initial image perceived, which only in the case of being positive will enhance their loyalty. Consequently, building a suitable image for a destination will determine its ability to attract and retain tourists.

Faced with this situation, the role of the agents and responsible of the destination to achieve the loyalty of the tourist is truly important, so they must, through their various actions, improve knowledge and image on the different tourist attractions of the destination. Only an adequate coordination and cooperation between these agents will be able to obtain the tourist satisfaction, satisfaction that will help to reinforce loyalty towards the destiny.

Regarding the limitations of the study, it would be interesting to have obtained more information from the point of view of hotel offer, since this research only covers the demand for such services. As future lines of research, we propose to cross-check information between offer and demand, as well as how to optimize the resources of the hotel sector that offers the all-inclusive modality and the product demanded by customers, which would lead them to repeat the visit, demonstrating the much sought after loyalty of the client.

References

Anderson, W., Juaneda, C. and Sastre, F. (2009). 'Influences of pro-all-inclusive travel decisions'. *Tourism Review*, 64 (2), pp. 4-18.

Anderson, W. (2012). 'Analysis of all-inclusive tourism mode in the Balearic Islands'. *Tourisms: An International Multidisciplinary Journal of Tourism*, 7 (1), pp. 309-323.

Çizel, R. B., Çizel, B., Sarvan, F. and Özdemir, B. (2013). 'Emergence and Spread of an All-Inclusive System in the Turkish Tourism Sector and Strategic Responses of Accommodation Firms'. *International Journal of Hospitality & Tourism Administration*, 14 (4), pp. 305–340.

Dick, A. S., and Basu, K. (1994). 'Customer loyalty: toward an integrated conceptual framework'. *Journal of the academy of marketing science*, 22 (2), pp. 99-113.

Enoch, Y. (1996). 'Contents of tour packages: a cross-cultural comparison'. *Annals of Tourism Research*, 23 (3), pp. 599-616.

Heung, V. and Chu, R. (2000). 'Important factors affecting Hong Kong consumers' choice of a travel agency for AI package tours'. *Journal of Travel Research*, 39, pp. 52-59.

Issa, J. and Jayawardena, C. (2003). 'The 'All-inclusive' concept in the Caribbean'. *International Journal of Contemporary Hospitality Management*, 15 (3), pp. 167-171.

Özdemir, B., Çizel, B. and Çizel, R. B. (2012). 'Satisfaction with all-inclusive tourism resorts: the effects of satisfaction with destination and destination royalty'. *International Journal of Hospitality & Tourism Administration*, 13 (20), pp. 109-130.

Reisinger, Y., and Turner, L. (1999). 'Structural equation modeling with Lisrel: application in tourism'. *Tourism Management*, 20 (1), 71-88.

Sucháček, J., Seďa, P., Friedrich, V. and Koutský, J. (2015). 'Regional Dimension of Security and Accidents and Their TV Reflection in the Czech Republic'. *Transformations in Business & Economics*, 14 (3C), pp. 544-563.

Wickens, E. (2002). 'The sacred and the profane'. *Annals of Tourism Research*, 29 (3), pp. 834-851.

Wong, C. and Kwong, W. (2004). 'Outbound tourists' selection criteria for choosing AI package tours'. *Tourism Management*, 25 (5), pp. 581-592.

Application of the Ordered Weighted Averaging (OWA) Method in Human Resources

Katerina Kashi[1]

Abstract. Competency models can be widely used by companies today for most human resources activities. Well-designed competency model can be used by the company and its HR in various ways. It can serve as a base for recruitment, performance management, succession planning, recognition and rewards, compensation and training and development. Competencies have to lead to effective performance, which means that the performance of a person with competency must be significantly better than that of a person without it. Competencies are components of a job, which are reflected in behavior that is observable in a workplace. Competency models, which should be designed for all key positions in the company. The goal of this paper is to present a competency model and an evaluation of key competencies for specific position. The ordered weighting averaging (OWA) is applied to assess the appraisal from optimistic to pessimistic perspectives. The results will be used to effectively plan recruitment, appraisal, training and development of employees.

Keywords: Competency models, key competencies, HRM, OWA.

JEL Classification: C49, M51

1 Introduction

Currently, employees' training and development play an integral part of human resources management. It is necessary for the company and its employees. Today, well-educated and trained employees present a significant value for any company. The times when the company's competitiveness depended only on tangible assets are long gone. Today, the companies are trying to concentrate not only on hiring and keeping qualified employees but also on their training and development, which can also be utilized by the company as an employees' motivation or benefit. In order to determine and provide needed activity which enables the employees to be more productive the author will use quantitative methods of economic analysis – methodology will be described in sixth chapter, to determine core competencies of key employees and then create a proposal for training and development program for the company. The goal of this paper is to present a competency model and an evaluation of key competencies for specific position. A starting point is obtained set of weights for selected competencies (Kashi, Horváthová, 2014). Ordered weighting averaging (OWA) method was used for evaluating employees according to selected competencies (criteria). The paper structured as follows: section 2 is focused on description of issues related to competencies and competency modelling; the section 3 deals with brief description of used multiple attribute decision making methods of analytic hierarchy process OWA and TOPSIS. In the section 4 author applies proposed methodology on performance appraisal in human resources management (HRM). Results are discussed and summarized in the last section.

---

[1] VŠB – Technical University of Ostrava, Faculty of Economics, Department of Management, Sokolská třída 33, Ostrava, Czech Republic, katerina.kashi@vsb.cz

2 Competency and Competency Models

Competence, a term, which has been first used in Great Britain as a basic part of the process for creating standards for the State Scottish System of Technical Qualification. Competence can be defined as "functional analysis", which determines what people in a specific roles have to be able to do and what work standards are expected of them. (Bartoňková, 2010). Boyatzis (2009) defines competency as a capability or ability. According to Veteška and Tureckiová (2008), the term competence can be defined also as a unique human ability to successfully act and further develop his/her potential on the basis of integrated set of own sources, that is in the specific context of various tasks and life situations connected with the possibility and willingness (motivation) to decide and take the responsibility for own decisions. Tureckiová (2004) states that competencies can be classified by several ways, i.e. there is an American concept that is aimed at individual characteristics of the job bearer, i.e. personal characteristics, or behavioral characteristics; British concept which is aimed especially at the outcomes deriving from the working position, i.e. determined competencies have to be compliant with the defined professional standards. Competence can be divided to "soft" and "hard" skills. Hard skills can usually include technical knowledge, skills, abilities, talent and attitude, which pertain to the technological, financial, economic and procedural aspects of work. On the other hand, soft skills include the area of behavior and ability to deal with people that includes everything pertaining to the work with people, that influence communication and dealing with individuals and groups (Prokopenko, Kubr et al., 1996).

A competency model is a framework, which lists the competencies required for effective performance in a specific job or group of jobs. When developing the competency model, the goal should be to identify the competencies, which are required for superior performance, not average or poor performance. People who are most likely to provide accurate data about the competencies that are required for superior job performance are those who perform the job the best (top performers).

Depending on the objectives, some models are meant to identify core competencies that are relevant and necessary to all organization's members; however the model can be designed for key employees only. The competency models are usually designed based on the employees' position and can be divided into three general groups: top management, middle management, line management and administrative (Sanghi, 2007).

Competencies have to lead to effective performance, which means that the performance of a person with competency must be significantly better than that of a person without it. Competencies are components of a job, which are reflected in behavior that is observable in a workplace (Sanghi, 2007).

3 Applied methods

Quantitative research will be executed through semi-structured interviews. For creation of competency models analytic hierarchy process (AHP) method has been used (see Kashi, Friedrich 2013). OWA method was used to evaluate group of five employees (managers) according to the competency model and performance in particular competencies.

3.1 Ordered Weighted Averaging (OWA)

One of the main objectives set by fuzzy theory was to develop a tool to model multiple attribute decision making (MADM) problems using linguistic variables. In this framework, the criteria are represented as fuzzy subsets over the space of decision alternatives and fuzzy set operators are used to aggregate the individual criteria to form overall decision function. It implicitly implies a requirement that all criteria must be satisfied by a solution to the problem. As Yager (1993) pointed out this condition may not always be appropriate relationship between the criteria. For example, a decision maker may be content if most of the criteria are satisfied. Yager (1988) suggested use of ordered weighted averaging operators as a tool to implement these aggregations. OWA is a class of multi-criteria operators (Yager, 1988). It involves two sets of weights: criterion importance weights and order weights. An importance weight is assigned to a given criterion (attribute) for all locations in a study area to indicate its relative importance (according to the decision-maker's preferences) in the set of criteria under consideration. The order weights are associated with the criterion values on a location-by-location (object-by-object) basis. They are assigned to a location's attribute values in decreasing order without considering which attribute the value comes from. The order weights are central to the OWA combination procedures. They are associated with the degree of "orness", which indicates the degree to which an OWA operator is similar to the logical connective or in terms of its combination behavior. The parameter is also associated with a trade-off measure indicating the degree of compensation between the parameters associated with the OWA operations serves as a mechanism to obtain results for different decision maker's perspectives. Thus, the "orness" measure allows for interpreting the results of OWA in the context of the behavioral theory of decision making.

Since its appearance, the OWA operator has been used in varied applications in decision making problems. Yager (2004) suggested a generalization of the OWA operator by using generalized means, known as the generalized OWA (GOWA) operator. With this generalization, it is possible to include the special cases found in the OWA operator like the maximum and the minimum, and the special cases found in the generalized mean such as the geometric and the harmonic mean. When using the OWA operator, it is assumed that the available information is exact numbers or singletons. However, this may not be the real situation found in the decision making problem. Sometimes, available information is vague or imprecise and thus it is not possible to analyze it with exact numbers. Then, it is necessary to use another approach that can assess the uncertainty such as the use of Fuzzy Numbers (FNs). With the use of FNs, the best and worst possible scenario can be analyzed with the possibility that the internal values of the fuzzy interval will occur.

The *OWA* operator provides a parameterized family of aggregation operators which are used in many applications. The definition of the *OWA* operator was introduced by Yager, (1988).

Definition: An *OWA* operator of dimension n is a mapping $OWA: R^n \rightarrow R$ that has an associated weighting vector $w = (w_1, w_2, ..., w_n)^T$ of dimension n having the properties,

$$w_j = Q\left(\frac{\sum_{k=1}^{j} u_k}{T}\right) - Q\left(\frac{\sum_{k=1}^{j-1} u_k}{T}\right), \tag{1}$$

$$w_j \in [0,1], \sum_{j=1}^{n} w_j = 1 \text{ and such that}$$

$$F_{OWA}(a_1, a_2, ..., a_n) = \sum_{j=1}^{n} w_j b_j , \tag{2}$$

where Q is linguistic quantifier "orness" (see Table 1), a_i is from R^n, b_j is the jth largest of the a_i, for all i, T is total sum of weights.

A fundamental aspect of this operator is the reordering of the arguments, based on their values. That is, the weights rather than being associated with a specific argument, as in the case of the usual weighted average, are associated with a particular position in the ordering. In the following Table 1 a family of linguistic quantifiers and their relevant values for optimistic coefficient and optimistic condition.

Linguistic quantifiers	Optimistic coefficient (degree of orness)	Optimistic condition
At least one	0.001	Very optimistic
At least a few	0.1	Optimistic
A few	0.5	Fairly optimistic
Half	1	Neutral
Most	2	Fairy pessimistic
Almost all	10	Pessimistic
All	0.001	Very pessimistic

Table 1 Linguistic quantifiers for OWA

Example 1: Assume $w = (0.4, 0.3, 0.2, 0.1)^T$, *where* T is "most"=2. Then,

$$F_{OWA}\ (0.7, 1.0, 0.2, 0.6) = (0.4 \cdot 1.0) + (0.3 \cdot 0.7) + (0.2 \cdot 0.6) + (0.1 \cdot 0.2) = 0.75 .$$

4 Results and discussion of applied MADM methods

In this section we will discuss results obtained from application of OWA method.

4.1 Evaluation of employees using OWA method

The evaluation of the criteria and sub-criteria has been done by one expert in each company. In large and medium size company it has been filled by the human resources (HR) manager, in small company by the executive/owner. All of them have filled in pre-prepared matrices for all levels of the competency model hierarchy. The results for individual matrices for each competency are described and evaluated below. Firstly, the HR managers/owner evaluated groups of competency based on pair comparison. Then the weights for individual group of competency were calculated based on the formulas. Then the consistency was checked. Consistency ratio index was fulfilled for all matrices in all three companies. The results of global weights for competencies for one position i.e. top manager is shown in Table 2.

Ranking	Competency	Global weight
1	Strategic thinking	19.04%
2	Business knowledge	13.30%
3	Change management	8.81%
4	Proactivity	7.77%
5	Mental agility	6.83%
6	Professional knowledge	6.76%
7	Leadership	6.62%

Table 2 Global weights for competencies for the position of top manager

Next, first seven core competencies were selected for the yearly appraisal of the employees. The employees were evaluated on all the competencies; however the most important competencies (seven first) i.e. professional knowledge, analytic thinking, proactivity, mental agility, team cooperation, effective communication and stress resilience will be linked to the employees' total reward. The data in Table 3 show what evaluation employees 1 to 5 received for the core (first seven) competencies. The ranking was on a scale 0 to 100, i.e. 100 is the highest possible score any employee can reach.

	C1	C2	C3	C4	C5	C6	C7
Alternative	Strate-gic thinking	Business knowledge	Change manage-ment	Proactivity	Mental agility	Profes-sional knowledg e	Leadership
Employee 1	87	64	87	74	68	65	63
Employee 2	95	75	88	75	65	58	68
Employee 3	88	78	67	66	70	67	58
Employee 4	75	68	71	73	68	60	56
Employee 5	78	55	72	68	58	65	78

Table 3 Evaluation of employees according to seven most important competencies

In the following Table 4 the initial global weights for seven most important competencies were normalized to calculate local weights.

Competency	Global weight	Local weight u_k (Normalized)
Strategic Thinking	19.04	0.275
Business Knowledge	13.3	0.192
Change management	8.81	0.127
Proactivity	7.77	0.112
Mental agility	6.83	0.099
Professional knowledge	6.76	0.098
Leadership	6.62	0.096

Table 4 Initial weights derived from AHP

Following Table 5 shows an example of OWA method application in evaluation of Employee 1 from the fairly pessimistic perspective (performs best in most criteria). Criteria are ordered according to respective performance of the employee in seven competencies. *Local criteria weights u_k are added up to make a cumulative total.* Then the ordered weights w_j are calculated. Finally, a weighted sum of ordered weights and employee performance is calculated.

Alternative/ criteria	**Employee 1**	u_k	***cumulative*** u_k	w_j	F_{owa} **(weighted sum)**
C1	87	0.275	0.275	0.076	6.600
C3	87	0.127	0.403	0.086	7.520
C4	74	0.112	0.515	0.103	7.636
C5	68	0.099	0.614	0.112	7.587
C6	65	0.098	0.712	0.130	8.428
C2	64	0.192	0.904	0.311	19.899
C7	63	0.096	1.000	0.182	11.488
				Total	**69.158**

Table 5 Example of Ordered Weighting Averaging method for „most criteria"

The applicant's ranking is, within the OWA method, determined based on value F_{OWA}, since it deals with distance minimization from the ideal variant, whereas the values are in descending order. The results of employees' rankings compared with Technique for Order Preference by Similarity to Ideal Solution (TOPSIS) (see Kashi, Horváthová, 2014) are shown in Table 6 and Table 7.

	At least one	**At least a few**	**A few**	**Half**	**Most**	**Almost all**	**All**	**TOPSIS**
Employee 1	86.82	85.30	79.70	74.79	69.16	63.43	63	0.60
Employee 2	94.75	92.65	85.15	78.84	71.78	61.06	58	0.88
Employee 3	87.78	85.94	79.48	74.22	68.64	61.03	58	0.57
Employee 4	74.91	74.17	71.44	68.94	65.72	58.40	56	0.31
Employee 5	77.87	76.72	72.41	68.44	63.41	55.60	55	0.19

Table 6 Employee evaluation based on OWA compared with TOPSIS

	At least one	**At least a few**	**A few**	**Half**	**Most**	**Almost all**	**All**	**TOPSIS**
Employee 1	3	3	2	2	2	1	1	2
Employee 2	1	1	1	1	1	2	2	1
Employee 3	2	2	3	3	3	3	3	3
Employee 4	5	5	5	4	4	4	4	4
Employee 5	4	4	4	5	5	5	5	5

Table 7 Employee evaluation based on OWA compared with TOPSIS

From the tables Table 6 and Table 7 above it is evident that based on TOPSIS employee 2 is the closest to the ideal variant, followed by employee 1 and employee 3. Employee 5 has received the worst evaluation with 0.19, which is very far from 1 – the ideal variant. However, the OWA method can be perceived as kind of sensitivity analysis of decision maker's attitude (from optimistic to pessimistic). Results show that the fairly optimistic, neutral and fairy pessimistic attitudes produce similar results to TOPSIS method.

Conclusion

AHP method helped to scale down the number of measures and helped to determine the most important competencies, which lead to the achievement of firm's strategic goals. According to study's findings, one may use the AHP to study the design of competency models as a HR strategic management system. Using OWA method the decision makers can choose appropriate optimistic coefficient and determine set of weights based on order of criteria. AHP and TOPSIS are also able to capture the consensus of a potentially divergent group of managers and can be quickly and easily updated as desired.

Acknowledgment

This paper is supported by the Student Grant Competition of the Faculty of Economics, VSB-Technical University of Ostrava, project registration number SP2017/125 Application of out-ranking methods with uncertainty in business economics and management and by the Education for Competitiveness Operational Programme, project registration number CZ.1.07/2.3.00/20.0296. All support is greatly acknowledged and appreciated.

References

Bartoňková, H. (2010). *Firemní vzdělávání.* Praha: Grada.

Boyatzis, R. E. (2009). 'Competencies as a Behavioral Approach to Emotional Intelligence'. *Journal of Management Development*, 28 (9), pp. 749-770.

Kashi, K. and Horváthová, P. (2014). 'MADM Methods in Practice: Linking Competencies to Employees' Appraisal and Total Reward'. *Conference Proceedings of the 15th European Conference on Knowledge Management*, vol. 3. 2014 Eds.: Vivas, Carla and Pedro Sequeira, pp. 1229-1239.

Michnik, J. (2013). 'Weighted Influence Non-linear Gauge System (WINGS) – An analysis method for the systems of interrelated components'. *European Journal of Operational Research.* 228 (3), pp. 536-544.

Prokopenko, J. and Kubr, M. et al. (1996). *Vzdělávání a rozvoj manažerů.* Praha: Grada.

Sanghi, S. (2007). *The Handbook of Competency Mapping.* London: Sage.

Tureckiová, M. (2004). *Řízení a rozvoj lidí ve firmách.* Praha: Grada.

Veteška, J. and Tureckiová, M. (2008). *Kompetence ve vzdělávání.* Praha: Grada.

Yager, R. R. (1993). 'Families of OWA operators'. *Fuzzy Sets and Systems*, 59, pp. 125-148.

Yager, R., R. (2004). 'Generalized OWA aggregation operators'. *Fuzzy Optimization and Decision Making*, 3, pp. 93-107.

Yager, R., R. (1988). 'On ordered weighted averaging aggregation operators in multi-criteria decision making'. *IEEE Transactions on Systems, Man, and Cybernetics*, 18, pp. 183-190.

Zarghami, M. and Szidarovszky, F. (2008). 'Fuzzy quantifiers in sensitivity analysis of OWA operator'. *Computers & Industrial Engineering*, 54 (4), pp. 1006-1018.

Improving the efficiency of the enterprise's activity based on the implementation of the controlling system

Tatyana Khudyakova[1], Andrey Shmidt[2]

Abstract. During the global economic instability, demand in developing toolkit which helps to mitigate the negative impact of environmental factors on efficiency of activity of the enterprise is increasing dramatically. But in practice implementation of any of the tools causes the growth of additional costs, which, for purposes of effective functioning of mini-economic system must be covered by the profit's increase from the introduction of this toolkit. The task's implementation was achieved by processing a significant amount of scientific and statistical literature and calculation of integral indicators of the effectiveness of controlling system's implementation at the enterprises. The analysis revealed a positive effect of the implementation of controlling system on the quality of decisions, efficiency of management, productivity, investment attractiveness, effectiveness of workflow and financial stability, and calculated the average integral efficiency indicators. The obtained results allow to make an unambiguous conclusion about the effectiveness of the controlling system's implementing, which is especially important during the period of economic globalization and the growth of perturbations in the external environment, the efficiency reserves identified in the operation of the controlling system can and should be a certain buffer to reduce the negative impact of external factors on the sustainability of the enterprise.

Keywords: stability of the enterprise, economic sustainability, financial sustainability, controlling system, risk, disturbing influences, effectiveness.

JEL Classification: C53, D81

1 Introduction

In conditions of the crisis phenomena caused by fluctuations of the external environment, the variability of the geopolitical and socio-economic space dramatically increases. Perturbations, coming from the outside, in large measure affect the state of the Russian industrial cluster, reducing its financial and economic stability. The system of controlling is directed to mitigate the impact of these disturbances on the operation of the terminal parts of the economy - enterprises. However, changes in the structure and functionality of an enterprise will entail the increase of costs. In this connection, before the design stage of controlling system stability, the stakeholders must understand the General trends of increasing efficiency of functioning of the enterprise from the event. In this case, the experience of leading Russian and foreign companies, which already use in their activities the system of controlling, comes to help. Analysis and synthesis of existing data about growth of efficiency of enterprise's activity and identification of common trends can in large extent facilitate the prediction step.

[1] South Ural State University, High School of Economics and Management, Russia, Chelyabinsk, Lenina av., 76, khudiakovata@susu.ru.

[2] South Ural State University, High School of Economics and Management, Russia, Chelyabinsk, Lenina av., 76, shmidtav@susu.ru.

2 Latest research and publications analysis

As part of the task the scientific works of Russian and foreign scientists regarding the stability of the enterprise were considered. Among them are the works of S.G. Falco, K. Russell and L. Levin (2015), O.V. Syuzeva (2010), Yusupova, S.Y. (2008), N.S. Necheukhina (2010), D.A. Yunusova (2009), A.N. Asaul, M.K. Starovoytov and R.A. Faltinsky (2009), E.A. Borgardt, V.M. Nosova (2014), K.A. Sakhovskaya, N.A. Tsaplina (2014), T. Hubert, S.G. Falco (2015), A.V. Shmidt and T.A. Khudyakova (2015) and others.

In addition, with the aim of obtaining initial data for analysis were reviewed and used information from various official sources, such as data management companies, Fund statistics and other. In total, the study was about 100 sources of information.

However, it should be noted that currently there is no accurate quantitative information on the impact of the introduction of the controlling system on the indicators of enterprise efficiency of its activities.

3 Analysis of scientific studies of the effects of the introduction of a controlling system in the enterprise efficiency

In the present time, there is not enough attention to the methodological issues in the field of formation and development of the controlling system as a basis for improving the sustainability of the economic entity by preventive control, aimed at reducing the negative impact of disturbances coming from the environment of the enterprise. Today there are no methodological approaches to the construction of the enterprise's controlling system which provides the maximum elimination of uncertainty of the external environment, aimed at improving its financial and economic stability. Controlling models, which are introduced at the enterprises, in the majority are reduced to the functions of accounting, control and planning without prediction of the degree of influence of external environment uncertainty on the financial and economic performance of the company. This is due to the evolution of controlling systems in the Russian Federation, as we have noted previously, the first mention of the introduction of controlling systems appeared only after restructuring in Russia. Only at the turn of the XXI century there is a beginning of forming approaches to strategic management of an economic entity that is beginning to dominate the concept of accounting. All these facts influenced the fact that in the scientific literature practically are no quantitative assessment of the impact of the introduction of a controlling system in the financial-economic activity of the enterprise. Only a small group of Russian researchers attempted to quantify the impact of the introduction of a controlling system in the performance of a business entity, despite the fact that the positive aspect of the implementation of controlling is discussed in practically all modern scientific works.

Some of the founders of Russian controlling Falco S., Russell K. and Levin L. in their article "Controlling in Russia" note that according to experts "it is possible to achieve the growth of the integral indicators of the efficiency by 15–30%" due to the introduction of the controlling system at the enterprise. And implementation of controlling at the enterprises engaged in innovative developments, can improve their efficiency by about 50–75% (Falco, Russell and Levin, 2015).

In the dissertation research Syuzeva O.V. (Syuzeva, 2010) and Yusupova S. Y. (Yusupova, 2008), basing on the official data of the chamber of Commerce, note the increase of efficiency of made decisions, calculated as the profit growth to the increase in costs as a result of implementation of controlling system on industrial enterprises, noting the fact that the growth from 11% to 18.9% (Syuzeva, 2010). Herewith, there is an increase in productivity of managerial staff from 9.6% to 16% (Syuzeva, 2010; Yusupova, 2008).

Another Russian scientific work, which deals with the effectiveness of the implementation of controlling system at the enterprise, is dissertation research of Necheukhina N. S., in which, despite the fact that the dissertation discusses the implementation at the industrial enterprises of the controlling system, only affecting primary production in the context of accounting, is noted the growth of efficiency of management, efficiency, decision-making, and increasing productivity (Necheukhina, 2010). The growth of these indicators is comparable with the values given in the work of Suseva O.V.

Yusupova S. Y. in her dissertation "Theory and practice of implementation of controlling system in the information society" notes that "the most effective application of controlling systems is application for a global, strategic decisions. In this case, due to a more careful studying, the quality of decisions and their performance increase that conditioned a significant increase of management efficiency" (Yusupova, 2008) (table 1).

Indicator	The rate of growth of decisions quality, %	The rate of growth of management efficiency, %
The range of values of the analyzed index	18.9–43.4	18.9–38.7
The average value of the indicator	34.02	30.98
Integral index, %	32.46	

* compiled by the author based on (Yusupova, 2008)

Table 1 The effectiveness of making long term financial decisions on the basis of controlling activities in Russian companies*

Analysis of impact of implementation of controlling system in foreign enterprises on the basis of research conducted by PricewaterhouseCoopers (table 2) carrying out activities in the field of consulting and audit, showed trends similar to Russian, although the increase of the resulting indicator of financial-economic activity of the enterprise and also the growth of the integral indicator, characterizing the generalized growth rates of indicators measured during the implementation of controlling system at the enterprise, in the foreign companies are lower than is Russian. This trend is explained by the fact that foreign companies are already using the tools of strategic management and controlling, but in the Russian practice, as we noted earlier, controlling a new phenomenon, so the first implementation causes a much greater return.

Analysis of changes of indicators of efficiency of activity of foreign industrial enterprises in the implementation of cost accounting systems (table 3) allows to follow positive trends in the development of these businesses. At first, as a result of implementing a particular type of controlling, companies managed to increase the investment attractiveness level on average, almost 9% (maximum increase of 34% was demonstrated by IBM (Yusupova, 2008)). At second, to increase the efficiency of paperwork on average to almost 10% (the maximum increase to

27.6% was demonstrated by the company Mazda (Yusupova, 2008)). At third, it was able to increase the level of financial stability on average by more than 8% (maximal increase of 22.5% showed Corporation Cristal Gross (Yusupova, 2008)).

Indicator	The rate of growth of management efficiency	The rate of growth of efficiency of the production process
The range of values of the analyzed index	7.2–25.0	8.4–31.9
The average value of the indicator	13.25	20.53
Integral index	16.49	

* compiled by the author based on 'The Pricewaterhouse Cooper's bulletin'; (Yunusova, 2009)

Table 2 The effectiveness of the implementation of controlling system in foreign industrial companies*

Other official sources, mentioning the impact of the implementation of controlling system in foreign enterprises, are the materials of analytical Department of the state Duma of the Russian Federation for control and financial monitoring (table 3). Based on the analysis of this source, we can conclude that the level of investment attractiveness as a result of introduction at the enterprise of the controlling system increases to an average of 8.9%, the efficiency of document flow – by 9.7%, the level of financial sustainability of 8.3%.

Indicator	The rate of growth of investment attractiveness level, %	The rate of growth of efficiency of document flow, %	The rate of growth of financial stability, %
The range of values of the analyzed index	1.2–33.9	0.96–27.6	0.45–22.5
The average value of the indicator	8.9	9.7	8.3
Integral index, %		8.95	

* compiled by the author

Table 3 Dynamics of indicators of foreign industrial companies as a result of implementation of controlling

Thus, the analysis of the growth of investment attractiveness, efficiency of document flow, financial sustainability of foreign industrial companies allows us to conclude that the introduction of a particular type of controlling helps to improve the situation at the enterprise and efficiency of its activities. Moreover, despite the fact that the growth rate varies in different enterprises, dynamic of changes in all 16 analyzed companies is positive. Therefore, we can conclude that the introduction of the controlling system at the enterprises allows to increase the level of sustainability of the entity, that is especially important in the period of crisis.

There is one more mention about the relationships between the introduction of industrial enterprise system of controlling and increasing financial and technical-economic indicators in the work of Asaul A. N., Starovoytov M. K. and Faltinsky R. A. (Asaul, Starovoytov and

Faltinsky, 2009). Despite the fact that the authors consider controlling in the context of budgeting, they note that the probability of growth of sales is 20%, the probability of the growth of joint stock capital is 100%, while the probability of growth of net profit varies only at the level of 2%. Borgardt E. A. and Nosova V. M. in their work, dedicated to the establishment of a controlling system in JSC "KAMAZ", note the following results from implementing this system: "the productivity of management personnel will increase by 9.6 %, the efficiency of the decision in the average will increase by 11%, the effect of the adoption of long-term financial decisions on the basis of controlling activities will account for almost 20 %" (Borgardt and Nosova, 2014).

The implementation of the controlling system in the Airbus Group has allowed to increase the profitability of turnover in 2015 by 10% (Hubert and Falco, 2015).

4 The main results of research of the effect of the introduction of the controlling system to increase the efficiency of the enterprise

On the basis of the analysis of the works, containing a quantitative assessment of the effectiveness of implementation of controlling system in the enterprise, it is possible to make the following conclusions (table 4).

The effectiveness indicators of implementation of controlling system	The range of variation of the indicator %	The average value of the indicator, %
The rate of growth of efficiency of the decision, %	8.7–18.9	13.6
The rate of productivity growth of management personnel %	9.6–17.2	13.4
The rate of growth of the management efficiency, %	7.2–38.7	18.5
The rate of growth of solutions quality, %	18.9–43.4	34.0
The rate of growth of efficiency of the production process, %	8.4–31.9	20.5
The rate of growth of financial stability, %	0.45–22.5	8.3
The integral indicator of the effectiveness of the implementation of the controlling system, %	16.42	

* compiled by the author

Table 4 The effectiveness indicators of implementation of controlling system at the enterprise

At first, all the researchers have noted the positive dynamics of financial and economic stability and indicators of the company as a result of use of the controlling system, despite the fact that controlling in most of the works considered in a truncated version of its functionality, acting as either control and accounting, or budgeting.

At second, the implementation of controlling allows to increase the effectiveness of the decision by 8.7%–18.9%, or an average by 13.6%.

At third, there is the productivity growth of managerial personnel by 9.6%–17.2% or an average of 13.4%.

At fourth, the increase of management efficiency is 7.2%–38.7%, the average for the group of industrial enterprises is 18.5%.

At fifth, the quality of decisions increases. This increase is an average by 34.0%, with variation according to analyzed enterprise from 18.9% to 43.4%.

At sixth, the implementation of a controlling system at the industrial enterprise causes an increase in the efficiency of the production process by 8.4%–31.9%, or an average by 20.5%.

At seventh, the use of controlling system at the enterprise, even if the functionality is incomplete, has a positive effect on the overall level of its financial stability. The average increase for this indicator is 8.3%, with a range from 0.45% to 22.5%.

On the basis of generalization of the obtained results we have calculated integral indicator of the effectiveness of the implementation of controlling system at industrial enterprise, which is 16.42%.

5 Conclusion

The obtained results allow to make an unambiguous conclusion about the effectiveness of the implementation of the controlling system at the enterprise, which is especially important in the period of globalization of the economy and the growth of perturbations in the external environment. The efficiency reserves, which were identified in the course of functioning of the controlling system, can and should become a certain buffer to reduce the negative impact of environmental factors on the sustainability of the enterprise.

Besides, in our opinion a comprehensive approach to implemented controlling system in the context of both financial and economic aspects, the use of the extended functionality, which combines not only the functions of control, accounting and budgeting, but also the function of preventive control activities of the enterprise in the conditions of variable environment (Khudyakova and Shmidt, 2015), the basis of which should be the science-based simulation models, will increasingly improve the efficiency of introduction of the controlling system at the industrial enterprise, and also to reduce the probability of loss of financial and economic stability of the minieconomic system Khudyakova and Shmidt, 2015).

Acknowledgements

South Ural State University is grateful for financial support of the Ministry of Education and Science of the Russian Federation (grant No 26.9677.2017/BP).

The work was supported by Act 211 Government of the Russian Federation, contract № 02.A03.21.0011.

References

Asaul, A.N., Starovoytov, M.K. and Faltinsky, R.A. (2009). *Cost management in construction*. St. Petersburg.

Borgardt, E.A. and Nosova, V.M. (2014). 'System of controlling management as management innovation of industrial organization'. *Vestnik VSU. Series: economy and management*, 1.

Falco, S., Russell, K. and Levin, L. (2015). Controlling in Corporate management, [Online]. Available at: http://www.cfin.ru/management/controlling/controlling.shtml [cited 2016-08-01].

Hubert, T. and Falco, S.G. (2015). 'Financial controlling in the European aerospace and defense Group Airbus S.A.S.'. *Controlling*, 55.

Khudyakova, T.A. and Shmidt, A.V. (2015). 'Methodological Approach to Forecasting Financial and Economic Enterprise Stability'. *Proceedings of the 26th International Business Information Management Association Conference.*

Materials of analytical Department of the state Duma of the Russian Federation for control and financial monitoring (catalogue No. 1-0233.89 of December 5, 2004).

Necheukhina, N.S. (2010). 'The modeling of accounting events in the system of controlling in industrial enterprises'. *Doctoral thesis*. Izhevsk.

'The data of the chamber of Commerce of the Russian Federation' (2006). *The Bulletin Information*, 5.

Shmidt, A.V. and Khudyakova T.A. (2015). 'Uncertainty of External Environment during the Construction of the Controlling System of Sustainability'. *Proceedings of the 26th International Business Information Management Association Conference.*

Shmidt, A.V. and Khudyakova T.A. (2015). 'Theoretical Approaches to the Essence and Economic Sustainability Evaluation of Industrial Enterprises'. *Proceedings of The 26th International Business Information Management Association Conference.*

Syuzeva, O.V. (2010). 'Organisational and methodical provision of formation and development of controlling in industrial enterprises'. *Doctoral thesis*. Moscow.

'The Pricewaterhouse Cooper's bulletin'. (2002), 2, London.

Yunusova, D. A. (2009). 'Organizational and economic mechanism of increase of economic stability of industrial enterprise (on the example of Republic Dagestan)'. *Doctoral thesis*.

Yusupova, S.Y. (2008). 'Theory and practice of implementation of controlling system in the information society'. *Doctoral thesis*. Moscow.

Examining the interrelationships between sustainability-oriented innovation practices and organizational performance

Matjaž Maletič[1], Damjan Maletič [2], Boštjan Gomišček [3]

Abstract. The purpose of this research was to empirically analyze the contribution of sustainability-oriented innovation practices on the various organizational performance dimensions. Drawing on sustainability-oriented innovation practices and organizational performance outcomes, this paper utilizes Partial Least Squares Path Modeling (PLS-PM) to estimate both the direct and the indirect effects upon economic performance.
Data were collected based on a large-scale survey among five countries (i.e., Germany, Poland, Serbia, Slovenia and Spain). The results demonstrate that the sustainability-oriented innovation practices directly and indirectly (through quality performance, innovation performance, environmental performance and social performance) influence economic performance. This paper contributes towards filling the gap in understanding the mechanism by which sustainability-oriented innovation enhances economic performance.

Keywords: sustainability-oriented innovation, organizational performance, economic performance, PLS-PM.

JEL Classification: M1, Q5

1 Introduction

Over the last decades, the literature has increasingly emphasized the importance of integrating the sustainable development and sustainability concept into organization's business models (Hahn and Scheermesser, 2006; Lozano, 2012; Matos and Silvestre, 2013) with the focus on creating the sustainable organization which aims to act pro-actively in implementing environmental and social practices (Hart and Milstein, 2003). Similar idea has been reinforced by several authors (e.g. Van Marrewijk and Were, 2003; Jonker and Karapetrovic, 2004) indicating that the objective of a business is the creation of value and synergies between the economic, social and ecological realms of corporate performance. Whereas organizations put the effort not only on the customers, but in all of the interested parties (stakeholders), they should begin to deal with broader sustainability factors that can impact on their medium to long-term success (Fairfield et al., 2011).

Therefore, in the current highly competitive context, the question arises whether engaging in sustainability can bring an advantage to the organization. In response to this question, Azapagic (2003) elaborates that for many industry leaders and corporations, corporate sustainability has become an invaluable tool for exploring ways to reduce costs, manage risks, create new products, and drive fundamental internal changes in culture and structure. In this sense, Delai

[1] University of Maribor, Faculty of Organizational Sciences, Enterprise Engineering Laboratory, matjaz.maletic@fov.uni-mb.si.
[2] University of Maribor, Faculty of Organizational Sciences, Enterprise Engineering Laboratory, damjan.maletic@fov.uni-mb.si.
[3] University of Wollongong in Dubai, Faculty of Business, BostjanGomiscek@uowdubai.ac.ae.

and Takahashi (2013) point out that sustainable development actions and initiatives have become vital aspects for any organization.

Prior studies have empirically investigated the relationship between sustainability-oriented innovation and sustainability management (e.g. Wagner, 2008). Nevertheless, this study is different from the previous ones in terms of exploring the benefits of sustainability-oriented innovations as it considers broader aspects of the organizational performance. In this regard, Maletič et al. (2016) have provided empirical evidence concerning the effect of sustainability-oriented innovation practices on the overall organizational performance. This study advances prior findings by investigating the role of intermediate variables (i.e. non-financial performance outcomes) on the link between sustainability-oriented innovation and economic performance. The latter can improve our understanding of the mechanisms through which sustainability-oriented innovation practices affect economic performance.

Therefore, the purpose of this paper is to empirically analyze the effects of sustainability-oriented innovation practices on the overall organizational performance. Further, this paper also aims to advance understanding of the measurement of corporate sustainability practices with the focus on innovation dimensions.

The paper is structured as follows: The following chapter 2 presents the literature review. The chapter 3 explains the research methodology; the chapter 4 present the data analysis and the results; in the chapter 5 discussion of the findings is presented and finally the chapter 6 conclusions as well research implications together with limitations of the study and future research suggestions are presented.

2 Sustainable innovation and organizational performance

Recently, literature has paid attention to the sustainability-related innovation practices, predominantly through the search of the ways on how to manage product development in a more sustainable way (Hallstedt et al., 2013). As stated by Klewitz and Hansen (2014), the debate on organizations that strive to achieve the goals of sustainable development through innovation was initially focused on eco-innovations. The ultimate goal of putting efforts to eco-innovations is to provide new business opportunities and contribute to a transformation towards a sustainable society (Carrillo-Hermosilla et al., 2010).

Lately, the debate on sustainability and innovation has expanded its focus to include a wide range of themes such as sustainability-related innovation (e.g. Wagner, 2008; Klewitz and Hansen, 2014), sustainable innovation (Boons et al., 2013), and CSR-driven innovation (e.g. Hockerts et al., 2008).

Whereas management literature suggests that sustainability-related innovation can be a source of competitive advantage for organizations, empirical results are not conclusive (Lopez-Valeiras et al., 2015). Accordingly, drawn upon several recent studies (Lopez-Valeiras et al., 2015; Rahman et al., 2015; Schrettle et al., 2014), one can identify a promising avenue for future research; in particular it is suggested that further research is needed to explore the link between sustainability-oriented innovation and organizational performance. Moreover, prior studies (Wagner and Llerena, 2008) have begun to challenge the assumption of a unidirectional relationship between sustainability-oriented innovation and economic performance by introducing arguments for bidirectional causality.

An improved understanding of the link between sustainability-oriented innovation practices and organizational performance does not just contribute to a debate about the business case for sustainability (Schaltegger and Wagner, 2006), but also contributes to the knowledge of measuring sustainability-oriented innovation activities (Pujari, 2006). However, few studies have empirically investigated the specific organizational performance outcomes concerning sustainability-oriented innovation.

3 Methodology

The following section delineates the research methodology and outlines the development of measures.

3.1 Sample and data collection

This cross-sectional study is based on a questionnaire survey. The questionnaire with the cover letter signifying the purpose of the study was emailed to target respondents. It was requested that questionnaire should be directed to employees who held a managerial position in relation to strategic and operational decision-making processes. The questionnaire was responded by organizations that were located in Germany, Poland, Serbia, Slovenia and Spain, in portion of 14.7%, 21.4%, 7.5%, 43.6% and 12.8%, respectively. A sample covers various sectors, including manufacturing industry, construction industry, retail industry, water supply and waste management industry, service industry etc. A total of 266 usable responses were collected during the research time frame.

3.2 Measures

The measures of sustainability-oriented innovation practices are based on those used in previous studies on similar topics in order to ensure their content validity. Hence, the domains of construct were identified via a thorough review of the literature (e.g. Maletič et al., 2016; Pujari, 2006; Wagner and Llerena, 2008).

The scales for organizational performance dimensions were derived from Maletič et al. (2016). While recognising that performance is multi-dimensional concept (Chenhall and Langfield-Smith, 2007), we designed our survey instrument to capture the most commonly studied dimensions of organizational performance (e.g. Baird et al., 2011; Antony and Bhattacharyya, 2010; Martensen et al., 2007). The corresponding items for measuring the sustainability-oriented innovation practices and organizational performance are presented in Appendix 1 and Appendix 2.

4 Results

The following section outlines the survey results. The section, therefore, presents the validity results of the measurement model and illustrates the findings regarding the structural model assessment.

4.1 Measurement Model Assessment

In order to assess the PLS-PM measurement model (outer model), loadings and communalities were checked. Principally, the loadings represent the correlations between a latent variable and its indicators. Furthermore, communalities are squared correlations and they measure the part of the variance between a latent variable and its indicator that is common to both (Sanchez, 2013). As suggested by Sanchez (2013) loadings should be above the value of 0.7. The outer model assessment results (loadings, weights and communalities) for studied constructs are presented in Appendix 1 and 2. As shown by the results, the measurement model appears to be acceptable with the majority of loadings above threshold criterion of 0.7. Additionally, cross-loadings were also checked to ensure validity of the model.

Regarding the block unidimensionality the following indices were used: Cronbach's alpha, Dillon-Goldstein's rho and eigenvalues (Table 1). The purpose of the Cronbach's alpha is to evaluate how well a block of indicators measure their corresponding latent construct (Sanchez, 2013). As shown by the results, the Cronbach's alpha values for each block of indicators (i.e. latent variable) were above the recommended value of 0.70 (Sanchez, 2013; Hair et al., 2010). Furthermore, composite reliability was assessed by Dillon-Goldstein's rho. According to the Sanchez (2013) the value of 0.7 and above suggests that the corresponding block is considered as unidimensional. The results show that the Dillon-Goldstein's rho values for all the constructs are above the cut-off point of 0.7. Additionally, eigenvalues were checked to assess the unidimensionality. The block is considered as unidimensional if the first eigenvalue is larger than 1.

	Mode	MVs	Cronbach's alpha	Dillon-Goldstein's rho	eig.1st	eig.2nd
SOICD (LV1)	A	6	0.907	0.929	4.11	0.640
SOPPD (LV2)	A	7	0.899	0.921	4.37	0.678
Quality performance (LV3)	A	4	0.806	0.873	2.53	0.673
Innovation performance (LV4)	A	3	0.806	0.886	2.16	0.434
Environmental performance (LV5)	A	4	0.740	0.837	2.25	0.697
Social performance (LV6)	A	4	0.717	0.827	2.21	0.838
Economic performance (LV7)	A	4	0.789	0.865	2.47	0.702

Note. MVs - manifest variables (no. of items). A – reflective mode. SOICD - sustainability-oriented innovation competencies deployment. SOPPD - sustainability-oriented process and product deployment.

Table 1 Summary of the results regarding the block unidimensionality

4.2 Structural Model Assessment

The results regarding the assessment of the structural (inner) model are presented in Table 2. Initially, coefficients of determination (R^2) of the endogenous latent variables are checked. For instance, the results indicate that 57.1 % of the variance in the "sustainability-oriented process and product deployment (SOPPD)" is explained by "sustainability-oriented innovation competencies deployment (SOICD)". Moreover, results suggest that 61.5 % of the variance in "Economic performance (LV7)" is explained by its independent variables.

	Type	R^2	Block Communality	Mean Redundancy	AVE
SOICD (LV1)	Exogenous	0.000	0.685	0.000	0.685
SOPPD (LV2)	Endogenous	0.571	0.624	0.356	0.624
Quality performance (LV3)	Endogenous	0.160	0.632	0.101	0.632
Innovation performance (LV4)	Endogenous	0.172	0.721	0.124	0.721
Environmental performance (LV5)	Endogenous	0.179	0.562	0.101	0.562
Social performance (LV6)	Endogenous	0.196	0.544	0.107	0.544
Economic performance (LV7)	Endogenous	0.309	0.615	0.190	0.615

Note. AVE - Average Variance Extracted. SOICD - sustainability-oriented innovation competencies deployment. SOPPD - sustainability-oriented process and product deployment.

Table 2 Summary of the results regarding the inner model assessment

Furthermore, average communality representing the average of all the squared correlations between each manifest variable and the corresponding latent variable scores in the model (Esposito Vinzi et al., 2010) are also show in Table 1. It appears that that the highest value corresponds to the "Innovation performance (LV4)", while the lowest value corresponds to the "Social performance (LV6)".

Mean redundancy characterizes the percentage of the variance in the endogenous block that is predicted from the independent latent variables. High redundancy emphasizes the ability to predict. For instance, "SOICD (LV1)" predicts 35.6 % of the variability of indicators of "SOPPD (LV2)" block.

Furthermore, convergent validity is defined as the extent to which the measurement items converge into a theoretical construct (Hair et al., 2010). For this purpose, the average variance extracted (AVE) was considered to measure the amount of variance that a latent variable captures from its indicators in relation to the amount of variance due to measurement error (Sanchez, 2013). The results indicate that AVE values for all blocks (i.e. latent variables) are above the conventional threshold of 0.5 (Sanchez, 2013).

Path analysis was further conducted to test the relationships among latent variables. The results regarding the inner model are presented in Table 3 and Figure 1. Generally, path coefficients are representing the strength and direction of the relations between the latent variables. According to the results, "SOICD (LV1)" has a strong effect on "SOPPD (LV2)" (0.7555). Moreover, "Organizational sustainability foundation (LV1)" also positively and directly affects the non-financial performance variables, namely "Quality performance (LV3)" (0.2457), "Innovation performance (LV4)" (0.1350) and "Social performance (LV6)" (0.2471). Considering the "SOPPD (LV2)", it can be seen that the strongest effect is on "Environmental performance (LV5)" (0.4229), while the lowest effect is on "Quality performance (LV3)" (0.1799).

Relationship	Direct effect	Indirect effect	Total
LV1 → LV2	0.7555	0.000	0.7555
LV1 → LV3	0.2457	0.136	0.3816
LV1 → LV4	0.1350	0.229	0.3641
LV1 → LV5	0.0000	0.319	0.3195
LV1 → LV6	0.2471	0.170	0.4173

LV1 → LV7	0.0000	0.261	0.2606
LV2 → LV3	0.1799	0.000	0.1799
LV2 → LV4	0.3032	0.000	0.3032
LV2 → LV5	0.4229	0.000	0.4229
LV2 → LV6	0.2252	0.000	0.2252
LV2 → LV7	0.0000	0.204	0.2042
LV3 → LV7	0.0916	0.000	0.0916
LV4 → LV7	0.3744	0.000	0.3744
LV5 → LV7	0.1037	0.000	0.1037
LV6 → LV7	0.1347	0.000	0.1347

Table 3 Path coefficients

Given the indirect effect, it can be emphasized that "OSOICD (LV1)" indirectly through "Quality performance (LV3)", "Innovation performance (LV4)" and "Social performance (LV6)" affects "Economic performance (LV7)". Furthermore, "SOPPD (LV2)" also indirectly affects "Economic performance (LV7)". Among the non-financial performance outcomes, "Innovation performance (LV4)" is considered as the most significant predictor of "Economic performance (LV7)".

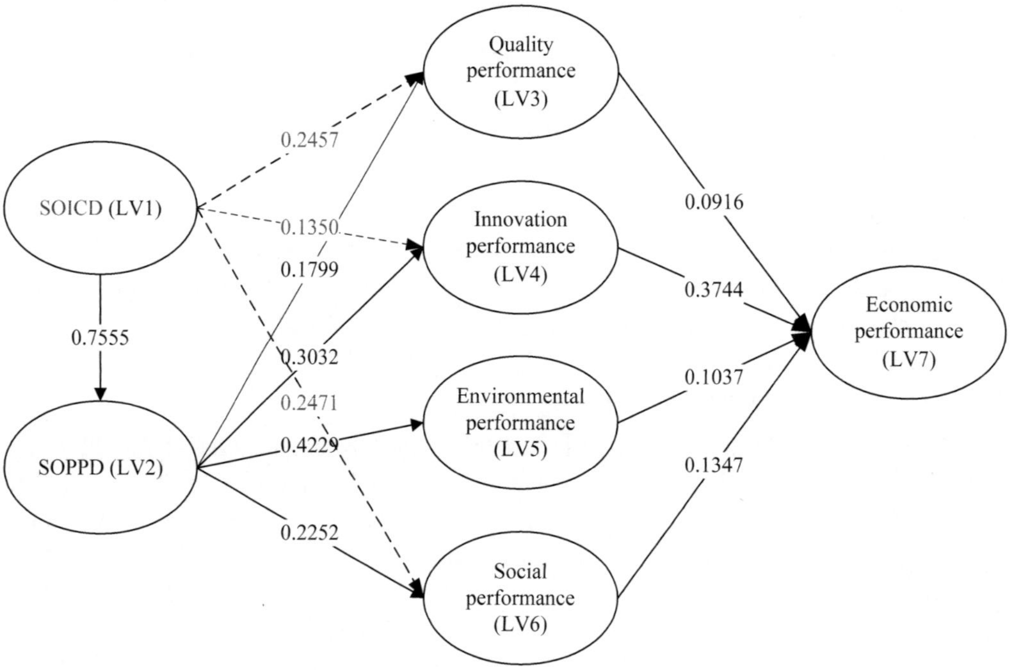

Figure 1 Inner model with path coefficients

5 Discussion

Debates relating to corporate sustainability are becoming important subjects of the wide range of management literature in this century (Asif et al., 2011). Although researchers have widely discussed the relevant issues of sustainability-oriented innovation (e.g. Wagner, 2008; Klewitz and Hansen, 2014), there is a lack of empirical evidence on the relationship between these activities and overall organizational performance. To fill this existing research gap, this study proposes a novel construct – sustainability-oriented innovation practices - and develops a research framework to further discuss the effect of these practices on the organizational performance.

Furthermore, our study underscores previous assertions that organizations can benefit from pursuing sustainability (e.g. Schaltegger and Wagner, 2006). The results of the regression analysis have confirmed the premise that sustainability practices positively influence the organizational performance. As such, the study provides empirical evidence indicating that organization can benefit by obtaining and deploying sustainability-oriented innovation practices. In particular, the results of this study suggest that organizational learning in terms of developing new sustainability-oriented innovation competencies can provide superior performance benefits to the organization. Indeed, several prior studies have suggested that organizational learning with regard to innovation can contribute positively to the sustainability (e.g. Lozano, 2014; Siebenhuner and Anold, 2007). In this regard we can argue that developing capabilities and, therefore, acquiring the intangible assets, is essential for future growth and it is needed to successfully integrate and embed the sustainability in every aspect of the organization.

Furthermore, the results of this study indicate that organizations can benefit from integrating sustainability aspects in their products and processes, as reflected by the positive and significant effect of SOPPD on the organizational performance. These findings are somewhat supporting the argument that incorporating sustainability activities in product and process development can provide tools and mechanisms to organizations to enhance their economic benefits without affecting environment and communities (Pujari, 2006; Schrettle et al., 2014). In this regard, stakeholder dialogue and stakeholder knowledge integration can be regarded as the capabilities necessary to capture stakeholder's requirements and transform them into innovative solutions (i.e. products, services, processes or strategies) (Ayuso et al., 2006). Moreover, recent study (Hahn, 2015) provided deepen understanding of this matter in terms of reciprocal stakeholder behaviour that aims to provide an explanation of why and under which conditions it makes good economic sense for companies to act proactively and beyond legal requirements.

Therefore, our study leads us to suggest that organizations should built sustainability aspects into tangible and intangible product/process quality characteristics, through a constant focus on stakeholders' wants and needs, and on the basis of principles of continuous improvement. However, one can argue that organizations are confronted with creating value by identifying an overlap between customer benefits and clearly defined (prioritized) sustainability goals, i.e., translating sustainability goals into product features that contribute to the customer value (Keskin et al., 2013). Owing to the above-explained complexities in managing sustainability, recent studies (e.g. Kuei and Lu, 2013) emphasize the integration of (total) quality management and sustainability, thereby enhancing the value and competitive position of organizations as well as contributing to the sustainable development. The latter also brings the debate on the relationship between integrated (total) management systems and sustainable development to the forefront (Mežinska et al., 2015).

6 Conclusion

This study contributes to the field of corporate sustainability management practice & implication by applying a PLS-PM based research on the relationship between sustainability-oriented innovation practices and organizational performance. Seen in this context, the main theoretical contribution of this study is reflected through the proposal of a novel construct – sustainability-oriented innovation practices - and the successful verification of the effect of these practices on the organizational performance by using the PLS-PM based study. This is significant because so far there are only a few empirically based studies that investigate sustainability-related innovations and its performance implications. In this regard, this work can contribute to a better understanding of the underlying dimensions of sustainability-oriented innovation and its relationship with the overall organizational performance.

As with all empirical studies, there are a number of limitations and directions for future research. First, the scales that were used to measure the construct 'sustainability-oriented innovation practices' capture only limited dimensions of innovation-related themes. Future research needs to examine the usefulness of additional measures. Secondly, future studies could improve the homogeneity of the sample to avoid potential bias in sampling as well as to further contribute to the generalization of the results.

References

Antony, J.P. and Bhattacharyya, S. (2010). 'Measuring organizational performance and organizational excellence of SMEs – Part 1: a conceptual framework'. *Measuring Business Excellence*, 14 (2), pp. 3-11.

Asif, M., Searcy, C., Zutshi, A. and Ahmad, N. (2011). 'An integrated management systems approach to corporate sustainability'. *European Business Review*, 23 (4), p.p. 353-367.

Azapagic, A. (2003). 'Systems approach to corporate sustainability. A general management framework'. *Process Safety and Environmental Protection*, 81 (5), pp. 303-316.

Ayuso, S., Rodríguez, M. A. and Ricartm, J. E. (2006). 'Responsible competitiveness at the 'micro' level of the firm. Using stakeholder dialogue as a source for new ideas: a dynamic capability underlying sustainable innovation'. *Corporate Governance*, 6 (4), pp. 475–490.

Baird, K., Hu, K.J. and Reeve, R. (2011). 'The relationships between organizational culture, total quality management practices and operational performance'. *International Journal of Operations & Production Management*, 31 (7), pp. 789-814.

Boons, F., Montalvo, C., Quist, J. and Wagner, M. (2013). 'Sustainable innovation, business models and economic performance: an overview'. *Journal of Cleaner Production*, 45, pp. 1-8.

Carrillo-Hermosilla, J., Río, P. and Könnölä, T. (2010). 'Diversity of eco-innovations: Reflections from selected case studies'. *Journal of Cleaner Production*, 18, pp. 1073-1083.

Chenhall, R. H. and Langfield-Smith, K. (2007). 'Multiple perspectives of performance measures'. *European Management Journal*, 25 (4), pp. 266–282.

Delai, I. and Takahashi, S. (2013). 'Corporate sustainability in emerging markets: insights from the practices reported by the Brazilian retailers'. *Journal of Cleaner Production*, 47, pp. 211-221.

Esposito Vinzi, V., Trinchera, L. and Amato, S. (2010). 'PLS path modeling: from foundations to recent developments and open issues for model assessment and improvement'. *Handbook of Partial Least*

Squares: Concepts, Methods, and Applications, Computational Statistics (vol. II), Springer, pp. 47–82.

Fairfield, K.D., Harmon, J. and Behson, S.J. (2011). 'Influences on the organizational implementation of sustainability: an integrative model'. *Organization Management Journal*, 8 (1), pp. 4–20.

Hahn, T. (2015). 'Reciprocal Stakeholder Behavior: A Motive-Based Approach to the Implementation of Normative Stakeholder Demands'. *Business & Society*, 54, pp. 9–51.

Hahn, T. and Scheermesser, M. (2006). 'Approaches to Corporate Sustainability among German Companies'. *Corporate Social Responsibility and Environmental Management*, 13, pp. 150–165.

Hair, J.F.Jr., Black, W.C., Babin, B.J. and Anderson, R.E. (2010). *Multivariate Data Analysis,* 7th ed., London: Pearson Prentice Hall.

Hallstedt, S.I., Thompson, A.W. and Lindahl, P. (2013). 'Key elements for implementing a strategic sustainability perspective in the product innovation process'. *Journal of Cleaner Production*, 51, pp. 277-288.

Hart, S.L. and Milstein, M.B. (2003). 'Creating sustainable value'. *Academy of Management Executive*, 17 (2), pp. 56-69.

Hockerts, K., Morsing, M., Eder-Hansen, J., Krull, P., Midttun, A., Halme, M. and Nurmi, P. (2008). CSR-driven innovation: Towards the social purpose business. Frederiksberg: Center for Corporate Social Responsibility, CBS, [Online]. Available at: http://samfundsansvar.dk/file/318859/csr_driven_innovation_towards_social_purpose_business_september_2008.pdf [cited 2017-01-17].

Jonker, J. and Karapetrovic, S. (2004). 'Systems thinking for the integration of management systems'. *Business Process Management Journal*, 10 (6), pp. 608-615.

Keskin, D., Diehl, J. C. and Molenaar, N. (2013). 'Innovation process of new ventures driven by sustainability'. *Journal of Cleaner Production*, 45, pp. 50–60.

Klewitz, J. and Hansen, E. G. (2014). 'Sustainability-oriented innovation of SMEs: A systematic review'. *Journal of Cleaner Production*, 65, pp. 57-75.

Kuei, C.H. and Lu, M.H. (2013). 'Integrating quality management principles into sustainability management'. *Total Quality Management & Business Excellence*, 24 (1-2), pp. 62-78.

Lopez-Valeiras, E., Gomez-Conde, J. and Naranjo-Gil, D. (2015). 'Sustainable Innovation, Management Accounting and Control Systems, and International Performance'. *Sustainability*, 7, pp. 3479-3492.

Lozano, R. (2012). 'Towards better embedding sustainability into companies' systems: an analysis of voluntary corporate initiatives'. *Journal of Cleaner Production*, 25, pp. 14-26.

Lozano, R. (2014). 'Creativity and Organizational Learning as Means to Foster Sustainability'. *Sustainable Development*, 22 (3), pp. 205-216.

Maletič, M., Maletič, D., Dahlgaard, J.J., Dahlgaard-Park, S.M. and Gomišček, B. (2016). 'Effect of sustainability-oriented innovation practices on the overall organisational performance: an empirical examination'. *Total Quality Management & Business Excellence*, 27 (10), pp. 1171–1190.

Martensen, A., Dahlgaard, J.J., Park-Dahlgaard, S.M. and Grønholdt, L. (2007). 'Measuring and diagnosing innovation excellence – simple contra advanced approaches: a Danish study'. *Measuring Business Excellence*, 11 (4), pp. 51-65.

Matos, S. and Silvestre, B.S. (2013). 'Managing stakeholder relations when developing sustainable business models: the case of the Brazilian energy sector'. *Journal of Cleaner Production*, 45, pp. 61-73.

Mežinska, I., Lapiņa, I. and Mazais, J. (2015). 'Integrated management systems towards sustainable and socially responsible organisation'. *Total Quality Management & Business Excellence*, 26 (5-6), pp. 469-481.

Pujari, D. (2006). 'Eco-innovation and new product development: Understanding the influences on market performance'. *Technovation*, 26, pp. 76–85.

Sanchez, G. (2013). *PLS Path Modeling with R*, Trowchez Editions. Berkeley, [Online]. Available at: http://www.gastonsanchez.com/PLS Path Modeling with R.pdf [cited 2016-12-10].

Schaltegger, S. and Wagner, M. (2006). 'Managing and measuring the business case for sustainability: Capturing the relationship between sustainability performance, business competitiveness and economic performance'. *Managing the business case for sustainability: The integration of social, environmental and economic performance (pp. 1–27)*. Sheffield: Greenleaf.

Schrettle, S., Hinz, A., Scherrer-Rathje, M. and Friedli, T. (2014). 'Turning sustainability into action: Explaining firms' sustainability efforts and their impact on firm performance'. *International Journal of Production Economics*, 147, pp. 73–84.

Siebenhuner, B. and Anold, M. (2007). 'Organizational learning to manage sustainable Development'. *Business Strategy and the Environment*, 16, pp. 339–353.

Van Marrewijk, M. and Were, M. (2003). 'Multiple levels of corporate sustainability'. *Journal of Business Ethics*, 44, pp. 107-19.

Wagner, M. (2008). Links between sustainability-related innovation and sustainability management. SFB 649 Discussion Paper 2008–046. Berlin: Technische Universität München, [Online]. Available at: http://sfb649.wiwi.hu-berlin.de/papers/pdf/SFB649DP2008–046.pdf [cited 2016-04-13].

Wagner, M. and Llerena, P. (2008). 'Drivers for sustainability-related innovation: A Qualitative analysis of renewable resources, industrial products and travel services'. *Working Paper*. Strasbourg, France.

Appendix 1 – Questionnaire items and outer model assessment statistics for sustainability practices

	weight	loading	communality	redundancy
SOICD - sustainability-oriented innovation competencies deployment (LV1)				
The organization upgrades employees' current knowledge and skills based on examples of best practices in corporate social responsibility	0.199	0.851	0.724	0.0000
The organization continuously strengthens employees' knowledge and skills to improve efficiency of current sustainability practices	0.212	0.865	0.748	0.0000
We develop new competencies supporting innovation in the organization	0.189	0.804	0.647	0.0000
We continuously try to strengthen innovation skills in key areas where we have no prior experiences	0.191	0.803	0.644	0.0000
The organization is characterised by a learning culture stimulating innovation for sustainability	0.228	0.887	0.787	0.0000
We search for external sources (e.g. partners, customers, research institutions) of knowledge in our search for innovative ideas related to sustainability	0.187	0.749	0.560	0.0000
SOPPD - sustainability-oriented process and product deployment (LV2)				
We acquire innovative environmental-friendly technologies and processes	0.181	0.746	0.556	0.3175
The organization undertakes regularly business process reengineering with a focus on green perspectives	0.200	0.836	0.699	0.3990

The organization integrates social aspects (e.g. health and safety aspects of employees and customers, fair operating practices) into product/service design	0.183	0.753	0.567	0.3235
Multiple departments (such as marketing, manufacturing, and purchasing) are working together on sustainability related initiatives	0.170	0.779	0.607	0.3466
We consider sustainability as an opportunity for product/service differentiation	0.180	0.790	0.623	0.3559
Preliminary market assessments are made to obtain customers' view of green product ideas	0.167	0.788	0.621	0.3545
The organization makes improvements to radically reduce environmental impacts of products and services' life-cycles	0.185	0.835	0.697	0.3977

Appendix 2 – Questionnaire items and outer model assessment statistics for organizational performance dimensions

	weight	loading	communality	redundancy
Quality performance (LV3)				
The quality of our products and services has been improved during the last 3 years	0.352	0.828	0.685	0.1093
Customer satisfaction has increased during the last 3 years	0.333	0.842	0.708	0.1130
Customer complaints has decreased during the last 3 years	0.284	0.776	0.603	0.0961
The cost of poor quality has decreased during the last 3 years	0.284	0.730	0.533	0.0851
Innovation performance (LV4)				
The organization has introduced more innovative products and services than our main competitors during the last 3 years	0.358	0.828	0.686	0.1180
The number of innovations that provide the organization with a sustainable competitive advantage has increased during the last 3 years	0.413	0.859	0.738	0.1269
The speed of adoption of new technology is faster than at our main competitors	0.406	0.859	0.738	0.1270
Environmental performance (LV5)				
The efficiency of the consumption of raw materials has improved during the last 3 years	0.302	0.740	0.547	0.0979
The resource consumption (thermal energy, electricity, water) has decreased (e.g. per unit of income, per unit of production, ...) during the last 3 years	0.376	0.804	0.646	0.1156
The percentage of recycled materials has increased during the last 3 years	0.340	0.711	0.505	0.0903
The waste ratio (e.g. kg per unit of product, kg per employee per year) has decreased during the last 3 years	0.313	0.742	0.551	0.0985
Social performance (LV6)				
Health and safety performance has improved during the last 3 years	0.366	0.626	0.392	0.0767
The turnover ratio has decreased during the last 3 years	0.229	0.637	0.406	0.0796
The employees' satisfaction has increased during the last 3 years	0.322	0.826	0.682	0.1335
The employees' motivation has increased during the last 3 years	0.431	0.835	0.697	0.1365
Economic performance (LV7)				
Return on investment (ROI) has increased above industry average during the last 3 years	0.274	0.694	0.482	0.1489
Sales growth has increased above industry average during the last 3 years	0.340	0.833	0.694	0.2142

Profit growth rate has increased above industry average during the last 3 years	0.309	0.845	0.714	0.2204
Market share has increased during the last 3 years	0.352	0.755	0.571	0.1763

Ownership's character as a factor determining perception of communication media in the gender context

Lucja Matusiková[1]

Abstract. In present time, the media significantly influence the events of everyday life. The nature of their ownership, i.e. their public or private character, may be an important factor when perceiving individual media. Main aim of this paper is to find out what is the opinion of the respondents towards the media, especially in the area of their credibility. In addition, there is an effort to determine whether the respondents prefer a certain type of media and which type it is. Subsequently, these re-search activities were focused on the fact whether the mentioned character of the medium ownership in respondents has the impact on its perceiving, whether this perception is also influenced by the gender division. The research was focused on the so-called Generation Z. The Chi-square test of independence served to confirm or reject the established hypotheses. Social media were not included in the currently conducted research, so that we could compare the research projects carried out with the benefit of hindsight.

Keywords: Mass media, public, private, gender, generation Z.

JEL Classification: D70, J16

1 Introduction

Marketing communication is carried out via a lot of channels. Media are one of the possibilities how to address potential customers. The effect of advertising impulses of broadcast media, i.e. communication media, depends on a lot of factors. They include for example their credibility. And right the media credibility in the context of their ownership character became the essential research artefact. With respect to the fact that a clear specification of private and public media may be implemented only in the case of television and radio media, the results of the research activities will be intended right and only for them.

2 Definition of Basic Terms

For the purposes of a correct interpretation of achieved results, we need to approach at least in basic dimensions the main notions that we will subsequently work with. Only the facts that are essential and more closely specifying or explaining individual concepts will be included.

2.1 Media

The Dictionary of Foreign Words (Linhart, 2008, p. 241) defines the notion Medium as "a mediation agent, environment, also as person arranging spiritistic information and, last but not least, as mass (collective) media printed (newspapers, magazines) as well as electronic (radio, television), mass medium".

The word medium is similarly characterized also by other authors (Jirák, Köpplová, 2003, p. 16), who state that "it is of the Latin origin and means a mediator, intermediating agent, that

[1]VSB-TU Ostrava, Departmant of Management, Sokolská 33, 701 21 Ostrava, lucja.matusikova@vsb.cz.

is anything that mediates, arranges something". Subsequently, the authors develop this idea with the fact that "the branches that deal with different manifestations of interpersonal, social communication mark the notion medium/media as something that mediates some information for somebody that is the communication medium".

An analogical characteristic may be also found with other authors (Reifová, 2004, p. 139) with that in this version the medium "does not have exactly and generally accepted borders". The medium is presented here as a direct individual means of communication as well as as labelling a technical means of communication. On the one hand, we encounter such characteristics as facial expressions, gestures or speech and, on the other hand, the computer network, cable television, etc. (Urban, Dubský, Murdza, 2011).

The notion mass media, whose content is more specific, forms a separate chapter. "Mass media mean means of communication and institutions that are able to produce in the large scale public notification and distribute it towards the scattered, varied and individually unidentified public." (Urban, Dubský, Murdza, 2011, p. 48)

2.2 Public and Private Media

In the Czech Republic, following the European model, at the beginning of the 1990s, the so-called dual system of television and radio broadcasting was elected, that is the co-existence of the public and private sectors. Concurrently, the rights and obligations of the radio and television broadcasting operators, licence procedures and registration of the operators of the taken-over broadcasting were determined. This state is regulated by Act No. 231/2001 Coll., on Operating Radio and Television Broadcasting, as amended.

Yet, talking about public broadcasting, we mean the Czech Television Company and the Czech Radio Company. These institutions operate on the media market on the basis of separate laws. It is Act No. 483/1991 Coll., on the Czech Television Company and Act No. 484/1991 Coll., on the Czech Radio Company, always as amended. The public character of financing these institutions is implemented by Act No. 348/2005 Coll., on Radio and Television Charges, as amended.

"The Czech Television Company and the Czech Radio Company are broadcasting operators by law with specific tasks of the public service. Both the operators are independent of the state, they do not receive any state subsidies and their activity is financed by the income from radio and television charges and the income from their own business activity (above all, it is the sales of advertising time as well as the revenues from copyrights, leases of equipment, etc.)" (The Ministry of Culture, 2012, [online]). The Czech Television Company and the Czech Radio Company fulfil their service for the public via own production and co-production and also by television and radio broadcasting and other services. Regarding the question of funding the Czech Television Company and the Czech Radio Company, the idea of financial security via the state budget was originally discussed. Yet, this idea was abandoned in connection with a threat of weakening the independence of the relevant medium of the state (Jirák, Köpplová, 2003).

2.3 Generation

According to the Dictionary of Foreign Words, the notion "generation" (Linhart a kol., 2008, p. 132) has a number of meanings. The generation is characterized first, that is a set of people born and living approximately at the same time. A generation sometimes means descendants of one pair of parents. The third semantic unit makes it possible to identify a generation as a specific set of concurrently living individuals of the same kind. A generation also means a membership of the type of technical equipment of a certain development stage.

From the viewpoint of perceiving communication media, we undoubtedly need to identify basic grounds that have had the impact on this age group of inhabitants, above all, from the sociological viewpoint. According to the Australian study of the labour market from 2007 (Bohutinská, 2008, [online]), currently, we may specify the following generationally differentiated groups of population:

- Born before 1946 = Pre Boomers
- Born from 1947 to1960 = Baby Boomers
- Born from 1961 to1975 = Generation X
- Born between 1976 and 1990 = Generation Y
- Born between 1995 and 2020 = Generation Z

For the purposes of presenting the results of the present research, only one generation cohort is specified in detail, that is Generation Z.

Born between 1991-2005 are marked as Generation Z (GZ). As the Grail Research study states (Grail Research a Division of Integreon, 2011), the GZ representatives include young people whose date of birth is usually determined by the middle 1990s and year 2010, whereas it should be noted that different studies e.g. Howe, Strauss (1991) freely work with this time factor, when they include the GZ into the period from 2000 to the present time.

With respect to the method of communication (they are constantly on-line via their mobile phones, they share a lot of information via You Tube etc.) and the ability of both the intensive and extensive use of the state-of-the-art technologies, they are also called the so-called "Digital Natives". Their relation to technologies may be even characterized as a certain form of addiction. They seek more and more sophisticated devices and appreciate particularly their simple and interactive design.

In spite of their currently low age in most cases, they appear to be socially more responsible than their predecessors. Owing to the sufficient amount of available information, far more intensively they are aware of the current problems, such as terrorism or climate changes.

If we summaries all the mentioned above, we may observe that the GZ is constantly on-line via a number of social networks and their decision-making processes are in many areas influenced by the ability to obtain information across the countries, cultures as well as religions.

3 Description of Used Methods

Inquiry is the most common form of receiving information from respondents. At the present time, the Internet and related social networks help this method. Currently, obtaining data is not a fundamental problem. What remains a problem is their processing, in particular, the assessment of set hypotheses using appropriate statistical methods.

3.1 Testing hypothesis

At this point it should be emphasized (Matusiková, Kashi and Zelinková, 2016) that in terms of practical application of statistical methods in analyzing empirical data, statistical hypothesis testing represents one of the most important parts of all. One of the basic statistic methods for the assessment of set hypotheses, is the Chi-square test of independence. The test is most often performed in MS Excel via the statistical function CHITEST.

The role of hypothesis testing is to decide about the basis of information obtained from random samples, whether we accept or reject a particular hypothesis concerning the master sample. The statistical hypothesis (Marek et al., 2007) can be understood as any statement that may involve unknown parameters, set functions of the parameters, but also the shape of the distributions and other characteristics of the master sample. A decision rule by which we assign a decision on the validity or invalidity of the hypothesis is called a statistical test.

The first step in statistical testing is always a statistical hypothesis formulation, i.e. a formulation of a research question in the experiment in the form of a zero and alternative statistical hypothesis, which are asked when testing against each other.

The second step in testing statistical hypotheses consists in determining a significance level of the test (error α selected by an expert), which is the probability that the null hypothesis will be rejected, although it is valid. We should be aware of the fact that the tested hypothesis is always accepted or rejected based on the results of the random selection and therefore, the rejection as well as the non-rejection of the H0 hypothesis can be correct, but also incorrect. As Table 1 shows, in general, we can commit one of two errors (Řezánková, 2011).

Test conclusion	**Reality** **H_0 is applicable**	**Reality** **H_0 is not applicable**
H_0 **will be accepted**	Correct decision	Error of type II
H_0 **will be rejected**	Error of type I	Correct decision

Table 1 Error of type I and II

The error of type I means the probability that the valid null hypothesis will be rejected, whereas the null hypothesis indicates that the model is accurate. The error of type II expresses the probability that the invalid null hypothesis will be accepted, which means that the inaccurate model will be accepted as accurate. There is an opposite relation between the error of type I and II. If the error of type I is minimized, the error of type II increases and vice versa. It should be noted that the adoption of the inaccurate model, the error of type II, is much worse than the rejection of the accurate model, the error of type I, it is better to be exposed to a higher error of the type I, thereby the error of type II will decrease.

The formulation of the test conclusion is the last step in statistical hypotheses testing, which can be done in two ways that is by comparing the calculated testing criterion with a critical value, which is determined in dependence on the selected significance level α. The p -value is used in statistical testing of the suitability of the model using different software. The P-value expresses the probability of rejecting the true null hypothesis and the error of type I. If p -value is less than the significance level α (α error), the null hypothesis H0 will be rejected. Symbolically, a conclusion can be used:

$p < 0.05$ statistically significant difference,

$p < 0.01$ statistically highly significant difference.

3.2 Concept of the Research, Determination of Objectives and Hypotheses

The research activities are part of the centrally organized research projects of the universities and individual faculties as well as the lecturers' individual activities. One of them is the research whose results are presented here.

Research objectives and hypotheses

The research set not only one but several objectives. They particularly concerned the efforts to:

- ascertain how often the respondents follow the surrounding events in media;
- determine whether the respondents prefer a certain type of media and which type;
- determine whether the nature of the ownership is a factor that has impact on media credibility.

For the purposes of the research to preserve unambiguousness of terms, two types of media were used, namely radio and television. There we could compare the impact of the ownership on the medium perception. Therefore, ČT1, ČT2 and ČT24 television stations represent public media. Concerning radio stations, they are Radiožurnál, Praha and Vltava. All remaining television and radio stations are private. In their responses, the respondents were also offered a possibility to supplement additional radio and television stations that they follow. Such media as the internet, social networks and others were disregarded.

In this connection the following hypotheses were determined:

1) H_0 Within the particular sample, the respondents' gender does not have impact on their responses.
2) H_1 The respondents' gender have impact on their responses within the particular sample.

From the methodological viewpoint, it was proceeded from theory to practice, from general to specific. Retrospectively, the knowledge obtained in the primary and secondary research is applied in the theoretical grounds.

During the research and evaluation activities, the methods of analysis, synthesis, induction, deduction and comparison were also used. The Chi-square test of independence in the contingency table will be used to confirm or reject the established hypotheses. The test was carried out in MS Excel via the statistical function CHITEST. Significance level is 5 %.

4 Results and Discussion of Perception of the Communication Medium in the Context of the Nature of its Ownership

At the Economic Faculty of VŠB – Technical University of Ostrava, a number of research activities are being continuously conducted within a wide spectrum of majors and also across these majors.

Yet, the original intention to carry out the project via the method of random sampling (the quota selection for the purposes of ensuring objectiveness) could not be implemented. Since the pilot project of the research showed that as far as media are concerned, the potential respondents are either too open and they are not willing to answer questions but on the contrary they raise questions themselves on the assumption that they will receive a satisfactory answer to them, or they will only wave it off with resignation and reject to continue in cooperation. In such a case, we needed to be satisfied with a much smaller sample and also with a sample of respondents that really wanted to answer the questions. Eventually, we conducted the re-search by a questionnaire enquiry. This way, we managed to receive 250 questionnaires. After checking their completeness, out of them we used 214 for further processing. The research was carried out in the streets of the city of Ostrava during February and September 2016.

4.1 Perception of the Communication Medium in the Context of the Nature of its Ownership in Practice

The questionnaires were completed by the respondents via standardized anonymous face-to-face dialogues with the respondents in public. After the experience from the pilot part of the project, the enquirers were instructed to address the individuals, when the willingness to answer and the year of birth (1995 and more) were the decisive criteria for addressing respondents. The completed questionnaires were subjected to the optic inspection, subsequently they were rewritten into the data matrices in MS Excel and processed with the use of MS Excel.
Target Group Identification

A total of 214 duly completed questionnaires from amongst the GZ representatives were received. The numerical representation of the enquired within genders in the form of the absolute value (hereinafter only A) and the percentage value (hereinafter only %) is shown in Table 2.

GZ	Male	Female	Total
A	96	118	107
%	45	55	100

Table 2 Division of Respondents according to Gender

In spite of the fact that due to a low number in individual categories the educational factor was not taken into account as an identification element, Table 3 shows the structure of the respondents' education. The structure of the respondents is undoubtedly affected by the time when the project was implemented. In the morning, more university students may be seen in the city centre when compared to secondary school students or apprentices or primary school pupils.

Education	Male	Female	Total A	Total %
Basic	4	4	8	4
Secondary vocational without school-leaving exam		6	6	6
Complete secondary sith school-leaving exam	92	108	200	93

Table 3 Respondents Distribution by Education

The residence or the region in which the respondents live became the third identification factor. Also several respondents from Slovakia were included into this category. The results are shown in Table 4.

Residence – Region	Male	Female	Total A	Total %
Ostrava	70	70	140	65
Olomouc	6	12	18	8
Brno	2	4	6	3
Pardubice	1	4	5	2
Hradec Královė	2	4	6	3
Zlín	2	16	18	8
Slovakia	14	8	22	10

Table 4 Respondents Distribution by Residence

Also the respondents' structure from the viewpoint of their residence reflects to a large extent the structure of the inhabitants or visitors of the city of Ostrava.

Questionnaire Enquiry Results of the GZ Sample

Within the research, a total of 8 questions of a different type were raised. The first two were of a closed character and the respondents needed to decide unambiguously for one of the options, which are shown in Table 5. The wording of the questions was as follows:

1) Do you follow the surrounding events in media, for example the television, newspaper, radio (circle one response only)?
2) Do you think that media provides true information?

Question No. 1	AM	AF	%M	%F	Question No. 2	AM	AF	%M	%F
Daily	46	46	48	39	**Yes**	12	44	12	37
Several times a week	14	44	15	37	**No**	68	52	71	44
From time to time	26	26	27	22	**I do not know**	16	22	17	19
I do not follow	10	2	10	2					
***p*-value**	0.0768		7.7		***p*-value**	0.0163		1.6	

Table 5 Frequency of Following Media and Confidence in them

In the case of the first question, the responses show that almost 50% men and 40% women follow media daily. More than 15% men and almost 40% women decided for the response "Several times a week". 30% enquired men and 22% women follow surrounding events in media "From time to time". The fact that 10% men and 2% women are not interested in sur-rounding events in media is definitely alarming. The question is whether they do not follow these events at all or they use different channels for it. In spite of these facts, we may observe that media are an integral part of our lives to a larger or smaller extent regardless of the con-tents we follow there.

The conducted statistical test of dependence of responses on respondents' age was not confirmed only minimally, see Table 5.

Whereas, the ratings of media at the investigated sample were relatively high, regarding credibility we could observe a significant difference in the results. Only 12% men and almost 40% women are convinced on the correctness of media information. More than 70% men and more than 40% women do not have confidence in them. Almost 20% enquired men and women cannot answer this question. Out of the number of previous research projects, we may work out that irresolution is very often connected with some negative experience, upon which the attitude towards a certain fact will change. In this case, the Chi-square test showed dependence of responses on respondents' age, see Table 5.

The subsequent four questions focused on following the television and radio stations and following news at these stations. For the purposes of the research, only basic television and radio stations were included in the offer, whereas the respondents had a possibility to supplement their preferences. Concurrently, the respondents could select from more options. For transparency, the results were adjusted according to the frequency of respondents' selective responses. The responses to questions or the frequency order are shown in Tables 6-9.

Question No. 3	ČT1	ČT2	ČT24	Nova	Cin-ema	Prima	Prima Cool	Prima Love	Bar-randov
Order M	3	8	4	2	5	6	1	7	9
Order F	5	8	7	1	4	3	2	6	9
p-value		0.5363 A					53.6%		

Table 6 Ratings of TV Stations

Table 6 shows that Prima Cool is number one for men and the same is Nova for women. The agreement showed in both genders in the case of the ČT2 and TV Barrandov stations, which the respondents put in two last places. As the table shows the remaining order was so jumbled that no correlations can be found. Like other stations that the respondents follow, the men mentioned the sports and music stations as well as the film and adventurous stations (HBO, Discovery). The same case is in women, who stated music channels Očko and MTV, also Zoom, HBO, Discovery and others. At this place, the internet as a source of information appeared for the first time. The fact is also interesting that the women did not mention any special programme directly focused on cooking, which was common at this cohort in the previous research projects. It may be also caused by the fact that there are relatively a lot of cooking programmes also on the existing stations and thus the specialisation is not unnecessarily needed. Also the Slovak and Polish broadcasting stations occurred there. The Slovak stations were mentioned not only by the Slovak respondents. Independence of the analyzed quantities on gender distribution was confirmed by the CHITEST, when the P-value was at the level of 53.6%.

Whereas men watch news on ČT1 most often, women choose Nova. Concerning the station at which the news is watched the least, both women and men placed the ČT2 station last. The male selection for their number one may be the result of a habit, the female selection may arise from the NOVA station programme concept, when for example the series with a high share of female public are on prior to the main evening news. Nor in this case did the CHITEST at the level of 80.9% confirm dependence of respondents' replies on respondents' gender. It is shown in Table 7.

Question No. 4	ČT1	ČT2	ČT24	Nova	Prima	Bar-randov
Order M	1	5	3	2	4	6
Order F	2	5	4	1	3	5
p-value		0.8087 A			80.9%	

Table 7 Ratings of News at TV Stations

Other questions focused on following radio stations and their news programmes. Evropa 2 took the first place among the radio station at both the genders, whereas also other two places were the same (Kiss rádio and Helax, for women also Orion). The fact is also interesting that the first public representative of the radio media – Radiožurnál – took only the 5th or 7th place. In addition, the respondents stated some other radio stations that they follow, for ex-ample Rock radio, BBC, Express, Funrádio. The presented results subjected to the CHITEST, whose value is 82.8%, showed that also in this case it is not gender dependence within the inquired group as it is shown in Table 8.

Question No. 5	Radiožurnál	Praha	Vltava	Frekvence 1	Impuls	Evropa 2	Čas	Orion	Kiss	Helax	Does not follow
Order M	7	8	8	5	6	1	6	4	2	3	-
Order F	6	7	7	4	3	1	5	3	2	3	-
p-value			0.832 A					83.2%			

Table 8 Ratings of Radio Stations

When analyzing the responses connected with following news on individual radio stations, the agreement occurred in the first place, when in both the cases Evropa 2, that is a private station, became "number one". The private stations Impuls and Orion or Kiss rádio took in women the second and third place. In men, these were Kiss rádio or Helax and Impuls. The first private Radiožurnál took only the 5th place among women and the 5th place among men. The results shown below in Table 9 were again subjected to statistical evaluation. As the CHTEST showed, the results are independent of respondents' gender, providing the value is 82.8%.

Question No. 6	Radiožurnál	Praha	Vltava	Frekvence 1	Impuls	Evropa 2	Čas	Orion	Kiss	Helax	Does not follow
Order M	5	6	6	4	3	1	5	4	2	2	-
Order F	6	7	7	4	2	1	5	3	3	6	-
p-value			0.8283A					82.8%			

Table 9 Ratings of News on Radio Stations

The last two questions were again of a closed character and the respondents needed to select unambiguously one of the options. The wording of the questions was as follows:

7) Do you have confidence in these news?
8) Is your confidence influenced by the ownership structure of the media (private, public)?

Question No. 7	AM	AF	%M	%F	Question No. 8	AM	AF	%M	%F
Yes	24	54	25	46	**Yes**	44	44	12	37
No	44	32	46	27	**No**	44	60	71	44
I do not know	28	32	29	27	**I do not know**	8	17	17	19
***p*-value**	0.0955 A		9.5%		***p*-value**	0.8154 A		81.5%	

Table 10 Confidence in News and its Impact by Ownership Structure of Medium

As Table 10 shows, there is a considerable difference between the way men and women respond, in particular, as long as the confidence in media is concerned. Interesting is also the fact that almost 30% enquired men and women do not know whether they have confidence in these news. Simultaneously, more women think that they are not influenced in their decision by the ownership structure of the medium. In both the cases, although with a significant difference, the responses of the inquired were at the level that shows independence of the analyzed variables, which was proved by the CHITEST. Regarding Question No. 7, the P-value was 9.5% and for Question No. 8, it was 81.5%.

5 Conclusion

In order to ensure a suitable way of communication with the client, by all means we need to utilise the most reliable communication medium. The ability of the medium to obtain credibility and maintain it may be characterized as a significant competitive factor.

On the basis of the questionnaire enquiry we have ascertained that the addressed GZ sample has a relatively intensive interest in surrounding events, whereas more than 60% men and almost 80% women follow TV or radio daily or several times a week. A significant percentage of respondents of both the genders follow the events in media only from time to time, it is almost 30% men and more than 20% women of the GZ. The fact is interesting that this age cohort includes a group of respondents that do not follow surrounding events in the selected media at all. The hypothesis that there is a dependence of respondents' replies on respondents' gender was not confirmed.

The GZ women have far more confidence in media that they follow when compared to their male opposites. Also, a high percentage of both the gender groups cannot answer the question of media credibility. And the following question "Do you think that media provide true information?" is the only question in which the hypothesis of dependence of the respondents' replies on their gender was proved by the Chi-square test. When analyzing the ratings of individual TV stations and related news at these stations, the GZ was able to unite across the gender in only the least followed stations in general as well as by news. In case of radio stations, it was not so dramatic. The ratings were same for both the genders right in the first three places and an absolute number one occurred at the station at which both the GZ gender groups follow the news.

The major areas of the research included news credibility in the followed medium and the impact of its ownership structure (private versus public) on such credibility.

If we review the GZ, then we may observe that credibility in the followed news was in the completely reverse order in the GZ men and GZ women. The percentage of the GZ women that have credibility in the followed news is identical with the percentage of the GZ men that do not have confidence in it. There is a significant percentage (almost 30%) of men and women that cannot answer this question.

So what is the impact of the media ownership structure on their credibility? Regarding the GZ men, the same percentage of them decided for both "yes" and "no". Regarding the GZ women, more than 50% of the enquired declared no effect of the ownership structure.

Of course, the conducted research has its limitations. It would be ideal to have a chance to collect the sample according to the quota selection, but, as mentioned earlier, respondents' willingness to cooperate decreases from year to year. In addition, there is a problem with a regional focus. Yet, for comparison it is positive that all the author's research activities have a regional focus and, therefore, the data may be compared even if there is a certain time between the research projects. If we wanted to compare the research results with the similar results, we would get into a difficult situation. For comparison, the categories that may be com-pared need to be determined and it is also purposeful. None of so far executed researches of GZ respondents dealt with the classic information channels (TV and radio). Prior generations has been researched much more. To name some of the recent projects, there was research focused on the impact of Facebook advertising on GY representatives' purchasing behavior in South Africa (Duffet, 2015) or on GY purchasing behavior in the area of luxury fashion, awareness of their brands and buying motivations (Giovannini, Xu and Thomas, 2015), earlier for example the research focused on GY opinions in the area of enterprise social applications (Boughzala, 2014) and many others. Social networks, their impact on decision-making in the area of education, purchasing behavior and employment became the alpha and omega of these research projects. Author realizes the problem of the frequency of respondents. Presented results, however, are the basis for the research that will be conducted within Standard Visegrad Project „The Customer Citizenship Behavior of V4 Citizens - An Empirical Perspective".

Above all, marketing companies (Grail Research a Division of Integreon, 2011) show an eminent interest in the GZ. For the time being, the Generation Z is at the very beginning of consumer-study-professional activities. If we take into account that today the oldest one is 20 years old and the youngest one, according to the statistics (Czech Statistical Office, 2016), is being born, then we have something to do with more than a two-million consumer potential in the Czech Republic. The scale of this cohort is unpredictable now and the information about it should be collected continuously and, above all, across the whole spectrum. In the future, we may be surprised not only by the scope, but particularly by the depth of enquired services ordered without the need of personal contact. Finally, it may have a principal effect on the employment and performance of economies.

The foregoing indicates that the traditional forms of communication transmission that is radio and television, have got to the side-lines of research activities. However, their influence does not fall, despite the presence of Facebook, Instagram and any other less or more specialized servers of the social networks does not fall. Even though the communication via social media is by its nature a complex concept (Ungerman, Myslivcová, 2014).

Continuously, their activities get connected and their results may be observed day in day out. Owing to social networks, the overview of the medium ownership structure is vanishing, it is very difficult to identify the real sources of information and attribute them someone's authorship. In the end, quite often we cannot say whether it is expert and relevant information of the public medium or an advertising message of private investors.

The last events both in Europe and the world show that media are a very significant, strong and never-ending source for investigating their impact on the society. They are also a noticeable way of addressing not only potential clients via marketing communication in the form of advertising spots but, presently, this is mainly the information of a safety character, on which basis a significant part of our life decision-making processes are made in the area of employment, portfolio of purchases, travelling, etc. It remains on us, our society, to whom and how large credibility we will attach to them, which is the substance of the present media events. "Like the society – like the media!"

Acknowledgements

This paper was supported within Operational Programme Education for Competitiveness – Project No. CZ.1.07/2.3.00/20.0296

References

Bohutínská, J. (2008). Generace Y – nový pojem také u podnikatelů, [Online]. Available at: http://www.podnikatel.cz/clanky/generace-y-novy-pojem-take-u-podnikatelu/.

Boughzala, I. (2014). 'You: What Generation Y thinks about Corporate Social Networking Applications?'. *Proceedings of the Annual Hawaii International Conference on System Sciences*. New York: IEEE, pp. 688 – 696.

Czech Statistical Office (2016), [Online]. Available at: https://www.czso.cz/csu/czso/1-population-and-families-and-households-gxb45zgg77.

Duffet, R. G. (2015). 'The influence of Facebook advertising on cognitive attitudes amid Generation Y'. *Elecronic Commerce Research*, 15 (2), pp. 243-267.

Giovannini, S., Xu, Y.J. and Thomas, J. (2015). 'Luxury fashion consumption and Generation Y consumers Self, brand consciousness, and consumption motivations'. *Journal of Fashion Marketing and Management*, 19 (1), pp. 22-40.

Grail Research a Division of Integreon. Consumers of Tomorrouw. Insights and Observations About Generation Z. (2011), [Online]. Available at: http://www.slideshare.net/baurzhan/consumers-of-tomorrow-insights-and-observations-about-generation-z-15753651.

Howe, N. and Strauss, W. (1991). *Generations: The History of America's Future, 1584 to 2069*. New York: William Morrow & Company.

Jirák, J. and Köpplová, B. (2003). *Média a společnost*. Praha: Portál.

Linhart, J. et al. (2008). *Slovník cizích slov pro nové století*. Litvínov: Dialog.

Marek, L. et al. (2007). *Statistika pro ekonomy*. Příbram: Professional Publishing.

Matusiková, L, Kashi, K. and Zelinková, K. (2016). *Intergeneration Comparison of Experiences in Product Complaints*. Ostrava: VŠB-TU Ostrava.

Reifová, I. (2004). *Slovník mediální komunikace*. Praha: Portál.

Řezanková, H. (2011). *Analýza dat z dotazníkových šetření*. Praha: Professional Publishing.

Urban, L., Dubský, J. and Murdza, K. (2011). *Masová komunikace a veřejné mínění*. Praha: Grada Pubishing.

Ungerman, O. and Myslivcová, S. (2014). 'Model of communication usable for small and medium sized companies for the consumer communication in social media'. *E+M*, 17, pp. 167-184. Available at: dx.doi.org/10.15240/tul/001/2014-1-013.

The Ministry of Culture. *Veřejnoprávní vysílání* (2012). [Online]. Praha: Ministerstvo kultury, [cited 2012-01-15]. Available at: https://www.mkcr.cz/.

Zákon č. 231 /2001 Sb., o provozování rozhlasového a televizního vysílání, ve znění pozdějších předpisů.

Zákon č. 483/1991 Sb., o České televizi, ve znění pozdějších předpisů.

Zákon č. 484/1991 Sb., o Českém rozhlase, ve znění pozdějších předpisů.

Zákon č. 348/2005 Sb., o rozhlasových a televizních poplatcích, ve znění pozdějších předpisů.

Analysis of Gross Wages in Moravian - Silesian Region according to Education Level

Lea Nedomova[1], Milos Maryska[2], Petr Doucek[3]

Abstract. Regional units' performance and importance for the state depends to some extent on the size of wages paid in regions. The article analyzes average real gross wages in the Moravian - Silesian region by achieved education during 2000 - 2015. For our analysis, we used data from the sample survey "Average Earnings Information System" conducted by Trexima, a.s. for the Czech Statistical Office on a yearly basis. We analyzed these data, using the functionality of MS Excel and IBM SPSS software. The analysis results show higher average wages in the Moravian - Silesian region in lower education categories (elementary and vocational school) but lower wages in higher education categories (high school and university) as compared to the average of the Czech Republic. We have also discovered that average real gross wages in the Moravian - Silesian region kept dropping from 2011 to 2014 in all analyzed categories. The year-to-year wage increase in 2015 indicates a turn for the better.

Keywords: Gross real wages, education level, basic education, high school education, university education.

JEL Classification: E24, J31

1 Introduction

The transformation of the Czech economy from a centrally planned economy to a market economy has changed both the structure of individual industries in regions and the structure of job positions (Bílkova, 2009; Bílková, 2012). One of the regions that has been going through such changes is NUTS II – the Moravian - Silesian region. Its original focus on heavy industry and mining is gradually shifting towards a large variety of light industry as well as towards a sufficient base for providing all kinds of services (Maryska, Doucek and Nedomova, 2015; Doucek, Nedomova and Maryska, 2015). The new freeway connecting this region with Brno and Polish regions has led to a great potential increase in work opportunities in the region. How did these changes reflect in the wages of workers in this region? (Malá, 2015) Did they improve their living standard or not too much? Based on the study (ESV, 2012), the Moravian - Silesian region placed third in an interregional comparison of wages. Prague placed first and the Central Bohemian region second (CZSO, 2012).

2 Research Questions

Based on the long-term research conducted at the Faculty of Informatics and Statistics, University of Economics, Prague (FIS), we wanted to analyze the wage trend in the Moravian - Silesian

[1] University of Economics, Prague/Faculty of Informatics and Statistics, Department of Systems Analysis, W. Churchill Sq. 4, 130 67 Prague 3, nedomova@vse.cz.

[2] University of Economics, Prague/Faculty of Informatics and Statistics, Department of Information Technologies, W. Churchill Sq. 4, 130 67 Prague 3, maryskam@vse.cz.

[3] University of Economics, Prague/Faculty of Informatics and Statistics, Department of Systems Analysis, W. Churchill Sq. 4, 130 67 Prague 3, doucek@vse.cz.

region during 2000 – 2015 by achieved education as well as to compare the wage trend in the Moravian - Silesian region with the average of the Czech Republic, including Prague, and to show and compare trends in real gross wages by achieved education (Marek, 2016; Marek and Doucek, 2016; Fischer et al, 2013).

3 Methodology Description

We obtained the data for our research from the ISPV (Average Earnings Information System) sample survey. The ISPV (ISPV, 2017) regularly monitors the earnings and work hours of employees in the Czech Republic. The ISPV contains data from regular statistical surveys that are called the "Average Earnings Quarterly Survey" and are included in the statistical surveys program announced by the Czech Statistical Office (CSO) in the collection of laws for the relevant calendar year. The statistical surveys program for the relevant year is always announced by a decree in the collection of laws. The main monitored earnings indicators include gross monthly wages and hourly wages. Besides the differentiation of gross monthly wages, other wage components, i.e. bonuses, extra pays and compensations, are monitored as well. In this set of data, the gross monthly wage is calculated as a multiple of hourly earnings in the second quarter and the average monthly work hours in individual years. The average work hours are rounded off to a whole number. The size of the analyzed sample gradually increased from over 154,000 in 2000 to approximately 250,000 in 2015 for the Moravian - Silesian region and from one million in 2000 to over two million in 2015 for the Czech Republic.

The data sample for each education category in the Moravian - Silesian region in 2015 is as follows: approximately 16,000 respondents for Elementary Schools, 87,000 respondents for Vocational Schools, 90,000 respondents for High Schools, 9,500 respondents for Bachelor, 40,000 respondents for Master and 3,000 respondents for Ph.D. This clearly shows that the data sample for employees with a bachelor degree and a Ph.D. degree is the smallest and thus also the least accurate. Approximately 246,000 data records were analyzed.

The limitation of the data sample is the fact that it includes enterprises that are registered in the Moravian - Silesian region regardless of their actual place of operation and that these enterprises have more than nine employees. It means that one-person or very small "enterprises," i.e. so-called micro-enterprises to use the taxonomy of the European Union, are not included in this data sample and thus not analyzed. Another limitation that should be pointed out is the fact that these data are for the second quarter. Therefore, the average wage in a certain year is actually the average wage in the second quarter of that year. This is why our data may somewhat differ from the official public statistics. We used the second quarter because in this quarter there are the least amount of national holidays, employee vacations and bonuses and therefore, the second quarter provides an ideal picture of the basic wages that are least distorted by other wage components. The data from which we calculated the average wages in the Czech Republic include the Moravian - Silesian region, and so the average wages actually represent all regions of the CR and not regions without the analyzed Moravian - Silesian region.

To determine the level of education, we used the highest achieved education criterion as well as the generally effective methodology and classified the level of education as follows:

- Elementary education (Elementary School);

- Secondary education;
  - Vocational School;
  - High School;
- University education;
  - Bachelor;
  - Master;
  - Ph.D. – meaning scientific preparation education.

To compare the results in individual years, we converted the average nominal wages to wages in 2015, using the annual inflation rate from the data of the Czech National Bank (CNB, 2017). We analyzed our data, using the statistical tools in MS Excel.

4 Results

Our results provide information about the overall trend in real wages in three basic categories of achieved education – elementary, secondary and university. The last two categories are sub-divided based on the usual classification in the Czech Republic.

Each figure, which compares the average real gross wages in the second quarter of the relevant year in the Moravian - Silesian region and the Czech Republic, also contains an index comparing wages between both time series, where the Czech Republic represents a basis for comparison, i.e. 100%. The figure also contains a linear function to smooth the trend in both analyzed values of the previous year.

4.1 Comparison of total average wages

The average wage trend in the Moravian - Silesian region during the last 16 years regardless of the level of education is shown in Figure 1. The trend shows that up to the year 2002 the average wages in the Moravian - Silesian region (in chart used Moravian – Silesian) were in line with the all-state average, and starting in 2003 were permanently below the average of average wages in the Czech Republic. By the year 2008, this gap increased by five percentage points and in the year 2009 by an additional two percentage points. After that, the average wages kept increasing towards the all-state average, reaching 94.2% of the all-state average in 2012. Between 2013 and 2015, the average wages in the region started dropping again, all the way to 92.89% of the all-state average in 2015.

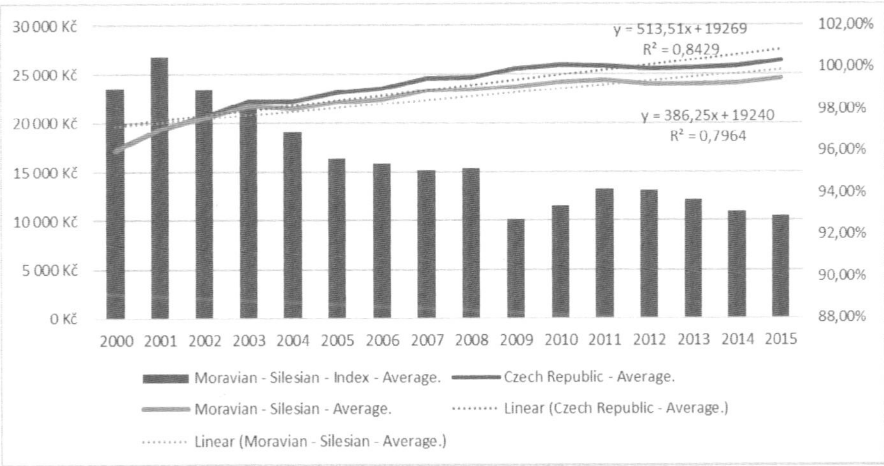

Figure 1 Trend in average wages [Own computation, data ISPV, 2017]

The real gross wages in the region dropped (as did the average wages in the Czech Republic) from 2011 until 2014. A slight year-to-year increase started between 2014 and 2015.

The trend line shows a faster trend in the all-state average wage (the slope of the line is 513.51, with 84.29% confidence) than in the Moravian - Silesian region (the slope of the line is 386.25, with 79.64% confidence).

4.2 Elementary education

We first analyzed in detail the average wages of workers with a completed elementary education. Their trend during the analyzed time period is shown in Figure 2.

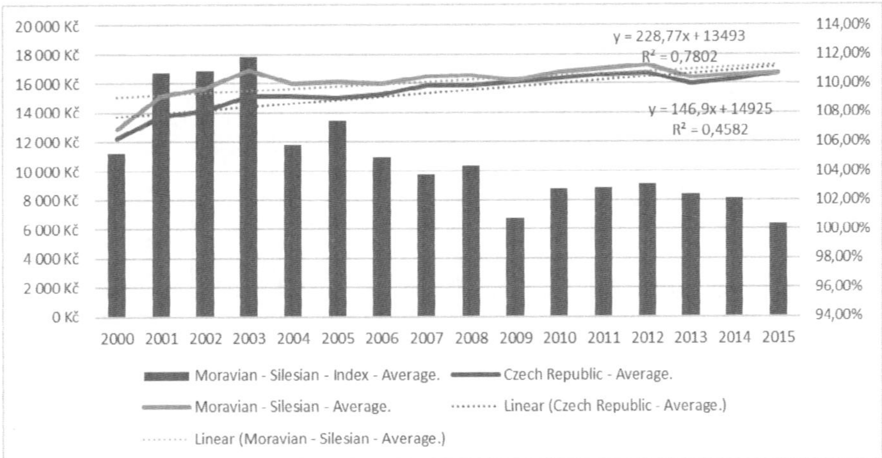

Figure 2 Trend in average wages – Elementary education [Own computation, data ISPV, 2017]

The wages of workers with an achieved elementary education are higher in the Moravian - Silesian region during the entire analyzed time period than the all-state average. The biggest difference was in 2003 – almost 12 percentage points. The lowest difference was in 2015 – only 0.31 percentage point. The slope of the trend line is higher for the Moravian - Silesian region (228.77, with 78.02% confidence); the all-state average was approximated with a slope of

146.90, with only 45.82% confidence. We will see how this trend will continue after we analyze the data for 2016.

The drop in average wages in 2009 was caused by the impact of the economic crisis, in particular on the industrial sector, i.e. mainly on exploitation and mining, which has a strong representation in the region (CZSO, 2012).

4.3 Secondary education

Secondary schools represent a special sector, the graduates of which are qualified for performing professional work. These are often graduates of technical or economic schools (vocational schools). There are also secondary schools, the graduates of which receive a general education without any profound specialization. All of them usually hold the lowest management positions in different organizations or are self-employed (small businessmen).

Vocational schools

The wage trend in this category is shown in Figure 3. The trend in this category is also favorable for the Moravian - Silesian region. The average wages in the Moravian - Silesian region were higher than the all-state average practically during the entire analyzed time period. The lowest difference was identified in 2009 where the average wage was higher by only 0.59%. The slope of the trend approximation line is also steeper in the Moravian - Silesian region (284.33, with 81.1% confidence) than the estimated trend in the average wage in the Czech Republic for this category of education (194.56, 66.36% confidence). Another interesting fact we discovered is a year-to-year drop in wages in 2009 and a year-to-year drop in wages between 2011 and 2014. A slight increase started between 2014 and 2015. We will see whether or not this trend will continue after we analyze the data for 2016.

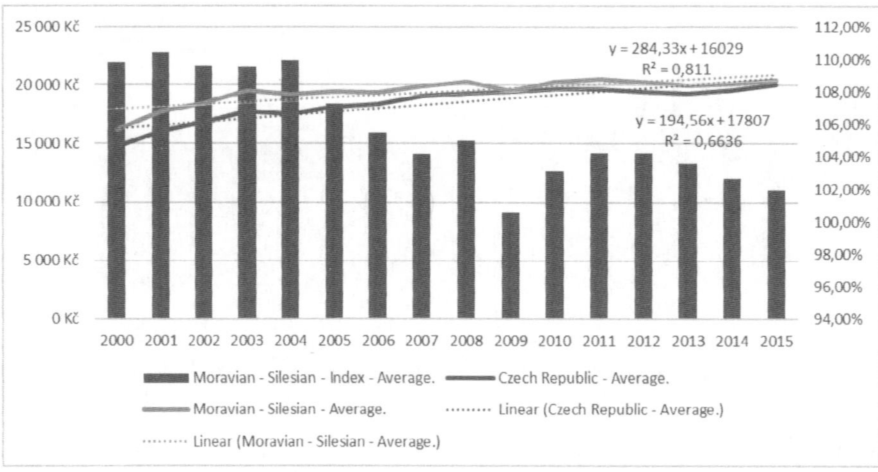

Figure 3 Vocational schools [Own computation, data ISPV, 2017]

High schools

The analyzed time series of wages in the "high school" category provide a rather different picture of wages as compared to the average of the Czech Republic. Workers with this type of education are represented in the analyzed statistical sample with the same frequency as workers with a vocational education. The wage trend during the analyzed time period is shown in Figure 4.

Figure 4 clearly shows that these workers have lower wages than the all-state average during the entire analyzed period. The wages in the Moravian - Silesian region most closely approached the all-state average in 2000 – 98.67% of the all-state average. On the other hand, the gap was the biggest in 2009 – 93.58%. In 2015, the wages in this category represented 94.54% of the all-state average. The wages in the Moravian - Silesian region show a decreasing trend between 2010 and 2014 and a slight increase between 2014 and 2015. The slope of the trend line is 413.35 for the average of the Czech Republic and 340.29 for the Moravian - Silesian region, with approximately 70% confidence.

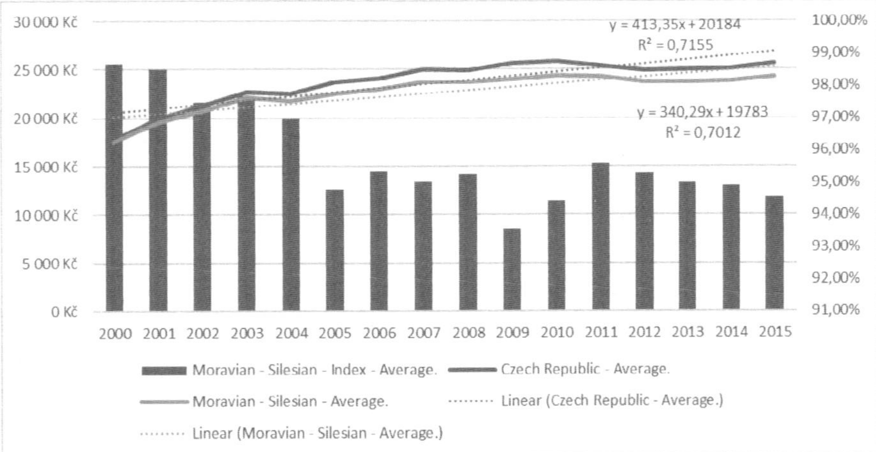

Figure 4 High schools [Own computation, data ISPV, 2017]

4.4 University education

University education represents the highest possible education in the Czech Republic. However, even university education has different levels. The model of the Bologna Declaration from 1995 suggests the lowest level to be the bachelor degree for the majority of study fields, then the former standard Master degree and finally the highest education in the form of scientific preparation, the so-called doctorate degree (in the figures shown as Ph.D.).

Bachelor level of education

The bachelor level of education is the lowest level of university education. These graduates do not often work in regular organizations because the majority of branches of business, especially technical or technically- oriented, require a five-year education at the master level. Therefore, this category mostly includes professionals in marketing and economic branches or some professions in information and communication technologies (multimedia, computer network operation, etc.). The wage trend in this category is shown in Figure 5.

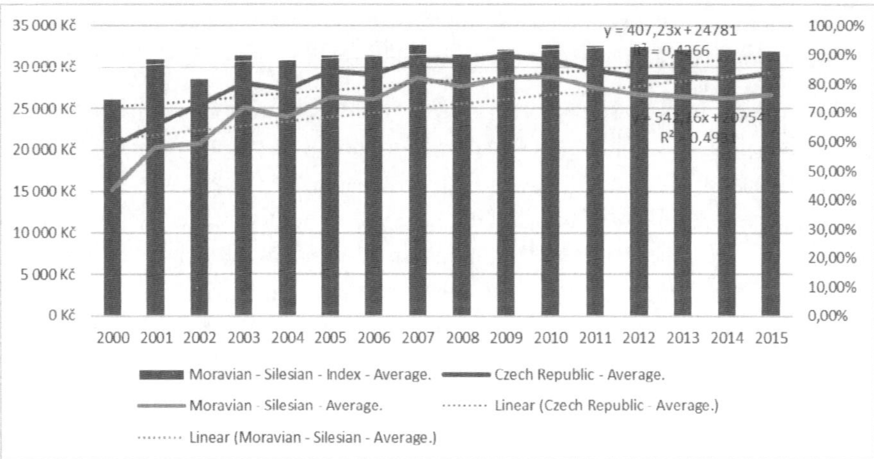

Figure 5 Bachelor level of education [Own computation, data ISPV, 2017]

Figure 5 demonstrates the average wage in this category in the Moravian - Silesian region. This average wage goes up and down from year to year. When analyzing its long-term trend, we can see that the average wage in the Moravian - Silesian region went up between 2000 (only 630 records) and 2010 (5,362 records), kept dropping after 2010 until 2014 and went slightly up between 2014 and 2015. The wages in the Moravian - Silesian region were lower during the entire analyzed time period as compared to the average of the Czech Republic. During 2013 – 2015, the wages were less than 92% of the all-state average. We did not approximate the trend in this category because it goes up and down in very short time periods (even between individual years). The estimate shows a permanently growing trend, but only with 42.66% confidence for the average of the Czech Republic and with 49.31% confidence for the Moravian - Silesian region.

Master level of education

A master level of education is the most usual in current economic practice. These graduates usually hold middle and high management positions in private companies and are top management members and/or owners. The wage trend in this category is shown in Figure 6.

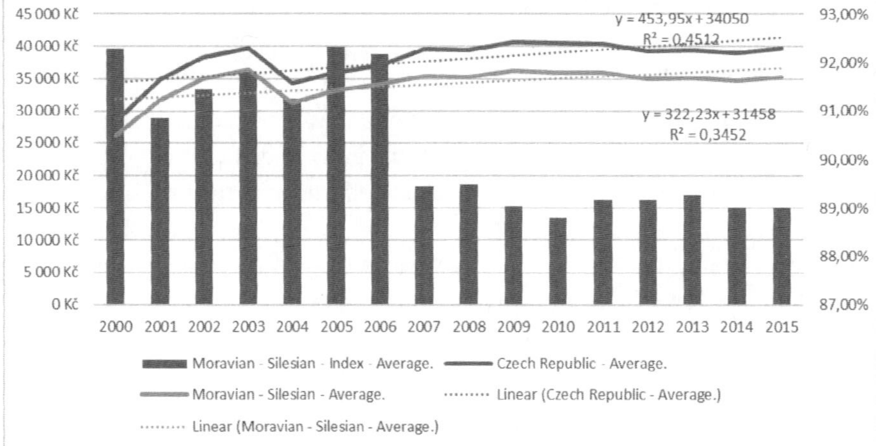

Figure 6 Master level of education [Own computation, data ISPV, 2017]

The average wages in this category in the Moravian - Silesian region did not reach the all-state average during the entire analyzed time period. They came the closest to the all-state average in 2005 (92.32%). During the last two years, they represented 89.01% of the all-state average. After a big slump in 2004, the average wages kept going up until 2011, started dropping after 2011 until 2014 and went slightly up in 2015. Because of the big slump in 2004 and the drop after 2011, the trend function does not have a great informative value. The confidence for the average of the Czech Republic is 45.12% and for the Moravian - Silesian region only 34.52%. The wage slump in this category in 2004 was caused by lower revenues in the mining industry and lower outputs of heavy industry during the second half of 2004 (CZSO, 2005).

Doctorate level of education – Ph.D.

In general, a doctorate level of education should be a gateway to top management positions that are very well paid. Another option is an academic career where the wages are rather low. Therefore, both these factors will affect the average wages during the analyzed period. The wage trend in the category of workers with a Ph.D. degree is shown in Figure 7.

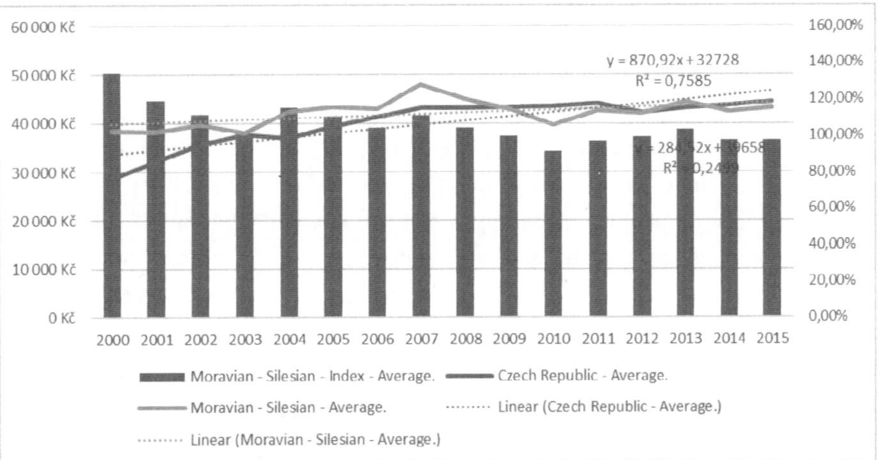

Figure 7 Doctorate level of education – Ph.D. [Own computation, data ISPV, 2017]

The trend in the wages of the Ph.D. category in the Moravian - Silesian region shows a big variability during the analyzed time period. The wage stagnation or slight drop between 2000 – 2003 (the sample includes only 300 – 400 records) turned into wage growth until 2007. After that, the wages dropped again approximately to the wage level of 2000. This drop stopped in 2010. Since then, the wages went up and down from year to year, while slightly growing. After 2011, the average wage of Ph.D. workers in the Moravian - Silesian region practically copies the averages wages in the Czech Republic. The approximation function predicts a slight increase for the average of the Czech Republic (with 75.85% confidence). We will not take into account the forecasted trend in the average wage in the Moravian - Silesian region since its confidence is below 25%.

4.5 Comparison of wages based on the level of education

A comparison of the average wages during the analyzed time period based on the level of education is another important outcome. This comparison is provided in Figure 8.

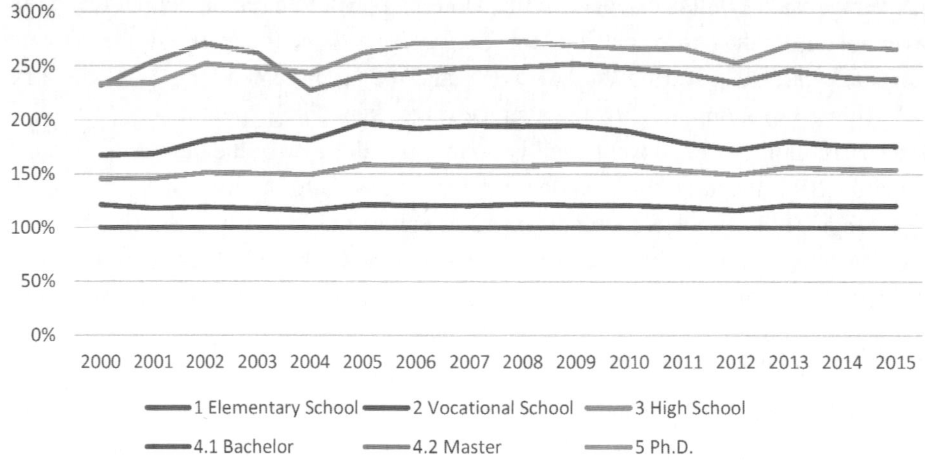

Figure 8 Comparison of wages based on the level of education [Own computation, data ISPV, 2017]

Figure 8 shows a relatively big difference between the wages of workers with an elementary education and workers with a high school education; the difference between the average wage in the high school education category and in the elementary education category represents approximately 50% of the wages of workers with an elementary education. Another huge difference is that between an elementary education and a master level of education - approximately 140%. On the other hand, we found it surprising that the difference between a high school education and a bachelor level of education was only 20 percentage points. The difference between the average wages of workers with a master's degree and workers with a Ph.D. degree was also small during the past five years – approximately 20 to 25 percentage points.

5 Conclusions

Based on the analysis of real gross wages in the Moravian - Silesian region by achieved education and their comparison with the all-state average, we can conclude the following:

- The average wage of workers with a lower level of education – an elementary and vocational education – is higher in the Moravian - Silesian region than the average wage of the Czech Republic in these two categories;
- The average wage of workers with a higher level of education – a high school education and bachelor and master level of education – is lower in the Moravian - Silesian region than the average wage of the Czech Republic in these categories;
- The average wage of workers with a Ph.D. degree is in line with the average wage of the Czech Republic in this category;
- The drop in the average wage in the Moravian - Silesian region as compared to the average wage in the Czech Republic in 2009 in the elementary and secondary education category was caused by an almost 8% year-to-year drop in the GDP of the region (CZSO, 2015). The average wages of workers with a higher level of education did not seem to be sensitive to this factor;
- The biggest wage differences are between an elementary education and high school education and between a bachelor level of education and master level of education.

On the other hand, the smallest differences are between an elementary education and vocational education and a master level of education and Ph.D. level of education.

Acknowledgements

Paper was processed with contribution of long term support of scientific work on Faculty of Informatics and Statistics, University of Economics, Prague (IP 400040).

References

Bílková, D. (2012). 'Recent Development of the Wage and Income Distribution in the Czech Republic'. *Prague Economic Papers,* 21 (2), pp. 233–250.

Bílková, D. (2009). 'Vliv délky praxe na výši mezd zaměstnanců v České republice od počátku hospodářské recese v roce 2009'. *Politická ekonomie,* 64 (6), pp. 674–694.

CNB. (2017). Roční míra inflace, [Online]. Available at: http://www.cnb.cz [cited 2017-01-17]

CZSO. (2015). Základní tendence demografického, sociálního a ekonomického vývoje Moravskoslezského kraje - 2015, [Online]. Available at: https://www.czso.cz/csu/czso/zakladni-tendence-demograficckeho-socialniho-a-ekonomickeho-vyvoje-moravskoslezskeho-kraje-2015 [cited 2017-01-11].

CZSO. (2012). Trh práce 1993–2011, [Online]. Available at: http://www.czso.cz/csu/2012edicniplan.nsf/p/3103-12 [cited 2017-01-05].

CZSO. (2005). Ekonomický vývoj, [Online]. Available at: https://www.czso.cz/csu/czso/13-2105-05-v_letech_2000_az_2004-5_4_prumysl [cited 2017-01-05].

Doucek, P., Nedomova, L. and Maryska, M. (2015). 'Is It Attractive To Be the ICT Professional in the Czech Economy?'. *Proceedings of IDIMT-2015 Information Technology and Society Interaction and Interdependence,* Poděbrady, Czech Republic, pp. 73–88.

ESV. (2012). Ekonomický a sociální význam průmyslu pro Moravskoslezský kraj – ve faktech, datech a skutečnostech, [Online]. Available at: http://www.socialnidialog.cz/images/stories/Vyznam_prumyslu_pro_MSK_final.pdf [cited 2017-01-17].

Fischer, J., Vltavská, K., Doucek, P. and Hanclová, J. (2013). 'Vliv informačních a komunikačních technologií na produktivitu práce a souhrnnou produktivitu faktorů v České republice'. *Politická ekonomie*, 61 (5), pp. 653–674.

ISPV. (2017). ISPV – informační systém o průměrném výdělku, [Online]. Available at: https://www.ispv.cz [cited 2017-01-11].

Malá, I. (2015). 'Vícerozměrný pravděpodobnostní model rozdělení příjmů českých domácností'. *Politická ekonomie*, 63 (7), pp. 895–908.

Marek, L. and Doucek, P. (2016). 'Vývoj mezd a příjmové nerovnosti u ICT odborníků v České republice'. *Politická ekonomie,* 64 (8), pp. 922–938.

Marek, L. (2016). 'Comparison of wages in the Czech Regions'. *Proceedings of 34th International Conference Mathematical Methods in Economics*, Liberec, Czech Republic, pp. 534–539.

Maryska, M., Doucek, P. and Nedomova, L. (2015). 'ICT professionals wages development'. *Proceedings of the 12th International Conference Liberec Economic Forum 2015,* Liberec, Czech Republic, pp. 101–111.

Approach to information support of the new product development process in the middle-sized companies

Matjaz Roblek, Tomaz Kern, Eva Krhac, Benjamin Urh[1]

Abstract. Companies make important decisions in changing business processes and information support when they are growing from small to medium-size (ME). One way of solving this problem is the introduction of a certain degree of formalization in business. This includes the identification and standardization of business processes. A particular challenge is the formalization of knowledge intensive processes, especially the formalization of the new product development (NPD) process. In this paper, we present an adapted approach to the business process reengineering, which is suitable for medium-sized companies. The approach was tested in a real company, and the results of renovation were measured by structural indicators.

Keywords: business process reengineering, new product development, information systems, medium-sized enterprises.

JEL Classification: M10, L20

1 Introduction

With the business growth, the company owns more and more business processes. That increases the need for *formalization*, which outputs in a detailed prescription of excetution of business processes. It increases the need for the *typization*, as the need for classify processes into different categories, with different management and information support. Also, it increases the level of *standardization*, as the need to execute the process according to a prescribed way, which is optimal from very different perspectives, for example from the view of efficient utilization of human resources, assets, information technology, and product quality assurance. Stevenson (Stevenson, 2015) argues that there should be a greater process formalization, typization and standardization to achieve more effective and efficient operations.

Policar (2008) found out that the organization of the companies that have 10 or fewer employees do not differ significantly from those having up to 50 employees. For start-up and small businesses it has also been proven (Kern, 1998), that they do not have the need for the formalization of business processes. He found out that the organization of companies is significantly different in large companies with 250 or more employees when their processes become complex and the interdependences among processes are often not transparent.

Medium-sized enterprises (or ME) are in transition between small and large companies and employ between 50 and 250 workers. Snidermann (2012) demonstrates that they are special group to study. They have advantages over micro companies: they easier tackle with business challenges, and they easier obtain financing. They have advantages over large companies as they are more agile to changes in the business environment, and they are closer to the customer. Basu at al. (2003) notes that the ME are also specific in approach to the process renovation. Their approach is much more rational than in the large companies, they have greater lim-

[1] University of Maribor, Faculty of Organizational Sciences, Enterprise Engineering Laboratory, Kidriceva 55a, Kranj, Slovenia, matjaz.roblek@um.si, tomaz.kern@um.si, eva.krhac1@um.si benjamin.urh@fov.uni-mb.si,

itation of financial resources and less time to introduce changes in the processes, and the renovation is often subordinated to the possibilities of modern IT solutions.

We want to understand with this research, what is the optimal rate of formalization of ME processes, how flexible should be their information support, and if the general methodological approach to renovation for ME should be the same as for the large enterprises.

1.1 Knowledge intensive processes and their formalization

Knowledge intensity of the business process is described by the dynamism and innovation of explicit, implicit and cultural knowledge (Drakos, 2014). In the start-up or small company the processes are controlled by implicit and cultural knowledge. The lack of explicit knowledge means more errors in the process, possible wrong decisions and unnecessary feedback loops in operations. If this happens the company needs to establish a certain degree of formalization and standardization in the processes. On the other side, the employees hardly understand that they will benefit on effectiveness from additional formalization (administration), especially employees in knowledge intensive processes of ME.

1.2 New product development process

The representative of a knowledge intensive process in the manufacturing companies is the process of new product development (NPD). In the NPD process of a small company we have great domination of implicit and cultural knowledge, because the organization of NPD process was mostly designed by the company founder (Policar, 2008). ME need to improve the amount and the quality of explicit knowledge if they are increasing the volume of work or are becoming part of global supply chains. The question is how to achieve the optimal level of formalization of NPD process in the ME to maintain its initial spirit as a start-up company, while ensuring effective massive development of new products, and achieve good synchronization between NPD and other repetitive processes of ME (e.g. manufacturing) which are dominated by rules and routine.

1.3 Information support of NPD process

The research of information systems of NPD processes, that was performed in 8 small companies and 7 ME in Slovenia (Roblek and Kern, 1998-2016) showed, that start-up and small companies in NPD process use mainly tools for computer-aided design (CAD), standard IT solutions to support communication (e-mail, web portals) and computer spreadsheets (MS Excel). While ME use CAD tools, tools for project management or project portfolio management, information systems for technical documentation (e.g. Windchill), document management systems for contracts, promotion material. ME show greater need for master data management and for data connection among the development information system and the enterprise resource planning system (ERP).

1.4 Formalization of NPD process

Horie and Ikawa (2014) concluded that the insistence on existing NPD process is the unfavourable factor for the company when it grows from a small to ME. The study (Woschke at al., 2016) notes that the ME begin to measure the losses in the NPD process, such as waiting times, duplication of work, additional material costs, and they seek for solutions in additional formalization and standardization of the NPD process. The study conducted in Ireland (Robbins, 2014) shows that the high efficiency of NPD process in small and ME generally depends on a well-defined business strategy, innovation and well-formalized NPD process. It demonstrates that the ME with well formalized NPD processes are showing higher yields and achieve a more radical innovations. The study Leithold at al. (2016) demonstrates that the essential feature of well-organized NPD process in ME is the capability of fast process adaptation. Other studies (Poetz and Schreier, 2012, Sosa at al., 2015, Woschke at al., 2016, Rajasekaran at al., 2016) also showed that the ME should further formalize the NPD process for its success.

ME have difficulties to recognize the positive impact of formalization of NPD process, we did not find research that suggests us how to carry out the transition of ME NPD process from a non-formal to a formal state. Small companies in the transition to ME do not have basic formalization of NPD process. Therefore, ME need a special approach to process reengineering.

2 Methodology

There are many approaches to process improvement in large companies (Harmon, 2015, Kern, 2003). The proper approach to the renovation of NPD process of the ME should consider the following features:

- responsiveness; high dynamics and speed in bringing changes to the NPD process;
- flexibility; NPD process has no standard output;
- process network; NPD process is based on good support of related processes;
- easy use of information system.

2.1 Pre-study

We performed a pre-study defined by Drakos (2014) first, where we analysed how employees of NPD process are ready for transition. In the pre-study, we figured out that the influence of historical thinking of employees has significant impact on the current organization of NPD process. We also created a model of rough processes (function tree model and value added chain model) and we asked key employees where they see the solutions for problems of current NPD process. The pre-study confirmed a huge gap between employees in understanding the formalization of NPD process. In general, employees disagreed with the recording and transferring of explicit knowledge. The result of the pre-study was used for a proper preparation of the renovation project.

2.2 Modelling ME As-Is processes

The analysed ME did not have defined processes before the renovation project (only sloppy records for the purpose of the ISO standards). So, it was necessary to establish a business process management first. In the first part of the project, we carried out the identification and recording of the detailed logic of all processes of ME, structural analysis of the competitive situation of the processes (internal and external problems, challenges and opportunities for improvement), and construction of the priority list of processes for renovation. Processes were classified into two sets according to recommendations of Kokalj (2012): the set of processes with radical renovation (renovated with the method of business process reengineering) and the set of processes that was renovated with small gradual steps.

2.3 The renovation of NPD process

We found that the NPD process is semi-structured and case-like process. This means that it has all features to be successfully managed as a project with a few particularities: set of available project activities is fixed, resources are always the same. Therefore, we used the concept of milestones as a guideline for renovation of NPD process (Roblek at al., 2012). This concept allowed us to monitor and manage very diverse requirements of the NPD process in form of the standard control points. Each milestone has a responsible person, a set of documents with their status, rules and criteria that controls the flow of the NPD process. Milestones also represent links to the support processes (such as procurement, payroll), which are highly structured and require more precisely structured data/information. Imprecise NPD process links are also very susceptible for generating the unnecessary new variants of supportive processes (data inconsistencies and impracticability, emergence of alternatives). The problem is that from the perspective of research and development staff in the NPD process of ME, the additional non R&D data are only an unnecessary bureaucracy. *Figure 1* shows the final conceptual version of renewed process.

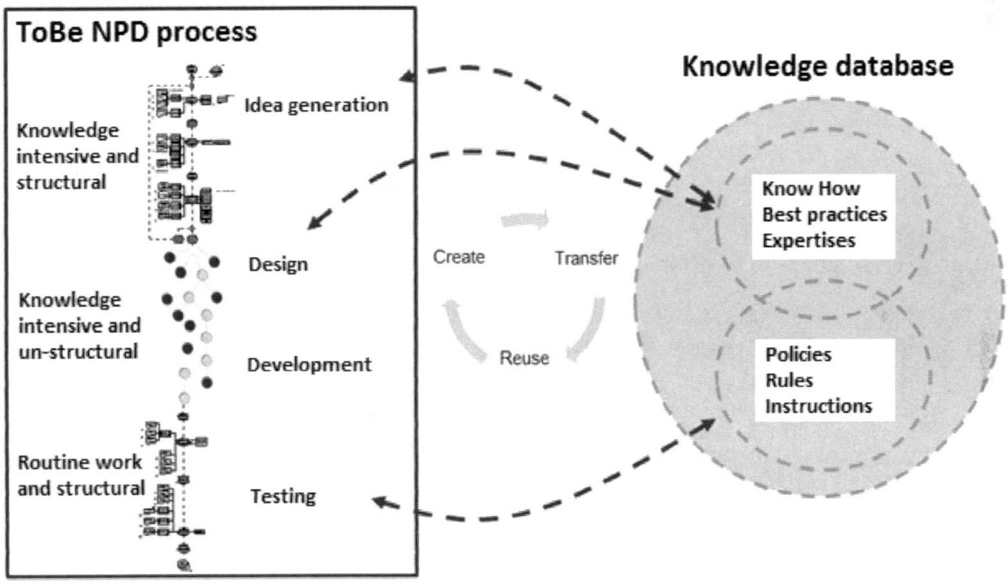

Figure 1 Final (To-Be) conceptual version of new NPD process

In the second step, we aligned the milestones with the main professional phases of NPD process (Kennet, 2013). Each activity inside each phase was professionally defined by best practice of Product lifecycle operations reference model (APICS, 2014). For the definition of required entities and data, we used the best practices from APQP method (Morris, 2012).

In the third step, we defined renovation of information support of the NPD process (which activity of the NPD process requires transaction mode of support, document mode of support, and support with knowledge information system (CAD / CAM, simulators).

3 Results

The suggested approach was tested in automotive ME in Slovenia, which is mainly export-oriented and it participates in the international supply chains. It passed half of the year since the completion of the renovation project, and according to McAfee (McAfee, 2002), we cannot credibly analyse the success of renovation by traditional economic indicators. Therefore, we tried to perform prediction of actual changes of traditional economic indicators with the calculation of structural indicators (Urh at al., 2015) in the analytical module of tool ARIS 9.8.

The analysis of changes of organizational elements

We counted, for all sequential activities (hereinafter referred to as functions) of NPD process, if there are the transitions between two functions in form of change of organizational unit, work position, role or person (*table 1*).

	The degree of organizational changes / improvements	As-Is	To-Be
a)	The number of functions	144	77
b)	The number of various organizational roles	43	38
c)	The number of function transitions	125	96
d)	Minimum no. of organizational changes	73	86
e)	Ratio of min. organiz. changes/function transitions	0,58	0,9
f)	Maximum no. of organizational changes	90	90
g)	Ratio of max. organiz. changes/function transitions	0.72	0.94

Table 1 Organizational change between As-Is and To-Be

The analysis of changes of information carriers

We calculated the changes in information carriers (e.g. Documents, e-mail, file) for all functions in the sequence of the NPD process. The transition exists where two successive functions in the process do not share at least one identical information carrier (*table 2*).

	The degree of the document changes / improvements	**As-Is**	**To-Be**
a)	The number of various information carriers	99	106
b)	The number of transitions of information carriers	50	81
c)	Function transitions with media breaks	20	28
d)	Ratio of media breaks/function transitions	0.4	0.35

Table 2 Information carriers change between As-Is and To-Be

The analysis of changes of information systems

We calculated supported information systems for all functions in the sequence of the NPD process. In addition, we checked all successive functions whether there is a replacement of the IS. Transition exists if two successive functions have not at least one identical information system (*table 3*).

	The degree of information changes / improvements	As-Is	To-Be
a)	The number of various info. systems or modules	44	17
b)	Functions with application system in %	45.65	62.34
c)	The number of function transitions	91	63
d)	Application system breaks	32	17
e)	Ratio of application system breaks/function transitions	0.35	0.27

Table 3 Information system change between As-Is and To-Be

4 Discussion

All To-Be values of structural indicators are the data of the real NPD process of the analysed company.

The *table 1* presents us that the renewed NPD process is unified: the number of functions in the new process has been reduced by 67 functions compared to the existing process (using the same modelling convention). The new process is leaner than As-Is process and thus more effective. This improvement was mostly made in the structured part of the NPD process by the unification and integration of work. The new process has 12% less different job roles. The ratio between the minimum and maximum number of job roles is unified according to the number of functions in the process, mainly due to elimination of the alternative routes and shortcuts. Since the relationships in both cases are greater in To-Be than in the As-Is process; it means that the responsibility for carrying out a specific activity in the process is clearly allocated to a specific employee.

The *table 2* shows that the number of information carriers was increased from 99 in As-Is to 106 in To-Be process. This warrants greater formalization of the process, and consequently a greater degree of explicit knowledge (which was the objective of the project). The ratio of number of changes of information carriers according to the number of functions in the process shows, that the degree of formalization has no impact on deterioration of the process as a whole (reduced by 5%). This means that despite the increase in the number of information carriers at each function, there is a relative reduction in the number of the document breaks through the process.

It is evident from the *table 3* that the To-Be process is unified according to use of information technology. The number of different information systems or modules was decreased by 61.5% (it is necessary to clarify that the modelling convention evaluated different Excel files as different IS elements!). The level of automation of the process with information systems was increased by 17%.

The achieved values of structural indicators shows, that we can confirm that the approach we used had positive impact on the new NPD process. We have succeeded in ensuring enough formalization considered particularities of ME, as recommended by Robbins (Robbins, 2014). We ensured that important tacit knowledge is recorded and is available as explicit knowledge. We left part of the NPD process in unstructured form, with which we retain the flexibility and agility of development activities, as recommended by Leithold at al. (2016).

5 Conclusions

We would like to emphasize that we performed only one application of this approach. Despite the presence of large number of good practices of renovation for large companies, there are few examples of best practice for companies in the transition from small to ME. We will continue with this research untill we achive a statisticaly important sample.

Acknowledgements

We would like to thank Laboratory of Enterprise Engineering on Faculty of Organizational Sciences.

References

APICS (2014). *PLCOR Product Lifecycle Operations Reference Model*. APICS Supply Chain Council.

Basu, S., Palvia P. and Chen, L. (2003). *Encyclopedia of Library and Information Science*, 2nd ed. Atlanta: Gorgia Institute of Technology.

Drakos, N. (2014). How to Choose the Right Technology for a Knowledge Management Program, [Online]. Available at: http://www.gartner.com [cited 2017-01-18].

Harmon, P. (2015). *Once More on Business Process Methodologies*. BPR Trends, [Online]. Available at: http://www.bptrends.com/bpt/wp-content/uploads [cited 2017-01-16].

Horie, N. and Ikawa, Y. (2014). Knowledge integration in a product development organization for new businesses: A case study of a precision device manufacturer. *Management of Engineering & Technology (PICMET)*, Portland International Conference.

Kennet, K. (2013). *The PDMA handbook of new product development*, 3rd ed. New Jersey: Wiley.

Kern, T. (2003). 'The model of dynamic adaptation of business structures to changing processes'. *Proceedings of the Fourth Annual Global Information Technology Management World Conference*, Calgary, Alberta, Canada, June 8-10, 2003. Greensboro (NC): Global Information Technology Management Association, pp. 278-281.

Kern, T. (1998). 'Procesna organizacija: oblikovanje organizacije poslovnih sistemov na osnovi modela strukturiranih organizacijskih procesov'. *Doctoral thesis*. Univarza v Mariboru Fakulteta za organizacijske vede Kranj, 202.

Kokalj, Š. (2012). 'Mehanizem za ocenjevanje strukturne učinkovitosti procesov'. *Master thesis*, Univerza v Mariboru Fakulteta za organizacijske vede, Kranj.

Leithold, N., Woschke, T., Haase, H. and Kratzer, J. (2016). 'Optimising NPD in SMEs: a best practice approach'. *Benchmarking: An International Journal*, 23, pp. 262 – 284.

McAfee, A. (2002). 'The impact of enterprise information technology adoption on operational performance: An empirical investigation'. *Production and Operations Management*, 11, pp. 33-53.

Morris, M. (2012). *Advanced Product Quality Planning and Control Plans based on APQP*, 2nd ed. ASQ Automotive Division.

Poetz, M.K. and Schreier, M. (2012). 'The Value of Crowdsourcing: Can Users Really Compete with Professionals in Generating New Product Ideas?'. *The Journal of Product Innovation Management* 29 (2), pp. 245-256.

Poličar, M. (2008). 'Organizacijska kultura v družinskih podjetjih'. *Diploma thesis*. Univerza v Mariboru Fakulteta za organizacijske vede, Kranj.

Rajasekaran, K.G., Bhaskar, G.B., Murali, S. and Chandrasekaran, M. (2016). 'Identification and Prioritisation of Supplier, Customer and Organization Collaborating Factors Influencing New Product Development'. *Indian Journal of Applied Research*, 7 (6), pp. 535-547.

Robbins, P. (2014). 'How having an innovation strategy and process can improve NPD outcomes for Irish SME's'. *The XXV ISPIM Conference – Innovation for Sustainable Economy & Society*, Dublin. Dublin, Ireland, pp. 1-40.

Roblek, M., Kern, T. and Zajec, M. (2012). 'Knowledge management of the new product development process with process-knowledge allocation model'. *The 6th IEEE International Conference on Management of Innovation and Technology*, Sanur Bali, Indonesia, pp. 214-219.

Roblek, M. and Kern, T. (1998-2016). 'ARIS procesni repozitoriji podjetij. LIPPS – Laboratorij za inženiring poslovnih in produkcijskih sistemov', Univerza v Mariboru Fakulteta za organizacijske vede. Interno gradivo.

Sinderman, B. (2012). Three Things Mid-Sized Companies Do Better. Forbes, [Online]. Available at http://www.forbes.com/sites/forbesinsights/2012/04/20/three-things-mid-size-companies-do-better.

Sosa, E. M., Gargiulo, M. and Rowles, C. (2015). 'Can Informal Communication Networks Disrupt Coordination in New Product Development Projects?'. *Organization Science*, 4, pp. 1059–1078.

Stevenson, W.J. (2015). *Operations Management* 12th ed. New York: McGraw-Hill, pp. 236-262.

Urh, B. and Kern, T. (2015). 'Is the structural efficiency of business processes connected to the effectiveness'. *Proceedings of the 34th International Conference on Organizational Science Development.* Moderna organizacija. Kranj, pp. 1221-1230.

Woschke, T., Haase, H. and Lautenschläger, A. (2016). 'Waste in NPD processes of German SMEs'. *International Journal of Productivity and Performance Management*, 4, pp. 532-553.

Impact of ISO 14001 standard on various aspects of sustainable development: a case study

Marjan Senegačnik[1], Matjaž Maletič[2], Eva Krhač[3], Damjan Maletič[4]

Abstract. Paper is concerned with the role of the ISO 14001 standard in the sustainable development in Slovenian companies. A qualitative research was performed and the method of semi-structured interview was used. Six Slovenian companies of different size and from various branches were included into research (four of them have implemented the ISO 14001 standard and two have not implemented ISO 14001). Various aspects of sustainable development were observed in the study (environmental performance, economic aspects and social efficiency). Results of the study confirm that ISO 14001 standard can be an efficient tool for improving environmental performance and social efficiency in the organization and can bring positive economic effects.

Keywords: ISO 14001 standard, sustainable development of organization, environmental performance, economic efficiency, social responsibility.

JEL Classification: I2, Q2

1 Introduction

Sustainable development and environmental protection present nowadays one of the most important areas for companies. Legislative demands on the field of environmental protection are becoming increasingly more restrictive and complex. Additionally, there should not be neglected the role of stakeholders as are business partners, customers, civil society etc. which also devote increasingly more attention to the environmental protection and sustainability. It is particularly demanding task to find a balance between environmental friendly behavior and economically successful operation.

Therefore in the scientific literature can be found many studies concerned with these problems and there has been formulated a term of sustainable organization (Hart and Milstein, 2003). The sustainable development is a comprehensive concept and can be described as so called "triple bottom line" including environmental, social and economical dimension (Dylik and Hockerts, 2002). In literature can be found studies which are focused in the economic viability and financial effects of sustainable development (Dylik and Hockerts, 2002; Salzmann et al., 2005) as well as those which are concerned with wider perspectives of sustainable development (Maletič et al., 2011). Nevertheless care for environmental responsibility and sustainable development present considerable obligation they offer also many opportunities for the compa-

[1] University of Maribor, Faculty of Organizational Sciences, Kidričeva cesta 55a, 4000 Kranj, Slovenia, marjan.senegacnik@fov.uni-mb.si.
[2] University of Maribor, Faculty of Organizational Sciences, Kidričeva cesta 55a, 4000 Kranj, Slovenia, matjaz.maletic@fov.uni-mb.si
[3] University of Maribor, Faculty of Organizational Sciences, Kidričeva cesta 55a, 4000 Kranj, Slovenia, eva.krhac@fov.uni-mb.si.
[4] University of Maribor, Faculty of Organizational Sciences, Kidričeva cesta 55a, 4000 Kranj, Slovenia, damjan.maletic@fov.uni-mb.si.

nies (Poksinska et al., 2003). Coordination of environmental responsibility with successful operation and effectiveness of the company presents considerable challenge and requires a systematic approach. In this process play important role legislative demands, situation on the market, area of activity as well as the size of the company (Maletič et al., 2015; Podpečan et al., 2014). According to Schaltegger and Synnestvedt (2002) there exists relatively strong correlation between environmental effectiveness of the organization and implementation of environmental standards.

Systems of environmental management can help the company to improve its environmental effectiveness as well as to lower its costs and improve the image of the organization (Chavan, 2005; da Silva and de Medeiros, 2004). The environmental management system also helps the company to accept environmental responsibility and to introduce the concept of continuous improvement (Poksinska et al., 2003, Psomas et al., 2013).

Eklington (1999) defines sustainable development as equilibrium between environmental protection (planet), economic success (profit) and social responsibility (people). This is in accordance with the above mentioned triple bottom line context and means successful market orientation and concurrent integration of environmental, social and economic aspects (Schlategger et al., 2013). Dyllick and Hockerts (2002) established the following three elements as necessary pillars of sustainable organization: a) sustainable organization besides economic aspects pays attention to environmental and social aspects, too; b) sustainable development of the organization requires a long-term orientation as a basis for providing current as well as future needs of the stakeholders; c) sustainable development must respect that its development is grounded on the income of the capital and not on the capital itself. Lozano (2008) proposes that various aspects and definitions of sustainable development should be interpreted from different perspectives: a) perspective of traditional economy, b) perspective of environmental economy, c) integrative perspective (including environmental, social and economic aspects), d) intergenerational perspective and e) holistic perspective.

Environmental management system ISO 14001 can be defined as guidelines for the introduction and management of environmental treatment system in the organization and can be implemented in small, medium and large companies (Poksinska et al., 2003). According to the constantly increasing importance of environmental responsibility of companies there can be observed an increase of organizations which implement environmental management systems (MacDonald, 2002; Neugebauer, 2012; Psomas et al., 2011).

In the literature prevail researches which study impact of environmental management systems on the environmental effectiveness of the company (Nawrocka and Parker, 2009; Perotto et al., 2008). Certain studies confirm positive correlation between environmental responsible behavior of the organizations and their competitive advantages (Gonzalez-Benito, 2005; Poksinska et al., 2003). Castka and Prajogo (2013) in their study confirmed positive impact of ISO 14001 standard implementation on the operational effectiveness of the organization. However there should be mentioned also that there exist also studies which give contradictory results and do not confirm a positive link between implementation of environmental protection activities and business success of organizations (Sarkis and Cordeiro, 2001; Wagner et al., 2002).

De Vries et al. (2012) observe that ISO 14001 implementation brings to the organization positive effects which can be reflected in the indicators of environmental performance as well as in business success indicators. Psomas et al. (2011) emphasize that positive effect of ISO 14001 implementation cannot be observed on short-term period but it become evident in the long run. De Vries et al.(2012) highlight as the main advantages of ISO 14001 standard for the company improvement of the competition advantages of the organization on the market, commitment of the top management to the environmental goals, clearly defined responsibilities, strong internal motivation, adequate training and involvement of employees as well as involvement of interested stakeholders in the business process.

Therefore, the majority of organizations after implementation of ISO 14001 have improved environmental performance. Employees present the crucial factor in this process according to their enhanced environmental awareness and improved understanding of company activities on the environment (Chavan, 2005; Psomas et al., 2011)

2 Methods

Plural or so called "multiple" case study has been chosen as an adequate method (Yin, 2009). Data were collected with the use of semi-structured interview which was performed among employees responsible for environmental protection or quality – therefore middle management or top management of the companies. Questions in the interview were concerned with the motives for the introduction of the ISO 14001 standard in the organization as well as with the positive results of ISO 14001 implementation where all the three dimensions of sustainable development were taken in consideration: environmental performance, social efficiency and economic performance (Maletič et al., 2015). For the organizations which have not implemented ISO 14001 standard questions have been adequately modified and the emphasis was given on the activities concerned with sustainable development performance. Questions included both close type questions as well as open type questions.

Six organizations have been included in the survey – four of them have implemented the ISO 14001 standard and two organizations which have not introduced ISO 14001. The four organizations which use ISO 14001 have implemented this standard more than 10 years ago. Ten years have been estimated as a sufficiently long period that effects of standard implementations for the organization can be clearly recognized. According to the review of the literature we have also taken into consideration a sample of 4 to 10 organizations is sufficient for a credible qualitative study (Curtis et al., 2000). General characteristics of organizations are shown in Table 1.

Organizations	Organizations with implemented ISO 14001				Organizations without implemented ISO 14001	
	Organization A	Organization B	Organization C	Organization D	Organization E	Organization F
Time of ISO 14001 implementation	13	10	10	13	0	0
Business area	Production of raw materials	Service and production	Manufacturing activity	Production	Fresh water supply, waste water treatment, remediation	Production

Table 1 General characteristics of organizations included in the study

3 Results and analysis

3.1 Motives for implementation of environmental activities

When considering motives for the introduction of the ISO 14001 standard or implementation of environmental activities in the company expectations and demands of customers are particularly emphasized as can be seen from Table 2.

Motives for implementation of environmental activities	Organizations with ISO 14001	Organizations without ISO 14001
Improved environmental performance	+++	++
Fulfillment of customers expectations and demands	+++	+++
Fulfillment of environmental legislation and regulations	+++	+++
Internal motives of organization	+++	++

Table 2 Motives for implementation of ISO 14001 or environmental activities

Those organizations which have implemented ISO 14001 emphasized as the most important motives:

- Environmental care
- Establishment of efficient environmental management system and
- Improvement of environmental performance of the processes.

According to the Bansal and Roth (2002) can be motives for introduction of the ISO 14001 divided into three groups: a) motives deriving from ethical aspects, b) motives deriving from relations with stakeholders and c) motives deriving from gaining of competitive advantages. Ethical motives are connected with environmental responsibility. Motives deriving from relations with stakeholders are concentrated both on primary stakeholders (customers, suppliers) as well as on secondary stakeholders (local communities, authorities).

In the organizations without ISO 14001 improvement of environmental performance does not present important motive for the introduction and implementation of environmental activities. In these organizations there is much more emphasized the role of external motives as are expectations of customers and fulfillment of legislative demands.

The most evident difference among both groups of organizations is connected with internal motives. The organizations with ISO 14001 defined internal motives as a very important element of introduction of environmental system.

3.2 Financial and nonfinancial aspects of business

A number of previous studies found that ISO 14001 implementation besides achievement of environmental objectives can bring also positive financial effects (de Vries et al., 2012; Heras-Saizarbitoria et al., 2010; Psomas et al., 2011; Sebhatu and Enquist, 2007). Also results of the present study that organizations with ISO 14001 observe increase of sales as well as lowering of operational costs. On the other hand, organizations without ISO 14001 have not detected any lowering of operational costs. This is in accordance with findings of other authors that environmental management system presents an efficient support for cost management (da Silva and de Medeiros, 2014; Paulraj and de Jong, 2011).

As can be seen from Table 3 both groups of organizations have observed improvement of customers satisfaction in the last years. However, the financial effects were more favorable for the organizations with ISO 14001.

Financial and nonfinancial effects of business	Organizations with ISO 14001	Organizations without ISO 14001
Increase of sales in the last three years (in comparision to sector average)	+++	++
Improved satisfactory of customers in the last three years	++	++
Lowering of operational costs in the last three years	++	+
Improved quality of our products in the last three years	++	+++

Table 3 Financial and nonfinancial aspects of business

All organizations included in the survey observe improved quality of their products in the last three years. There can be observed that organizations try to combine the concerns for quality and sustainable development.

3.3 Environmental performance

The results of study show that organizations have observed increased efficiency of raw material use as can be seen from Table 4. Particularly organizations with the implemented ISO 14001 emphasized improved efficiency of the resource use and reduced waste quantity.

Environmental performance	Organizations with ISO 14001	Organizations without ISO 14001
Improved efficiency of raw materials use in the last three years	++	++
Lowering of use of resources (electric energy, water, heat) on the product unity	+++	++
Increased per cent of use of recycled materials in the last three years	++	++
Lowered waste quantity (kg/product or kg/employee) in the last three years	+++	++

Table 4 Environmental performance

One of the organizations included in the survey stated that they achieve environmental performance through clearly defined and realistically achievable goals, measurement of goals achievement and timely action. Organizations often combine areas of environmental protection and quality assurance and about such observations report also many other authors (Corbett and Klassen, 2006; Kleindorfer et al., 2005; Proto and Supino, 2000).

3.4 Social performance

When regarding aspects of social responsibility the results of survey show that organizations devoted the main attention to the following areas:

- safety and health at work,
- improvement of motivation and satisfaction of employees and
- increased extent of education.

Also Ronnenberg et al. (2011) emphasize in their study the importance of inclusion of employees in training and education as one of the most important factors in the introduction of environmental management system. The answers on questions regarding the area of social effectiveness are shown in Table 5.

Social performance	Organizations with ISO 14001	Organizations without ISO 14001
Improved efficiency of health and safety assurance at work (in the last three years)	+++	+++
Improved level of satisfaction of employees (in the last three years)	++	+++
Improved motivation of employees (in the last three years)	++	+++
Increased extent of education and training of employees (in the last three years)	++	+++
Improved reputation of the organization (in the last three years)	++	+++

Table 5 Social performance

From the Table 5 can be seen that also organizations which have not implemented ISO 14001 are aware that sustainable development of organization depends especially on employees. Therefore also these organizations pay a lot of attention to the education of their employees.

Nevertheless, organizations without ISO 14001 have not exceeded as high degree of environmental performance as organizations with implemented ISO 14001.

4 Conclusion

The present research is concerned with the role of ISO 14001 in the process of sustainable development of organization. The results of our study support the assumption that ISO 14001 standard serves not only to achieve better environmental performance but helps also to improve other aspects of sustainable development.

One of the important findings is that organizations without ISO 14001 are concerned mainly with external motives as are expectances of customers and other stakeholders. On the other hand, internal motives play important role in the organizations with implemented ISO 14001 standard.

Some important differences were observed also when regarding economic aspects. Organizations with implemented ISO 14001 emphasized positive effects as are increased sales as well as lowered operation costs. This was not the case in organizations without ISO 14001.

In the area of social efficiency organizations with ISO 14001 highlighted environmental awareness of their employees and the introduction of internal communication. Organizations without ISO 14001 are also aware of the importance of care for their employees and for safe and healthy working environment.

At the end should be mentioned certain limitations of the present research. The number of organizations included in the study is relatively small and for more general conclusion a wider research is necessary. There should be included greater number of organizations of different size (small, medium, large) and from various areas.

References

Bansal, P. and Roth, K. (2000). 'Why Companies go Green? A Model of Ecological Responsiveness'. *Academy of Management Journal*, 43(4), pp. 717-736.

Castka, P. and Prajogo, D. (2013). 'The effect of pressure from secondary stakeholders on the internalization of ISO 14001'. *Journal of Cleaner Production*, 47, pp. 245-252.

Chavan, M. (2005). 'An appraisal of environment management systems: a competitive advantage for small businesses'. *Management of Environmental Quality: An International Journal*, 16 (5), pp. 444-463.

Corbett, C.J. and Klassen, R.D. (2006). 'Extending the Horizons: Environmental Excellence as Key to Improving Operations'. *Manufacturing & Service Operations Management*, 8 (1), pp. 5–22.

Curtis, S., Gesler, W. and Smith, G. in Washburn, S. (2000). 'Approaches to Sampling and Case Selection in Qualitative Research: Examples in the Geography of Health'. *Social Science & Medicine*, 50 (7 – 8), pp. 1001 – 1014.

Elkington, J. (1999). 'Triple bottom line revolution: reporting for the third millennium'. *Australian CPA*, 69, pp. 75-77.

da Silva, G.C.S. and de Medeiros, D.D. (2004). 'Environmental management in Brazilian companies'. *Management of Environmental Quality: An International Journal*, 15 (4), pp. 380-388.

De Vries, H.J. and Bayramoglu, D.K. in van der Wiele, T. (2012). 'Business and environmental impact of ISO 14001'. *International Journal of Quality & Reliability Management*, 29 (4), pp. 425-435.

Dyllik, T. and Hockerts, K. (2002). 'Beyond the business case for corporate sustainability'. *Business Strategy and the Environment*, 11(2), pp. 30-141.

González-Benito, J. and González-Benito, Ó. (2005). 'Environmental proactivity and business performance: an empirical analysis'. *Omega*, 33 (1), pp. 1-15.

Hart, S.L. in Milstein, M.B. (2003). 'Creating sustainable value'. *Academy of Management Executive,* 17 (2), pp. 56-69. http://www.jstor.org/stable/4165956

Heras-Saizarbitoriaa, I., Dogui, K. and Boiral, O. (2010). 'Shedding light on ISO 14001 certification audits'. *Journal of Cleaner Production*, 51, pp. 88-98.

Kleindorfer, P., Singhal, K. and Van Wassenhove, L. (2005). 'Sustainable Operations Management'. *Production and Operations Management*, 14 (4), pp. 482–492.

Lozano, R. (2008). 'Envisioning sustainability three-dimensionally'. *Journal of Cleaner Production*, 16, pp. 1838–1846.

MacDonald, J.P. (2002). 'Strategic sustainable development 1 using the ISO 14001 Standard'. *Journal of Cleaner Production*, 13, pp. 631 – 643.

Maletič, M., Maletič, D. and Gomiščck, B. (2011). 'Can sustainable quality management contribute to the organizational performance?'. *African Journal of Business Management*, 5 (9), pp. 3723–3734.

Maletič, M., Podpečan, M. and Maletič, D. (2015). 'ISO 14001 in a corporate sustainability context: a multiple case study approach'. *Management of Environmental Quality: An International Journal*, 26 (6), pp. 872-890.

Nawrocka, D. and Parker, T. (2009). 'Finding the connection: environmental management systems and environmental performance'. *Journal of Cleaner Production*, 17, pp. 601–607.

Neugebauer, F. (2012). 'EMAS and ISO 14001 in the German industry e complements or substitutes?'. *Journal of Cleaner Production*, 37, pp. 249- 256.

Paulraj, A. and de Jong, P. (2011). 'The effect of ISO 14001 certification announcements on stock performance'. *International Journal of Operations & Production Management*, 31 (7), pp. 765-788

Perotto, E., Canziani, R., Marchesi, R. and Butelli, P. (2008). 'Environmental performance, indicators and measurement uncertainty in EMS context: a case study'. *Journal of Cleaner Production*, 16, pp. 517-530.

Podpečan, M., Maletič, M., Maletič, D. and Senegačnik, M. (2014). 'Ali standard ISO 14001 spodbuja organizacije k doseganju ciljev trajnostnega razvoja? = Does standard ISO 14001 encourages organizations to achieve the sustainable development goals? '. *Fokus 2020 : zbornik 33. mednarodne konference o razvoju organizacijskih znanosti = Focus 2020 : proceedings of the 33rd International Conference on Organizational Science Development*. Kranj: Moderna organizacija, pp. 571-583.

Poksinska, B., Dahlgaard, J.J. and Eklund, J.A.E. (2003). 'Implementing ISO 14000 in Sweden: motives, benefits and comparisons with ISO 9000'. *International Journal of Quality & Reliability Management*, 20 (5), 585–606.

Proto, M. in Supino, S. (2000). 'Ecomanagement quality system: ISO 14000. The state-of-the-art in Italy'. *Total Quality Management & Business Excellence*, 11 (4), pp. 767-72.

Psomas, E.L., Fotopoulos, C.V. in Kafetzopoulos, D.P. (2011). 'Motives, difficulties and benefits in implementing the ISO 14001 Environmental Management System'. *Management of Environmental Quality: An International Journal*, 22 (4), pp. 502-521.

Ronnenberg, S.K., Graham, M.E. and Mahmoodi, F. (2011). 'The important role of change management in environmental management system implementation'. *International Journal of Operations & Production Management*, 31 (6), pp. 631-647.

Salzmann, O., Ionescu-Somers, A. and Steger, U. (2005). 'The Business Case for Corporate Sustainability: Literature Review and Research Options'. *European Management Journal*, 23 (1), pp. 27–36.

Sarkis, J. and Cordeiro, J.J. (2001). 'An empirical evaluation of environmental efficiencies and firm performance: Pollution prevention versus end-of-pipe practice'. *European Journal of Operational Research*, 135, pp. 102-113.

Schaltegger, S., Beckmann, M. and Hansen, E.G. (2013). 'Transdisciplinarity in Corporate Sustainability: Mapping the Field'. *Business Strategy and the Environment*, 22, pp. 219–229.

Schaltegger, S. and Synnestvedt, T. (2002). 'The link between ''green'' and economic success: Environmental management as the crucial trigger between environmental and economic performance'. *Journal of Environmental Management*, 65 (4), pp. 339–346.

Sebhatu, S.P. and Enquist, B. (2007). 'ISO 14001 as a driving force for sustainable development and value creation'. *The TQM Magazine*, 19 (5), pp. 468-482.

Wagner, M., Van Phu, N., Azomahou, T. and Wehrmeyer, W. (2002). 'The relationship between the environmental and economic performance of firms. An empirical analysis of the European paper industry'. *Corporate Social Responsibility and Environmental Management*, 9, pp. 133–146.

Yin, R. K. (2009). *Case Study Research: Design and Methods*, 4th ed. Thousand Oaks, CA: SAGE.

Performance-based management of public utility organizations

Mariann Veresné dr. Somosi[1], György Dr. Koczіszky[2]

Abstract. In Hungary after 2010, based on economic policy concepts, not only the number of state-owned public utility organizations was increased significantly but also the expectations against them. The authors in their research examine the characteristics of public utility organizations' performance management, with special regards on the organizations' performance-oriented and proper operation; and they make recommendation for applying a complex model.

Keywords: public utility organizations, performance-based management, compliance, performance models.

JEL Classification: L25, L32

1 Introduction

Nowadays the business organizations of the private sector apply a more complex performance measurement and evaluation methodology than before; they provide information from the performance of a given department, or college, and also the employees get feedback from the adequacy and quality of their work. This complex method supports the decision making, and on the other hand promotes the professional and human development of the employees.

In the last years the performance management gets more emphasis also in the operation of public utility organizations. The need is not occasional, hence the efficiency and effectivity of the public utility organizations (in most of the cases) does not reach the values of the private sector.

In order to make performance measurement and evaluation as a really supportive tool for the management, there is a need for processes which make the organizational and individual performance measureable.

The aim of this recent research is to examine the characteristics of public utility organizations' performance management and make recommendation for applying a complex, integrated model for their evaluation.

2 The frames of performance management

The performance management is a necessary criterion of strategy-oriented leadership, and the following factors give significant importance to it: resource allocation related to public tasks, and high quality fulfilment of the population's needs. That is why the organizational and individual performance management and evaluation has to be integrated in a process structure, which leads from the strategic planning through the implementation to the achievement of goals

[1] University of Miskolc, Faculty of Economics , Institute of Management Sciences, 3515 Miskolc-Egyetemváros, szvvsm@uni-miskolc.hu.

[2] University of Miskolc, Faculty of Economics, Institute of World-and Regional Economics, 3515 Miskolc-Egyetemváros, regkagye@uni-miskolc.hu.

(IFUA, 2010). Molnar (2016) introduces a useful framework for modern process development of public organizations.

The framework is partially standardisable, and partially contains organization-specific elements.

The essential meaning of the integrated management approach is that it handles the following as a uniform, complex process: strategy creation, organizational level determination of strategic goal hierarchy, indicator system (quantitative, qualitative) which monitors the realization of goals, determination of implementation supporting actions (and dismantling them to departments and individuals). The process is cyclical, the potential modifications and corrections can be made based on the obtained results and experiences with the help of feedbacks.

The frames of the performance-based management supporting system are determined by the requirement system of the 5E regulation applied in the public sphere (Figure 1).

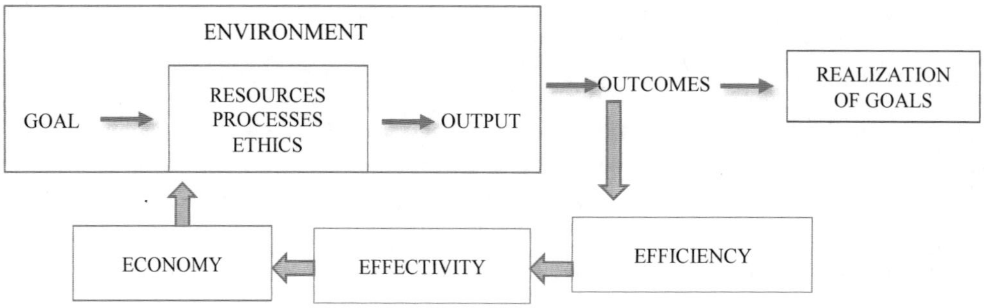

Figure 1 Complex requirement system of the public utility organizations' operation [Own compilation]

The model is suitable for the complex determination of the organizational performance, also for examining causal relationship, and linking past, present and future performances.

2.1 Expectations related to the performance-based management

The expectations related to the performance-based management framework are complex; they have to meet at the same time the following requirements (Veresné Somosi, 2013):

- goal orientation,
- measurability of goals,
- flexibility,
- clarity,
- actuality,
- comparability,
- process-orientation,
- consistence,
- possibility of further development,
- sustainability,
- integrity,
- transparency.

2.2 Method orientation

The performance measurement and evaluation practice of organizations has been changed significantly from the 1980s; it can be characterized by decreasing dominancy of financial performance measurement, by the usage of non-financial indicators, appearance of strategic performance measurement systems and value creation (Wimmer, 2000).

The literature suggests several models (e.g.: performance prism, Hoshin management, EFQM, Balanced Scorecard, etc.), which are all adequate for measuring organizational, group level or individual performance. There are several similarities and differences among the models, and furthermore their practical applicability is different (e.g.: similar future orientation, integrated indices, structures, their relation to customers and employees, definition of core processes, appearance and measurement of "invisible" assets, etc.).

According the typology of methods (Table 1) can be made a conclusion that based on the evaluation of advantages and disadvantages there is a need for a combined, more complex model, which integrates the advantages of CAF and BSC models, and gives an opportunity for managing knowledge. So the combined application of CAF (widespread in the public sphere) and BSC models creates on the one hand the breakdown of organizational performance expectations to the level of individuals, and on the other hand it guides the organization towards the realization of the formulated strategic goals and actions. Beside these we think the knowledge management as a high priority issue. Beside the continuous development of the employees' knowledge and competence also the improvement of problem solving and initiative capacity is relevant, because in this case also the goals of employees can be prevailed in a higher level, which strengthens their satisfaction and commitment. The transfer of the employees' knowledge and experience can have significant effects on the organizational strategy; it may result the definition of such goals which are responding for internal and external effects.

The joint application of these three methods can improve the organization's efficiency in goal realization, and also the quality of the organizational operation. It is important to emphasize that this framework functions not alone, and not for itself, but it improves the organizational and individual efficiency, development and motivation in a system and process approach.

3 Comparison of performance models and recommendations

The compliance management gives our model's framework, which creates opportunity to monitor compliance with the on the one hand internal and on the other hand external regulations of public utility organizations.

3.1 Comparison of performance models

Methods / Aspects	PERFORMANCE PRISM	HOSHIN MANAGEMENT	EFQM/CAF MODEL	BALANCED SCORECARD / SKANDIA NAVIGATOR (SN)
Methods' relevance	Involvement of stakeholders in the evaluation of organizational performance – reciprocity (owners, employees, customers, suppliers, social environment).	The activity of the organization's employees → realization of goals which have significant importance; short reaction time for environmental changes.	Most efficient usage of resources to reach the stakeholders' satisfaction and to increase effectivity.	The organization monitors its processes, clientele, and rates on returns, value of employees, and the context of its financial situation. SN: exploring and applying intellectual capital.
Orientation of methods	▪ Three dimensional model. ▪ Satisfaction and contribution of stakeholders. ▪ Strategies; processes; capabilities.	Definition of expected results for a given time period. Planning tools. Harmonization of the operation (3xPDCA cycle) HOSHIN performance method. Supporting the organizational study.	Capabilities (leadership, strategy, management of employees, resources, partner-relations, processes). Results (satisfaction of employees, customers and consumers, social image, result of core processes).	Financial perspective. Customers' perspective. Operational perspective. Development, learning perspective. SN: People.
Consequence of the methods' application	The protection and creation of owner's value can be realized, when the organization provides satisfaction also for the other stakeholders.	Changes of breakthrough character → for critical problems.	Examination of the organizational activity and results periodically and in a complex, system approach; comparison with the EFQM model.	Translating the strategy into indices. Exploring the effect relationship among the indices. The BSC evaluation system will be a management system.
Problems of clarity	When the selection of performance indices related to internal process is occasional. The performance indices will be not built in an integrated system.	It is harder to follow up the periodically changing system, it draws up learning pressure.	The possible follow up of critical processes' high priority; coordination problems of innovation and learning.	The uncertainty of performance expectations in all levels of hierarchy.

Methods / Aspects	PERFORMANCE PRISM	HOSHIN MANAGEMENT	EFQM/CAF MODEL	BALANCED SCORECARD / SKANDIA NAVIGATOR (SN)
Some „reality” of the method's application	The needs and expectations of and against the stakeholders are not handled adequately.	It concerns not always with the critical problems of the company.	The lack of commitment worsens the efficiency of the model application.	Through the „balance dimensions” the performance indices of the organization's important fields cannot be balanced.
The method's problems in the aspect of the system, and the organization	The application of such indicators, which do not allow the monitoring of the selected strategy's implementation. Using the indices for a „malformed” communication of strategies inside the organization. The strategy realization's incentives are not/ or only partly incorporated in the individual performance evaluation.	The improper dismantling of objectives / target values along the inner vertical and horizontal hierarchy. The diagnosis distortions of Hoshin management system.	The subjectivity of questionnaire making and of the text evaluation.	The pressure for perfect indices can make the system as impenetrable.
Problems of consistency	The performance indices do not correspond the strategies, processes and capabilities which are made to fulfil the stakeholders' needs.	The new system uses the previous year's „Hoshin results and system elements” not adequately.	Campaign actions coming from the cyclic character of self-evaluation.	▪ Wrong evaluation of results. ▪ Partial or complete absence of actions.

Table 1 Comparison of performance models [Own compilation based on Gyökér – Finna, 2008; Kaplan – Norton, 1998; Szintay, 2005]

3.2 The compliance model

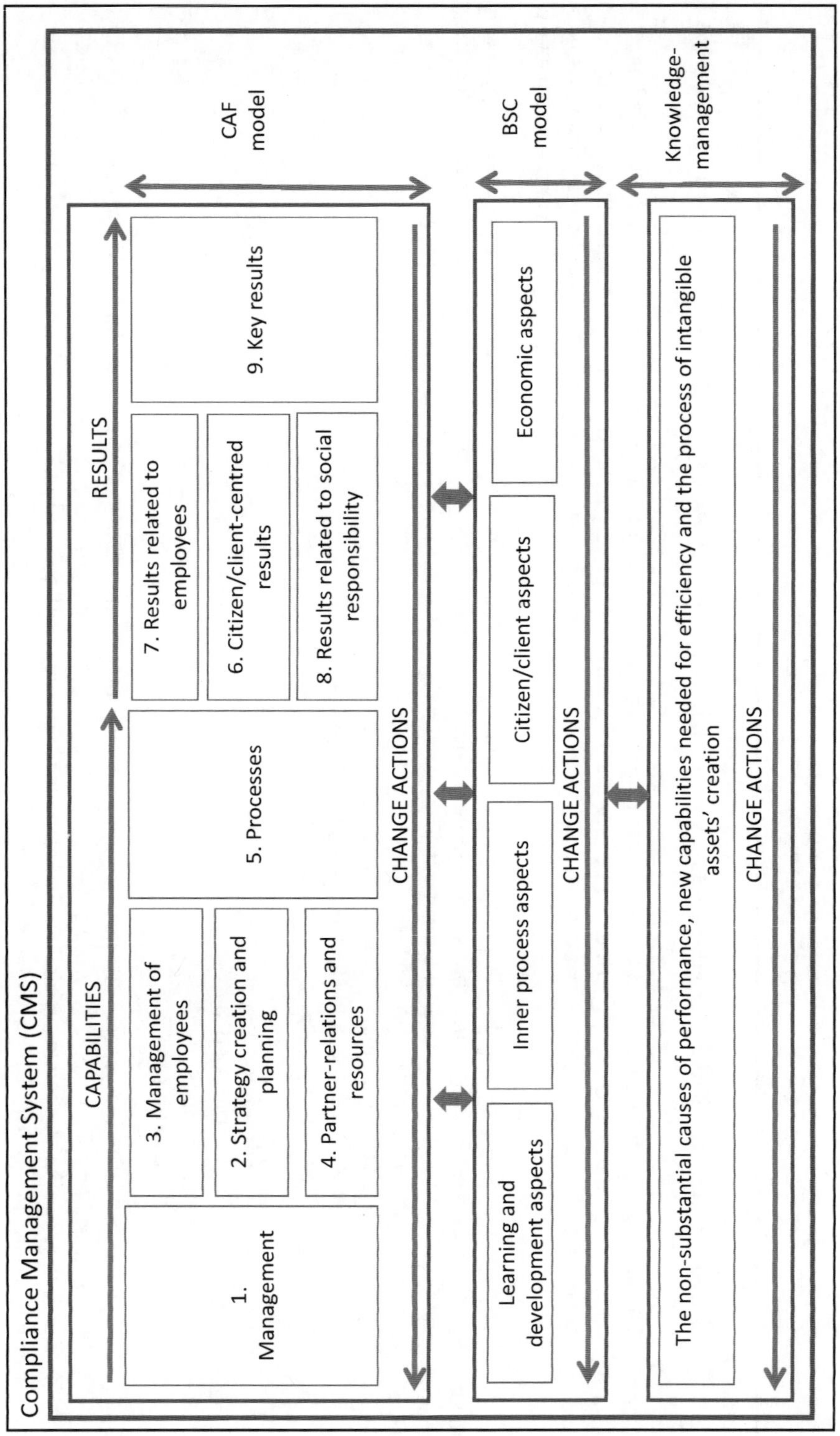

Figure 2 Performance-based management framework of public utility organizations [Own compilation]

To make the monitoring easier we have created a questionnaire which has got 6 question groups, and as a sum of 43 aspects. The questionnaire can be made with a help of a 5 graded ordinal scale (with points from one to five) (Table 2).

	Examined area	**Organization's evaluation**					$\overline{\Sigma}$
		1	**2**	**3**	**4**	**5**	
1.	Testing the complexity of legislative background						
2.	Testing the actuality of legislative background						
3.	Testing the compliance inner communication						
4.	Testing the control system						
5.	Testing the efficiency of compliance education						
6.	Testing the organizational requirements of compliance						
	Summa						

Table 2 Structure of the monitoring/controlling aspects of compliance system [own compilation]

Acknowledgement

"The described study was carried out as part of the EFOP-3.6.1-16-00011 "Younger and Renewing University – Innovative Knowledge City – institutional development of the University of Miskolc aiming at intelligent specialization" project implemented in the framework of the Szechenyi 2020 program. The realization of this project is supported by the European Union, co-financed by the European Social Fund."

References

Gyökér, I. and Finna, H. (2008). *Teljesítménymenedzsment.* Budapest: Oktatási segédanyag.

IFUA Horváth & Partners Kft. (2010). A szervezeti és egyéni szintű teljesítményértékelési rendszer továbbfejlesztése, [Online]. Budapest Főváros XVII. kerület Rákosmente Polgármesteri Hivatala. Available at: http://www.rakosmente.hu [cited 2017-01-30].

Kaplan, R. S. and Norton, D. P. (1998). *The balanced scorecard.* Budapest: Közgazdasági és jogi Könyvkiadó.

Molnar, V. (2016). 'Non-production process controlling, Six Sigma approach'. *Controller Info,* 4 (2), pp. 37-44.

Szintay, I. (2005). *Minőségmenedzsment I-III.* Miskolc: Bíbor Kiadó.

Veresné Somosi, M. (2013). *Teljesítményalapú szervezetalakítás elmélete és módszertana.* Miskolc: Miskolci Egyetemi Kiadó.

Wimmer, Á. (2000). *A vállalati teljesítménymérés az értékteremtés szolgálatában, a működési és a pénzügyi teljesítmény kapcsolatának vizsgálatában.* Budapest: Budapesti Közgazdaságtudományi és Államigazgatási Egyetem.

Do gender and personality traits influence use of deal sites? A replication

František Sudzina[1,2], Antonín Pavlíček[3]

Abstract. There is a growing body of literature on impact of personality traits on technology adoption. But majority of these studies are never replicated and, therefore, it is hard to estimate how general are their findings. The focus of this paper is adoption of deal sites, and its aim to replicate in the Czech Republic a research of deal sites use originally conducted in Denmark. While in Denmark, agreeableness, neuroticism, and gender significantly influenced use of deal sites, in the Czech Republic, it was the remaining traits - extraversion, conscientiousness, and openness to experience, and gender. In both surveys, women used deal sites more than men. If usage is defined as at least one purchase within last six months, then only gender and extraversion are significant and conscientiousness is borderline significant.

Keywords: adoption, deal sites, personality traits, empirical research.

JEL Classification: L86, M31, C12

1 Introduction

Coupons sold through deal sites are used in marketing mix of a variety of companies. According to a recent study cited by Kotler et al. (2017), "digital coupons now outpace printed newspaper coupons 10 to 1". Although some people first recall Groupon as a representative of deal sites, group-buying is not the main, nor the mandatory feature of deal sites. From a business model perspective, deal sites can be classified as affinity club (Johnson, 2010), round-up buyers (like Linder and Cantrell's (2000) buying club), and trade show (like Timmers' (1998) third-party marketplace) in the framework compiled by Taran et al. (2016).

According Delina (2014), transparency of price and demand plays a significant role in achieving fair market prices. Deal sites use transparency for accumulating marginal acceptable demand which provide possibility to offer bargain price. Smutný (2015) presents importance and the use of online marketplaces (e.g. AppStore, Groupon) for marketing activities by Czech companies that conduct business over the Internet.

In the Czech Republic, deal sites exist since 2009; a major increase in use of deal sites started in 2010 in connection with Slevomat.cz that is a still market leader and whose name became a synonym for group-buying in the Czech Republic. Till 2015, the market grew 50% year-by-year. In the last two years, the growth slowed down, revenue stabilized, and the number of competitors decreased. Nowadays, there are 45 active deal sites, of which top 5 have 90 % of market, the market leader has 40 %. The highest number of deal sites - 204 - existed in August 2011, there was a 78 % since then. The market cleared itself and deal sites strengthen their

[1] University of Chemical Technology, Department of Economics and Management, Studentská 6, 166 28 Praha, Czech Republic, sudzinaf@vscht.cz.
[2] Aalborg University, Faculty of Social Sciences and The Faculty of Engineering and Science, Department of Business and Management, A. C. Meyers Vænge 15, 2450 Copenhagen, Denmark, sudzina@business.aau.dk.
[3] University of Economics Prague, Faculty of Informatics and Statistics, Department of System Analysis, Nám. W. Churchilla 4, 130 67 Praha, antonin.pavlicek@vse.cz.

positions and brands since 2015. Digital coupons are still the fourth most common product sold on the Czech web.

Revenue of the market leader – Slevomat.cz – was over 1.2 billion Czech crowns in 2015, i.e. about a billion more than remaining deal sites. Pepa.cz, Vykupto.cz, Nákupvakci.cz, Hyperslevy.cz and Slever have revenue up to 300 million Czech crowns. In the process of consolidation, there were mergers of smaller deal sites, and bankrupcies of relatively large deal sites (Kouzelnydeda.cz, Zapakatel.cz, Nakupvakci.cz).

The most purchased product categories through Czech deal sites are Gastronomy, Fashion, Experiences, Weight Loss, Skin Care, Massage, Hair-dressing, Wellness, Language and education courses. Slevomat.cz offers the widest range of experiential services, such as cultural and adrenalin events, gastronomy, and weekend stays. Slevomat.cz does not sell coupons for fashion products and products anymore because it believes that services have higher values, esp. in relation to current increase of buying through mobile phones. The deal site also provides assurance to its customers - if dissatisfied, they will get the money back. Therefore, it is often safer to buy through Slevomat.cz than through an actual partner because customers get their money back immediately if there is any problem.

A list of top Czech deal sites is provided in Table 1.

	revenue 2012 (mil CZK)	**revenue 2015 (mil CZK)**	**Employees**	**Page visits daily**
Slevomat.cz	758	1200	160	200000
Vykupto.cz	320	300	35	33000
Zapakatel.cz	260		Bankruptcy 6/2014	
Hyperslevy.cz	159	300	40	30000
Pepa.cz	138	300	43	66000
Nakupvakci.cz	102		Bankruptcy 12/2016	
Slevoteka.cz	60	105	10	130000

Table 1 Top Czech deal sites

There is an increasing body of literature on deal sites but so far, there is only one paper on impact of gender and personality traits on use of deal sites in the Web of Science database. According to (Sudzina, 2015), gender, agreeableness, and neuroticism influence use of deal sites. The research was conducted in 2014 in Denmark, respondent were university students.

The aim of this paper is to replicate the study in the Czech Republic, also surveying university students. Some regular deal sites in the Czech Republic accidentally sold coupons for non-existing services. Stories about such fraud were published in Czech newspapers. So, results of the analysis could be influenced by the fact that respondents may have heard about such problems and may be more careful because of it. Therefore, different personality traits may be significant compared to Denmark where there was no negative experience reported so far.

The rest of the paper is organized in the following way: In the next section, there is a description what data were collected and how, and how they were analyzed. In the following section, results of the analysis are presented. The last section offers conclusions.

2 Data and methodology

Data were collected in December 2016-January 2017 using an on-line questionnaire. Respondents were 264 university students from the Czech Republic, of which 117 were male (coded as 1) and 147 female (coded as 2). Overall, 140 respondents indicated that they use deal sites (coded as 1), and 124 do not (coded as 2) - this is the dependent variable for model 1 (the replication). Moreover, there was another question that asked about how many coupons respondents bought in the last six months. Overall, 110 respondents indicated at least one purchase (coded as 1), and 154 either stated zero or were not asked the question as they indicated before that they do not use deal sites (coded as 2) - this is the dependent variable for model 2. In both cases, the software changed codes from 1 and 2 to 0 and 1, i.e. regression coefficients link to non-use. In other words, a negative (significant) regression coefficient for extraversion means that high extraversion leads to "low non-use" of deal sites, i.e. a negative (significant) regression coefficient for extraversion means that high extraversion leads to high use of deal sites.

Personality traits were measured using Rammstedt and John's (2007) Big Five Inventory-10, i.e. a 10-item version of the Big Five Inventory questionnaire developed by John and Srivastava (1999), and translated to Czech by Hřebíčková et al. (2016). The instruction was to rate "How well do the following statements describe your personality" with statements "I see myself as someone who..."

- ... is reserved,
- ... is generally trusting,
- ... tends to be lazy,
- ... is relaxed, handles stress well,
- ... has few artistic interests,
- ... is outgoing, sociable,
- ... tends to find fault with others,
- ... does a thorough job,
- ... gets nervous easily,
- ... has an active imagination

on a 1-5 Likert scale where 1 meant strongly disagrees and 5 stood for strongly agree. Extraversion was calculated as an average of the 1st (reversed-scored) and the 6th answer, agreeableness as an average of the 2nd and the 7th (reversed-scored) answer, conscientiousness as an average of the 3rd (reversed-scored) and the 8th answer, neuroticism as an average of the 4th (reversed-scored) and the 9th answer, and openness to experience as an average of the 5th (reversed-scored) and the 10th answer.

Authors are aware of the new version of Big Five Inventory - Big Five Inventory-2 (Soto and John, in press) but there is no validated translation available yet.

The questionnaire contained additional questions which were not used in the analysis presented in this paper.

Binary logisitic regression was used to analyze impact of gender and five personality traits (extraversion, agreeableness, conscientiousness, neuroticism, openness to experience) on use of deal sites in both models. A multivariate approach was used. SPSS software was used for the analysis.

3 Results

The research question is if gender, extraversion, agreeableness, conscientiousness, neuroticism, and openness to experience influence use of deal sites. Usage for model 1 is measured using a direct question on whether a respondent uses deal sites. Binary logistic regression results for the full model are provided in Table 2. Cox&Snell R^2 is 0.120, Nagelkerke R^2 is 0.160 and p-value is lower than 0.001.

	B	S.E.	Wald	Df	Sig.	Exp(B)
Gender	-1.253	.301	17.333	1	.000	.286
Extraversion	-.465	.152	9.385	1	.002	.628
Agreeableness	.070	.168	.174	1	.677	1.072
Conscientiousness	.413	.167	6.121	1	.013	1.512
Neuroticism	.040	.133	.090	1	.764	1.041
Openness to experience	.305	.154	3.918	1	.048	1.357
Constant	.555	1.134	.240	1	.625	1.742

Table 2 Binary logistic regression for the full model 1

Gender, extraversion, conscientiousness, and openness to experience significantly influence use of deal sites by university students in the Czech Republic, while it was gender, agreeableness, and neuroticism in case of university students in Denmark in the study conducted in 2014 (Sudzina, 2015). In both countries, there is a higher percentage of women using deal sites. It remains unclear if and to what extent the difference in findings may be due to deal site-related fraud stories in the Czech Republic and no such experience in Denmark. It is worth noting that, in Danish sample, frequency of use for users was significantly influenced by openness to experience, and there was a borderline impact of extraversion (Sudzina, 2016).

Classification table is provided in Table 3. Overall, the model is able to correctly predict 63.3 % of cases. It is somewhat more precise for predicting users than non-users. The percentage is similar to the one reported in (Sudzina, 2015).

Observed\Predicted	Use	Non-use	Total
Use	102	38	72.9
Non-use	59	65	52.4
Total			63.3

Table 3 Classification table for the full model 1

Carlson and Wu (2012) suggest to exclude independent variables that are not significant. Binary logistic regression results for the reduced model are provided in Table 4. Cox&Snell R^2 is 0.119, Nagelkerke R^2 is 0.159 and p-value is lower than 0.001.

	B	S.E.	Wald	Df	Sig.	Exp(B)
Gender	-1.207	.277	19.053	1	.000	.299
Extraversion	-.468	.151	9.564	1	.002	.626
Conscientiousness	.406	.166	5.969	1	.015	1.501
Openness to experience	.307	.154	3.971	1	.046	1.360
Constant	.887	.919	.933	1	.334	2.429

Table 4 Binary logistic regression for the reduced model 1

Classification table for the reduced model is provided in Table 5. The overall percentages of correctly predicted cases dropped to 61.4 %, only marginally less compared to the full model.

Observed\Predicted	Use	Non-use	Total
Use	99	41	70.7
Non-use	61	63	50.8
Total			61.4

Table 5 Classification table for the reduced model 1

To sum up, when it comes to personality traits, it is more extrovert, less conscientious and less open-to-experience people who use deal sites in the Czech Republic.

In model 2, the research question is if gender, extraversion, agreeableness, conscientiousness, neuroticism, and openness to experience influence whether a respondent purchased at least one coupon within last six months. In other words, there is a stronger requirement on who is a user. Binary logistic regression results for the full model are provided in Table 6. Cox&Snell R^2 is 0.081, Nagelkerke R^2 is 0.109 and p-value is 0.001.

	B	S.E.	Wald	Df	Sig.	Exp(B)
Gender	-1.099	.300	13.441	1	.000	.333
Extraversion	-.353	.148	5.670	1	.017	.702
Agreeableness	.020	.167	.015	1	.903	1.021
Conscientiousness	.302	.165	3.371	1	.066	1.353
Neuroticism	.094	.131	.514	1	.473	1.099
Openness to experience	.206	.153	1.822	1	.177	1.229
Constant	1.146	1.133	1.023	1	.312	3.146

Table 6 Binary logistic regression for the full model 2

Considering the stricter definition of use, gender and extraversion significantly influence use of deal sites, and the influence of conscientiousness is borderline significant. Compared to model 1, openness to experience is not significant.

Classification table is provided in Table 7. Overall, the model is able to correctly predict 60.6 % of cases. Unlike model 1, it is somewhat more precise for predicting non-users than users.

Observed\Predicted	Use	Non-use	Total
Use	46	64	41.8
Non-use	40	114	74.0
Total			60.6

Table 7 Classification table for the full model 2

Carlson and Wu (2012) suggest to exclude independent variables that are not significant. Binary logistic regression results for the reduced model are provided in Table 8. Cox&Snell R^2 is 0.073, Nagelkerke R^2 is 0.098 and p-value is lower than 0.001.

	B	S.E.	Wald	Df	Sig.	Exp(B)
Gender	-.964	.270	12.745	1	.000	.381
Extraversion	-.335	.146	5.277	1	.022	.715
Conscientiousness	.284	.163	3.025	1	.082	1.329
Constant	2.084	.800	6.790	1	.009	8.040

Table 8 Binary logistic regression for the reduced model 2

Classification table for the reduced model is provided in Table 9. The overall percentages of correctly predicted cases marginally dropped to 60.2 %.

Observed\Predicted	Use	Non-use	Total
Use	40	70	36.4
Non-use	35	119	77.3
Total			60.2

Table 9 Classification table for the reduced model 2

Since significance of conscientiousness did not improve, it will be excluded; binary logistic regression results for the reduced model are provided in Table 10. Cox&Snell R^2 is 0.062, Nagelkerke R^2 is 0.084 and p-value is lower than 0.001.

	B	S.E.	Wald	Df	Sig.	Exp(B)
Gender	-.879	.263	11.165	1	.001	.415
Extraversion	-.313	.145	4.668	1	.031	.731
Constant	2.843	.684	17.294	1	.000	17.174

Table 10 Binary logistic regression for the second reduced model 2

Classification table for the reduced model is provided in Table 11. The overall percentages of correctly predicted cases dropped to 58.7 %.

Observed\Predicted	Use	Non-use	Total
Use	40	70	36.4
Non-use	39	115	74.7
Total			58.7

Table 11 Classification table for the second reduced model 2

To sum up, when it comes to a stricter definition of use, it is women, more extrovert, and possibly less conscientious people who purchased at least one coupon within the last six months.

4 Conclusion

Although deal sites exist for many years now in the Czech Republic and Denmark now, they are used only by about one half of the surveyed respondents. The aim of the paper was to investigate the influence of gender and Big Five Inventory personality traits (extraversion, agreeableness, conscientiousness, neuroticism, openness to experience) on use of deal sites in the Czech Republic and compare results with a previous study conducted in Denmark.

With regards to the results of the conducted survey, gender, extraversion, conscientiousness, and openness to experience significantly influence use of deal sites in the Czech Republic, while in Denmark, it was gender and the remaining traits - agreeableness, and neuroticism. While significance of particular personality traits differed in both studies, both binary logistic regression models were able to correctly classify about two thirds of respondents as either users or non-users.

When a stricter definition of use is used, i.e. only respondents who purchased at least one coupon within last six months are considered to be users, only gender and extraversion are significant, and conscientiousness is borderline significant.

A somewhat surprising finding is that women in both studies were more likely to use deal sites than men, though in general men are more likely to adopt any (other) technology. It would appropriate for future studies focusing on adoption of deal sites to include gender and all five personality traits as independent, possibly control, variables.

References

Carlson, K. D. and Wu, J. (2012). 'The illusion of statistical control: Control variable practice in management research'. *Organizational Research Methods*, 15 (3), pp. 413-435.

Delina, R. (2014). 'Transparency in electronic business negotiations: Evidence based analysis'. *Quality Innovation Prosperity*, 18 (2), pp. 79-89.

Hřebíčková, M., Jelínek, M., Blatný, M., Brom, C., Burešová, I., Graf, S., Mejzlíková, T., Vazsonyi, A. T. and Zábrodská, K. (2016). 'Big Five Inventory: Základní psychometrické charakteristiky české verze BFI-44 a BFI-10'. *Československá Psychologie*, 60 (6), pp. 567-583.

John, O. P. and Srivastava, S. (1999). 'The Big Five trait taxonomy: History, measurement, and theoretical perspectives'. *Handbook of personality: Theory and research*, 2nd ed. New York: Guilford Press, pp. 102-138.

Johnson, M. W. (2010). *Seizing the White Space: Business Model Innovation for Growth and Renewal*. Boston: Harvard Business School Press.

Kotler, P., Armstrong, G., Harris, L. C. and Piercy, N. (2017). *Principles of Marketing*, 7th European ed. New Jersey: Pearson Publishing.

Linder, J. and Cantrell, S. (2000). *Changing Business Models: Surfing the Landscape*. Cambridge: Accenture Institute for Strategic Change.

Rammstedt, B. and John, O. P. (2007). 'Measuring personality in one minute or less: A 10-item short version of the big five inventory in English and German'. *Journal of Research in Personality*, 41 (1), pp. 203-212.

Smutný, Z. (2015). 'Challenges in online marketing management: A study of Czech companies in the environment of Internet-based services'. *11th International Conference on Strategic Management and its Support by Information Systems*, Uherské Hradiště, Czech Republic, pp. 100-107.

Soto, C. J. and John, O. P. (in press). 'The next Big Five Inventory (BFI-2): Developing and assessing a hierarchical model with 15 facets to enhance bandwidth, fidelity, and predictive power'. *Journal of Personality and Social Psychology*.

Sudzina, F. (2015). 'Do gender and personality traits influence use of deal sites?'. *IDIMT-2015, Information Technology and Society Interaction and Independence*, Poděbrady, Czech Republic, pp. 133-138.

Sudzina, F. (2016). 'Do gender and personality traits influence frequency of use of deal sites?' *29th Bled eConference: Digital Economy*, Kranj, Slovenia, University of Maribor, pp. 266-274.

Taran, Y., Nielsen, C., Montemari, M., Thomsen, P. and Paolone, F. (2016). 'Business model configurations: a five-V framework to map out potential innovation routes'. *European Journal of Innovation Management*, 19 (4), pp. 492-527.

Timmers, P. (1998). 'Business models for electronic markets'. *Electronic Markets*, 8 (2), pp. 3-8.

Satisfaction Assessment with the Process and Result of Online Dispute Resolution in B2B Relationships

Nikola Šimková[1], Zdeněk Smutný[2]

Abstract. Paper deals with a comparison of two methods of online dispute resolution – the first is previously proposed e-NeGotiAtion method and the second method is using e-mail communication for negotiation. For this purpose, it was carried out multiple case study. In this paper is presented the first part of the multiple case study focused on selected characteristics of a participant (e.g. age, sex, personality factors, positive and negative affectivity) and their impact on the process, result and satisfaction with online dispute resolution. It can be concluded that the process of e-negotiation, regardless of the type of used method, brings satisfaction respondents with lower Extroversion and also females with higher Agreeableness. In a case of satisfaction with the overall solution, sex does not play an important role. All respondents negotiating through e-NeGotiAtion method were satisfied with the overall solution.

Keywords: Multiple case study, Alternative dispute resolution, B2B relationships, ICT, Internet.

JEL Classification: M15, M16

1 Introduction

Internet technologies bring new communication possibilities, which support not only human but also company activities and bring social change (Pattnaik, 2013). At the same time, these technologies contribute to the globalization of economic activities, which take place in Internet-based services. With the new possibilities come the new restrictions, which are commonly associated with the nature of communication that is indirect and takes place in the Internet-based environment. In connection with communication between companies based on B2B relationship also raises the issue of conflict resolution among these companies. Such conflict is most often associated with the business activities of involved companies. There are many ways how to solve the conflicts at different levels (e.g. personal negotiation, mediation, arbitration), including various mixed approaches. These approaches, which try to solve conflicts outside the courts, are collectively called Alternative Dispute Resolution (ADR). The goal of these approaches is to come to an understanding for a reasonably short time and avoid expensive solution in the form of court proceedings (Cortés, 2011; Tang, 2007).

The subfield of ADR deals with conflicts resolution and using Internet-based technologies is called Online Dispute Resolution (ODR). According to (Lodder and Zeleznikow, 2005), ODR moves ADR from a physical to a virtual environment and mainly consists of ADR processes. This field is mainly focused on conflict resolution in the B2C and C2C relationships and conflicts between people in general (e.g. divorce). In this field is used a variety of more or less automated approaches that are often built on the principles of artificial intelligence (Carneiro et

[1] Technical University of Košice, Faculty of Economics, Department of Banking and Investment, Nemcovej 32, 040 01 Košice, Slovakia, nikola.simkova@tuke.sk; Masaryk University, Žerotínovo nám. 617/9, 601 77 Brno, Czech Republic, nikola.simkova@mail.muni.cz.

[2] University of Economics, Prague, Faculty of Informatics and Statistics, Department of Systems Analysis, W. Churchill Sq. 4, 130 67 Prague 3, Czech Republic, zdenek.smutny@vse.cz.

al., 2014). Article (Xu and Yuan, 2009) distinguishes four main types of ODR systems: automated negotiation, assisted negotiation, mediation, and arbitration. In the paper (Simkova and Smutny, 2016) was introduced a conceptual design of ODR process using a genetic algorithm, which is focused on B2B relationships. This conceptual design consists of a method (assisted negotiation), in which is used a genetic algorithm for selection of the most appropriate resolution to the dispute from the perspective of involved parties.

As a part of our further research, this conceptual design was implemented into artifact – the method where is the proposed genetic algorithm used. In order to evaluate the relevance of the proposed solution was prepared multiple case study, where is compared traditional negotiation using only e-mail communication and proposed method using a genetic algorithm.

The aim of this paper is to introduce and discuss the first results of this case study related to satisfaction assessment with the process and result of online dispute resolution. This paper assesses the negotiation process in terms of selected characteristics of participants and addresses the question: What effect have selected characteristics of participants (e.g. age, sex, country of study, personality factors, positive and negative affectivity) on the process, result and satisfaction with ODR?

2 Methodology

To carry out multiple case study research was selected the procedure described in (Yin, 2014). A case study is very similar to experiment, which requires full control of systematic and precision of execution by given researcher, what is connected to the deterministic behavior of the studied system. In the case of the social component involvement, the system becomes non-deterministic and it is preferable to use the specific research methods such as a case study. In this research, we used multiple case design, which is composed of several equally executed case studies.

For simulating negotiations between the companies were selected students from two universities in two different countries. It was carried out 20 individual case studies. Half of the case studies was conducted using e-NeGotiAtion method introduced in (Simkova and Smutny, 2016) and the second half in the form of free communication via e-mail (e-Mail method). For each of these forms were two completely different scenarios (case study scenario 1 or 2) of the dispute between buyer and seller. Case study had the following six phases which description is shortened due to the length of the paper:

- *Plan* – set of objectives for the case study research and process design of its implementation;
- *Design* – preparation of detailed plan of case studies execution (e.g. introduce participants with the task, schedule of questionnaires sending);
- *Prepare* – creation of program that uses a genetic algorithm described in (Simkova and Smutny, 2016) and preparation of questionnaires or other background materials;
- *Collect* – realization of individual case studies;
- *Analyze* – evaluation and interpretation of the acquired data;
- *Share* – preparation of specific outcomes of multiple case study for different audiences or conferences and journals.

Although this paper only presents the first results of the multiple case study, which is indirectly related to the evaluation of the proposed artifact in the form of the method, so it brings interesting findings regarding to the approach of participants in the negotiating process. This paper provides general results of behavioral research that is always connected with the design science research (Kampling et al., 2016). These findings will be used in further research dealing with the psychological aspects of the negotiation (personal level) using ODR approaches.

3 Multiple case study

The participants in the study were 40 students (mean age 23.6; SD=2.3) who formed pairs. Each pair was tasked to negotiate online and consists of one participant from Faculty of Economics, Technical University of Košice in Slovakia and one participant from Faculty of Informatics and Statistics, University of Economics, Prague in the Czech Republic. Participants were randomly assigned a role (buyer/seller), a method (e-NeGotiAtion/e-Mail) and a type of case study scenario (1/2). This case study was also part of two different courses in Slovakia and the Czech Republic, where the aim was to simulate real conditions (as a business game) in the negotiations between companies as a part of teaching – see a similar approach to teaching described e.g. in (Mildeova and Capek, 2015).

Before negotiation students filled in an initial questionnaire. This questionnaire had as the main goal to determine if there were any differences between the randomly generated pairs. We measured the participant's personality in terms of the Big-Five dimensions (Extroversion, Agreeableness, Conscientiousness, Emotional Stability and Openness). To identify these values participants before reading the case study were asked to which extent they agree or disagree with 10 statements on a 7-point scale (1-Disagree strongly, 7-Agree strongly). This instrument is called the Ten Item Personality Measure (TIPI) (Cobb-Clark and Schurer, 2012). We were also interested in measuring emotions after reading the case study. For this purpose, we used the Positive and Negative Affect Schedule (PANAS) instrument (Watson, Clark and Tellegen, 1988). To determine positive and negative affects participants were asked to rate the extent to which they experienced each of the 20 emotions on a 5 point scale (1-Very slightly, 5-Very much).

3.1 Characterization of the population

The box plots (Figure 1) summarize the measured values of personality and affects. As can be seen, positive affect is higher than negative affect, what is expected in a healthy population.

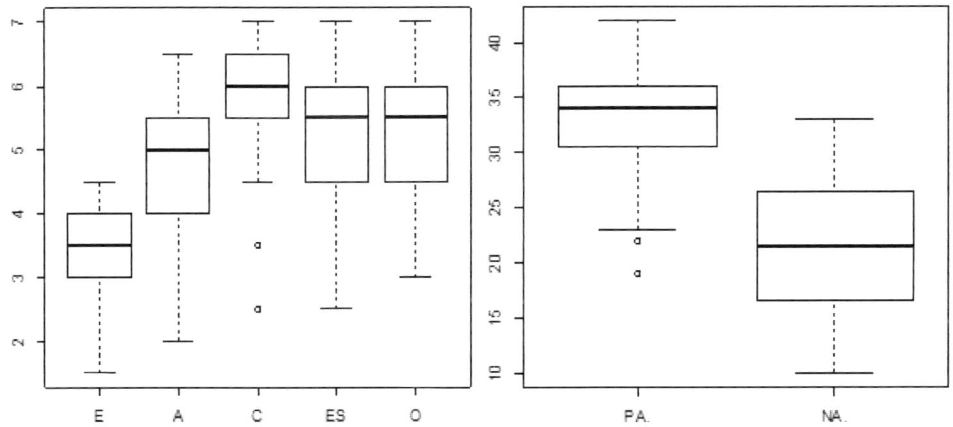

Figure 1 Measured values of personality, positive and negative affects

The Mann-Whitney nonparametric test was used to identify eventual differences in personality and emotional state of respondents. At a significance level ($\alpha = 0.05$), we tested the following hypotheses:

- H_0: The medians for personality/emotional measure (E/A/C/ES/O/PA/NA) of the two groups (buyers/sellers, e-NeGotiAtion/e-Mail method, case study scenario 1/case study scenario 2, students from Slovakia/students from the Czech Republic, males/females) are equal.
- H_1: The medians for personality/emotional measure of the two groups are not equal.

As a result, we obtained p-values of the Mann-Whitney test, which are shown in Table 1.

	Buyers vs. Sellers	e-NeGotiAtion vs. e-Mail	Case study scenario 1 vs. 2	Students from SK vs. CZ	Males vs. Females
E	0.07131	0.6875	0.0592	0.3599	0.4035
A	0.848	0.2918	0.6029	0.004215	0.02824
C	0.945	0.4643	0.07047	0.214	0.01476
ES	0.1405	0.1442	0.1519	0.8592	0.1325
O	0.8155	0.0639	0.1786	0.5368	0.4006
PA	0.2067	0.4718	0.5871	0.2217	0.9448
NA	0.8283	0.2074	0.4239	0.7245	0.2931

Table 1 *p*-values of the Mann-Whitney test

Regard to the aspects that were randomly assigned to participants (role, method and type of case study scenario) we obtained in all cases (E/A/C/ES/O/PA/NA) p-value exceeding the significance level, so we do not reject the null hypothesis. This means that possible different results of the negotiation between the two groups are not caused by statistically significant differences in personalities or their emotional state after reading a case study.

The aspects such as the country of study and sex, which were not assigned randomly, brought slightly different results. If we focus on the country of the study, we do not reject the null hypothesis of equal medians for personal predispositions and temporary mood fluctuations except for agreeableness of the participants. For this personality factor we adjusted alternative hypothesis as the one-sided:

- H_0: The medians for Agreeableness of the students in Slovakia and in the Czech Republic are equal.
- H_1: The median for Agreeableness of the students in Slovakia is higher than in the Czech Republic.

The result of the test brought p-value equal to 0.002108, based on which we reject the null hypothesis of equal medians for Agreeableness in favor of the alternative hypothesis that students in Slovakia have higher statistically significant Agreeableness compared with students in the Czech Republic.

In our research appear 24 males and 16 females. The null hypothesis of equal medians for personality factors and emotional state we do not reject excluding Agreeableness and Conscientiousness. In these cases, we formulated one-sided alternative hypotheses:

- H_0: The medians for Agreeableness/Conscientiousness of males and females.
- H_1: The median for Agreeableness/Conscientiousness of males is lower than females.

In these two tests are p-values (0.01412 and 0.007382) less than the specified significance level, therefore we reject the null hypothesis of equal medians for these two personality factors in favor of the alternative hypotheses, that males have lower Agreeableness and Conscientiousness than females. There are a lot of studies about gender differences in the personality. Researchers found that the magnitude of gender differences varied across cultures, but women reported themselves to be higher in Neuroticism (Emotional Stability) and Agreeableness, while in other personality dimensions there are no significant gender differences (Costa, Terracciano and McCrae, 2001). Weisberg, DeYoung and Hirsh (2011) showed the largest gender difference in Agreeableness.

3.2 Results

When the negotiations are completed, respondents filled in a final questionnaire that had a possibility to assess the process and results of the e-negotiation. We analyzed data obtained from initial and final questionnaires together with results of the negotiations in SPSS software Clementine 11.1 and we used C5.0 algorithm for creating decision trees and rules.

We were interested in what would be the impact of the respondent characteristics - age, sex, country of study, five personality factors (Extroversion, Agreeableness, Conscientiousness, Emotional Stability and Openness), positive and negative affects - on the satisfaction with the process of e-negotiation. Participants rated this indicator on a scale from 1 (very dissatisfied) to 7 (very satisfied). For creation a decision tree and rules we assigned values 1-3 dissatisfied (N), 4 - neither dissatisfied nor satisfied (N/Y) and values 5-7 we identified as satisfied with the process of e-negotiation (Y).

Using C5.0 algorithm, we obtained decision tree and three decision rules with 90% confidence:

1) rule: if it is a female with Extroversion more than 3 and with Agreeableness less than or equal to 4.5, then she is not satisfied with the process of e-negotiation (instance: 3, confidence: 0.8);
2) rule: if a person has an Extroversion less than or equal to 3, then he/she is satisfied with the process of e-negotiation (I: 14, C: 0.938);

3) rule: if a female has an Agreeableness more than 4.5, then she is satisfied with the process of e-negotiation (I: 11, C: 0.923).

If we included the method as input, we got the same results, so satisfaction with the process of e-negotiation is not related to the method used by the respondents.

We used again the same inputs (the respondent characteristics), but we chose as output satisfaction with the overall solution, which values were grouped into three categories: values 0-4 are identified as not satisfied (N), 5 as neither dissatisfied nor satisfied (N/Y) and values 6-10 are labeled as satisfied with the overall solution (Y), where the evaluation scale was from 0 (absolutely unsatisfactory solution) to 10 (maximum satisfactory solution).

The result was a decision tree with 97.5% confidence and three decision rules with 95% confidence:

1) rule: if negative affect of a person exceeds 25 and he/she is older than 23 years, then he/she is neither dissatisfied nor satisfied with the overall solution (I: 6, C: 0.625);
2) rule: if a person has a negative affect less than or equal to 25, then he/she is satisfied with the overall solution (I: 26, C: 0.964);
3) rule: if a person is younger than 23 years, then he/she is satisfied with the overall solution (I: 23, C: 0.96).

Considering the method as an input to the model, other factors are shown relevant for satisfaction with the overall solution. We got a decision tree and five decision rules with 100% confidence:

1) rule: if a person negotiates via e-Mail and has an Agreeableness less than or equal to 3, then he/she is neither dissatisfied nor satisfied with the overall solution (I: 2, C: 0.5);
2) rule: if a person is older than 23 years, negotiates via e-Mail and Emotional Stability has more than 5.5, then he/she is neither dissatisfied nor satisfied with the overall solution (I: 2, C: 0.75);
3) rule: if Agreeableness is higher than 3 and Emotional Stability is less than or equal to 5.5, then the person is satisfied with the overall solution (I: 23, C: 0.96);
4) rule: if he/she is younger than 23 years, then the person is satisfied with the overall solution (I: 23, C: 0.96);
5) rule: if a person uses a new method e-NeGotiAtion, he/she is is satisfied with the overall solution (I: 20, C: 0.955).

Especially the fifth decision rule brings to us valuable information that all participants using the method e-NeGotiAtion presented in (Simkova and Smutny, 2016) are satisfied with the overall solution.

4 Discussion

We found that the process of e-negotiation, regardless of the type of used method, brings satisfaction respondents with lower Extroversion (less than or equal to 3) and also females with higher Agreeableness (more than 4.5).

In a case of satisfaction with the overall solution, sex does not play an important role. Without considering the method as an input, we identified that participants with lower negative affect (less than or equal to 25) together with younger respondents (less than 23 years) are satisfied with the overall solution. Including the type of the method, higher Agreeableness (more than 3) and lower Emotional Stability (less than or equal to 5.5) means satisfaction with results of e-negotiation. Moreover, all respondents negotiating through e-NeGotiAtion method are satisfied with the overall solution.

An important advantage of the proposed method e-NeGotiAtion compared to other approaches to negotiation is its scalability in the case of negotiation between multiple parties. Genetic algorithm used in the method can be easily adapted for this purpose, while still providing relevant solutions taking into account views of all parties involved in the negotiation.

Limitation of the carried out case study is the involvement of students, who simulated the work of account managers. In practice, it is common, that the contracts and the associated potential conflicts solves more commonly senior account managers. For this reason, we see as limiting the age of the students and their experiences in the field. However, we believe that the case study results are relevant because the objective of both students and account managers is to maximize their profits (or minimize losses) during the negotiation.

In connection with the practical deploying of e-NeGotiAtion method has to be always taken into account the contextual conditions of the deployment. If we assume that the method will be deployed globally thanks to ICT, so its potential preference over other ADR approaches will be connected to the particular cultural context in which a given company trades. Based on experience from other fields e.g. (Sudzina, 2014), it can be assumed, that the trust in the mediated negotiation will be related to the particular cultural context.

Acknowledgement

Authors would like to thank all students from the both countries, which participated in this case study research.

References

Carneiro, D. et al. (2014). 'Online dispute resolution: An artificial intelligence perspective'. *Artificial Intelligence Review*, 41 (2), pp. 211-240. DOI: 10.1007/S10462-011-9305-Z

Cobb-Clark, D. A. and Schurer, S. (2012). 'The stability of big-five personality traits'. *Economics Letters,* 115 (1), pp. 11-15.

Cortés, P. (2011). 'Developing online dispute resolution for consumers in the EU: A proposal for the regulation of accredited providers'. *International Journal of Law and Information Technology*, 19 (1), pp. 1-28. DOI: 10.1093/IJLIT/EAQ011

Costa, P. T. Jr, Terracciano, A. and McCrae, R. R. (2001). 'Gender differences in personality traits across cultures: robust and surprising findings'. *J Pers Soc Psychol.*, 81 (2), pp. 322-31.

Kampling, H., Klesel, M. and Niehaves, B. (2016). 'On Experiments in Design Science Research and Theory Development: A Literature Review'. *Proceedings of the 49th Hawaii International Conference on System Sciences*, New York, IEEE, pp. 4454-4463. DOI: 10.1109/HICSS.2016.554

Lodder, A. R. and Zeleznikow, J. (2005). 'Developing an Online Dispute Resolution Environment: Dialogue Tools and Negotiation'. *Harvard Negotiation Law Review*, 10, pp. 287-337.

Mildeova, S. and Capek, M. (2015). 'Business Games for Management Trainings: An Illustration by the Game Dynacorp?'. *Proceedings of the 12th International Conference on Efficiency and Responsibility in Education*, Prague, Czech Republic, pp. 363-369.

Pattnaik, B. K. (2013). 'Globalization, ICT Revolution in India and Socio-cultural Changes: Sociological Explorations'. *Polish Sociological Review*, 181, pp. 39-62.

Simkova, N. and Smutny, Z. (2016). 'Conceptual Design of Online Dispute Resolution in B2B Relationships'. *Proceedings of the 24th Interdisciplinary Information Management Talks*, Podebrady, Czech Republic, pp. 303-310.

Sudzina, F. (2014). 'Does Trust Influence the Extent of Inter-Organizational Barter?'. *Proceedings of the 14th International Conference on Finance and Banking*, Ostrava, Czech Republic, pp. 394-400.

Tang, Z. (2007). 'An effective dispute resolution system for electronic consumer contracts'. *Computer Law and Security Report*, 23 (1), pp. 42-52. DOI: 10.1016/J.CLSR.2006.11.002

Watson, D., Clark, L. A. and Tellegen, A. (1988). 'Development and validation of brief measures of positive and negative affect: the PANAS scales'. *J Pers Soc Psychol.*, 54 (6), pp. 1063-70.

Weisberg, Y. J., DeYoung, C. G. and Hirsh, J. B. (2011). 'Gender Differences in Personality across the Ten Aspects of the Big Five'. *Front Psychol.*, 2 (178), pp.

Xu, Z. and Yuan, Y. (2009). 'Principle-based dispute resolution for consumer protection'. *Knowledge-Based Systems*, 22 (1), pp. 18-27. DOI: 10.1016/J.KNOSYS.2008.04.009.

Yin, R. K. (2014). *Case Study Research: Design and Methods*. Los Angeles: SAGE Publications.

SECTION B

Project management

Project templates draft based on an analysis of the current state of the implementation and application of IFRS in the Czech Republic

Hana Bartková[1], Hana Štverková[2], Jitka Baňařová[3]

Abstract. Currently, IFRS are the world's most widely used standard for compilation and publication of financial statement. That is the reason why companies decide to transition to these standards. The transition could be described as a standardized process that can define a sequence of the steps. Project templates draft based on an analysis of the current state of the implementation and application of IFRS in the Czech Republic as performance enhancers for support of SMEs. The activities that need to be implemented to fulfill the objective of implementation and use of IFRS in the SMEs are described in this paper.

Keywords: IFRS, small and medium-sized enterprise, project, template.

JEL Classification: M2, M41

1 Introduction

In today's turbulent and dynamic business environment occurs - due to the globalization – the cooperation with the foreign companies or networking of small and medium-sized enterprises in different sectors and countries. On the basis of the pilot survey was found - through the market research and secondary analysis of data - that 60% of large businesses already use international financial reporting standards (the parent company, interconnected companies, etc.). Because of this fact the field survey aimed at small and medium-sized enterprise (hereinafter "SME"), which are considered the backbone of national economies - they constitute 99.6% of all enterprises in the Czech Republic. For identification and addressing of SMEs was primarily chosen typology according to Eurostat, i.e. business with up to 99 employees. (Stverkova, 2013; SBA, 2015)

It was examined whether they are using or planning to implement International Financial Reporting Standards (hereinafter "IFRS"). In the questionnaire survey the typology was adapted according to the Accounting Act and according to the law on support for SMEs, so the results of inquiries and proposals would be relevant. Based on the survey results the project template draft was carried out for implementation and use of IFRS in terms of legislation of the Czech Republic. (Matoskova et al, 2013; Malerova et al, 2014; Pokorny and Gondek, 2016) Part of the project templates proposal is to use project management methodology (Mutinova and Banarova, 2013), especially capturing the process by using algorithms, Work Breakdown Structure (hereinafter "WBS") and Gantt diagram.

[1] VŠB-TU Ostrava, Faculty of Economics, Department of Accounting and Taxes, Sokolská třída 33, 701 21 Ostrava 1, Czech Republic, hana.bartkova@vsb.cz.

[1] VŠB-TU Ostrava, Faculty of Economics, Department of Business Administration, Sokolská třída 33, 701 21 Ostrava 1, Czech Republic, hana.stverkova@vsb.cz.

[1] VŠB-TU Ostrava, Faculty of Economics, Department of Systems Engineering, Sokolská třída 33, 701 21 Ostrava 1, Czech Republic, jitka.banarova@vsb.cz.

2 Theoretical basis of International Financial Reporting Standards (IFRS) a Small and Medium Sized Enterprises (SMEs)

IFRS are one form of international harmonization of accounting with the broadest international application and with a long tradition. The basic objective is to achieve worldwide harmonization of financial accounting and reporting. These are high quality accounting rules, which offer quick and effective solutions to the problems of the companies operating in the capital markets. They are not binding, they are only a recommendation for the accounting professional organizations in each country, so they can applied those in their national standards or accounting modifications. Standards are formulated in general, including the possibility of alternative procedures, ensuring their wide international acceptability (e.g. in a non-inflationary as well as in a hyperinflationary economy, etc.). (KACR, 2016)

Currently are these accounting rules the world´s most widely used standard for compilation and publication of financial statement. Their use is not limited only to Europe but they are - or will be - gradually used both in North and South America, Australia, Asia and Africa. If there will be differences of interpretation during the application of standards, comments on them will be issued by so called Standing Interpretations Committee of the Committee on International Accounting Standards, respectively nowadays "IFRS Interpretations Committee" and the interpretations issued by the Committee (formerly SIC – "Standing Interpretations Committee", now IFRIC – "International Financial Reporting Standard(s)"). Interpretations form a part of the mandatory literature of IASB.

Accounting problems in the Czech Republic are above all because of detailed and complicated legislative regulations, where you can find variants that although suit to the law, but goes against the essence of the problem. If there was only the basic principle which has been checked here would be less room for circumvention.1 However, the results of foreign studies show that the adoption of IFRS becomes always an asset for the company, but it can be expected over a long period of time.

It is obvious that the impacts of harmonization of accounting for Czech companies will become stronger and that the timely solution of issues will provide some competitive advantage in the future. For many companies transition to IFRS will mean major changes that will affect all business transactions from relations with investors to everyday procedures and can affect not only the viability of some products, but also the reported profitability of the whole company.

The small companies have been often presented as a hidden giant. The SMEs have the key position in the national economy in terms of creating of healthy entrepreneurial surroundings; they are of high importance for the development of the national economy, regions, individual towns and villages. They help to create the healthy entrepreneurial surroundings and increase the market dynamics. The development of small and medium-sized enterprises is generally regarded as a main factor of economic development and this in disregard of economic advancement of the country. (Stverkova, 2013; Blecharz and Stverkova, 2014)

SMEs represented 99.9% of businesses in the Czech non-financial business economy. The proportion of micro-companies stood at 96.1%, around 3.4 percentage points above the EU average. (SBA, 2015)

The knowledge of deeper classifications aspects of SMEs as "EU Recommendations" has been essential in claiming of different benefits, which EU for SMEs in its member states provides. The small and medium-sized enterprise has been defined in the legislation of Czech Republic and in the European Union for purpose of its support. In the Czech Republic has been this definition mentioned in the Act on Promotion of Small and medium-sized entrepreneurship No. 47/2002 Col., as amended. Since January 1st, 2005 has been in force also the definition of SMEs for purposes of granting of aid from public funds in the sphere of EU. According to recommendation of European Commission, EU recommendation 2003/361 have been the enterprises classified this way:

- micro-enterprise – employing up to 10 employees, net sales for the last closed accounting period does not exceed EUR 2 million and the assets, in the balance sheet, does not exceed EUR 2 million (this category has been earmarked within the small enterprises);
- small enterprises – employing up to 50 employees, net sales for the last closed accounting period and the assets, in the balance sheet, does not exceed EUR 10 million;
- medium-sized enterprises – employing up to 250 employees, net sales for the last closed accounting period does not exceed EUR 50 million and the assets, in the balance sheet, does not exceed EUR 43 million.

For all mentioned categories of enterprises has been the independence another necessary condition, i.e. no other person or more people together, who fulfill above mentioned requirements, cannot have 25% or larger share in fixed capital of enterprise or its voting rights.

The determination of SMEs has not been usually clear, because the sorting aspects of each institution have been different. The most common using has been the sorting according to number of employees, assets, performance, added value and other criteria.

The next possibility how to classify the enterprises is according to the Czech Statistical Office. Except of above mentioned classification of small and medium-sized entrepreneurship, which represents the quantitative classification, exist also the qualitative aspect of SMEs. The qualitative determination of SMEs has been an important prerequisite for a correct understanding and definition of this group. The small and medium-sized enterprise has been affected by the owner of this enterprise, who usually performs three roles. In contrast to the big enterprises have been by the small and medium-sized enterpriser unified individual tasks: the owner, managing of property rights, the general manager, professional managing of enterprise, and the professional specialist of the enterprise, performing the profession. The management has been practiced mainly by the enterpriser, i.e. the owner and therefore has been based not so much on knowledge, but rather on the intuition and the improvisation. The organizational structure has been mostly flat, which means an easier and faster communication between the management and the employees and also the individual workers. (Stverkova and Humlova, 2016) The marketing has been realized only in a limited space and because it's easy adaptability have been the SMEs able to react quickly to the market changes. The human resources have been practiced primarily by the owner or the management. The employees must be universally specialized so that they can better adapt to any change in the production process. (Stverkova, 2013)

The SMEs ensure on the market the competition and counteract the monopolistic tendencies. The enterprises have been forced to try to search for the most optimal market finding. They ensure to the consumers the possibility of a choice in consumption; the competition allows operating to reduce prices. The high flexibility of small enterprises has been an impulse for an innovation and structure changes.

The SMEs ensure the social stability and the freedom. They give a chance to free finding of entrepreneurs, to a self-realization of citizens in the economic sphere. The employment has been together with the ensuring of economic growth, acceptable inflation and balanced payment balance the basic aim of the economic policy. The SMEs have been creating the available employment, especially for the group of job applicants, who have been entering firstly to the labour market, for women (part-time work), the freed manpower from the secondary sector etc. The importance of an existence of SMEs has been also given by their contributing to fulfillment of the main aims of economic and social policy (especially of labour policy), the price stability, the balance of the payment balance etc.

3 The results of the field survey

During the months of October 2016 to January 2017 conducted polling the companies related to the use of IFRS. Approached was approximately 350 companies. On the survey answered 154 respondents, which is a 44% return.

Based on the survey were found the following facts:

- Respondent´s companies are based in the Czech Republic at 100% and all are up to 25% owned by a foreign entity;
- Connection to the foreign entities is shown in Graph 1. In terms of the main study examined subjects, 30% of businesses in the service sector, 50% in manufacturing, 10% in trade and the remainder in other activities, as shown in Graph 2.

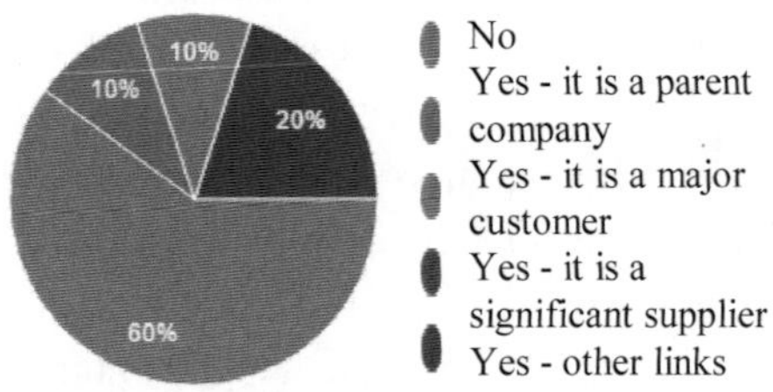

Graph 1 Connection to the foreign entities [Own elaboration]

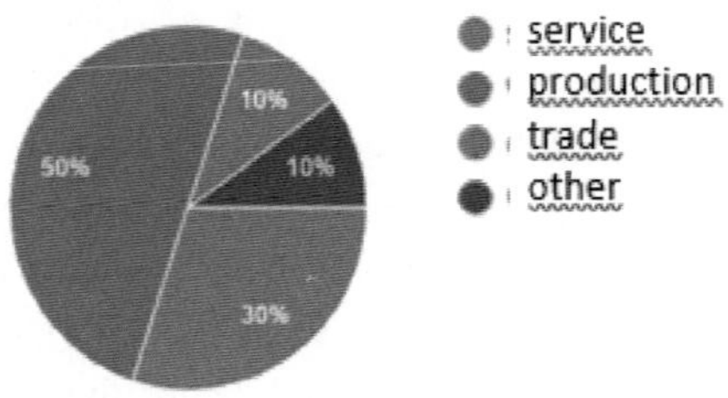

Graph 2 Terms of the main study examined subjects [Own elaboration]

Analyzed was also the representation of companies by number of employees (micro, small, medium and large enterprise), as defined by the law on the promotion of entrepreneurship, mentioned in chapter one of this paper. Percentage representation by number of employees is captured in Graph 3. Another aspect for the typology of the company is turnover, the survey results are depicted in Graph 4. From a quantitative point of view the typology of SMEs according to the law on the promotion of entrepreneurship is important aspect of the amount of assets in the company. Shown in Graph 5.

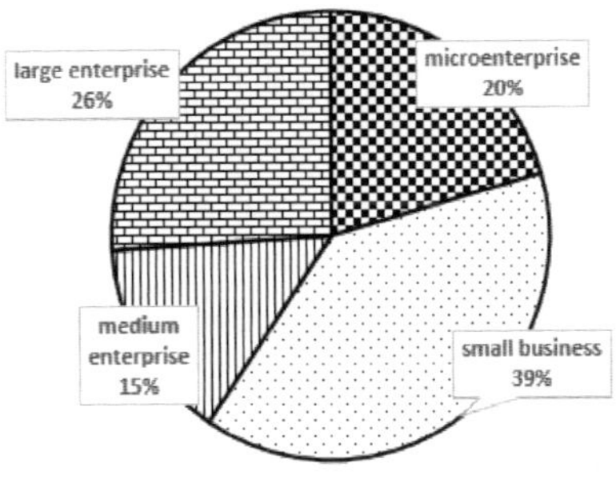

Graph 3 Number of employees [Own elaboration]

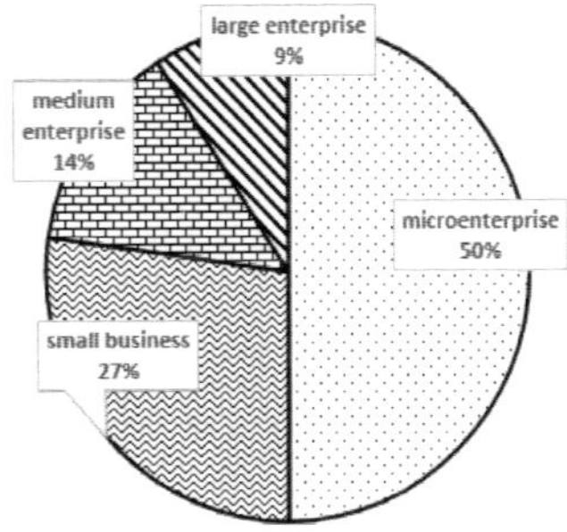

Graph 4 Typology according to the company turnover [Own elaboration]

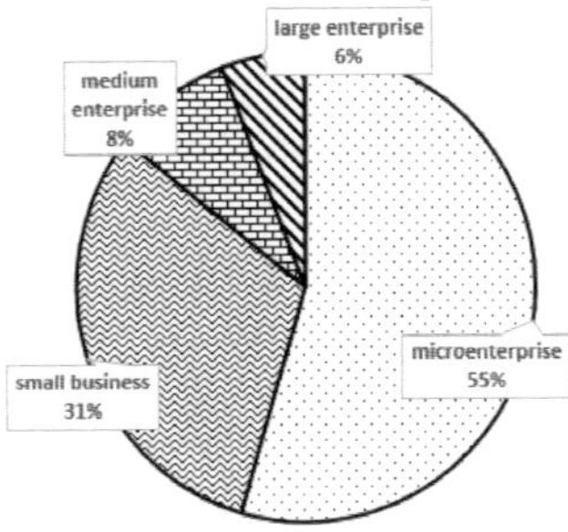

Graph 5 The amount of assets in the company [Own elaboration]

The survey showed that only 21% of respondents show results by a different accounting system than national. Of these 21% is 11% in a system of IAS / IFRS, and 10% use international standard US GAAP.

In the analysis it was found that the biggest adjustments are carried out during the transition from national accounts to another accounting system while editing:

- value of property,
- depreciation,
- leasing,
- grants,
- temporal resolution,
- claims,
- revenues,
- costs,
- stock.

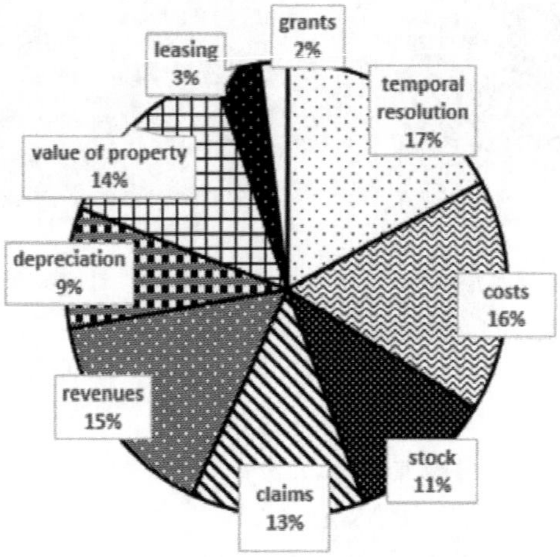

Graph 6 Types of adjustments during the transition from national accounts to another accounting system [Own elaboration]

4 Project templates draft

Based on the survey 21% of respondents use international accounting standards and further 20% of businesses plan to introduce IFRS within 2 years. Because of this can be assumed that this is not an isolated element, but can be predicted generalization of this trend also in terms of globalization tendencies. Therefore it is a system process.

This process can be expressed on the basis of systematic follow-up steps that can be formalized using general project templates. This can be expressed using an algorithm that expresses a logical sequence of individual phases, which can be then atomized into individual activities, shown in Figure 1. This so called "WBS structure" (Figure 2), which describes the activities that need to be implemented to fulfill the objective of the project, in this case implementation and use of IFRS in the company. (Rehacek, 2015; Banarova, 2011)

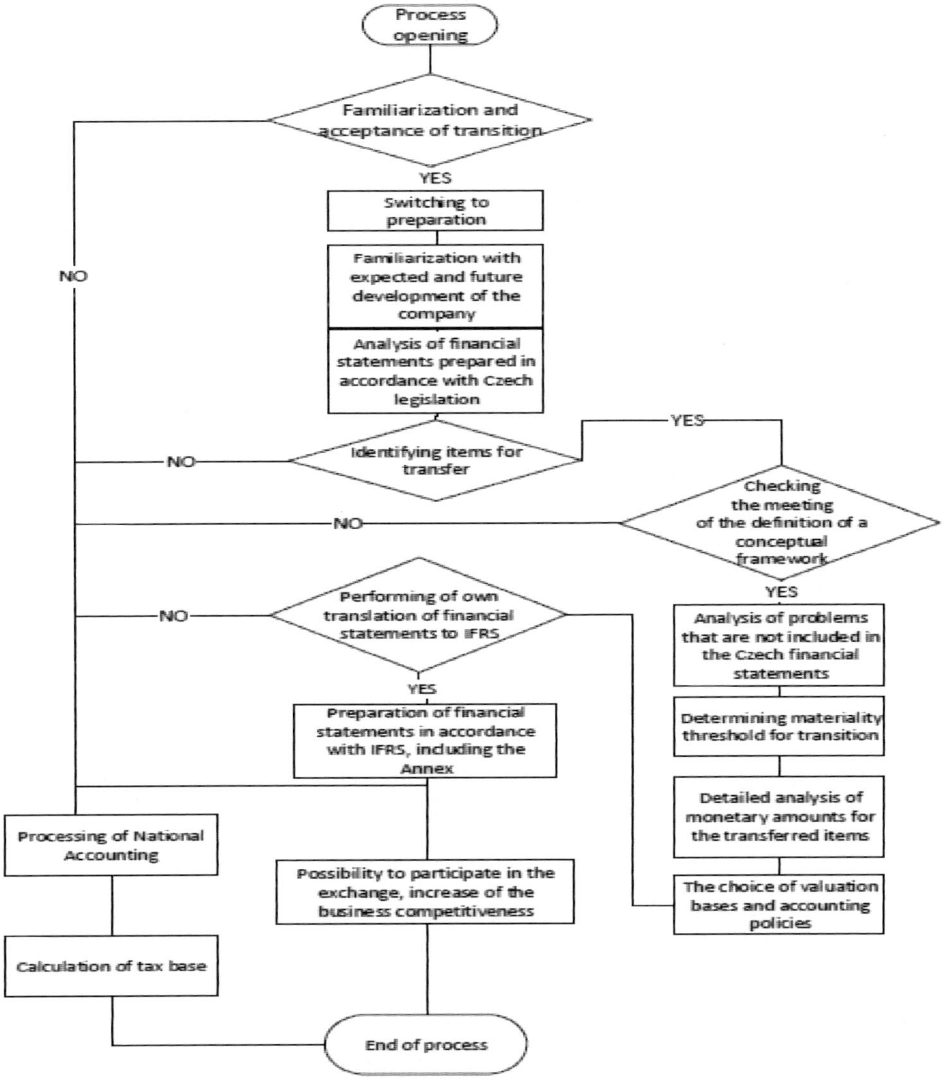

Figure 1 Algorithm [Own elaboration]

PROJECT TEMPLATE FOR DESIGN PROCESS OF TRANSITION TO IFRS

- **1 Process opening**
- **2 Familiarization and acceptance of transition**
- **3 Switching to preparation**
- **4 Familiarization with expected and future development of the company**
  - *4.1 Creating a team of concerned employees*
  - *4.2 Familiarization and training in IFRS*
- **5 Analysis of financial statements prepared in accordance with Czech legislation**
  - *5.1 Identifying items for transfer*
  - *5.2 do not meet the definition of assets, liabilities or equity according to IFRS -> elimination during the transfer from the balance sheet*
  - *5.3 do not meet the definition of revenues according to IFRS -> deferred or eliminated from the profit and loss statement*
  - *5.4 meet the definition of property investment in accordance with IAS 40 -> will be reported according to standard*
  - *5.5 meets the definition of short-termism according to IAS1 -> separate from the fixed assets or liabilities*
  - *5.6 the intangible asset with so called indefinite useful life -> by IAS38 cease to depreciate*
  - *5.7 are long-term assets held for sale -> reported in accordance with IFRS5*
  - *5.8 may have after the transfer another purchase pricet as per IFRS compared to the national adjustment*
- **6 Checking the meeting of the definition of a conceptual framework**
- **7 Analysis of problems that are not included in the Czech financial statements**
  - *7.1 distinguish between finance leases and operating leases*
  - *7.2 provide: a related parties, events after the balance sheet date, pending litigation, guarantees, the functional currency of the company*
- **8 Determining materiality threshold for transition**
- **9 Detailed analysis of monetary amounts for the transferred items**
- **10 The choice of valuation bases and accounting policies**
  - *10.1 evaluate standards -> any change in accounting policy has to be addressed retrospectively*
  - *10.2 evaluate - choice of the pricing models for standards*
- **11 Performing of own translation of financial statements to IFRS**
  - *11.1 cancellation of accounting according to Czech legislation*
  - *11.2 replacing with amounts required by IFRS (or differential method)*
  - *11.3 show a new level of deferred taxes, resulting from the new accounting values reported in accordance with IFRS*
- **12 Preparation of financial statements in accordance with IFRS, including the Annex**
  - *12.1 balance sheet*
  - *12.2 prrofit and loss statament*
  - *12.3 annex*
  - *12.4 statement of changes in equity*
  - *12.5 cash flow*
- **13 Possibility to participate in the exchange, increase of the business competitiveness**
- **14 Processing of National Accounting**
  - *14.1 balance sheet*
  - *14.2 profit and loss statement*
  - *14.3 annex*
  - *14.4 voluntary part*
    - *14.4.1 statement of changes in equity*
    - *14.4.2 cash flow*
- **15 Calculation of tax base**
  - *15.1 profit from ordinary activities*
    - *15.1.1 Profit from operating activities*
    - *15.1.2 Profit from financial activities*
  - *15.2 adjustment of deductibels and imputed items*
  - *15.3 tax calculation*
  - *15.4 re-incorporation into national accounting*
    - *15.4.1 balance sheet*
    - *15.4.2 profit and loss statement*
    - *15.4.3 annex*
- **16 End of process**

Figure 2 Work breakdown structure (WBS) [Own elaboration]

Visualization of WBS and algorithm for implementation and application of IFRS is caught in the Gantt chart (Figure 3). Project duration is individual based on the extent of the transfer. But should not exceed three months.

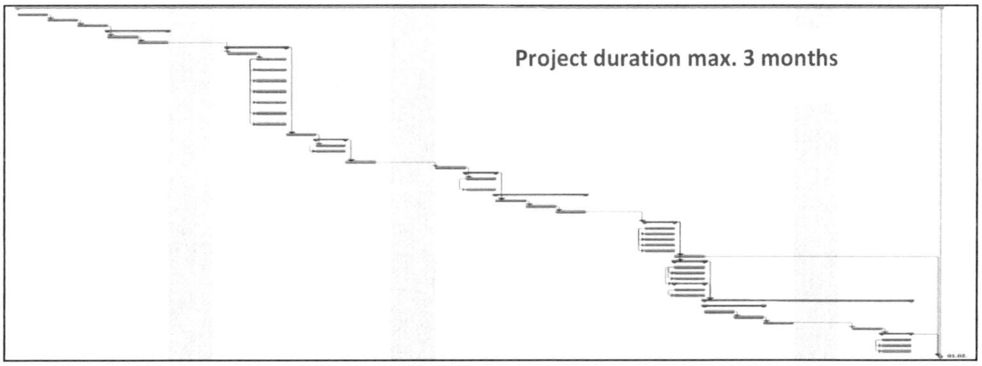

Figure 3 Gantt chart of the project templates [Own elaboration]

5 Conclusion

In terms of predictability of generalization of the trend of implementation of IFRSs has been prepared algorithm of implementation and application of IFRS in the Czech companies. Based on the analysis made at the SMEs was found an increase of the introduction of IFRS in the Czech Republic. Entrepreneurs saw the problem in the harmonization of Czech and international standards, which should be removed if they will proceed on the basis of defined steps that are captured in the WBS structure in this paper. Due to the introduction of IFRS, it is possible to predict the potential competitive advantage for businesses, particularly in terms of selection procedures, the possibility to enter the global capital markets. Enterprises operating in the border areas respectively expanding to the foreign markets are struggling with foreign banks that require financial statements according to IFRS methodology. Indisputable advantage of the introduction and use of IFRS is a single financial language. However, it is also necessary to point out exacting preparation for the introduction of IFRS and the related costs of its implementation. The transition to IFRS helps companies enter the global capital markets, helps to reduce costs and become a full-fledged participant in international markets. The existence of a common international language worldwide increases confidence in the companies which use it - it improves their ability to raise funds etc. From the perspective the created methodology will be topical for all businesses if there is a convergence of Czech accounting rules with IFRS. Currently, this article is especially beneficial for companies focusing on foreign markets, cooperating in an international context and considering capital ties with foreign partners.

Acknowledgements

This work was supported by Institutional Development Project at VSB-Technical University of Ostrava with reference number 165/2017/RPP-TO-1/a.

References

Act on Promotion of Small and medium-sized entrepreneurship No. 47/2002 Col., as subseguently amended.

Banarova, J. (2011). 'New Tools and Options for Multi-Criteria Decision Making'. *Proceedings of 9th International Conference on Strategic Management and its Support by Information Systems*, Celadna, Czech Republic, pp. 11-17.

Mutinova, T. and Banarova, J. (2013). 'Evaluation of SWOT Analysis Using AHP Method'. *Proceedings of 10th International Conference on Strategic Management and its Support by Information Systems*, Valasske Mezirici, Czech Republic, pp. 124-134.

Blecharz, P. and Stverkova, H. (2014). 'Assessing the service quality in small and medium-sized companies'. *Actual Problems of Economics,* 154 (4), pp. 206- 2017.

KACR, The Chamber of Auditors of the Czech Republic (2016). International Financial Reporting Standards (IFRS), [Online]. Available at: http://www.kacr.cz/ifrs [cited 2017-01-20].

Malerova, L., Smetana, M. and Drozdova, M. (2014). 'Decreasing aftermath large extraordinary situations via the simulations'. *Advanced Materials Research,* 1001, pp. 453-457.

Matoskova, J., Mikeska, M., Polcaková, M., Sobotkova, E., Jurasek, M. and Banarová, M. (2013). 'Knowledge sharing as a competitive advantage of SMEs'. *Creating Global Competitive Economies: 2020 Vision Planning and Implementation - Proceedings of the 22nd International Business Information Management Association Conference, IBIMA 2013*, Rome, Italy, pp. 856-869.

Pokorny, J. and Gondek, H. (2016). 'Comparison of theoretical method of the gas flow in corridors with experimental measurement in real scale'. *Acta Monranistica Slovaca,* 21 (2), pp. 146-153.

Rehacek, P. (2015). 'Organization Forms for Project Management'. *Proceedings of 25th International-Business-Information-Management-Association*, Amstrerdam, Netherlands, pp. 2092-2101.

SBA, Czech Republic (2015). *Malé a střední podnikání,* [Online]. Available at: http://www.mpo.cz/cz/podnikani/ male-a-stredni-podnikani/studie-a-strategicke-dokumenty/ [cited 2016-08-24].

Stverkova, H. (2013). *The SMEs competitiveness & service quality evaluating not only in the CZ.* Saarbrücken: LAP LAMBERT Academic Publishing.

Stverkova, H. and Humlova, V. (2016). 'Assessment of the Competitiveness of SMEs through BEE Model in the Moravian-Silesian Region'. *Proceedings of 1st international conference contemporary issues in theory and practice of management: CITPM 2016*, Czestochawa, Poland, pp. 423-429.

An early warning system for monitoring new product development projects

Marcin Relich[1]

Abstract. This paper is concerned with developing methodology of designing an early warning system for monitoring R&D projects. The proposed methodology consists of three steps: planning values of a NDP project, carrying out an earned value analysis for a NDP project, and proposing alternative variants of the project completion. The planned values of a NDP project are predicted with the use of computational intelligence techniques, taking into account variables that significantly impact the project time and cost. These variables and constraints are specified in terms of a constraint satisfaction problem.

Keywords: cost management, earned value analysis, project management, R&D projects, decision support system.

JEL Classification: C63, D81

1 Introduction

New product development (NPD) projects are seen as a key factor in maintaining and increasing the competitiveness of organisations (Ernst, 2002; Cooper and Edgett, 2008; Ulrich and Epinger, 2011). Nevertheless, there are needed some conditions to gain the advantage over competitors. Firstly, new products should be designed according to customers' desires what requires the market research in the early phase of the NPD process (Chan and Ip, 2011). Secondly, a NPD project requires the effective management of NDP projects in the perspective of time, cost, and quality (Cooper and Edgett, 2008). The effective management of NDP projects allows companies to be competitive through cost reduction, shorter time-to-market, and greater customer satisfaction resulting from product reliability. Thirdly, the unit production cost of a new product should be reasonable to compete in the market and to ensure the return of investment as soon as possible (Anderson, 2001). However, the estimation of the unit production cost and future profits of a new product is a challenging task in the phase of designing a product, before the manufacturing and commercialisation phase. This study focuses on the second above-mentioned issue, i.e. improving management of NPD projects through comprehensive monitoring of the NPD process.

Despite the large interest among organisations in project management techniques, the success rate for NPD projects in various industries is low (Cooper and Edgett, 2008; Kormancová, 2012). The main features that determine project success are twofold: managing costs to achieve efficiencies, and creating and enhancing value (Venkataraman and Pinto, 2008). Significant cost and time overruns often take place in all types of projects, including NPD projects. Partially, this results from the uncertain nature of a project. Nevertheless, there are also some significant organisational factors that hinder the project performance, for example, insufficient support from the top management, missing decisions, dwindling motivation and lack of engagement within the project team (Kuster et al., 2015). Despite the fact that tools for cost efficiency

[1] University of Zielona Gora, Faculty of Economics and Management, Licealna 9, 65-417 Zielona Gora, Poland, m.relich@wez.uz.zgora.pl

are widely used by companies, the lack of an integrated cost and value management framework may also be the factor that these problems persist (Venkataraman and Pinto, 2008). Therefore, this study focuses on developing an early warning system that could help organisations monitoring the cost and time of a NPD project, and taking into account their information systems in order to retrieve the data of past projects.

Early warning systems (EWS) should predict as early as possible potential performance deviations by monitoring measurable determinant factors, and propose appropriate actions to prevent or reduce the forecasted deviations (Li et al., 2010). EWS monitor a broad spectrum of natural and man-made hazards. In organisations, EWS are used e.g. in identifying enterprise decline in a life cycle (Cao et al., 2011) and project problems (e.g. in the context of scheduling, cost-related, financial, and delivery problems) (Nikander and Eloranta, 2001). In general, early warning sources are related to risk analysis (Nikander and Eloranta, 2001), project assessment methods (Cooper et al., 1997), and earned value management (Vanhoucke, 2012). The goal of this research is to propose a methodology of designing an early warning system that bases on an earned value analysis to monitor a NPD project, and that generates alternative variants of the project completion using a knowledge base that is specified in terms of a constraint satisfaction problem.

The remaining sections of this paper are organised as follows: Section 2 presents a model of knowledge base that is specified in terms of a constraint satisfaction problem. The proposed method for designing of an early warning system is presented in Section 3. Finally, some concluding remarks are contained in Section 4.

2 Model of knowledge base for describing NPD projects

The NPD process consists of phases such as identifying customers' requirements about new product(s), generating ideas for new product(s), selecting a portfolio of the most promising concept(s), designing the selected product(s), manufacturing and testing prototype(s) of the designed product(s), and launching new product(s). Today's information systems support the employees in managing these phases of the NPD process, and also register and store the performance of past NPD projects (e.g. customer desires, cost and time of designing a new product, materials required to manufacture prototypes of a new product, cost and time of testing prototypes, and the unit production cost).

Nowadays, more and more organisations use enterprise resource planning (ERP) software that helps manage company's business processes in the field of purchasing, manufacturing, sales, and accounting. ERP software supports employees in purchasing goods, material requirements planning, advanced planning and scheduling, taking sales order, cost allocation, planning and budgeting. In addition, today's ERP software provides integrated tools that refer to customer relationship management (CRM) and computer-aided design (CAD). CRM system provides solutions towards the customer support (e.g. create service order, track product problems) and identification of customer requirements, wants, and desires that can be used to improve existing products. CAD software allows designers to put together complex assemblies directly on the computer without ever building a costly physical part or prototype (Ptak and Schragenheim, 2004). ERP, CRM, and CAD systems register product performance in pre-sales and post-sales phases, and participate in product life-cycle management (PLM). The improvement of the collaborative design process has initiated the development of a product data management (PDM) system.

A PDM system facilitates the design release, distributes the design data to multiple manufacturing sites, and manages changes to the design in a closed loop fashion (Ptak and Schragenheim, 2004). Moreover, PDM provides the data and tools to control the design cycle and manages changes, including changes in the cost and schedule of a project. The database of an integrated enterprise information system can be used to identify key factors that impact the time and cost of a NPD project. Consequently, these factors can be used to predict project values. Figure 1 illustrates a framework of acquiring knowledge about NPD projects with the use of the data from an enterprise information system.

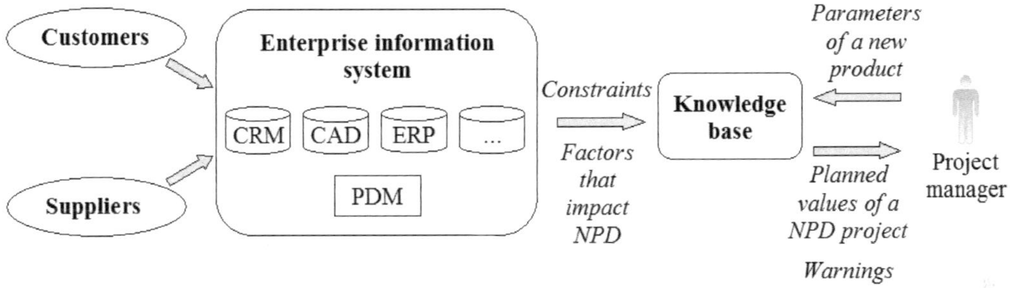

Figure 1 Framework of acquiring knowledge about NPD projects [own work]

The knowledge base consists of relationships between the cost/time of past NPD projects and the factors that strongly impact the project cost and time. These relationships can be identified with the use of econometric and computational intelligence methods, including artificial neural networks that are able to identify complex nonlinear patterns in a data set. Generating warnings by an EWS requires determining some constraints, e.g. the project budget. These constraints, relationships, and facts, which are stored in the knowledge base, create a model that encompasses the company's restrictions related to the prediction of the project cost and time. This model can be described in terms of constraint satisfaction problem (CSP) as follows:

$$CSP = (V, D, C) \qquad (1)$$

where: V is a finite set of variables, D is a finite set of discrete domains of variables, and C is a finite set of constraints limiting and linking variables.

Constraints can refer to the project budged, cost of materials, unit production cost, price of the product that depends on substitutive products, etc. An example of key factors (variables) that can be acquired from an enterprise database to predict the time and cost of a NPD project, is as follows:

- number of interviewed clients to survey clients' desires
- number of clients' desires for a new product
- number of clients' desires translated into product specification
- number of components in the product
- number of completely new components in the product
- number of modified components in the product

- number of project team members

Some variables can be used to predict the project time and cost for a single phase of the NPD process (e.g. the number of interviewed clients to survey clients' desires for estimating the cost of the phase refers to market research), whereas other variables can be used to evaluate project values in a few phases of the NPD process (e.g. the number of components in the product for estimating the cost of designing and testing of a new product).

The model formulation in terms of a CSP integrates technical parameters, available resources, identified relationships and client's desires in the form of knowledge base, and facilitates the development of a decision support system (Relich, 2016). Knowledge base described as a CSP can be considered as a platform for query formulation and obtaining answers (Bocewicz et al., 2014; Sitek and Wikarek, 2016). The problem solution is related to looking for the answer to the following questions: what is the cost of NPD project? or which values should have a NPD project so as not to exceed the budget? As knowledge is the most comprehensive resource that help developing the company's wealth (Grzybowska and Łupicka, 2016), there is the need to elaborate a method that supports project managers in acquiring knowledge from an enterprise information system, and uses the knowledge to monitor the project performance. The next section presents the methodology of designing an early warning system for monitoring NPD projects.

3 The proposed method for designing an EWS for NPD projects

The proposed method consists of the following steps:

1) planning values of a NDP project
2) carrying out an earned value analysis for a NDP project
3) proposing alternative variants of the project completion

In the first step, the planned values (time and cost) of a NDP project are predicted with the use of the econometric modelling and computational intelligence techniques on the basis of variables (factors) that significantly impact the project time and cost. The planned value is calculated with the use of the data refers to past projects that have developed similar products to a new product, i.e. products that are in the same product line. Computational intelligence techniques include structures such as artificial neural networks and fuzzy-neural system that cope with identifying complex non-linear relationships in a data set (Relich, 2016). Taking into account the imprecise information related to a project, structures based on fuzzy logic can be successfully used in evaluating project parameters (Hudec, 2015; Doskočil, 2016). In the proposed method, the quality of forecasting is compared between the econometric modelling and fuzzy-neural system in order to select the most appropriate forecasting method.

The second step refers to an earned value analysis (EVA), in which the planned value (PV) is compared with the actual value (AV). If the actual cost exceeds the margin of safety for the planned cost, then an EWS generates warning signals about the over-budget. Figure 2 illustrates an example of an earned value analysis for the case if the budget "burned".

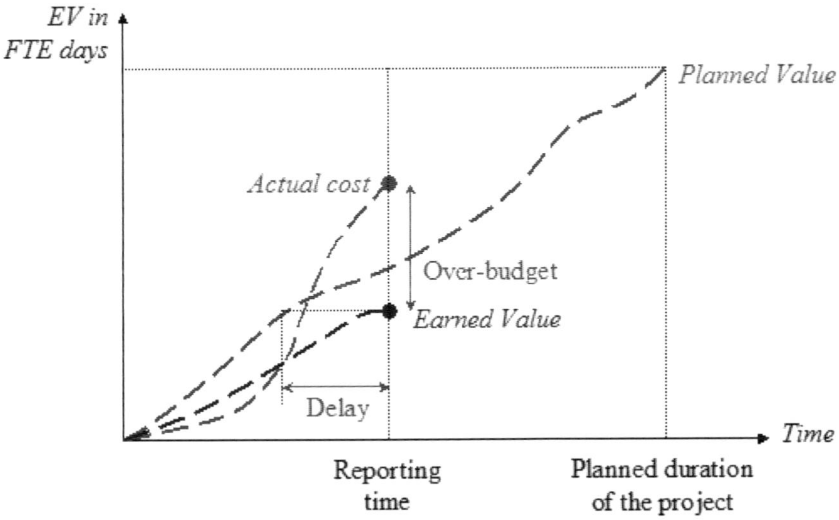

Figure 2 Example of an earned value analysis [own work based on Kuster et al., 2015]

An earned value analysis also illustrates the schedule variance, for which time delay is especially important from the perspective of an EWS. The budget (cost) variance can be measured in full-time equivalent (FTE) days.

The third step of the proposed method is concerned with identifying alternative variants of the project completion, taking into account constraints (e.g. the project budget and deadline, the availability of team members in each time unit) and the actual values of the cost and time related to completed tasks. This step requires the selection of variable(s), for which solutions are sought, and related domain(s). For example, if the planned values of the NPD project take into consideration the development of 10 prototypes of a new product, then alternative variants can include the planned values (time and cost) for the number of prototypes between 6 and 9. Figure 3 illustrates the structure of the proposed early warning system.

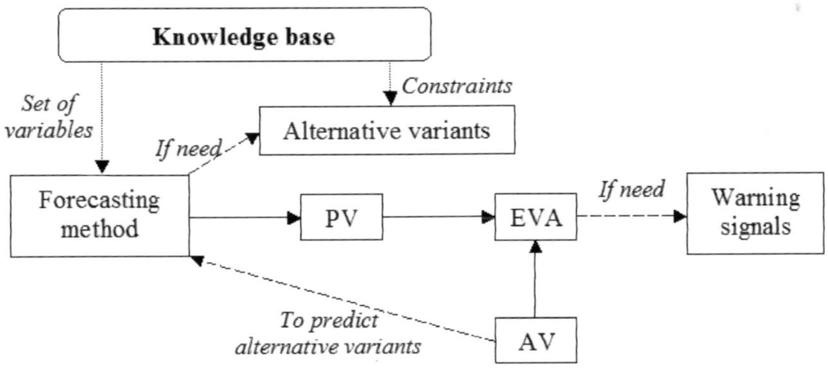

Figure 3 The structure of the proposed EWS [own work]

Knowledge base includes variables and constraints that are identified by an expert and/or data mining techniques from an enterprise information system. The specification of knowledge base in terms of a CSP facilitates its implementation in a constraint programming (CP) environment. A CP seems to be particularly well suited to modelling real-life and day-to-day decision-making processes at an enterprise. A CP is qualitatively different from the other programming paradigms, in terms of declarative, object-oriented and concurrent programming. A CP approach tackles with CSPs with the use of paradigms such as propagate-and-search or propagate-and-distribute. A CSP can always be solved with brute force search, where all possible values of all variables are enumerated and each is checked to in the context of a solution. Except for trivial problems, the number of candidates is usually too large to enumerate them all. A constraint programming has embedded ways to solve CSPs with greatly reduction of the amount of search needed (Van Roy and Haridi, 2004). This is sufficient to solve many practical problems such as supply chain problem (Nielsen et al., 2014; Sitek et al., 2014; Grzybowska, 2015), scheduling problem (Banaszak, 2006; Relich, 2013; Kłosowski et al., 2016; Rudawska et al., 2016), or the problem of generating alternative variants considered in this study. To sum up, a CP is a pertinent framework for a declarative CSP description and it can be used to develop a decision support system.

4 Conclusion

New product development is one of the most important activities in an organisation, influencing the client's satisfaction, the product success, and finally, business competitiveness. The NPD process is long-term and costly; hence, project-oriented companies are forced to the effective management of NPD projects in order to increase their chance of success. The effective project management requires persistent monitoring of the NDP process in the perspective of the project time and cost. Early warning systems support the project manager to predict as early as possible potential performance deviations by monitoring measurable factors, and propose appropriate actions to prevent or reduce the forecasted deviations.

The main contribution of this study is concerned with specifying a framework of acquiring knowledge about NPD projects in terms of a constraint satisfaction problem. This specification enables the use of a constraint programming that solves a constraint satisfaction problem in an effective way, and the design of the proposed EWS as an interactive task-oriented decision support tool. Another contribution of this study refers to identifying key factors from an enterprise system that impact project values, and using these factors (variables) to predict project values (time and cost). Hence, the planned cost of a NPD project is calculated in an earned value analysis according to the identified factors instead the average value of past similar projects. To increase the forecast quality, results from the econometric modelling are compared with results from computational intelligence techniques that are able to identify complex nonlinear relationships among the data. Moreover, the proposed methodology includes the possibility of proposing alternative variants of the project completion.

References

Anderson, D.M. (2001). *Design for manufacturability: Optimizing cost, quality and time-to-market.* Cambria: CIM Press.

Banaszak, Z. (2006). 'CP-based decision support for project driven manufacturing'. *International Series in Operations Research & Management Science*, 92, pp. 409-437.

Bocewicz, G., Nielsen, I. and Banaszak, Z. (2014). 'Automated guided vehicles fleet match-up scheduling with production flow constraints'. *Engineering Applications of Artificial Intelligence*, 30, pp. 49-62.

Cao Y., Chen, X., Wu, D. and Mo, M. (2011). 'Early warning of enterprise decline in a life cycle using neural networks and rough set theory'. *Expert Systems with Applications*, 38, pp. 6424-6429.

Chan, S.L. and Ip, W.H. (2011). 'A dynamic decision support system to predict the value of customer for new product development'. *Decision Support Systems*, 52, pp. 178-188.

Cooper, R.G., Edgett, S.J. and Kleinschmidt, E.J. (1997). 'Portfolio management in new product developments: Lessons from the leaders'. *Research Technology Management*, 40, pp. 16-28.

Cooper, R.G. and Edgett, S.J. (2008). 'Maximizing productivity in product innovation'. *Research Technology Management*, 51, pp. 47-58.

Doskočil, R. (2016). 'An evaluation of total project risk based on fuzzy logic'. *Business: Theory and Practice*, 17 (1), pp. 23-31.

Ernst, H. (2002). 'Success factors of new product development: A review of the empirical literature'. *International Journal of Management Reviews*, 4, pp. 1-40.

Grzybowska, K. and Kovács, G. (2015). 'Supply chain coordination between autonomous agents – A game-theory approach'. *Proceedings of the Federated Conference on Computer Science and Information Systems, ACSIS*, vol. 5, pp. 1623-1630.

Grzybowska, K. and Łupicka, A. (2016). 'Knowledge acquisition in complex systems'. *Advances in Computer Science Research*, 57, pp. 262-266.

Hudec, M. (2015). 'Managing fuzziness of real world in business informatics'. *Proceedings of the 11th International Conference on Strategic Management and its Support by Information Systems*, Uherské Hradiště, The Czech Republic, pp. 221-228.

Kłosowski, G., Gola, A. and Świć, A. (2016). 'Application of fuzzy logic in assigning workers to production tasks'. *Distributed Computing and Artificial Intelligence, Advances in Intelligent Systems and Computing*, 474, pp. 505-513.

Kormancová, G. (2012). 'Project success and failure'. *Theory of Management 6: The Selected Problems for the Development Support of Management Knowledge Base*, pp. 117-119.

Kuster, J., Huber, E., Lippmann, R., Schmid, A., Schneider, E., Witschi, U. and Wust, R. (2015). *Project management handbook*. Berlin: Springer.

Li, Y., Kramer M., Beulens, A. and van der Vorst, J. (2010). 'A framework for early warning and proactive control systems in food supply chain networks'. *Computers in Industry*, 61, pp. 852-862.

Nielsen, P., Michna, Z. and Do, N.A.D. (2014). 'An empirical investigation of lead time distributions'. *IFIP Advances in Information and Communication Technology*, 438, pp. 435-442.

Nikander, I.O. and Eloranta, E. (2001). 'Project management by early warnings'. *International Journal of Project Management*, 19, pp. 385-399.

Ptak, C. and Schragenheim, E. (2004). *ERP tools, techniques, and applications for integrating the supply chain*. London: CRC Press Company.

Relich, M. (2013). 'Fuzzy project scheduling using constraint programming'. *Applied Computer Science*, 9 (1), pp. 3-16.

Relich, M. (2016). 'Computational intelligence for estimating cost of new product development'. *Foundations of Management*, 8 (1), pp. 21-34.

Relich, M. (2016). 'A knowledge-based system for new product portfolio selection'. *New Frontiers in Information and Production Systems Modelling and Analysis, Intelligent Systems Reference Library*, 98, pp. 169-187. Springer.

Rudawska, A., Čuboňova, N., Pomarańska, K., Stanečková, D. and Gola, A. (2016). 'Technical and organizational improvements of packaging production processes'. *Advances in Science and Technology. Research Journal*, 10 (30), pp. 182-192.

Sitek, P., Nielsen, I. and Wikarek, J. (2014). 'A hybrid multi-agent approach to the solving supply chain problems'. *Procedia Computer Science*, 35, pp. 1557-1566.

Sitek, P. and Wikarek, J. (2016). 'A hybrid programming framework for modeling and solving constraint satisfaction and optimization problems'. *Scientific Programming*, Article ID 5102616. DOI: 10.1155/2016/5102616.

Ulrich, K.T. and Eppinger, S.D. (2011). *Product design and development*. New York: McGraw-Hill.

Vandevoorde, S. and Vanhoucke, M. (2006). 'A comparison of different project duration forecasting methods using earned value metrics'. *International Journal of Project Management*, 24, 289-302.

Van Roy, P. and Haridi, S. (2004). *Concepts, techniques and models of computer programming*. Massachusetts Institute of Technology.

Venkataraman, R.R. and Pinto, J.P. (2008). *Cost and value management in projects*. New Jersey: Wiley.

EVM modification based on human factor influence to project budget estimate at completion

Tomáš Šubrt[1], Jan Bartoška[2], Petr Kučera[3]

Abstract. Any project as a unique sequence of tasks is a subject to the human agent impact. This article aims to analyze the design and use of nonlinear modification of BCWS (Budgeted Cost for Work Scheduled) parameter within EVM (Earned Value Management) for monitoring project planned progress respecting human factor impact on the actual work effort. The EVM tools very often measure duration of project activities, where the BCWS is a key parameter. In our previous approach, we focused on human factor influence to BCWS only now we focus on its influence to a more complex EVM parameter estimating final project budget – EAC (Estimate at Completion). Work effort of a resource is hidden beyond majority of project parameters, including EVM. Such influence generates nonlinearity, which is usually ignored in estimations. Linear estimation can be doubtful and thus to express the BCWS, consequently EAC, non-linear mathematical models are used. Correct nonlinear estimate proposed in this paper helps to reduce cone of uncertainty in initial stage of the project. At the same time, the human agent impact manifests itself in the form of the Student Syndrome phenomenon beside for instance Parkinson's Law.

Keywords: Project management, Earned Value Analysis, Non-Linear mathematical model, Work contour, Work effort, Estimate at Completion.

JEL Classification: C44

1 Introduction

Work effort of a resource is hidden beyond majority of project parameters, including EVM. Such influence generates nonlinearity, which is usually ignored in estimations. The estimation and continuous refinements of project budget are mostly based on BCWS, derived from the work effort in a project, influenced by various forms of the Student Syndrome phenomenon, Parkinson's law, multitasking and others. The BCWS is not the final result of nonlinear modifications based on work effort agent (Bartoška, Kučera and Šubrt, 2016), we continue to project this principle to EAC estimations. Later in the paper, we would like to proof, that our nonlinear estimates of EAC will significantly reduce cone of uncertainty at the beginning of project realizations.

Earned Value Management (Vandevoorde and Vanhoucke, 2005, Project Management Institute, 2013, Kim and Kim, 2014) is based on comparing the Baseline and Actual plan of the project realization. Baseline and Actual plan is determined by the partial work of single resources in the particular project activities. Baseline is always based on expected resource work contours and the impact of human agent is usually not included. The impact of human agent is

[1] Czech University of Life Sciences in Prague, Department of Systems Engineering, Kamýcká 129, Prague, Czech Republic, email: subrt@pef.czu.cz
[2] Czech University of Life Sciences in Prague, Department of Systems Engineering, Kamýcká 129, Prague, Czech Republic, email: bartoska@pef.czu.cz
[3] Czech University of Life Sciences in Prague, Department of Systems Engineering, Kamýcká 129, Prague, Czech Republic, email: kucera@pef.czu.cz

usually expected only in the actual course of the project. The versatility of the human agent in projects can be described also by the first "Parkinson's first law" (Parkinson, 1991). It is natural for people to distribute work effort irregularly to the whole time sequence which was determined by the deadline of the task completion. The questions of "Parkinson's first law" in project management are further dealt with in e.g. Gutierrez and Kouvelis (1991).

Work effort of an allocated resource has very often been researched in projects from the area of information technologies and software development, as these projects contain a high level of indefiniteness, and even common and routine tasks are unique. At the same time, it concerns the area where it is possible to find a great number of approaches to estimate how work-intensive the project will be or how long the tasks will take, and also case studies. The proposal for mathematical apparatus for planning the course of tasks within a case study is dealt with for instance in Özdamar and Alanya (2001) or Barry, Mukhopadhyay and Slaughter (2002). The authors Özdamar and Alanya (2001) propose a particular pseudo-heuristic approach to estimate the tasks course where the indefiniteness in the project is expressed by fuzzy sets. Barry, Mukhopadhyay and Slaughter (2002) concentrate on the existence and expression of the relation between project duration and total effort and in their theoretical starting points they point out the dynamics of the relation between the effort and project duration when a self-strengthening loop can be expected. The work effort can be described also using system dynamic models as presented e.g. in a study from project management teaching by Svirakova (2014). The others who research the project complexity and work effort are for instance Clift and Vandenbosh (1999), who point out a connection between the length of life cycle and project management structure where a key factor is again a human agent.

The aim of this paper is to propose and analyze an application of a non-linear modification of the BCWS parameter within EVM and use of it for more precise estimation of budget estimate at completion. The paper builds on the previous authors' works.

2 Materials and methods

2.1 Student Syndrome phenomenon

If there is a deadline determined for the completion of a task and a resource is a human agent, the resource makes its effort during the activity realization unevenly and with a variable intensity. Delay during activity realization with human resource participation leads to stress or to tension aimed at the resource or the tension of the resource him/herself. The development and growth of the tension evokes the increase in the work effort of the human agent allocated as a resource. For more details see previous paper (Bartoška, Kučera and Šubrt, 2015).

2.2 Mathematical model of the Student Syndrome

Authors in previous paper (Bartoška, Kučera, and Šubrt, 2015) propose a mathematical expression of the Student Syndrome. Its brief description follows: First, a function expressing the proper Student Syndrome denoted by p_1 is introduced. It has three minima $p_1(t) = 0$ in $t = 0$, $t = 0.5$, and $t = 1$; and two maxima: former one close to the begin and latter one close to the end of the task realization. Beside this, functions denoted by p_2 expressing the resource allocation according to single standard work contours of flat, back loaded, front loaded, double peak, bell and turtle are proposed. All these functions are in the form of 4th degree polynomial. To express the strength of the Student Syndrome manifestation during the realization of a task the rate r of the Student Syndrome is introduced. It acquires values between 0 and 1 ($r = 0$ represents a situation when the Student Syndrome does not occur at all and the resource keep the work contour exactly; $r = 1$ means that the Student Syndrome manifests in its all strength and the resource absolutely ignore the work contour). As a result, the resource work effort during a real task realization can be modeled using function $p = rp_1 + (1-r)p_2$. For more details see previous paper (Bartoška, Kučera and Šubrt, 2015).

2.3 Modification of the BCWS by Work Effort

The EVM extension in the form of *BCWS* parameter modification for different work contours (turtle, bell, double peak, back loaded, front loaded, etc.) which is described below and applied in a case study is based on previous work of the authors of this paper (Bartoška, Kučera, and Šubrt, 2015 Kučera, Bartoška and Šubrt, 2014).

This approach can be applied when computing the *BCWS* of an activity in the project. It is computed in the classical way using the formula:

$$BCWS = \%PC \,.\, BAC \tag{1}$$

where *%PC* is the percentage of the work planned by the work calendar (planned completion percentage) and *BAC* is Budget at Completion of the project. The share of the whole work effort as a part of task duration requires can be calculated for a single resource as:

$$\int_0^a p(t)dt = 1 \tag{2}$$

Let there are n resources, indexed by 1, 2, …, n, allocated at the task. Let r_k, p_{1k}, p_{2k} denotes r, p_1, p_2 for k-th resource. Then the *BCWS* can be calculated:

$$BCWS = \left(\sum_{k=1}^{n}\int_0^a (r_k p_{1k}(t) + (1 - r_k)p_{2k}(t))dt\right).BAC \tag{3}$$

The resource work effort affects the growth of *BCWS*. It is not possible to expect uniform increase of *BCWS* in general and in case of all project tasks. In case of changing *BCWS*, EVM may provide fundamentally different results for the assessment of the state and development of the project ((Bartoška, Kučera and Šubrt, 2016),

2.4 Prediction of the project budget estimate at completion

Thanks to its parameters, EVM allows and then calculates CPI and SPI estimate of the remaining budget to complete the project (Estimate at Completion). In Project Management Institute (2013) we can find three different ways of calculating this estimate, for short-term fluctuation (EAC1) to capture the trend of rising costs (EAC2) and to capture the effect of delaying (EAC3):

$$EAC1 = ACWP + BAC - BCWP \tag{4}$$

$$EAC2 = BAC / CPI \quad (5)$$

$$EAC3 = ACWP + (BAC - BCWP) / (CPI . SPI) \quad (6)$$

where ACWP is the actual project costs and BCWP is a created value, calculated as follows (Project Management Institute, 2013)

$$BCWP = \%WP . BAC \quad (7)$$

where % WP is the estimated percentage of actual work (% Work Performed) of resources allocated to the project. In the expression (6) CPI and SPI are used, calculated as follows:

$$CPI = BCWP / ACWP \quad (8)$$

$$SPI = BCWP / BCWS \quad (9)$$

Of these formulas, it is obvious that a different method of calculating BCWS will have a major impact on the value of both CPI and SPI and on estimation of future value of project budget (EAC3).

2.5 Cone of uncertainty - uncertainty estimations in the project

Cone of uncertainty is a phenomenon of NASA (1990), when during tracking project progress uncertainty of the estimates on effort, deadlines or the allocation of resources decrease. At the beginning of the project the uncertainty of the estimates is up to 4-times higher (in the case of costs and budget) than final reality, i.e. the estimates made at the beginning of the project during its preparation or planning can vary by up to 400% compared to the estimate later in the project.

The budget estimate at completion (EAC) is often used and similarly to other estimates of the project, it subjects to the cone of uncertainty. This may result a significant distortion of the budget estimates for the completion and it can considerable disadvantage the project as a whole.

3 Results and Discussion

The Student Syndrome phenomenon influences resource work effort, changes the work contour shape and transfers itself into the whole project EVM parameters. The work contours of the resources and the Student Syndrome impact may have a significant effect on both the actual and planned course of the project. As far as calculations in EVM are based on unrealistically expectations of *BCWS*, EVM may be unsuccessful. Finally, EAC estimate derived from non-linear BCWS significantly improves quality of project financial management reducing cone of uncertainty during the initial project phase.

3.1 Case Study

An illustrative fictitious case is described in Table 1. It is an IT project of a small extent. Planned tasks are differentiated by the type of work contour and by the human factor impact (Student Syndrome rate). IT projects are typical by a higher degree of procrastination, in particular in the last part of the project duration. Analytical work at the beginning is usually realized with the active participation of the customer side of the project.

	Student Syndrome Rate	**Work Contour**	**Start**	**Man-day**
Business Requirements	0.3	Front Loaded	0	5
End-User Requirements	0.3	Front Loaded	0	7
Conceptual Design	0.3	Front Loaded	7	5
Architectural Design	0.3	Front Loaded	7	8
Database Components	0.5	Back Loaded	13	10
Code/Logic Components	0.5	Back Loaded	13	17
GUI Interface Components	0.5	Back Loaded	13	15
User Acceptance Test	0.5	Back Loaded	30	5
Performance Test	0.5	Back Loaded	32	6
Product Release	0.5	Back Loaded	35	5
			Total Scope	83

Table 1 Case Study – The Project Plan

The project is planned for 40 working days. The total scope of the planned work is 83 man-days. As well, the project plan (see Figure 1) can be subjected to time analysis by Critical Path Method, etc.), however, this paper does not further follow up these results.

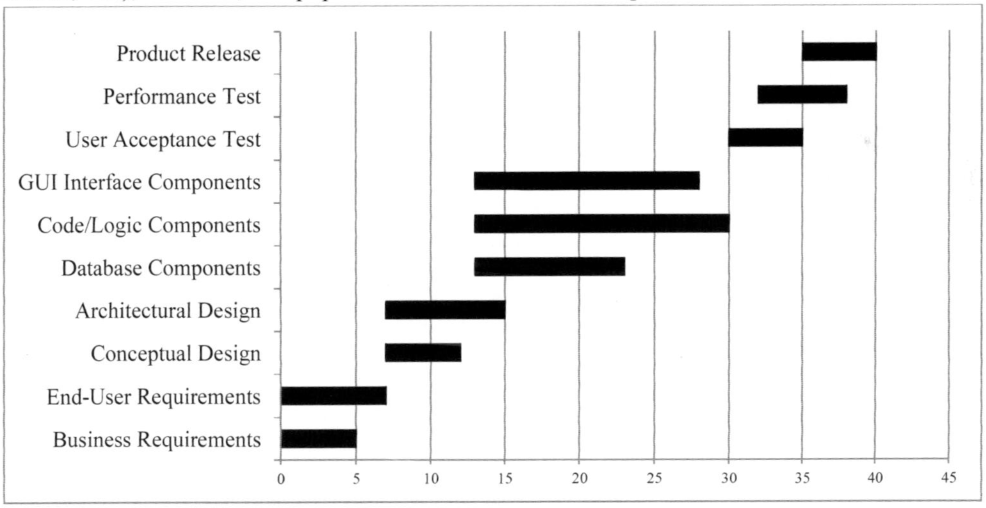

Figure 1 Case Study – Gantt Chart [Bartoška, Kučera and Šubrt, 2016]

In case of the first 4 tasks we expect the work accumulation at the beginning and a lower Student Syndrome phenomenon impact; therefore these tasks work contour is front loaded (see Figure 2) and the Student Syndrome rate value $r = 0.3$ (see Table 1). The reason may be a higher level of cooperation with stakeholders in the project, i.e. e.g. the analysis and collection of information with the participation of the contracting authority and end users (the meetings are planned in advance and their terms are fulfilled, which has a positive impact on tasks duration). In case of the remaining 6 tasks, it is possible to expect the work accumulation at the end and a higher impact of procrastination; therefore these tasks work is back loaded (see Figure 3) and the value $r = 0.5$ (see table 1). The reason may be more technologically demanding nature of these tasks (programming and expert work).

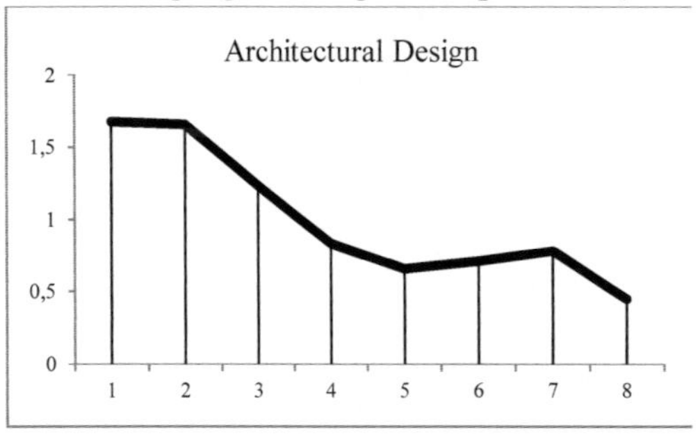

Figure 2 Case Study – a task with front loaded work contour and r=0,3 [Bartoška, Kučera and Šubrt, 2016]

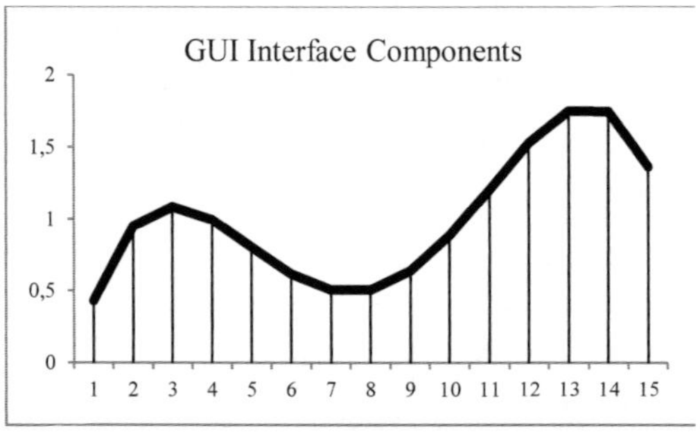

Figure 3 Case Study – a task with back loaded work contour and r=0,5 [Bartoška, Kučera and Šubrt, 2016]

The application of the work contour of front loaded at the project beginning leads to a higher work effort rate of resources planned. The application of the back loaded work contour and a higher human factor impact causes significantly lower work effort rate than planned. The resulting difference may be a reason of EVM failures.

3.2 Linear and Non-Linear BCWS

The *BCWS* curves (formula 3 and Figure 4) bring two parts of information: 1) the area below the curve expresses the expended work effort by the resource; 2) the function value determines the fulfilled project extent (e.g. on 40th day it is 83 man-days). The whole planned work effort course is higher than the identified course comprising the task nature and human resource impact (Bartoška, Kučera and Šubrt, 2016).

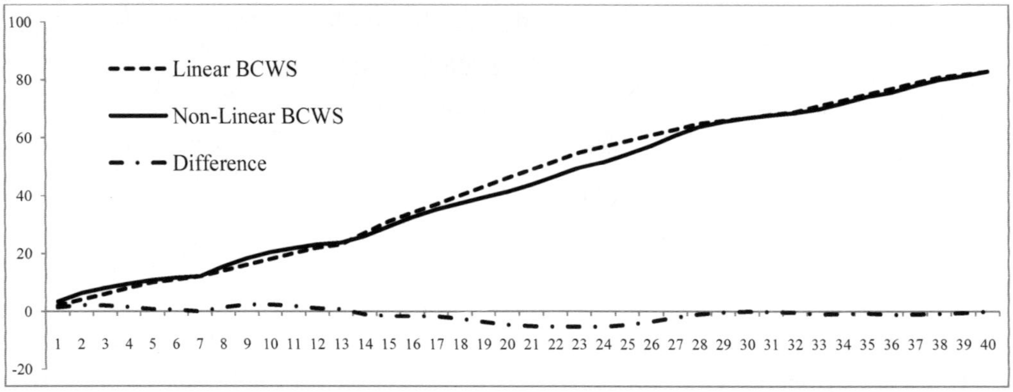

Figure 4 Case Study – difference between Linear and Non-Linear BCWS [Bartoška, Kučera and Šubrt, 2016]

From Figure 4 it can be evidently seen that since 13th day **the work is carried out with a lower work effort**. The overall difference between the Linear *BCWS* and the Non-Linear *BCWS* is –39.283 man-days (the difference between the areas below the curves). The observed difference is not an absent work in the project extent, but the work spent by the resources inefficiently due to the human factor impact. The reason lies in the nature of the tasks (back loaded versus front loaded) and the expected human factor impact (Student Syndrome phenomenon). Although the extent of the project (83 man-days) is completed through 40th day of duration, **the allocated resources do not make the expected work effort to the project during its realization**. The original work plan for single tasks is primarily based on the assumption of uniform work plan and work effort. When including the Non-Linear course of work plan and work effort, a decline of the work effort occurs. At the same time, this work effort decline affects the Earned Value and increases the Actual Costs. What is more, the project completion date may be threatened. These conclusions should be subjected in further research.

3.3 Disillusionment in EVM by Linear BCWS

Including Actual Cost of Work Performed (ACWS) and the value of the actual work performed (% Work Performed per day) to the case study, the different progression of the values of the Linear BCWS and Non-Linear BCWS impacts significantly also other EVM parameters. The assessment of project status and development becomes inconsistent. Thus, the value of actual work performed may be affected by the Student Syndrome phenomenon e.g. in the following way (see Figure 5; for each day, an estimate of the work performed in relation to the plan is calculated).

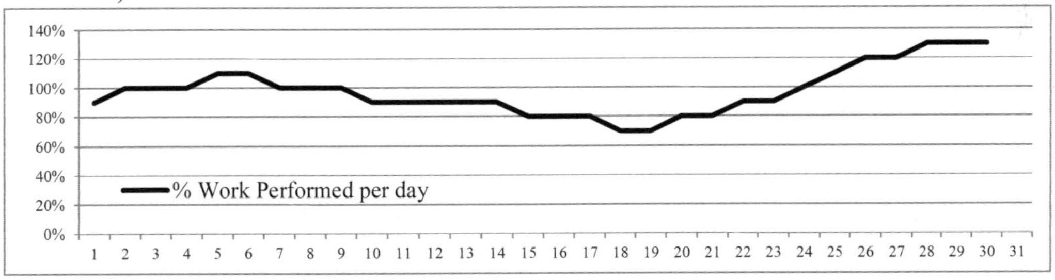

Figure 5 Case Study – % Work Performed per day [Bartoška, Kučera and Šubrt, 2016]

Further, to illustrate, let us expect that the project is in 30th day of its duration at this moment and the Actual Cost of Work Performed development is as follows (Figure 6, indicated in Man-days):

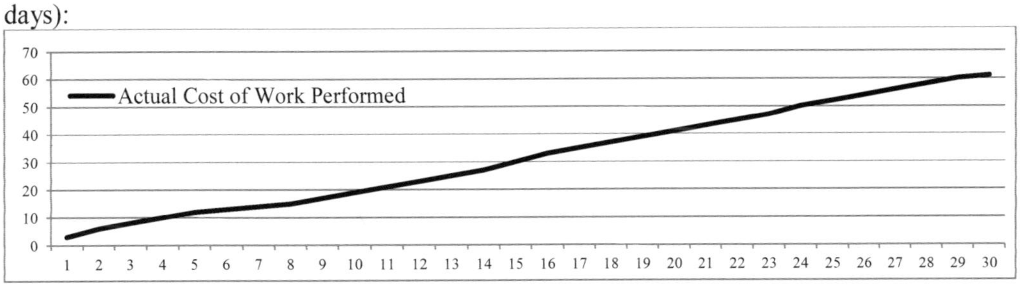

Figure 6 Case Study – Actual Cost of Work Performed (ACWP) [Bartoška, Kučera and Šubrt, 2016]

Other derived EVM parameters especially CV% (Cost Variance %) and SV% (Schedule Variance %), express the relative deviation of the project from its budget or plan (Figure 7 and 8):

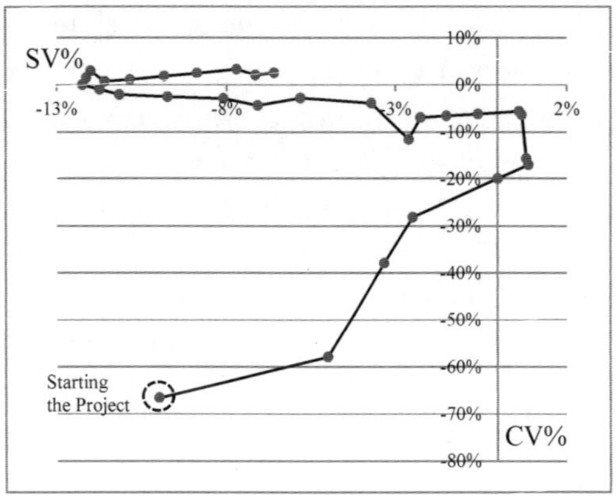

Figure 7 Case Study – Within using Linear BCWS [Bartoška, Kučera and Šubrt, 2016]

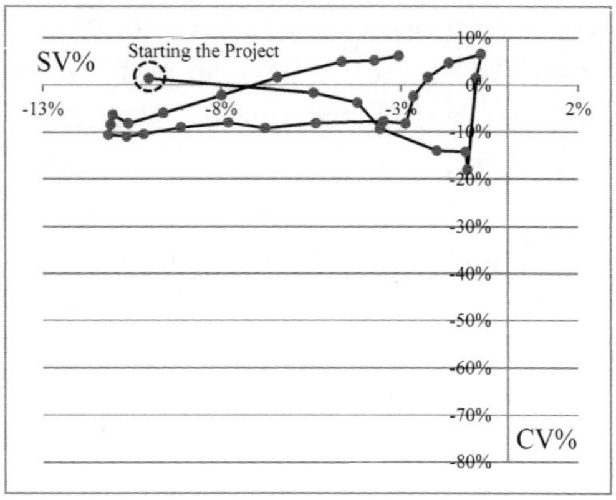

Figure 8 Case Study – Within using Non-Linear BCWS [Bartoška, Kučera and Šubrt, 2016]

From Figures 7 and 8 it is apparent that the observed project progress in case of the Linear BCWS values application differs completely form the identified progress in case of the Non-Linear BCWS values application. When including the human factor impact and various shapes of the work contour for single activities (Non-Linear BCWS, Figure 8), the project is assessed better at the beginning; however, during the course it often gets into a negative misalignment – it is more often in delay or over budget comparing to observing the duration with the Linear BCWS values (Figure 7). In case of the Linear BCWS values application the project would be assessed positively too: after the first five days mistakenly significant improvement of the state occurs (furthermore, it seems that from 6th to 9th day the project is ahead of time as the SV% values are greater than 0). The project is assessed completely differently. The inclusion of the human factor and work contours leads to discovery of a deeper crisis in the project.

3.4 Adjusting budget estimates of cone of uncertainty influence

To the EAC it is possible to include nonlinear form BCWS. It means that current allocation of resources is included in the budget i.e. it contains the actual work effort of the resource affected by human factors (Student Syndrome e.t.c.).

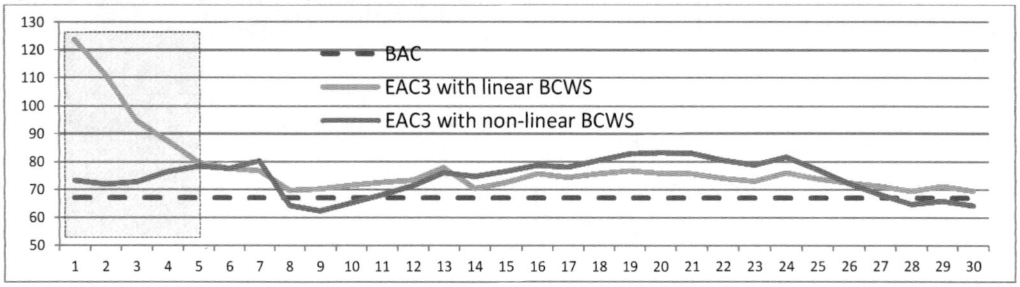

Figure 9 Case Study – Estimate at Completion 3[authors]

Budget estimate at completion (Figure 9, EAC3 with linear and non-linear BCWS) usually moves away from the planned budget (BAC). Based on the calculation made in this case study, it is evident that the inclusion of non-linear BCWS adjusts the project budget estimate at completion of the cone of uncertainty. The initial estimate is not distorted, but it is close to real effort of resources.

The value of estimates in case of nonlinear BCWS (EAC3 with nonlinear BCWS) in the first 5 days of the project is not distorted, the project may be in term and its management's prediction is rated positively. While in case of original EAC (EAC3 with linear BCWS) the budget estimate amplitude is evident and the project could be rated negatively. Negative estimation and evaluation of the project at its beginning can lead, under certain conditions, to a chain reaction of negative expectations, e.g. if the budget is estimated or drawn badly (the estimate is significantly higher than planned budget), we can expect further deterioration during the project progress and its possible failure.

4 Conclusion

The article discusses an application of a newly proposed *BCWS* nonlinear calculation for monitoring the project duration within EVM and for improving of budget estimate at completion during project progress, significantly during its initial phase. As the case study shows, as far as the task nature (work contour) and the human resource impact (Student Syndrome phenomenon) is comprised, the planned course of work effort (Non-Linear *BCWS*) may significantly differ from the commonly expected one (Linear *BCWS*). A possible decline or increase of resources work effort is used for reducing cone of uncertainty and helps to eliminate future project failures due to wrong budgeting.

References

Barry, E., Mukhopadhyay, T. and Slaughter, A. S. (2002). 'Software project duration and effort: An empirical study'. *Information Technology and Management*, 3, pp.113–136.

Bartoška, J., Kučera, P. and Šubrt, T. (2015). 'Modification of the BCWS by Work Effort'. *Proceedings of the 33rd International Conference Mathematical Methods in Economics MME 2015*. University of West Bohemia, Plzen, pp. 19-24.

Clift, T. and Vandenbosh, M.(1999). 'Project complexity and efforts to reduce product development cycle time'. *Journal of Business Research*, 45, pp. 187–198.

Gutierrez, G.J. and Kouvelis, P. (1991). 'Parkinson's law and its implications for project management'. *Management Science*, 37 (8), pp. 990-1001.

Kim, B., C. and Kim, H., J. (2014). 'Sensitivity of earned value schedule forecasting to S-curve patterns'. *Journal of Construction Engineering and Management*, 140 (7) pp. 14-23.

Kučera, P., Bartoška, J. and Šubrt, T. (2014). 'Mathematical models of the work contour in project management'. *Proceedings of the 32nd International conference on Mathematical Methods in Economics*, Palacký University, Olomouc, pp. 518-523.

Özdamar, L. and Alanya, E. (2001). 'Uncertainty modelling in software development projects (with case study)'. *Annals of Operations Research*, 10, pp. 157–178.

Parkinson, C.N. (1991). *Parkinson's Law and Other Selected Writings On Management*. Federal Publications (S) Pte Ltd, Singapore.

Project Management Institute (2013). *A Guide to the Project management body of knowledge (PMBOK® Guide)*, 5th ed. Newtown Square: Project Management Institute Inc.,

Svirakova, E. (2014). 'System dynamics methodology: application in project management education'. *Proceedings of the 11th International Conference on Efficiency and Responsibility in Education*. CULS, Prague, pp. 813-822.

Vandevoorde, S. and Vanhoucke, M. (2005): 'A comparison of different project duration forecasting methods using earned value metrics'. *International Journal of Project Management*, 4 (4) pp. 289-302.

Bartoška, J, Kučera, P. and Šubrt, T. (2016). 'Modification of the EVM by Work Effort and Student Syndrome phenomenon'. *34th International Conference Mathematical Methods in Economics (MME 2016)*, Liberec, Technical University Liberec, pp. 25-30.

NASA (1990). *Manager's Handbook for Software Development, Revision 1*. Document number SEL-84-101. Greenbelt, Maryland: Goddard Space Flight Center, NASA

Dysfunctions in the work of team

Renata Winkler[1]

Abstract. Dysfunctions have diverse nature and form. Dysfunctions affect, among others, reduction in performance and efficiency of the organization's system, decrease in potential and quality of the work resources, and increase in costs of operation. The most common dysfunctions of the team's functioning (lack of trust, fear of conflict, lack of involvement, avoidance of responsibility, lack of attention to the results, and groupthink) were discussed. Author focused on possibility of reducing the risk of occurrence these dysfunctions or minimizing the consequences of their occurrence.

Keywords: dysfunction, work team, trust, involvement, conflict, groupthink.

JEL Classification: D23

1 Introduction

Cooperation within teams, regardless of the potential opportunities and benefits, is a tremendous challenge for the people involved. Success of a team largely depends on how the individuals forming this team function and cooperate. Ensuring proper level of cooperation requires the bond between the members of the team to be properly shaped and strengthened. This is especially challenging in the case of project teams, which are established for a determined period of time for the needs of a specific project, and the makeup of which often changes throughout the project (since some people are involved in the team's work only at a specific stage of the project). Therefore, the interest in the issues of improving, developing and integrating the team grows. In connection with the above, the purpose of the article is indicate the types of actions that can restrict the risk of occurrence of dysfunctions in team or increase the chance to minimizing the consequences of their occurrence. To achieve this aim necessary is look at the reasons of dysfunction and in the context of them search for adequate solutions. The deliberations contained in this article have been conducted on the basis of desk research.

2 Teamwork dysfunctions

The notion of dysfunction was introduced to social sciences by R. Merton (Kosikowski, 2012) to distinguish adverse impact of a phenomenon on modification or adaptation of the social system. In general, dysfunction is understood as lack of functionality[2], failure to adjust to the needs and goals, or as disorder in activities (or as an incorrect activity) (Słownik Wyrazów Obcych – płyta, 2001). The notion of dysfunction can refer both to each disorder (disturbance or abnormality) of the normal operation of a system (organization, unit, team), which results in undesirable effects and prevents full execution of the adequate functions[3] (Listwan, 2005), as well as to a dependent and non-preferred (undesirable) consequence of the existence or operation of a system element or the entire system (Stanowski, 1983). In the opinion of Penc (2011), appearance of a dysfunction is reflected not only in impossibility to adapt to perform-

[1] Cracow University of Economics, Department of Organizational Behaviours, ul. Rakowicka 27, 31-510 Kraków, Poland, e-mail: renata.winkler@uek.krakow.pl

2 The prefix 'dys' indicates impediment or denial of something (from Greek: dys-~ non-, bad).

3 And thus causes deviations from the condition specified as the pattern.

ing certain functions properly (correctly), but also in reluctance to adapt in such a way. The effects of a dysfunction (though often extensive) can be difficult to identify. Dysfunctions affect, among others (Cewińska, Wojtaszczyk, 2005): reduction in performance and efficiency of the organization's system, decrease in potential and quality of the work resources, increase in operating costs. According to Kieżun (1997), each relatively permanent form of dysfunction, which causes wastefulness exceeding the limits of social tolerance, should be considered a pathology. On the other hand, Stocki (2005) suggests to use the notion of pathology to refer to each dysfunction appearing in an organization, which does not allow for achieving realistic goals appointed in this organization within the assumed time and using the specified measures, consistent with the social interest.

Dysfunctional phenomena can be observed every day. Additionally, the nature and form of dysfunctions is so diverse that it is not possible to create their finite index; it is also difficult to clearly state what is a dysfunction, and what is merely its cause, since some dysfunctions create others or constitute their basis. Lencioni (2012) has identified the following types of the common and most frequently occurring dysfunctions:

- lack of trust,
- fear of conflict,
- lack of involvement,
- avoidance of responsibility,

Sztompka (2002) pointed out, that there is also groupthink.

2.1 Lack of trust

Terminological issues

The trust – in the opinion of Sztompka (1999) – is a special type of *resource/asset* that allows for making a specific assumption concerning formal properties of actions of other people (such as their: regularity, correctness, degree of predictability, as well as their rationality, efficiency – or effectiveness) without taking into account the content of these actions [4]. Trust allows for reducing the constraints existing in interpersonal cooperation. Appearance of trust in the established (existing) relationship relieves from the need to verify the intentions and actions of the partner. It gives us the basis for creating open communication, which is a constitutive factor conditioning effective shaping of cooperation. Thanks to trust, the "external costs" of interactions are significantly reduced, the level of work satisfaction is increased and the team is able to generate measurable economic benefits. Trust is particularly important in difficult and crisis situations. It is the necessary binding material for interpersonal relations in many aspects and on various levels. Betrayal of trust is never forgotten. Additionally, trust is not something you can own, which very important. It is not something you "have" or "possess". Trust is given. Very important is that the mere absence of trust stem from the fact that there is no cause for reliance (Faulkner, 2017).

[4] At the same time, it should be emphasised that the issue of trust is interdisciplinary (it is the domain of, among others, such sciences as ethics, theology, social psychology, sociology and political science, as well as management sciences) - thus (depending on the adopted approach) the notion of trust can be understood as: reliability, hope, belief (set of beliefs), predisposition, variable (situational, structural or interpersonal) (Lewicka-Strzałecka, 2003).

Consequences and reason - theoretical background

Lack of trust increases the uncertainty level of actions of other people, reflects reduce credibility of the addressees (partners). It involves the faith that persons will exploit our weaknesses (Głuszek, 2002). Lack of trust makes us maintain high level of caution, constant vigilance and makes us distance ourselves. It fosters alienation and atomisation, suppresses the necessary criticism, limits freedom of action, demobilises, makes us refrain from taking action (generates passiveness), reinforces opportunism, and contributes to creation of protective barriers (Sztompka, 1999). Unjustified distrust substantially limits contacts with others, limits communication openness, creates secrets, closed and confrontational attitudes, cripples operations, results in inertia, destroys any opportunity for potentially favourable interactions. Constant control causes people to feel threatened and makes them refrain from taking initiatives aiming to improve efficiency. Furthermore, with no trust people are reluctant to share knowledge and are substantially more willing to use their knowledge as a weapon or protection against threats (Latusek-Jurczak, 2012), which substantially hinders their mutual cooperation and limits the team's functioning.

Absence of trust appear when inside organization we can observe (Latusek-Jurczak, 2012; Żarczyńska-Dobiesz, 2008):

- lack of organizational transparency – namely lack of clarity and openness in area of: (1) the assumed goals, (2) expectations towards the employees, (3) principles/rules concerning behavior (acceptable and unacceptable), and (4) the system's rules, behavior in certain situations;
- absence of normative reliability – which should be understood as lack of consistency in compliance with and enforcement of the binding rules (including compliance with the rights and obligations) with respect to all people, regardless of their position;
- lack of organizational stability – namely absence of stability and cohesion of the organizational policy with regard to the key areas;
- absence of responsibility of the authorities – which means that the actions of the leaders not only can be unreasonable, but can be also without undergo verification and control (although it take place in this kind of situation that it should be check);
- lack of respect for dignity, integrity and autonomy in the organization members.

2.2 Fear of conflict

Terminological issues

Conflict we can define as interactive process manifested in incompatibility, disagreement, or dissonance within or between social entities (Rahim, 2011). Conflict may be both constructive and destructive (Johnson, Johnson and Tjosvold 2005). Most usually depends on the context of the conflict. A constructive dispute is possible in the context of cooperation. In the rivalry context, we have a destructive dispute. So far, it has not been proven that occurrence of a conflict is less beneficial than lack of conflict, and the opinion that high-quality problem-solving depends on a constructive conflict between the group members is prevalent in the subject literature. As stated by Johnson, Johnson and Tjosvold (2005), a constructive dispute is the starting point for the cooperation goal the group is supposed to achieve. Popular opinions also state that "innovation creates conflict" and that "creativity needs conflict" (Gruber, 2005).

Consequences and reason - theoretical background

Although workplace conflict is unavoidable consequence of professional life, in most cases of interpersonal situations and situations inside and between groups, conflicts are more often avoided and suppressed than encouraged or formed. Conflict is perceived mainly as a source of threat. Therefore, the appearance of a conflict is feared, and hence emphasizing, expression and/or propagation of differences is met with resistance. It may give rise to an illusory sense of unanimity within the team, cause intensification of internal animosities and reduction in decision quality. Teams that fear of conflict often have boring meeting, create environments where back-channel politics and personal attack existing, ignore controversial topics that are critical to the team's success, waste time and energy with posturing and interpersonal risk management (Carraher, Smith and DeLisle, 2017; Love, 2014).

Conflict appears wherever there is diversity and inconsistency of values, goals, interests of individuals, groups or organizations, of which those entities are aware (Bernard, 1951). Conflict in the workplace are created for example because of existing inside organization competitive tensions, power struggles, jealousy, performance discrepancies, compensation issues, etc. Of course the grounds for conflict can constitute also: personal psychology, group norms, stereotypes and prejudice (Doherty and Guyler, 2008). Conflict is ultimately the drive for some kind of change in the staus quo. Avoiding, ignoring or suppressing conflicts certainly very often take place because the vast majority of people forming the group do not have the proper skills necessary to give a constructive aspect to the conflict.

2.3 Lack of involvement

Terminological issues

Employee involvement is most often defined as emotional and intellectual commitment to the organization or the amount of discretionary effort exhibited by employees in their jobs (Saks, 2006). Involvement[5] in a way emotionally, mentally and behaviourally "binds" the organization with the employee, which allows for turning their potential into economic results (Kwiecień, 2012). As proven by the research conducted by Haday (2003), the results of the employees' work depend to a greater extent on their involvement than on their level of work satisfaction. Permanent change and development can be achieved only through authentic involvement in the sphere of values, beliefs, emotions (Rzycka, Porosło, 2010).

Consequences and reason - theoretical background

Lack of involvement may lead to reduction in the employees' tendency to expend effort for the organization, their initiative level and discipline (which, in turn, leads to: increased level of absence, tardiness, delays in performance of the assigned tasks, missing of internal deadlines, lower diligence). As a result, not only the work efficiency is lower, but we can also ob-

[5] Involvement is examined through the prism of three dimensions: emotional (feelings), rational (thoughts), motivational (actions).

serve an increase in the amount of opportunistic behaviour and an increase level of personnel fluctuation (Carraher, Smith and DeLisle, 2017).

Frequent reasons for the lack of involvement include unclearly formulated expectations, defective communication, lack of feedback, lack of the possibility of professional development (trainings, promotions), no respect for the work done by the employee, impossibility to find balance between professional and private life, and impossibility to openly express own opinions. Lack of involvement may also appear if the team member divides their work time between participating in the project and working full-time.

2.4 Avoidance of responsibility

Terminological issues

The sense of obligation and readiness to bear the consequences of the undertaken actions constitute the essence of responsibility (Kurpiewski, 1993). A responsible action is the opposite to a reckless action, i.e. acting based on the view that "things will work out somehow" (Półtawski, Maciejszczak, 2012). A broadly understood responsibility constitutes an element of the contemporary canon of management. Responsibility requires involvement. However, the *sine qua non* condition of elementary responsibility is recognising the existence of a value (Rogoziński, 2012) that may be realised (concretised) into real items and situations. Very important is, that avoidance of responsibility involves lack of attention to the results

Consequences and reason

Non-existent responsibility or low level of responsibility can facilitate various negative effects, like reducing the feeling of sense of work and satisfaction of work, minimum effort (efforts at the level of survival), negligent performance, wasting time and resources, low quality of decisions, reduction of employee loyalty (Bugdol, 2006).

The grounds for lack of responsibility include: ambiguity (of rules, roles, tasks), lack of delegation of authority, lack of the possibility to participate in decision-making, no sense of community, and the sense of objectification and injustice.

2.5 Groupthink

Terminological issues

The phenomenon of teams making exceptionally inapt decisions is called, after I.L. Janis, "groupthink" (Janis, 1972). In a group threatened by groupthink, some symptomatic phenomena can usually be seen (Fuller, Aldag, 1997; Turner et al, 2006):

- an illusory sense of unanimity appears within the group – among others: blocked internal criticism and exchange of counterarguments; persons, who try to spread ideas contradictory to the group's position, are pressured to adopt the point of view of the majority; individual persons, in order to avoid recurring negative reactions of the group, minimise their own doubts and do not disclose differing beliefs,
- there is an evident presence of "mindguards" (some persons begin to, on their own initiative, filter information reaching the group from the outside, preventing the information that negate the position adopted by the group from reaching the group).

- collective rationalisation is formed, allowing for marginalisation of information, which should induce the group to reformulate their position,
- the group is convinced of the moral indisputability of its actions, which fosters ignoring of external standards and ethical aspects of decisions,
- the stereotyping process is activated, as a result of which the leaders of competitive groups and the achievements of people from outside the group are assessed as smaller, worse[6].

Consequences and reason

As a result of groupthink the team is making wrong decisions because because in the team we can observe (Stankiewicz, 2003): reducing the discussion to deliberations on just a few actions, without analysing the full range of alternatives, neglecting ideas and solutions that have been assessed by majority of the group as unsatisfactory already at the very beginning; avoiding repeated, thorough analysis of the solution that has been favoured by the majority from the very beginning; low utilisation of the possibilities of obtaining information from experts, who could estimate profits and losses; emergence of a selective bias in the way the group responds to information, depending on whether the information are in accordance with the previously made decisions – and – preparation of only one (the only right one) solution.

Syndrome of groupthink appears only with specific psychological conditions of the group members. Specifically, when the team's motivation to maintain its cohesion dominates the motivation to make a decision, resulting in the group members voluntarily limiting their intellectual capacity. This takes place, above all, if the group members are under strong decision-making pressure, under which the group itself is often the only point of reference, providing a sense of mental comfort for the group members. Such pressure appears when (George, 1997):

- persons responsible for solving the problem and making the decision are involved in a conflict of moral, ethical and utilitarian values (for instance: economic, professional, organizational, political). In particular, when pursuing some of these values excludes keeping the others.
- there is a high level of decision-making uncertainty. The problem is complex and, it is impossible to predict the decision's consequences, the group has insufficient access to information, the available information are of low quality, the team members do not have proper competences, and the criteria of the assessment of the created solution are unknown.

3 Conclusion

Taking into account the reasons of dysfunction that was discussed (table 1) possible is indicate the possibility of reducing the risk of occurrence these dysfunctions or minimizing the consequences of their occurrence.

Considering the specified reasons for the lack of trust, we can indicate that development of trust is possible if: (1) organizational policy with regard to the key areas are consistent, (2) goals, expectations towards the employees and principles concerning behavior are formulated

[6] Obviously, not in all situations will all the symptoms listed above be observed.

clearly, (3) the binding rules are effective and reliable enforcement – and (4) the integrity and autonomy of team's members are respected. It is also worth mentioning that conducted by Kwiecień [2012, p. 267] research shows that the important factor Influencing trust is internal communication.When employees feel that they are the treated fairly and consistently, when we can tell about open communication between team's members - possibility of avoiding lack of trust (or minimalize possible consequence of lack of trust) exists.

Dysfunction	Reasons
Lack of trust	Lack of organizational transparency. Absence of normative reliability. Lack of organizational stability. Absence of responsibility of the authorities. Lack of respect for dignity, integrity and autonomy in the organization members. Errors in internal communication.
Fear of conflict	Perceiving conflict as a source of threat. Lack of skills necessary to give a constructive aspect to the conflict.
Lack of involvement	Unclearly formulated expectations. Defective communication. Lack of the possibility of professional development. No respect for the work impossibility to find balance between professional and private life. Impossibility to openly express own opinions.
Avoiding responsibility	Ambiguity (of rules, roles, tasks). Lack of delegation of authority. Lack of the possibility to participate in decision-making. No sense of community. The sense of objectification injustice
Groupthink	Specific psychological conditions of the group members that makes that inside team the motivation to cohesion is stronger than motivation to make a decision

Table 1 Reasons of dysfunctions

How to reduce the fear of conflict? The most important is develop adequate skills that are necessary to achieve a constructive aspect to the conflict. When members of team acquire this kind of skill, they: will be able to listen to all ideas (also from antagonistic people), will be critical towards the idea (not towards the people); will be able to separate the criticism addressed at them from their personal value; will be able focus on the possibility to make possibly the best decision; gain the ability to look at a problem from another perspective and back off from their position and change their opinion if the collected evidence indicate such a need. Acquiring a set of the aforementioned skills is not easy – they are highly connected to communication skills. But it allow them overcome the fear of conflict. Thereby it will be easier for them overcome the fear of conflict. They will achieve ability to engage in constructive conflict, focus on discussing important topics and solve real problems quickly (minimalizing politics). Good solution will be build conflict management system also (Proksch, 2016; Budd and Colvin, 2014).

Involvement has many sources. However, involvement above all requires trust. The atmosphere of mutual trust is necessary to create, maintain or increase the level of employee involvement. It also requires a proper employee motivation system, a reliable and fair employee evaluation system, an effective and supportive leader, and a functional participation system. Important factors shaping involvement also include the level of the employees' sense of safety (also financial), the possibility to use own skills and abilities, the possibility of individual development.

What is important if we want to overcome avoidance of responsibility? Taking into account the reasons of this dysfunction – we can indicate development of a system of participation or/and empowerment, because people need the delegation of authority and the possibility of participating in decision-making. But – and its really important (and we should it stressed) – achieving accountability is not possible without the development of commitment and trust.

When we take into account the causes of the groupthink syndrome which was discussed[7], we can tell that reducing the risk of this syndrome to a minimum, we can achieve if:

- the team leader will avoid declaring his/her preferences,
- the group leader will encourage the team members to perform a critical evaluation of the proposed solutions and to openly express their doubts,
- several independent will be groups appointed within the team to solve the problem (each working with another leader), tasked not only with proposing a solution, but also with assessment of the solutions proposed by other groups8
- each member of the decision-maker group will not only have the right to discuss the prepared solutions with people from outside the group, but will also be encouraged to exercise this right,
- experts from outside the group, well-versed in the subject, will be invited to the group meetings,
- at least one group member at each group meeting will play the role of "devil's advocate",
- no warning sign will be ignored and appropriate amount of time will be provided for its examination,
- after working out a compromise and before making the final decision, a "last chance meeting" will be organized, where each team member will clearly express all their doubts and reflections.

Minimisation of the risk of the discussed types of dysfunctions in team work (in particular with regard to project teams) is achieved, among others, through creation of an adequate organizational policy, ensuring organizational transparency, consequent enforcement of the binding rules, responsible management, construction of an effective employee motivation system and a reliable and fair employee assessment system, as well as introduction of a functional participation system. It is strongly recommended to focus on respecting the dignity, integrity and autonomy of the team members, developing their communication skills, providing them with individual development opportunities, and building their sense of safety. It is also important to appoint an effective and supportive team leader.

---

[7] Including studies Littlejohn and Foss (2005).

[8] If it is possible to appoint only one group, this group will be in certain time intervals divided into subgroups, working separately, which will then be merged again.

Acknowledgements

The publication was financed from the funds granted to the Faculty of Management of the Cracow University of Economics, within the framework of the subsidy for the maintenance of research potential in 2016.

References

Bernard, J. (1951).'The Conceptualization of Intergroup Relations with Special Reference to Conflict'. *Social Forces*, 29 (3), pp. 243-251.

Budd, J.W. and Colvin, A.J. (2014). 'The Goals and Assumptions of Conflict Management in Organizations'. *The Oxford Handbook of Conflict Management in Organizations*. Oxford: Oxford University Press.

Bugdol, M. (2006). *Wartości organizacyjne: szkice z teorii organizacji i zarządzania*. Kraków: Wydawnictwo Uniwersytetu Jagiellońskiego.

Carraher, E., Smith, R.E. and DeLisle, P. (2017). *Leading Collaborative Architectural Practice*. New Jersey: Wiley.

Cewińska, J. and Wojtaszczyk, K. (2005).'Dysfunkcje w zarządzaniu zasobami ludzkimi w przedsiębiorstwach regionu łódzkiego w świetle badań pilotażowych'. *Dysfunkcje zarządzania zasobami ludzkimi*. Łódź: Wydawnictwo Uniwersytetu Łódzkiego.

Doherty, N. and Guyler, M. (2008), *The Essential Guide to Workplace Mediation & Conflict Resolution: Rebuilding Relationships*. London-Philadelphia: KoganPage.

Faulkner, P. (2017). *The Problem of Trust. The Philosophy of Trust*. New York: Oxford University Press.

Fuller, S.R. and Aldag, R.J. (1997). 'Challenging the Mindguards: Moving Small Group Analysis beyond Groupthink'. *Beyond Groupthink: Political Group Dynamics and Foreign Policy Making*. Michigan: University of Michigan.

George, A.L (1997). 'From Groupthink to Contextual Analysis of Policy – making Groups'. *Beyond Groupthink: Political Group Dynamics and Foreign Policy Making*. Michigan: University of Michigan.

Głuszek, E. (2002). 'Zaufanie jako istotny składnik kapitału intelektualnego przedsiębiorstwa'. *Prace Naukowe Akademii Ekonomicznej we Wrocławiu*, 963, pp. 122-131.

Gruber, H.E. (2005). 'Rozwiązywanie konfliktu a twórczość: Rola punktu widzenia'. *Rozwiązywanie konfliktów*. Kraków: Wydawnictwo Uniwersytetu Jagiellońskiego.

Hadaj, S. (2003).'Staff commitment is the key to an improved performance', *Personnel Today*, 6 (10), [Online], Available at: http://www.personneltoday.com/hr/staff-commitment-is-the-key-to-an-improved-performance/ [cited 2016-12-28].

Janis, I.L. (1972).*Victims of Groupthink: A Psychological Study of Foreign – Policy Decisions and Fiascoes*. Boston: Houghton Mifflin.

Johnson, D.W., Johnson, R.T. and Tjosvold, D. (2005). 'Konstruktywny spór: Wartość intelektualnej opozycji'. *Rozwiązywanie konfliktów*. Kraków: Wydawnictwo Uniwersytetu Jagiellońskiego.

Kieżun, W. (1997). *Sprawne zarządzanie organizacją. Zarys teorii i praktyki*. Warszawa: Oficyna Wydawnicza Szkoły Głównej Handlowej.

Kosikowski, C. (2012). 'Dysfunkcje finansów publicznych'. *Instytucje: konflikty i dysfunkcje*. Warszawa: Oficyna Naukowa.

Kurpiewski, W. (1993). 'Zagadnienie odpowiedzialności w buddyzmie'. *O odpowiedzialności: moralny wymiar odpowiedzialności w życiu publicznym: materiały III Jagiellońskiego Sympozjum Etycznego*. Kraków: Uniwersytet Jagielloński.

Kwiecień, A. (2012). 'Zaufanie kluczem do realizacji strategii'. *Determinanty potencjału rozwoju organizacji*. Kraków: Mfiles.pl.

Latusek-Jurczak, D. (2012). 'Rola kultury organizacyjnej w zarządzaniu wiedzą'. *Zarządzanie wiedzą*. Warszawa: Wolters Kluwer.

Lencioni, P. (2012). *The Five Dysfunctions of a Team: Participant Workbook for Team Leaders*. San Francisco: Wiley.

Lewicka-Strzałecka, A. (2003). 'Zaufanie w relacji konsument-biznes'. *Prakseologia*, 143, pp. 195-208.

Listwan, T. (2005). 'Dysfunkcje personalne w organizacjach międzynarodowych w Polsce'. *Dysfunkcje zarządzania zasobami ludzkimi*. Łódź: Wydawnictwo Uniwersytetu Łódzkiego.

Littlejohn, S.W. and Foss, K.A. (2005). *Theories of Human Communication*. Australia–Canada–Mexico–Singapore–Spain–United Kingdom–United States: Thomson Wadsworth.

Love, A. (2014). *The Manager's Guide to Mediating Conflict*. Birmingham: Impackt Publishing Ltd.

Penc, J. (2011), *Zachowania organizacyjne w przedsiębiorstwie. Kreowanie twórczego nastawienia i aspiracji*. Warszawa: Wolters Kluwer Polska.

Półtawski, A. and Maciejszczak, M. (2012), 'Husserl a Ingarden'. *Metafizyka. Fenomenologia. Realizm*. Wrocław: Polskie Forum Filozoficzne.

Proksch, S. (2016). *Conflict Management*. Switzerland: Springer.

Rahim, M.A. (2011). *Managing Conflict in Organizations*. New Brunswick-London: Transaction Publisher.

Rogoziński, K. (2012), *Zarządzanie wartością z klientem*. Warszawa: Wolters Kluwer.

Rzycka, O. and Porosło, W. (2010), *Menedżer coachem: jak rozmawiać, by osiągnąć rezultaty*. Warszawa: Wolters Kluwer.

Saks, A.M. (2006).'Antecedents and consequences of employee engagement'. *Journal of Managerial Psychology*, 21 (7), pp. 600-619.

Słownik Wyrazów Obcych – płyta (2001). Warszawa: Wydawnictwo Naukowe.

Stankiewicz, J. (2003). 'Kryzys decyzji jednostkowych i grupowych – uwarunkowania'. *Zachowania organizacji wobec zjawisk kryzysowych*. Wrocław: Katedra Projektowania Systemów Zarządzania Akademii Ekonomicznej we Wrocławiu.

Stanowski, A. (1983). 'Dysfunkcja'. *Encyklopedia katolicka. Tom 4*. Lublin: Towarzystwo Naukowe KUL.

Stocki, R. (2005). *Patologie organizacyjne – diagnoza i interwencja*. Kraków: Oficyna Ekonomiczna.

Sztompka, P. (1999). 'Prolegomena do teorii zaufania'. *Idee a urządzanie świata społecznego*. Warszawa: Wydawnictwo Naukowe PWN.

Sztompka, P. (2002). *Socjologia: Analiza społeczeństwa*. Kraków: Znak.

Turner, M.E., Pratkanis, A.R., Probasco, P. and Leve, C. (2006). 'Threat, Cohesion, and Group Effectiveness: Testing a Social Identity Maintenance Perspective on Groupthink'. *Small Groups: Key Readings*. Hove – London – New York: Psychology Press.

Żarczyńska-Dobiesz, A. (2008). *Adaptacja nowego pracownika do pracy w przedsiębiorstwie*. Warszawa: Wolters Kluwer.

SECTION
C

Quantitative methods and their applications in management issues

An Influence of Remittances on the Aggregate Consumption Growth – Evidence from Central America

Ondřej Badura[1], Jana Závacká[2]

Abstract. The impact of remittances on aggregate consumption behaviour has been proven for many times already, yet these international transfers still often remain on the edge of macroeconomic analysis, which is one of the most important supports for making economic policy – a state management. This approach can be acceptable for fully developed countries, where aggregate aspect of remittances would be barely visible. But in environment of the developing world, where remittance inflows may be an important source of national income, we would hardly be able to create accurate a realistic aggregate consumption function without the knowledge of remittances' influence. The aim of this study is to analyze the aggregate consumption growth in terms of remittance flows using data from countries of Central America. To achieve this objective, we use a panel data regression, which results firstly confirm the direct influence of remittance growth on the growth of aggregate consumption and secondly they provide a basic view of consumption effect of remittances in the specific environment of the Central America region.

Keywords: remittances, consumption, panel regression, Central America.

JEL Classification: E21, F24

1 Introduction

To earn more money, it has been always one of the most important reasons for migration or just for working abroad. Now, in the time of the globalized world, it is easier and easier to take such working opportunities. But working abroad does not have to mean spending the money abroad. In many cases, especially when the worker comes from developing country, he has left his family in his home country, and they are desperately dependent on the money he sent them back. This is what we call remittances – income received by family members abroad. Though it does not have to include just family members itself, it is still the most common example. But the really important thing here is the income nature of remittances. Since the simple Keynesian consumption function, there is no doubt among the professional economic circles that it is income, what drives and determines the level of consumption spending of an individual household as well as of the whole economy. In consumption analysis, we usually take income as one uniform variable that explains the level of consumption. But taking into account that different sources of household financial budget may influence consumption behaviour differently, it could be beneficial to study these parts of income separately. In other words, to explore the consumption-income relationship in terms of more income determinants. As it was indicated above, in countries, where a lot of people migrate for work abroad, remittances may represent the significant source of income. Beside the benefit of such an analysis in the theoretical field, it could help the state strategic management to make appropriate and effective economic policy,

[1] VŠB - Technical University Ostrava, Department of Economics, Sokolská třída 33, 701 21 Ostrava, Czech Republic, e-mail: ondrej.badura@vsb.cz
[2] VŠB - Technical University Ostrava, Department of Systems Engineering, Sokolská třída 33, 701 21 Ostrava, Czech Republic, e-mail: jana.zavacka1@vsb.cz

especially concerning migration and international transfer laws. The aim of this study is to analyze the aggregate consumption growth in terms of remittance flows.

The importance of remittances for the consumption behaviour of a household is logically determined by the share of this kind of income on the whole budget. When thinking in macroeconomic scale, it is not different. There are some factors in macroeconomic environment that may indicate the potential of remittances to influence the aggregate level of consumption, like the relative amount of emigrants (relative to the country's population) or a simple economic level, but all of these factors actually indicate the same thing – the share of remittances on aggregate income of receiving country. The higher is the share, the higher is the possibility of finding and proving the effect. Thus, we use this share as a criterion for choice of the receiving countries and so we analyze only economies with high share of remittances in gross domestic product (GDP). We focus particularly on the region of Central America, so the panel regression is driven on the data from countries with similar macroeconomic environment. We compare the results with the results from similar studies analyzing the same effect in different parts of the developing world, for example with Badura and Závacká (2016) who did so in the context of Asian economies.

As it was already mentioned, the condition of the high level of received remittances relative to the GDP leads us to the environment of the developing world. And that is also where we should look for the existing evidence of the consumption effect of remittances. This simple premise is then supported by many empirical studies concerning the consumption – income analysis in the terms of remittances, almost all of them focused on the less developed countries with a high number of emigrants. We can divide those studies into two categories. The first one includes papers that examine the influence of remittances on income distribution and its aspects. The second category concerns on the direct influence on aggregate consumption spending.

From the first category, which de facto reflects the indirect effect of remittances on consumption, we can mention, for example, publications based on data from one particular country such as Lazarte et al (2014), who deals with the impact of this type of international transfers on income distribution a thus poverty in Bolivia or Hobbs and Jameson (2012), analyzing the same problem for Nicaragua. The same issue is often examined also worldwide, not only on example of one country. That kind of paper could be represented by Gibson, Mc Kenzie and Stillman (2013), who on one hand prove the positive effect of emigration and remittance inflows on income poverty in developing world, on the other hand, the widely discuss problems and difficulties in modelling those effects. The clear link between income inequality and remittances was also confirmed in the study of Koechlin and Gianmarco (2007), who use a wide panel of 78 countries worldwide.

To the second category of studies, which major goal was to analyze the direct effect of remittances on consumer behaviour, belongs, for example, Ahmad, Khan and Atif (2013) or Yousafzai (2015) who analyze the influence of remittances on the aggregate consumption function and also on particular types of consumer expenditures. Further, we can mention Incaltarau Maha (2012), who deals with the relation of remittances and consumption in a macroeconomic context of Romania, Zhu (2014) examining the same issue on the example of rural households in China, or Gallegos and Mora (2013), who moreover proved that higher consumption expenditure from received remittances leads also to long term economic and human development, at least in the case of Mexico. Combes and Ebeke (2011) is then an example of a study, which does not focus only on one particular country and so they can conclude more generally. The main contribution of their panel analysis is the finding that consumption instability can be significantly reduced by sufficient inflows of remittances.

The aim of this study is not to come up with a new and entirely original pattern. As you could see, the impact of remittance inflows on the level of aggregate consumption spending (and income distribution) has been proven for many times already. But most of these studies concentrate either on one particular country or on the panel of countries worldwide. But the consumption effect of remittances could be also different in different macroeconomic environments, which are given not only by national characteristic, but also by the specifics of the region. The main goal of this paper is then to bring another little contribution to this topic doing so for environment of developing world of Central America.

The paper is organized as follows. The description of the input data and the model is introduced in Section 2. The estimation results are presented in Section 3. In the last Section we conclude.

2 The model

2.1 The data

The significance of remittances on the consumption growth was tested in Stata using the yearly data from 1996 to 2014 from American countries: Dominican Republic, El Salvador, Guatemala, Honduras, Nicaragua, St. Kitts and Nevis. In case of Nicaragua the data were available from 1999. We have chosen these countries because their share of remittances on GDP was high (except the Dominican Republic all the shares were around 10%) and because of the availability of the data. Their share of remittances on GDP with its mean value are presented in Figure 1.

To achieve the stationarity of the time series all the variables were expressed in their growth rates. For the analysis the following time series were considered:

- growth of remittances (*growth_remitt*) – the annual growth of received remittances (expressed in current US$), transformed into the growth of the real remittances by division by the consumer price index (with respect to the baseline year 2010);
- growth of consumption (*growth_c*) – the annual growth of the household final consumption expenditure (expressed in current US$), transformed into the growth of real household final consumption expenditure by division by the consumer price index (with respect to the baseline year 2010);
- growth of GDP (*growth_gdp*) – the annual growth of GDP (expressed in current US$), transformed into the growth of GDP by the division by consumer price index (with respect to the baseline year 2010);
- consumer price index – the time series of the Consumer price index (CPI, expressed to the baseline year 2010).

Besides these variables, we have also tried to estimate the model with an influence of the short term interest rate, the growth of CPI, the rate of unemployment and the lagged values of model variables, however, the importance of all these variables were rejected at the 10% level of statistical significance. All the data were downloaded from the World Bank database. There is the graphical presentation of the time series of the real consumption growth in the next section. The time series of other data from the model could be found in the Appendix.

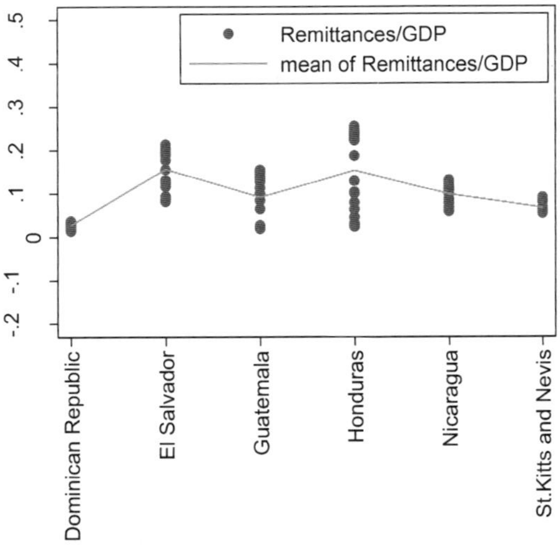

Figure 1 The share of remittances on GDP and its mean value [own computations].

2.2 The model

Firstly, the real consumption growth across countries was analyzed. The observations together with the mean values are presented in Figure 2. We can see that despite the different variability (high in the Dominican Republic and St. Kitts and Nevis) the mean value seems to be similar for all of these countries.

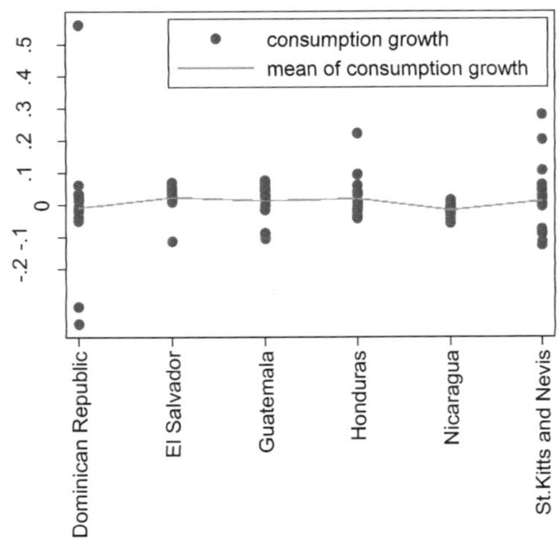

Figure 2 Consumption growth and its mean value [own computations].

However, we have started with the panel data regression. According to Hausman test, the hypotheses that the difference in coefficients is not systematic was strongly rejected at the 10% of significance. Thus, the model with random effects were estimated. Following the test for time effects, we have found that the model could be improved with the dummy variables for the year 2008. The following model was estimated:

$$growth\_c_{it} = \beta_0 + \beta_1 growth\_gdp_{it} + \beta_2 growth\_remitt_{it} + \beta_3 I^{2008}{}_{it} + u_{it}^{RE} + \varepsilon_{it}^{RE}. \quad (1)$$

$\beta_0, \beta_1, \beta_2, \beta_3$ are model parameters, $I^{2008}{}_{it}$ dummy variable for the year 2008 and u_{it}^{RE} the between-entity and ε_{it}^{RE} the within-entity errors. Following the results of Breusch-Pagan Lagrange multiplier test we failed to reject the hypotheses that there is no significant difference across units at 5% level of significance. Thus the model was also estimated by the ordinary least square regression (OLS).

$$growth\_c_{it} = \beta_0 + \beta_1 growth\_gdp_{it} + \beta_2 growth\_remitt_{it} + \beta_3 I^{2008}{}_{it} + \varepsilon_{it}^{OLS}. \quad (2)$$

ε_{it}^{OLS} is the error term from OLS regression. There was no significant heteroscedasticity neither autocorrelation of residuals at the 5% level of significance.

3 Estimation results

The estimation results of both models (1) and (2) are presented in Table 1. The estimations are quite stable, the use of OLS regression differs only slightly in their standard error estimations.

Variable	Random effects GLS regression	OLS regression
growth_gdp	**0.990**	**0.990**
	0.181	0.181
	(0.000)	(0.000)
growth_remitt	**0.108**	**0.108**
	0.050	0.050
	(0.030)	(0.033)
I^{2008}	**0.108**	**0.108**
	0.035	0.035
	(0.002)	(0.003)
const.	**0.024**	**0.024**
	0.010	0.010
	(0.018)	(0.020)
Number of observations	105	105
R^2		0.286

Table 1 Estimation results

We can see that the growth of the real consumption spending is estimated to be very similar to the growth of the real GDP. The significance of the growth of the remittances is statistically significant at the 5% level of significance. The estimation of the coefficient by the dummy variable in 2008 (the global crisis in the US) is positive, the ad hoc increase in the consumption growth could be probably explained by the prompt fall of the dollar.

We have already driven similar estimations for the Asian economies in Badura and Závacká (2016). The estimation of the impact of the growth of the real GDP on the growth of the real consumption spending was 0.968, thus very similar to our result. The impact of the growth of the remittances was 0.028, thus smaller than our result now which is 0.108. The coefficient of determination of the OLS estimation was small, 0.286 only. The F-test confirmed the statistical significance of the model at the 5% level of significance and the Ramsey RESET test did not reject the hypothesis that the model has no omitted variables at the 5% level of significance too. The importance of the growth of remittances on the modelling of the growth of the real consumption spending was confirmed, thus the model was sufficient for the purpose of this paper. According to the data it seems that the reason of the lower ability of the model to explain the variability in the growth of the real consumption spending will be particular to each country.

4 Conclusion

The primary goal of this paper was to examine the growth of aggregate consumption of households in term of remittance growth and thus to verify the initial hypothesis that in the environment of Central America, remittances belong among the important determinants of aggregate consumption function. This assumption has been actually confirmed through a statistically significant and robust coefficient for remittance growth. It is necessary to note that the explanatory ability of the model itself is quite low, in other words, it doesn't represent complete consumption function, but just a simple evidence of consumption effect of remittances. However, the achieved results are much in line with the results from the similar study driven in the environment of Asian economies (Badura and Závacká, 2016).

We have to mention further that the explanatory ability of the model wasn't influenced only by the low value of coefficient of determination, but also by the selection of countries. The results are not fully general, but valid only for specific environment of Central America with high share of remittances in national income. The economies of the chosen countries and their historical evolvements are always specific. However, we believe that state management and policy makers could benefit from the results of this study, since when the influence of remittances is now confirmed, it seems profitable and effective to support work emigration (within some limits, of course) and thus to firstly raise the aggregate consumption and also to unburden the local labor market, suffering from high unemployment. It is also useful to realize that remittances themselves aren't naturally part of the GDP, but they often significantly contribute to the household income and through consumption spending they can regularly increase GDP of the economy and so to contribute to real economic convergence. And in the cases where remittances aren't just consumed, but used also for investments, this effect of long term economic growth and development could be even accelerated. Despite the fact that most of remittances received are spent for necessary goods and so this channel must be analyzed at the first place, it would be useful to distinguish the consumption and the investment channel of use of remittances a thus to describe the positive effect of emigration in more detail.

Although the influence of remittances on the aggregate consumption growth in Central America has been clearly confirmed in this study, the low coefficient of determination (R^2) could be a signal for more possible hidden influences in these economies. Was the low share of explained variability caused by changing variables of economic environment across the time?

Or is it just a result of too big heterogeneity of the chosen countries and their specific economics environment? Looking for the answers of these questions and improving this model could be a relevant motive for extension of this work.

Acknowledgements

This paper has been funded by SGS project No. SP2016/112 "Remittances and their influence on macroeconomic and microeconomic indicators" and the Operational Programme Education for Competitiveness – Project CZ.1.07/2.3.00/20.0296.

References

Ahmad, N., Khan, Z. U. and Atif, M. (2013). 'Econometric Analysis of Income, Consumption and Remittances in Pakistan: Two Stage Least Square Method'. *Journal of Commerce,* 5 (4), pp. 1-10.

Badura, O. and Závacká, J. (2016). 'Are remittances important for the aggregate consumption growth'? *34th International Conference on Mathematical Methods in Economics,* Liberec, Czech Republic, pp. 13-18.

Combes, J. L. and Ebeke, Ch. (2011). 'Remittances and Household Consumption Instability in Developing Countries'. *World Development,* 39 (7), pp. 1076-1089.

Gallegos, J. L. C. and Mora, J. A. N. (2013). 'Remittances, Consumption and Human Development: Evidence of Mexico's Dependence'. *Análisis Económico,* 28, pp. 93-121.

Gibson, J., Mc Kenzie, D. and Stillman, S. (2013). 'Accounting for Selectivity and Duration-Dependent Heterogeneity When Estimating the Impact of Emigration on Incomes and Poverty in Sending Areas'. *Economic Development and Cultural Change,* 61, pp. 247-280.

Hobbs, A. W. and Jameson, K. P. (2012). 'Measuring the Effect of Bi-directional Migration Remittances on Poverty and Inequality in Nicaragua'. *Applied Economics,* 44, pp. 2451-2460.

Incaltarau, C. and Maha, L. G. (2012). 'The Impact of Remittances on Consumption and Investment in Romania'. *Journal of European Studies,* 3 (2), pp. 61-86.

Koechlin, V. and Gianmarco, L. (2007). 'International Remittances and Income Inequality: An Empirical Investigation'. *Journal of Economic Policy Reform,* 10 (2), pp. 123-141.

Lazarte, A., et al (2014). 'Remittances and Income Diversification in Bolivia's Rural Sector'. *Applied Economics,* 46 (8), pp. 848-858.

Yousafzai, T. K. (2015). 'The Economic Impact of International Remittances on Household Consupmtion and Investment in Pakistan'. *Journal of Developing Areas,* 49 (6), pp. 157-172.

Zhu, Y., et al (2014). 'Where Did All the Remittances Go? Understanding the Impact of Remittances on Consumption Patterns in Rural China'. *Applied Economics,* 46 (12), pp. 1312-1322.

Appendix

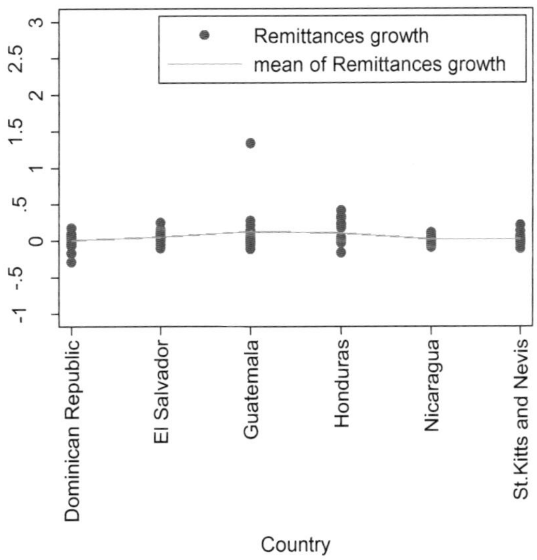

Figure 3 The growth of received remittances and its mean value [own computations].

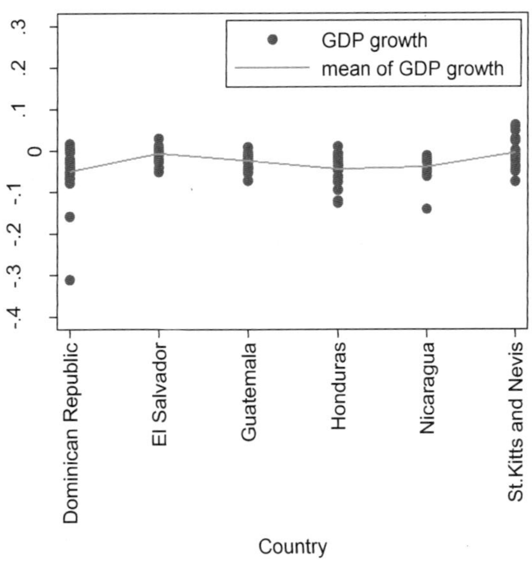

Figure 4 The growth of real GDP and its mean value [own computations].

A discrete variant of Farkas' Lemma: an addendum

David Bartl[1]

Abstract. We have established a discrete variant of Farkas' Lemma [Bartl, D. and Dubey, D. (2017). *Operations Research Letters*, 45, pp. 160–163] in the setting of a module over a linearly ordered commutative ring, which may contain zero divisors, and need not be associative nor unital. However, a certain hypothesis about the ring has been essential there, leaving some questions open. This paper supplements the aforementioned one. We prove the same discrete variant of Farkas' Lemma under a different hypothesis about the ring. Moreover, we present four examples of rings to show that the two hypotheses (the former one and the new one) about the ring are independent of each other.

Keywords: Farkas' Lemma, systems of linear inequalities, linearly ordered modules, linearly ordered rings.

JEL classification: C65

1 Introduction

In the literature, many variants of Farkas' Lemma (Farkas, 1902) can be found. See Dinh and Jeyakumar (2014a), Li and Ng (2014), López (2014), Mordukhovich (2014), Yang and Meng (2014), Dinh and Jeyakumar (2014b) for a recent survey. A particular generalization of Farkas' Lemma, due to Bartl (2007), is in the setting of a vector space (of finite or infinite dimension) over a linearly ordered (commutative or skew) field; shorter algebraic proofs of this result can be found in Bartl (2008, 2012a,b). Considering the very short algebraic proof (Bartl, 2012b) thoroughly, we could report a discrete variant of Farkas' Lemma (Bartl and Dubey, 2017), which is stated in the setting of a module over a linearly ordered commutative ring.

For simplicity, we illustrate the result in the setting of the module $\mathbb{Z}^n$ over the linearly ordered ring $\mathbb{Z}$ of the integer numbers. Let $\boldsymbol{A} \in \mathbb{Z}^{m \times n}$ be a matrix and let $\boldsymbol{c} \in \mathbb{Z}^n$ be a vector. Assume that the Farkas condition holds, i.e., for all $\boldsymbol{x} \in \mathbb{Z}^n$, if $\boldsymbol{A}\boldsymbol{x} \le \boldsymbol{o}_m$, then $\boldsymbol{c}^T\boldsymbol{x} \le 0$. The question is whether there exists a non-negative $\boldsymbol{u} \in \mathbb{Z}^m$ such that $\boldsymbol{A}^T\boldsymbol{u} = \boldsymbol{c}$. Actually, we simplify the question: we conclude that there exist a non-negative $\boldsymbol{u} \in \mathbb{Z}^m$ and a *positive* $r \in \mathbb{Z}$ such that $\boldsymbol{A}^T\boldsymbol{u} = \boldsymbol{c}r$, i.e., the vector $\boldsymbol{c}$ also gets scaled to its "proper length".

We established a more general result in Bartl and Dubey (2017). First, we considered an arbitrary linearly ordered commutative ring R instead of the ring $\mathbb{Z}$. The ring R might contain zero divisors and might not be associative nor unital. The ring R had to satisfy a certain hypothesis, however. Second, we did not consider the Farkas condition in the free module R^n or $\mathbb{Z}^n$, as above, but we considered it in the setting of an arbitrary module W over the ring R.

The purpose of this paper is to prove the result of Bartl and Dubey (2017) under a *different* hypothesis about the ring R. Moreover, we shall present four examples of linearly ordered commutative rings to demonstrate that the certain hypothesis of Bartl and Dubey (2017) and the hypothesis used in this paper are independent of each other.

[1]ORCID: http://orcid.org/0000-0003-1313-035X, david.bartl@post.cz.

2 Notation

To present our result, we use the notation of Bartl and Dubey (2017); we recall the notation here for the convenience of the reader.

The symbol R denotes a commutative ring and V denotes a module over the ring R. We assume that a binary relation "$\leq$" and "$\preceq$" is given on the ring R and the module V, respectively. We say that V is a *linearly ordered module* over the *linearly ordered ring* R iff, for all $\lambda, \mu \in R$ and for all $u, v \in V$, it holds

$$
\begin{aligned}
&\lambda \geq 0 \lor \lambda \leq 0\,, && u \succeq 0 \lor u \preceq 0\,,\\
&\lambda \geq 0 \land \lambda \leq 0 \implies \lambda = 0\,, && u \succeq 0 \land u \preceq 0 \implies u = 0\,,\\
&\lambda \geq 0 \land \mu \geq 0 \implies \lambda + \mu \geq 0\,, && u \succeq 0 \land v \succeq 0 \implies u + v \succeq 0\,,\\
&\lambda \geq 0 \land \mu \geq 0 \implies \lambda\mu \geq 0\,, && \lambda \geq 0 \land u \succeq 0 \implies \lambda u \succeq 0\,,\\
&\lambda \leq \mu \iff \lambda - \mu \leq 0\,, && u \preceq v \iff u - v \preceq 0\,,
\end{aligned}
$$

where we have used the usual convention that $\lambda \geq \mu$ or $u \succeq v$ iff $\mu \leq \lambda$ or $v \preceq u$, respectively. An element $\lambda \in R$ is *positive*, *negative*, *non-negative*, *non-positive*, and *non-zero*, iff $\lambda > 0$, $\lambda < 0$, $\lambda \geq 0$, $\lambda \leq 0$, and $\lambda \neq 0$, respectively. These five concepts are defined for elements of the module V analogously.

For a vector $u \in V$ and for a scalar $\lambda \in R$, we let $\iota u\lambda = \lambda u$, the λ-multiple of the vector u. That is, the symbol "ι" (Greek letter iota) means the next two elements of the module and ring are to be transposed and multiplied in the new order. Notice that, for a fixed $u \in V$, we thus obtain a linear mapping or homomorphism $\iota u \colon R \to V$ with $\iota u \colon \lambda \mapsto \lambda u$.

Let W be another module over the commutative ring R. Given a linear form $\alpha \colon W \to R$ and a vector $u \in V$, we can compose the form α with $\iota u \colon R \to V$. We denote the composition by $\iota u\alpha$, and we have $\iota u\alpha x = (\alpha x)u$ for any $x \in W$. Consider a linear mapping or homomorphism $\gamma \colon W \to V$. Given a constant $r \in R$, then $r\gamma$ is the r-multiple of the mapping γ. We have $r\gamma x = r(\gamma x)$ for any $x \in W$. Notice that $r\gamma$ is a linear mapping, because the ring R is commutative, and that we drop parentheses around the argument "x" if they are unnecessary. That is $\alpha x = \alpha(x)$ and $\gamma x = \gamma(x)$ for all $x \in W$.

3 A discrete variant of Farkas' Lemma

In this section, we recall the former result of Bartl and Dubey (2017) and we prove the same result under a *different* hypothesis about the linearly ordered ring R. We present the common assumptions first.

Let R be a linearly ordered commutative ring. The ring R need not be associative and need not be unital (i.e., need not possess the unit element, neutral with respect to multiplication). Recall that an element $a \in R$ is a *zero divisor* iff $a \neq 0$ and there exists a non-zero $b \in R$ such that $ab = ba = 0$. The ring R may contain zero divisors.

Furthermore, let V be a linearly ordered module over the linearly ordered ring R. Although the ring R need not be associative, we assume that $(\lambda\mu)u = \lambda(\mu u)$ for all $\lambda, \mu \in R$ and for all $u \in V$.

Finally, let W be a module over the ring R with $(\lambda\mu)x = \lambda(\mu x)$ for all $\lambda, \mu \in R$ and for all $x \in W$. Last but not least, let $\alpha_1, \dots, \alpha_m \colon W \to R$ be linear forms, where m is a non-negative natural number, and let $\gamma \colon W \to V$ be a linear mapping.

3.1 Our former result

Given two positive elements $a, e \in R$, the element $a \in R$ is *infinitely less* than e iff $a < e$ and $ta < e$ for all $t \in R$.

Here, we assume the following properties of the linearly ordered commutative ring R: the ring may contain zero divisors, need not be associative, need not be unital, and it satisfies Hypothesis 1.

Hypothesis 1. There exists a positive element $e \in R$ such that $ee > 0$ and, for any element $a \in R$, if $e > a > 0$ and a is a zero divisor, then a is not infinitely less than e.

Our former result is as follows.

Lemma 1 (A discrete variant of Farkas' Lemma, Bartl and Dubey, 2017)**.** *Under the above assumptions and Hypothesis 1, the next statement* (A) *implies the subsequent statement* (B)*:*

(A) *For each $x \in W$, it holds*

$$(\alpha_1 x \leq 0 \wedge \cdots \wedge \alpha_m x \leq 0) \implies \gamma x \preceq 0\,. \tag{1}$$

(B) *There exist an $r \in R$ and $u_1, \dots, u_m \in V$ such that $r > 0$ and $u_1, \dots, u_m \succeq 0$, and*

$$r\gamma = \iota u_1 \alpha_1 + \cdots + \iota u_m \alpha_m\,. \tag{2}$$

See Bartl and Dubey (2017) for the proof, further remarks and discussion.

3.2 Our new result

We stipulate that the square of an element takes precedence over the multiplication, that is, we let $\delta a^2 = \delta(a^2) = \delta(aa)$ for any $\delta, a \in R$. Notice that, since the ring R need not be associative, we may have $\delta a^2 = \delta(aa) \neq (\delta a)a$.

Here, we assume the following properties of the linearly ordered commutative ring R: the ring may contain zero divisors, need not be associative, need not be unital, and it satisfies Hypothesis 2.

Hypothesis 2. There exists a positive element $\delta \in R$ such that $\delta a > 0$ implies $\delta a^2 > 0$ for any element $a \in R$.

Remark 1. Assume that Hypothesis 2 holds. Notice that, if $\delta a > 0$ and $\delta b > 0$ for some $a, b \in R$, then $\delta(ab) > 0$ too. Indeed, it holds $\delta a^2 > 0$ and $\delta b^2 > 0$, and we may assume wlog that $a \geq b > 0$. Then $aa \geq ab \geq bb > 0$, hence $\delta(ab) \geq \delta(bb) = \delta b^2 > 0$.

Remark 2. If the ring R contains some zero divisors, then δ must be a zero divisor. Let $a, b \in R$ be non-zero and such that $ab = 0$. We may assume wlog that $a \geq b > 0$. Then $ab \geq bb \geq 0$, hence $b^2 = 0$. Should δ not be a zero divisor, then $\delta b > 0$, but $\delta b^2 = 0$, a contradiction.

Remark 3. If the ring R contains no zero divisors, then δ can be any positive element and its existence means that the ring R is non-trivial.

Lemma 2 and Lemma 3, which follow, are our new results.

Lemma 2 (A discrete variant of Farkas' Lemma, a new result)**.** *Under the above assumptions and Hypothesis 2, the next statement* (A) *implies the subsequent statement* (B)*:*

(A) *For each $x \in W$, it holds*

$$(\alpha_1 x \leq 0 \ \wedge \ \cdots \ \wedge \ \alpha_m x \leq 0) \implies \gamma x \preceq 0\,. \tag{3}$$

(B) *There exist an $r \in R$ and $u_1, \ldots, u_m \in V$ such that $r > 0$ and $u_1, \ldots, u_m \succeq 0$, and*

$$r\gamma = \iota u_1 \alpha_1 + \cdots + \iota u_m \alpha_m\,. \tag{4}$$

Lemma 3. *Under the above assumptions and Hypothesis 2, the next statement* (A′) *implies the subsequent statement* (B′)*:*

(A′) *For each $x \in W$, it holds*

$$(\delta\alpha_1 x \leq 0 \ \wedge \ \cdots \ \wedge \ \delta\alpha_m x \leq 0) \implies \delta\gamma x \preceq 0\,. \tag{5}$$

(B′) *There exist an $r \in R$ and $u_1, \ldots, u_m \in V$ such that $r > 0$ and $u_1, \ldots, u_m \succeq 0$, and*

$$r\gamma = \iota u_1 \alpha_1 + \cdots + \iota u_m \alpha_m\,, \tag{6}$$

moreover, either $r = \delta$ or $r = \delta s$ for some $s \in R$.

It is easy to see that Lemma 2 follows from Lemma 3. Indeed, if statement (A) is satisfied, i.e., formula (3) holds for any $x \in W$, then formula (3) holds for $x := \delta x$ too. Since the forms $\alpha_1, \ldots, \alpha_m$ and the mapping γ are linear, we have $\alpha_i(\delta x) = \delta\alpha_i x$ and $\gamma(\delta x) = \delta\gamma x$ for any $x \in W$, whence statement (A′) follows. Next, once statement (B′) is established, then statement (B) is obvious.

We now prove Lemma 3 by induction. The proof is based upon the very short algebraic proof of Farkas' Lemma (Bartl, 2012b). It is similar to the proof of Lemma 1 by Bartl and Dubey (2017) therefore.

Proof. Assume that $m = 0$ and let statement (A′) hold. Then the logical conjunction "$\delta\alpha_1 x \leq 0 \ \wedge \ \cdots \ \wedge \ \delta\alpha_m x \leq 0$" in (5) is empty, hence logically true by convention. It follows that $\delta\gamma = o$, the zero mapping $o\colon W \to V$. Furthermore, the logical conjunction "$u_1, \ldots, u_m \succeq 0$" is also empty, thus logically true by convention. The sum "$\iota u_1 \alpha_1 + \cdots + \iota u_m \alpha_m$" in (6) being empty, it equals the zero mapping $o\colon W \to V$ by convention. Putting $r = \delta$, we conclude that statement (B′) holds. We have proved the statement of Lemma 3 for $m = 0$ thus.

Assume that the statement of Lemma 3 has been proved for a non-negative natural number m. We shall prove it for $m + 1$. Thus, assume that it holds

$$\forall x \in W\colon \ (\delta\alpha_1 x \leq 0 \ \wedge \ \cdots \ \wedge \ \delta\alpha_m x \leq 0 \ \wedge \ \delta\alpha_{m+1} x \leq 0) \implies \delta\gamma x \preceq 0\,. \tag{7}$$

If it holds even

$$\forall x \in W\colon \ (\delta\alpha_1 x \leq 0 \ \wedge \ \cdots \ \wedge \ \delta\alpha_m x \leq 0) \implies \delta\gamma x \preceq 0\,, \tag{8}$$

then we are done: there exist an $r > 0$ and non-negative $u_1, \ldots, u_m \in V$ such that $r\gamma = \iota u_1 \alpha_1 + \cdots + \iota u_m \alpha_m$ with $r = \delta$ or $r = \delta s$ for some $s \in R$ by the induction hypothesis; put $u_{m+1} = 0$. Assume now that (8) does not hold. Then

$$\exists x_{m+1} \in W\colon \ (\delta\alpha_1 x_{m+1} \leq 0 \ \wedge \ \cdots \ \wedge \ \delta\alpha_m x_{m+1} \leq 0) \ \wedge \ \delta\gamma x_{m+1} \succ 0\,. \tag{9}$$

Since (7) holds, it follows $\delta\alpha_{m+1}x_{m+1} > 0$.

Now, observe that

$$\begin{aligned} &\alpha_{m+1}\big((\alpha_{m+1}x_{m+1})x - (\alpha_{m+1}x)x_{m+1}\big) = \\ &\quad = (\alpha_{m+1}x_{m+1})(\alpha_{m+1}x) - (\alpha_{m+1}x)(\alpha_{m+1}x_{m+1}) = 0 \end{aligned} \tag{10}$$

for any $x \in W$ by the commutativity of the ring R. Notice that it holds $\gamma\big((\alpha_{m+1}x_{m+1})x - (\alpha_{m+1}x)x_{m+1}\big) = \big((\alpha_{m+1}x_{m+1})\gamma - \iota(\gamma x_{m+1})\alpha_{m+1}\big)(x)$ and it also holds $\alpha_i\big((\alpha_{m+1}x_{m+1})x - (\alpha_{m+1}x)x_{m+1}\big) = \big((\alpha_{m+1}x_{m+1})\alpha_i - (\alpha_i x_{m+1})\alpha_{m+1}\big)(x)$ for $i = 1, \ldots, m$. Hence and by (7) and (10), we have

$$\forall x \in W\colon \left\{ \begin{aligned} \delta\big((\alpha_{m+1}x_{m+1})\alpha_1 \ &- \ (\alpha_1 x_{m+1})\alpha_{m+1}\big)(x) \leq 0 \\ &\vdots \\ \delta\big((\alpha_{m+1}x_{m+1})\alpha_m \ &- (\alpha_m x_{m+1})\alpha_{m+1}\big)(x) \leq 0 \end{aligned} \right\} \implies$$

$$\implies \delta\big((\alpha_{m+1}x_{m+1})\gamma - \iota(\gamma x_{m+1})\alpha_{m+1}\big)(x) \preceq 0\,.$$

Then, by the induction hypothesis, there exist an $r' > 0$ and non-negative $u'_1, \ldots, u'_m \in V$ such that

$$\begin{aligned} r'\big((\alpha_{m+1}x_{m+1})\gamma - \iota(\gamma x_{m+1})\alpha_{m+1}\big) = \quad & \iota u'_1\big((\alpha_{m+1}x_{m+1})\alpha_1 \ - \ (\alpha_1 x_{m+1})\alpha_{m+1}\big) + \cdots + \\ & + \iota u'_m\big((\alpha_{m+1}x_{m+1})\alpha_m - (\alpha_m x_{m+1})\alpha_{m+1}\big)\,, \end{aligned}$$

equivalently

$$\begin{aligned} \big((\alpha_{m+1}x_{m+1})r'\big)\gamma = \iota\big((\alpha_{m+1}x_{m+1})u'_1\big)\alpha_1 + \cdots + \iota\big((\alpha_{m+1}x_{m+1})u'_m\big)\alpha_m \\ + \iota\big(r'(\gamma x_{m+1}) - (\alpha_1 x_{m+1})u'_1 - \cdots - (\alpha_m x_{m+1})u'_m\big)\alpha_{m+1}\,, \end{aligned} \tag{11}$$

moreover, either $r' = \delta$ or $r' = \delta s'$ for some $s' \in R$. We distinguish two cases.

First, if $r' = \delta$, simply put $r = (\alpha_{m+1}x_{m+1})r' = (\alpha_{m+1}x_{m+1})\delta = \delta\alpha_{m+1}x_{m+1} > 0$, see above, below (9).

Second, if $r' = \delta s'$ for some $s' \in R$, then, for any $x \in W$, we have

$$\begin{aligned} \big((\alpha_{m+1}x_{m+1})r'\big)\gamma x &= [r'(\alpha_{m+1}x_{m+1})]\gamma x = r'[(\alpha_{m+1}x_{m+1})\gamma x] = \\ &= (\delta s')[(\alpha_{m+1}x_{m+1})\gamma x] = \delta\big(s'[(\alpha_{m+1}x_{m+1})\gamma x]\big) = \\ &= \delta\big([s'(\alpha_{m+1}x_{m+1})]\gamma x\big) = \big(\delta[s'\alpha_{m+1}x_{m+1}]\big)\gamma x\,. \end{aligned}$$

Put $r = \delta(s'\alpha_{m+1}x_{m+1})$. It holds $\delta\alpha_{m+1}x_{m+1} > 0$, see above, and $r' = \delta s' > 0$, hence $r > 0$ by Remark 1.

Finally, put $u_i = (\alpha_{m+1}x_{m+1})u'_i$ for $i = 1, \ldots, m$ and $u_{m+1} = r'(\gamma x_{m+1}) - (\alpha_1 x_{m+1})u'_1 - \cdots - (\alpha_m x_{m+1})u'_m$. Since $r > 0$ and noticing that $u_i \succeq 0$ for all $i = 1, \ldots, m, m+1$, we are done. □

4 Examples

In this section, we present four examples of linearly ordered commutative rings to show that Hypothesis 1 and Hypothesis 2 are independent of each other.

Example 1 presents a linearly ordered commutative ring R that satisfies Hypothesis 2 and does not satisfy Hypothesis 1.

Example 1. Let R be the ring of the sums $a + b\delta$ for $a, b \in \mathbb{R}$, say. (Alternatively, we can consider $\mathbb{Q}$ or $\mathbb{Z}$ instead of $\mathbb{R}$. This remark applies to the subsequent three examples as well.) The addition and multiplication are defined in the usual way, using the rule that $\delta^2 = \delta\delta = 0$. That is, we have $(a' + b'\delta) + (a'' + b''\delta) = (a' + a'') + (b' + b'')\delta$ and $(a' + b'\delta)(a'' + b''\delta) = (a'a'') + (a'b'' + b'a'')\delta$. Finally, the ordering is lexicographical ($1 \gg \delta$), that is, we have $a + b\delta \geq 0$ if and only if $a > 0$ or $a = 0$ and $b \geq 0$. This ring possesses an element δ to satisfy Hypothesis 2, but does not possess any element e to satisfy Hypothesis 1.

Example 2 presents a linearly ordered commutative ring R that satisfies Hypothesis 2 and satisfies Hypothesis 1.

Example 2. Let R be the ring of the formal series of the form $\sum_{n=-1}^{\infty} a_n x^n$ with $a_n \in \mathbb{R}$, say, where only finitely many of a_n's are non-zero. The addition and multiplication are defined in the usual way with the rule that $x^{-2} = x^{-1}x^{-1} = 0$. That is, we have $\sum_{n=-1}^{\infty} a'_n x^n + \sum_{n=-1}^{\infty} a''_n x^n = \sum_{n=-1}^{\infty}(a'_n + a''_n)x^n$ and $\left(\sum_{n=-1}^{\infty} a_n x^n\right)\left(\sum_{n=-1}^{\infty} b_n x^n\right) = \sum_{n=-1}^{\infty} c_n x^n$ with $c_n = \sum_{k=-1}^{n+1} a_k b_{n-k}$. Lastly, the ordering is lexicographical ($\cdots \gg x^2 \gg x^1 \gg x^0 \gg x^{-1}$), that is, it holds $\sum_{n=-1}^{\infty} a_n x^n \geq 0$ if and only if there exists an $n_0 \geq -1$ such that $a_{n_0} > 0$ and $a_n = 0$ for all $n > n_0$, or $a_n = 0$ for all $n \geq -1$. This ring possesses an element δ to satisfy Hypothesis 2 and possesses an element e to satisfy Hypothesis 1; consider $\delta = x^{-1}$ and $e = x^0$, say.

Remark 4. Any non-trivial linearly ordered commutative ring R without zero divisors also satisfies both Hypothesis 2 and Hypothesis 1. See Remark 3 above and Bartl and Dubey (2017), Remark 1, respectively.

Example 3 presents a linearly ordered commutative ring R that does not satisfy Hypothesis 2 and satisfies Hypothesis 1.

Example 3. Consider the index set $N = (0, +\infty)$, the set of positive real numbers. (Alternatively, let $N = (0, +\infty) \cap \mathbb{Q}$ so that the index set is countable.) Let the ring R consist of the formal sums of the form $\sum_{n \in N} a_n x^n$ with $a_n \in \mathbb{R}$, say, where only finitely many of a_n's are non-zero. The addition is defined in the usual way. We have $\sum_{n \in N} a'_n x^n + \sum_{n \in N} a''_n x^n = \sum_{n \in N}(a'_n + a''_n)x^n$. The multiplication is defined as follows.

Let us multiply $a_m x^m$ with $b_n x^n$. If $m+n \leq 1$, then the result is zero, we have $a_m x^m \cdot b_n x^n = 0$. If $m + n > 1$, then we have $a_m x^m \cdot b_n x^n = a_m b_n x^{m*n}$ where $m * n = m + n - 1$, cf. the Łukasiewicz t-norm. That is, we have $\left(\sum_{m \in N} a_m x^m\right)\left(\sum_{n \in N} b_n x^n\right) = \sum_{k \in N} c_k x^k$ with $c_k = \sum_{m \in N} \sum_{n \in N, m*n=k} a_m b_n$.

The ordering is lexicographical ($x^m \ll x^n$ iff $m < n$), that is, we have $\sum_{n \in N} a_n x^n \geq 0$ if and only if there exists an $n_0 \in N$ such that $a_{n_0} > 0$ and $a_n = 0$ whenever $n_0 < n \in N$, or $a_n = 0$ for all $n \in N$.

Observe that an element x^n with $n \in N$ is a zero divisor if and only if $n < 1$. Considering the element $e = x^1$, say, we can see that this ring satisfies Hypothesis 1. Indeed, no zero divisor is infinitely less than e. To see that, given a zero divisor $a_m x^m$, it is enough to multiply it by x^n with $n > 2 - m$. Since the ring contains an element e and zero divisors, it is not associative (Bartl and Dubey, 2017, Remark 1).

We now show that the ring does not possess any element δ to satisfy Hypothesis 2. By Remark 2, any element δ satisfying Hypothesis 2 must be a zero divisor. Thus, considering $\delta = x^n$ with $0 < n < 1$, find an m so that $1 - n < m \leq 1 - n/2$. Then $m + n > 1$, hence $\delta x^m = x^n x^m = x^{m*n} = x^{m+n-1} > 0$. If $2m \leq 1$, then $x^m x^m = 0$, hence $\delta(x^m)^2 = 0$. Assume that $2m > 1$ now. Then $\delta(x^m)^2 = x^n x^m x^m = x^n x^{m*m} = x^n x^{2m-1}$. Since $n + 2m - 1 \leq 1$, we have $\delta(x^m)^2 = 0$.

Example 4 presents a linearly ordered commutative ring R that does not satisfy Hypothesis 2 and does not satisfy Hypothesis 1.

Example 4. Consider the ring R introduced in Example 3 with the index set restricted to the open interval $N = (0, 1)$, alternatively $N = (0, 1) \cap \mathbb{Q}$. Notice that the ring R consists of zero divisors only, and the zero element. The ring does not possess any element δ to satisfy Hypothesis 2 (see Example 3). And the ring does not possess any element e to satisfy Hypothesis 1 either. If $e = x^n$ and $m \in N$ is such that $0 < m < n < 1$, then x^m is infinitely less than e. Indeed, we have $x^m x^p \ll x^m$ for any $p \in N \subseteq (0, 1)$, because $m * p = m + p - 1 = m - (1 - p) < m$ whenever $0 < p < 1$. Thus, the element $e = x^n$ does not have the required properties. Note also that this ring R is associative because the Łukasiewicz t-norm $*$ is.

5 Conclusions

In Bartl and Dubey (2017), we proved Lemma 1 under the assumptions given at the beginning of Section 3 and Hypothesis 1. The question whether Lemma 1 can be proved or disproved if Hypothesis 1 does not hold was left open.

In this paper, we have proved the same result under the assumptions given at the beginning of Section 3 and Hypothesis 2. Moreover, we demonstrated in Section 4 that Hypothesis 1 and Hypothesis 2 are independent of each other. We thus have a partial answer to the question posed in Bartl and Dubey (2017): yes, the result (Lemma 1 or Lemma 2) can be proved even if Hypothesis 1 does not hold, provided that Hypothesis 2 holds.

Now, the open question is reduced to the case when neither Hypothesis 1 nor Hypothesis 2 holds. Put differently, we ask whether it is possible to prove the result when neither Hypothesis 1 nor Hypothesis 2 is satisfied, or whether a counterexample disproving the result can be found in this case.

References

Bartl, D. (2007). 'Farkas' lemma, other theorems of the alternative, and linear programming in infinite-dimensional spaces: a purely linear-algebraic approach'. *Linear and Multilinear Algebra*, 55 (4), pp. 327–353.

Bartl, D. (2008). 'A short algebraic proof of the Farkas lemma'. *SIAM Journal on Optimization*, 19 (1), pp. 234–239.

Bartl, D. (2012a). 'A note on the short algebraic proof of Farkas' lemma'. *Linear and Multilinear Algebra*, 60 (8), pp. 897–901.

Bartl, D. (2012b). 'A very short algebraic proof of the Farkas lemma'. *Mathematical Methods of Operations Research*, 75 (1), pp. 101–104.

Bartl, D. and Dubey, D. (2017). 'A discrete variant of Farkas' lemma'. *Operations Research Letters*, 45 (2), pp. 160–163.

Dinh, N. and Jeyakumar, V. (2014a). 'Farkas' lemma: three decades of generalizations for mathematical optimization'. *Top*, 22 (1), pp. 1–22.

Dinh, N. and Jeyakumar, V. (2014b). 'Rejoinder on: Farkas' lemma: three decades of generalizations for mathematical optimization'. *Top*, 22 (1), pp. 41–44.

Farkas, J. (1902). 'Theorie der einfachen Ungleichungen'. *Journal für die reine und angewandte Mathematik*, 124 (1), pp. 1–27.

Li, C. and Ng, K.F. (2014). 'Comments on: Farkas' lemma: three decades of generalizations for mathematical optimization'. *Top*, 22 (1), pp. 23–26.

López, M.A. (2014). 'Comments on: Farkas' lemma: three decades of generalizations for mathematical optimization'. *Top*, 22 (1), pp. 27–30.

Mordukhovich, B.S. (2014). 'Comments on: Farkas' lemma: three decades of generalizations for mathematical optimization'. *Top*, 22 (1), pp. 31–37.

Yang, X.Q. and Meng, K.W. (2014). 'Comments on: Farkas' lemma: three decades of generalizations for mathematical optimization'. *Top*, 22 (1), pp. 38–40.

Evaluation of Efficiency in Insurance Industry with use of Balanced Scorecard Frame

Blanka Bazsová[1]

Abstract. The Balanced Scorecard is an effective method used within strategic management for creation and realization of strategic goals. It places emphasis on personal and social responsibility of managers for enterprise development. The Balanced Scorecard system increases transparency of these goals, personal responsibility for the strategy, and it causes the growth of competitiveness and expansion of the enterprise. The Balanced Scorecard (BSC) defines financial and non-financial goals and indicators, which serve for measurement of performance and – after all – the successfulness of the enterprise. The data envelopment analysis (DEA) model is a model, which measures the efficiency by means of the rate of expended inputs to the produced outputs. The goal of this paper is to compare the technical efficiency of 13 insurance companies in Czech Republic with help of the non-parametric approach DEA, specially the input-oriented model with the use of Balanced Scorecard frame. Outputs of the paper will be determined by BSC indicators in the sphere of insurance industry and then will be compared with the technical efficiency by using DEA approach. Results showed that 4 insurance Czech companies were efficient, 4 highly and moderately efficient and 5 little efficient and inefficient.

Keywords: analysis, efficiency, evaluation, insurance, performance.

JEL Classification: G22, L25

1 Introduction

Successfulness of each enterprise depends on the established strategy and effectiveness of its realization of this strategy. For whatever enterprise in the world, it is valid that if they want to be successful in whatever market, their performance must be at least equal to the best worldwide companies in the given sphere. The ascending performance of the company, and thereby its ascending successful depends on many factors, which are often hidden and don't need to be included (seen) in the financial analyses. For example, information technologies. At present, they are boisterously discussed phenomenon, that's why it is necessary to take a think about possibilities of their usage. Computers already played the role both in operational activity and in the whole supplier-customer chain. We can see the accelerating trend in companies' investment supporting the ICT (Ministr and Pitner, 2014). ICT cannot replace top manager decision making, but they can support it significantly, especially propagation of knowledge (Smida, 2003). Analysis of the ICT factors which supports innovation processes in the company were the research area of many authors, e.g. Hanclova and Ministr (2013).
On the other hand, the information technologies put increasingly higher demands for enterprise managers. Their work is often very difficult, what is also caused by responsibility for the whole enterprise, or by permanent necessity to learn new knowledge from the sphere of enterprise management. The manager has to consider farther than the enterprise borders. The manager has to be able to plan, organize, govern, check, as well as motivate to acceptation of demanding

[1] VŠB-Technical University of Ostrava/Faculty of Economics/Department of Systems Engineering, 17. listopadu 15/2172, Ostrava, 708 33, blanka.bazsova@vsb.cz

tasks. The strategic vision helps the managers to think permanently of the enterprise and its possibilities, its environment, activities and results (Jirasek, 2004). The strategy of each enterprise cannot be static, but has to be permanently revised and actualize in dependence on changes in the extern and inner environment (Grasseova et al, 2010). The enterprise strategy comes from the analysis of the position and conditions of its acting within the market. However it is necessary to consider the global developmental tendencies, which are characterized by some factors, such as: high general uncertainty, possible unpredictable interventions of the state, ascending consumption, growing possibilities of automation and possibilities of occurrence of new untraditional organization structures within the worldwide ubiquity of the Internet, and so on. As says Soucek (2003) „The most important ratio scale for the strategy quality is whether it will bring to approaching the worldwide competitiveness" (Soucek, 2003).

1.1 Balanced Scorecard

The important role in the strategic management plays the measurement. The Balanced Scorecard method is a frame for the complex system of the strategic management of an enterprise and measurement of their performance. The BSC supports a straight responsibility of employees for the strategic targets of the enterprise. The base of this method is mutual cohesion of performance indicators configured in four perspectives. BSC helps to companies in fulfilment of the strategic targets and connects the company strategies with operation management (Management Mania, 2013). The start of this method relates to the annual developmental project "Measuring Performance in the Organization of the Future". The head of this project was David Norton, and a consultant was Robert Kaplan from Harvard Business School. The project has supported by KPMG and Institute Nolan Norton, the president of which was David Norton. The goal of the project was to find a better method of evaluation of company performance, which wouldn't be based only on financial indicators. Within the project, several tens of American companies from different spheres of activities has analyzed (Kaplan, Norton, 2007). There are more goals, which can be devided according to the perspectives. These goals have to be measurable by indicators.

Indicators selected using the Balanced Scorecard were part of the research group of authors Correa, Prochnik, Ferreira and Vianna, which was published in 2014. This assessment is carried out within the perception of employees at two hospitals in Brazil, where the method was implemented BSC. The research tended to focus on the organizational aspects of the hospitals, especially in the perspective of learning and growth and internal processes. Their data have obtained through interviews with staff, and questionnaire. The results have evaluated statistically, and have made a comparative analysis. Such indicators were selected competence of employees, which can´t be compared with the results obtained from this research. The selected indicators will the starting point in this research in the insurance industry too. The technical efficiency will be evaluated by data envelopment analysis. Bentes, Carneiro da Silva Ferreira and Kimura (2012) chose two factors - the BSC framework and method of multi-criteria evaluation of AHP for purpose of measuring organizational performance integrating. On the example of telecommunication companies in Brazil judged using these frameworks performance of three organizational units. For evaluation, with only selected organizational side - the criteria and sub-criteria that have related to organizational performance.

To evaluate the performance using the BSC and DEA approach were conducted two studies. The first study's authors from Wu and Liao (2014), who assessed the performance of 38 international airlines. Rated operational efficiency in the airline industry. Another performance evaluation was performed using the BSC-model DRF-DEA again authored by Wu and Li (2009), which was assessed higher education. Targets and indicators in the sphere of insurance industry.

DEA method has been used statistically in the evaluation of technical efficiency in banking and healthcare, as evidenced by the research of many authors, for example Toloo (2015), Chytilova (2014). Grmanova and Hostak (2016) evaluate efficiency of national insurance markets using a two stage model of data envelopment analysis. They conducted comparison in the efficiency of national insurance in post-communist countries with particular emphasis of efficiency in the Czech Republic. Grmanova and Hostak (2016) statistically evaluated efficiency score by using the U-statistics and p-values.

2 Data Analysis

The insurance industry is the sphere, which is focusing on protection of property, vehicles, people health, life and roads. Most of insurance companies classify the insurance to life and general ones. It is also reflected in the balance sheet. Thirteen insurance companies act in the domestic market. Information of them is collected by Czech association of insurance companies. For the purpose of financial perspective, same as in other spheres, it is important to monitor expenses and revenues. However, revenues in some branches, such as education system or health service, can be hardly measured, because they are in violation of financing this sphere. They always were considered in these spheres as noneconomic ones. The financial perspective is at the forefront of interests of controlling. Controlling prepares not only reports from the sphere of accounting, calculation and budgeting, but also submits proposals for enterprise strategy and entrepreneurial schedule (Jirasek, 2004).

We consider 13 insurance companies. They provide a broad spectrum of insurance because of a danger to life, health and property of citizens in the Czech Republic. The management makes an effort to improve the position on the insurance market. The goal of the paper is to suggest measurable goals by using BSC method to measure the effectiveness and efficiency of the insurance companies. The Balanced Scorecard method (BSC) and data envelopment analysis (DEA) approach will be applied. At first, it is necessary to choose the measurable goals, which are involved by using the Balanced Scorecard method. The second step is to measure the chosen indexes by using DEA. It is important to determine, which variables are inputs and which of them are outputs. The data about the chosen parameters had been collected from the annual reports in 2015.

If we want to choose the indicators, we have to collect all information about the insurance companies. Annual report contains two important financial documents - the balance sheet and cash flow. We start with the goals´ hierarchy, which is shown in figure 1. The goal on the top in the first position is improving the position on the insurance market. This goal is divided into financial perspective, customer perspective, learning and growth and processes perspective. The increasing level of income is the most important issue in financial perspective. If the insurance company wants to increase the level of income, it should increase written premiums.

Through the increasing of the income, it can increase the profit after tax. Profit after tax is the item in the balance sheet, which is listed on the liabilities side.

The partial strategic goal in customer perspective can be even the increasing of a number of contracts. This goal is difficult to track in partial companies, because annual reports don´t involve this issue. Publication of this item is mandatory, not included in the income statement or balance sheet. That is why it is more appropriate to measure the volume of contracts. We can identify two groups – volume of contracts for life insurance and the volume of contracts in general insurance. The impact of advertising on insurance products and the number of clients, causes an increasing market share.

If we track the increasing of the availability of services in the perspective learning and growth, we can establish more branches and recruit more staff. Therefore the measurable index will be the number of employees.

By tracking the internal processes perspective, we make an effort to reduce the cost of processing contracts, the expenses for insurance benefits cleared from provision.

According to these four perspectives and their measurable indicators, we can specify the input and output variables for evaluating of efficiency by using Data Envelopment Analysis (see table 1).

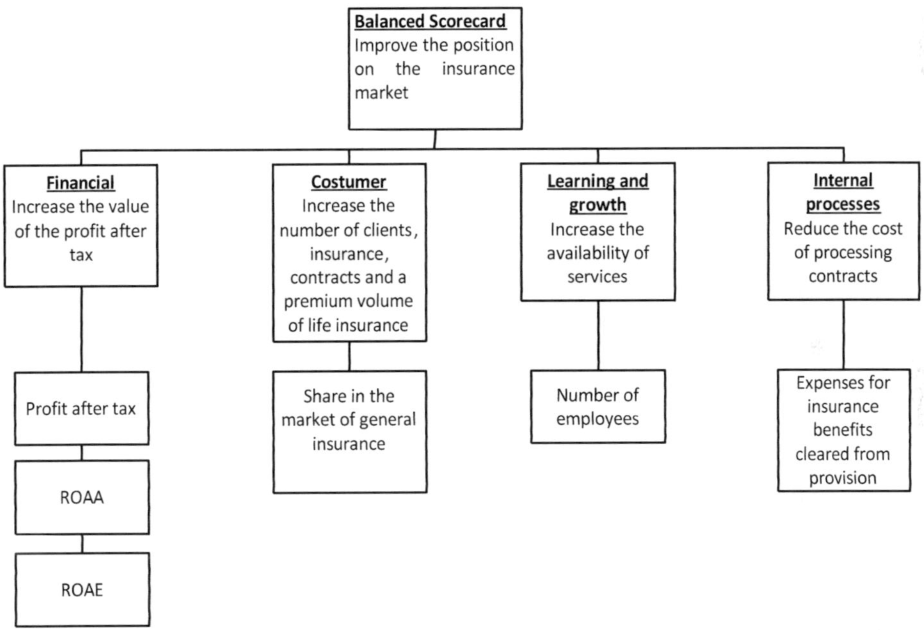

Figure 1 Balanced Scorecard perspectives in the insurance industry (source: own)

Indicator or variable name	Variable marking	Perspective	Description
Profit after tax	O2	Financial perspective	Variable means profit for the current accounting period. Insurance on the technical account in 2015 from Annual reports (Dluhosova, 2006)
ROAA	O3	Financial perspective	Average return on Assets. Indicator of profitability measures the profit with the assets regardless of what resources are funded. (Dluhosova, 2006).
ROAE	O4	Financial perspective	Return on equity. Indicator of profitability.
Number of employees	I1	Learning and growth	The number of employees on permanent employment. Employees are the important resources of the organization (Rehacek, 2015)
Expenses for insurance benefits cleared from provision	I2	Internal processes	Expenses are in the balance-sheet in the income statement.
Share in the market of general insurance	O1	Customer	It was calculated by using Herfindahl-Hirschman index (HHI).

Table 1 Variables description in each perspective (source: own)

Return on assets and equity are based on this calculation (Dluhosova, 2006):

$$ROAA = \frac{profit}{assets} \tag{1}$$

$$ROAE = \frac{profit}{equity} \tag{2}$$

Share in the market is based on the Herfindhal – Hirschman Index calculation (Borovcova, 2016):

$$HHI = \sum_{i=1}^{n} x_i^2, \tag{3}$$

where n is number of the all insurers, x_i^2 is share of i-insurer on the total turnover of the sector. The data about the 13 insurance companies includes six following (above mentioned) parameters, which are involved to measure their efficiency.

3 Data Envelopment Analysis (DEA)

Data Envelopment Analysis (DEA) is a method of multi-criterion assessment for assessing the efficiency of production units (DMU – Decision Making Units) which use an identical input to produce an identical output (Toloo, 2015). Efficiency of production units is based on a mathematical expression of efficiency. The philosophy behind the calculation of efficiency is based on the assumption that one unit of production generates one input and output. The calculation of effectiveness is expressed as an output-input ratio:

$$Efficiency = \frac{output}{input}$$

$$Efficiency = \frac{\sum weighted\ sum\ of\ outputs}{\sum weighted\ sum\ of\ inputs} \tag{4}$$

$$\theta_k = \frac{\sum_{j=1}^{n} u_j y_{jk}}{\sum_{i=1}^{m} v_i x_{ik}},$$

with u and v expressing the weights of inputs and outputs, where $k = 1,..,n$ and express the efficiency of the k-th DMU.

Efficient units are those that reach the maximum value of the given ratio (Fiala and Dlouhy, 2006). As DMU makes use of a variety of inputs in production, it generates different outputs, and each of these inputs and outputs differs in the value: efficiency on the basis of weighed inputs and outputs needs be defined. If we indicate inputs as the variable $x_1, \ldots, x_m$ and outputs as the variable $y_1, \ldots y_n$, for DMUs whose amount is $j = 1, \ldots n$, then the calculation of the production units' efficiency is:

Efficiency can reach values within the interval <0,1>. The DMU is efficient if the ratio result equals 1. The more the value approaches 0, the less the DMU is efficient in its use of inputs. Efficiency assessment of DMU can also be visualized graphically. Charnes, Cooper and Rhodes (1978) devised the following input-oriented CCR model:

$$\max \theta = \sum_{r=1}^{s} u_r y_{r0}$$

$$\sum_{i=1}^{m} v_i x_{i0} = 1 \tag{5}$$

$$\sum_{r=1}^{s} u_r \times y_{rj} - \sum_{i=1}^{m} v_i x_{ij} \leq 0, \text{ where } j = 1, \ldots, n$$

The conditions of non-negativity apply for variables u and v are $v_i, \geq 0 \quad i = 1, \ldots, m$ and $u_r \geq 0 \quad r = 1, \ldots, s$ Variables u and v are unknown weights in this model. These weights are calculated by means of the DEA CCR model (Toloo, 2015).

4 Results and discussion

Based on the available data from annual reports, the efficiency of individual 13 insurance companies was calculated (see table 2). There are involved two input variables based on BSC and four BSC output variables. The results in Table 2 showed efficient and inefficient insurance companies. The efficient DMUs are C4, C6, C8 and C12 (with $\theta = 1.000$). C4 represents Cardif pojišťovna, C6 is Česká pojišťovna, C8 is ČSOB and C12 is Kooperativa.

DMU	Efficiency	v1	v2	u1	u2	u3	u4
C1	0.379	0.000855	0.000002	0.337824	0.000000	0.000000	0.000000
C2	0.390	0.000082	0.000000	0.032296	0.000000	0.000000	0.000000
C3	0.827	0.022727	0.000000	0.497960	0.000000	0.000000	0.027828
C4	1.000	0.013699	0.000000	0.300140	0.000000	0.000000	0.016773
C5	0.326	0.000033	0.000000	0.012907	0.000000	0.000000	0.000000
C6	1.000	0.000000	0.000012	1.562500	0.000000	0.000000	0.000000
C7	0.491	0.000160	0.000000	0.063580	0.000000	0.000000	0.000000
C8	1.000	0.000000	0.000005	0.147904	0.000000	0.000000	0.000011
C9	0.667	0.000000	0.000000	0.000000	0.000000	0.028254	0.000000
C10	0.217	0.020408	0.000000	0.446261	0.000000	0.000000	0.024943
C11	0.648	0.018868	0.000000	0.413401	0.000000	0.000000	0.023102
C12	1.000	0.001757	0.000000	0.038430	0.000000	0.000000	0.002148
C13	0.315	0.000035	0.000000	0.013805	0.000000	0.000000	0.000000

Table 2 Technical Efficiency of the insurance companies (source: own calculation)

The least efficient DMUs are C5, C10 and C13 insurers. C5 is Česká pojišťovna, C10 is Česká podnikatelská pojišťovna, C10 is ERGO pojišťovna and C13 is Generalli pojišťovna (see Table 2). This low efficiency is caused by high input variables – high number of employees and expenses for insurance benefits cleared from provision.

The results of the analysis, carried out using the CCR input oriented model showed that the significant influence at the efficiency score have the weights *u1*, *u3* and *u4*.

If we look at the results C10 DMU, we can see, that this unit has the efficiency 0.217. If the DMU C10 increases its share in the market by one unit, then it is expected that efficiency will increase by *0.44* (*u1*) to *0.217 + 0.44*. The results of efficiency will be *0.667*, since the denominator of does not change and retains the value *1*. If we interpret variable *u2* with zero value, that means, that one unit increase in profit has no effect on efficiency score.

For the statistical evaluation, it is useful to arrange the efficiency evaluation of the insurance companies into intervals, determining the efficiency level, visualized in table 3. Only four companies (30.77%) are efficient. Highly efficient and moderately efficient are four companies (30.77%) and little efficient and inefficient are 5 companies (38.46%).

Efficiency level		
1.00	Efficient	4
(1.00-0.45]	Highly and moderately efficient	4
(0.45-0.00]	Little efficient and inefficient	5

Table 3 Efficiency level (source: own calculation)

5 Conclusion

The efficiency evaluation in the Czech insurance companies was based on model of Data Envelopment Analysis. By using of Balanced Scorecard indicators and input oriented CCR model, the possibility to measure the efficiency of the companies in insurance industry in the Czech Republic has been demonstrated. There were selected six indicators to ensure the success in efficiency of each DMUs on the market. Results showed that there were efficient four insurance companies in the Czech Republic. The significant indicators are: share in the market, number of employees and index number ROAE. By applying of Balanced Scorecard method and CCR model we can join the efficiency and the strategic goals and indicators in insurance companies.

Acknowledgements

This paper was supported within SGS Project No. SP2017/141 "Diskriminační analýza versus analýza datových obalů " and Operational Programme Education for Competitiveness – Project No. CZ.1.07/2.3.00/20.0296.

References

Bentes, A. V., Carneiro, J., da Silva JF and H. Kimura (2012). 'Multidimensional assessment of organizational performance: Integrating BSC and AHP'. *Journal of Business Research*, 65 (12), pp. 1790-1799.

Borovcova, M. (2016). 'Insurance Market Assessment in the Czech Republic'. *Conference Proceedings from 8th International Scientific Conference Managing and Modelling of Financial Risks,* Ostrava, Czech republic, pp. 114-122.

Correa, M.G., Prochnik, V., Ferreira, A. C. and Vianna, D.S. (2014). 'Brazilian Hospital Employee Perceptions of the BSC'. *Latin American Business Review,* 15, pp. 141-166.

Charnes, A., W. W. Cooper and Rhodes, E. (1978). 'Measuring the efficiency of decision making units'. *European Journal of Operational Research*, 2, pp. 429–444.

Dluhosova, D. (2006) *Finanční řízení a rozhodování podniku. Analýza, investování, oceňování, riziko, flexibilita*. Praha: Ekopress.

Grmanova, E. and Hostak, P. (2016). 'Evaluation of the efficiency of national insurance markets using a two-stage model of data envelopment analysis'. *Proceedings of the 10th International Days of Statistics and Economics*, Prague, Czech Republic, pp. 504-513.

Fiala, P. and Dlouhy, M. (2006). *Základy kvantitativní ekonomie a ekonomické analýzy*. Praha: Oeconomica.

Grasseova, M. et al (2010). *Analýza v rukou manažera. 33 nejpoužívanějších metod strategického řízení.* Praha, Computer Press.

Hanclova, J. and Minitr, J. (2013). 'The Use of ICT Tools as Innovations in SMES in the Czech-Polish border Areas'. *Proceedings of the 21th Interdisciplinary Information Management Talks, IDIMT-2013*, Prague, Czech Republic, pp. 129-136.

Chytilova, L. (2014). 'Analysis of Bank Efficiency: An Application of DEA Approach in the Czech Commercial Banks'. *Proceedings of 32nd International Conference Mathematical Methods in Economics*, Olomouc, Czech Republic, pp. 118 - 123.

Jirasek, J. A. (2004). *Strategie. Umění podnikatelských vítězství*. Professional Publishing, Praha.

Kaplan, R.S. and Norton, D.P. (2007). *Balanced Scorecard. Strategický system měření výkonnosti podniku.* Praha: Management Press.

Management mania (2013). *Balanced Scorecard,* 2013, [Online]. Available at: https://managementmania.com/cs/balanced-scorecard [cited 2017-01-09].

Ministr, J. and Pitner, T. (2014). 'Towards an Ecosystem for Academic-Industrial Cooperation'. *Proceedings of the 22nd Interdisciplinary Information Management Talks (IDIMT) Conference*, Prague, Czech Republic, pp. 71-78.

Rehacek, P. (2015). 'Organization Forms for Project Management'. *Proceedings of the 25th International Business Information Management Association Conference IBIMA 2015*, Amsterdam, Netherlands, pp. 2092-2101.

Soucek, Z. (2003). *Úspěšné zavádění strategického řízení firmy*. Praha: Professional Publishing.

Smida, F. (2003). *Strategie v podnikové praxi*. Praha: Professional Publishing.

Toloo, M. (2015). *Data Envelopment Analysis*. Ostrava: Ekonomická fakulta, VŠB-TU Ostrava.

Wu, Y.X., and Li, C.D. (2009). 'Research on Performance Evaluation on Higher Education Based on the Model of BSC-DRF-DEA'. *2009 IEEE16th International Conference on Industrial Engineering and Engineering management, Vols 1 and 2*, Beijing, China, pp. 2030-2034.

Wu, W.Y and Liao, Y. K. (2014). 'A balanced scorecard envelopment approach to assess airlines′ performance'. *Industrial Management and Data Systems*, 114 (1), pp. 123-143.

Risk and Uncertainty in Decision-making about Agricultural Insurance

Helena Brožová, Jana Křečková[1]

Abstract. Rational decision-making is limited by the rationality of decision-maker, complexity of the decision problem, and the incomplete information about the problem. One specific case of this incompleteness is measure of knowledge of risk or uncertainty. Transition from uncertainty to risk helps to improve our decision process and gives a great competitive advantage. This is important mainly if the decisions are influenced by specific type of event, for instance crisis, situation which can revise the decisions outcome in situation with unknown or only estimated probability of realization. This type of situation can be called key state of nature.

The article discusses the decision-making process on the agricultural insurance in relation to the expectation of the key state of nature – environmental and other threats.

Keywords: Decision-making, key state of nature, EMV, stochastic dominance, probability threshold.

JEL Classification: C79, Q19

1 Introduction

The decision-making is very complex and difficult process and good decision has an important impact on positive economic results. Often the decision maker behaviour, knowledge and information negatively influenced the decisions (Hammond et al., 1998). Therefore, it is important to support the decision makers and the decision-making process using appropriate models, especially operations research models. For instance the theory of games is used to model conflict situations where each participant wants to find the best decision (Neumann, Morgenstern, 1944). One of them is decision model or game against nature (Pratt et al., 1964).

The decision maker selects one of at least two alternatives that are available. The result depends on alternatives outcome under possible future states of nature. The payoffs - outcome are associated with each combination alternative – state of nature. The future result of selected alternative depends also on the probabilities of realization of states of nature (Pratt et al., 1964, Bonini et al., 1997, Raiffa, 1997).

Estimation of probability of the states of nature is very complicated task (Špička, Vilhelm, 2012). Therefore, the decision-making under uncertainty is often supposed. Transition from uncertainty to risk helps to improve our decisions and gives a great competitive advantage. It would require that the decision maker could be able to estimate the probability of the states of nature or anticipate the development of decision-making situations. For these type of problems there are many solutions process. For instance, Hurwicz criterion can be used for analysis of future expected outcome. Another one is commonly used effort to obtain so called additional

[1] Czech University of Live Sciences in Prague, Faculty of Economics and Management, Department of Systems Engineering, Kamycka 129, 165 21 Praha 6 – Suchdol, brozova@pef.czu.cz, kreckova@pef.czu.cz

information (Pratt et al., 1964, Bonini et al. 1997, Raiffa, 1997). However this approach is again based on using of probability estimation and not analysing of sensitivity.

Suppose now the promising state of nature exists. If this promising state of nature is expected with higher probability, then the result of alternative could be expected better and vice versa (Brožová, Flégl, 2011). If the probability of some state of nature is changed then the stochastic dominance of alternatives can be also changed.

In this paper, we analyse the stability of the best decision based on the changes of states nature probabilities especially on the probability of the key state of nature, type of event which has a great impact on the solution of the decision problem. We use the Expected Monetary Value criterion (EMV) and stochastic dominance approach. The paper is organised as follow: the first part consists of a description of the decision-making model, EMV criterion and stochastic dominance, the second part consists of the explanation of the sensitivity analysis of the results, and the third part shows its practical application to the agricultural insurance.

2 Decision-making with the key state of nature

2.1 EMV criterion and stochastic dominance

The aim of the decision-making model under risk (game against nature) is to select the best alternative from set of alternatives that are available. Possible future states of nature have an impact on the outcome of selected decision which is expressed as payoffs associated with each combination alternative/state of nature. This outcome depends also on the probabilities with which the states of nature are realized. The decision model under risk (Neumann, Morgenstern, 1944, Pratt et al., 1964, Bonini et al., 1997, Raiffa, 1997) is describe on the following table (Table 1).

		States of nature			
		S_1	S_2	...	S_n
	A_1	v_{11}	v_{12}	...	v_{1n}
Alternatives	A_2	v_{21}	v_{22}	...	v_{2n}
	...	...	...	...	...
	A_m	v_{m1}	v_{m2}	...	v_{m3}
Probabilities		p_1	p_2	...	p_n

A_i is the i-th alternative, $i = 1, ..., m$
S_j is the j-th state of nature, $j = 1, ..., n$,
v_{ij} is the payoff of alternative A_i and state of nature S_j combination
p_j is probability of state of nature S_j.

Table 1 Decision table

The appropriated alternative in the decision under risk is typically chosen according to the commonly used criterion the Expected monetary value (*EMV*), the alternative is selected if it has the maximal mean value of payoff (1)

$$EMV_i = \sum_{j=1}^{n} p_j v_{ij} \quad i = 1, \dots, m$$
$$A_l: \quad EMV_l = \max_{i=1,\dots,m} EMV_i \tag{1}$$

Another approach is the analysis of the dominance of the alternatives – outcome dominance, event dominance and stochastic dominance. An interesting case of dominance of decision alternatives under risk is the canonical first-order stochastic dominance. The alternative A_i has a first-order stochastic dominance over alternative A_j for the required outcome x if A_i gives at least as high probability of receiving at least x as does A_j, and for some x, A_i gives a higher probability of receiving at least x

$$P(v_{A_i} \geq x) \geq P(v_{A_j} \geq x) \qquad (2)$$

This weakest form of dominance describes an overall behaviour of alternative payoffs. It can be graphically displayed as a graph of cumulative probability $P(v_A \geq x)$, which is called a risk profile (Pratt et al., 1964, Bonini et al., 1997, Raiffa, 1997).

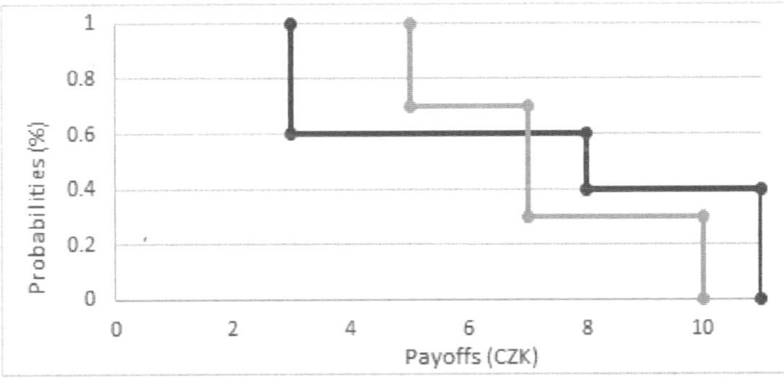

Figure 1 Risk profile - example (source: authors)

2.2 Sensitivity analysis according to the key state of nature probability

Decision under risk assumes probabilities estimation of the state of nature. Changing one of these probabilities may affects the solution of the problem, because the best alternative may changes. Very often, there is a specific key state of nature, which probability would be analysed to receive the best alternative of the problem for changing situation (Brožová, Flégl, 2011).

Let the state S_n is the key state of nature. If the probability p_n of the key state of nature increases, probabilities of other states of nature have to decrease and vice versa (Brožová, Flégl, 2011). Suppose this relation is proportional, increasing or decreasing of probabilities of other states of nature are directly proportional to their initial values (3).

$$p_j = p_j - p_n \frac{p_j}{\sum_{j=1}^{n-1} p_j}, \quad j = 1,\dots,n-1 \qquad (3)$$

The *EMV* in relation to the probability of the key state of nature EMV^{KSN} will be calculated as follows (4) and again the best alternative A_l must maximize this value.

$$EMV_i^{KSN} = \sum_{j=1}^{n-1} (p_j - p_n \frac{p_j}{\sum_{j=1}^{n-1} p_j}) v_{ij} + p_n v_n, \quad i = 1,\dots,m$$
$$A_l : EMV_l^{KSN} = \max_{i=1,\dots,m} EMV_i^{KSN} \qquad (4)$$

The values of the EMV^{KSN} can be shown graphically, on the axe $\boldsymbol{x}$ is probability of the key state of nature and on the axe $\boldsymbol{y}$ is the corresponding EMV^{KSN} values. Each alternative is represented by one line. The best alternative corresponds to the upper line segment, so the best alternative is changed in all breakdown points of the EMV^{KSN} lines. It is possible to set intervals of the probability of the key state of nature in which one of decision alternatives is the best according to the EMV criterion. These threshold probabilities of the key state of nature can be calculated using MS Excel Solver for goal model with changing value of probability of the key state of nature and the goal $EMV_i^{KSN} = EMV_j^{KSN}$.

If we assume the change of probability of the key state of nature and the following changes of the probability of the others then it is obvious that the cumulative probability $P(v_A \geq x)$ will also change. As the consequence, change of the dominance of the alternatives is also possible. Intervals of probability of the key state of nature for which each decision alternative is stochastically dominant could be stated. For this calculation was again used MS Excel Solver and goal model with changing value of probability of the key state of nature, the constraints $P(v_{A_i} \geq x) \geq P(v_{A_j} \geq x)$ for all possible payoffs and the goal $\min(P(v_{A_i} \geq x) - P(v_{A_j} \geq x)) = 0$.

3 Decision of Agricultural Insurance according to the Key State of Nature

3.1 Agricultural insurance decision model under risk

Analysis of the best alternative in the problem of agricultural insurance was developed on the data of one of the largest Czech insurance companies providing agricultural insurance. The active annual insurance policies of insurance of animals, crops and forests for the period 2010 - 2015 were processed (Křečková, Brožová, 2017).

We assume that the decision-maker chooses the alternative either "To get insured" or "Not to get insured". The impact of both decisions depends on the future situation, on whether an insured event occurs or not.

Individual states of nature are formed by the types of the insured event and were divided into four categories: "No claim"; "Small claim"; "Medium claim" and "High claim". A small claim is such whose insurance settlement does not exceed half of the premium paid by a specific client. The amount of insurance settlement for a medium claim is in the interval from half of the premium to the whole premium of a specific client and the amount of insurance settlement in case of a high claim exceeds the value of the given premium.

Table 2 contains information on the distribution of selected types of damage, their average premium and the average insurance settlement for each group of damages.

Type of damage		**No claim**	**Small claim**	**Medium claim**	**High claim**
Interpretation		**No insurance settlement**	**Insurance settlement at maximum 1/2 of the premium**	**Insurance settlement from 1/2 of the premium up to the premium**	**Insurance settlement higher than the premium**
Frequency (%)		91.33	2.78	2.13	3.76
Premium (CZK)	Min	360	1,676	1,063	500
	Avg	61,222	373,898	491,751	265,210
	Max	2,888,988	5,700,051	6,141,176	2,041,188
Insurance settlement (CZK)	Min	0	759	768	800
	Avg	0	89,685	356,870	553,142
	Max	0	2,593,651	3,622,259	6,871,716

Table 2 Types of damages according to the premium of individual clients and their premium and damages (source: authors)

The decision-making model contains individual payoffs for combinations of decision alternatives and states of nature. In this case, the payoffs are determined based on the difference between costs associated with the payment/non-payment of premium and the paid/unpaid insurance settlement. The actual amount of damage/claim is not necessary to take into consideration because payoffs for each state of nature would be changed in both alternatives by an equal value. If the decision-maker is insured, the payoff is equal to the difference between the insurance settlement and paid premium. If the decision-maker is not insured, the payoff is equal to the loss of the expected but not received insurance settlement.

The decision-making model is in Table 3 where the resulting payoffs are set out as well as objective probabilities of each of the state of nature (the risk vector) that have been determined based on the occurrence of damages in the previous years. It is most likely (91.33%) that the client will not sustain any damage and unlikely (3.76%) that the client will sustain high claim.

	No claim	Small claim	Medium claim	High claim	EMV
To get insured	-61,222	-284,213	-134,881	287,932	**-55,865**
Not to get insured	0	-89,685	-356,870	-553,142	**-30,881**
Probability of the occurrence	91.33%	2.78%	2.13%	**3.76%**	(in CZK)

Table 3 Decision-making model and EMV criterion (source: authors)

Result of the model is in the last column in Table 3, the best decision according to the EMV criterion is alternative "Not to get insured". In the case that the decision-maker decides "Not to get insured" and there is "No claim", he or she has no costs but, in the opposite extreme case, he or she can sustain a loss of more than CZK 0.5 million (not receiving insurance settlement). The any damage will probably have to be covered only using own funds. That is the common reason for decision "To get insured".

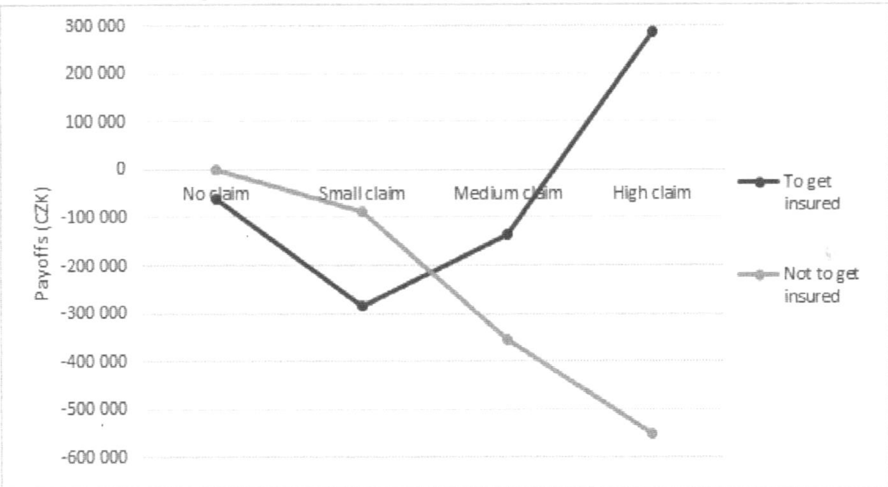

Figure 2 Payoffs according to the alternatives and states of nature (source: authors)

From the data presented in Table 3, it is possible to construct the risk profile of the alternatives - a graph of cumulative probabilities of achieving a certain level of payoffs.

Figure 3 shows that no alternative dominates based on stochastic dominance. There is a 97% probability that if the client is insured, he or she will sustain a loss of more than CZK 134,000. And there is an almost zero probability that the client would be paid the insurance settlement for the damage that would be twice the value of the premium the client paid. On the other hand, if the client does not get insured, he or she risks a big loss but the probability of this loss drops rapidly to zero. It is true that the client may sustain a loss of more than CZK 0.5 million with the probability of 96% but, at the same time, with 91% probability he or she will not sustain any damage.

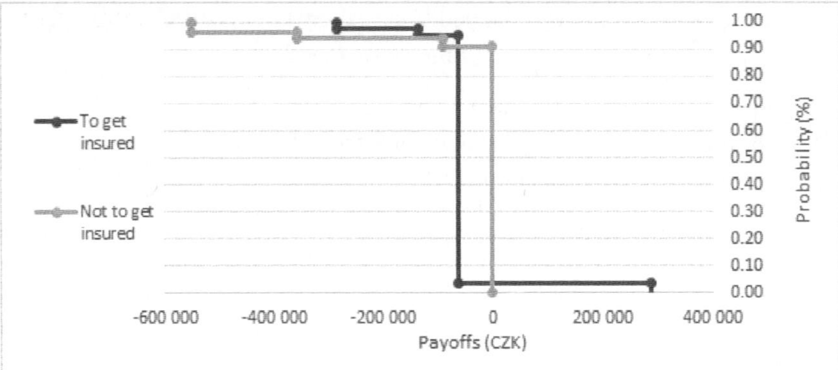

Figure 3 Stochastic dominance (source: authors)

3.2 Analysis of the best decision according to the probability of the key state of nature "High claim"

Because of the threat of large damage is very significant in terms of financial results, we will further consider the state of nature "High claim" as the key state of nature. Table 4 and Figure 4 shows the threshold probability of this key state of nature for which both decisions are identical in terms of EMV^{KSN}.

	No claim	Small claim	Medium claim	High claim	EMV
To get insured	-61,222	-284,213	-134,881	287,932	**-45,948**
Not to get insured	0	-89,685	-356,870	-553,142	**-45,948**
Probability of the occurrence	88.7%	2.7%	2.1%	**6.5%**	(in CZK)

Table 4 Threshold probability of the key state of nature "High claim" - EMV criterion is equal for both alternatives (source: authors)

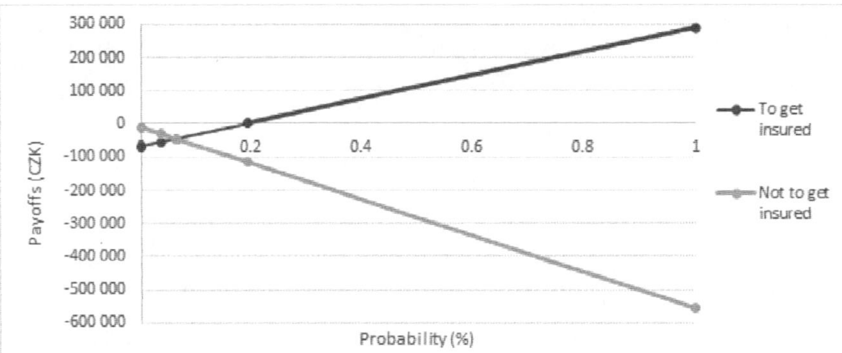

Figure 4 EMV values according to the probability of the key state of nature "High claim" (source: authors)

It is therefore possible to say that the alternative "Not to get insured" is the best alternative if the probability of "High claim" is less than or equal to 6.5%, while the initial evaluation of this probability is 3.76%. It means that the alternative "Not to get insured" is the best alternative for probability of the key state of nature in interval $\langle 0\,\%; 6.5\,\% \rangle$ and the alternative "To get insured" is the best alternative for this probability in interval $\langle 6.5\,\%; 100\,\% \rangle$.

Further, using Solver, the probability of key state of nature "High claim" was calculated for which the expected monetary value of the decision "To get insured" is equal to zero. This will happen when the key state of nature "High claim" probability will be equal to 19.4% (Figure 4 and Table 5).

	No claim	Small claim	Medium claim	High claim	EMV
To get insured	-61222	-284213	-134881	287932	**0**
Not to get insured	0	-89685	-356870	-553142	**-115746**
Probability of the occurrence	76.5%	2.3%	1.8%	**19.4%**	(in CZK)

Table 5 Threshold probability of the key state of nature "High claim" - EMV criterion for alternative "To get insured" is equal to 0 (source: authors)

As shown the risk profile in Figure 3 and Figure 5 and corresponding data in the Table 6, the decision "To get insured" dominated if the probability of the key state of nature "High claim" is at least 48.7%. The alternative "To get insured" is the dominating alternative for probability of the key state of nature in interval $\langle 48.7\,\%; 100\,\% \rangle$.

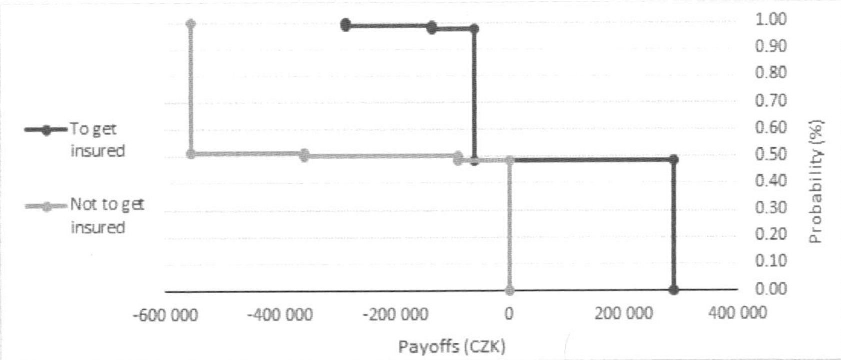

Figure 5 Risk profiles of both alternatives corresponding to the probability 48.7 % of the key state of nature "High claim" (source: authors)

	No claim	Small claim	Medium claim	High claim	EMV
To get insured	-61222	-284213	-134881	287932	**104644**
Not to get insured	0	-89685	-356870	-553142	**-274710**
Probability of the occurrence	48.7%	1.5%	1.1%	**48.7%**	(in CZK)

Table 6 Threshold probability of the key state of nature "High claim" - alternative "To get insured" is dominating (source: authors)

Decision model with EMV criterion states as the best decision the alternative "Not to get insured". It corresponds for instance to finding of Liu et al. (2016) which identified the need for more state support of agricultural insurance.

The analysis of stochastic dominance shows that there is no dominant alternative and prevailing common decisions in practice is "To get insured". It corresponds to the bounded rationality in decision-making, the perspective of the decision maker, who does not have complete information about the whole problem.

The sensitivity analysis with respect to the change of probability of key state of nature were provided shows that the alternative "To get insured" changes to better than "Not to get insured" only if the probability of "High claim" increases. This is position of the risk averse or pessimistic decision-maker.

4 Conclusion

The problem of agricultural insurance is highly dependent on the occurrence of large damage of agricultural production. The success of agricultural activity is dependent on environmental influences and the weather. These threats can destroy entire crop or livestock. Possible protection for farmers can be the agricultural insurance.

Therefore the results of analysis of the decision-making model in connection to changes of the probability of the key state of nature are very important. That is the appropriate approach in the case of the decision-making under uncertainty with unknown probabilities or under risks with hard determined probabilities of the states of nature. It could be also used for the purpose of incorporating the impact of bounded rationality, optimism, or pessimism of the decision maker or risk aversion of the decision-maker.

Acknowledgements

This work was supported by the grant project of the Internal Grant Agency of the FEM CULS Prague "Evaluation of tariff procedures in general insurance", No. 20151036.

References

Bonini, Ch. P., Hausmann, W. H. and Bierman, H. (1997). *Quantitative analysis for management*. Boston: Irwin,

Brožová, H. and Flégl, M. (2011). 'Analysis of Decision-Making Problems with Key State of Nature'. *Proceedings of the 29th International Conference on Mathematical Methods in Economics,* Jánská Dolina, Slovakia, pp. 70-75.

Hammond, J.S., Keeney, R.L. and Raiffa, H. (1998). 'The hidden traps in decision making'. *Harvard business review*, 76 (5), pp. 47-48.

Křečková, J. and Brožová, H. (2017) 'Insurance and Bounded Rationality'. *AGRIS on-line Papers in Economics and Informatics,* 9 (1), (in print).

Liu, F., Corcoran, Ch.P., Tao, J. and Cheng, J. (2016). 'Risk perception, insurance recognition and agricultural insurance behavior–An empirical based on dynamic panel data in 31 provinces of China'. *International Journal of Disaster Risk Reduction*, 20, pp.19-25.

Pratt, J.W, Raiffa, H. and Schlaifer, R. (1964). 'The Foundations of Decision under Uncertainty: An Elementary Exposition'. *Journal of the American Statistical Association*, 59 (306), pp. 353-375.

Raiffa, H. (1997). *Decision Analysis: Introductory Readings on Choices under Uncertainty*. New Jersey: McGraw Hill.

Špička, J. and Vilhelm, V. (2012). *Problematika řízení rizik v zemědělských podnicích ČR*, 109/2012, Praha: UZEI.

von Neumann, J. and Morgenstern, O. (1944). *Theory of Games and Economic Behavior*. New York: Princeton University Press.

A comparison of two kinds of failures in M/E_n/1/m queueing system

Michal Dorda[1], Dušan Teichmann[2], Vojtěch Graf[3]

Abstract. In the article two kinds of server failures are compared. The first type of failures does not interrupt service of the customer that is currently being served – the failures are non-preemptive. The second type of failures interrupts service of the customer immediately, all the customers found in the system leave the system and no customers enter the system when the server is under repair. The comparison is done for a single-server queueing system with the Poisson input process and Erlang distributed service times. On the basis of numerical experiments differences in values of selected performance measures are presented in the article.

Keywords: Queueing system, server failures, non-preemptive, catastrophic, Matlab.

JEL Classification: C44

1 Introduction

Queueing systems with servers that are subjected to breakdowns (or failures) have been studied in many publications for decades. Such queueing systems can be applied for modelling many service systems we can meet in economics, logistics, informatics or transport.

The article is focused on a comparison of two types of random failures in a single-server queueing system with a finite capacity. The first type of the failures does not interrupt service of the customer that is currently being served – we say the failures are non-preemptive. In literature, we can often meet with non-preemptive priority queueing systems, that means there are at least two classes of the customers entering the system and one class of the customers has non-preemptive priority over the other classes – see for example Dudin and Dudin (2016). The difference between the non-preemptive priority customers and the non-preemptive failures (as defined in the article) lies in the fact that the non-preemptive customers can be usually queued (the non-preemptive customers can wait in the queue) whilst the non-preemptive failures cannot be queued.

If the non-preemptive failure occurs in the system when a customer is being serviced, then it is possible to finish service of the customer before we begin to repair the non-preemptive failure. The concept of the non-preemptive failures is also close to so-called server vacations – see for example (Doshi, 1986). But both concepts differ in the fact, that server can usually go on vacation only when the system is empty. In our case the repair of the non-preemptive failure can start even if there are some customers in the system.

[1] VŠB – Technical University of Ostrava, Faculty of Mechanical Engineering, Institute of Transport, Ostrava – Poruba, 17. listopadu 15/2172, 708 33, Czech Republic, michal.dorda@vsb.cz.

[2] VŠB – Technical University of Ostrava, Faculty of Mechanical Engineering, Institute of Transport, Ostrava – Poruba, 17. listopadu 15/2172, 708 33, Czech Republic, dusan.teichmann@vsb.cz.

[3] Czech Technical University in Prague, Faculty of Transportation Sciences, Department of Logistics and Management of Transport, Praha 2, Horská 3, 128 03, Czech Republic, grafvojt@fd.cvut.cz.

The second type of the failures does interrupt service of the customer immediately, all the customers found in the system leave the system (they are rejected) and all customers coming to the system when the server is under repair are rejected as well. That means the system is always empty when the second type of the failure is under repair. Such failures are often called the catastrophic failures (or catastrophes) in specialized literature devoted to queueing systems subject to failures – see for example (Dimou and Economou, 2013).

And finally, the article continues in our previously published articles. In the article (Dorda and Teichmann, 2015) a mathematical model which is employed in the article to demonstrate differences between the types of the failures has already been presented.

2 Assumptions and Notation

Let us consider a single-server queueing system with a finite capacity. Let us denote the capacity of the queueing system m. That means the capacity of the queue intended for waiting customers is m-1. Let us assume that the waiting customers are served according to the standard FCFS (first come first served) discipline.

Let the input process of the customers coming to the system be the Poisson process which is defined with the input rate (intensity) λ. Therefore, inter-arrival times between the consecutive customers follow the exponential probability distribution defined with the same parameter λ. Please note that because of the finite capacity of the queueing system some customers cannot enter the system – the customers are rejected (or lost we can say) if they are coming to the system when the system is full (that means m customers are found in the system).

Let us consider that service of each customer consists of n phases, where n is an integer greater or equal to 2. Time duration of each phase is exponentially distributed with the same parameter $n\mu$. Each customer undergoes the individual phases of service one by one and leaves the system after terminating the last phase. Service of another customer can be initiated only when the last service phase of the preceding customer is finished. Because the Erlang probability distribution with the parameters n and $n\mu$ arises from n mutually independent exponential distributions with the same parameter $n\mu$, we can say that total service times are Erlang distributed with the parameters n and $n\mu$.

Now let us consider that the server is subjected to random failures. Let times between the failures and times to repair be distributed exponentially. Because we assume two failure concepts, we have two models – the first model works with the non-preemptive failures, whilst the second model works with the catastrophic failures. Table 1 summarizes all the random variables used in the models.

Random variable	Probability distribution	Parameters – 1st model	Parameters – 2nd model
Customer inter-arrival times	Exponentially distributed	$\lambda > 0$	$\lambda > 0$
Customer service times	Erlang distributed	$n \geq 2$, $n\mu > 0$	$n \geq 2$, $n\mu > 0$
Times between failures – non-preemptive failures	Exponentially distributed	$\eta_1 > 0$	$\eta_1 = 0$
Times to repair – non-preemptive failures	Exponentially distributed	$\zeta_1 > 0$	$\zeta_1 = 0$
Times between failures – catastrophic failures	Exponentially distributed	$\eta_2 = 0$	$\eta_2 > 0$
Times to repair – catastrophic failures	Exponentially distributed	$\zeta_2 = 0$	$\zeta_2 > 0$

Table 1 Summary of the random variables used in the models

3 Mathematical model

In this section we would like to present a mathematical model which incorporates both concepts of the failures into a common mathematical model. To create the mathematical model of the modelled queueing system we must identify individual states the system can be found in. In order to do it three discrete random variables must be defined – let us denote them K, P and F.

The first variable K describes how many customers are found in the system. The variable can take its values k from the set $\{0,1,...,m\}$. The variable P takes its values p from the set $\{0,1,...,n\text{-}1\}$; the values of p express how many phases of service the server has already terminated. The last variable F must be defined to model individual states of the server; the variable can take 4 values f from the set $\{0,1,2,3\}$ with the following meaning:

- If f equals 0, then no failure is found in the system – the server is idle or busy depending on the number of the customers found in the system. The states are common for both modifications of the modelled system.
- If f is 1, then the non-preemptive failure has occurred in the system but the failure is waiting to be repaired because service of the customer that is currently being served must be terminated before we can start to repair the non-preemptive failure – the server is busy. The server can be found in the states with $f = 1$, only if the non-preemptive failures are assumed.
- If f is 2, then the non-preemptive failure is under repair – the server is broken. The server can be found in the states with $f = 2$, only if the non-preemptive failures are assumed.
- If f equals 3, the catastrophic failure is under repair – the server is broken. The server can be found in the states with $f = 3$, only if the catastrophic failures are assumed.

Using the defined random variables, we can depict the individual states of the system and possible transitions between the states in infinitesimal time including individual transition rates – see Figure 1.

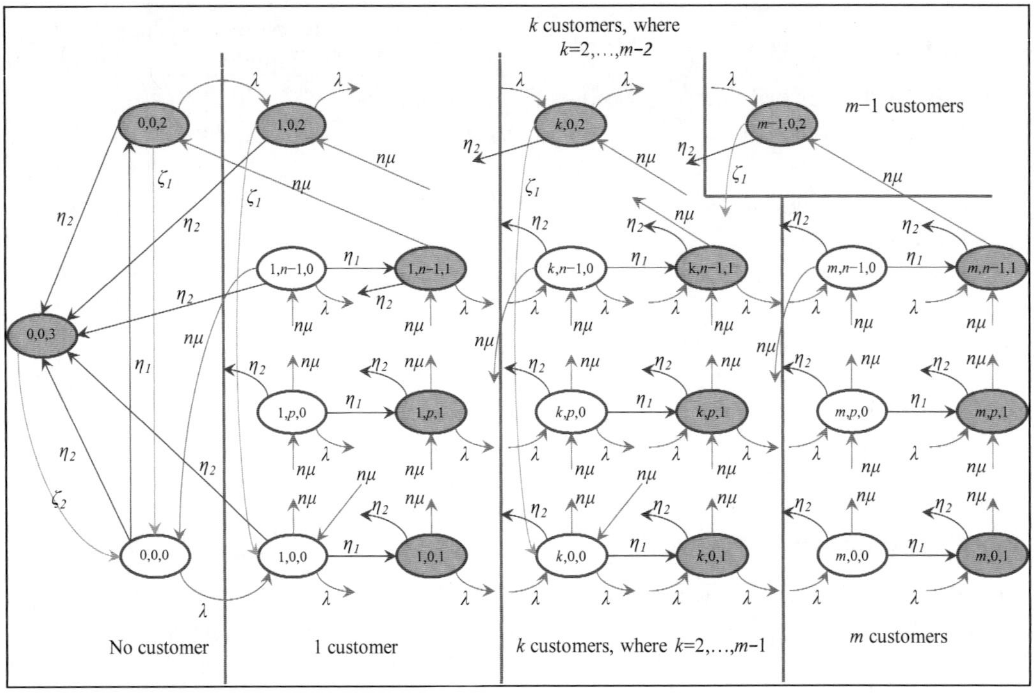

Figure 1 State transition diagram of the system [Dorda and Teichmann, 2015]

Please note that the states that correspond to the non-preemptive failures are highlighted purple, the state (0,0,3) is highlighted red and corresponds to the catastrophic failures. Other states are common for both classes of the failures. If $\eta_1 > 0$, $\zeta_1 > 0$, $\eta_2 = 0$ and $\zeta_2 = 0$, then only the non-preemptive failures can occur in the system. If $\eta_1 = 0$, $\zeta_1 = 0$, $\eta_2 > 0$ and $\zeta_2 > 0$, then only the catastrophic failures can occur. If we substituted $\eta_1 > 0$, $\zeta_1 > 0$, $\eta_2 > 0$ and $\zeta_2 > 0$, then both classes of failures would be considered in the model.

On the basis of the state transition diagram we can write down linear equations for the individual stationary probabilities. The linear equation system describing the common model has the following form (Dorda and Teichmann, 2015):

$$(\lambda+\eta_1+\eta_2)\cdot P_{(0,0,0)} = n\mu\cdot P_{(1,n-1,0)} + \zeta_1\cdot P_{(0,0,2)} + \zeta_2\cdot P_{(0,0,3)}, \quad (1)$$

$$(\lambda+n\mu+\eta_1+\eta_2)\cdot P_{(k,0,0)} = \lambda\cdot P_{(k-1,0,0)} + n\mu\cdot P_{(k+1,n-1,0)} + \zeta_1\cdot P_{(k,0,2)}$$
$$\text{for } k=1,\dots,m-1, \quad (2)$$

$$(n\mu+\eta_1+\eta_2)\cdot P_{(m,0,0)} = \lambda\cdot P_{(m-1,0,0)}, \quad (3)$$

$$(\lambda+n\mu+\eta_2)\cdot P_{(1,0,1)} = \eta_1\cdot P_{(1,0,0)}, \quad (4)$$

$$(\lambda+n\mu+\eta_2)\cdot P_{(k,0,1)} = \eta_1\cdot P_{(k,0,0)} + \lambda\cdot P_{(k-1,0,1)} \text{ for } k=2,\dots,m-1, \quad (5)$$

$$(n\mu+\eta_2)\cdot P_{(m,0,1)} = \eta_1\cdot P_{(m,0,0)} + \lambda\cdot P_{(m-1,0,1)}, \quad (6)$$

$$(\lambda+n\mu+\eta_1+\eta_2)\cdot P_{(1,p,0)} = n\mu\cdot P_{(1,p-1,0)} \text{ for } p=1,\dots,n-1, \quad (7)$$

$$(\lambda+n\mu+\eta_1+\eta_2)\cdot P_{(k,p,0)} = \lambda\cdot P_{(k-1,p,0)} + n\mu\cdot P_{(k,p-1,0)} \text{ for } k=2,\dots,m-1 \text{ and } p=1,\dots,n-1, \quad (8)$$

$$(n\mu+\eta_1+\eta_2)\cdot P_{(m,p,0)} = \lambda\cdot P_{(m-1,p,0)} + n\mu\cdot P_{(m,p-1,0)} \text{ for } p=1,\dots,n-1, \quad (9)$$

$$\left(\lambda+n\mu+\eta_2\right)\cdot P_{(1,p,1)}=\eta_1\cdot P_{(1,p,0)}+n\mu\cdot P_{(1,p-1,1)} \text{ for } p=1,\ldots,n-1, \tag{10}$$

$$\left(\lambda+n\mu+\eta_2\right)\cdot P_{(k,p,1)}=\eta_1\cdot P_{(k,p,0)}+\lambda\cdot P_{(k-1,p,1)}+n\mu\cdot P_{(k,p-1,1)}$$
$$\text{for } k=2,\ldots,m-1 \text{ and } p=1,\ldots,n-1, \tag{11}$$

$$\left(n\mu+\eta_2\right)\cdot P_{(m,p,1)}=\eta_1\cdot P_{(m,p,0)}+\lambda\cdot P_{(m-1,p,1)}+n\mu\cdot P_{(m,p-1,1)} \text{ for } p=1,\ldots,n-1, \tag{12}$$

$$\left(\lambda+\zeta_1+\eta_2\right)\cdot P_{(0,0,2)}=\eta_1\cdot P_{(0,0,0)}+n\mu\cdot P_{(1,n-1,1)}, \tag{13}$$

$$\left(\lambda+\zeta_1+\eta_2\right)\cdot P_{(k,0,2)}=n\mu\cdot P_{(k+1,n-1,1)}+\lambda\cdot P_{(k-1,0,2)} \text{ for } k=1,\ldots,m-2, \tag{14}$$

$$\left(\zeta_1+\eta_2\right)\cdot P_{(m-1,0,2)}=n\mu\cdot P_{(m,n-1,1)}+\lambda\cdot P_{(m-2,0,2)}, \tag{15}$$

$$\zeta_2\cdot P_{(0,0,3)}=\eta_2\cdot P_{(0,0,0)}+\eta_2\cdot\sum_{k=1}^{m}\sum_{p=0}^{n-1}\sum_{f=0}^{1}P_{(k,p,f)}+\eta_2\cdot\sum_{k=0}^{m-1}P_{k,0,2}\,. \tag{16}$$

Equations (4) – (6) and (10) – (15) corresponds to the model with the non-preemptive failures, equation (16) to the model with the catastrophic failures. Equations (1) – (3) and (7) – (9) are common for both models.

In order to get a unique solution of common equation system (1) – (16), it is necessary to add the normalization condition of probability. The condition replaces an equation of equation system (1) – (16) and can be expressed in the form:

$$P_{(0,0,0)}+\sum_{k=1}^{m}\sum_{p=0}^{n-1}P_{(k,p,0)}+\sum_{k=1}^{m}\sum_{p=0}^{n-1}P_{(k,p,1)}+\sum_{k=0}^{m-1}P_{k,0,2}+P_{(0,0,3)}=1. \tag{17}$$

The first and the second term of equation (17) are common for the both models, the third and the fourth term correspond to the model with the non-preemptive failures and the last term is for the model with the catastrophic failures.

The common equation system consists of $2\cdot m\cdot n+m+2$ linear equations with the same number of the stationary probabilities. The model with the non-preemptive failures consists of $2\cdot m\cdot n+m+1$ linear equations whilst the model with the catastrophic failures has $m\cdot n+2$ linear equations. The equation system can be solved numerically using a suitable software tool, we can use for example Matlab. After calculating the stationary probabilities, we are able to compute some performance measures of the modelled queueing systems. Let us focus on the following performance measures.

For the mean number of the customers in the service *ES* we can write:

$$ES=\sum_{k=1}^{m}\sum_{p=0}^{n-1}P_{(k,p,0)}+\sum_{k=1}^{m}\sum_{p=0}^{n-1}P_{(k,p,1)}, \tag{17}$$

The first term on the right side of formula (17) is common for the both models, the second term is unique for the model with the non-preemptive failures.

The mean number of the customers waiting in the queue *EL* is given by formula (18):

$$EL=\sum_{k=2}^{m}(k-1)\cdot\sum_{p=0}^{n-1}P_{(k,p,0)}+\sum_{k=2}^{m}(k-1)\cdot\sum_{p=0}^{n-1}P_{(k,p,1)}+\sum_{k=1}^{m-1}k\cdot\sum_{p=0}^{n-1}P_{(k,p,2)}\,. \tag{18}$$

The first term on the right side of formula (17) is common for the both models, the second and the third term are unique for the model with the non-preemptive failures.

The mean number of the broken servers EF can be expressed with formula (19):

$$EF = \sum_{k=0}^{m-1} P_{(k,0,2)} + P_{(0,0,3)}. \tag{19}$$

Please note that the first term on the right side of equation (19) corresponds to the non-preemptive failures and the second term to the catastrophic failures.

4 Computational experiments

In the section we present some results of numerical experiments in order to compare selected performance measures of both models. Table 2 summarizes the values of the individual parameters of both models applied in the numerical experiments. As you can see, for each model we used 10 different failure rates (η_1 or η_2) and 10 repair rates (ζ_1 or ζ_2). That means 100 numerical experiments were carried out with each model in order to get graphical dependencies of the performance measures on the failure rate and the repair rate.

Parameter	1st model	2nd model
Capacity of the system	$m = 10$	$m = 10$
Customer inter-arrival times	$\lambda = 10\ h^{-1}$	$\lambda = 10\ h^{-1}$
Customer service times	$n = 5$ $n\mu = 50\ h^{-1}$	$n = 5$ $n\mu = 50\ h^{-1}$
Times between failures – non-preemptive failures	$\eta_1 = 0.1\ h^{-1}$ up to $1\ h^{-1}$ with step $0{,}1\ h^{-1}$	$\eta_1 = 0$
Times to repair – non-preemptive failures	$\zeta_1 = 0.1\ h^{-1}$ up to $1\ h^{-1}$ with step $0{,}1\ h^{-1}$	$\zeta_1 = 0$
Times between failures – catastrophic failures	$\eta_2 = 0$	$\eta_2 = 0.1\ h^{-1}$ up to $1\ h^{-1}$ with step $0{,}1\ h^{-1}$
Times to repair – catastrophic failures	$\zeta_2 = 0$	$\zeta_2 = 0.1\ h^{-1}$ up to $1\ h^{-1}$ with step $0{,}1\ h^{-1}$

Table 2 Summary of the random variables used in the models

Figure 2 depicts the dependence of the measure ES on the failure rate η_1 (or η_2) and the repair rate ζ_1 (or ζ_2). Please note, that the left-sided graph corresponds to the model with the non-preemptive failures whilst the right-sided graph to the model with the catastrophic failures. We can see that ES decreases with the increasing failure rate (the failures are more frequent) and increases with the increasing repair rate (a shorter time is needed to repair the server). One can notice that differences between both models are not noticeable in this case. Subtle differences would be observable if we looked at the results in tabular form (not presented in the article). In general, we can say that the model with the non-preemptive failures gives slightly greater values of ES than the model with the catastrophic failures.

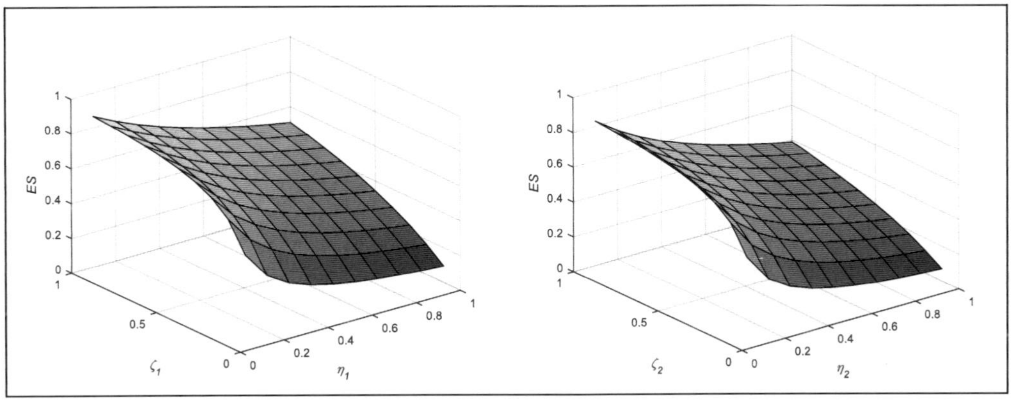

Figure 2 The dependence of *ES* [Own elaboration]

Figure 3 depicts dependencies of *EL* on the failure rate η_1 (or η_2) and the repair rate ζ_1 (or ζ_2). In contrary with the measure *ES*, in this case we can see an essential difference. This is because of different behaviour of the customers when the server is under repair. In the model with the non-preemptive failures the customers are waiting in the queue until the server is repaired. Moreover, new customers can enter the system when the server is broken. That means the value of *EL* increases with the increasing failure rate and decreases with the increasing repair rate. On the other hand, for the model with the catastrophic failures it holds that the system is always empty when the server is under repair. Therefore, the measure *EL* decreases with the increasing catastrophe rate and increases with the increasing repair rate.

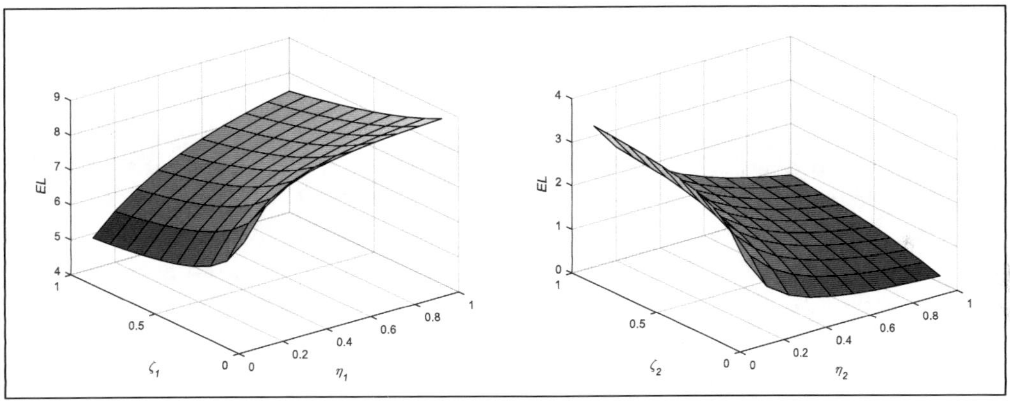

Figure 3 The dependence of *EL* [Own elaboration]

Figure 4 shows the dependence of *EF* on the failure rate η_1 (or η_2) and the repair rate ζ_1 (or ζ_2). In this case we can see there is no visible difference in both graphs. The measure *EF* increases with the increasing failure rate and decreases with the increasing failure rate. It holds in the case of *EF* that the model with the catastrophic failures gives slightly higher values of *EF*.

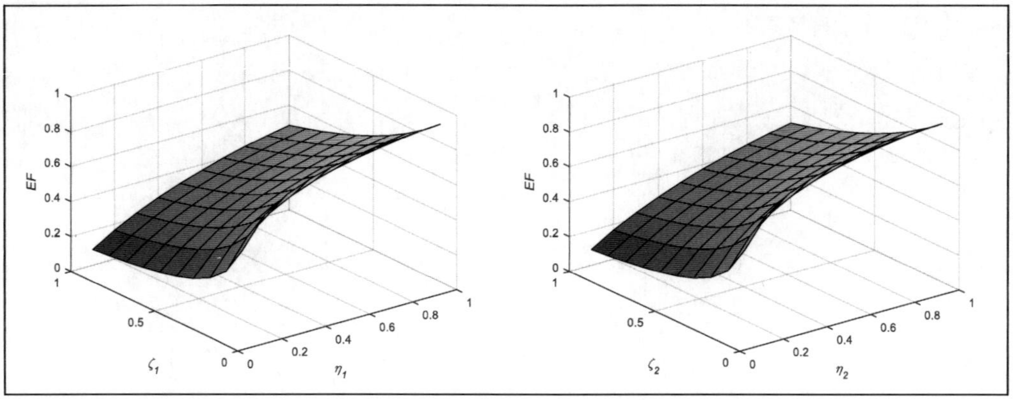

Figure 4 The dependence of *EF* [Own elaboration]

5 Conclusions

The article is aimed at the comparison of two types of the failures – the non-preemptive failures and the catastrophic failures. The comparison was carried out on the single-server queueing system with the finite capacity of the queue.

We focused on three performance measures – the mean number of the customers in the service *ES*, the mean number of the customers waiting in the queue *EL* and the mean number of the broken servers *EF*. On the basis of the numerical experiments we carried out with the presented mathematical models, we found out that the differences in the values of *ES* and *EF* are practically negligible. The most noticeable differences were reached for the values of *EL*. This is because of different behaviour of the customers when the server is under repair.

References

Dimou, S. and Economou, A. (2013). 'The single server queue with catastrophes and geometric reneging'. *Methodology and Computing in Applied Probability*, 15 (3), pp. 595-621. DOI: 10.1007/s11009-011-9271-6.

Dorda, M. and Teichmann, D. (2015). '$M/E_n/1/m$ queueing system subject to two types of failures'. *Proceedings of the 33rd International Conference Mathematical Methods in Economics (MME 2015)*, Cheb, Czech Republic, pp. 139-144.

Doshi, B. T. (1986). 'Queueing systems with vacations – a survey'. *Queueing systems*, 1.1, pp. 29-66.

Dudin, A. and Dudin, S. (2016). 'Analysis of a Priority Queue with Phase-Type Service and Failures'. *International Journal of Stochastic Analysis*, 2016, pp. 1-11. DOI:10.1155/2016/9152701.

Hybrid OWA COPRAS-G approach to startup evaluation using BLUES tool

Jiri Franek[1]

Abstract. This paper is focused on presenting an enhanced start-up firms assessment method based on original BLUES approach. This novel approach combines ordered weighted averaging (OWA) generated weights for different evaluators attitudes represented by the OWA operator's degree of orness and Complex Proportional Assessment with grey numbers (COPRAS-G) method with interval data. Proposed multiple criteria decision making approach (MCDM) was applied on an example of two start-up firms Projektove.cz and Czech Cool Trade. Results were compared with the OWA approach. Both MCDM approaches showed similar change of ranking that occurs when the evaluator's attitude (the degree of orness) changes from optimistic to pessimistic.

Keywords: MCDM, OWA, COPRAS-G, startup, performance evaluation.

JEL Classification: C49, M12

1 Introduction

New businesses are an important source of economic growth (Fritsch, 2013). The knowledge spillover theory of entrepreneurship (Acs et al. 2009) assumes that starting an innovative venture requires a combination of knowledge and entrepreneurial talent. Innovative institutions such as research and technology centres and business incubators are necessary for reaching viability of start-ups and spin-offs. Contemporary situation of innovative enterprise in the Czech Republic requires significant support and development. One possibility is to establish and support innovatively focused enterprises and organizations such as spin-offs and start-ups. These entities contribute to transfer new findings and innovative solutions (Peterková et al., 2014). Business incubators offer consulting and other services, they provide support to start-up firms. To evaluate success factors of new ventures Peterkova et al. (2015) performed a study using BLUES (Brain Logistics Start Up Evaluator) methodology in the case of two selected start-up companies from the IT sector. BLUES methodological framework is based on a set of evaluation criteria and the resulting score is then used for comparison of startup success. The South Moravian Innovation Centre has developed this methodology as a simple and repeatable tool to evaluate start-ups that can be used as a basis for creating their annual development plan and assessment of their viability by investors or other stakeholders (e.g. entrepreneurial incubators). The output of an evaluation done according to BLUES provides the opportunity to compare company's ratings to possible optimal points and to monitor development over time within the firm or to other firms in the database according to selected criteria.

This paper is focused on enhancing the BLUES methodology by multiple criteria decision making (MCDM) approach with uncertainty to capture the subjectivity of the evaluation. Also, proposed hybrid methodology gives the evaluator an option to change the perspective from

[1] VŠB – Technical University of Ostrava, Faculty of Economics, Department of Business Administration, Sokolská třída 33, Ostrava, 702 00, jiri.franek@vsb.cz

which the evaluation is made. The existing BLUES methodology adopts similar distribution of weights as well as known EFQM (European Foundation for Quality Management) Excellence Model and the committee that has developed the model itself has determined the weights. To give the evaluator more options, the ordered weighted averaging (OWA) operator can be used. The evaluator can change his perspective from pessimistic (an alternative must fulfill all criteria) to optimistic (an alternative must fulfill some criteria). By using OWA operator the evaluation can have different results according to evaluator's perspective. To capture the vagueness of evaluation of each alternative, an interval approach to MCDM is used in form of COPRAS (Complex Proportional Assessment) method developed by Zavadskas et. al (1994) and later developed with grey numbers as COPRAS-G by Zavadskas et al. (2008). However, it is possible to apply other MCDM methods that can be well employed to solve the problem. This paper is focused only on the COPRAS approach but it does not limit further application of other suitable MCDM approaches with interval data. The goal of this paper is to present a hybrid MCDM approach combining existing BLUES methodology with OWA generated weights and MCDM method of COPRAS-G using interval data.

2 Summary of selected methods and description of applied MCDM approach

This section deals with description of selected MCDM methods and applied approach for evaluation of start-up firms with hybrid BLUES methodology based on OWA and CORPAS-G. Firstly, the existing BLUES methodology, as used by Peterková et al. (2015), will be introduced. Then OWA operator as well as the COPRAS-G method will be presented. Finally, the applied novel MCDM approach will be described.

2.1 Brain Logistics Start-Up Evaluator (BLUES)

BLUES evaluates a start-up's survival potential and development plan based on seven key areas: product, customers, finance, information, people, processes, and motivation (Brain Logistics, 2016). The BLUES model awards weighted points to the company based on its success in each area. The result is a number from 0 to 300. If the company exceeds 200 points, it has a good potential to be successful. These points are then compared to the maximum possible points for each category to assess the company's viability. The start-up's points are also compared to those awarded to a selected competitor to determine the start-up's competitive position. Participating start-up companies receive the possibility to feed into the database and to get additional feedback and rating through a tailor-made benchmarking report, which highlights the key success factors and immanent weaknesses of the emerging enterprise. BLUES uses web-enabled analytical benchmarking database of key data extracted from start-up companies.

In following Table 1, the BLUES tool is presented based on Peterková et al. (2015). The table includes the evaluation criteria and weights in points that were allocated to them in the original form. There is no information about the process of the weights allocation and the decision-making process behind its creation. The most important groups of criteria are finance (80 points), product (50 points) and customers (50 points). The most important sole criteria are sufficient capital, winning of customers and ability to make product (all with maximum 35 points). The total number of points allocated to all criteria is 300.

Area	Local weight (points)	No.	Criterion	Global weight (points)
Product	50	C01	Ability to make product	35
		C02	Feasibility of the concept	15
Customers	50	C03	Awareness of customers' needs	15
		C04	Winning of customers	35
Finance	80	C05	Sufficient capital	35
		C06	Sufficient cash for individual needs	15
		C07	Plan of costs and revenues	10
		C08	Plan of cash flow	10
		C09	Calculation of break-even point	5
		C10	Prices and cost calculations	5
Information	30	C11	Information network of partners	20
		C12	Business planning	10
People	40	C13	Family support	15
		C14	Selection and recruitment of employees	10
		C15	Motivation and fluctuation of employees	10
		C16	Ability to delegate	5
Processes	30	C17	Process and control mechanisms	5
		C18	Level of ICT use	15
		C19	Capacity planning	10
Motivation	20	C20	Owner's motivation	20

Table 1 BLUES startup evaluation tool with weights based on Peterková et al. (2015)

BLUES methodology provides information in seven areas based on given criteria. It provides mainly qualitative information obtained by comparing the maximum points with the average number of points of the selected sample. The BLUES start-up evaluation tool will be used for evaluating two consultancy start-ups *Projektove.cz* and *Czech Cool Trade* (CCT). They will be compared with the benchmarking *sample* of companies that are listed in BLUES database.

2.2 Ordered weighted averaging OWA operator

The OWA operator was introduced by Yager (1988) and it provides a parameterized family of aggregation operators between maximum and minimum, reflecting the fact that the operator is commutative, monotonic, bounded and idempotent. Different families of OWA operators can be used by choosing a different manifestation of the weighting vector (Yager, 1988; 1996; Merigo and Gil-Lafuente, 2009; Merigo and Casanovas, 2011). When using the OWA operator, it is assumed that the available information is in the form of exact numbers. However, this may not be the real situation found in the decision making problem. Sometimes, available information is vague or imprecise and thus it is not possible to analyze it with exact numbers. Recently, researchers focused on combining the OWA and other MCDM methods of VIKOR (Chen et al., 2011) and ELECTRE (Heravi et al., 2015).

The OWA operator provides a parameterized family of aggregation operators which are used in many applications. Essentially, in this approach, it is assumed that we desire an acceptable solution, where all the criteria can be satisfied. One then selects, as the best solution, the alternative with the highest aggregated value. Yager (1988) suggested a generalization of this approach which he called *quantifier guided aggregation*. The OWA aggregation operator is defined as follows:

An aggregation operator F,

$$F : I^n \rightarrow I, \tag{1}$$

is called an Ordered Weighted Averaging operator of dimension n if it has associated with it a weighting vector W,

$$W = \begin{bmatrix} w_1 \\ . \\ . \\ . \\ w_n \end{bmatrix}, \tag{2}$$

such that $w_i \in [0,1]$ and $\sum_{i=1}^{n} w_i = 1$ where,

$$F(a_1, ..., a_n) = \sum_{j=1}^{n} w_j b_j, \tag{3}$$

where b_j is the jth largest of the a_i.

The formal procedure used to evaluate this decision function is expressed as follows. The quantifier is used to generate an OWA weighting vector W of the dimension n. This weighting vector is then used in an OWA aggregation to determine the overall evaluation for each alternative. For each alternative, the argument of this OWA aggregation is the satisfaction of the alternative to each of the criteria: $A_i(x),\ i = 1, ..., n$.

Thus, the process used in quantifier guided aggregation is as follows:

- Use Q (criteria are satisfied by a good solution) to generate a set of OWA weights w.
- For each alternative x calculate the overall evaluation value:

$$D(x) = F(A_1(x), ..., A_n(x)). \tag{4}$$

The procedure used for generating the weights from the quantifier depends on the type of quantifier provided. In our case, we shall consider the case in which Q is a regular increasing monotone (RIM) quantifier. In this case, the weights are generated as:

$$w_i = Q\left(\frac{i}{n}\right) - Q\left(\frac{i-1}{n}\right) \text{ for } i = 1, \dots, n. \tag{5}$$

The use of a RIM quantifier to guide the aggregation essentially implies that the more criteria is satisfied the better is the solution. This condition seems to be one that is naturally desired in criteria aggregation.

A fundamental aspect of the OWA operator is the reordering of the arguments, based on their values. That is, the weights rather than being associated with a specific argument, as in the case of the usual weighted average, are associated with a relevant position in the ordering. Yager associated with any OWA aggregation a measure of its degree of *orness*. In particular, if we have a weighting vector W of dimension n then this represents the measure of *orness*. In Table 2, we can see the linguistic quantifiers and degrees of *orness* used in this paper.

Linguistic quantifiers	Optimistic coefficient (degree of orness)	Optimistic condition
At least one	0.001	Very optimistic
At least a few	0.1	Optimistic
A few	0.5	Fairly optimistic
Half	1	Neutral
Most	2	Fairy pessimistic
Almost all	10	Pessimistic
All	0.001	Very pessimistic

Table 2 Linguistic quantifiers and relevant coefficients. Source: own elaboration based on Zarghami and Szidarovszky (2008)

2.3 COPRAS-G method

The COPRAS (COmplex PRoportional ASsessment) method is presented by Zavadskas et al. (1994). Description of COPRAS methods and possibilities of its application are published in several papers (Zavadskas et al., 1994; Zavadskas et al., 2008). Ranking alternatives by the COPRAS method assumes direct and proportional dependence of significance and priority of investigated alternatives on a system of criteria (Zavadskas et al. 1994). The determination of significance and priority of alternatives, by using COPRAS method, can be expressed concisely using three stages (Zavadskas et al. 1994; Zavadskas et al. 2008). However, many decisions are made in real-world situations where the values of criteria are not precisely known. Then they can be expressed in the form of intervals (Zavadskas et al., 2008). For this reason, a new method of multiple-criteria complex proportional assessment with values determined in intervals, the COPRAS-G was developed (Zavadskas et al., 2008).

In step 1, the use of intervals has effects on the normalization of criterion values. The normalized values of decision-making matrix whose elements are intervals are calculated as follows (Zavadskas et al., 2008) for the lower bound (the same implies for the upper bound):

$$\underset{\sim}{\tilde{x}}_{ij} = \frac{\underline{x}_{ij}}{\frac{1}{2}\left(\sum_{i=1}^{m}\underline{x}_{ij} + \sum_{i=1}^{m}\overline{x}_{ij}\right)} = \frac{2\underline{x}_{ij}}{\sum_{i=1}^{m}\underline{x}_{ij} + \sum_{i=1}^{m}\overline{x}_{ij}}, \tag{6}$$

In formula (6), $\underline{x}_{ij}$ and are the lowest (or highest) performance of the *i-th* alternative with respect to the *j-th* attribute; and $\tilde{\underline{x}}_{ij}$ (upper bound) and $\tilde{\overline{x}}_{ij}$ (upper bound) are its normalized values. In step 2, the use of intervals has impact on formulas used for calculation of S_{+i} and S_{-i}. Then, the sum of maximizing attributes S_{+i} of *i-th* alternative is calculated as:

$$S_{+i} = \frac{1}{2}\sum_{j=1}^{k}(\tilde{\underline{x}}_{ij} + \tilde{\overline{x}}_{ij}) \cdot q_j, \tag{7}$$

The third step is calculation of the score for each alternative Q_i. To calculate the Q_i for interval data in COPRAS-G Replacement of the crisp x_{ij} with the interval value $[\underline{x}_{ij}, \overline{x}_{ij}]$, where $\underline{x}_{ij}$ is the lower limit and $\overline{x}_{ij}$ is the upper limit of interval, requires some modifications in the ranking procedure.

$$Q_i = S_{+i} + \frac{\sum_{i=1}^{m} S_{-i}}{S_{-i}\sum_{i=1}^{m}\frac{1}{S_{-i}}}. \tag{8}$$

The detailed procedure for ranking alternatives using COPRAS or COPRAS-G method is shown in (Zavadskas et al., 2009).

2.4 Description on new hybrid MCDM approach

The new hybrid MCDM approach is based on combination of ordered weighted averaging (OWA) and COPRAS-G. OWA generated weights are used for both lower and upper bound of interval data that come from the evaluation of alternatives and then the final scores are calculated to create ranking of alternatives. The procedure is illustrated in following Figure 1.

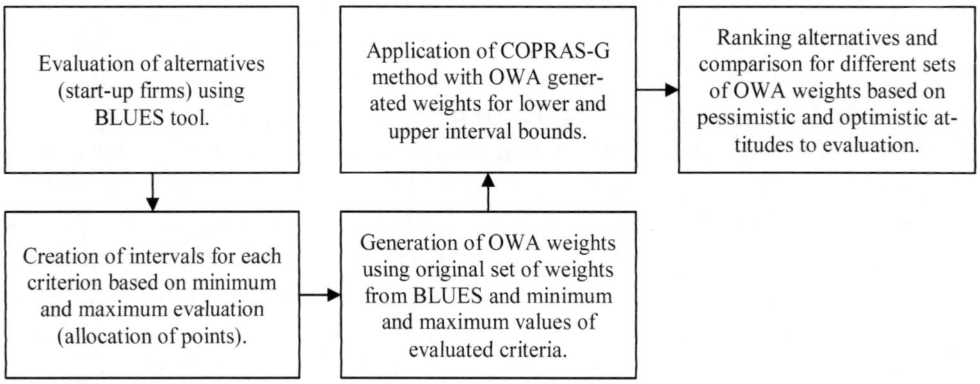

Figure 1 Hybrid MCDM approach for start-up evaluation based on BLUES methodology

3 Application of the proposed hybrid MCDM approach

For proposed methodology application, an evaluation of two consultancy firms Projektove.cz and Czech Cool Trade was performed as an example. In addition, average data of the BLUES benchmarking sample of firms was used to investigate how different evaluator's attitudes described by OWA operator can influence final ranking of alternatives and thus, evaluation of selected start-ups.

3.1 Application of proposed MCDM approach and results

The original BLUES tool uses rigid set of weights (v_{ij}), but using OWA operator, the evaluator can choose how well does the alternative fulfill evaluation criteria (c_i), hence its optimistic (some criteria are fulfilled) or pessimistic attitude (most criteria must be fulfilled). These attitudes are presented in Table 2 in previous section 2.1. Using OWA operator and its procedure described in section 2.1, new set of weights (w_{ij}) for lower (minimum values of evaluated criteria of relevant alternative) and upper (maximum values of evaluated criteria of relevant alternative) bounds can be generated as follows. These values must be generated separately for each alternative and its lower (a_j^-) and upper (a_j^+) bounds so it means for three alternatives x_1, x_2 and x_3 generating 6 sets of weights. The Table 3 shows the set of OWA generated weights for upper bound of evaluation of Projektove.cz (x_2).

c_i	(v_{ij})	**OWA generated weights w_{ij} for upper bound Projektove.cz**						
		At least one	**Few**	**Some**	**Half**	**Many**	**Most**	**Almost all**
C01	0.117	0.000	0.026	0.092	0.117	0.095	0.000	0.000
C02	0.050	0.000	0.021	0.055	0.050	0.021	0.000	0.000
C03	0.050	0.000	0.006	0.028	0.050	0.078	0.051	0.000
C04	0.117	0.000	0.021	0.081	0.117	0.123	0.004	0.000
C05	0.117	0.998	0.807	0.342	0.117	0.014	0.000	0.000
C06	0.050	0.000	0.008	0.032	0.050	0.061	0.006	0.000
C07	0.033	0.000	0.004	0.018	0.033	0.054	0.054	0.000
C08	0.033	0.000	0.004	0.018	0.033	0.057	0.078	0.000
C09	0.017	0.000	0.004	0.014	0.017	0.011	0.000	0.000
C10	0.017	0.000	0.002	0.008	0.017	0.033	0.133	0.000
C11	0.067	0.000	0.009	0.039	0.067	0.096	0.034	0.000
C12	0.033	0.000	0.004	0.018	0.033	0.059	0.110	0.000
C13	0.050	0.000	0.017	0.049	0.050	0.026	0.000	0.000
C14	0.033	0.000	0.004	0.017	0.033	0.061	0.153	0.000
C15	0.033	0.000	0.003	0.017	0.033	0.063	0.211	0.000
C16	0.017	0.000	0.002	0.008	0.017	0.033	0.155	1.000
C17	0.017	0.000	0.002	0.010	0.017	0.023	0.005	0.000
C18	0.050	0.000	0.014	0.045	0.050	0.031	0.000	0.000
C19	0.033	0.000	0.005	0.021	0.033	0.043	0.007	0.000
C20	0.067	0.000	0.037	0.087	0.067	0.020	0.000	0.000

Table 3 OWA generated weights for upper bound of evaluation of Projektove.cz (x_2)

By weights generated by OWA operator, the alternatives can be evaluated by using the OWA overall value $D(x_i)$ as it stands in formula (4). Table 4 contains values of D(x) calculated from average values of lower and upper bounds to be comparable with results from COPRAS-G method. Results show the values and ranking of alternatives using different evaluators attitudes simulated by the OWA operator degree of *orness* (see Table 1).

$D(x_i)$	At least one	Few	Some	Half	Many	Most	Almost all
Sample	23.595	23.022	20.308	17.168	13.106	8.553	4.700
Projektove.cz	33.961	30.474	21.546	16.350	11.920	4.556	3.000
CCT	18.992	18.267	16.511	15.621	14.873	10.763	4.500

Table 4 Comparison of overall values of OWA based sum of scores from BLUES assessment

In following Figure 2 we can see the resulting ranking of three alternatives (benchmarking sample of firms, Projektove.cz and CCT).

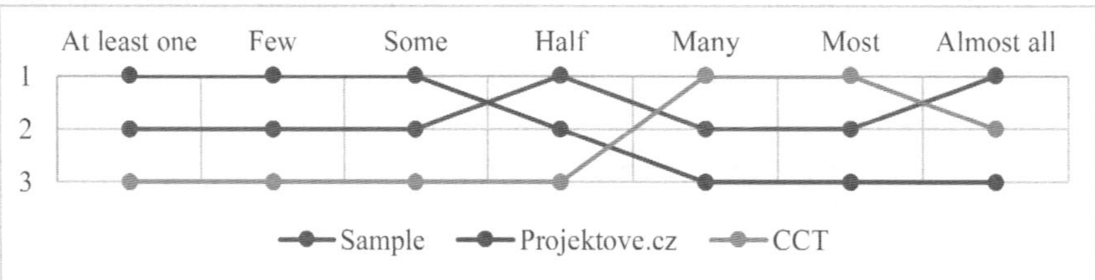

Figure 2 Comparison of ranking based on OWA overall score *D(x)* and different evaluators attitudes

In the next step, OWA generated weights for lower and upper bound of intervals based on BLUES assessment were used to calculate ranking with COPRAS-G method. Resulting normalized values Q_i are shown in Table 5.

Q_i	At least one	Few	Some	Half	Many	Most	Almost all
Sample	0.413	0.482	0.767	1	1	1	1
Projektove.cz	0.413	0.474	0.714	0.899	0.871	0.726	0.601
CCT	1	1	1	0.985	0.844	0.727	0.699

Table 5 Comparison of overall values of OWA COPRAS-G based sum of scores from BLUES assessment

Following Figure 3 illustrates the changes in ranking of three evaluated start-up firms using interval data and hybrid OWA COPRAS-G approach.

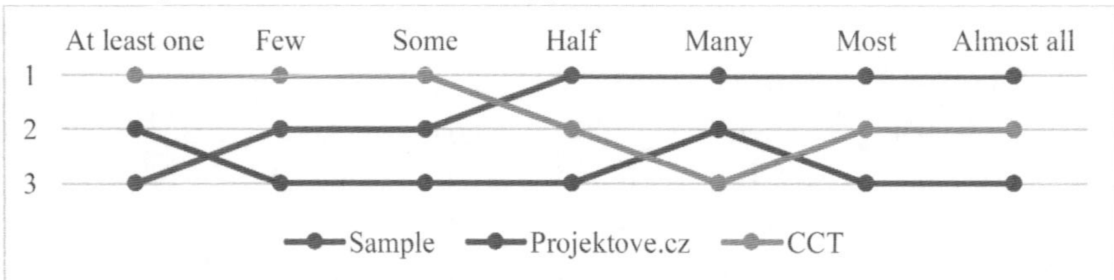

Figure 3 Comparison of ranking based on hybrid OWA COPRAS-G for different evaluators attitudes

Both approaches (overall OWA score and hybrid OWA COPRAS-G) clearly produced diverse results. This is because both approaches are based on different assumptions and are coming from two distinctive MCDM groups of methods. However, what can be compared is the influence of evaluators' attitudes towards the assessment simulated by the *orness* degree of OWA operator. This can be perceived as a kind of sensitivity analysis of evaluators' attitudes. This gives the evaluator a possibility to see how the results differ, when he or she chooses, for example, an attitude to evaluate alternatives so that he or she expects the best alternative to satisfy all or just a few criteria. Figures 2 and 3 show the final ranking of alternatives (start-up firms). Results that were obtained from calculation of overall OWA score $D(x_i)$ are more straightforward. Start-up firm *Projektove.cz* is evaluated using the BLUES methodology as the best one when the evaluator's attitude is focused on satisfying just one or some or all criteria. Evaluator's attitude towards satisfying half criteria is a turning point where the ranking changes. There the *benchmarking sample of firms* is the best alternative. In the case of many-to-most attitude the best alternative is *CCT*. However, if the evaluator's attitude is to find the alternative that satisfies almost all criteria, the benchmarking sample is selected as the best but CCT is close to that too. Based on the hybrid OWA COPRAS-G approach (Table 5 and Figure 3), the results show a different picture. CCT is ranked as the best from the at least one to some attitude (more optimistic). Then, from the half to almost all attitude (more pessimistic), the benchmarking sample is ranked as the best with both start-up firms being close to each other.

The results point to a question, which of those MCDM approaches should be selected for evaluation and why. To choose correct MCDM approach or model is a topic for a separate research. However, there can be some suggestions which approach can be used for certain task or utilization of results. The OWA overall score calculation is easier to use and understand for an evaluator or a committee with less experience in MCDM methodology. Also, it is a non-compensatory approach. On the other hand, COPRAS-G method is suitable for non-commensurable data and the evaluator can exchange the weights and use the tool for larger number of alternatives. So, based on this assessment of both approaches the hybrid OWA COPRAS-G method has more properties available that can be exploited by the evaluator, than the OWA overall score method.

4 Conclusions

This paper was focused on presenting an enhanced start-up firms assessment method based on original BLUES approach. This novel approach combines OWA generated weights for different evaluators' attitudes represented by the OWA operator's degree of *orness* and COPRAS-G methods with interval data. The proposed MCDM approach was applied on an example of two start-up firms *Projektove.cz* and *Czech Cool Trade*. Results were compared with the original OWA approach developed by Yager (1996). Both MCDM approaches showed similar change of ranking that occurs when the evaluator's attitude (the degree of *orness*) changes from optimistic to pessimistic. This poses a question how much such attitude changes or sensitivity of evaluators' judgement can change the ranking of alternatives (in this case start-up firms). In most of MCDM applications, a sensitivity analysis is performed to see how change in criteria weights influences the result. Using OWA operator, this sensitivity analysis can be enlarged to include the influence of evaluator's attitude as well. Also, it can be mentioned that presented combination of OWA and COPRAS-G method is novel and requires more testing and assessment.

Acknowledgements

This paper was supported by grant No. GA 17-22662S of the Czech Science Foundation, SGS project No. SP2017/125 and the Operational Programme Education for Competitiveness Project CZ.1.07/2.3.00/20.0296. The support is greatly acknowledged and appreciated.

References

Acs, Z. J., Braunerhjelm, P., Audretsch, D. B. and Carlsson, B. (2009). 'The knowledge spillover theory of entrepreneurship'. *Small Business Economics*, 32, pp. 15-30.

Brain Logistics (2016), [Online]. Available at: http://www.brainlogistics.cz/ [cited 2016-12-20].

Chen, Y., Kevin, L.W. Dr and Liu, S-F. (2011). 'An OWA-TOPSIS method for multiple criteria decision analysis'. Expert Systems with Applications, 38 (5), pp. 5205-5211.

Fritsch, M. (2013). 'New business formation and regional development – a survey and assessment of the evidence'. *Foundations and Trends in Entrepreneurship*, 9, pp. 249-364.

Heravi, G., Fathi, M. and Faeghi, S. (2015) 'Evaluation of sustainability indicators of industrial buildings focused on petrochemical projects'. *Journal of Cleaner Production*, 109, pp. 92-107.

Merigó, J.M. and Gil-Lafuente, M. A. (2009). 'The induced generalized OWA operator'. *Information Sciences*, 179 (6), pp. 729-741.

Merigó, J.M. and Casanovas, M. (2011). 'Induced aggregation operators in the Euclidean distance and its application in financial decision making'. *Expert Systems with Applications*, 38 (6), pp. 7603-7608.

Peterková, J., Wozniaková, Z. and Stefanovová, Z. (2014). 'Innovative entrepreneurship by start-ups and spin-offs in the Czech Republic'. *Actual problems of economics*, 154 (4), pp 247-257.

Peterková, J., Wozniakova, Z. and Skopalová, D. (2015). 'Performance Evaluation of Start-Ups by Using BLUES Methodology'. *Proceedings of the 11th European Conference on Management, Leadership*, Lisbon, Portugal, pp. 314-322.

Yager, R. R. (1988). 'On ordered weighted averaging aggregation operators in multicriteria decision making'. *IEEE Transactions on Systems, Man and Cybernetics*, 18, pp. 183-190.

Yager, R. R. (1996). 'Quantifier guided aggregation using OWA operators'. *International Journal of Intelligent Systems*, 11, pp. 49-73.

Zarghami, M. and Szidarovszky, F. (2008) 'Fuzzy quantifiers in sensitivity analysis of OWA operator'. *Computers & Industrial Engineering,* 54 (4), pp. 1006–1018.

Zavadskas, E. K., Kaklauskas, A. and Sarka, V. (1994). 'The new method of multi-criteria complex proportional assessment of projects'. *Technological and Economic Development of Economy*, 1 (3), pp. 131-139.

Zavadskas, E.K., Kaklauskas, A., Turskis, Z. and Tamosaitiene, J. (2008). 'Selection of the effective dwelling house walls applying attributes determined in intervals'. *Journal of Civil Engineering and Management*, 14 (2), pp 85-93.

Two-factor Outranking Approach to MCDM Methods for the Lagging Regions Determination

Roman Guliak[1]

Abstract. The determination of lagging regions is a problem of high importance, especially in the context of Regional Cohesion policy. MCDM methods are commonly applied as the possible tool for solving of this problem. The outranking elements were embedded into the selected MCDM methods (VIKOR, TOPSIS) to avoid highlighted drawbacks of original methods. Suggested two-factor outranking approach decreases the compensating effect and provides clear determination of lagging regions by the hybrid MCDM methods. To define well-grounded lagging cluster of regions the combination of MCDM and PrincipalComponent Analysis is proposed. The ranks obtained by the hybrid versions of MCDM methods according to the Kendall's Tau coefficient are found to be almost identical. However the VIKOR method appeared to be more distinctive and less sensitive one, producing more incomparable alternatives sharing the same rank. In addition, the patterns of the Visegrad countries were defined highlighting priorities in the development of NUTS 2 regions.

Keywords: lagging regions, multiple criteria, MCDM, TOPSIS, VIKOR, outranking principles.

JEL Classification: C44, R15

1 Introduction

Determination of lagging regions is an important issue especially in the context of Regional Cohesion policy. In the current practice, the only basis for the decision making underlying the allocation of Cohesion Policy funds is the economic status of the regions determined in the most extent by the GDP per capita level. There is some research in the economic literature suggesting alternative basis different from the single GDP criterion, but constructed from the set of indicators leading to such multidimensional indices, as competitiveness, development, inequality, efficiency and other similar ones. The application of the latter ones mostly represents the current concern in the paper due to their ability to rank alternatives being evaluated, not just to classify them.

Having analyzed the variety of MCDM methods used, we concluded that one group of authors (Annoni, Dijsktra, 2013; Gábor, Ottaviano, 2015) prefers the usage of synthetic methods based on a linear aggregation, the other group is in favour of DEA (Zhu, 2001; Melecký, Staníčková, 2011; Ramík, Hančlová, 2012; Charles, Zegarra, 2014). Less scholars applied MCDM methods based on Multi-attribute utility theory (MAUT): Mahmad, S., Yusop, Z. (2010), Dai, X., Zhang, J. (2011), Sánchez-Domínguez, Á., Ruiz-Martos, M.J. (2014), Polednikova, E. (2014), Önay, O. & Yıldırım, B. F. (2016), Savić D., Bogetić Z., Dobrota M., Petrović N. (2016), Marković M., et al. (2016).

The application of MCDM methods from outranking family, such as ELECTRE (ELimination and Choice Expressing the Reality) (Roy, 1968; Roy, Bouyssou 1993) or

[1] VŠB - TU Ostrava, Faculty of Economics, Sokolská třída 33, 70121 Ostrava 1, e-mail: roman.guliak@vsb.cz

PROMETHEE (Preference Ranking Organisation Method for Enrichment Evaluations) (Brans, 1982; Brans et al., 1984) is almost absent in the regional research. Contrary to the outranking methods, traditional ones based on the MAUT suffer from the criticism aimed at the compensatory nature of the methods.

Relying on this, the purpose of our paper is twofold. The aim is to improve MAUT based methods in the light of compensatory effect being decreased due to the introduced two-factor outranking (TFO) approach including regret factor and comprehensive preference model underlain by thresholds for the pair wise comparison, strong and weak preference relationships and the net flow usage.

The remaining part of the paper is organized as follows. Section 2 describes the basic MAUT methods applied. The following section introduces the TFO approach consisting of the element attributed to the outranking methods. Section 4 presents the application of MCDM methods to a real-world decision-making problem related to the lagging regions determination among Visegrad countries. Section 5 summarizes the paper and gives some concluding points.

2 Description of original MCDM methods

Below we describe the basis methods stressing out some disadvantages, which will be eliminated due to the suggested in the following section TFO approach. As the methodological basis in this research, two MAUT based methods (TOPSIS, VIKOR) are going to be used. All of them are related to the distant based methods, and their utility function consists of more than one parameter (distance from ideal point).

Let us suppose that MCDM problem can be described by *m* alternatives $(A_1, A_2, ..., A_m)$ presenting the NUTS 2 regions and *n* criteria $(C_1, C_2, ..., C_n)$ characterizing the performance of the regions. Performance matrix $X = \lfloor x_{ij} \rfloor_{m \times n}$ shows all values assigned to the alternatives relating to an each criterion. The weights of criteria have been denoted by $W = [w_1, w_2, ..., w_n]$ under the condition of $\sum_{j=1}^{n} w_j = 1$.

Both methods presented provide the different background for the compromise solution. The VIKOR method considers the mutual concession between a maximum utility of the majority and a minimum individual regret of the opponent calculated using Lp-metric. The TOPSIS method seeks for the compromise solution based on the shortest distance to the ideal point and the farthest to the negative ideal one. All the methods presented below work with the initial (given) weights, which in this current research will be calculated by Entropy method, as we assume that a decision maker in this problem has no strong reason to prefer one criterion over others (Hwang and Yoon, 1981; Zanakis et al., 1998).

The first method to describe is the VIKOR (VIseKriterijumska Optimizacija I Kompromisno Resenje). It is a compromise ranking method developed by Opricovic (1998). Its role is to find multi criteria raking index base on particular measure of closeness to the ideal solution (Opricovic, 1998), providing a maximum group utility of the majority and a minimum of the individual regret of the opponent (Opricovic, Tzeng, 2004). However, the balance parameter inherent in the VIKOR method leaves the space for changes and not stable results influencing the final score of the alternatives. In this research the equal importance is given to the both strategies (v=0.5). The presence of this parameter is considered as the drawback of the method on the way of its application for the lagging regions determination.

The last but not least method is the TOPSIS (Technique for Order Preference by Similarity to Ideal Solution) (Hwang, Yoon, 1981) method, determining the similarity to "double-side" ideal solution. Therefore, it introduces the criteria space in which every alternative A_i represented by a point in the n-dimensional criteria space and coordinates of those points are attribute values of decision-making matrix X. The method finds the alternative with the closest Euclidean distance from the ideal point, but at the same time, the farthest Euclidean distance from the anti-ideal point. Meanwhile the formula for the calculation of final relative closeness to the ideal solution does not consider the relative importance of these distances, what is believed to be the shortage of the method (Hwang, Yoon, 1981; Yoon, 1987).

The presented methods are based on the distance function but with the differences in the dealing with the ideal point. The compromise solution is based on the negotiation leading to an agreement established by mutual concessions. The TOPSSIS method is suitable for cautious decision maker not only making as much profit as possible, but also avoiding risk as much as possible. The VIKOR method considering just "closeness" to the positive ideal solution is influenced by the minimum of individual regret and suitable for the decision makers more aimed at the maximum profit than risk avoidance.

3 Introduction of two-factor outranking approach

It is customary to distinguish two schools of thoughts, producing the different basis for the decision-making process, in particular, French school (Roy,1968) propagating outranking concept and American school based on the multi-attribute value functions and multi-attribute utility theory (MAUT) (Keeney, Raiffa, 1976). In this section in some extent we will combine two these groups, enriching the methods from the first one (original methods) by outranking elements from the second one. The outranking methods are designed to decrease the compensatory effect and that is why are characterized by the limited degree to which a disadvantage on a particular viewpoint may be compensated by advantages on other viewpoints (Pirlot, 1997).

In such way, the compensatory effect being present in MAUT methods is considerably decreased. This advantage of outranking methods in the light of binary preference relations can enrich practice of the lagging regions' determination. The advantage of outranking methods can be transferred to the MAUT methods due to the approach presented hereinafter.

Outranking methods indicate the degree of dominance of one alternative over another (Rogers, Bruen, 1998). Providing the set of preference relations between alternatives, the outranking methods reveal the very different from MAUT logic. The question is, whether there is enough info to state that one alternative is at least as good as another. The rational of outranking methods is similar to the voting theory (Vincke, 1992), where the alternative a is considered to be better than alternative b if the number of votes (or criteria) in favour of alternative a exceeds the number of votes supporting the opposite statement. Preferences in ELECTRE methods are modelled by using binary outranking relations, S, whose meaning is "at least as good as". Considering two actions a and b, three situations may occur: P - strictly preferred, I – indifferent, R – incomparability (Roy, 1991).

It seems that exploitation of expressed preference relations can give principally new results in comparison to the MAUT MCDM methods. In this research, such approach will be utilised in not full extent, as it is done in the outranking methods, but just partially for two factors underlying corresponding outranking extension for the basic methods. The steps of mentioned two factors outranking (TFO) approach will be introduced hereinafter.

Step 1. The main purpose of the suggested extension is to decrease the compensatory effect inherent in the MAUT methods. It is going to be done first at expense of Regret (R) criterion introduced as the additional factor. It serves to eliminate compensating effect. This factor accounts the worst criterion influencing the estimation of the alternative. In this way apart from the main index produced by the basic method, we equally care about the minimization of the regret that the ideal solution cannot be reached. The basic idea of the Regret additional factor originates from the VIKOR method, but its calculation depends on the basic method: for the TOPSIS method, it is the farthest distance from negative ideal solution and for the VIKOR method, it is regret factor suggested in original formulation.

Step 2. To make comparison between alternatives stricter we conduct it simultaneously for both main and additional criteria. Let us denote values of i-th criteria ($i = 1,\ldots,m,$ where in our case m=2, namely main factor – M and regret factor – R) for j-th alternative as y_{ji}, j=1,...N. Thus, for each pair of alternatives j, k the set of criteria I={1,..m} is divided into three groups corresponding to the mentioned above binary outranking relations:

$I^+_{jk} = \{ i \in I | y_{ji} \succ y_{ki} \}$, includes criteria for which j-th alternative is better than k-th;

$I^-_{jk} = \{ i \in I | y_{ji} \prec y_{ki} \}$, includes criteria for which j-th alternative is worse than k-th;

$I^\circ_{jk} = \{ i \in I | y_{ji} \approx y_{ki} \}$, includes criteria for which j-th and k-th alternatives are equal.

The ELECTRE III method, in which the criteria of the set of decisional alternatives are compared by means of a binary relationship, defined as "outranking relationship", are more "flexible" than the ones based on a multi-objective approach (Maystre L. et al, 1994).

An economical interpretation of the development scores for all methods is measured from 0 to 1 and maximum value in this interval indicates the highest level of development (in VIKOR vice versa). Speaking in terms of M and R nature, for VIKOR method they both are going to be minimized. In contrast, M indicator at the TOPSIS method is presented as benefit criterion. The transfer of M and R indicators from the methods is the following. Within the frame of the TOPSIS method separation ideal $M_i = S_i^*$ and negative-ideal $R_i = S_i^-$ measures correspondingly are as follows:

$$S_i^* = \sqrt{\sum_{j=1}^{n} (v_{ij} - v_j^*)^2} \rightarrow \min \tag{1}$$

$$S_i^- = \sqrt{\sum_{j=1}^{n} (v_{ij} - v_j^-)^2} \rightarrow \max \tag{2}$$

where: v_j^* and v_j^- are the best (desired) and the worst (tolerable) weighted normalized values respectively.

In relation to the VIKOR method the maximum utility of the majority $M_i = S_i$ and minimum individual regret of the opponent R_i are measured as:

$$S_i = \sum_{j=1}^{n} w_j (f_j^* - f_{ij}) / (f_j^* - f_j^-) \to \min, \tag{3}$$

$$R_i = \max_j \left[w_j (f_j^* - f_{ij}) / (f_j^* - f_j^-) \right] \to \min, \tag{4}$$

where: f_j^* and f_j^- are the best (desired) and the worst (tolerable) values of all criterion functions respectively.

Thus, the alternatives are pair wise compared with respect to two criteria keeping the following conditions for the VIKOR method:

$a \succ b,\ if\ M_a < M_b \wedge R_a < R_b$ (alternative a outranks b);

$a \sim b,\ if\ M_a < M_b \wedge R_a > R_b$ or $M_a > M_b \wedge R_a < R_b$ (alternative a indifferent to b);

$a \prec b,\ if\ M_a > M_b \wedge R_a > R_b$ (alternative b outranks a).

As for TOPSIS method, this preference model for two criteria can be easily adjusted just changing the orientation of the R criterion from the minimization to the maximization by analogy to the shown above idea.

Step 3. If the decision maker takes into account the imperfect character of the evaluation of actions, it is necessary to use the discrimination indifference and preference thresholds. This leads to a pseudo-criterion model on each criterion helping account imperfect nature of the evaluations and avoid a small difference between values, which can influence the decision making process. An increase of the accuracy of the comparisons between alternatives is reached due to the introduction of pseudo-criteria (Brans et al., 1986) with intrinsic preference (p) and indifference (q) thresholds. In our case, we use the same formula for the M and R criteria having indifference and preference thresholds equal:

$$q(M) = p(M) = \frac{M_j^{\max} - M_j^{\min}}{n-1}. \tag{5}$$

Eventually the comprehensive model of preferences will provide us tree types of relations, in particular Strong preference (P), Weak preference (Q), and Indifference (I), which together with pseudo-criterion were adopted from the outranking methods. Speaking of each type of preference, we have the following preferences conditioned (table 1):

Preferences	Two-factor threshold condition
aPb, iff	$M_a < M_b - p(M) \wedge R_a < R_b - p(R);$
bPa, iff	$M_a > M_b + p(M) \wedge R_a > R_b + p(R);$
aQb, iff	$M_a < M_b - p(M) \wedge R_b - p(R) \leq R_a \leq R_b + p(R) \vee$ $M_b - p(M) \leq M_a \leq M_b + p(M) \wedge R_a < R_b - p(R);$
bQa, iff	$M_a > M_b + p(M) \wedge R_b - p(R) \leq R_a \leq R_b + p(R) \vee$ $M_b - p(M) \leq M_a \leq M_b + p(M) \wedge R_a > R_b + p(R);$
aIb, iff	$M_a < M_b - p(M) \wedge R_a > R_b + p(R) \vee$ $R_a < R_b - p(R) \wedge M_a > M_b + p(M).$

Table 1 Conditions of preferences [author]

Step 4. To measure the preference degree of the statements about relations between alternatives we need to quantify outranking relations or define their values. The preference degree or the strength of alternative is computed based on the preference function giving four types of degrees rising from the accounting both *M* and *R* criteria:

$$F(a,b) = \begin{cases} 1 \ \ if \text{ aP}^+\text{b or } 0.5 \ if \text{ aQ}^+\text{b;} \\ 0 \ \ if \text{ aIb;} \\ -1 \ \ if \text{ bP}^-\text{a or } -0.5 \ if \text{ bQ}^-\text{a.} \end{cases} \tag{6}$$

Step 5. Step is specified to aggregate the preference degrees between alternatives using "net flow" concept, which was introduced in the PROMETHEE method by Brans, Mareschal and Vincke (1984). Aggregation is done by the calculating of the positive or dominance (Φ_J^+) and negative or subdominance flows (Φ_J^-) and resulting net preference flow or global (Φ_J), what leads to the complete ranking. Comparing to ELECTRE method, the incomparable status does not exist here. Based on this, the aggregating utility function is calculated as the row summation of preference degrees within the matrix of alternatives $N \times N$:

$$\Phi_J = \Phi_J^+ + \Phi_J^-, \ j=1,\ldots N, \tag{7}$$

Step 5.The final 6th step is to define the relative net flow ($\Phi_J^{+/-}$) showing the percent of the dominance or sub dominance of the alternatives. In the context of the regional development the closer to the -100 %, the less region is developed.

$$\Phi_J^{+/-} = \frac{\sum_{j=1}^{n} F_j^{P+/-} + \sum_{j=1}^{n} F_j^{Q+/-}}{n-1}. \tag{8}$$

Al in all, it should be noticed, that the standard aggregation functions (Lp-metric) in original methods are substituted by the TFO approach presented above.

4 Application of MCDM methods for the lagging regions determination

The initial list of 10 essential economic, social and innovative indicators being used for the analysis of performance of 35 NUTS 2 regions from Visegrad group countries is given in the appendix (table 1). The entire indicators are benefit ones apart the *UN* (cost one). The suitability of the data sample for the regional development measurement is checked (KMO > 0.6 and sig.

< 0.05) by the Kaiser-Meyer-Olkin indicator and Bartlett's test. The *EAR* is considered to be redundant, because of its high correlation with *ER* (0.94) and the lowest variance coefficient (6 %). Thus from 10 initial indicators the 9 essential one are left for the further analysis.

Having applied the selected MAUT based methods and their hybrid modification we obtained the six orders of rank for 35 NUTS 2 regions (appendix, table 4). The relatively high degree of consistency is present for many regions being considered as robust relating to the MCDM methods applied. Looking at the ranks from the hybrids methods, we can notice that in the frame of VIKOR Hybrid method the decision making process is less sensitive making some alternatives incomparable. We conclude that hybridization is empowered to decrease a compensatory effect of original MAUT MCDM methods by introducing into them new outranking elements.

To measure the correspondence between the initial ranking and the hybrid ranking the Kendall's Tau correlation coefficient was chosen (appendix, table 5). It is obvious, that the difference in ranks is almost missing. There is a high correlation (>0.965) between the original rankings and hybrid versions. It means that TFO works similar to the initial aggregating function (distance to the ideal and negative) applied in TOPSIS and VIKOR methods. The sufficient difference (0.647) in the ranks within the original methods is found between methods; similar can be said about their hybrid versions (0.672).

The concluding step is to use the advantage of the TFO approach for the lagging regions determination. It is done in a very simple way just looking at the net flow value (form. 8). If it takes a negative value, the region is mostly dominated by the rest of regions and classified as lagging region. Having provided that, it is necessary to choose among the hybrid methods the most effective one using some criteria of cluster's quality. For this purpose, we propose the criterion corresponding to the results of PCA method. Form the table 1 (appendix) we see that two components (economic and socio-innovative) were extracted, after what they were explored against the ranks obtained by Hybrid VIKOR and TOPSIS methods. We have found that TOPSIS Hybrid method mixes enough regions from different clusters (fig. 2a). The VIKOR Hybrid method (fig. 2 b) in contrast gives the most appropriate and easy to interpret placement of the lagging cluster.

a. Lagging regions by TOPSIS Hybrid (TH) method **b.** Lagging regions by VIKOR Hybrid (VH) method

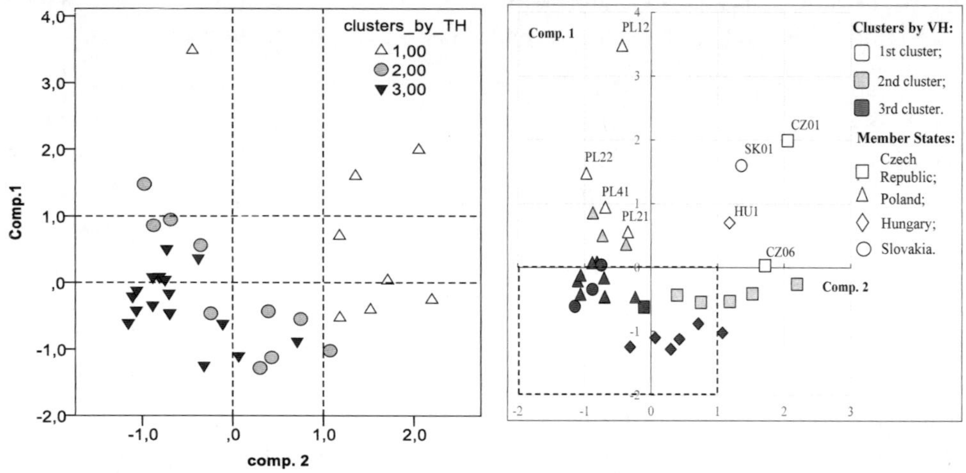

Figure 2 Clustering of lagging NUTS 2 regions by PCA and hybrid methods, 2013 year [author]

From the figure 2.b, we can state that the socio-innovative component is not critical factor in the regional clustering. Improvements in the socio-innovative direction are not so efficient to change the cluster. Such situation can be quite beneficial to lagging regions supporting innovative and social development (Czech Republic and Hungary), as these activities will not necessarily change the cluster of the region or will do it much slower keeping the "funding faucet" open.

Regions from Poland are distinctly characterized by the economic way of development what makes them more efficient compare to regions from the other countries paying more attention to social-innovative direction. From the other hand, Polish regions being efficient might be suffering from high level of unemployment and necessity to be improved technologically by providing innovations. Relying mostly on the high level of innovativeness does not necessarily mean the high level of the regional development.

5 Conclusions

From the methodological point of view, the application of the TFO approach reveals and forms new clustering perspectives for the MCDM methods, left behind the curtains of their initial formulation. In this way, aggregating function in the view of the TFO approach is appeared to be more advantageous in the light of the lagging regions determination. The compensating effect of original MCDM methods was decreased by the introduction of the Regret factor in the outranking comprehensive model based on the binary relationships, pseudo-criteria and thresholds. Such a new extension to the selected methods helps identify the lagging regions based on dominated alternatives defined by the negative net flow indicator utilising cardinal properties coming from the ordinal ones.

From the practical point of view due to the fruitful combination of the PCA, MCDM methods and TFO approach the cluster of lagging regions was defined. The hybrid version of VIKOR method appeared to be the most effective relating to the current data sample. Lagging cluster obtained by this method is characterised by the lowest economic and medium socio-innovative aspects of regional development. In addition, it is easily interpretable and clearly structured. The transition to the 2nd and 1st clusters is determined in the higher extent by the economic factor of the development, not by socio-innovative factor. Thus, the economic factor is more important relating to cluster affiliation. For example, the Polish regions, taking the minimum socio-innovative vector of the development, are closer to the more developed 2nd and 1st clusters. In contrast, the patterns of the Czech Republic and Hungary show that they prefer the way of socio-innovative development, what gives them slower transition to the second cluster and longer way to stay under the Regional Cohesion funding. The balanced development is more attributed to the highly developed regions presenting mostly the capital cities.

Acknowledgements

This article has been funded by INFINITY project in the framework of the EU Erasmus Mundus Action 2 and by Student Grant Competition project SGS SP 2017/125 of Faculty of Economics, VŠB-Technical University of Ostrava.

References

Annoni, P. and Dijsktra, L. (2013). *EU Regional competitiveness Index RCI 2013*. Brussels: European Commission.

Brans, J.P. (1982). L'ingenierie de la decision: l'elaboration d'instruments d'aide a la decision. *Colloq. d'aide a la decision, Universite Laval*, Quebec, Canada, Aou't.

Brans, J.P., Mareschal, B. and Vincke, Ph. (1984). 'Promethee: A new family of outranking methods in multicriteria analysis'. *Operational Research*, 84, pp. 408–421.

Brans, J.P., Vincke, Ph. and Mareschal, B. (1986). 'How to select and how to rank projects: the PROMETHEE method'. *European Journal of Operational Research*, 24, pp. 228–238.

Charles, V. and Zegarra, F. (2014). 'Measuring regional competitiveness through Data Envelopment Analysis: A Peruvian case'. *Expert Systems with Applications*, 41, pp. 5371-5381.

Dai, X. and Zhang, J. (2011). 'The TOPSIS Analysis on Regional Disparity of Economic Development in Zhejiang Province'. *Canadian Social Science*, 7 (5), pp. 135-139.

Gábor, B. and Ottaviano, G. (2015). *Micro-founded measurement of regional competitiveness in Europe*. Mimeo, CERS-HAS.

Hwang, C.L. and Yoon, K.P. (1981). *Multiple Attribute Decision Making, Methods and Applications*. Berlin: Springer-Verlag.

Ishizaka, A. and Nemery, Ph. (2013). *Multi-criteria decision analysis: methods and software*. West Sussex: Wiley.

Keeney, R. L. and Raiffa, H. (1976). *Decision with multiple objectives: Preferences and value tradeoffs*. New York: Wiley.

Mahmad, S. and Yusop, Z. (2010). 'Regional Development Disparities in Malaysia'. *Journal of American Science*, 6 (3), pp. 70-78.

Marković, M., Zdravković, S., Mitrović, M. and Radojičić, A. (2016). 'An Iterative Multivariate Post Hoc I-Distance Approach in Evaluating OECD Better Life Index'. *Social Indicators Research*, 126, pp. 1–19.

Maystre L., Pictet, J. and Simos, J. (1994). *Méthodes multi - critères Electre:* Description, *conseils pratiques et cas d'application à la gestion environnementale*. Lausanne: Presses polytechniques et universitaires romandes.

Melecký, L. and Staníčková, M. (2011). 'The Competitiveness of Visegrad Four NUTS 2 Regions and its Evaluation by DEA Method Application'. *Proc. 29th Inter. Conf. on Mathematical Methods in Economics*, pp. 474-479.

Morrison, D. F. (2005). *Multivariate Statistical Methods*. California: Thompson Brooks.

Önay, O. and Yıldırım, B. F. (2016). 'Evaluation of NUTS Level 2 Regions of Turkey by TOPSIS, MOORA and VIKOR'. *International Journal of Humanities and Social Science*, 6 (1), pp. 212-221.

Opricovic, S. (1998). *Multi-Criteria Optimization of Civil Engineering Systems*. Belgrade: Faculty of Civil Engineering.

Opricovic, S. and Tzeng, G.H. (2004). 'Compromise solution by MCDM methods: a comparative analysis of VIKOR and TOPSIS'. *European Journal of Operational Research*, 156 (2), pp. 445–455.

Polednikova, E. (2014). 'Comparing Regions' Ranking by MCDM methods: the Case of Visegrad Countries'. *WSEAS Transactions on Business and Economics*, 11, pp. 496-507.

Ramík, J. and Hančlová, J. (2012). 'Multicriteria Methods for Evaluating Competitiveness of Regions in V4 Countries'. *Multiple Criteria Decision Making´12,* Katowice: The University of Economics in Katowice, pp. 169-178.

Roy, B. (1968). 'Classement et choix en présence de points de vue multiples (la méthode ELECTRE)'. *Revue Française d'Informatique et de Recherche Opérationnelle,* 8, pp. 57–75.

Roy, B. and Bouyssou, D. (1993). 'Aide Multicrit`ere `a la D´ecision: M´ethodes et Cas'. *Economica*, Paris.

Roy, B. (1991). 'The outranking approach and the foundations of ELECTRE methods'. *Theory and Decision*, 31 (1), pp. 49–73.

Rogers, M. and Bruen, M. (1998). 'Choosing realistic values of indifference, preference and veto thresholds for use with environmental criteria within ELECTRE'. *European Journal of Operational Research,* 107, pp. 542–551.

Sánchez-Domínguez, Á. and Ruiz-Martos, M.J. (2014). 'A progressive approach to the measurement of regional performance in the European Union'. *Journal for a Progressive Economy*, 3, pp. 62-65.

Savić, D., Bogetić, Z., Dobrota, M. and Petrović, N. (2016). 'A Multivariate Approach in Measurement of the Sustainable Development of European Countries'. *Management*, 78. pp. 73-86.

Vincke, Ph. (1992). *Multi-criteria decision aid.* New York: Wiley.

Yoon, K. (1987). 'A reconciliation among discrete compromise solutions'. *Journal of the Operational Research Society,* 38 (3), pp. 277-286.

Zanakis, S. H., Solomon, A., Wishart, N. and Dublish, S. (1998). 'Multi-Attribute Decision Making: A Simulation Comparison of Selected Methods'. *European Journal of Operational Research*, 107, pp. 507-529.

Zhu, J. (2001). 'Multidimensional quality-of-life measure with an application to Fortune's best cities'. *Socio-Economic Planning Sciences*, 35, pp. 263-284.

Appendix

#	Abbrev.	Indicators
1	*DI*	Disposable Income (net) of households by NUTS 2 regions, in purchasing power standard based on final consumption per inhabitant, PPS/inhab.
2	*EAR*	Economic Activity Rates by sex, age (from 15 to 64 years) and NUTS 2 regions, %.
3	*ER*	Employment Rates by sex, age (from 15 to 64 years) and NUTS 2 regions, %.
4	*TE*	Tertiary Education (levels 5-8), %.
5	*UN*	Total Unemployment (%), %.
6	*PROD*	Regional productivity measured as the ratio between Gross Value Added at basic prices and the number of the persons employed, euro/pers.
7	*GFC*	Gross Fixed Capital formation by NUTS 2 regions, euro/per.
8	*TRD*	Total intramural R&D expenditure (GERD) by sectors of performance and NUTS 2 regions (Percentage of gross domestic product (GDP), %.
9	*JVR*	Job Vacancy Rate activities (except activities of households as employers and as own use producers; activities of extra-territorial organizations and bodies), %.
10	*BRD*	Total intramural R&D expenditure by business enterprise sector, %.

Table 1 Indicators describing the socio-economic development of NUTS 2 regions from Visegrad group in 2013 year [*Eurostat base available from: http://ec.europa.eu/eurostat*]

Compo-nent	Initial Eigen values			Extraction Sums of Squared Loadings			Rotation Sums of Squared Loadings		
	Total	% of Var.	Cumul. %	Total	% of Var.	Cumul. %	Total	% of Var.	Cumul. %
1	4.762	52.915	52.915	4.762	52.915	52.915	3.339	37.101	37.101
2	1.883	20.920	73.835	1.883	20.920	73.835	3.306	36.734	73.835
…									
9	.015	.169	100						

Table 2 Variance explanation by PCA division [author]

# of regions	Abbrev.	Comp. 2	Comp. 1	# of regions	Abbrev.	Comp. 2	Comp. 1
1. Czech Republic				3. Poland			
1	CZ01	2.052	1.993	18	PL21	-0.352	0.556
2	CZ02	2.195	-0.256	19	PL22	-0.975	1.479
3	CZ03	1.523	-0.407	20	PL31	-0.812	0.08
4	CZ04	-0.108	-0.619	21	PL32	-0.240	-0.463
5	CZ05	1.184	-0.527	22	PL33	-1.103	-0.209
6	CZ06	1.714	0.032	23	PL34	-0.707	-0.164
7	CZ07	0.750	-0.545	24	PL41	-0.689	0.942
8	CZ08	0.390	-0.431	25	PL42	-0.883	0.077
2. Hungary				26	PL43	-0.701	-0.465
9	HU1	1.180	0.699	27	PL51	-0.875	0.855
10	HU21	1.075	-1.022	28	PL52	-0.697	-0.457
11	HU22	0.712	-0.879	29	PL61	-1.058	-0.121
12	HU23	0.065	-1.103	30	PL62	-1.062	-0.419
13	HU31	-0.318	-1.252	31	PL63	-0.378	0.361
14	HU32	0.298	-1.285	**4. Slovakia**			
15	HU33	0.426	-1.125	32	SK01	1.357	1.602
3. Poland				33	SK02	-0.751	0.039
16	PL11	-0.731	0.499	34	SK03	-0.884	-0.342
17	PL12	-0.442	3.486	35	SK04	-1.148	-0.609

Table 3 The scores of principal components for the NUTS 2 regions of Visegrad group [author]

region #	abbrev.	Original methods		Hybrid methods		Relative net flows from Hybrid methods, %		Clusters	
		T	V	TH	VH	TH	VH	TH	VH
1	CZ01	3	1	3	1	89.71	95.59	1	1
2	CZ02	4	10	4	9	86.76	48.53	1	2
3	CZ03	8	11	8	12	60.29	30.88	1	2
4	CZ04	25	28	25	27	-39.71	-36.76	3	3
5	CZ05	7	12	7	11	61.76	38.24	1	2
6	CZ06	5	5	5	4.5	79.41	66.18	1	1
7	CZ07	14	15	14	15	26.47	1.47	2	2
8	CZ08	16	16	16	16	10.29	0.00	2	2
9	HU1	2	2	2	2	91.18	94.12	1	1
10	HU21	9	18	10	18	42.65	-11.76	2	3
11	HU22	17	20	19.5	20	-2.94	-17.65	3	3
12	HU23	22	29	23	29	-29.41	-57.35	3	3
13	HU31	21	31	21	31	-22.06	-70.59	3	3
14	HU32	12	22	13	24.5	32.35	-29.41	2	3
15	HU33	15	25	15	24.5	11.76	-29.41	2	3
16	PL11	23	13	22	14	-25.00	20.59	3	2
17	PL12	1	3	1	3	94.12	92.65	1	1
18	PL21	13	6	12	6.5	35.29	61.76	2	1
19	PL22	10	7	9	4.5	47.06	66.18	2	1
20	PL31	28	23	29	22.5	-63.24	-27.94	3	3
21	PL32	11	19	11	19	38.24	-14.71	2	3
22	PL33	35	35	33	35	-88.24	-80.88	3	3
23	PL34	32	32	31	32.5	-86.76	-73.53	3	3
24	PL41	18	8	18	8	1.47	52.94	2	1
25	PL42	29	24	29	22.5	-63.24	-27.94	3	3
26	PL43	31	33	33	32.5	-88.24	-73.53	3	3
27	PL51	19	9	17	10	8.82	44.12	2	2
28	PL52	34	34	35	34	-89.71	-79.41	3	3
29	PL61	30	21	29	21	-63.24	-23.53	3	3
30	PL62	33	30	33	30	-88.24	-66.18	3	3
31	PL63	20	14	19.5	13	-2.94	25.00	3	2
32	SK01	6	4	6	6.5	70.59	61.76	1	1
33	SK02	24	17	24	17	-35.29	-7.35	3	3
34	SK03	26	26	26	26	-45.59	-32.35	3	3
35	SK04	27	27	27	28	-54.41	-39.71	3	3

Table 4 Ranks, relative net flows and clusters based on the Hybrid methods [author]

Methods	T	TH	V	VH
T (TOPSIS)	1			
TH (TOPSIS Hybrid)	0.967	1		
V (VIKOR)	0.647	0.666	1	
VH (VIKOR Hybrid)	0.655	0.672	0.965	1
average correl.	0.756	0.768	0.759	0.764

Table 5 Correlation between methods (Kendall's Tau, two sided) [author]

An application of convex nonparametric least squares to estimation banks (in)efficiency in the Visegrad countries

Jana Hanclova [1], Lucie Chytilova [2]

Abstract. The paper examines analyses of (in)efficient banks in the Visegrad countries in year 2013. We use the convex nonparametric least squares (CNLS) estimation as a nonparametric regression method that does not require a priory specification of functional form. We evaluate banks performance using additive CNLS model under different conditions for return to scale. The model of banks efficiency is extended by banking specific factors that enter the model as contextual variables. The corresponding parameters represent the marginal effects of the asset quality ratio (capital ratios, operating ratios, liquidity ratios). The results provide an assessment of (in)efficiency 55 banks and compare the performance of banks in the Visegrad countries countries in year 2013.

Keywords: Convex nonparametric least squares, contextual variables, bank (in)efficiency, Visegrad countries, additive models.

JEL classification: C14, C51

1 Introduction

Nowadays, analysis of banks efficiency in the Visegrad countries is very popular, many researchers are working in this topic, for example: Boda and Zimkova (2015), Hanclova (2016), Chytilova (2016), Kocisova Kristina (2014), Svitalkova (2014), Repkova (2014). They are asking questions as: Which bank has the best performance? What are the key sources of bank efficiency? What are the basic approaches to assessing the efficiency of banks? Efficiency analysis is a multidisciplinary approach that combines methods of operative research, econometrics, economics, management science and system engineering. The application of these methods lies both in micro and macroeconomics, especially in manufacturing, banking, education, transport, healthcare, energy and so on.

Methodology of efficiency analysis is divided into two basic approaches. Data Envelopment Analysis (DEA) and Stochastic Frontier Analysis (SFA). DEA is an axiomatic, mathematical programming approach that represents the nonparametric treatment of the frontier in terms of axioms of production theory (disposability), convexity (concavity), and homogeneity (constant return to scale). The advantage of DEA is that it does not require the prior knowledge of the functional form of the frontier estimation or the distribution of inefficiency. It is a data-driven approach.

SFA belongs to parametric approaches. SFA uses probabilistic modeling of the deviation from the frontier. This deviation is decomposed into a nonnegative inefficiency term and an idiosyncratic error term. This includes the omitted factors such as heterogeneity of production units and their operating environments. SFA estimates predefined functional forms. The

[1]VSB - Technical university of Ostrava, Department of Systems Engineering, Sokolska 33, Ostrava, Czech Republic, jana.hanclova@vsb.cz.
[2]VSB - Technical university of Ostrava, Department of Systems Engineering, Sokolska 33, Ostrava, Czech Republic, lucie.chytilova@vsb.cz.

disadvantage is that the axioms of production theory may not be met.

The link between the gap of axiomatic DEA and stochastic SFA is a nonparametric least squares (CNLS). Kuosmanen (2008), Kuosmanen and Johnson (2010) and Kusomanen and Kortelainen (2012) have led to the full integration of DEA and SFA into a unified framework of productivity analysis. It is known as stochastic nonparametric envelopment of data (StoNED).

The main objective of this paper is to compare the results of (in) efficiency with help of different versions of the CNLS models. These models will be applied into 55 banks of the Visegrad countries in 2013.

The rest of this paper is organized as follows. Section 2 presents the CNLS regression as a quadratic programming problem under different return to scale conditions and the possibility of implementation of contextual variables that represent operational conditions or practices. The attention is paid to the additive form of production function. Section 3 focuses on the application of the CNLS models for evaluation of (in)efficiency banks in the V4 countries. Finally, Section 4 includes a discussion of some results and presents options for future research.

2 CNLS estimation with multiple regressor

In this part of the paper, different variants of CNLS additive models with multiple inputs will be specified as quadratic programming tasks under different return to scale conditions.

The production envelope function estimated by CNLS is the lower concave envelope of the function. We can consider a production function (f) with restrictions that is estimated by CNLS, and we specify a regression model $y = f(\mathbf{x}) + \epsilon$, where y is the dependent variable (output), $\mathbf{x}$ is a vector of inputs and ϵ is a random term satisfying $E(\epsilon|\mathbf{x}) = 0$ We use *additive specification* of the random term. We estimate the production function applying OLS method.

CNLS estimates an unknown production function $f(\mathbf{x})$ belonging to he set of continuous, monotonic increasing and globally concave functions F. We obtain the CNLS estimator of $f(\mathbf{x})$ as the optimal solution to the infinite-dimensional least squares problem (Kuosmamen (2008)):

$$\min_f \sum_{i=1}^{N} (y_i - f(\mathbf{x_i}))^2 \tag{1}$$

subject to $f \in F_2$. We solve (1) for observed data points $(\mathbf{x_i}, y_i)$ for $i = 1, \dots, n$ by solving the finite-dimensional Quadratic Programming (QP) problem:

$$\begin{aligned} &\min_{\alpha,\beta,\epsilon} \sum_{i=1}^{N} (\epsilon_i)^2 \\ \text{s.t.}\quad & y_i = \alpha_i + \beta_{\mathbf{i}}'\mathbf{x_i} + \epsilon_i && i = 1, \dots, n \\ & \alpha_i + \beta_{\mathbf{i}}'\mathbf{x_i} \leq \alpha_h + \beta_{\mathbf{h}}'\mathbf{x_i} && h, i = 1, \dots, n \text{ and } i \neq h \\ & \beta_i \geq 0 && i = 1, \dots, n. \end{aligned} \tag{2}$$

Where y_i is the output, $\mathbf{x_i} = (x_{i1}, \dots, x_{in})'$ is input vector and ϵ_i is disturbance term that represents the deviation of units i from the estimated function. First constraint is a basic linear hyperplane with estimates intercept α_i and slope $\beta_{\mathbf{i}} = (\beta_{i1}, \dots, \beta_{in})'$ parameters characterizing the marginal products of inputs for each observation. Second constraint impose concavity using Afriats inequalities (Afriat, 1972). Finally, third constraint include monotonicity on the underlying unknow production function. The fitted value $(\hat{\alpha}_i, \hat{\beta}'_{\mathbf{i}})$ using CNLS are unique (Lee et al. (2013). Using the results from problem (2), Kuosmanen and Kortelainen (2012) propose to solve problem (3) to estimate the lower concave envelope:

$$\begin{aligned} \min_{\alpha_{le}\beta_{le}} &= \alpha_{le,i} + \beta'_{\mathbf{le,i}}\mathbf{x_i} \\ \text{s.t.} \quad & \alpha_{le,i} + \beta'_{\mathbf{le,i}}\mathbf{x_i} \geq \hat{y}_i \qquad i = 1, \ldots, n, \end{aligned} \tag{3}$$

where $\alpha_{le,i}$ and $\beta'_{\mathbf{le,i}}$ indicate these parameters which are reestimated in (3) to find the lower concave envelope and may be distinct from the parameters estimated in (2). Typically the number of unique hyperplane segments is much lower than n, Kuosmanen and Johnson (2010) presented an opportunity to reduce the number of constraints and decrease the time required to solve problem (2).

So far, we have focused on a concave production function with no particular scaling properties imposed. The most common scaling property is *constant* return to scale (CRS) which impose the additional restriction in problem (2)

$$\alpha_i = 0 \, \forall \, i = 1, \ldots, n. \tag{4}$$

We can used also *nondecreasing* return to scale (NDIRS) with assumption $\alpha_i \leq 0 \, \forall \, i = 1, \ldots, n$ or *nonincreasing* return to scale (NIRS) with restriction $\alpha_i \geq 0 \, \forall \, i = 1, \ldots, n$ or *variable* return to scale (VRS) without restriction of parameter α_i.

Another option to extend the problem (2) is to introduce contextual variables $\mathbf{z_i}$ into the production function $y = f(\mathbf{x}, \mathbf{z}) - u$ and to reformulate the model (2) to the following problem:

$$\begin{aligned} & \min_{\alpha,\beta,\epsilon,\delta} \sum_{i=1}^{N} (\epsilon_i)^2 \\ \text{s.t.} \quad & y_i = \alpha_i + \beta'_{\mathbf{i}}\mathbf{x_i} + \delta'_{\mathbf{i}}\mathbf{z_i} - u_i && i = 1, \ldots, n \\ & \alpha_i + \beta'_{\mathbf{i}}\mathbf{x_i} + \delta'_{\mathbf{i}}\mathbf{z_i} \leq \alpha_h + \beta'_{\mathbf{h}}\mathbf{x_i} + \delta'_{\mathbf{h}}\mathbf{z_i} && h, i = 1, \ldots, n \text{ and } i \neq h \\ & \beta_i \geq 0, \delta_i \geq 0, u_i \geq 0 && i = 1, \ldots, n. \end{aligned} \tag{5}$$

Contextual variables characterize specific operational conditions and practices.

3 Empirical study

In this section, we will apply the CNLS method to assess the performance of 55 banks in Visegrad countries (Czech Republic (CZ), Hungary (HU), Poland (PL) and Slovakia (SK)) by selected data for year 2013.

3.1 Data

In accordance with the transitional approach to assess efficiency of banks (Hanclova, 2016), there have been selected three input variables (x_1 = personnel costs, x_2 = deposits and short-term financing, x_3 = interest expense on client deposits), one output variable (y = loans and advances to banks) and eight contextual variables (z_1 = equity/total assets, z_2 = net interest margin, z_3 = return on average assets (ROAA), z_4 = return on average equity (ROAE), z_5 =

cost to income ratio, z_6 = net loans/total assets, z_7 = net loans/deposits and short-term fundings and z_8 = liquid assets/deposits and short-term funding).

	Mean	**Median**	**Std. Deviation**	**Minimum**	**Maximum**
X1	83672	42803	124752	2143	686796
X2	6291691	3292296	8142494	63289	31888107
X3	100346	57136	141830	90	671724
Y	546770	151600	1100379	400	6977311
Z1	10.63	9.52	5.23	4.05	32.36
Z2	3.13	2.74	1.66	0.59	8.28
Z3	0.52	0.66	1.74	-6.89	4.43
Z4	3.91	7.14	21.31	-81.60	80.93
Z5	63.57	56.21	31.22	26.68	229.88
Z6	59.47	64.18	16.26	14.50	92.93
Z7	81.46	78.91	49.25	15.92	341.63
Z8	18.08	11.77	17.39	1.81	82.55

Table 1 Descriptive statistics of used variables

Contextual variables specify assest quality ratios capital ratio (z_1), operations ratios ($z_2, \ldots, z_5$) and liquidity ratios (z_6, z_7, z_8). Input and output variables are in thousands of euros, contextual variables are in $\%$. There have been analyzed 55 banks (14 from the Czech Republic, 8 from Hungary, 24 from Poland and 9 from Slovakia). The data samples in this empirical research were extracted from the Bank Scope Bureau van Dijk database[1] for the year 2013. Table 1 presents the descriptive statistics of used variables.

3.2 CNLS estimation

Based on the specification of input and output variables there were estimated four efficient lower concave production frontiers by CNLS as the optimal solution of problem by solving the finite-dimensional Quadratic Programming (QP) problem (2) under various return to scale conditions (constant - CRS, nondecreasing - NDIRS, non-increasing - NIRS and variable - VRS). For each of these models, we have received estimated values $\hat{\alpha}_i$, $\hat{\beta}_\mathrm{i}$, $\hat{\epsilon}_i = e_i$, $\hat{y}_i$. The estimation of bank performance with inclusion of contextual variables under VRS conditions was performed using a formulated problem (5) and estimates of $\hat{\alpha}_i$, $\hat{\beta}_\mathrm{i}$, $\hat{\delta}_\mathrm{i}$, $\hat{u}_i$ $\hat{y}_i$ were obtained. Calculations were programmed and implemented using GAMS software.

The estimation of the probability distribution of the error term $\hat{\epsilon}_i$, which expresses the deviation of the output from the efficient frontier, is presented in Figure 1. The results show that the distribution for CRS, NDIR and NIRS models are almost the same. The case of variable return to scale shows that the distribution shifts slightly to the right. If we also include contextual variables we can see that kurtosis is reduced and skewness is moving to the left.

Figure 2 shows the estimated distribution density for output deviations from the efficient frontier for banks in four surveyed countries and for three different models according to return to scale assumption. The results for the Czech Republic show that the skewness is going to left compared to Hungary. There is also a higher peak for the VRS model with contextual variables. This is, on the contrary, in Hungary, below the density level for the CRS model and on the same level in the Slovak Republic.

[1] https://bankscope.bvdinfo.com/version-2016419/home.serv?product=scope2006

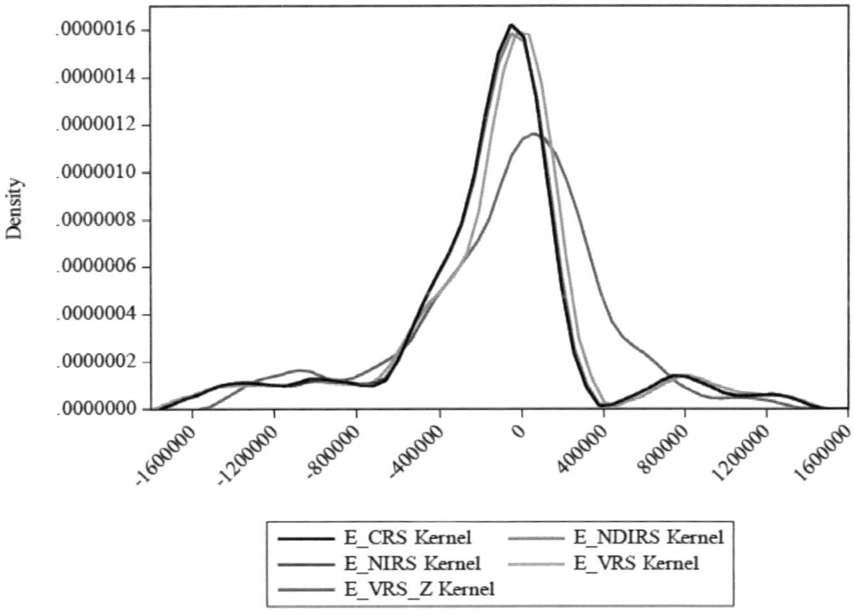

Figure 1 Kernel density for error term for estimated models

It turns out that it is advisable to look for sources of inefficiency also through contextual variables. Estimated parameters $\hat{\delta}$ reveal that the performance that the deviation from the efficient frontier is relatively positively effected by the indicators from the group of operations ratios z_4 = return on average equity (ROAE) (3894) and also from the group of liquidity ratios z_8 = liquid assets/deposits and short-term funding (1090). Conversational variables have also negative effect, more precisely, variables as operations ratios z_3 = return on average assets (ROAA) (-409563) and z_2 = net interest margin (-14391). From the group of liquidity ratios we talk about z_6 = net loans/total assets (-124). For models with contextual variables we can see that the estimations $\hat{\alpha}_i$ are positive and in range from 233730 to 407338. This means that the *nonincreasing* return to scale (NIRS) is prefered. The only one exception is the Polish bank B52 (Bank of Tokyo - Mitsubishi). This bank prefer *nondecreasing* return to scale (NDIRS) and $\hat{\alpha}_{B52} = -6221230$. The influence of other regional factors is reported by Suchacek (2015).

Figure 3 compares the absolute deviations of observed values of outputs (loans and advances to bank) by the Visegrad countries for 3 selected key models (CRS, VRS and VRS with contextual variables). The effect of contextual variables is evident for Hungary, where deviations have been reduced. On the other hand, these variables have led to an increase in these imbalances, especially for Slovak banks and moderately for Polish banks. Otherwise, according to the absolute comparison, these deviations are higher for Czech banks compared to banks from other V4 countries. Outlying negative deviations can be observed for all three models according to the yield range for the Hungarian bank B03 (OTP Bank) and for Polish banks B05 (Bank Zachodni WBK) and B07 (ING Bank Slaski). From the point of view of variability of variance, the highest variability is in Czech banks and the lowest in Slovak banks. This is influenced by the number of representative banks in the selection (CZ-14, SK-9).

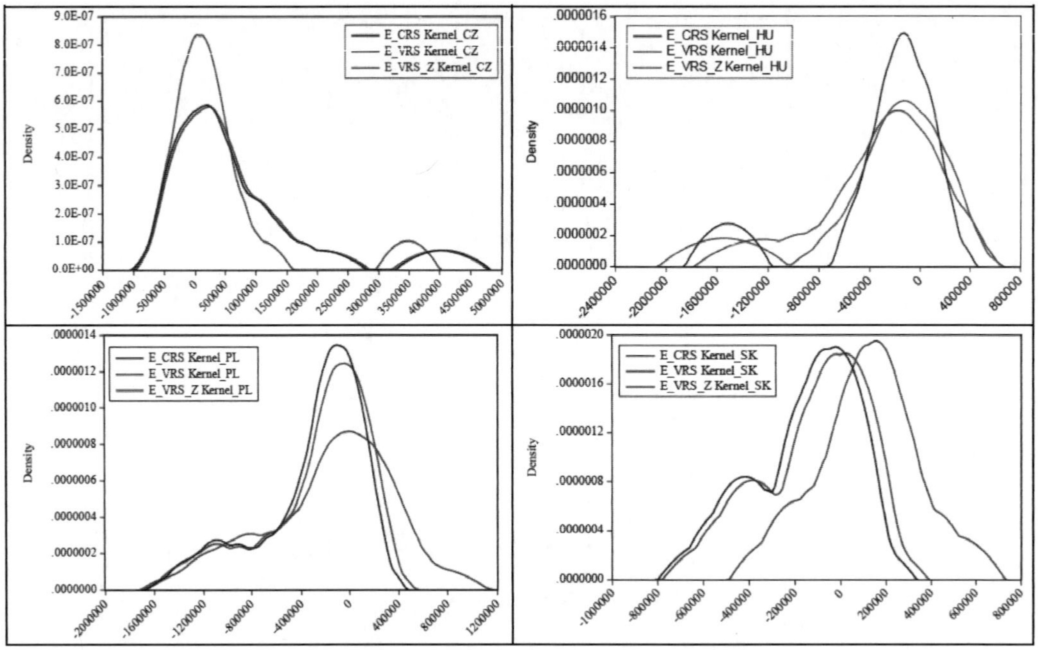

Figure 2 Estimation of Kernel density for output deviations from efficient frontier by country

Table 2 presents inefficiency sources from the point of view of input variable. There is a strong influence of variable x_2 (deposit and short-term funding), which operates in almost all models. With the release of revenue restrictions, both staffing and personal expenses (x_1) increase. The effect of input variable x_3 (interest expense on customer deposits) is significant in the model with nondecreasing return to the scale of production function and model with contextual variables.

	CRS	NDIRS	NIRS	VRS	VRS_Z
x_1	no	B35, B39	B09	B09	B08, B09, B29-B31, B34, B35, B39, B44-B46,B49, B51-B55
x_2	B01-B55	B01-B55	B01-B08, B09-B55	B01-B08, B10-B55	B01-B08, B10-B51, B53-B55
x_3	no	B33, B35, B36, B37, B39, B43, B44	no	no	B30, B31, B33, B39, B44, B45, B48, B50

Table 2 Impact of input factors on bank performance by model

4 Conclusion and discussion

The article was devoted to evaluate the performance of 55 banks from the Visegrad countries using the CNLS method under different return to scale conditions. There has also been a further widening of contextual variables.

The results show that comparing the empirical density of the distribution of true output deviations from the efficient frontier causes a deflection to the right if we are working with assumption of variable return to scale and we introduce contextual variables evaluating asset quality. Also, there are differences in the kernel density estimation for output deviations from the effective frontier by country. In the case of Czech and Hungarian banks, there are remote groups of banks, but in the Czech Republic it is on the right side and in the Hungarian banks on the left side of the empirical division.

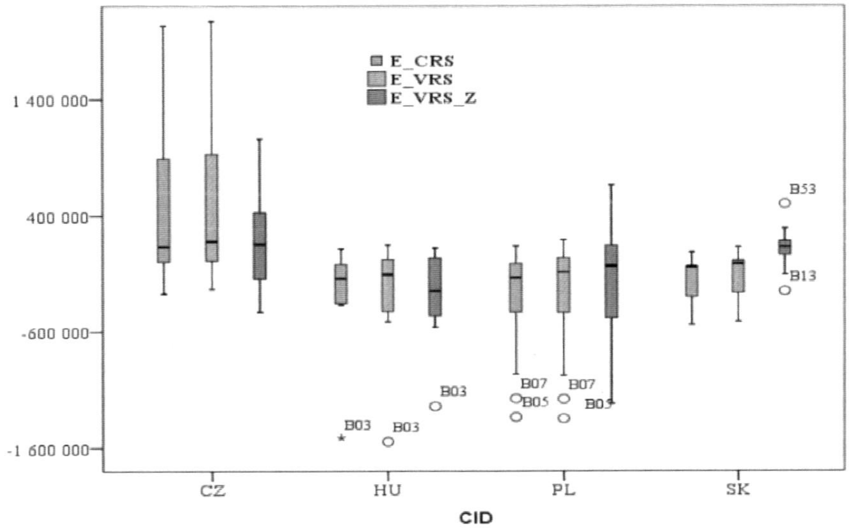

Figure 3 Boxplots for error term for selected models and V4 countries

Sources of inefficiency were detected as very strong influence of return on average equity (ROAE) and liquid assets/deposits, at least from the point of view of contextual variables. From the viewpoint of input variables, there is a strong influence of the variable deposits and short-term funding, which operates in almost all models.

The future work should focus on panel data, so we can analyze more year and changes over time. Another important research should be done in terms of different types of distribution and decomposition on single components. It is also possible to use the multiplier form of production function.

Acknowledgements

This article was supported by Student Grant Competition project (SP2017/114) of Faculty of Economics, VŠB-Technical University of Ostrava and the Czech Science Foundation through project No. 17-23495S.

References

Afriat, S. N. (2008). ‘Efficiency estimation of production functions’. *International Economic Review*, 13 (3), pp. 568-598.

Boda, M. and Zimkova, E. (2015). ‘Efficiency in the Slovak banking industry: A comparison of three approaches’. *Prague Economic Papers*, 24 (4), pp. 434-451.

Chytilova, L. (2016). ‘Banking efficiency in the Visegrad Group according to Data Envelopment Analysis’. *Proceedings of 34th International Conference Mathematical Methods in Economics (MME)*, Liberec, Czech Republic, pp. 325-230.

Hanclova, J. (2016). 'A two-stage Data Envelopment Analysis Model with application to banking industry in the Visegrad Group'. *Proceedings of 34th International Conference Mathematical Methods in Economics (MME)*, Liberec, Czech Republic, pp. 254-259.

Kocisova, K. (2014). 'Application of Data Envelopment Analysis to Measure Cost, Revenue and Profit Efficiency'. *Statistika*, 94 (3), pp. 47- 57.

Kuosmanen T. and Kortelainen, M. (2012). 'Stochastic non-smooth envelopment of data: Semi-parametric frontier estimation subject to shape constraints'. *Journal of Productivity Analysis*, 38 (1), pp. 11-28.

Kusomanen, T. (2008). 'Representation theorem for convex nonparametric least squares'. *Econometric Journal*, 11 (3), pp. 308-325.

Kusomanen, T. and Johnson, A. L. (2010). 'Data envelopment analysis as nonparametric least-squares regression'. *Operations Research*, 58 (1), pp. 149-160.

Lee, Ch. Y., Johnson, A.L., Moreno-Centeno, E. and Kuosmanen, T. (2013). 'A more efficient algorithm for Convex Nonparametric Least Squares'. *Journal European Journal of Operational Research*, 227 (2), pp. 391-400.

Repkova, I. Z. (2014). 'Efficiency of the Czech banking sector employing the DEA window analysis approach'. *Procedia Economics and finance*, 12 (2014), pp. 644-653.

Suchacek, J. (2015). 'Large Enterprise Branches: The Case of the Czech Republic'. *Economics and Sociology*, 8 (4), pp. 82-93.

Svitalkova, Z. (2014). 'Comparison and evaluation of bank efficiency in selected countries in EU'. *Procedia Economics and finance*, 12 (2014), pp. 587-596.

Relationship of the regional growth and volatility: Spatial econometric analysis for the V4 regions

Michaela Chocholatá[1]

Abstract. This paper deals with the analysis of the relationship between the regional growth and volatility for a sample of 114 NUTS 3 regions of V4 countries over the period 2000-2013. Since the existence of the spatial dependence was confirmed, besides traditional non-spatial analysis were the estimated models enriched by inclusion of the spatial dimension. Although the results based both on non-spatial and spatial models confirmed on average the positive relationship, after the inclusion of country dummies it was proved the significantly negative relationship for the regions of the Czech Republic and Hungary.

Keywords: growth, volatility, spatial econometrics, region.

JEL Classification: R11, C21

1 Introduction

The analysis of relationship between the regional growth and its volatility has attracted attention of researchers especially during the last few decades. As pointed out by Ezcurra and Rios (2013), there are several arguments supporting the relationship (either positive or negative) between the economic growth and volatility. Several empirical studies investigating whether the volatility has a positive or negative impact on regional growth yielded different results.

Ramey and Ramey (1995) using data from 92 countries as well as data from OECD countries presented that countries with higher growth volatility have a lower growth rate. Martin and Rogers (2000) tested the growth-volatility relationship based on cross-country regressions and proved the strong significantly negative growth-volatility relationship both for OECD countries and 90 European regions. Chatterjee and Shukayev (2006), analysing the same data as Ramey and Ramey (1995), based on various definitions of the growth rate as well as different sample compositions, concluded that there is no robust significant relationship between the economic growth and its volatility. Imbs (2006), dealing with different sets of the UNIDO (United Nations Industrial Development Organization) data, presented that the link between economic growth and volatility depends on the level of the data aggregation. Since the results implied that the relationship between aggregate growth and aggregate volatility is negative, it was proved significantly positive growth-volatility relationship at the sectoral level.

Concerning the growth-volatility relationship, the empirical studies often include some control variables (e.g. initial GDP per capita, population density or population growth, investment ratio, unemployment rate) into the estimations. Another important factor, the geographical proximity, is often being neglected and regions are considered as isolated units. However, nowadays there have been published various studies dealing with the growth-volatility relationship taking into consideration the location of a region as well as the fact that there are strong spatial relationships among neighbouring regions (see e.g. Falk and Sinabell, 2009, Ezcurra and Rios,

[1] University of Economics in Bratislava, Faculty of Economic Informatics, Department of Operations Research and Econometrics, Dolnozemská cesta 1/b, 852 35 Bratislava, michaela.chocholata@euba.sk.

2013, Chocholatá and Furková, 2016). Falk and Sinabell (2009) using the data for 1084 European regions (EU15) estimated the growth-volatility relationship allowing for spatial effects. Their results indicating that the regional growth rate and volatility are significantly positively related showed relevance of the spatial aspect. Furthermore, by inclusion of country interaction variables they were able to identify countries with significantly positive as well as significantly negative relationship. The empirical model of Ezcurra and Rios (2013) accounts for spatial dependence in investigation of the relationship between volatility and economic growth in the 279 European regions. Their results imply the existence of a positive growth-volatility relationship and are robust to inclusion of various explanatory variables. Chocholatá and Furková (2016) analysed regional income disparities of the net disposable income of households across 82 regions of Austria, Czech Republic, Slovakia, Poland, Hungary and Germany. Concerning the growth-volatility relationship they proved the negative impact of volatility on the growth (both non-spatial and spatial).

The aim of this paper is to analyse the relationship between the average annual growth of GDP per capita (expressed in current market prices in Purchasing Power Standards – PPS) from 2000 to 2013 and the growth volatility based on regional data of 114 NUTS 3(Nomenclature of Territorial Units for Statistics) regions of V4 countries (Czech Republic, Hungary, Slovak Republic and Poland). Both non-spatial and spatial models will be estimated and the dummy variables will be used to test the uniformity of the relationship across countries.

The paper is organized as follows. After the introduction it follows section 2 which characterizes the methodology and models of the growth-volatility relationship, section 3 presents the data and empirical results and section 4 concludes with indications for further work.

2 Methodology and Models

In order to test the growth-volatility relationship based on cross-sectional data, the basic empirical linear model can be formulated as follows:

$$\bar{g}_i = \alpha + \beta\sigma_i + \gamma_{CZ} D_{iCZ}\sigma_i + \gamma_{HU} D_{iHU}\sigma_i + \gamma_{SK} D_{iSK}\sigma_i + \varepsilon_i, \tag{1}$$

where $\bar{g}_i = \frac{1}{T}\ln\left(\frac{GDP_{i,T}}{GDP_{i,0}}\right)$ denotes the average annual growth of the GDP per capita in the i-th region during the period $(0,T)$, symbol σ_i denotes the volatility variable (measured as the standard deviation of the growth over the analysed period), α and β are unknown parameters. Since Poland is chosen as a reference country, dummy variables $D_{iCZ}, D_{iHU}, D_{iSK}$ indicate whether the region i belongs to a corresponding country (CZ-Czech Republic, HU-Hungary, SK-Slovakia) or not – taking a value of 1 or 0, respectively, $\gamma_{CZ}, \gamma_{HU}, \gamma_{SK}$ are corresponding parameters and ε_i is an error term. The inclusion of the dummy variables in the multiplicative form with the volatility variable σ_i enables to analyse whether the impact of volatility on growth differs across countries (Falk and Sinabell, 2009).

Model (1) supposes that the analysed regions are geographically independent units. To avoid the possibly biased results and hence misleading conclusions in the presence of spatial dependence, it is necessary to include the spatial effects into the econometric modelling. The first insight into the existence of mutual interactions among regions gives the preliminary analysis usually based on Exploratory Spatial Data Analysis (ESDA) which includes inter alia various tests of global and local spatial autocorrelation, enabling to check if there is a spatial pattern present in the analysed data or not. The linkages among regions are described by the appropriate spatial weight matrix **W** (see e.g. Fischer and Getis, 2010). Since the global Moran's *I* statistics informs about the strength of the spatial association across neighbouring regions, the LISA (Local Indicators of Spatial Association) are useful for identifying of spatial clusters (see e.g. Anselin, 1995, Fischer and Getis, 2010). Based on the ESDA results, the regression residuals of the model (1) are tested for spatial autocorrelation. In case that the spatial autocorrelation of the regression residuals is confirmed, the Lagrange Multiplier (LM) tests are usually used to decide whether to estimate a spatial autoregressive (SAR) or a spatial error (SEM) model.

The SAR model of the growth-volatility relationship is as follows:

$$\bar{g}_i = \alpha + \beta\sigma_i \; + \rho\sum_{j\neq i} w_{ij}\bar{g}_i + \gamma_{CZ}D_{iCZ}\sigma_i + \gamma_{HU}D_{iHU}\sigma_i + \gamma_{SK}D_{iSK}\sigma_i + \varepsilon_i, \tag{2}$$

where ρ denotes the spatial lag parameter, w_{ij} are the elements of the row-standardized matrix of spatial weights **W** and all the other symbols have already been defined above. An alternative way to capture the spatial effects is to estimate the SEM model:

$$\begin{aligned} \bar{g}_i &= \alpha + \beta\sigma_i + \gamma_{CZ}D_{iCZ}\sigma_i + \gamma_{HU}D_{iHU}\sigma_i + \gamma_{SK}D_{iSK}\sigma_i + u_i, \\ u_i &= \lambda\sum_{j\neq i} w_{ij}u_j + \varepsilon_i, \end{aligned} \tag{3}$$

where parameter λ is a spatial error coefficient indicating the extent of the spatial autocorrelation between regression residuals.

3 Data and empirical results

The empirical part of the paper is based on the data from 114 NUTS 3 regions of V4 countries (14 Czech regions, 20 Hungarian regions, 8 Slovak regions and 72 Polish regions) received from the database REGIO of the Eurostat. The GDP per capita expressed in current market prices in Purchasing Power Standards (PPS) from 2000 to 2013 was used to calculate the average annual growth (based on natural logarithmic definition of the growth rate – see above). Volatility is calculated as the standard deviation of the annual growth rates. The whole analysis was carried out in the software GeoDa (Geographic Data Analysis). The corresponding shapefile (.shp) was downloaded from the web page of Eurostat and thereafter 114 NUTS 3 regions were selected in GeoDa. Figure 1 depicts the box maps of (a) the average annual growth of GDP per capita (2000-2013) and of (b) volatility for individual analysed regions in order to gain an insight into the regional structure of the growth and the volatility. This type of map enables to see the location of outliers in the growth and volatility distribution, respectively. Concerning the average annual growth of GDP there were identified neither lower nor upper outliers. Regions with lowest growth rates are situated mainly in the Czech Republic and Hungary, the regions with highest growth rates are the Slovak regions as well as several Polish regions and one Hungarian region. The diversity in case of growth volatility is much higher. Since there were no lower outliers, 4 Polish regions, 1 Slovak and 1 Hungarian region could be characterized as upper outliers with extremely high growth volatility. The highest volatility was typical for the Slovak regions, followed by Hungarian regions.

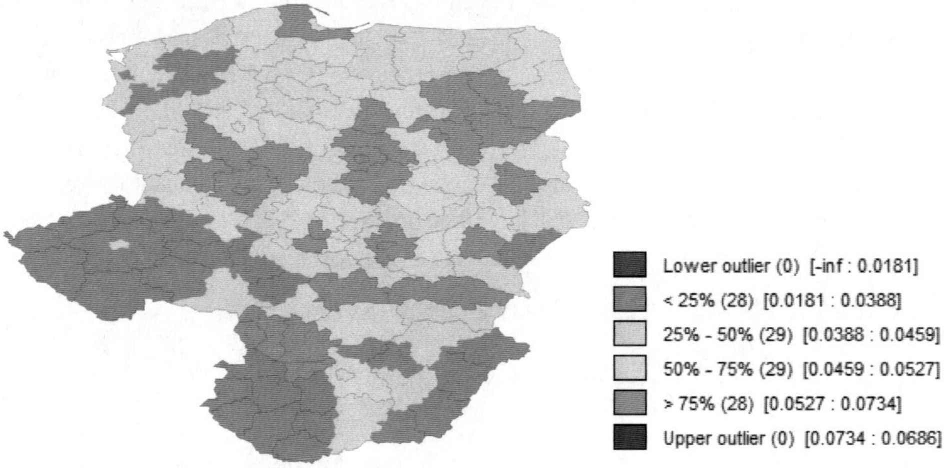

(a) average annual growth of GDP per capita

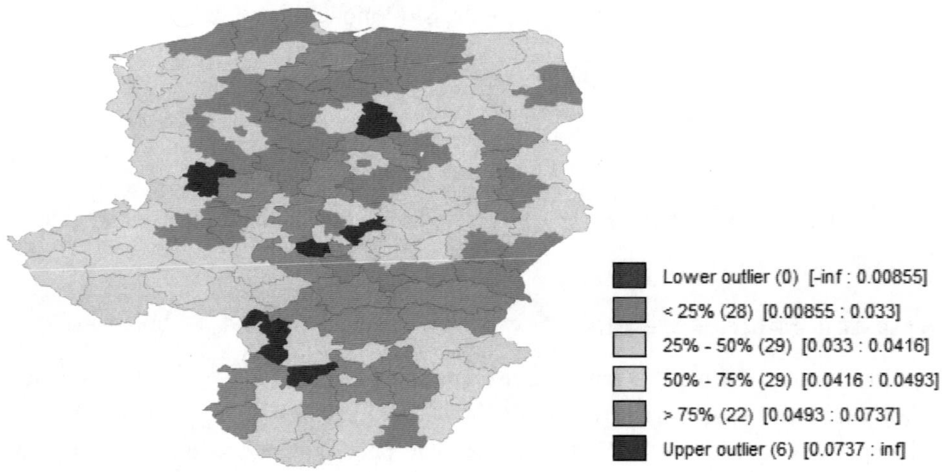

(b) volatility of growth

Figure 1 Box maps of average annual growth of GDP per capita and of volatility of growth

Mean values of both the average annual growth and volatility for individual countries are graphically presented in Figure 2. The average annual growth of GDP per capita in PPS from 2000 to 2013 was 4.5 %, the volatility of growth measured as the standard deviation of growth was 4.3 % on average. The highest values of both the growth and volatility of 5.5% and 5.9 %, respectively, were reached for the Slovak regions, the Polish regions exhibit the second highest average annual growth of 4.9 %, but the lowest volatility of about 4 %.

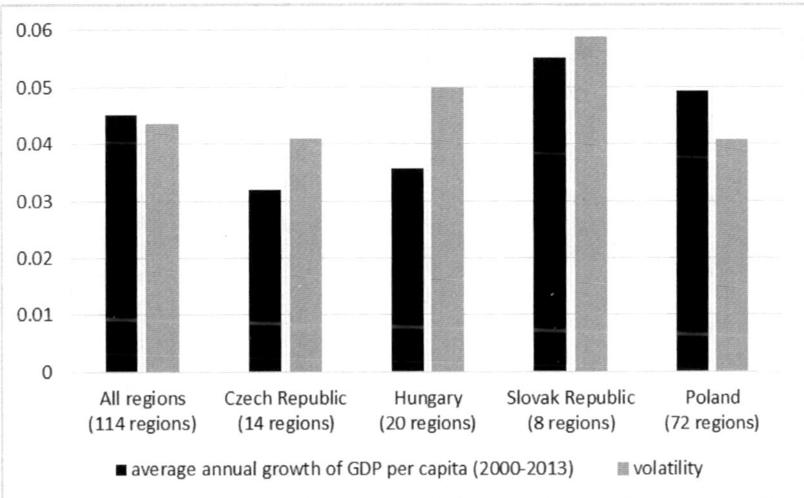

Figure 2 Mean values of average annual growth of GDP per capita and volatility of growth

Based on the figures above, it is clear that there are quite huge regional differences both in the growth and volatility values. Figure 3 presents a scatterplot of volatility and average annual growth indicating the positive link between them in NUTS 3 regions of V4 countries.

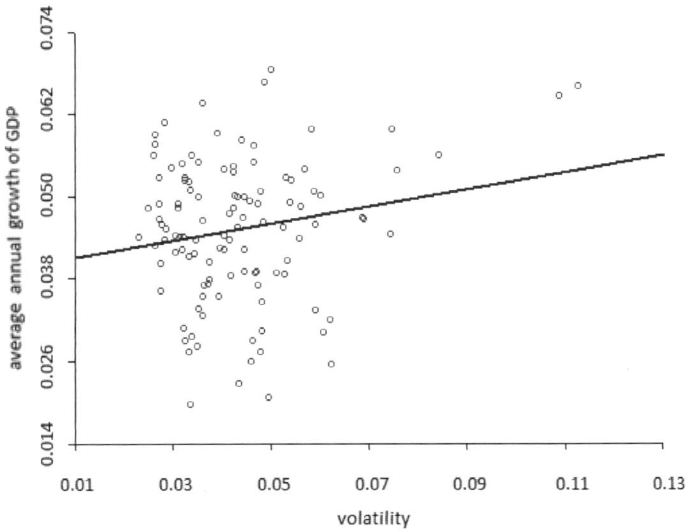

Figure 3 Scatterplot of volatility and average annual growth of GDP per capita (2000-2013)

Before doing an econometric analysis it is useful to investigate the relevance of the spatial aspect. Although based on the Figure 1 it is possible to identify both the spatial clusters and the extreme values (outliers), the box maps do not give any information about statistical significance of the clustering. The presence of positive spatial autocorrelation in the average annual growth of GDP was confirmed by the value of the global Moran's I statistics of 0.508 (Figure 4)[2]. The LISA cluster map on Figure 4 indicates that there are statistically significant clusters

[2] All the calculations in the paper, taking into account the space aspect, are based on queen case definition of the spatial weight matrix **W**.

of regions with high values of average annual growth located across 12 Polish regions surrounded by other high growth regions and clusters of slow growing regions surrounded also by slow growing regions in the Czech Republic and Hungary. Statistically significant negative association was confirmed for Sandomiersko-jedrzejowski region in Poland[3].

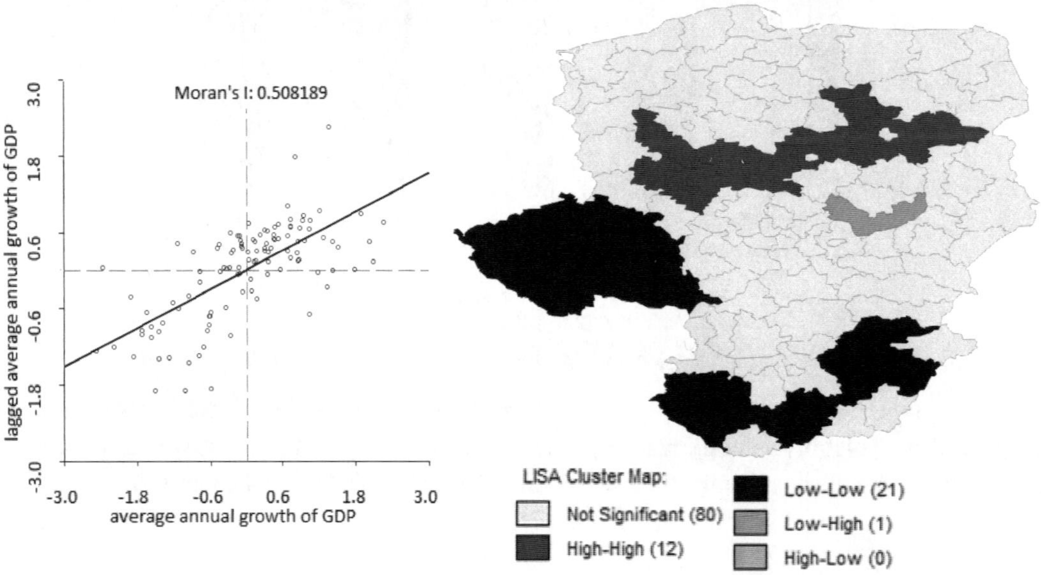

Figure 4 Moran's *I* and LISA cluster map for average annual growth of GDP per capita (2000-2013)

Since presence of the positive spatial autocorrelation was confirmed, we would expect that spatial dependence does matter and therefore the spatial aspect should not be neglected at econometric modelling. Following the classical approach, we do not start with the estimation of the spatial model directly, but we begin with the OLS (Ordinary Least Squares) estimation of the linear model (1) without consideration of country dummies (estimation results see the first column of the Table 1). Based on the results of LM tests and their robust versions it follows the ML (Maximum Likelihood) estimation of SEM model (3) without consideration of country dummies (estimation results see the second column of the Table 1). The estimation results of both models have yielded statistically significant estimations of all the parameters (corresponding *p*-values are in parentheses) indicating the positive impact of volatility on the growth variable. The statistical significance of the spatial parameter in the SEM model confirmed the relevance of the location consideration in the econometric modelling.

In the second step of the econometric analysis we decided to consider the differences between regions in individual countries. The econometric models were therefore enriched by inclusion of country dummies (Poland was taken as a reference country) in the multiplicative form with the volatility variable enabling to analyse whether the impact of volatility on growth differs across countries. Estimation results of corresponding models are summarized in last two columns of Table 1 – linear model with included dummy variables (1) and with regard to its diagnostic check – SAR model with included dummy variables (2). To eliminate the misleading

[3] Positive spatial autocorrelation was confirmed also for the volatility variable. The results can be provided by the author upon request.

conclusions based on linear model without spatial component included, we will focus on the interpretation of the estimation results of SAR model (2). Positive sign of the β parameter indicates that the relationship between the volatility and the growth is significantly positive on average (taking Poland as a reference country). However, we furthermore found out that, similar as presented by Falk and Sinabell (2009), the impact of volatility on growth is not uniform across analysed countries, since in case of two countries the relationship was significantly negative – for the Czech regions and for the Hungarian regions reaching the magnitudes of -0.0961 and -0.0272, respectively.[4]

	Linear model	**SEM**	**Linear model**	**SAR**
Method	**OLS**	**ML**	**OLS**	**ML**
Dummies	**No**	**No**	**Yes**	**Yes**
α	0.0398 (0.0000)	0.0392 (0.0000)	0.0406 (0.0000)	0.0240 (0.0000)
β	0.1244 (0.0505)	0.1336 (0.0053)	0.2064 (0.0001)	0.1765 (0.0001)
λ	-	0.6859 (0.0000)	-	-
ρ	-	-	-	0.3635 (0.0004)
γ_{CZ}	-	-	-0.4044 (0.0000)	-0.2726 (0.0000)
γ_{HU}	-	-	-0.2877 (0.0000)	-0.2037 (0.0000)
γ_{SK}	-	-	0.0298 (0.5380)	0.0531 (0.2318)
		Test results		
LM (lag)	66.5026 (0.0000)	-	11.5947 (0.0007)	-
Robust LM (lag)	0.6515 (0.4196)	-	7.3894 (0.0066)	-
LM (err)	69.4788 (0.0000)	-	5.7377 (0.0166)	-
Robust LM (err)	3.6277 (0.0568)	-	1.5324 (0.2158)	-

Table 1 Estimation results (p-values in parentheses)

4 Conclusion

The central point of the analysis presented in this paper was to investigate the growth-volatility relationship in a sample of 114 NUTS 3 regions of V4 countries (Czech Republic, Hungary, Slovak Republic and Poland) over the period 2000-2013. Since the existence of the spatial dependence was confirmed, besides traditional non-spatial analysis were the estimated models enriched by inclusion of the spatial dimension. In order to investigate the heterogeneity of the growth-volatility relationship across analysed countries, the dummy variables in interaction with the volatility variable were used. Since we identified on the average the positive relationship between volatility and growth, based on the use of dummy variables it was proved that the

[4] The robustness of presented results was tested based on inclusion of the further explanatory variable, the initial GDP in 2000 in natural logarithm, into estimated equations with no impact on the positive sign of β parameter. The whole analysis was also done separately for a subgroup of 72 Polish NUTS 3 regions supporting the positive growth-volatility relationship.

relationship is for two countries (Czech Republic and Hungary) significantly negative. To consider the impact of additional control explanatory variables in the analysis of the growth-volatility relationship as well as subsequent analysis of spillover effects across regions are the interesting areas of future research. Finally, it can be concluded, that the results of our study are in line with other studies (e.g. Chatterjee and Shukayev, 2006, Falk and Sinabell, 2009 and Ezcurra and Rios, 2013) asserting that the character of the growth-volatility relationship, i.e. positive or negative, strongly depends on the analysed group of countries/regions, choice and definition of data, analysed data period and used methodology.

Acknowledgements

This work was supported by the Grant Agency of Slovak Republic – VEGA grant No. 1/0248/17 "Analysis of Regional Disparities in the EU based on Spatial Econometric Approaches".

References

Anselin, L. (1995). 'Local Indicators of Spatial Association – LISA'. *Geographical Analysis*, 27 (2), pp. 93-115.

Chatterjee, P. and Shukayev, M. (2006). 'Are Average Growth and Volatility Related?'. *Bank of Canada Working Paper*, 2006-24.

Chocholatá, M. and Furková, A. (2016). 'Income disparities and convergence across regions of Central Europe', [Online]. *Croatian Operational Research Review*, 7 (2), pp. 303–318. Available at: http://hrcak.srce.hr/ojs/index.php/crorr/article/view/4539 [cited 2017-01-30].

Ezcurra, R. and Rios, V. (2013). Volatility and Regional Growth in Europe: Does Space Matter?, [Online]. Available at: http://www-sre.wu.ac.at/ersa/ersaconfs/ersa13/ERSA2013_paper_00133.pdf [cited 2017-01-30].

Falk, M. and Sinabell, F. (2009). 'A Spatial Econometric Analysis of the Regional Growth and Volatility in Europe'. *Empirica*, 36, pp. 193-207.

Fischer, M. M. and Getis, A. (2010). *Handbook of Applied Spatial Analysis. Software Tools, Methods and Applications*. Berlin: Springer Verlag.

Imbs, J. (2006). 'Growth and volatility', [Online]. Available at: http://www.jeanimbs.com/papers2_files/JMEjuly2006.pdf [cited 2017-01-30].

Martin, P. and Rogers, C.A. (2000). 'Long-Term Growth and Short-term Economic Instability'. *European Economic Review*, 44, pp. 359-381.

Ramey, G. and Ramey, V. A. (1995). 'Cross-Country Evidence on the Link between Volatility and Growth'. *American Economic Review*, 85, pp. 1138-1151.

http://ec.europa.eu/eurostat/ [cited 2017-01-05].

http://ec.europa.eu/eurostat/web/gisco/geodata/reference-data/administrative-units-statistical-units [cited 2017-01-05].

https://geodacenter.asu.edu/software/downloads [cited 2017-01-05].

Effectiveness of the Hill-Climbing Algorithm for Robust Emergency System Design

Jaroslav Janáček[1], Marek Kvet[2]

Abstract. A robust emergency service system is usually designed so that the deployment of given number of service centers minimizes the maximal value of objective functions corresponding with the specified scenarios. If the problem is solved by the branch-and-bound method, the min-max link-up constraints represent an undesirable burden of the computational process. Within this paper, we try to overcome the drawback following from the link-up constraints by usage of an iterative process applied to a surrogate problem, objective function of which represents convex combination of objective functions corresponding to individual scenarios. We provide the reader with a comparison of the original min-max approach to the suggested approach based on the convex combination of scenario objective functions.

Keywords: Robust emergency service system design, integer linear programming, convex combination, iterative algorithm.

JEL Classification: C61, C63

1 Introduction

Designing facility deployment of an emergency service system, a responsible designer must comply with randomly occurring events endangering the accessibility of the service for the system users (Janáček, 2015), (Marianov and Serra, 2002). The uncertainty caused by the detrimental events can be handled by a robust system design, where robustness is achieved by taking into account the various detrimental scenarios caused by the random events, which can appear in the road network. The events may be consequence of random failures due to congestion, disruptions or blockages. In this case, the emergency system is designed so that the resulting center deployment minimizes the maximal objective function value over all considered scenarios (Correia and Saldanha da Gama, 2015), (Janáček and Kvet, 2016a).

The scenarios for emergency system design are usually described by particular matrices of time distances from possible center locations to users' locations. This way, a possible detrimental scenario corresponds with evaluated consequence in the form of extended travel times. A robust emergency system design has to comply with all specified scenarios. The usual way of taking into account all scenarios is based on minimizing the maximal objective function of the individual instances corresponding with the particular scenarios. The min-max link-up constraints represent a computational burden due to bad convergence of branch-and-bound method embedded inside most available IP-solvers. Thus these approaches to the robustness constitute a big challenge to family of operational researchers and professionals in informatics.

Within this paper, we focus on the min-sum robust emergency service system design considering a given finite set of scenarios. To model the design problem, we make use of the radial

[1] Prof. RNDr. Jaroslav Janáček, CSc., University of Žilina, Faculty of Management Science and Informatics, Univerzitná 8215/1, 010 26 Žilina, Slovakia, e-mail: jaroslav.janacek@fri.uniza.sk
[2] Ing. Marek Kvet, PhD., University of Žilina, Faculty of Management Science and Informatics, Univerzitná 8215/1, 010 26 Žilina, Slovakia, e-mail: marek.kvet@fri.uniza.sk

formulation, which has proved to be able to considerably accelerate the associated solving process (Avella, Sassano and Vasil'ev, 2007), (García, Labbé and Marín, 2011), (Janáček and Kvet, 2012) comparing to the standard location-allocation formulation. Within this paper, we focus on complying bad convergence of the branch-and-bound method. We present the original approach (Pan, Du and Wei, 2014) to the robust design using an iterative approach based on convex combination of the detrimental scenarios.

The remainder of the paper is organized as follows: Section 2 is devoted to the description of standard model of the emergence system design with min-sum objective including the radial formulation. The robust emergency system design model is described in Section 3. The convex approach is explained in Section 4 and the associated numerical experiments are performed in Section 5. The results and findings are summarized in Section 6.

2 Radial formulation of the emergency system design

The weighted p-median problem, which corresponds to a simple emergency system design, is a task of location of at most p centers so that the sum of individual distances from each user's location to the nearest located center multiplied by the number of users sharing the location is minimal. To describe the problem, we denote I a set of possible center locations and J the set of possible users' locations. The symbol b_j denotes population of users located at $j \in J$. The symbol d_{ij} denotes the integer distance between a user at j and the possible center location i.

The weighted p-median problem is broadly discussed from the viewpoint of solving techniques suggested for fast solving of large instances. Within this paper, we make use of radial formulation (Avella, Sassano and Vasil'ev, 2007), (Current, Daskin and Schilling, 2002), (García, Labbé and Marín, 2011), (Janáček and Kvet, 2012).

The strategic decision in the problem concerns location of centers at possible center locations from the set I. To model this decision at the particular location i, we introduce a zero-one variable $y_i \in \{0, 1\}$, which takes the value of 1, if a center should be located at the location i, and it takes the value of 0 otherwise. To express a distance between a user location and the nearest located center, we partition the range of considered distances from 0 to $v+1$ into $v+1$ zones, where the width of every zone is equal to one. In addition, auxiliary zero-one variables x_{js} for $s = 0, \ldots, v$ are introduced. The variable x_{js} takes the value of 1, if the distance of the user at $j \in J$ from the nearest located center is greater than s and it takes the value of 0 otherwise. Then the expression $x_{j0} + x_{j1} + x_{j2} + \ldots + x_{jv}$ constitutes the distance d_{j*} from users' location j to the nearest located center. Further we introduce a zero-one constant a_{ij}^s for each $i \in I, j \in J$ and $s = 0, \ldots, v$. The constant a_{ij}^s is equal to 1, if the distance d_{ij} between the user location j and the possible center location i is less than or equal to s, otherwise $a_{ij}^s = 0$. Then the radial model can be formulated according to Janáček and Kvet (2012) as follows:

$$\text{Minimize} \quad \sum_{j \in J} b_j \sum_{s=0}^{v} x_{js} \tag{1}$$

$$\text{Subject to:} \quad x_{js} + \sum_{i \in I} a_{ij}^s y_i \geq 1 \quad j \in J, \ s = 0, \ldots, v \tag{2}$$

$$\sum_{i \in I} y_i \leq p \tag{3}$$

$$x_{js} \geq 0 \quad j \in J, \ s = 0, \ldots, v \tag{4}$$

$$y_i \in \{0, 1\} \quad i \in I \tag{5}$$

The objective function (1) gives the sum of weighted distance values. The constraints (2) ensure that the variables x_{js} are allowed to take the value of 0, if there is at least one center located in radius s from the user location j. The constraint (3) puts a limit p on the number of located centers. Even if only zero-one values of variable x_{js} are meaningful in the above model, constraints (4) are sufficient to ensure it due to partial integrality property of the model.

It can be easily found that the above-presented model contains $|J|*(v+1) + |I|$ variables and $|J|*(v+1)+1$ structural constraints. These figures can be rounded to $|J|*v+|I|$ and $|J|*v$ respectively. As concerns the number of non-zero items on the left-hand-sides of the structural constraints, it can be estimated by the expression $|J|*v*|I|$.

3 Robust emergency system design using detrimental scenarios

The robust emergency system design problem with radial formulation can be described using the above mentioned denotations J, I, b_j and p. In addition, let symbol U denote the set of possible failure scenarios. The distance between locations i and j under a specific scenario $u \in U$ is denoted here as d_{iju}. Besides the above defined location variables $y_i \in \{0,1\}$ for $i \in I$, the variable h is used as the upper bound of the objective function issues for individual scenarios. To formulate the radial model, the range of all considered distances from the matrix $\{d_{iju}\}$ is partitioned into $v+1$ unit zones according to Janáček and Kvet (2012). Then, auxiliary zero-one variables x_{jus} for $s = 0, \ldots, v$ and $u \in U$ are introduced. The variable x_{jus} takes the value of 1, if the distance of the user at $j \in J$ under scenario $u \in U$ from the nearest located center is greater than s and it takès the value of 0 otherwise. Then the expression $x_{ju0} + x_{ju1} + x_{ju2} + \ldots + x_{juv}$ constitutes the distance d_{ju*} from user location j to the nearest located service center under scenario $u \in U$. Similarly to the section 2, we introduce a zero-one constant a_{iju}^s under scenario $u \in U$ for each triple $i \in I$, $j \in J$, $s = 0, \ldots, v$. The constant a_{iju}^s is equal to 1, if the distance d_{iju} between the user location j and the possible center location i is less than or equal to s, otherwise a_{iju}^s is equal to 0. Then the radial-type min-sum robust emergency service system design problem can be formulated as follows:

$$\text{Minimize} \quad h \tag{6}$$

$$\text{Subject to:} \quad x_{jus} + \sum_{i \in I} a_{iju}^s y_i \geq 1 \quad j \in J, \ s = 0, \ldots, v, \ u \in U \tag{7}$$

$$\sum_{i \in I} y_i \leq p \tag{8}$$

$$\sum_{j\in j} b_j \sum_{s=0}^{v} x_{jus} \leq h \quad u \in U \tag{9}$$

$$x_{jus} \geq 0 \quad j \in J, \ s = 0, \ldots, v, \ u \in U \tag{10}$$

$$y_i \in \{0,1\} \quad i \in I \tag{11}$$

$$h \geq 0 \tag{12}$$

In this model, the objective function (6) represented by single variable h gives the upper bound of all objective function values over the individual scenarios. The constraints (7) ensure that the variables x_{jus} are allowed to take the value of 0, if at least one center is located in radius s from the user location j under scenario u and constraint (8) limits the number of located service centers by p. The link-up constraints (9) ensure that each particular scenario objective function value is less than or equal to the upper bound h. The constraint (3) puts a limit p on the number of located centers. Even if only zero-one values of variable x_{jus} are meaningful in the above model, constraints (10) are sufficient to ensure it due to partial integrality property of the model.

It can be easily found that the subscript u accompanies the subscript j in the model (9)-(12). It follows that the number of non-zero items on the left-hand-sides of the structural constraints can be estimated by the expression $|J|*v*|I|*|U|$. Obviously the robust emergency system model size is $|U|$ times bigger than the size of the original emergency system design model.

4 Concept of the convex approach

A design of robust emergency system based on direct solving of the mathematical programming problem described by the model (6)-(12) is limited by two factors. The first one is generally bad convergence of branch-and-bound methods applied to problems with the link-up constrains (9). The second factor consists in the size of the problem, which grows proportionally to the number of considered scenarios. These two drawbacks motivated suggestion of the following iterative approach, which avoids both the link-up constraints and size growth depending on cardinality of the scenario set.

The suggested approach is based on a convex combination of the objective functions associated with the individual scenarios. To explain the idea, we introduce the following denotations, where we consider that each scenario u influences only coefficients of the objective function. The associated objective function of a solution $\mathbf{y}$ is denoted as $f^u(\mathbf{y})$. We distinguish scenario $b \in U$, which is the basic scenario corresponding to the standard conditions. We consider that finite set Y of feasible solutions is the same for an arbitrary scenario u. Let $\mathbf{y}^u$ minimize the objective function $f^u(\mathbf{y})$. We define $f^r(\mathbf{y}) = max\{f^u(\mathbf{y}): u \in U\}$. The approaches presented in (Correia and Saldanha da Gama, 2015), (Janáček and Kvet, 2016a), (Janáček and Kvet, 2016b) and (Pan, Du and Wei, 2014) search for such solution $\mathbf{y}^r \in Y$ which minimizes $f^r(\mathbf{y})$, what is non-linear problem, even if the problem formulated for only one scenario is linear (see Fig. 1).

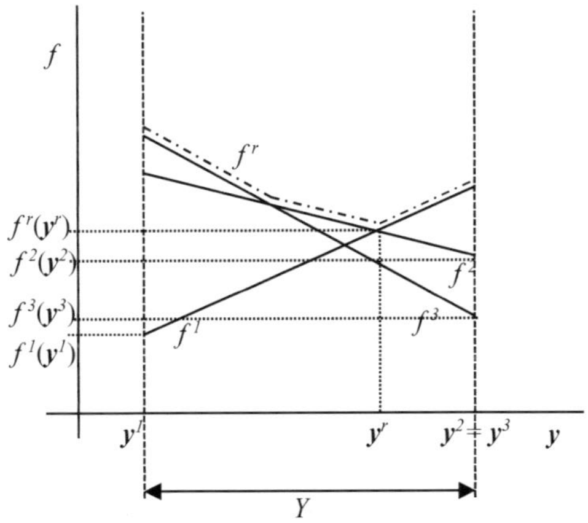

Figure 1 Three scenario objective functions and their maximum together with particular optimal solutions.

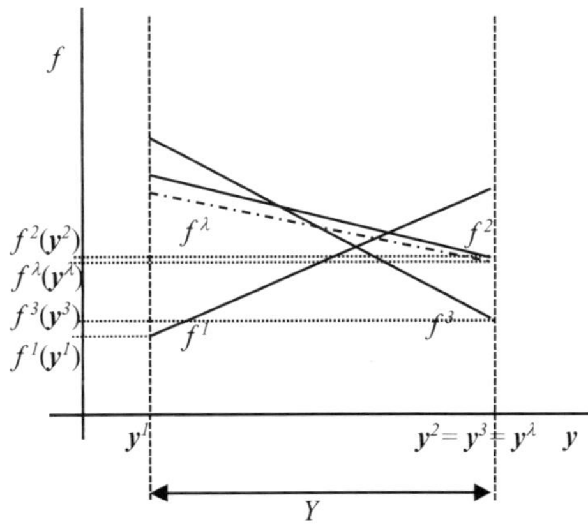

Figure 2 Three scenario objective functions and their convex combination together with particular optimal solutions.

The convex combination of the scenario objective function for the given set of nonnegative multipliers $\lambda_u \geq 0$ for $u \in U$ satisfying the condition that their sum equals to one can be defined using convex combination of considered matrices $\{d_{iju}\}$ for $u \in U$. The distance between i and j according to the convex combination is defined by (13).

$$d_{ij}(\lambda) = \sum_{u \in U} \lambda_u d_{iju} \qquad i \in I, j \in J \tag{13}$$

If we define a zero-one constant $a_{ij}^s(\boldsymbol{\lambda})$ which is equal to 1 in the case that the time distance $d_{ij}(\boldsymbol{\lambda})$ is less or equal to s, otherwise $a_{ij}^s(\boldsymbol{\lambda})$ equals to 0, then we can easily obtain the optimal solution for the convex combination objective function f^{λ} (see Fig. 2) by solving problem (1)-(5), where the incidental coefficients $a_{ij}^s(\boldsymbol{\lambda})$ are used instead of the original coefficients a_{ij}^s. As the solving process of the problem (1)-(5) is very fast in comparison to the solving process of (6)-(12), it can be performed several times during an iterative process, in which the multipliers λ_u are adjusted with the goal to approximate $f^r(y^r)$ by $f^{\lambda}(y^{\lambda})$ as closely as possible. The multiplier values are ever computed from a current solution $\boldsymbol{y}$ for a positive parameter β according to (14).

$$\lambda_u(\boldsymbol{y}) = \frac{(f^u(\boldsymbol{y}) - f^b(\boldsymbol{y}^b))^{\beta}}{\sum_{u \in U}(f^u(\boldsymbol{y}) - f^b(\boldsymbol{y}^b))^{\beta}} \qquad u \in U \tag{14}$$

The iterative process is described by the following steps:

0) Compute the optimal solution y^b for the objective function f^b and the multipliers λ_u associated with $\boldsymbol{y}^b$. Set $\boldsymbol{y} = \boldsymbol{y}^b$. Initialize the best found solution $\boldsymbol{y}^* = \boldsymbol{y}^b$. Set noFails=0.
1) Solve the problem (1) - (5) for the current $a_{ij}^s(\boldsymbol{\lambda})$ and obtain current solution $\boldsymbol{y}$.
2) If $f^r(\boldsymbol{y}) < f(\boldsymbol{y}^*)$, then update $\boldsymbol{y}^*$, otherwise set noFails= noFails +1.
3) Determine new values of λ_u for the current solution $\boldsymbol{y}$ according to (14).
4) If noFails >MaxFails, then terminate, otherwise go to 1).

We have to comment on β adjustment in the above algorithm. In the case of updating $\boldsymbol{y}^*$, we set β at the value of 1 and in the opposite case, we used the strategy of incrementing current value of β by 1.2, if the worst scenario was the same as in the previous step and we decremented the value of β by 0.2, when the worst scenarios differed.

5 Numerical experiments

To study the characteristics of suggested method, we performed the series of numerical experiments. The optimization software FICO Xpress 8.0 (64-bit, release 2016) was used and the experiments were run on a PC equipped with the Intel® Core™ i7 5500U processor with the parameters: 2.4 GHz and 16 GB RAM.

The used benchmarks were derived from the road network of Slovakia for eight self-governing regions, i.e. Bratislava (BA), Banská Bystrica (BB), Košice (KE), Nitra (NR), Prešov (PO), Trenčín (TN), Trnava (TT) and Žilina (ZA). All cities and villages with corresponding number b_j of inhabitants were taken into account. The set of communities represents both the set J of users' locations and also the set I of possible service center locations. The cardinalities of these sets vary from 87 to 664. The number p of located centers was derived from real emergency health care system, which has been originally implemented in studied regions and it varies from 9 to 67. The matrix $\{d_{ij}\}$ of the time distances from possible center locations to individual users' locations obtained from the associated road network represents so-called basic scenario in each solved instance. The scenarios used in our computational study were created in the following way. We chose 25 percent of matrix rows so that these rows correspond to the biggest cities concerning the number of system users. Then we chose randomly from 5 to 15 rows and the associated time distance values in the individual rows were multiplied by the randomly chosen integer from the range 2, 3, 4. This way, additional 10 different scenarios were generated for each self-governing region.

Preliminary experiments with convex algorithm were performed for maximal 9 iterations. Progresses of step-by-step obtained objective function values are depicted in the Figure 3. It can be observed that the best found value is obtained mostly in the three first iterations. The remaining iterations cause that the current solutions are either stuck at a local minimum or alternate between two solutions. Based on this founding, we set the maximal number of iterations at the value of 3 in the suggested algorithm.

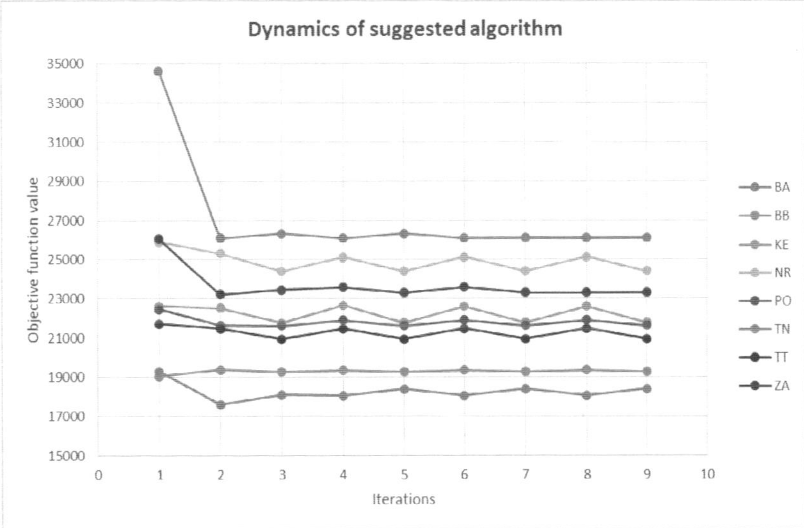

Figure 3 Graphs of progress of the objective function values according to iterations for the individual self-governing regions of Slovakia.

To compare the standard and suggested approaches, an individual experiment was organized so that the model (6) - (12) was used to obtain the optimal solution of the problem. The computational time in seconds is denoted by CT. The value of the objective function (6) is reported in the column denoted by h in the table column sections denoted by STANDARD. The same notation is used also for the suggested convex approach described in the Section 3, where the maximal number of iterations was 3. The column section LAMBDA contains the results of the convex approach. This section is enlarged by the column denoted by Dif, in which the differences between the optimal and the resulting solution of the convex approach are reported in percentage of the optimal objective function value.

Region	$\|I\|$	p	STANDARD		LAMBDA		
			CT [s]	h	CT [s]	h	Dif [%]
BA	87	9	17.8	25417	0.7	26102	2.7
BB	515	52	1259.3	18549	8.0	19056	2.7
KE	460	46	2032.9	21286	7.2	21756	2.2
NR	350	35	2991.8	24193	4.9	24402	0.9
PO	664	67	1866.6	21298	18.0	21607	1.5
TN	276	28	1710.5	17524	2.5	17605	0.5
TT	249	25	793.6	20558	2.6	20947	1.9
ZA	315	32	1404.4	23004	3.2	23224	1.0

Table 1 Comparison of the standard approach to convex algorithm with 3 permitted iterations

6 Conclusions

The main goal of this paper was to introduce an effective solving technique for robust emergency system design. The robustness follows the idea that the designed system should comply with specified scenarios by minimizing the maximal value of objective functions corresponding with the particular scenarios and thus it should be resistant to various detrimental events occurring randomly. We have presented an iterative approach, which can considerably outperform the exact approach as concerns computational time, whereas the resulting objective function value of the iterative approach does not differ from the exact value by more than two percent on average. Presented algorithm can be easily implemented without the necessity of developing special software tool. Future research in this field may be aimed at usage of special constraints, which prevent the iterative process from sticking at a local minimum or alternating between two solutions. Also settings of parameters of the approach deserve some additional research.

Acknowledgements

This paper was supported by the research grants VEGA 1/0518/15 "Resilient rescue systems with uncertain accessibility of service", VEGA 1/0463/16 "Economically efficient charging infrastructure deployment for electric vehicles in smart cities and communities", APVV-15-0179 "Reliability of emergency systems on infrastructure with uncertain functionality of critical elements".

References

Avella, P., Sassano, A. and Vasil'ev, I. (2007). 'Computational study of large scale p-median problems'. *Mathematical Programming*, 109, pp. 89-114.

Correia, I. and Saldanha da Gama, F. (2015). 'Facility locations under uncertainty'. *Location Science*, Springer, pp. 177-203.

Current, J., Daskin, M. and Schilling, D. (2002). 'Discrete network location models'. *Facility location. Applications and theory*, Berlin, Germany, pp. 81-118.

García, S., Labbé, M. and Marín, A. (2011). 'Solving large p-median problems with a radius formulation'. *INFORMS Journal on Computing*, 23 (4), pp. 546-556.

Janáček, J. (2015). 'Public service system design with fuzzy parameters of perceived utility'. *Central European Journal of Operations Research*, 23 (3), pp. 595-606.

Janáček, J. and Kvet, M. (2012). 'Relevant Network Distances for Approximate Approach to Large p-Median Problems'. *Operations research proceedings 2012: selected papers of the international conference on operations research,* Hannover, Germany, pp. 123 – 128.

Janáček, J. and Kvet, M. (2016a). 'Designing a Robust Emergency Service System by Lagrangean Relaxation'. *Proceedings of Mathematical Methods in Economics 2016*, Liberec, Czech Republic, pp. 349-353.

Janáček, J. and Kvet, M. (2016b). 'Min-Max Robust Emergency Service System Design'. *Communications: Scientific Letters of the University of Žilina*, 8 (3), pp. 12-18.

Marianov, V. and Serra, D. (2002). 'Location problems in the public sector'. *Facility location. Applications and theory*, Berlin, Germany, pp. 119-150.

Pan, Y., Du, Y. and Wei, Z. (2014). 'Reliable Facility System Design Subject to Edge Failures'. *American Journal of Operations Research*, 4, pp. 164-172.

Impact of the parameters on the number of stations of the Emergency Medical Services

Marta Janáčková[1], Alžbeta Szendreyová[2]

Abstract. The aim of our paper is to test the setting of parameters that affect the calculation of the appropriate number of stations of the Emergency Medical Services (EMS). The proposal how to determine the number of the EMS stations is based on the hypothesis that says: to add another EMS station to the current number of the stations is important only when the benefit is not less than the average asset calculated from the various options. A problem is solved in the different regions of the Slovak Republic. We compare the results that we get on the hypothesis with the real number of the stations that are located in different regions of the Slovakia today.

Keywords: integer programming, *p*-median problem, public service system, facility location problem, optimal number of stations.

JEL Classification: C61

1 Introduction

Stations of the Emergency Medical Service (EMS) provide services to the citizens which need help and each citizens has a right to get the provision of these services. The location of EMS stations and the proposal of their number are therefore a very important strategic decision in the planning of the public services (Janáček et al, 2010). A design of the EMS stations placements should follow the best availability of the provided service to the customers. The availability of the service can be measured by several criteria. Given to the chosen criteria, we can optimize the appropriate location of the stations and we can also optimize the number of stations.

In this article we use a hypothesis that proposes a suitable number of stations. We compare the real number of the EMS stations in different regions of the Slovak Republic with the number of located station that is obtained in accordance with the tested hypothesis.

2 A proposal to determine the appropriate number of stations

In our proposal, the minimization of the average service availability for the customer is the criterion of service. We measure the service availability in kilometers. In practice, The EMS stations are not built on green meadow. They are located mostly in the areas of the hospitals or in the localities with good transport availability and with flexible exit into surroundings.

The number of stations would be able to service the existing customers. However, the needs of the customers are random. Therefore, the required number of the stations may vary. The number of the costumers, the transport accessibility, the condition of the roads but also the random events influence the number of the EMS stations. We can estimate the limit below which the number of the stations would not fall. We solve the decision on the suitable location

[1] University of Žilina, Department of Applied Mathematics, Univerzitná 1, 01026 Žilina, Slovak Republic, e-mail: marta.janackova@fstroj.uniza.sk.
[2] University of Žilina, Department of Mathematical Methods and Operations Research, Univerzitná 1, 010 26 Žilina, Slovak Republic, e-mail: Alzbeta.Szendreyova@fri.uniza.sk.

of the required number as a p-median problem. The choice of the optimization criterion is important too (Janáčková and Szendreyová, 2015). In this paper we make use of the minimization of the total distance among customers and their associated stations. The model can be constituted as follows.

$$\text{Minimize} \quad \sum_{i \in I} \sum_{j \in J} d_{ij} z_{ij} \tag{1}$$

$$\text{Subject to} \quad \sum_{i \in I} z_{ij} = 1 \qquad for\ j \in J \tag{2}$$

$$z_{ij} \le y_i \qquad for\ i \in I, j \in J \tag{3}$$

$$\sum_{i \in I} y_i = p \tag{4}$$

$$z_{ij} \in \{0,1\} \qquad for\ i \in I, j \in J \tag{5}$$

$$y_i \in \{0,1\} \qquad for\ i \in I \tag{6}$$

Coefficients and variables in the model have the following meanings: I is the set of possible facility locations (stations), J denotes the set of customers, d_{ij} introduces the distance between station $i \in I$ and customer $j \in J$ and p is the required number of stations. The decision on locating or not locating a station i at a place $i \in I$ is modeled by a variable y_i and it takes the value of 1, if the station is located at place i and it takes the value of 0 otherwise. The decision on allocation of the customer from node $j \in J$ to the station at the place $i \in I$ is modeled by a variable z_{ij}. It takes the value of 1 if the customer j will be served from the station i and takes the value of 0 otherwise.

There exists also another model for solving the p-median problem, e.g. a radial formulation (Janáček and Kvet, 2015).

It is evident, that an adding even a single station to the lower bound improves the availability of the EMS. That means, if no condition goes against the location of the station, the optimal solution of the p-median problem on the interval $< p_{min}, p_{max} >$ is p_{max}. On the other side, the improvement of the objective value decreases step by step when we add another stations. The question is how long the increase of the number of the located stations will be effective. We declare the following hypothesis:

Let p_{ef} from the interval $< p_{min}, p_{max} >$ denotes the effective number of the EMS stations. p_{ef} occurs the value, where the decline of the objective value with increase of the value p by one unit is approximately equal to the average decrease on the interval. The relation (7) specifies the average decrease of the objective value (OV) on the interval $< p_{min}, p_{max} >$.

$$\frac{OV_{p_{min}} - OV_{p_{max}}}{p_{max} - p_{min}} \tag{7}$$

The principle of the pronounced hypothesis is shown graphically in Figure 1. The graph in Figure 1 represents the dependency of the objective value on the number of the EMS stations for the Trnava region in the Slovak Republic. The average decrease is represented by the line segment which connects the points with coordinates $[p_{min}, OV_{p_{min}}]$ and $[p_{max}, OV_{p_{max}}]$ In the case of Trnava region $p_{min} = 1, OV_{p_{min}} = 9735, p_{max} = 249$ and $OV_{p_{max}} = 0$. The value of p_{ef} is determined from the contact point of the line parallel to line that represents the average decrease.

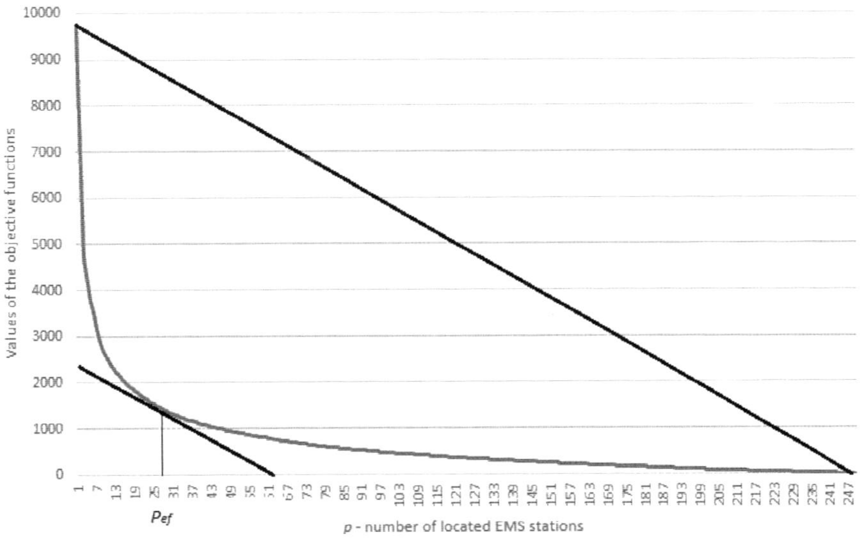

Figure 1 Dependence of the objective value on the number of the located stations

3 Experiments

We selected the individual regions of the Slovak Republic to test the hypothesis. Each municipality of the region was considered as the candidate of the station location and also as a customer. Then we solved a set of task as a *p*-median problem separately for each region. We started on the value of $p = 1$ and we increased sequentially the value of p by one. The criterion of the optimization was to minimize of the average distance between the customer and his associated station. The optimization was solved by using a professional solver XPRESS-MP (Xpress-MP Manual, 2005).

In Table 1 we present selected results obtained from the design of the optimal location of p stations for the Trnava region. We see that the task reaches the value of the average decrease of the objective value in the location of 26-30 stations in the region. This result may vary for the different setting of parameters, e.g. for another scope of the interval for the value of p.

Regions differ in the number of municipalities and in population density as well. To determine p as the lower limit of the possible number of EMS stations in the region, we chose the estimation that at least one station enter for every 50,000 inhabitants of the region. With increasing value of p, the objective values declined and the decrease of the objective value for two consecutive $p \in < p_{min}, p_{max} >$ was still smaller. When the decrease of the objective value for two consecutive p fell below 1% of the maximum decrease of the objective value, we stopped the cycle of calculations in processed set of the task.

p	OV	Decrease	p	OV	Decrease	p	OV	Decrease
1	9735	0	15	2064	75	29	1374	38
2	6641	3094	16	1989	75	30	1336	38
3	4692	1949	17	1925	64	31	1305	31
4	4141	551	18	1870	55	32	1276	29
5	3786	355	19	1817	53	33	1249	27
6	3466	320	20	1765	52	34	1226	23
7	3169	297	21	1714	51	35	1203	23
8	2860	309	22	1664	50	36	1181	22
9	2678	182	23	1617	47	37	1159	22
10	2536	142	24	1573	44	38	1138	21
11	2437	99	25	1530	43	39	1118	20
12	2331	106	26	1490	40	40	1098	20
13	2233	98	27	1450	40	41	1079	19
14	2139	94	28	1412	38	42	1060	19

Table 1 Trnava region, 249 municipalities, $p_{min} = 1$, $p_{max} = 249$, average decrease 39.254

We named p_{max} the last value of p which we solved the set of the task for. We calculated the average decrease of the objective value for the interval $< p_{min}, p_{max} >$ for the given region. Subsequently, we also found out one or more values of p in which the actual decrease of the objective value roughly corresponds to the value of the average decrease for the given interval. According to the hypothesis, the effective value of p_{ef} is from range$< p^*_{min}, p^*_{max} >$ that is specified in this way. Although, the objective value can improve by increasing of the value of p_{ef}, but it improve only by statistically insignificant values. We compared the obtained results with the number of the municipalities, where the EMS stations are located today. The results and the comparison are in Table 2.

Region	p^*_{min}	p^*_{max}	Decrease of the OV	Average decrease	Interval p_{ef}	Real number of stations (p_{real})
BA	12	31	266	14.00	19-21	15
BB	**13**	**29**	**2448**	**153.00**	**20-22**	**36**
KE	**16**	**26**	**1112**	**111.20**	**21-24**	**32**
NR	14	37	1452	63.13	23-26	27
PO	**16**	**36**	**3080**	**154.00**	**23-29**	**32**
TN	12	35	1214	52.78	21-26	22
TT	11	32	1161	55.29	17-23	17
ZA	**14**	**26**	**902**	**75.17**	**19-21**	**29**

Table 2 Estimation of the interval to determine p_{ef}

Table 2 shows that the design of the effective number of p_{ef} according to the hypothesis expects significantly lower values in regions with the highest number of real located stations (p_{real}). For the regions Banská Bystrica (BB), Košice (KE) and Žilina (ZA), even the value of p_{max} was less than p_{real}. In contrary, the value of p_{real} belongs to the interval $< p^*_{min}, p^*_{max} >$ in regions with a smaller number of municipalities in which there is located an EMS station. The facts led us to the question, what percentage of the improvement (effectiveness by hypothesis) matches the present state (p_{real}). For this purpose, we calculated the average decrease of the objective value for all theoretical possibility of the EMS station location, i.e. for the interval $< p_{min} = 1, p_{max} = M >$ where M is the number of candidates for the location of the station (number of the municipalities in region). We found out, what part of percentage from the maximal decrease introduces the decrease, which appertains to the value of p_{real}. The results are presented in Table 3.

Region	p_{max}	Maximal decrease	Average decrease	Decrease for p_{real}	p_{real} in % from maximal decrease	Real number of EMS stations (p_{real})
BA	87	778	25.895	21	2.70	15
BB	**515**	**9851**	**55.356**	**77**	**0.78**	**36**
KE	**460**	**8115**	**52.861**	**58**	**0.71**	**32**
NR	350	3352	37.926	51	1.52	27
PO	**664**	**9751**	**53.833**	**108**	**1.11**	**32**
TN	276	2892	37.775	51	1.76	22
TT	249	3094	39.254	64	2.07	17
ZA	**315**	**4754**	**45.72**	**44**	**0.93**	**29**

Table 3 Calculation of effectiveness for p_{real}

4 Conclusion

As shown in Table 3, the real number of municipalities with located EMS station in the region with fewer number of the stations shows an effectiveness at a level from 1.52% to 2.7% from the maximal possible (not real) decrease of the objective value, that corresponds to the increase of the value of p by one unit. In regions with a greater number of the EMS stations, the effectiveness for p_{real} and for the interval $< p_{min} = 1, p_{max} = M >$ varies in the range of 0.7 through 1.11, while M is the number of the municipalities of the region.

We must say that the borders of the values p_{min} and p_{max} are not quite well adjusted. It should be noted that the order of the regions according to the number of stations also does not correspond completely with the order according to the total number of the municipalities in region. We expect, that the number of the EMS stations will be affected not only by the number of the municipalities but also by geographical distribution of the population into municipalities. The result may be influenced by fact, that in some municipalities are located more than one EMS stations. Our model cannot that fact take into account.

The estimation of the effective number of the EMS stations nearly coincides with the real number of the EMS stations in regions with fewer stations. The design of the effective number of the stations is significantly lower in regions with higher number of the stations. This may be due to the fact that these are regions with the largest populations (Janáčková and Szendreyová, 2016). It was not taken into account in the optimization, because the distance between the customer and stations from the same municipality is equal to the value of zero. A verification of these assumptions will be discussed later.

Acknowledgements

This work was supported by the research grants VEGA 1/0518/15 "Resilient rescue systems with uncertain accessibility of service" and APVV-15-0179 "Reliability of emergency systems on infrastructure with uncertain functionality of critical elements" and VEGA 1/0463/16 – "Economically efficient charging infrastructure deployment for electric vehicles in smart cities and communities".

References

Janáček, J. et al (2010). *Design of the areas of large service systems*. Žilina: University of Zilina.

Janáček, J. and Kvet M. (2015). 'Emergency system design with temporarily failing centers'. *Proceedings of the 13th International Symposium on Operational Research*, Bled, Slovenia, pp. 490-495.

Janáčková, M. and Szendreyová, A. (2015). 'Time-distance versus utility in the public service system design'. *Proceedings of the 13th International Symposium on Operational Research*, Bled, Slovenia, pp. 446-451.

Janáčková, M. and Szendreyová, A. (2016). 'An importance of the population density for the location of the Emergency Medical Service stations'. *Proceedings of 34th international conference: Mathematical methods in economics*, Liberec, Czech Republic, pp. 354-358.

Xpress-MP Manual 'Getting Started' (2005). Blisworth: Dash Associates.

LTPDvar: A decision support tool for LTPD sampling plans

Nikola Kaspříková [1]

Abstract. LTPDvar is an R extension package which has been developed for the calculation and evaluation of the LTPD and AOQL variable sampling plans minimizing the mean inspection cost per lot of the average process quality when the remainder of the rejected lots is inspected. We recall the design of the recently proposed LTPD plans based on the usage of the exponentially weighted moving average statistic for the known standard deviation case and then compare the economic efficiency of the plans with attributes sampling plan using a cost model considering differences in variable and fixed cost.

Keywords: Acceptance sampling, LTPD, EWMA, cost optimization, inspection by variables.

JEL classification: C44

1 Introduction

The LTPDvar software (Kasprikova, 2016a) is an extension package for the R computing environment (R Core Team, 2017) developed for computation and evaluation of optimal plans for statistical acceptance sampling. Sampling inspection is one of the tools of industry statistics. The acceptance sampling plans are designed and used to improve the economic efficiency of business process. There exist many types of such acceptance sampling plans. New rectifying lot tolerance percent defective (LTPD) plans for sampling inspection by variables based on the exponentially weighted moving average statistic have been recently introduced. (Kasprikova, 2016b) addresses the case of known standard deviation and the plans for the unknown standard deviation case are introduced in (Kasprikova, 2017). This paper recalls the design of the plans for the known standard deviation case and focuses on new approach to the comparative economic efficiency evaluation of these plans. The LTPDvar (Kasprikova, 2016a) package which implements the algorithms for the calculation of the plans and which has been published on the Comprehensive R Archive Network can be used for the calculation of such plans.

The LTPD sampling plans minimizing the mean inspection cost per lot of process average quality when the remainder of rejected lots is inspected were originally designed by Dodge and Romig for the inspection by attributes - see (Dodge and Romig, 1998). Plans for the inspection by variables and for the inspection by variables and attributes (all items from the sample are inspected by variables, the remainder of rejected lots is inspected by attributes) were then proposed and it was shown that these plans are in many situations more economical than the corresponding Dodge-Romig attribute sampling plans. The LTPD plans for the inspection by variables and attributes have been introduced in (Klufa, 1994), using an approximate calculation of the plans. Exact plans, using non-central t distribution in the calculation of the operating characteristic, have been reported in (Klufa, 2010) and implemented in

[1] University of Economics in Prague, Department of Mathematics, Nám. W. Churchilla 4, Praha, Czech Republic, nb33@tulipany.cz.

the LTPDvar R package (Kasprikova, 2016a). It has been shown that these plans are in many situations superior to the original attribute sampling plans and similar results have been obtained for the AOQL plans – the analysis is provided in (Kasprikova and Klufa, 2015) and in (Kasprikova and Klufa, 2011). An economic model considering difference in variable cost is used in (Kasprikova and Klufa, 2015) and (Kasprikova and Klufa, 2011).

The plans proposed in (Kasprikova, 2016b) and (Kasprikova, 2017) reflect the recent development in the field of the design of the acceptance sampling plans and make use of the exponentially weighted moving average (EWMA) statistic for the inspection by variables. The EWMA statistic has often been used in the process monitoring applications, nevertheless its application in the design of the acceptance sampling plans (see e. g. (Sankle and Singh, 2012)) is rather new.

The recently proposed LTPD plans for the inspection by variables and attributes which are designed to use the EWMA statistic in the decision procedure are addressed in the present paper and the discussion of the economic performance of such plans is provided. The case of the known standard deviation is considered in this paper. The structure of the paper is as follows: the LTPD plans for the inspection by attributes minimizing the mean inspection cost per lot of the process average quality when the remainder of the rejected lots is inspected are recalled first, then the LTPD plans for the inspection by variables and attributes using EWMA statistic are calculated using the LTPDvar package and the evaluation of the comparative economic efficiency is shown, using a simple economic model which considers differences in both variable and fixed costs.

1.1 LTPD attribute sampling plans

First we recall the attribute sampling plans. Dodge and Romig in (Dodge and Romig, 1998) consider the case, where each inspected item is to be classified as either good or non-conforming (acceptance sampling by attributes) and they search for the sampling plans which minimize the mean number of the items inspected per lot of the process average quality

$$I_s = N - (N - n) \cdot L(\bar{p}; n; c) \tag{1}$$

under the condition

$$L(p_t; n; c) \leq \beta, \tag{2}$$

where $L(p, n, c)$ is the operating characteristic (the probability of accepting a submitted lot with the proportion defective p when using the plan (n, c) for acceptance sampling),
N is the number of the items in the lot (an input parameter),
$\bar{p}$ is the process average proportion defective (an input parameter),
p_t is the lot tolerance proportion defective (an input parameter, $P_t = 100p_t$ is the lot tolerance per cent defective, denoted LTPD),
n is the number of items in the sample $(n < N)$,
c is the acceptance number (the lot is rejected when the number of defective items in the sample is greater than c).

Condition (2) provides a guarantee for the consumer that the lots of the unsatisfactory quality level, with the proportion defective p_t are going to be accepted only with the specified probability β at most (the so-called consumer's risk). The standard value 0.1 is used for the consumer's risk in (Dodge and Romig, 1998).

1.2 Sampling plans for the inspection by variables

We recall the recently introduced LTPD plans for the inspection by variables and attributes - see (Kasprikova, 2017). The plans have been designed in (Kasprikova, 2017) under the following assumptions: The measurements of a single quality characteristic X are independent and identically distributed normal random variables with parameters μ and σ^2. We consider the known σ case. For the quality characteristic X, either an upper specification limit U (the item is defective if its measurement exceeds U), or a lower specification limit L (the item is defective if its measurement is smaller than L), is given.

For the design of the rectifying LTPD plans minimizing the mean inspection cost per lot of the process average quality we shall use a procedure based on the EWMA statistic. The procedure is as follows: draw a random sample of n items from the lot and compute the sample mean $\bar{x}$ and the statistic Z at time t as

$$Z_t = \lambda \bar{x} + (1-\lambda) Z_{t-1}, \tag{3}$$

where λ is a smoothing constant (between 0 and 1). Accept the lot if

$$\frac{U - Z_t}{\sigma} \geq k \quad \text{or} \quad \frac{Z_t - L}{\sigma} \geq k. \tag{4}$$

The operating characteristic is (see e.g. (Sankle and Singh, 2012))

$$L(p) = \Phi((u_{1-p} - k)A), \tag{5}$$

where

$$A = \sqrt{\frac{n(2-\lambda)}{\lambda}}, \tag{6}$$

Φ is the standard normal distribution function and u is the corresponding quantile function.

The plan parameters (n, k) are to be determined so that the plan has optimal economic characteristics and satisfies the requirement (2), when (5) is used as the operating characteristic.

Regarding the economic optimality, Klufa in (Klufa, 1994) uses the economic model, described in more detail in (Kasprikova and Klufa, 2015) and searches for the acceptance plan (n, k), minimizing the mean inspection cost per lot of the process average quality C_{ms} under the condition (2). We are going to use this model for the design of the plans too. The inspection cost per lot, assuming that the remainder of the rejected lots is inspected by attributes (the inspection by variables and attributes), is $n\, c_m^*$, with the probability $L(p; n, k)$, and $[n\, c_m^* + (N-n)\, c_s^*]$ with the probability $[1 - L(p; n, k)]$, where c_s^* is the cost of the inspection of one item by attributes, and c_m^* is the cost of the inspection of one item by variables. The mean inspection cost per lot of the process average quality is then

$$C_{ms} = n \cdot c_m^* + (N-n) \cdot c_s^* \cdot [1 - L(\bar{p}; n, k)]. \tag{7}$$

Let us denote

$$c_m = \frac{c_m^*}{c_s^*}. \tag{8}$$

Instead of C_{ms} we shall look for the acceptance plan (n, k) minimizing

$$I_{ms} = n \cdot c_m + (N - n) \cdot [1 - L(\bar{p}; n, k)] \tag{9}$$

(both functions C_{ms} and I_{ms} have a minimum for the same acceptance plan ($C_{ms} = I_{ms} \cdot c_s^*$)) under the condition (2).

For the discussion of the c_m parameter, see (Kasprikova and Klufa, 2015). The value of this parameter must be estimated based on the real cost calculation in practice. Usually it is $c_m > 1$.

2 Calculation and evaluation of the plans with LTPDvar package

The LTPD acceptance sampling plan based on the EWMA model for sampling inspection by variables when the remainder of rejected lots is inspected by attributes, as implemented in (Kasprikova, 2016a) will be calculated in the example below. The solution for the known σ case will be searched for, using the operating characteristic given by (5). The resulting sampling plan will then be evaluated with regard to the economic characteristics and compared with the corresponding LTPD attributes sampling plan as discussed in (Dodge and Romig, 1998).

Example 1. A lot with $N = 1000$ items is considered in the acceptance procedure. The lot tolerance proportion defective is given to be $p_t = 0.01$, and the process average quality is $\bar{p} = 0.001$. It is known that the cost of the inspection of one item by variables is 2 times higher than the cost of the inspection of one item by attributes, so parameter c_m equals 2. Find the LTPD acceptance sampling plan for sampling inspection by variables when remainder of rejected lots is inspected by attributes with the EWMA statistic with smoothing constant $\lambda = 0.85$.

The plan can be calculated using the functions available in the LTPDvar package for the R software (R Core Team, 2017), see the documentation of the package for a more detailed description. The implementation is based on the following principles: the k corresponding to particular sample size n is obtained using the condition (2) and the cost-optimizing n is searched for using numerical methods, where the approximate solution, which is calculated first, is used for setting the bounds of the intervals to be searched in.

The resulting plan may be obtained using the following call in the LTPDvar package:

```
planLTPD(N=1000, pbar=0.001, pt=0.01,cm=2,method="ewmaSK",
lam=0.85,intdif=70)
```

and the output of the calculation is as follows.

```
An object of class "ACSPlan"
Slot "n":
[1] 18
```

```
Slot "k":
[1] 2.586041
```

So the resulting solution is $n = 18$, $k = 2.586041$.

The corresponding Dodge-Romig attributes sampling plan is $n = 250$, $c = 0$.

For the comparison of these two plans - the EWMA plan for inspection by variables and attributes ($n = 18$, $k = 2.586041$) and Dodge-Romig plan ($n = 250$, $c = 0$) from an economic point of view we use a simple economic model of cost difference (measured in the c_s^* units) in which we consider the difference of the mean inspection costs per lot of the process average quality of the particular plans and the effect of the difference in fixed costs:

$$c = I_{ms}(18, 2.586041) - I_s(250, 0) + f, \tag{10}$$

where f is the increase in fixed cost (measured in c_s^*) in case that we opt for the plan for the inspection by variables and attributes. The decision to implement the plan for the inspection by variables and attributes may bring higher fixed cost in some cases in practice in comparison with performing just the attribute inspection due to presumably more difficult preparation of the inspection procedure.

The I_{ms} function is implemented in the LTPDvar package too and (for plan $n = 18$, $k = 2.586041$) may be called as shown below.

```
Ims(n= 18, k=2.586041, N= 1000, pbar=0.001, cm=2, type="ewmaSK",
lam=0.85)
```

In this case we obtain $I_{ms} = 42.30547$. The cost measure c then represents the cost difference (measured in the c_s^* units) in the mean inspection cost per lot of the process average quality in case that the EWMA based plan for the inspection by variables and attributes is used in place of the corresponding attribute sampling plan. The guidelines for the application and interpretation of the measure are as follows: in case that the resulting c value is negative, then one should preferably choose the plan for the inspection by variables and attributes.

Let's suppose that in our example situation $f = 150c_s^*$, then we get $c = -175.7$, which shows that there can be expected savings in the mean inspection cost per lot of the process average quality if the EWMA plan is used in place of the corresponding attribute inspection plan.

3 Conclusion

The EWMA-based known standard deviation case LTPD plans for the sampling inspection by variables when the remainder of the rejected lots is inspected by attributes minimizing the mean inspection cost per lot of the process average quality in many cases bring significant economic advantages over the corresponding attribute inspection plans. The improvement in economic efficiency can be assessed using simple model considering difference in variable and fixed cost and the LTPDvar package for the R computing environment can be conveniently used for the calculation of the optimal acceptance sampling plan. Future development of the LTPDvar tool could include implementation of other sampling schemes designs.

Acknowledgements

This paper has been produced with contribution of long term institutional support of research activities by Faculty of Informatics and Statistics, University of Economics, Prague.

References

Dodge, H. F. and Romig, H. G. (1998). *Sampling Inspection Tables: Single and Double Sampling*. New York: John Wiley.

Kasprikova, N. (2016a). *LTPDvar: LTPD and AOQL plans for acceptance sampling inspection by variables*. R package. URL http://CRAN.R-project.org/package=LTPDvar.

Kasprikova, N. (2016b). 'Calculation of the LTPD Variables Sampling Plans in R Computing Environment'. *15th Conference on Applied Mathematics (Aplimat 2016)*, Bratislava, Slovak Republic, pp. 661-667.

Kasprikova, N. (2017). 'Rectifying LTPD Plans Minimizing Mean Inspection Cost Per Lot of Process Average Quality Using EWMA Statistics'. *Journal of Testing and Evaluation*, 45 (4), DOI: 10.1520/JTE20150259.

Kasprikova, N. and Klufa, J. (2011). 'Calculation of LTPD single sampling plans for inspection by variables and its software implementation'. *International Days of Statistics and Economics*, Praha, Czech Republic, pp. 266-276.

Kasprikova, N. and Klufa, J. (2015). 'AOQL sampling plans for inspection by variables and attributes versus the plans for inspection by attributes'. *Quality technology and quantitative management*, 12 (2), pp. 133-142.

Klufa, J. (1994). 'Acceptance sampling by variables when the remainder of rejected lots is inspected'. *Statistical Papers*, 35, pp. 337-349.

Klufa, J. (2010). 'Exact calculation of the Dodge-Romig LTPD single sampling plans for inspection by variables'. *Statistical Papers*, 51 (2), pp. 297-305.

R Core Team. (2017) *R: A language and environment for statistical computing*. R Foundation for Statistical Computing, Vienna, Austria, URL http://www.R-project.org.

Sankle, R. and Singh, J.R. (2012). 'Single sampling plans for variables indexed by aql and aoql under EWMA model'. *Journal of Reliability and Statistical Studies*, 5 (2), pp. 11-20.

Time coordination of bus arrivals on a set of bus stops

Petr Kozel[1], Šárka Michalcová[2]

Abstract. This paper deals with a time coordination of bus arrivals on a set of bus stops. A quality criterion of this problem is to minimize the waiting time of passengers to make public transport more attractive. One possible solution to this problem is to coordinate bus arrivals. This problem can be formulated as a mathematical model with the quadratic objective function and a set of equality or inequality constraints. Nevertheless, this quadratic programming model can be difficult to solve. Our approach introduced in this paper is based on a piecewise linearization of the quadratic objective function. This integer programming model enables to include to the problem some other significant aspects of time coordination of bus arrivals. Therefore, the attention is aimed at the importance of continuity of bus arrivals on a set of bus stops. Integer programming model of the above mentioned problem will be presented in the following text and associated numerical experiments with real data will be presented too.

Keywords: public transport, coordination of bus arrivals, waiting time of passengers, integer programming.

JEL Classification: C44, C61

1 Introduction

Time coordination of bus arrivals can often be solved in public transport. One approach to problem-solving of this situation is to create an integer programming model. The really important question is: What may be the quality criteria? The first of these criteria can be formulated as a minimal time difference among successive arrivals of buses (Černý and Kluvánek, 1991). Furthermore, an iterative method can improve this basic approach. This so-called "cascade approach" is discussed in (Kozel and Kohání, 2010). The second criterion can be the total waiting time of passengers who need to wait at a bus stop (in passenger-minutes). The last named criterion is used in this case.

In general, n arrivals of vehicles at a stop can be considered in the designated period. Let t_i be an arrival time of vehicle i at the stop. The earliest possible arrival time of the vehicle i is denoted by a_i. This time may increase at most until the time $a_i + c_i$, where c_i is the maximum of possible shift of arrival at the stop. It is important to find such time positions of the individual arrivals, that the total passengers' waiting time has to be minimal.

Arrival times t_0 and t_n are fixed. The aim is to shift times t_i for $i = 1, ..., n-1$, so that the total waiting time of passengers (in passenger-minutes) must be minimal. Fig. 1 shows how the waiting time depends on the arrival time distribution in the time period $\langle t_0, t_n \rangle$. The grey colored

[1] Technical University of Ostrava/Faculty of Economics, Department of Mathematical Methods in Economics, Sokolská třída 33, 701 21 Ostrava 1, Czech Republic, petr.kozel@vsb.cz.
[2] Technical University of Ostrava/Faculty of Economics, Department of Mathematical Methods in Economics, Sokolská třída 33, 701 21 Ostrava 1, Czech Republic, sarka.michalcova@vsb.cz.

area represents the total waiting time of passengers who come at the stop in a given time period and wait for a bus.

The total waiting time of passengers in the period $\langle t_0, t_n \rangle$ can be expressed as:

$$\sum_{i=1}^{n} \frac{1}{2} f \left(t_i - t_{i-1}\right)^2 = \sum_{i=1}^{n} f \frac{1}{2} v_i^2 \ , \tag{1}$$

where the variable v_i represents the length of time interval between two succeeding arrivals t_{i-1} and t_i (for $i = 1, ..., n$) assuming that passengers arrive at the stop equally and uniformly with intensity f.

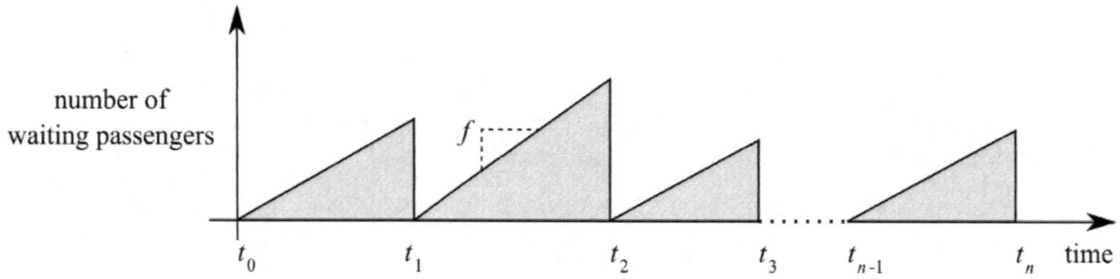

Figure 1 Waiting time of passengers during time period $\langle t_0, t_n \rangle$

2 Mathematical model of the basic problem

Firstly, our attention is focused on presentation of the basic problem. The introduce variable x_i (for $i = 1, ..., n-1$) represents a time shift of the arrival t_i from the earliest possible arrival time a_i. Then the mathematical model of this problem can be formulated as follows:

Minimize $$\frac{1}{2} f \sum_{i=1}^{n} v_i^2 \tag{2}$$

Subject to $$x_1 + a_1 - t_0 = v_1 \tag{3}$$

$$x_i + a_i - x_{i-1} - a_{i-1} = v_i \qquad \text{for } i = 2, ..., n-1 \tag{4}$$

$$t_n - x_{n-1} - a_{n-1} = v_n \tag{5}$$

$$x_i \le c_i \qquad \text{for } i = 1, ..., n-1 \tag{6}$$

$$x_i \in \mathbb{Z}_0^+ \qquad \text{for } i = 1, ..., n-1 \tag{7}$$

$$v_i \ge 0 \qquad \text{for } i = 1, ..., n \tag{8}$$

The condition (2) represents the objective function as the total waiting time of passengers who arrived at the stop. However, this objective function is non-linear. In this paper, the quadratic non-linear function (2) will be approximated by a piecewise linear function. This linearization approach has been analyzed in details in (Gábrišová, 2010), (Gábrišová and Kozel, 2010) and (Kozel and Gábrišová, 2011). The conditions (3) – (5) determine the shift between two consecutive arrivals as the relation between the values of the variables v_i and x_i. The conditions (6) provide that the shift of individual arrivals of buses does not exceed the allowed limit. The conditions (7) and (8) are obligatory and define the domain of variables.

The following issue follows the basic problem logically and corresponds with the requirements of practice. If there is a shift in arrival of a certain bus at one stop, it must also be a shift of the same bus at other stops. Hence, at the time coordinating, it is appropriate to take into account all stops that are operated by a specific vehicle and then to define necessary linkages.

3 Mathematical modeling of time coordination of bus arrivals on a set of bus stops

In the context of our problem solving, variable $n(k)$, where $k \in K$ and represents arrivals of vehicles at a stop in the considered time period. K is a set of bus stops in a traffic area and it is true that $k = 1, ..., p$, therefore $|K| = p$. Let $t_i(k)$ be an arrival time of vehicle i at the stop k, where $i = 1, ..., n(k)$, $k = 1, ..., p$. The earliest possible arrival time of the vehicle i is denoted by a_{ki}, where $i = 1, ..., n(k)-1$, $k = 1, ..., p$. This time may be increased until the time $a_{ki} + c_{ki}$, where c_{ki} is maximum of possible arrival shift at the stop, where $i = 1, ..., n(k)-1$, $k = 1, ..., p$. It is necessary to find such time positions of the individual arrivals, so that the total passengers' waiting time has to be minimal. The average value of incoming passengers at the stop is defined for each bus stop. The average value (intensity) of incoming passengers at the stop is denoted as f_k, where $k = 1, ..., p$.

The necessary linkages among individual bus arrivals, which are operated by the same vehicle, can be defined on the basis of bivalent matrix $b_{i(k)j(r)}$. If $b_{i(k)j(r)} = 1$, then the arrival time of vehicle i at stop k is dependent on the arrival time of vehicle j at stop r and it is necessary that $i = 1, ..., n(k)-1$, $j = 1, ..., n(r)-1$, where $k = 1, ..., p$, $r = 1, ..., p$ and $k \neq r$. If $b_{i(k)j(r)} = 0$ then the necessary linkages are not defined. Arrival times $t_0(k)$ and $t_n(k)$ are fixed. The aim is to shift times $t_i(k)$ for $i = 1, ..., n(k)-1$, $k = 1, ..., p$, so that the total waiting time of passengers at all bus stops (in passengers-minutes) is minimal. In the following text, there is shown the linearized mathematical model of time coordination of bus arrivals on a set of bus stops.

Variables x_{ki} (for $i = 1, ..., n(k)-1$, $k = 1, ..., p$) represent shift of $t_i(k)$ from the earliest possible arrival time a_{ki}. Consequently, mathematical model of the given problem solving can be defined as follows:

$$\textit{Minimize} \quad \frac{1}{2}\sum_{k=1}^{p} f_k \sum_{i=1}^{n(k)} \sum_{j=1}^{m(k,i)} (2j-1)u_{kij} \tag{9}$$

$$\textit{Subject to} \quad x_{k1} + a_{k1} - t_0(k) = \sum_{j=1}^{m(k,1)} u_{k1j} \qquad \text{for } k = 1, ..., p \tag{10}$$

$$x_{ki} + a_{ki} - x_{ki-1} - a_{ki-1} = \sum_{j=1}^{m(k,i)} u_{kij} \qquad \text{for } i = 2, ..., n(k)-1,\ k = 1, ..., p \tag{11}$$

$$t_n(k) - x_{kn(k)-1} - a_{kn(k)-1} = \sum_{j=1}^{m(k,n(k))} u_{kn(k)j} \qquad \text{for } k = 1, ... p \tag{12}$$

$$x_{ki} \le c_{ki} \qquad \text{for } i = 1, ..., n(k)-1, k = 1, ..., p \tag{13}$$

$$x_{ki} = x_{rj} \qquad \text{for } i = 1, ..., n(k)-1, j = 1, ..., n(r)-1,\ k = 1, ..., p,\ b_{i(k)j(r)} = 1 \tag{14}$$

$$u_{kij} \le 1 \qquad \text{for } i = 1, ..., n(k), j = 1, ..., m(k,i),\ k = 1, ..., p \tag{15}$$

$$x_{ki} \in \mathbb{Z}_0^+ \qquad \text{for } i = 1, ..., n(k)-1, k = 1, ..., p \tag{16}$$

$$u_{kij} \ge 0 \qquad \text{for } i = 1, ..., n(k), j = 1, ..., m(k,i),\ k = 1, ..., p \tag{17}$$

The quadratic function (2) is approximated by a piecewise linear function (9) with introducing new variables u_{kij} for $i = 1, ..., n(k)$, $j = 1, ..., m(k,i)$, $k = 1, ..., p$, subject to $\sum_{j=1}^{m(k,i)} u_{kij} = v_i$ for $i = 1, ..., n(k)$, $k = 1, ..., p$. Index notation $m(k,i)$ expresses maximal time between two arrivals i and $i-1$ at bus a stop k. The objective function (9) determines the total waiting time of passengers at all bus stops (in passengers-minutes). The conditions (10) – (12) determine the shift between two consecutive arrivals of bus links. The conditions (13) ensure that the shift of arrival time x_{ki} is limited by input constants c_{ki}. The conditions (14) ensure respecting of necessary linkages due to problem solving. The conditions (15) determine accuracy of auxiliary variable u_{kij}. Inequality $u_{kij} \le 1$ shows the accuracy of minutes. Remaining conditions (16) and (17) are obligatory.

4 Numerical experiment

Computational experiments, which were realized under practical conditions, are briefly described in the following text. Time coordination of bus arrivals on the set of bus stops was implemented in selected public transport area in Frýdek-Místek. Calculations were made for two parallel directions: 1) Frýdek-Místek – Dobrá – Raškovice and 2) Frýdek-Místek – Skalice – Raškovice. Each of two mentioned directions contains three significant stops (thus in total six stops), at which the time coordination of bus arrivals was implemented at the same time. There were defined some necessary linkages for each triples of stops (namely continuity of bus arrivals) that had to be preserved. Moreover, the necessary linkages among parallel directions at the bus stop Raškovice were defined. Furthermore, passengers transfer in individual directions at this stop. Whole problem is captured in detail in Fig. 2 and Fig. 3.

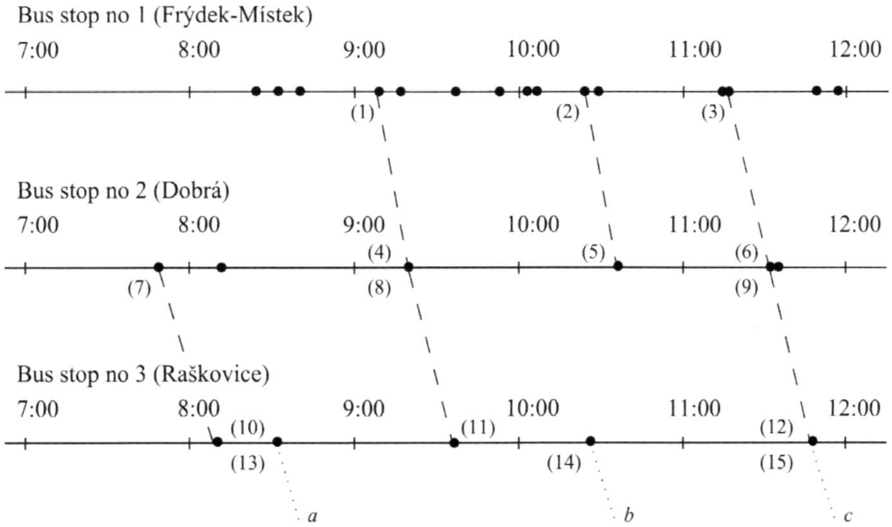

Figure 2 Transport direction F-M - Dobrá - Raškovice

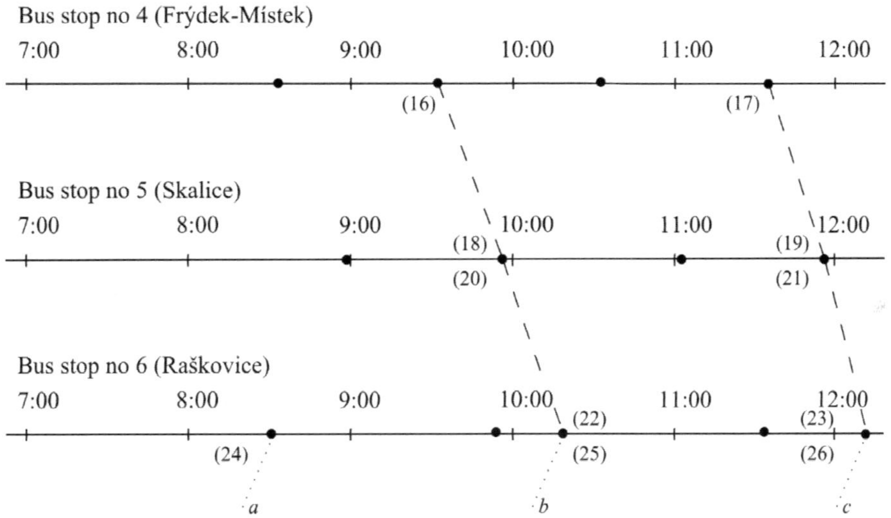

Figure 3 Transport direction F-M - Skalice - Raškovice

Each of the stops is shown by a horizontal line with time interval limitation. The black dots show arrival times of buses at each stop. In addition to the above, arrivals of buses, feasible shift of which is intertwined (the necessary linkage), are indicated by dashed lines. Each of the necessary linkages is marked with a serial number in a bracket. As already mentioned above, passengers may transfer in both directions at the bus stop. So, the arrivals of some buses are intertwined in both directions at this stop. This is indicated by dotted lines labelled as *a*, *b* and *c*.

Table 1 summarizes details regarding to the individual bus stops, at which the time coordination of bus arrivals was implemented. This table contains the number of a bus stop k, the average intensity of arrival passengers at the bus stop (per time unit) f_k, bus arrivals at the stop $n(k)$ and the number of necessary linkages $l(k)$.

Bus stop no. k	f_k **[pass/min]**	$n(k)$	$l(k)$
1	1.25	15	3
2	0.4	6	6
3	0.14	5	6
4	0.34	4	2
5	0.1	4	4
6	0.14	5	5

Table 1 Description of individual bus stops

Table 2 summarizes the results of numerical experiments. In each table we can find information about the specific bus stop. Evaluation criterion for comparing of the obtained results is the total number of waiting passengers-minutes at the bus stop (calculated according to (1)). Moreover, three options have been compared at each bus stop: the default variant – before process coordination, the variant A – time coordination of bus arrivals at the specific stop, model (2) – (8), the variant B – time coordination on a set of stops, model (9) – (17). Percentage improvement is also shown in the options A and B towards the default variant.

Bus stop no. k	**Variants**	**Total waiting time [pass.* min]**	**Improvement of default variant [%]**
1	Default variant	5591.25	-
	Variant A	4620	17.37
	Variant B	4851.25	13.23
2	Default variant	4357	-
	Variant A	3355.4	22.99
	Variant B	3619	16.94
3	Default variant	1507.24	-
	Variant A	1376.06	8.7
	Variant B	1402.52	6.95
4	Default variant	2925.53	-
	Variant A	2919.07	0.22
	Variant B	2930.63	-0.17
5	Default variant	911.05	-
	Variant A	906.05	0.55
	Variant B	909.35	0.19
6	Default variant	1219.61	-
	Variant A	1057.49	13.29
	Variant B	1065.47	12.64

Table 2 Results of numerical experiments

5 Conclusion

The present paper has been devoted to the time coordination of bus arrivals on a set of bus stops. As first there has been introduced mathematical model of the basic problem in the text and then mathematical model for the time coordination of bus arrivals on a set of stops. Computational experiment with both mathematical models was specifically realized for conditions of public transport in Frýdek-Místek. In fact, it was the time coordination of bus arrivals at 6 selected stops, which were operated by the same vehicles. There were used 39 bus arrivals and 26 necessary linkages for the time coordination. Computational experiment was realized in optimization software FICO Xpress. To compare both variants: obtained results of the mathematical model for time coordination of bus arrivals on a set of stops have been better in 5 cases in comparison with the default state. The result has been worse only in one case: the bus stop no. 4. It has been caused by necessary linkages, which reduce a set of feasible solutions. Admittedly, a significant benefit of our approach is that the solution is completely real with the restrictions from the practice. And finally in the context of time: all computational times for solved problems were under 1 second.

Acknowledgements

This paper was supported within Operational Programme Education for Competitiveness – Project No. CZ.1.07/2.3.00/20.0296 and programme for the support of applied research and experimental development, Technology Agency of the Czech Republic (EPSILON): 'Effective approaches to economical and adaptable systems of maintenance and operation of transport networks' TH02010930.

References

Černý, J. and Kluvánek, P. (1991). *Basis of Mathematical Transport Theory.* Bratislava: VEDA, (in Slovak).

Gábrišová, L. (2010). 'Accuracy of Solution of Some Non-linear Problems by a Piecewise Linear Approximation'. *Proceedings of workshop 'Problems of Discrete Optimization for Transport'*, Pardubice, Czech Republic, pp. 43-51, (in Slovak).

Gábrišová, L. and Kozel, P. (2010). 'Accuracy of Linear Approximation Used in Non-linear Problem Optimization'. *Journal of Information Control and Management Systems of the University of Žilina,* 6 (4), pp. 301-310.

Janáček, J. (2003). *Mathematical Programming.* Žilina: EDIS (in Czech).

Kozel, P. and Gábrišová, L. (2011). 'Minimization of Passengers Waiting Time by Vehicle Shedule Adjustment'. *Proceedings of 9th European Conference of Young Research and Scientific Workers TRANSCOM,* Žilina, Slovak, pp. 103-106.

Kozel, P. and Koháni, M. (2010). 'Using Cascade Approach to the Coordination of Bus Arrivals'. *Proceedings of 'Problems of Discrete Optimization for Transport'*, Pardubice, Czech Republic, pp. 119-130, (in Czech).

Kozel, P. (2012). 'Traffic of Public Mass Transport System Time Network Coordination'. *Thesis.* Technical University of Ostrava, (in Czech).

Xpress-MP Manual (2005). 'Getting started'. Dash Associates, UK: Blisworth.

Xpress-Mosel (2005). 'User Guide. Dash Associates, UK: Blisworth.

Advanced setting of supply policies by discovering knowledge from data using Orange

Eva Krhač, Benjamin Urh, Matjaž Maletič, Matjaž Roblek [1]

Abstract. In this paper we analyzed the needs for inventory in enterprises and presented the optimal method for managing inventory in the case of Gumitehna Ltd. In the selection and analysis of criteria that affect the determination of the optimal policy of supply and inventory management we used the business intelligence tool Orange. We have found that the model is useful in practice.

Keywords: Inventory Management, Supply Policies, Knowledge Discovery from Data.

JEL Classification: M15, O14

1 Introduction

Inventory management in trading enterprises is dedicated to avoiding under- and over-inventory. The aim is to find inventory levels which allowing to achieve a high level of customer servicing and at the same time does not significantly increase the volume of funds tied in inventory (Grčar, 2010). From the perspective of warehouse management, inventory is understood as a certain quantity of goods, deferred or stored at a designated place - the warehouse in the enterprise (Ljubič, 2000). Optimal inventory should be with minimal inventory costs at maximum business reliability (Završnik, 2008). The level of optimal inventory is constantly changing and is dependent on the several of changing factors which have an impact on inventory (Grčar, 2010). So, when product comes through the various stages of its life cycle, one static and once specified model of inventory management is not optimal.

From the perspective of the level of servicing customers are important individual parameters of each product by which we provide desired level. From the perspective of inventory management of enterprise, it is important that inventory of products with similar characteristics, is determined by the same purchasing policy, because we want to unify ordering procedures and only automate ordering (increase the efficiency of inventory management). The aim is to consume as little as possible sources for determining the most optimal inventory. In this case, we need criteria according to which the products will be defined and classified in the groups and then will be identified the most appropriate inventory management policies for them. It is also important to detect timely changes in parameters (market or supply) and on the basis of these changes to choose other supply policy of individual products so that they will be classified in a more optimal group.

In the literature, there are models which on the basis of different criteria classify products and distribute supply policies. The models determine the size of inventory and provide the optimum level in accordance with best practice (Stevenson, 2015). The aim of the research was

[1] University of Maribor, Faculty of Organizational Sciences, Enterprise Engineering Laboratory, Kidriceva 55a, Kranj, Slovenia, eva.krhac1@um.si, benjamin.urh@fov.uni-mb.si, matjaz.maletic@fov.uni-mb.si, majaz.roblek@um.si.

to find a more advanced way of processing information about the products and the determination of inventory management policies. For this purpose, we tested the adequacy of the tool Orange, which is an open-source tool for the visualization and data analysis. The tool Orange has been developed at the University of Ljubljana, Faculty of Computer Science, Laboratory of Bioinformatics and is useful for supporting Knowledge Discovery from Data - nontrivial process of discovering implicit, previously unknown and potentially useful knowledge from data (Kljajić, 2015). The basic idea is to develop a system or tools for review of big data, discovering patterns and legality in these data, and on the basis of this forecasting future value.

As a real example, we used an enterprise Gumitehna Ltd., whose primary activity is the sale of industrial rubber products (retail, wholesale) in Slovenia, the European Union and in the former Yugoslavia (Kovač, 2012). The main problem of the enterprise is inventory management – they are faced with excessive inventory of certain products and also with shortages in the inventory of other products. The overstock causes them unnecessary inventory costs and storage costs and on the other side, the understock causes the cost of a lack of stock and consequently loss of customers. Current practice in inventory management policy is on the basis of qualitative method, which is primarily based on the subjective assessment of the enterprise director, sales staff and managers. When the stock of the product is reduced, they ordered new stocks based on a consideration of the delivery time and price of the product. With the help of tool Orange we wanted to get a set of inventory management policies, suitable for enterprise Gumitehna Ltd.

2 Methodology

In the first part we carried out theoretical study of the scientific literature and materials in the area of inventory management, in which we studied their meaning, types and possible costs. We have also studied inventory management policies and indicators of inventory management. In the second, empirical part, we suggested appropriate inventory management policies for specific groups of products. First, we made an analysis of the current state of inventory management in the enterprise Gumitehna d.o.o.: we demonstrated business model, explained the existing inventory management policies, and demonstrated the current state of inventory (Krhač, 2016). The necessary data were obtained from enterprise - part of the data from interviews with employees in the enterprise and the second part of the data (about products) we exported from enterprise information system VASCO to the Microsoft Excel tool. Products were categorized on the basis of eight criteria. Then we used the tool Orange for basic statistics and identifying the order of importance of the selected criteria. We proposed inventory management policies on the basis of theoretical research, comparisons with existing cases, researched quantitative methods of forecasting, and on the experiences and suggestions of employees in the enterprise.

3 Results

Based on previous research, we have decided to split products on the basis of the following criteria: A-B-C analysis, x-y-z analysis, seasonal changes, size of the product, product life cycle, the origin of the supplier, product delivery time and continued delivery of the product. We wanted to know which criteria are most important for the division of products? The assumption was that we could make two groups regarding the importance of the following criteria:

- very important criteria: A-B-C analysis, x-y-z analysis, product life cycle, product delivery time;
- less important criteria: seasonal changes, the size of the product, the origin of the supplier, continued delivery of the product.

First, we developed a data model in the tool Orange, which was composed of discrete data - attributes (our eight criteria) and three decision-making classes:

- products ordered on the basis of statistical calculations;
- products ordered on the basis of past experience;
- products are not ordered in stock.

Table 1 shows the rules according to which we made classes.

Decision classes	A-B-C	x-y-z	Life cycle	Delivery time
Products ordered on the basis of statistical calculations	for A products; for B products; for C products	x, y and z; x, y and z; x and y	all 3 phases	all delivery times
Products ordered on the basis of past experience	C	z	Z, P	all delivery times
Products are not ordered in stock	C	z	P	1 - 4 weeks

Table 1 Characteristics specific criteria for the decision-making classes

Decisional classes were determined on the basis of four criteria (attributes), which we assumed to be more important. "Rules" for the selected four criteria (attributes) have been identified on the basis of the researched literature. Selected data are consistent and the data model does not contain the missing or unknown values - all these values were replaced with the most probable, because that impose rules for the preparation of data to import them into the tool Orange. Designed data model was imported into the tool Orange.

Then we used the visualization Linear Projection, which visually shows the criteria (attributes) which affect on individual decisions class (Figure 1). On class "ordering on the basis of past experience" particularly have impact A-B-C analysis and x-y-z analysis and less, seasonal changes and continued delivery of the product. A-B-C analysis and x-y-z analysis have primarily impact when the product are not ordered in stock. On class "ordering on the basis of statistical calculations" have affect all of the selected criteria (attributes).

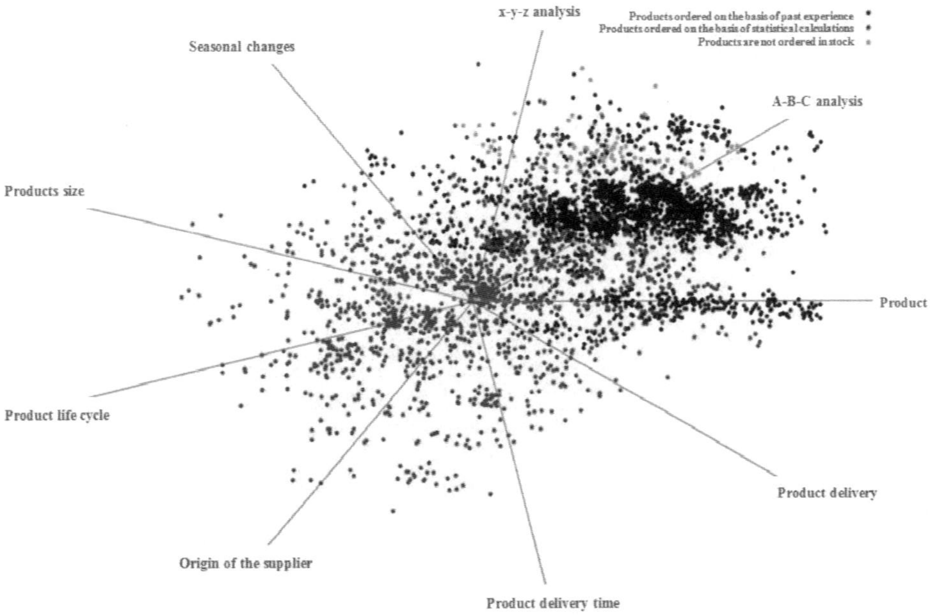

Figure 1 Linear Projection

Then we used the nomogram through which we found answers to questions about the importance of individual criteria. For products which can be ordered (in the future) based on past experience (Figure 2), more important criteria are: A-B-C analysis, x-y-z analysis, product delivery time and product life cycle. For products which can be ordered on the basis of statistical calculations, more important criteria are: A-B-C analysis, x-y-z analysis, product life cycle, and product delivery time. For products which do not need to be ordered on stock, more important criteria are: seasonal changes, product life cycle, the size of the product and product delivery time. When products are ordering on stock, continued delivery of the product and seasonal changes are less important:

- ordering based on past experience – last and penultimate criteria;
- ordering based on statistical calculations – penultimate and last criteria.

In the case that the products are subscribed on stock, more important are A-B-C analysis, x-y-z analysis, product delivery time and product life cycle.

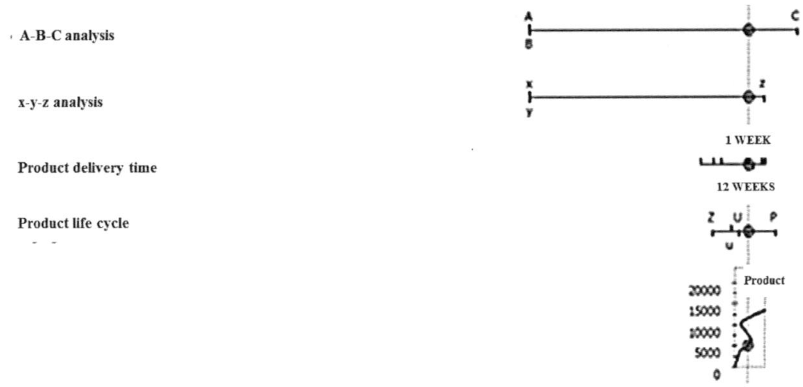

Figure 2 Nomogram

Then we used the algorithm CN2, which on the basis of case studies, showing the rules for further ordering stock and regularly ordering. Based on the data model, we found that 100% of the orders are made on the basis of past experience, where the product is C, z and not seasonal. 100% of the orders are made on the basis of statistical calculations, where product is B or A. 99% of orders are not subscribed to the stock when the product is C, seasonal, declining and its delivery time is one week.

We measured the accuracy of the classifiers which are used for classifying new cases based on a plurality of already classified cases. We used four classifiers (Naive Bayes, CN2 Rules, KNN and Classification Tree) and three dimensions for the assessment of learning (CA, AUC, Brier). CA (classification accuracy) shows the ratio between the number of correctly predicted examples and the total number of predicted examples. In numbers, this means that the objective of classification accuracy is to obtain higher rating, because higher rating means a better quality of predicted examples. AUC (area under the ROC curve) displays the probability that a classifier correctly distinguish between positive and negative examples - again, the aim is to get the highest rating (closer to the number 1.0000). Brier rating across all test cases evaluates the difference between the target and actual predicted distribution. The ideal situation is when classifier always accurately predicts the correct class, which shows us the number 0.0000. Therefore, an objective is that the Brier rating is closer to 0.0000. In the case of classifier CN2 rules and kNN, we identified overfitting (if the CA and AUC are equal to 1.0000 and Brier is equal to 0.0000), which means that classifiers too adapted to data from the training set and they made the bad results for the new data (Kljajić, 2015). As we can see in Table 2, the best rating has the Naive Bayes classifier, which calculates the conditional probability for each class (given values for all attributes) for the new example.

Method	**CA**	**AUC**	**Brier**
Naive Bayes	0.9981	1.0000	0.0104
CN2 rules	1.0000	1.0000	0.0000
kNN	1.0000	1.0000	0.0000
Classification Tree	0.9803	0.9988	0.0241

Table 2 The accuracy of classifiers

Then we used the Confusion Matrix, which contains information about actual and classified prediction of the system. The matrix is quality assessment of classification model, which in our case is represented by Naive Bayes. Confusion Matrix is for class "ordering on the basis of past experience" achieved 100% correct answers, for "ordering on the basis of statistical calculations" achieved 96% correct answers and for "not ordering in stock" achieved 100% correct answers.

	Products ordered on the basis of past experience	Products ordered on the basis of statistical calculations	Products are not ordered in stock	
Products ordered on the basis of past experience	100.0%	0.4%	0.0%	1.302
Products ordered on the basis of statistical calculations	0.0%	99.6%	0.0%	1.204
Products are not ordered in stock	0.0%	0.0%	100.0%	80
	1.297	1.209	80	2.586

Table 3 Confusion Matrix

In the end we made prediction, which helped us to establish how well the model predicts, how well the model is reliable. For this we used 12 random examples of products - four for each type of ordering. Based on the prediction, it was found that all three classifiers (KNN, Naive Bayes and Classification Tree) are accurately predicted all 12 randomly selected examples.

4 Discussion

The classification of material items in groups x, y, z in combination with classification in classes A, B, C is important in the (Roblek, 2013) planning of material needs, determining the quantities of supply, ordering in the renewal of inventories, issuing material in the manufacturing operations and record the accounting of consumption. In the effective management of inventories, we are interested about two pieces of information - when to order and how much to order (Ljubič, 2000).

On the basis of theoretical research, we learned the characteristics of individual inventory management policies and this has helped us in determining which policy is suitable for managing individual inventories. The following is a proposal of changes in the management of inventories in the enterprise Gumitehna Ltd., which includes the use of both, qualitative and quantitative methods to predict demand. For individual products we suggest the use of quantitative methods, which should give sufficiently precise forecast of demand. The suggestion is presented in Table 3. Example of the interpretation of Table 3: For A, x products, mature or declining, and with all delivery times we recommend the model of optimal economic quantity of order by considering of quantity discounts.

For all other combinations we propose the use of both, qualitative and quantitative methods of forecasting in demand. For enterprise is mainly useful sales staffs forecast, who predict by the use of knowledge and experience. Of course, it is necessary protecting enterprise against partiality staff, so we suggest the use of specific tools and utilities to obtain data and information on individual occurrences. For the enterprise we consider that the most useful and simple are market research of the products, life cycle analysis and the analogy with the past, the same or similar products. We suggest that in the prediction of demand, they use both methods and then compare the results. In the case that the results are very different, they can be sure that it was wrong prediction (or that the selected method is imprecise). Then, they can choose another way of forecasting demands or can be applied to any additional method.

	Deterministic planning		
	X	**Y**	**Z**
A	Model economically optimal quantity of order by considering of quantity discounts *Mature, declining; all delivery times* *(90.36 % Ax products)*	Model economically optimal quantity of order based on the average *Mature, declining; all delivery times* *(78.67 % Ay products)*	
B	Sourcing small quantities, which covering the needs of each of the forward units *Mature, declining; delivery time to 1 week (27.50 % Bxvz products)* Sourcing large quantities, which cover the needs of more forward units *Mature, declining; delivery time of at least 2 weeks (28.93 % Bxyz products)*		
C	*Stohastic planning*		*Deterministic planning*
	Q model - continuous monitoring of stock *Mature, declining; shorter delivery times* *(22.22 % Cx products)*	Q model - continuous monitoring of stock *Mature, declining; shorter delivery times* *(44.12 % Cy products)*	Ordering the actual needs *Mature, declining; shorter delivery times* *(61.25 % Cz products)*
	P model - periodic monitoring of stock *Mature, declining; longer delivery times* *(55.56 % Cx products)*		

Table 4 Appropriate inventory management policies for specific characteristics of criteria

In the end, we have examined in what percentages can be improved inventory management and found that the proposed changes accurately manage inventory in at least 44% of the products from the group. We considered only the changes in the use of quantitative methods. In management of the remaining inventories helps the use of two types of methods.

5 Conclusion

With the model and algorithms within the tool Orange, we can correctly predict more than 99.6% of cases. The objectives that we set ourselves at the beginning of work with the tool have been achieved, which means that the model is useful in practice.

We must not forget the potential to improve the data model in the future, which we see in most relevant sample - all the decision classes should have the same number of examples (currently, the first two decisions of the class had far greater number of examples than has an third decision-making class.

For the introduction of the proposed changes, some conditions should be completed. For good inventory management, it is necessary to know characteristics of the products, so it is necessary to have access to quality information about products. It is also important to constantly conducting statistics about forecasts in the past, which provides an overview of forecast accuracy and enables rapid adaptation to changes.

In the management of inventories it is necessary to consider all changes in inventories and several times repeat the procedure from empirical work - we suggest that the procedure is repeated once per year. In repetition of the procedure can be introduced changes. The first change, which would make sense, is change in the determination of criteria - criteria, which have proved to be less important, may be excluded from the study and it may also be used a new criterion. It would also be necessary to prepare a table of individual analysis and calculations (eg. Microsoft Excel). For the needs of this research most analysis has been performed in Microsoft Excel, for which we need a lot of time, because we are set up all tables for the first time. We should also mention the fact that we had the most difficulties in preparing the data for the empirical part in current information system VASCO, because it does not allow access to the necessary information or employees are spending more time than had been anticipated for searching data. Therefore, as the last amendment, which would in the future have contributed to faster and higher quality analysis, we suggest investment in upgrading the information system. Upgrading of the information system should allow easy and quick access to all information about past products.

Acknowledgements

We would like to thank Laboratory of Enterprise Engineering on Faculty of Organizational Sciences and Gumitehna Ltd.

References

Grčar, G. (2010). 'Inventory management in the enterprise Toko d.o.o.'. *Bachelor thesis*. Ljubljana: University of Ljubljana, Faculty of Economics, pp. 9.

Kovač, E. (2012). 'Analysis of the financial statements with indicators'. *Bachelor thesis*. Bled: Higher Vocational College for Hospitality and Tourism, pp. 5.

Krhač, E. (2016). 'Inventory management policies at Gumitehna Ltd.'. *Master thesis*. Kranj: University of Maribor, Faculty for Organizational Sciences, pp. 21-34.

Ljubič, T. (2000). *Planning and production management: models, methods, data*. Kranj: Moderna organizacija, pp. 347-361.

Stevenson, J. S. (2015). *Operations Management: Inventory Management*. New York: McGraw-Hill, pp. 546-582.

Kljajić Borštnar, M. (2015). *Knowledge Discovery from Data - lecture notes*. Kranj: University of Maribor, Faculty for Organizational Sciences.

Roblek, M. (2013). *Predicting, planning and operational business management - lecture notes*. Kranj: University of Maribor, Faculty for Organizational Sciences.

Završnik, B. (2008). *Management of purchasing and supply chains*. Maribor: Faculty of Economics and Business, pp. 61.

Comparison of logistic regression and decision tree for customer churn prediction in Telecommunications

Jan Manďák[1]

Abstract. Customer churn, loss of customers due to switch to another service provider or non-renewal of commitment, is very common in highly competitive and saturated markets such as telecommunications. In order to solve this problem, predictive models need to be implemented to identify customers who are at risk of churning and also key drivers of churn need to be identified. In this study, two models for prediction of customer churn in next 45 days are compared – logistic regression and decision tree. The dataset used contain 16 variables and 50,000 customers in both training and testing data set. Decision tree outperformed in predictive performance logistic regression with hit rate 81.1% and specificity 94%. The most important variables in both classification models were customer duration and contract duration and in logistic regression model also value added services played a big role.

Keywords: Churn Prediction, Telecommunications, Logistic Regression, Decision Tree, Predictive Performance, Variable Importance.

JEL Classification: C38

1 Introduction

The term "customer churn" is used to indicate those customers who are about to leave for a new competitor, or end their subscription. It is an expensive problem in many industries since acquiring new customers' costs five to six times more than retaining existing ones (Hudaib et al., 2015). Retaining existing customers is important, because it is easier to sell to an existing customers, than to attract and sell a new one. Building customer loyalty is also a key performance indicator for all businesses. There are two types of churn - *voluntary churn* is defined in the first sentence, while *involuntary churn* means customer disconnected by the operator, typically due to nonpayment or fraud reasons. Customer churn in telecommunications industry is really hot topic, because it is saturated market and it is therefore difficult to attract new customers and because it is relatively easy to switch to another company (Canale and Lunardon, 2014).

With the still decreasing costs of data storage, telecommunications companies have access to various data sources, which can be beneficial for analysis of customer churn. Traditional transactional data stored in databases can be combined with unstructured data such as complaints or feedback scraped from social networks or call recordings. These data are used to create predictive models with the use of algorithms such as logistic regression, decision trees, random forests or neural networks. Predictive models can help decision makers to identify customers who are likely to churn, and when (Balasubramanian and Selvarani, 2014). Telecommunication companies can then offer customers new incentives to stay. But it is not sufficient to only predict, which customers will likely churn, but also what are the key factors causing churn. With this knowledge in hands marketing departments can target retention campaigns to the right customer groups and can also change the whole base of services.

[1] VŠB-Technical University of Ostrava/Faculty of Economics, Department of Systems Engineering, Sokolská třída 33, 701 21 Ostrava, jan.mandak@gmail.com

2 Exploratory Data Analysis

Data for this study were obtained from European telecommunications operator. Raw input data for this task are stored in various production systems. The process of preparing data into the form suitable for modelling consists of the three traditional steps (ETL) – extract data from source systems, transform it and load it into data warehouse. There are two types of input variables, according to its original systems – demographic data and data related to the usage of various services. Into the demographic group we can assign variables listed in Table 1.

Variable name	Description
birthYear	Customer's year of birth
delinquent	Whether a customer has problem with paying bills
duration	How long a customer is customer of the company
accType	Type of account
creditLimit	Amount of money, which can customer utilize over regular payment
contractDuration	Date when contract ends

Table 1 Demographic variables

There are following variables in the service usage group of input variables, see Table 2. It is important to note that all averages are monthly averages.

Variable name	Description
avgInvoice	Average amount of invoice
avgExtra3	Average overpayment for last 3 months
avgExtra6	Average overpayment for last 6 months
avgExtra12	Average overpayment for last 12 months
avgData	Average data consumed (GB's)
avgVoice	Average voice consumed (min's)
avgSMS	Average number of SMS consumed
avgMMS	Average number of MMS consumed
VAS	Whether the customer has value added services
portout	Whether the customer left company or not

Table 2 Service usage variables

It is common in creation of predictive model to divide data sets into training data set and testing data set. In this task, data sets were created with respect to the time to simulate behaviour of predictive model in real world application. At first, explanatory variables were computed in time X. Because in time X we know the date of future portout, we can easily compute, which customers will leave company in 45 days after the date X and which won't. Then the same proccess was applied to create testing data set (see Fig. 1). In each data set there are approximately 50,000 customers. Finally, training data set is used to create predictive model and testing data set is used to test the predictive performance.

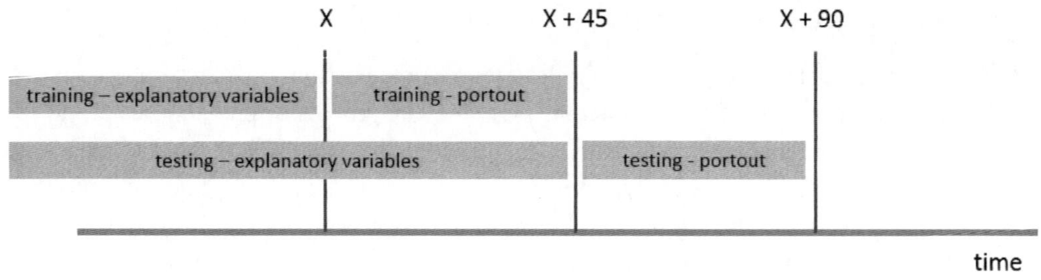

Figure 1 Training and testing data sets

In this chapter, variables in training data set are graphically analyzed to explore some interesting patterns and to get a view of how the data look like. This step is typically applied before modeling and can help inform the development of more complex predictive models. Two density plots for variables, where the differences between churners and non-churners are the biggest are shown (see Fig. 2). Blue density curve represents customers, which ported out, pink density curve represents customer, which stayed. It is evident that churned customers are younger and are with company lower time. It is also important to note, that the proportion of customers which left in the training data set is very low (785 out of 51,130, it means 1.535%). The reason is that we are looking at limited time period of 45 days, annual churn rate is higher.

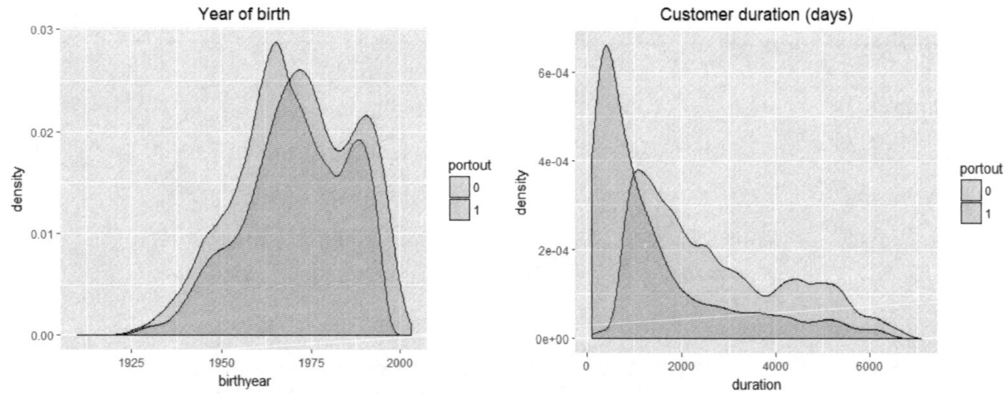

Figure 2 Kernel density plots (own calculation)

From the left chart in the Fig. 3 we can see that customers with account types BG and TM didn't churn (portout = 0). The majority (779 out of 785) of customers, which left company, had account type P. In the right chart it is clear that all churned customers didn't have value added services. It is evident that quality of value added services is not a reason for churn.

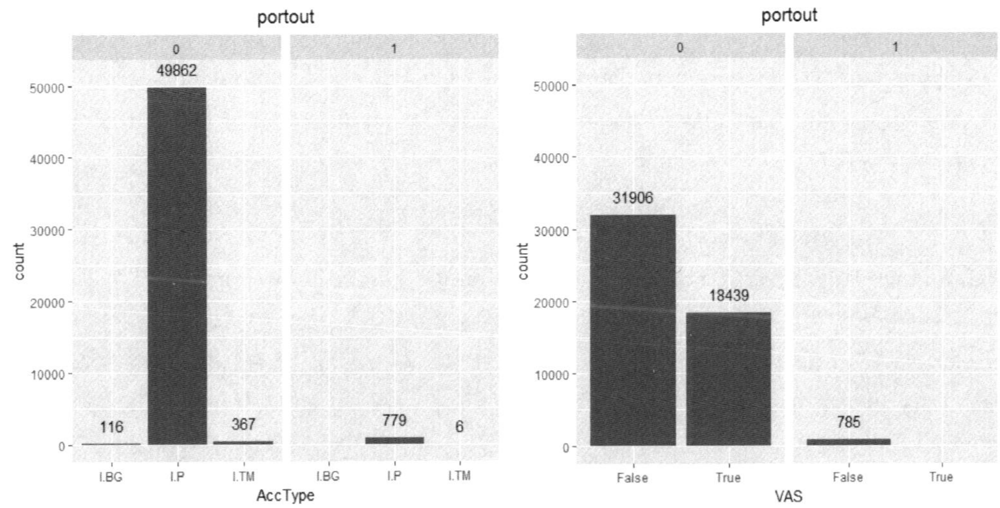

Figure 3 Differences between categorical variables (own calculation)

3 Classification models and performance metrics

In this chapter the theory of two classification models, compared in this study, logistic regression and decision trees, is shortly explained. Then from variety of performance metrics these metrics are chosen and described: *accuracy*, *hit rate (precision)* and *sensitivity (recall)*.

Logistic regression is a regression model where the dependent variable is categorical (James, 2013). The logistic regression model is used to estimate the probability of binary/categorical response based on one or more predictors. The logistic regression model is of the form of logistic function. Form with *n* explanatory variable is the following (1):

$$log\left(\frac{p(X)}{1-p(X)}\right) = \beta_0 + \beta_1 X_1 + \dots + \beta_n X_n, \tag{1}$$

where the left hand side is called *logit* or *log odds*. Increasing *X* by one unit changes the log odds by β_1, or equivalently it multiplies the odds by e^{β_1}. If β_1 is positive then increasing *X* will be associated with increasing *p(X)*, and if β_1 is negative then increasing *X* will be associated with decreasing *p(X)*. In logistic regression, parameters β are estimated to maximize the *likelihood function*.

Decision trees use a tree-logic to make predictions and can be expressed as a set of IF-THEN rules (Ledolter, 2013). The tree is generally presented upside down, with the root at the top and the leaves at the bottom. Starting from the root, the tree splits from the single trunk into two or more branches. Each branch itself might further split into two or more branches. This continues until we reach a leaf, which is a node that is not further split. We refer to the split of a branch as a node of the tree. The root and leaves are also referred to as nodes (Williams, 2011).

Recursive binary splitting is a method to grow a classification tree. Criterion for the splitting is the classification error rate (2). Classification error rate is simply the fraction of the training observations in that region that do not belong to the most common class:

$$E = 1 - \max_{k}(\hat{p}_{mk}) \tag{2}$$

In the equation (2) $\hat{p}_{mk}$ represents the proportion of training observations in the *m-th* region that are from the *k*-th class. More sophisticated measure for growing the tree is e.g. Gini index (3):

$$G = \sum_{k=1}^{K} \hat{p}_{mk}(1 - \hat{p}_{mk}) \tag{3}$$

Gini index is referred to as measure of node purity – a small value indicates that a node contains predominantly observations from a single class.

Advantages of decision trees are e.g. that they are easy to understand, can be displayed graphically or can handle both numerical and categorical variables (James, 2013). *Disadvantages* of decision trees are e.g. problem of over fitting or that value of numerical variables is to some extent lost.

In this study the most known performance metric – *accuracy* – is not sufficient. Two other metrics, *hit rate (precision)* and *sensitivity (recall)*, are much more important. All these metrics can be computed from information available in *confusion matrix* (Lantz, 2013). It is a table that categorizes predictions according to whether they match the actual value in the data (see Table 3). One dimension indicates the possible categories of predicted values while the other dimension indicates the same for actual values. There are four categories in 2 x 2 confusion matrix:

- True Positive (TP): Correctly classified as the class of interest;
- True Negative (TN): Correctly classified as not the class of interest;
- False Positive (FP): Incorrectly classified as the class of interest;
- False Negative (FN): Incorrectly classified as not the class of interest.

Confusion matrix		**Actual**	
		stay	**leave**
Prediction	**stay**	TN	FN
	leave	FP	TP

Table 3 Confusion matrix (Lantz, 2013)

As a logical following step, performance metrics, which can be computed from confusion matrices, are described and computed for our three scenarios (Lantz, 2013).

- Accuracy – the proportion of predictions, which were right. It is the sum of true positives and true negatives divided by the total number of customers (4):

$$Accuracy = \frac{TP+TN}{TP+TN+FP+FN}. \tag{4}$$

- Hit rate – the proportion of predictions of the class of interest, which were right. In our case it is a proportion of customers, where model predicted that they should churn, and they really churned. The company will focus its retention activities to these customers. Formally it is ratio of true positives and sum of true positives and false positives (5):

$$Hit\ rate\ (precision) = \frac{TP}{TP+FP}. \tag{5}$$

- Sensitivity - the proportion of churned customers which were correctly classified. Formally it is calculated as the ratio of true positives and sum of true positives and false negatives (6):

$$Sensitivity\ (recall) = \frac{TP}{TP+FN}. \tag{6}$$

4 Description of estimated models

In this chapter predictive models created using training data set are described. For logistic regression there are no parameters to tune, but for decision tree there is one tuning parameter – complexity parameter *cp*. Therefore *10-fold cross validation* is used to tune this parameter (Kuhn, 2016). The process of parameter tuning has the following steps (see Fig. 4).

```
Define sets of model parameter values to evaluate
for each parameter set do
    for each resampling iteration do
        Hold–out specific samples
        [Optional] Pre–process the data
        Fit the model on the remainder
        Predict the hold–out samples
    end
    Calculate the average performance across hold–out predictions
end
Determine the optimal parameter set
Fit the final model to all the training data using the optimal parameter set
```

Figure 4 Parameter tuning (Kuhn, 2016)

First model created for churn prediction was logistic regression model. Regression coefficients estimated using maximum likelihood method are in Fig. 5.

```
Coefficients:
                    Estimate Std. Error z value Pr(>|z|)    
(Intercept)       -3.149e+01  1.598e+03  -0.020  0.98428    
birthyear          8.000e-03  2.764e-03   2.894  0.00380 ** 
contractDuration   4.530e-03  1.672e-04  27.101  < 2e-16 ***
delinquenttrue     7.945e-01  2.712e-01   2.930  0.00339 ** 
duration          -4.148e-04  3.395e-05 -12.218  < 2e-16 ***
AccTypeI.P         1.486e+01  1.598e+03   0.009  0.99258    
AccTypeI.TM        1.596e+01  1.598e+03   0.010  0.99203    
averageInvoice12  -1.120e-04  1.383e-04  -0.810  0.41794    
averageExtra12    -4.854e-04  1.048e-03  -0.463  0.64327    
averageExtra6     -3.016e-04  1.155e-03  -0.261  0.79394    
averageExtra3      6.611e-04  5.387e-04   1.227  0.21970    
averageData        1.834e-06  1.500e-06   1.222  0.22170    
averageVoice      -1.028e-03  4.188e-04  -2.455  0.01409 *  
averageSms         4.569e-03  2.420e-03   1.888  0.05907 .  
averageMms        -4.972e-02  5.802e-02  -0.857  0.39148    
VASTrue           -1.904e+01  1.822e+02  -0.105  0.91675    
---
Signif. codes:  0 '***' 0.001 '**' 0.01 '*' 0.05 '.' 0.1 ' ' 1
```

Figure 5 Estimates of logistic regression coefficients (own calculation)

According to *p-values* < 0.05, there are 5 explanatory variables, which are statistically significant. Estimated regression coefficients suggest, that higher values of *contractDuration*, *birthyear* increases the probability of churn. Also when the customer has variable *delinquent* equal to TRUE, than there is higher probability of churn. On the other hand, higher values of *duration* and *averageVoice* decreases the probability of churn.

To avoid problem of overfitting, complexity parameter *cp* was tuned using *10-fold cross validation* to achieve the biggest *Accuracy* and set to value 0.011 (Fig. 6).

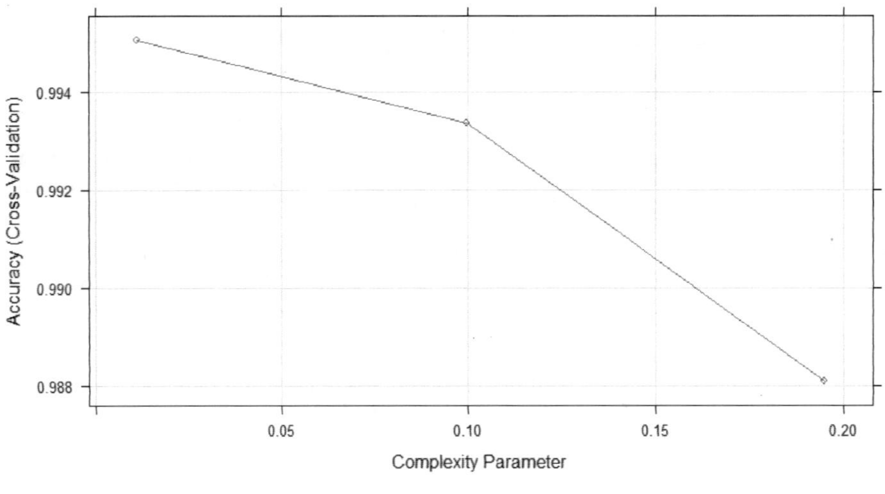

Figure 6 Tuning of complexity parameter (own calculation)

In the following Figure 7 we can see final decision tree. Final chart was created using function *fancyRpartPlot* from the *Rattle* package (Williams, 2011).

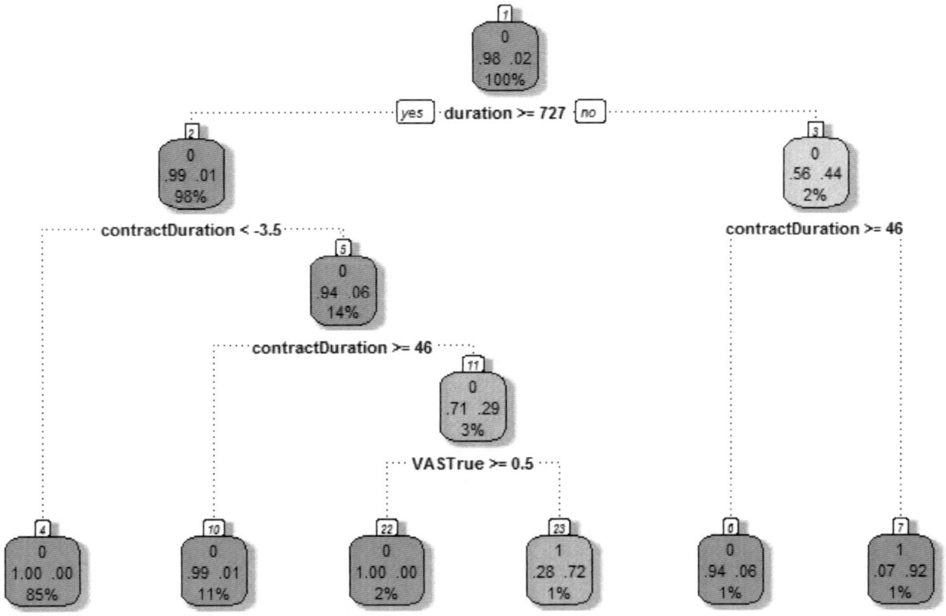

Figure 7 Decision tree model (own calculation)

Big advantage of *caret* package in *R* is possibility to compute importance of explanatory variables and therefore see, which factors drives the customer churn. For logistic regression absolute value of the *t-statistic* and for decision tree *impurity* are computed. Measures of importance are scaled to have a maximum value of 100 (see Fig. 8). The results are quite similar, both algorithms are mainly based on duration of customer and duration of his contract. One big difference is also visible, importance of value added services for decision tree is the second highest whereas for logistic regression this variable is unimportant.

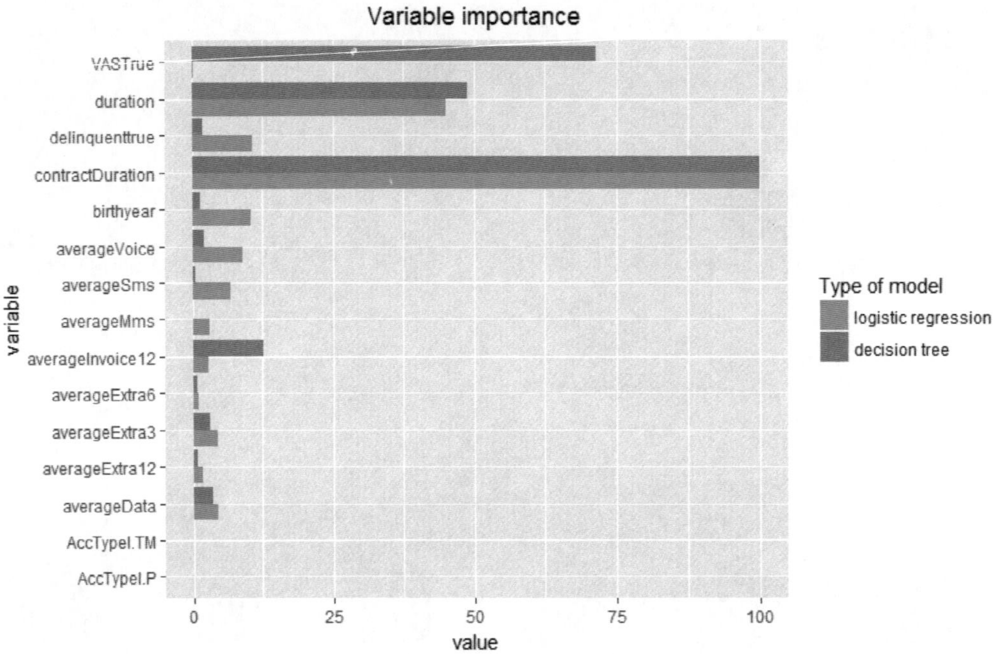

Figure 8 Comparison of variable importance (own calculation)

5 Assessment of predictive performance of models

Logistic regression and decision tree models, described in the previous chapter, are used to predict churn of customers in the testing data set. This step is really important, because in production use the models will predict on data unseen in the phase of model building. The ratio of churned customers in testing data set is similar to the ratio in training data set – 966 out of 50,446, it means 1.915%.

Below there are three confusion matrices, two for logistic regression model, one for cutoff value 0.5 and one for cutoff value 0.25, and one for decision tree model. The cutoff of logistic regression model was decreased to 0.25, because as you can see in Table 4, model with cutoff 0.5 predicted only a minimum of churned customers as they should churn. After this decrease of cutoff more customers are predicted to leave company.

Logistic regression (cutoff 0.5)		**Actual** stay	**Actual** leave	**Logistic regression (cutoff 0.25)**		**Actual** stay	**Actual** leave	**Decision tree**		**Actual** stay	**Actual** leave
Prediction	**stay**	49479	959	**Prediction**	**stay**	49185	540	**Prediction**	**stay**	49269	58
	leave	1	7		**leave**	295	426		**leave**	211	908

Table 4 Confusion matrices (own calculation)

Performance metrics of logistic regression model and decision tree are compared in Table 5. The reason for high accuracy in both models is caused by imbalanced data set. It is necessary to focus on hit rate and specificity. It is clear that the performance of logistic regression model is weak and this model is not suitable for this data set. On the other hand, results for decision tree are pretty good. 81.1% from the predictions for customer churn were correct, and decision tree was able to identify 94% of customers, which in reality really churned.

Model type	Accuracy	Hit Rate	Specificity
Logistic regression (cutoff 0.5)	0.9810	0.8750	0.0072
Logistic regression (cutoff 0.25)	0.9834	0.5908	0.4410
Decision tree	0.9947	0.8114	0.9400

Table 5 Performance statistics (own calculation)

6 Conclusion

Two data mining classification models, logistic regression and decision tree, were used to create predictive models for prediction of which customers will churn in next 45 day. Complexity parameter *cp* was tuned for decision tree model using *10-fold cross validation*. Performance results for decision tree outperformed results of logistic regression. 81% of decision tree predictions for churn were correct and decision tree was able to identify 94% of customer, who in reality really left. Most important variables in both models were customer duration and contract duration.

In further research the author will study the effect of removing outliers and replacing them with mean/median/k-nearest neighbor on predictive ability and because of the imbalanced data set also the effect of various sampling techniques like up-sampling, down-sampling or SMOTE (synthetic minority over-sampling technique) on predictive ability of models. From the algorithm perspective, it seems that tree-based models work fine for this type of data mining task, so complicated tree-based models like random forests and gradient boosting machine will be tested.

Acknowledgements

This research was supported by Student Grant Competition of Faculty of Economics, VŠB-Technical University of Ostrava within project (SP2016/116).

References

Balasubramanian, M. and Selvarani, M. (2014). 'Churn Customer in Mobile Telecom System Using Data Mining Techniques'. *International Journal of Scientific and Research Publications*, 4 (4), pp. 1-5.

Canale, A. and Lunardon, N. (2014). 'Churn Prediction in Telecommunications Industry. A Study Based on Bagging Classifiers'. *Statistica Applicata - Italian Journal of Applied Statistics*, 24 (3), pp. 279-290.

Hudaib, A., Dannoun, R., Harfoushi, O., Obiedat, R. and Faris, H. (2015). 'Hybrid Data Mining Models for Predicting Customer Churn'. *Communications, Network and System Sciences*, 8, pp. 91-96.

James, G. R. (2013). *An introduction to statistical learning: with applications in R*. New York: Springer.

Kuhn, M (2016). Contributions from Jed Wing, Steve Weston, Andre Williams, Chris Keefer, Allan Engelhardt, Tony Cooper, Zachary Mayer, Brenton Kenkel, the R Core Team, Michael Benesty,

Reynald Lescarbeau, Andrew Ziem, Luca Scrucca, Yuan Tang and Can Candan. caret: Classification and Regression Training. R package version 6.0-71. https://CRAN.R-project.org/package=caret

Lantz, B. (2013). *Machine learning with R*. Birmingham: Packt Publishing.

Williams, G. J. (2011), *Data Mining with Rattle and R: The Art of Excavating Data for Knowledge Discovery*. New York: Springer.

Cost Efficiency of EU Funded Projects: Case of Selected SMEs in the Moravian-Silesian Region

Lukáš Melecký[1], Michaela Staníčková[2]

Abstract. The organization, region or country development depends on the level of investment that affect the sales of products or services and new jobs creation at least. To the main problems related to investment projects funded from European Union Funds to which companies are experiencing belong sources of financing and the cost-benefit ratio of the project. Even if the literature offers several guides to prepare a project plan, the managers still encounter some constraints in doing this project cycle phase. After an introduction about the project management and Cost-benefit analysis approach and its importance for EU funded projects evaluation, the paper focuses on the cost efficiency evaluation of investment projects implemented by manufacturing Small and Medium-sized Enterprises in the Moravian-Silesian Region under selected Czech Operational programmes co-financed from the European Regional Development Fund in programming periods 2007–2013 and 2014–2020. Empirical analysis of cost efficiency is based on Data Envelopment Analysis approach.

Keywords: CBA, DEA-Cost efficiency, ESIF, Investment projects, Project management, Operational programmes, SME.

JEL Classification: C67, G17

1 Introduction

The European Union (EU) is a heterogeneous unit with significant disparities between its Member States and mainly among their regions in many areas of the modern economy (Hančlová, 2013). The support of cohesion and balanced regional development together with increasing level of EU, national and regional competitiveness belong to the temporary EU's key spatial development objectives. The process of European integration is thus guided by striving for two different objectives: to foster economic competitiveness and to reduce national/regional differences. The EU Cohesion policy has an important role in enhancing the regional competitiveness and prosperity. From the long-term perspectives, regional competitiveness requires paying attention not only to economic but also to social and environmental factors, in recent years especially to territorial characteristics of areas – cohesion and competitiveness are thus partly complementary EU goals (Molle, 2007). In the EU, emerging and re-emerging differentiating dimensions are combined; these dimensions are associated with the EU enlargement on the one hand and with the recent crisis impact on the other hand. This leads not only to transformation of economic stratification, but also to uneven manifestations and impacts of economic activities in European area. As a result of spatially selective effects of economic processes is then the newly forming spatial differentiation of the EU, which should be solved and minimize by the financing activities from the *European*

[1] VŠB-Technical University of Ostrava/ Faculty of Economics, Department of European Integration, Sokolská třída 33, 702 00 Ostrava 1, Czech Republic, lukas.melecky@vsb.cz.
[2] VŠB-Technical University of Ostrava/ Faculty of Economics, Department of European Integration, Sokolská třída 33, 702 00 Ostrava 1, Czech Republic, michaela.stanickova@vsb.cz.

Structural and Investments Funds (ESIF) through implementation of various projects based on common project and subsidy management rules and procedures.

The EU Member States and their regions are founded on the principles of solidarity, democracy, respect for human rights, fundamental freedoms and the rule of law. Among these fundamental freedoms is also the right of citizens and companies to participate actively in society, what is a significant component of the EU and as such constitute an increasingly important channel for EU investments made by SMEs in European Single market. However, it can be extremely challenging for individuals, companies and also public sector which are trying to understand how investment decisions are made within EU institutions and how to successfully apply for EU Funds implemented in the frame of the EU Cohesion policy. The EU distributes its funds in a number of ways: through individual projects and grant scheme, via a sector approach or by budget support to recipient governments. The project approach is particularly used to support initiatives outside the public sector, such as through subjects of civil society and the private sectors. Thus, it is essential for all entities to understand the concept of 'the project' and to have the capacity to design and implement projects, and especially to manage them strategically (Melecký, 2016). All projects, especially the investments projects, need to be related to the internal and external organization's environmental factors by exploring practice and distributed knowledge through interaction.

Context above just confirms common need for project management in terms of EU. What is the reason for high level of popularity of subsidy management in the EU and activities co-financed by ESIF? The programming period 2014–2020 presents opportunities to fund innovative ideas and development projects. The architecture of the EU Funds and direct subsidies continues to offer a wide range of funding opportunities in the EU Member States, and especially NUTS 2 regions by making available more than EUR 450 billion allocated for reformed EU Cohesion policy 2014-2020 through development programmes that enable to fully exploit their potential to achieve the Europe 2020 strategy objectives, while ensuring sound contribution to the Fund-specific purposes of the ESIFs (Staníčková, 2016).

The paper is focused on application of quantitative approach to analysis of financial flows from the viewpoint of costs presented first part of Cost-Benefit Analysis (CBA) approach. The main aim of the paper is the cost efficiency evaluation of selected investment projects implemented by Small and Medium-sized Enterprises (SMEs) in the Moravian-Silesian Region, based on Data Envelopment Analysis (DEA) approach. DEA-Cost efficiency is computed for 11 manufacturing companies' implemented 17 projects under two Czech Operational programmes (OP) financed from the European Regional Development Fund (ERDF) in programming period 2007–2013 and 2014–2020.

2 Cost-Benefit Analysis and Efficiency of Investments

Supporting the best quality project plans which offer best value for investments and impact significantly on jobs and growth is a key ingredient of the EU Cohesion policy. Evidence-based and successful policy requires making investment decisions based on objective and verifiable methods. Therefore, *Cost-Benefit Analysis* is explicitly required, among other elements, as a basis for decision making on the co-financing of projects included in OPs of the ERDF and the

Cohesion Fund. This tool could be used in decision-making in several domains, such as: opportunity studies, feasibility studies, change evaluation, staff hiring in projects, training programmes and others. However, the tool has become popular being imposed in the investment projects financed by the EU Structural Funds in programming period 2007–2013 and the ESIF in programming period 2014–2020 according to a specific guideline (EC, 2008, 2014).

CBA is an analytical tool to be used to appraise an investment decision in order to assess the welfare change attributable to it and, in so doing, the contribution to EU Cohesion policy objectives. The purpose of CBA is to facilitate a more efficient allocation of resources, demonstrating the convenience for society of a particular intervention rather than possible alternatives. CBA is about measuring in monetary terms all the benefits and costs of the project with tangible products as well as with non-tangible products and thus become a real management tool for national and regional authorities. Officially, CBA is an analytical tool for judging the economic advantages or disadvantages of an investment decision by assessing its costs and benefits in order to assess the welfare change attributable to it (EC, 2014).

The analytical framework of CBA refers to a list of underlying concepts which is as follows: opportunity cost, long-term perspective, calculation of economic performance indicators expressed in monetary terms, microeconomic approach, and incremental approach. First part of CBA procedure leads to the *financial analysis* of the project that involves examining the activities and resource flows of individual entities (e.g., an industrial or commercial firm, public institution, etc.) or groups of entities (e.g., artisans, farmers, retailers) (EC, 1997). For each of the entities taking part in a project, financial analysis involves comparison of *costs* (e.g., an operating and investment expenses) and *benefits* (e.g. a sales revenues, new jobs) resulting from the project activity. Cost and benefits thus present a project`s effects on financial and economic objectives of project. Evaluation of cost-benefit ratio is under way of efficiency analysis by comparing the results obtained with the resources used in every investment activities. CBA distinguish criteria for efficiency evaluation of effects *(E)* arising from investments in form (1):

$$E = B - C \geq 0 \ or \ E = \frac{B}{C} \geq 1. \qquad (1)$$

The formula (1) is based on logical reasoning that the benefits of the project *(B)* must be greater than the costs *(C)* associated with it. Any investment activity is thus effective when the cost-benefit ratio is greater than 1, i.e. each invested monetary units generate profit. Following part of the paper explore criteria mentioned above from the perspective of cost efficiency score.

3 DEA Approach to Cost Efficiency Analysis

Productivity management is one of the major sources of sustainable organizational efficiency, and a systematic understanding of the factors that affect productivity is very important. The measurement and analysis of productivity change is always a controversial topic and has enjoyed a great deal of interest among researchers and practitioners. Farrell had already investigated the question of how to measure efficiency and highlighted its relevance for economic policy makers in 1957. It is important to know how far a given industry can be expected to increase its output by simply increasing its efficiency without absorbing further resources (Farrell, 1957). Since that time the techniques to measure efficiency have improved and investigations of efficiency have become more frequent, particularly in industry and business sector. The evaluation and comparison of the performance of similar units is an important part of the management of a complex organization. *Data Envelopment Analysis* (DEA) is one of the powerful management techniques that empowers researchers to estimate organization' performance in comparison with other competitors and make better decisions.

DEA is an approach for providing a relative efficiency assessment and evaluating the performance of a set of peer entities called decision-making units (DMUs), which convert multiple inputs into multiple outputs. DEA is thus a multi-criteria decision-making method for evaluating the efficiency and productivity of a homogeneous group (DMUs). The definition of a DMU is generic and flexible. DEA is convenient for determining the efficiency of DMUs that are mutually comparable – using the same inputs and producing the same outputs but with different performances. Determining whether a DMU is efficient from the observed data is equivalent to testing whether the DMU is on the *frontier of the production possibility set*. DMU is efficient if the observed data correspond to testing whether the DMU is on the imaginary *production possibility frontier* (Cooper, Seiford and Zhu, 2011). All other DMUs are simply inefficient. The best-practice units are used as a reference for the evaluation of the other group units. The efficiency score of a DMU in the presence of multiple input and output factors is defined by the following equation (2):

$$efficiency = \frac{weighted\ sum\ of\ outputs}{weighted\ sum\ of\ inputs}. \tag{2}$$

If a performance measure (input/output) is added to or deleted from consideration, it will influence the relative efficiencies. Empirically, when the number of performance measures is high in comparison with the number of DMUs, then most of the DMUs are evaluated as efficient. Hence, the obtained results are not reliable. There is a rough rule of thumb (Cooper, Seiford and Zhu, 2011) that expresses the relation between the number of DMUs and the number of performance measures as follows (3). Suppose that there are n DMUs, which consume m inputs to produce s outputs:

$$n \geq \max\{3(m+s), m \cdot s\}. \tag{3}$$

In some applications the numbers of performance measures and DMUs do not meet the mentioned formula (3). To tackle this issue, some performance measures should be selected in a manner that complies with (3) and imposes a progressive effect on the efficiency scores. These selected inputs and outputs are called selective measures. Formula (3) needs more consideration. Toloo, Barat and Masoumzadeh (2015) checked more than 40 papers containing practical applications and found statistically that, in nearly all of the cases, the number of inputs and outputs does not exceed 6. Simple calculation shows that, when $m \leq 6$ and $s \leq 6$, then $3(m + s) \geq m \times s$. As a result, in this paper, instead of using (3), the following formula (4) is applied:

$$n \geq 3(m+s). \tag{4}$$

In the case of this paper, the rule of thumb is met, because the number of DMUs is three times higher than the sum of input and outputs, that is, $17 \geq 3\ (2 + 3)$, $17 \geq 3\ (5)$, $17 \geq 15$.

If price data are available then it is possible to measure allocative, technical efficiency as well as overall cost, revenue and profit efficiency. To calculate these main types of efficiency, a set of linear programs should be solved.

The input-oriented DEA model under the assumption of variable return to scale can be used for calculation of input-oriented technical efficiency and cost efficiency. Input-oriented model under the assumption of variable return to scale is often termed as BCC model, which can be written in the following form (5):

$$\min \theta_q, \tag{5}$$

subject to
$$\sum_{j=1}^{n} x_{ij} \lambda_j \leq \theta_q x_{iq}, i = 1,2,..., m,$$

$$\sum_{j=1}^{n} y_{rj} \lambda_j \geq y_{rq}, r = 1,2,..., s,$$

$$\sum_{j=1}^{n} \lambda_j = 1,$$

$$\lambda_j \geq 0, j = 1,2,..., n.$$

Where θ_q is input-oriented technical efficiency (TE_q) of Decision Making Unit (DMU_q) in the input-oriented DEA model, y_{rq} is produced amounts of rth output (r = 1,2,..., s) for DMU_q, x_{iq} is consumed amounts of ith input (i = 1,2,..., m) for DMU_q, y_{rj} is produced amounts of rth output (r = 1,2,..., s) for DMU_j (j = 1, 2,..., n), x_{ij} is consumed amounts of ith input (i = 1,2,..., m) for DMU_j (j = 1, 2,..., n), λ_j is weight assigned to the DMU_j (j = 1,2,..., n).

To calculate cost efficiency is necessary to solve the cost minimisation DEA model (6):

$$\min \sum_{i=1}^{m} w_{iq} x_{iq}^{*}, \tag{6}$$

subject to
$$\sum_{j=1}^{n} w_{iq} \lambda_j \leq x_{iq}^{*}, i = 1,2,..., m,$$

$$\sum_{j=1}^{n} y_{rj} \lambda_j \geq y_{rq}, r = 1,2,..., s,$$

$$\sum_{j=1}^{n} \lambda_j = 1,$$

$$\lambda_j \geq 0, j = 1,2,..., n.$$

Where w_{iq} is a vector of input prices of DMU_q and x^{*}_{iq} is the cost minimising vector of input quantities for DMU_q given the input prices w_{iq} and the output levels y_{rq}.

The overall cost efficiency (CE_q) is defined as the ratio of minimum cost of producing the outputs to observed cost of producing the outputs for the DMU_q (7) (Coelli et al., 2005):

$$CE_q = \frac{\sum_{i=1}^{m} w_{iq} x_{iq}^*}{\sum_{i=1}^{m} w_{iq} x_{iq}}. \tag{7}$$

The overall cost efficiency can be expressed as a product of technical and allocative efficiency measures. Therefore, the allocative efficiency of the DMU_q can be calculated as ratio of overall cost efficiency (CE_q) to input-oriented technical efficiency (TE_q). These three measures (technical, allocative and overall cost efficiency) can take values ranging from zero to one, where a value of one in case of TE, AE and CE indicates full efficiency. If production unit is fully technically efficient ($TE_q = 1$) and displays allocative efficiency ($AE_q = 1$); it is also overall cost efficient ($CE_q = 1$). This production unit uses minimum amount of inputs for producing of given outputs, while the proportion of inputs will guarantee the minimum possible costs. The production unit which is technically efficient ($TE_q = 1$) but does not demonstrate allocative efficiency ($AE_q<1$) is not also overall cost efficient ($CE_q<1$). This production unit uses minimum amount of inputs for producing the given outputs, but the proportion of inputs will not guarantee the minimum possible costs. The production unit which reaches allocative efficiency ($AE_q = 1$), but does not reach technical efficiency ($TE_q<1$) cannot be marked as overall cost efficient ($CE_q<1$). The proportion of inputs will guarantee the minimum possible costs, but this combination of inputs is not minimal for a producing of given outputs. If the production unit fails to demonstrate any of these three types of efficiency ($TE_q<1$; $AE_q<1$; $CE_q<1$), then the value of overall cost efficiency can be interpreted as a potential costs saving that can be achieved if the production unit uses the inputs in optimal combination. Potential costs saving can be calculated by subtracting the value of overall CE_q from the number one.

There is a great variety of applications of DEA for evaluating the performances of many different kinds of entities as banks (e.g. Chytilová, 2015; Camanho and Dyson, 2005), spatial units (e.g. Hančlová, 2013) or projects (e.g. Staníčková, Melecký and Navrátil, 2013) engaged in many different activities. Because of the low assumption requirements, DEA has also opened up possibilities for use in cases that have been resistant to other approaches because of the complex (often unknown) nature of relations between multiple inputs and multiple outputs involved in DMUs. DEA method is a convenient method for comparing evaluated DMUs presented by projects, because it evaluates not only one factor but a set of different factors that determine the degree of efficiency. DEA method used for our evaluation is based on a particular set of input and output indicators.

4 Cost Efficiency of EU Funded Projects: Evaluation of Projects Implemented by Selected SMEs in Moravian-Silesian Region

Empirical part of the paper describes application of DEA approach for measuring cost efficiency of selected projects realized by SMEs in the Moravian-Silesian Region. Case study based on DEA-Cost efficiency evaluates a cross-projects level data of 11 companies' in manufacturing sector implemented 17 projects under two Czech OPs co-financed from ERDF. The sample of investment projects presents actual projects on which the authors of the paper collaborated or still collaborate in the role of project managers during initialization and implementation phase. Dataset present objectively verifiable indicators that give an adequate picture of the situation and be measurable in a consistent way at an acceptable cost. In programming period 2007–2013, SMEs have been funded through the OP Entrepreneurship and Innovation (OP Podnikání a inovace, OPPI) – Programme Development (Rozvoj). In programming period 2014–2020, SMEs are subsidised from the OP Entrepreneurship and Innovation for Competitiveness (OP Podnikání a inovace pro konkurenceschopnost, OPPIK) – Programme Technology (Technologie). Both OPs and their Programmes support technological development of companies through acquisition and of new machinery and technological equipment for expansion of production capacity and diversification of production. Companies getting support from the given OPs must have their business and production activities in the manufacturing industry based on CZ NACE (Nomenclature of Economic Activities Classification) sectoral classification. Characteristics of evaluated projects supported by the ERDF under selected Czech OPs are presented in Annex in Table 1 and Table 2.

For each project in each SME in the sample, it was necessary to select inputs, outputs, input prices and output prices. We consider 17 DMUs, i.e. projects and two inputs, namely, number of eligible costs (tangible and intangible fixed assets) (I-1) and its price: eligible costs in CZK (IP-1), number of ineligible costs (e.g. value added tax, public tenders, project publicity, administrative costs) (I-2) and its price: ineligible costs in CZK (IP-2). On the output side we consider three types of outputs, namely number of acquired technologies (O-1) and its price: total price of acquired technologies in CZK (OP-1), number of newly created jobs, resp. number of new employees (O-2) and its price: average monthly labour cost per employee in CZK (OP-2), changes in beneficiary`s sales based on subsidy in % (O-3) and its price: changes in beneficiary`s sales in CZK (OP-3). Descriptive statistics of variables are shown in Table 1.

Indicator	N	Range	Minimum	Maximum	Mean	Std. Deviation
I-1	17	1.00	1.00	2.00	1.29	0.47
I-2	17	3.00	2.00	5.00	3.65	0.86
IP-1	17	33,518,002.64	397,565.60	33,915,568.24	12,669,685.52	10,760,163.96
IP-2	17	7,457,280.67	88,488.66	7,545,769.33	2,823,092.36	2,356,130.52
O-1	17	80.00	2.00	82.00	16.65	18.28
O-2	17	9.00	1.00	10.00	4.24	2.73
O-3	17	155.99	5.35	161.34	36.92	42.62
OP-1	17	33,518,002.64	397,565.60	33,915,568.24	12,669,744.34	10,760,139.65
OP-2	17	17,916.00	15,000.00	32,916.00	21,970.29	4,483.99
OP-3	17	213,926,290.70	574,750.00	214,501,040.70	21,898,967.62	50,125,167.97

Table 1 Descriptive statistics of input and output variables used for cost efficiency evaluation [Own calculation in IBM SPSS 24 and own elaboration, 2017]

By solving the cost minimization problem using the DEA Frontier software, we obtain overall cost efficiency of evaluated projects presented in Table 2. In Table 2, Coefficient of efficiency (CE) results are highlighted by the traffic light method. Range of colours of this method changes from green colour, through shades of yellow colour to red colour. Projects with the highest and higher CE values mean better level of efficiency and are highlighted by green colour – the higher CE value, the darker shadow of green colour. On the contrary, projects with the lowest and lower CE values mean worse level of efficiency, resp. it represents level of inefficiency, and these projects are highlighted by red colour – the lower CE value, the darker shadow of red colour. Projects with CE values between group of efficient (shadows of green colour) and inefficient projects (shadows of red colour) are highlighted by shadows of yellow colour and can be named as highly efficient and slightly inefficient based on range.

Input oriented CE model singled out projects which are efficient (CE = 1); to this group belong projects 2, 3, 7, 12, 13, and 14. Efficient projects are highlighted by bold and grey colour in Table 2. In this case, the efficiency boundary is a straight line cutting through these DMUs. All other units are inefficient (CE<1), i.e. they fall short of the efficiency curve. The most inefficient DMUs are projects 10, 8, 1, and 15. Their CE values achieve the worst levels of all projects; inefficient projects are highlighted by italics and red colour in Table 2. However assess that all other projects are simply inefficient, it would be too simplistic. We can say that rest of projects (between the group of efficient and inefficient ones) belong to the group of highly efficient (projects 6, 17, 9, 11, and 4) – CE values are higher than 0.7 and lower than 1.0; or slightly inefficient projects 16 and 5 – CE values are higher than 0.6 and lower than 0.8. Let is note that DEA approach allows us to determine how DMU should change its behaviour to become efficient and rise to the efficiency curve. In Table 2, for inputs of inefficient projects are calculated optimal quantities of inputs getting optimal setting of inputs. Optimal dataset could serve to SMEs as instruction how realized the projects efficiently and for improving input-output ratio.

DMU	**VRS CE**	**Initial Inputs**		**Optimal Inputs**		**Results Arrangement**		
		I-1	*I-2*	*I-1*	*I-2*	*Rank*	*DMU*	*VRS CE*
Project_1	0.537	2.000	5.000	**1.000**	**3.000**	1.	**Project_2**	1.000
Project_2	1.000	1.000	2.000	1.000	2.000		**Project_3**	1.000
Project_3	1.000	1.000	3.000	1.000	3.000		**Project_7**	1.000
Project_4	0.828	1.000	4.000	**1.000**	**2.143**		**Project_12**	1.000
Project_5	0.746	1.000	4.000	**1.000**	**2.000**		**Project_13**	1.000
Project_6	0.905	1.000	4.000	**1.173**	**2.494**		**Project_14**	1.000
Project_7	1.000	1.000	4.000	1.000	4.000	2.	Project_6	0.905
Project_8	0.581	2.000	4.000	**1.000**	**3.013**	3.	Project_17	0.891
Project_9	0.858	1.000	4.000	**1.114**	**2.383**	4.	Project_9	0.858
Project_10	0.601	2.000	4.000	**1.143**	**2.654**	5.	Project_11	0.848
Project_11	0.848	1.000	4.000	**1.041**	**2.494**	6.	Project_4	0.828
Project_12	1.000	2.000	4.000	2.000	4.000	7.	Project_16	0.747
Project_13	1.000	1.000	2.000	1.000	2.000	8.	Project_5	0.746
Project_14	1.000	1.000	2.000	1.000	2.000	9.	*Project_10*	0.601
Project_15	0.523	2.000	4.000	**1.000**	**2.286**	10.	*Project_8*	0.581
Project_16	0.747	1.000	4.000	**1.000**	**2.055**	11.	*Project_1*	0.537
Project_17	0.891	1.000	4.000	**1.073**	**2.858**	12.	*Project_15*	0.523

Table 2 Cost efficiency of evaluated projects [Own calculation in the DEA Frontier and own elaboration, 2017]

*** Formatting Issue - Best Available Paper/Graphic ***

5 Conclusion

CBA or different modification of this approach such as input-output cost efficiency approach used in this paper has the reason to emphasize whether the sample of selected investment projects focusing on purchasing new innovative technologies leading to ensure production growth and corporate sales are simply efficient, or not. Different guides, according to the EU or national principles and regulations and the specific literature, are available for investment project evaluations, as well. But the evaluation process of investment project supported from the EU Funds is much more complicated and presents one of the most serious and complex problem of the EU Cohesion policy implementation in the Czech Republic during last decade. Cost efficiency input-output ratio findings of surveyed examples of projects realized in the Moravian-Silesian region is also influenced by other aspects such as beneficiary`s CZ NACE determining sectors of the Czech economy for SME`s entrepreneurship. This is one of the key factors affecting cost of production and possible increase in sales. The SME size can definitely be another aspect need to be reflected in presented cost efficiency results in each project and play the key role in determining the amount of support from ERDF to concrete SME. Analysis of these and other aspects, however, is beyond the scope of this paper.

Acknowledgements

This paper was created under SGS project (SP2017/111) of Faculty of Economics, VŠB-TUO, and Operational Programme Education for Competitiveness – Project CZ.1.07/2.3.00/20.0296.

References

Camanho, A.S. and Dyson, R. (2005). 'Cost efficiency measurement: DEA application to bank branch assessment'. *European Journal of Operations Research*, 161 (2), pp. 432-446.

Chytilová, L. (2015). 'Analysis of Factors of Cost Efficiency/inefficiency and its Components of Banks in the Visegrad Group'. *Financial Management of Firms and Financial Institutions: 10th International Scientific Conference*, Ostrava, Czech Republic, pp. 435-443.

Coelli, T., Rao, D. S. P., O´Donnell, CH. J. and Battese, G. E. (2005). *An Introduction to Efficiency and Productivity Analysis*. New York: Springer.

Cooper, W.W., Seiford, L.M. and Zhu, J. (2011). *Handbook on Data Envelopment Analysis*. New York: Springer.

European Commission. (1997). *Financial and Economic Analysis of Development Projects (Manual)*. Luxembourg: EC.

European Commission. (2008). *Guide to Cost-Benefit Analysis of Investment Projects*. Brussels: EC.

European Commission. (2014). *Guide to Cost-Benefit Analysis of Investment Projects*. Brussels: EC.

Hančlová, J. (2013). 'Econometric Analysis of Macroeconomic Efficiency Development in the EU15 and EU12 Countries'. *Proceedings of the 11th International Conference on Liberec Economic Forum 2013*, Liberec, Czech Republic, pp. 166-175.

Melecký, L. (2016). 'Changing of EU Project and Grant Management Approach in Response to New Trends of Programming Period 2014–2020'. *Proceedings of the 3rd International Conference on European Integration 2016*, Ostrava, Czech Republic, pp. 605-614.

Molle,W. (2007). *European Cohesion Policy*. London: Routledge.

Staníčková, M. (2016). 'Practical Aspects of EU Project and Grant Management in Programming Period 2014-2020'. *Proceedings of the 3rd International Conference on European Integration 2016*, Ostrava, Czech Republic, pp. 898-907.

Staníčková, M., Melecký, L. and Navrátil, B. (2013). 'Measuring the Student Research Projects' Efficiency Using DEA Method'. *Proceedings of the Conference on Efficiency and Responsibility in Education 2013*, Prague, Czech Republic, pp. 573-580.

Toloo, M., Barat, M. and Masoumzadeh, A. (2015). 'Selective measures in data envelopment analysis'. *Annals of Operations Research*, 226 (1), pp. 523-642.

*** Formatting Issue - Best Available Paper/Graphic ***

P	Programme	PP	Period of project realization	Project realization (in months)	Eligible costs (in CZK)	Ineligible costs (in CZK)	Subsidy rate (in %)	Subsid (in CZK
PI	Rozvoj III	2007-2013	1.6.2010-31.8.2011	14.0	19,617,840.00	4 524 568.00	60	11,770,00
PI	Rozvoj III	2007-2013	1.10.2012-31.5.2014	8.0	14,815,400.00	2 981 080.00	40	5,926,16
PI	Rozvoj III	2007-2013	1.10.2012-1.12.2013	15.0	32,515,965.00	7 001 193.00	40	13,006,38
PI	Rozvoj III	2007-2013	1.10.2014-15.6.2015	8.5	7,094,000.00	1 048 180.00	50	3,547,00
PIK	Technologie II	2014-2020	9.5.2015-31.12.2015	3.7	2,920,000.00	752 350.00	45	1,314,00
PIK	Technologie II	2014-2020	11.9.2015-31.12.2015	3.7	8,483,600.00	2 016 296.00	45	3,817,62
PIK	Technologie III	2014-2020	22.6.2016-30.4.2017	12.3	27,135,330.00	6 061 419.30	45	12,210,89
PIK	Technologie III	2014-2020	18.1.2016-30.6.2017	17.5	10,017,290.00	2 375 056.89	45	4,507,78
PIK	Technologie III	2014-2020	22.2.2016-31.10.2016	8.3	6,400,000.00	1 561 800.00	35	2,240,00
PIK	Technologie III	2014-2020	22.6.2016-30.4.2017	14.3	12,727,000.00	2 978 800.00	45	5,727,15
PIK	Technologie III	2014-2020	20.1.2016-31.5.2017	14.4	21,692,395.00	4 692 102.95	35	7,592,33
PIK	Technologie IV	2014-2020	17.1.2017-31.12.2017	11.5	33,915,568.24	7 545 769.33	45	15,262,00
PIK	Technologie V	2014-2020	9.12.2016-30.4.2017	4.7	462,739.96	102 175.39	45	208,23
PIK	Technologie V	2014-2020	9.12.2016-31.3.2017	3.7	397,565.60	88 488.66	45	178,90
PIK	Technologie IV	2014-2020	1.1.2017-31.12.2017	12.0	10,140,956.00	2 407 900.76	45	4,563,43
PIK	Technologie IV	2014-2020	2.1.2017-31.12.2017	12.0	3,078,666.00	834 069.86	45	1,385,39
PIK	Technologie IV	2014-2020	11.1.2017-31.12.2017	11.7	3,970,338.00	834 069.86	45	1,786,65

cision-Making Unit, OP = Operational Programme, PP = Programming Period.

Characteristics of Implemented Projects Supported by the ERDF under selected Czech OPs [SMEs' statistics; own elaboration

acteristics	N	Range	Minimum	Maximum	Mean	Std. De
zation (Months)	17	13.80	3.70	17.50	10.31	4.
CZK)	17	40,975,283.31	486,054.26	41,461,337.57	15,481,763.16	13,119
(%)	17	25.00	35.00	60.00	44.41	5.
K)	17	15,083,101.18	178,904.52	15,262,005.70	5,590,821.09	4,770,

Table 2 Descriptive statistics: Project characteristics [Own calculation in IBM SPSS 24 and own elaboration, 2017]

Robust DEA for banks' efficiency under uncertainty

Emmanuel Kwasi Mensah[1], Mehdi Toloo[2]

Abstract. The Data Envelopment Analysis (DEA) has been the benchmarked model for measuring the efficiency of banks over the years. However, inherent noise and uncertainties in the data are hardly considered for robust efficiency scores. The disadvantage is that a small perturbation in the uncertain parameters can lead to high infeasibility of the efficient solutions. This paper introduces a robust DEA into the measurement of banks efficiency. The proposed robust approach is based on the robust counterpart optimization of Ben-Tal & Nemirovski (2000), and it is implemented in the traditional DEA models germane to the performance measurement of banks. A preliminary result from data on banks in the Czech Republic indicates that efficiency scores measured with the robust DEA model provides a true and stable performance measure than the normal DEA model.

Keywords: Robust optimization, DEA, Robust DEA, Banks efficiency, Uncertainty.

JEL Classification: C6, G2

1 Introduction

Measurement of relative efficiency of banks is one of the primary concern and major research in the banking sector. For an excellent performance reference indicator, the appropriate ways of measurement are critical. Multi-criteria decision making approaches via the Data Envelopment Analysis (DEA) (Barr & Seiford (1993); Jemric & Vujcic (2002); Grigorian & Manole (2002); Jablonsky, Petr, Yannis, & Dimitris (2004)) and the Analytical Hierarchy Process (AHP) (Saaty (2008); Hunjak & Jakovčević (2001)) have been the main tools employed towards this end. Whiles these methods yield desired efficiency scores for ranking of banks, they have been used so with the assumption of certain inputs and outputs data. Given that technology reliance, forecasting data among others could be uncertain, the true efficiency measures could be missing.

A possible path to treat uncertainty in input/output data is to rely on the probability distribution or the imprecision of the data. On the former, stochastic DEA has been considered to measure the inherent randomness in the data. The latter approach has, however, stimulated research centered on fuzzy DEA and interval DEA. Applications to precise measuring of banking performance have been made in literature (See Jablonsky et al. (2004); Wanke, Barros, & Emrouznejad (2016)). The shortcoming with these approaches, however, is that whiles historical data of input/output values are seldom known and hence difficult to determine the distribution of data for the stochastic analysis, the following approaches are computationally expensive in implementation.

In this paper, we introduce a proposed robust DEA for the measurement of banks' efficiency. The robust DEA is based on the robust counterpart optimization using the uncertainty set

[1]Department of Economics, University of Insubria, Varese, Italy, email: ekmensah@uninsubria.it

[2]Department of Systems Engineering, Technical University of Ostrava, Czech Republic, email: mehdi.toloo@vsb.cz , webpage: http://homel.vsb.cz/~tol0013/

introduced by Ben-Tal & Nemirovski (2000). A practical yield of this approach is that efficiency results are robust whenever the uncertain inputs and outputs are feasible in the defined uncertainty. The robust optimization in DEA (herein called RDEA) for robust performance measure was proposed by Sadjadi & Omrani (2008) with application to the efficiency assessment of electricity distribution companies. Other applications have since been made also considering the robust counterpart of Bertsimas & Sim (2004). However, application of the RDEA for the robust efficiency of banks has been lacking. As a novelty, this paper presents a robust solution for the two most important traditional DEA models germane to the efficiency analysis of banks. A conscious effort is made by comparing the results of the robust DEA solution and the (uncertain) DEA solution.

The rest of paper is organized as follows: Section 2 gives an overview of uncertainties in the banking sector. Sections 3 and 4 describe the efficiency assessment with DEA and RDEA, respectively. The application of the RDEA to the Czech Republic banks data is provided in Section 5. Concluding remarks are made in Section 6.

2 Uncertainties in the banking sector

Period of banking uncertainties are times during which the likelihood of future events or direction of investment cannot be determined. As a result, forecast of future performance of borrowers or the volume of liabilities that must be issued to fund assets become difficult to ascertain (Dinger & Craig (2013); Buch, Buchholz, Tonzer, & Buch (2014)). Banking sector uncertainties are created following shocks in the global market (e.g. shocks in oil price, global financial crises, etc.). On the other hand, uncertainties in moderate form is a daily operational phenomenon in the financial sector. Information processing or information asymmetry between lenders and borrowers can create internal uncertainties that could result in behavioral changes among financial partners. Banks which face uncertainties tend to restrict lending to borrowers. If the uncertainty level is high, investors may also demand high funding premium for their investment which apparently reduces the ability of banks to provide loans (Buch et al. (2014)). Dinger & Craig (2013) identify these uncertainties as a determinant of bank 's liability structure. Thus, depending on the insurance position of a bank, its fortune in uncertainty rely partially on how it leverages its liability structure to meet returns on assets and profit objectives.

Uncertainties in the banking sector imply that planning on both inputs and outputs data becomes unreliable. Financial data including banks data are undoubtedly random and uncertain all the time. As a measure, Buch et al. (2014) compute uncertainty among banks as a cross-sectional dispersion of volatilities to bank's specific variables. Most of the uncertainties in data are idiosyncratic in nature, observable by bank insiders who are privy to detailed knowledge of bank's portfolio, data, and its dynamics. Among many of the sources are listed below

- *Prediction error*: Banks are occasionally involved in forecasting of financial data. For instance, projections on returns on investment, liabilities, loans, etc., are made towards preparation of balance sheet and financial report. These variables are subject to prediction errors.
- *Measurement error*: Banks record data assuming away random errors, many of which cannot be measured exactly. Measured data revolved around their mean value and has inherent errors.

- *Implementation errors:* Some of the banking data used for analysis cannot be implemented exactly as computed. These data are subject to implementation error. e.g. the intensity of technological usage of banks equipment.

3 Data Envelopment Analysis

Data envelopment analysis is a non-parametric mathematical programming approach for assessing the efficiencies of homogenous Decision Making Units (DMU). The approach was introduced by Farrell (1957) and operationalized as a linear programming by Charnes, Cooper, & Rhodes (1978). As a data-oriented methodology, DEA allows for efficient determination of multiple inputs and multiple outputs weight without any specification on the functional form of the production relationship or pre-assigned weights. There are two main DEA models discussed in literature which we shall consider for analysis in this paper; the CCR model after Charnes et al. (1978) and the BCC model after Banker, Charnes, & Cooper (1984). The main difference between these models lies in their scale assumption. The CCR model is built on radial measurement and hence constants return to scale assumption. On the other hand, the BCC model which includes but not limited to radial measurement uses piecewise linear and concave frontiers that result in different production scale such as decreasing, constant, and increasing returns to scale.

Both CCR and BCC model can be analyzed under the input or output orientation of production. Thus, there two types of traditional DEA models: input-oriented and output-oriented. In an *input-oriented* model, inputs are minimized whiles the desired output level is satisfied. The *output-oriented* model seeks to maximize output with a given level of inputs. While an output-oriented model may be appropriate for banking operations, it is unlikely that banks outputs would be increased simply to promote efficiency. As a cost minimization strategy, we consider in input-oriented CCR and BCC models. The CCR model is particularly useful when all DMUs (banks)[3] are operating at optimal scale. Both models are considered believing that some banks operate at optimal scale while others operate at sub-optimal including decreasing returns to scale. Factors that can cause sub-optimal scale include imperfect competition, prudential requirements and leverage concerns (Grigorian & Manole (2002)).

3.1 The CCR and BCC models

Charnes et al. (1978) proposed the CCR model which measure relative efficiency of DMUs as a maximum weighted sum of outputs to maximum weighted sum of inputs. To relate the efficiency score of each bank to the performance of others, the ratio of these virtual inputs and outputs are restricted to less than one or equal to one. The CCR model permits only efficiency measure in constant returns to scale; however, Banker et al. (1984) extended the following BCC model[4] in order to allow variable returns to scale assumption:

[3] Without loss of generalization, throughout this paper, DMUs and banks shall be used interchangeably.

[4] The stated model is called the multiplier form of the BCC model. The envelop form can be derived by writing its dual.

$$\begin{array}{ll} \max \sum_{r=1}^{s} u_r y_{ro} + u_o & \\ \text{s.t.} & \\ \sum_{i=1}^{m} v_i x_{io} = 1 & \\ \sum_{r=1}^{s} u_r y_{rj} + u_o - \sum_{i=1}^{m} v_i x_{ij} \leq 0 & j = 1, \dots, n \\ v_i \geq 0 & i = 1, \dots, m \\ u_r \geq 0 & r = 1, \dots, s \\ u_o \;\; \text{free in sign} & \end{array} \tag{1}$$

where $j = 1, \dots, n$ denotes the number of banks, u_r and v_i are the respective output and input weights corresponding to the amount of outputs y_{ij} and inputs x_{ij} evaluated at $r = 1, \dots, s$ and $i = 1, \dots, m$, and free variable u_o indicates where the under-evaluation unit find itself in the returns to scale (RTS). As a result, the CCR model is a special case of the BBC model where $u_0 = 0$. Suppose θ is the optimal value of the objective function corresponding to the unit under evaluation $\text{Bank}_{o \in \{1,\dots,n\}}$. Banks with $\theta < 1$ are called inefficient and are distance apart from the efficient frontier. The efficient frontier is spanned by banks with $\theta = 1$. For more details about basic DEA models see Toloo (2014).

4 Robust Data Envelopment Analysis

In this section, the proposed robust DEA for robust efficiency measure is described. We begin with the idea of robust optimization. The robust optimization approach deals with uncertainties and noisy data in many linear programming problems (Ben-Tal & Nemirovski (2000); Bertsimas & Sim (2004)) such as the DEA (Sadjadi & Omrani (2008); Lu (2015)). The approach is based on an uncertainty set defined for all uncertain data and a tractable robust counterpart derived from the nominal problem. For simplicity, we consider only the robust approach of Ben-Tal & Nemirovski (2000). According to the authors, the true values of the uncertain input and output data is obtained from the nominal values by random perturbation

$$\begin{aligned} \tilde{x}_{ij} &= (1 + \varepsilon\eta_{ij})\bar{x}_{ij} \\ \tilde{y}_{ij} &= (1 + \varepsilon\eta_{ij})\bar{y}_{ij} \end{aligned} \tag{2}$$

where $\varepsilon > 0$ is given uncertainty level and the perturbation $\{\eta_{ij}\}_{ij \in J_i}$ are the independent random variables which takes values in [-1, 1]. Without loss of generality, the uncertain component $\eta_{ij} = 0$ for each $j \in J_i$ where J_i is the index for the uncertain coefficients in row i. In this study, we consider uncertainty in some part of the output parameter. Each uncertain data of a DMU is assumed to perturb in an ellipsoidal uncertainty set $\mathcal{U}_{ell}$. For simplicity, the set $\mathcal{U}_{ell}$ is normalised to the ball of radius Ω centred at the origin. i.e. $\mathcal{U}_{ell} = \text{Ball}_{\Omega} = \{\eta \in \mathcal{R}_{[-1,1]} : \parallel \eta \parallel_2 \leq \Omega\}$. Then, the set of uncertain outputs of each DMU_j can be described by the ellipsoid as

$$\mathcal{U}_{\Omega}^{y_{ij}} = \{\mathbf{Y} | \; \tilde{y}_{ij} = \bar{y}_{ij} - \varepsilon\eta_{ij}\bar{y}_{ij} \;\; \forall i,j, \;\; \textstyle\sum_{(i,j)\in J} |\eta_{ij}| \leq \Omega^2, \;\; \eta_{ij} \in [-1, 1] \; \} \tag{3}$$

where $\mathbf{Y}$ is a vector of the output data. The uncertainty set described above provides a realisation for the uncertain output data to be immunized along the parameter Ω regardless of any perturbation in the interval [-1,1]. Thus, as a condition for feasibility of the tractable solution, we require that the ith constraint of the contaminated output data are satisfied. The contaminated data for the CCR model in (1) can therefore be expressed below.

$$\begin{aligned}
&\max \textstyle\sum_{r=1}^{s} u_r(1+\varepsilon\eta_{ij})\bar{y}_{io} \leq 0 \\
&\text{s.t.} \\
&\textstyle\sum_{i=1}^{m} v_i x_{io} = 1 \\
&\textstyle\sum_{r=1}^{s} u_r(1+\varepsilon\eta_{ij})\bar{y}_{ij} - \sum_{i=1}^{m} v_i x_{ij} \leq 0 \quad j = 1, \dots, n \\
&v_i \geq 0 \quad i = 1, \dots, m \\
&u_r \geq 0 \quad r = 1, \dots, s
\end{aligned} \tag{4}$$

Reinjecting equation (3) into model (4) and following closely the robust counterpart formulation of Ben-Tal & Nemirovski (2000), the robust input oriented CCR model is proposed as follows:

$$\begin{aligned}
&\max \textstyle\sum_{r=1}^{s} u_r y_{ro} - \sum_{j\in J_i} u_r \hat{y}_{ro} - \Omega\sqrt{\sum_{j\in J_i} u_r^2 \hat{y}_{ro}^2} \\
&\text{s.t.} \\
&\textstyle\sum_{i=1}^{m} v_i x_{io} = 1 \\
&\textstyle\sum_{r=1}^{s} u_r y_{rj} - \sum_{i=1}^{m} v_i x_{ij} - \sum_{j\in J_i} u_i \hat{y}_{ij} - \Omega\sqrt{\sum_{i=1}^{m} u_i^2 \hat{y}_{ij}^2} \leq 0 \quad j = 1, \dots, n \\
&v_i \geq 0 \quad i = 1, \dots, m \\
&u_r \geq 0 \quad r = 1, \dots, s
\end{aligned} \tag{5}$$

A similar analogy can be made to derive the robust BCC model. Note that the differences lies in the returns to scale variable u_o. In model (5), the role of $0 \leq \Omega \leq 1$ is to adjust the level of uncertainty according to the risk averseness of the decision maker. For $\Omega = 0$, no protection is sought against uncertainty. The higher the value of Ω, the more risk averseness.

Data		Mean	SD	Min	Max
Input	Assets	267693	344216.15	8985	937174
	Employees	2693.21	3682.13	59	10760
Outputs	Deposits	189561.14	246958.35	2940	688624
	Loans	140507.71	189912.94	1762	489103

Table 1. Summary statistics of data

5 Case study of banks in the Czech Republic

We consider 14 active banks which are the main legally mandated banks in the Czech Republic. All the banks are known to operate under a common set of rules and regulations. For assessing the relative efficiencies of these banks, there are two approaches; (i) operating approach (ii) intermediary approach. The former is a cost revenue management approach while the later considers the banks as intermediaries transmitting capital and labor to loans and securities (Jemric & Vujcic (2002)). The RDEA approach uses the second approach. The data for the banks is adapted from Toloo & Tichý (2015) for the 2014 accounting year. Table 1 shows the summary statistics of the data. Two inputs data made of employees and assets and two output data made of deposits and loans comprises the data. These inputs and outputs indicators were considered following common consensus in literature (See Jablonsky et al. (2004); Jemric & Vujcic (2002); Wanke et al. (2016)). For the purpose of this study, deposits and loans data were considered as uncertain. The empirical analysis is discussed in the subsection.

5.1 DEA Results

This section illustrates the relative efficiency measures described in section 3.1 and 3.2. The result for both the input-oriented CCR model and input-oriented BCC model are respectively shown in Table 2. As observed from the Table 2, there are five efficient banks technically; CMZRB, EQB, FIO, RB and UCB[5]. These are banks with non-zero weights and efficiency score of 1. The other inefficient banks can, however, radially decrease their inputs by an appropriate margin to ensure efficiency using the efficient banks as a reference point.

There are comparative differences among the results in CCR and BCC model. Under the variable returns to scale, pure technical efficiencies are measured whiles scale inefficiencies are left out. This is evidenced by the efficiency of 11 banks from the BCC model. In general, the efficiency of DMUs under the BCC model is higher than the CCR. The efficiency score of the CCR runs from a minimum of 0.2233 (ERB bank) to 1 whiles LBBW bank records the minimum efficiency of 0.703 under the BCC model. Surprisingly, the two banks are counter efficient to each other under the two models. Though it looks more plausible to consider the BCC model, for banking operations, the CCR model seems likely to generate good estimates of capacity output. Note that in measuring the efficiency of banks, other determining factors such as the size of bank, level of capitalization, type of ownership, structure of the financial industry, etc. can influence the bank's performance.

Banks	θ^*	v_1^*	v_2^*	u_1^*	u_2^*
AIR	0.99 (1)	0 (0.11)	0.29 (0.29)	0.32 (0.29)	0 (0.11)
CMZRB	1 (1)	20.5 (5.48)	0.50 (0.08)	0.01 (0.03)	0.05 (0.08)
CS	0.91 (1)	0.02 (0.01)	0.01 (0.01)	0.01 (0.01)	0.01 (0.01)
CSOB	0.89 (1)	0.28 (0.38)	0.01 (0.01)	0.01 (0.01)	0.01 (0.01)
EQB	1 (1)	0.60 (0.74)	1.09 (1.09)	0.88 (0.74)	0.60 (0.74)
ERB	0.22 (0.82)	139 (139)	0 (0)	0 (0)	1.27 (0)
FIO	1 (1)	36.4 (15.9)	0.42 (0.49)	0.42 (0.49)	0.42 (0.49)
GEMB	0.99 (0.99)	0 (0)	0.07 (0.07)	0 (0)	0.09 (0.09)
ING	0.88 (1)	11.3 (31)	0.05 (0.01)	0.09 (0.43)	0 (0.01)
JTB	0.96 (1)	20 (3.34)	0.02 (0.10)	0 (0.10)	0.24 (0.10)
KB	0.92 (1)	0.02 (0.35)	0.01 (0.01)	0.01 (0.01)	0.01 (0.01)
LBBW	0.7 (0.7)	0 (0)	0.32 (0.32)	0.34 (0.35)	0 (0)
RB	1 (1)	0.03 (0.04)	0.05 (0.05)	0.03 (0.04)	0.03 (0.04)
UCB	1 (1)	0.87 (0.75)	0.03 (0.03)	0.02 (0.03)	0.03 (0.03)

weights are multiplied by 10^{-4}

Table 2 Optimal weights and CCR- (BCC-) efficiency score (input-oriented)

5.2 RDEA Results

The result for the main contribution of this paper is presented in this section. The result focuses on the robust solution proposed by Ben-Tal & Nemirovski (2000). The perturbation of the output data is set to 0.1 of the uncertain output. For each $j \in J_i$, the uncertain output $\tilde{y}_{ij}$ is modelled as a symmetric and bounded random variable taking values in the interval $[y_{ij} - \hat{y}_{ij}, y_{ij} + \hat{y}_{ij}]$. Therefore $\tilde{y}_{ij}$ changes in the interval $[0.9y_{ij}, 1.1y_{ij}]$. As seen in Table 3, the level of uncertainty is set for different values of Ω. The robust score (R-score) in the 2nd and 5th column indicates when $\Omega = 0$. Under this consideration, no protection is made to any ith-row of the uncertain constraints. The worse-case scenario considers full protection for the uncertain parameters. Here $\Omega = 1$ and is most conservative and highly risk-aversive.

[5] Note that the efficiency scores are only relative in magnitude and they are subjected to the number of banks used.

BANKS	Robust CCR efficiency			Robust BCC efficiency		
	R-score	$\Omega = 0.5$	$\Omega = 1$	R-score	$\Omega = 0.5$	$\Omega = 1$
AIR	0.8976	0.6864	0.5354	0.9827	0.7060	0.5901
CMZRB	0.8905	0.7477	0.6737	0.9254	0.7669	0.7004
CS	0.8390	0.7175	0.5677	1.0000	0.7176	0.5679
CSOB	0.7810	0.6523	0.5121	1.0000	0.6932	0.5492
EQB	0.9246	0.7002	0.5526	1.0000	1.0000	1.0000
ERB	0.2233	0.1489	0.1117	0.8194	0.8194	0.8194
FIO	1.0000	0.7477	0.6695	1.0000	1.0000	1.0000
GEMB	0.9001	0.7388	0.5858	0.9048	0.7405	0.5897
ING	0.7252	0.6515	0.5834	0.7700	0.6655	0.5843
JTB	0.8682	0.7041	0.5727	0.9371	0.7042	0.5751
KB	0.8446	0.7388	0.5858	1.0000	0.7392	0.5871
LBBW	0.6364	0.4756	0.3570	0.6466	0.5448	0.4865
RB	0.8182	0.7156	0.5430	0.8235	0.7184	0.5512
UCB	1.0000	0.7067	0.5691	1.0000	0.7068	0.5696

Table 3 Robust efficiency scores for CCR and BCC

Observe that the efficiency score of each bank decreases as the conservativeness level increases. This fact established in literature (See Ben-Tal & Nemirovski (2000); Sadjadi & Omrani (2008); Lu (2015)) is mainly as a result of the worse-case protection of uncertainties for the objective function in model (5). The efficiency scores ultimately diminish in magnitude in both the CCR and BCC model as the level of conservatism increases. For instance, under the robust CCR model, when $\Omega = 0.5$, the efficiency score for AIR bank is recorded at 0.6864 and decrease to 0.5354 when $\Omega = 1$. The robust efficiency score of the banks, practically and differentially in the two different models are analogous to the traditional DEA models.

However, the robust DEA scores and different from the DEA scores. In the robust case, only few banks are efficient when the real output data are used. It can be observed that the robust efficiency scores are lower compared to the DEA scores. Two banks, i.e., FIO and UCB, are robust efficient under the CCR model whiles CS, CSOB, EQB, FIO, KB and UCB banks have robust efficient scores under the BCC model. The underlying intuition to these discrepancies arises from two reasons. (i) the normal DEA solution contains errors from the uncertain loans and deposits data. By robustifying the model, we ensure only efficiency scores from the 'true' data. (ii) the inefficiencies resulting from randomness in the data are disentangled in the robust measure. Thus, by measuring not only the averages but also variations (uncertainty) in the data, we are in a better position to provide efficient solutions that are stable for the ranking of banks.

6 Concluding remarks

This paper investigated the efficiency of banks under significant uncertainties in the output data. We have introduced a robust DEA model into the measurement of banks efficiency when the underlying data has noise in it. The proposed robust approach is based on the robust counterpart optimization of Ben-Tal & Nemirovski (2000) and it is implemented in the CCR and BCC DEA models. The preliminary result from data on banks in Czech Republic indicates that, efficiency scores measured with the robust DEA model provides a true and stable performance measure than the normal DEA model. When the data under consideration is uncertain and its distribution parameters is unknown but known to be symmetric in an interval, the robust DEA is best to measure efficiency of banks. The flexibility of proposed model is that, it allows the decision maker to define robustness of solution according to the level of risk-averseness.

Acknowledgement

The research was supported by the Czech Science Foundation through project No. 16-17810S.

References

Banker, R.D., Charnes, A. and Cooper, W.W. (1984). 'Some models for estimating technical and scale'inefficiencies in data envelopment analysis'. *Management Science*, 30 (9), pp. 1078–1092.

Barr, R.S. & Seiford, L.M. and Siems, T. F. (1993). 'An envelopment-analysis approach to measuring the managerial efficiency of banks'. *Annals of Operations Research*, 45 (1), pp. 1-19.

Ben-tal, A. & Nemirovski, A. (2000). 'Robust solutions of linear programming problems contaminated with uncertain data'. *Mathematical programming*, 88 (3), pp. 411-424.

Bertsimas, D. and Sim, M. (2004). 'The Price of robustness'. *Operations Research*, 52 (1), pp. 35–53.

Buch, C.M. et al. (2014). 'Uncertainty and International Banking'. *Conference paper for the conference on" International Banking: Microfoundations and Macroeconomic Implications" organized by the International Monetary Fund (IMF) and the Dutch National Bank (DNB).*

Charnes, A., Cooper, W.W. and Rhodes, E. (1978). 'Measuring the efficiency of decision making units'. *European Journal of Operational Research*, 2 (6), pp. 429–444.

Dinger, V. and Craig, B. (2013). 'Uncertainty and bank wholesale funding'. *Deutsche Bundesbank*, No 39/2013(November), pp. 1–31.

Farrell, M.J. (1957). 'The Measurement of Productive Efficiency'. *Journal of the Royal Statistical Society. Series A (General)*, 120 (3), pp. 253–290.

Grigorian, D. a. and Manole, V. (2002). 'Determinants of commercial bank performance in transition: an application of data envelopment analysis'. *IMF Working Paper Series*, (WP/02/146).

Hunjak, T. and Jakovčević, D. (2001). 'Ahp Based Model for Bank Performance'. In *Proceedings of 6th International Symposium on Analytic Hierarchy Process (ISAHP 2001)*. pp. 149–158.

Jablonsky, J. et al. (2004). 'Dea with interval data: An illustration using the evaluation of branches of a czech bank'. *Central European Journal of Operations Research*, 12 (4), p. 323.

Jemric, I. and Vujcic, B. (2002). 'Efficiency of Banks in Croatia: A DEA Approach'. *Comparative Economic Studies*, 44 (2–3), pp. 169–193.

Lu, C.-C. (2015). 'Robust data envelopment analysis approaches for evaluating algorithmic performance'. *Computers & Industrial Engineering*, 81, pp. 78–89.

Saaty, T.L. (2008). 'Decision making with the analytic hierarchy process'. *International Journal of Services Sciences*, 1 (1), p. 83-98.

Sadjadi, S.J. and Omrani, H. (2008). 'Data envelopment analysis with uncertain data: An application for Iranian electricity distribution companies'. *Energy Policy*, 36 (11), pp. 4247–4254.

Toloo, M. (2014). *Data Envelopment Analysis with selected models and applications*, SAEL, Vol. 30. Ostrava: VSB-TU Ostrava.

Toloo, M. and Tichý, T. (2015). 'Two alternative approaches for selecting performance measures in data envelopment analysis'. *Measurement*, 65, pp. 29–40.

Wanke, P., Barros, C.P. and Emrouznejad, A. (2016). 'Assessing productive efficiency of banks using integrated Fuzzy-DEA and bootstrapping: A case of Mozambican banks'. *European Journal of Operational Research*, 249 (1), pp. 378–389.

Determination of Coefficients of Multi-Attribute Utility Function with Attribute Breakdown

Viktor Molnar[1], Dora Diana Horvath[2]

Abstract. Multi-attribute decision-making requires a relatively considerable effort from decision-makers, which leads among others to the abandonment of utility-based decision procedures. Many researchers have worked on proposals that help in simplifying the decision-making process. A model is recommended in the paper, with the help of which difficult utility-based estimations can be reduced into a preference-based weighting. The latter is proven to be satisfactory and meanwhile includes the decision-makers' preference structure. The model substitutes a non-additive multi-attribute utility function with an additive one but the number of attributes increase in return, which is still considered as a less difficult method. In the last chapter we introduce the results of a non-representative test of the elaborated model in a case study form. It can be stated on the basis of the results that attribute breakdown helps in reaching a more realistic outcome.

Keywords: MAUT, AHP, MCDM, variable interaction.

JEL Classification: C60, D81

1 Introduction

One of the most significant difficulties in multi-criteria decision-making is the fact that decision-makers are not able to express their preferences exactly, which results in a long decision process. This problem is remarkable if the decision itself is complex or includes attributes of which measurement based mostly on subjective elements. The literature of managerial decision-making collects several useful publications which advise complicated mathematical models or easy-to-use but not perfectly appropriate ones to support decisions have to be made either on a higher significance level or within a short time, respectively.

Many publications attempt to propose a practical model for the simplification of the decision-making process but in several cases simplification results in a less reliable outcome. The first part of this study summarizes some main points and academic milestones of the above detailed problem. In the next part a useful model, which we consider as reliable despite the simplification, is introduced.

2 Literature review

In multi-criteria decision-making (MCDM) utility theory plays a significant role because several decision problems cannot be expressed by numerical data but only by preferences (Fishburn, 1970). Bouyssou and Vincke (1998) summarized the main theory and methods of preference modelling. At the same time conventional areas of decision-making use the latest results of MCDM society to improve their more and more complicated solutions of which

[1] University of Miskolc / Institute of Management Science, H-3515 Miskolc-Egyetemvaros, e-mail: szvmv@uni-miskolc.hu

[2] University of Miskolc / Institute of Management Science, H-3515 Miskolc-Egyetemvaros, e-mail: szvhdora@uni-miskolc.hu

objectives are the description of real-life mechanisms (Musinszki, 2016). Researchers in other specific topics have started to apply complex decision support models in their works, for example eco-industrial parks (Leong et al., 2017), portfolio optimization (Koksalan and Tuncer Sakar, 2016), employee performance management (Ishizaka and Pereira, 2016), monitoring of heart patients' behavior (Doumpos M. et al., 2016) or social accounting (Demeny and Musinszki, 2016).

Business decisions, however, include so many influencing factors that model-building for a complex decision problem is always challenging. Models which contain preference-based elements have to be constructed with an increased accuracy because of the nature of subjectivity and behavioral or personality factors. Outcomes of managerial decisions, for example, highly depend on personality (Kunos, 2016). In the model of organization competence building (Veres-Somosi, 2013) the method selection and competence analysis blocks include critical points in which only utility-based decision-making methods can ensure the desired outcome of decision. Due to the aforementioned complexity, in many decision support processes in practice interactive methods are applied to map decision-makers' preference systems. Some of the latest industrial applications of interactive process are described by Kaliszewski (2016) or Koksalan and Tuncer Sakar (2016).

Wide range of decision support solutions help decision-makers in specific problems. Researchers compare similar methods from time to time in order to refine the preliminary conditions of their applications. For example, Zanakis et al. (1998) compared the well-known Analytic Hierarchy Process (AHP) to Characteristic Objects Method (COMET). Salabun, Ziemba and Watrobski (2016) introduced a simulation procedure to support method selection. It also can be stated that linked methods as hybrid solutions can sometimes only be the ones that reflect the real situation in an appropriate manner. Chen, Tzeng and Ding (2008) combined AHP with Multi-Dimensional Scaling (MDS) procedures and there are many researchers like Gupta and Mohanty (2016) who approach the problems on the basis of fuzzy logic.

AHP (Saaty, 1994) is one of the most cited ranking methods and its weaknesses are known by many professionals. A comprehensive summary is given about advantages and disadvantages of the procedure by Forman (1993). One of the rarely cited weaknesses is that the base of ranking alternatives is not utility function but a simple pairwise comparison which, though, expresses preferences. Some researchers like Lai (1995) combined Multi-Attribute Utility Theory (MAUT) with AHP for additive multi-attribute utility functions. Following parts of the paper attempt to extend this direction of combination.

3 Extension of MAUT and AHP combination to general multi-attribute utility functions

3.1 Coefficients of multi-attribute utility functions

In construction of multi-attribute utility functions, determination of coefficients of a decomposition form is based on comparisons of certain outcome vectors with the reference lottery. As the result of these comparisons, decision-makers designate certain utility levels for the given outcomes (*Figure 1*). This process is relatively uncomplicated in case of comparing outcomes in which one attribute is fixed on the most preferred and the rest on the least preferred level. The task can be more difficult if two or more attributes are fixed on the most preferred level. To express the utility exactly, decision-makers need a lot of practice but consistence is not guaranteed.

$$(x_1^+; x_2^-; x_3^-) \sim \begin{cases} \beta_1 & (x_1^+; x_2^+; x_3^+) \\ 1-\beta_1 & (x_1^-; x_2^-; x_3^-) \end{cases} \qquad (x_1^+; x_2^-; x_3^+) \sim \begin{cases} \beta_{13} & (x_1^+; x_2^+; x_3^+) \\ 1-\beta_{13} & (x_1^-; x_2^-; x_3^-) \end{cases}$$

$$\lambda_1 = u(x_1^+; x_2^-; x_3^-) = \beta_1 \qquad \lambda_{13} = u(x_1^+; x_2^-; x_3^+) = \beta_{13} - \lambda_1 - \lambda_3$$

$$u(x) = \lambda_1 u_1(x_1) + \lambda_2 u_2(x_2) + \lambda_3 u_3(x_3) + \lambda_{12} u_1(x_1) u_2(x_2) + \lambda_{13} u_1(x_1) u_3(x_3) + \\ + \lambda_{23} u_2(x_2) u_3(x_3) + \lambda_{123} u_1(x_1)\, u_2(x_2)\, u_3(x_3)$$

Legend:
+, −: the most and the least preferred value of x_i attribute; u: utility; (x_1, x_2, x_3): output vector; $u(x)$: MAUF
λ: constant in decomposition form of MAUF; β: decision-maker's judgement for likelihood as the result of indifference comparison

Figure 1 Example for determination of some coefficients of a three-attribute quasi-additive type utility function (own construction)

3.2 AHP and additive utility functions

If additive independence condition is valid, the form of multi-attribute utility function is additive. It means that the algebraic form of the function contains only terms in which there are no interacting variables. AHP weights of attributes correspond to the coefficients of these terms. According to Lai (1995, p. 454.): "Although weights and priorities are conceptually different fundamental constructs in MAUT and AHP, they refer mathematically to the coefficients in the additive decision rules. Weights and priorities, as well as attributes and criteria, are therefore used interchangeably here."

This logic results in the fact that in case of additive-independent attributes it is not necessary to ask decision-makers to compare some multi-attribute outcomes to a reference lottery but they can only apply a simpler pairwise comparison or other weighting techniques.

3.3 Utility functions containing interacting variables

If attributes interact with each other, application of the additive form results in a distorted outcome. We found that in many practical applications a more profound breakdown of attributes can help in avoiding the problem of interactions with applying an additive function with more attributes. This logic can be visualized by use of AHP structure given in *Figure 2*.

In this example the decision problem contains two attributes of which importance are expressed by weighting. These weights cannot be the coefficients of an additive multi-attribute function because it is obvious that the value of the first depends on the value of the second one. The obvious solution of the given specific example is that the two attributes have one or more sub-attributes. If a decision problem can be broken down to influencing attributes which are additively independent from each other, the importance and therefore the weights of the lowest level of attributes correspond to the coefficients of an additive multi-attribute utility function in which the single-attribute utility functions represent the utilities of the considered attributes. Following this procedure the decision-maker faces a more complicated model, namely one with more variables, but determination of importance of single attributes results in more exact judgements than attempting that for interactions of variables. Moreover we consider this cognitive procedure as simpler than the reference lottery comparisons mentioned above.

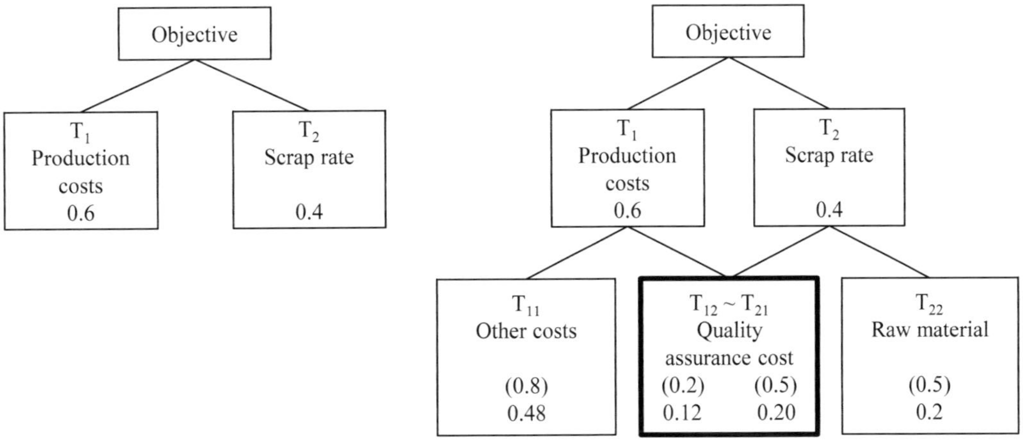

Figure 2 Example for interacting attributes (left) and breakdown of them (right) in order to construct additively independent attributes (own construction)

If two or more attributes are in interaction with each other, the number of attributes increases. In case of interaction one attribute has to be broken down to at least two attributes. If there are n attributes and there are total k interactions (two or more attributes interact with each other), the decision-maker has to give or has to perform at least $n+k$ weights or pairwise comparisons, respectively. In realization of attribute breakdown, it is more realistic that there will be more than k extra attributes as the result of a thorough consideration. Let the number of extra attributes m. Therefore the algebraic interpretation of the multi-attribute utility function can be given by *Equation 1*.

$$u(x_1; \ldots; x_n)_{\text{non-addtive}} \sim u(x_1; \ldots; x_{n+m})_{\text{additive}}, \qquad (1)$$

where multi-attribute utility is symbolized by u and attributes are symbolized by x_i.

A simple experiment was performed and we found that the 'shared weighting' as an estimation of coefficients of multi-attribute utility function is suitable to be used. The results are detailed in the case study below. Shared weighting means that the weights of the common attributes are summarized.

4 Case study - a CSR choice problem

A non-representative experiment was performed to test the elaborated model. Three middle-level managers were asked about a given decision problem. They had to rank given CSR actions (A_1-A_5) on the basis of given attributes. Both the group of actions and attributes were chosen by us from a published paper (Gligor and Muntenau, 2015). The structure of the decision problem is demonstrated in *Figure 3*. The decision structure contained interacting attributes: cost and quality of the CSR actions.

The experiment was divided into three sessions. In the first one subjects determined the performance values of the attributes for each alternative as the result of a group work (*Table 1*). The alternatives were the potential CSR actions of an imaginary company of which CSR-relevant characteristics were previously determined by the group. The subjects constructed their orders independently without any other information. Results are introduced in the first row of *Table 4*.

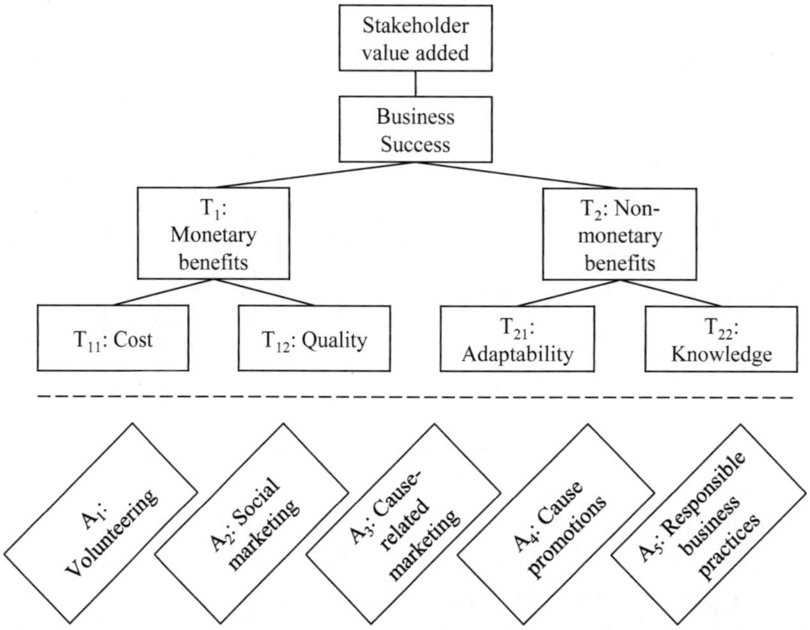

Figure 3 Decision structure on the basis of 'CSR potential positive impact model' [Gligor-Muntenau, 2015]

CSR action	Cost (Low: 1; High: 5)	Quality	Adaptability (Poor: 1; Excellent: 5)	Knowledge
Volunteering	1	5	2	5
Social marketing	5	1	3	4
Cause-related marketing	3	4	2	4
Cause promotion	2	4	4	4
Responsible business practices	5	3	2	4

Table 1 Performance of alternatives (own construction)

In the next phase they weighted the first-level attributes (T_1, T_2) and then the second-level ones (T_{11}, T_{12}, T_{21}, T_{22}). The weights and the weighted performances of alternatives (normalized performance values were weighted) are given in *Table 2*. The calculated ranking can be found in the second row of *Table 4*. In the third session when the experiment leaders explained the nature of interaction between attributes, they reconstructed the attributes and repeated the weighting procedure.

CSR action	Decision-Maker 1					Decision-Maker 2					Decision-Maker 3				
	Cost	Quality	Adaptability	Knowledge	Sum	Cost	Quality	Adaptability	Knowledge	Sum	Cost	Quality	Adaptability	Knowledge	Sum
	Weights														
	.4	**.1**	**.4**	**.1**		**.3**	**.25**	**.3**	**.15**		**.3**	**.15**	**.5**	**.05**	
A_1	.03	.03	.06	.02	*.141*	.02	.07	.05	.04	*.175*	.02	.04	.08	.01	*.153*
A_2	.11	.01	.09	.02	*.224*	.08	.01	.07	.03	*.193*	.08	.01	.12	.01	*.214*
A_3	.08	.02	.06	.02	*.184*	.06	.06	.05	.03	*.194*	.06	.04	.08	.01	*.182*
A_4	.05	.02	.12	.02	*.219*	.04	.06	.09	.03	*.220*	.04	.04	.15	.01	*.239*
A_5	.13	.02	.06	.02	*.232*	.10	.04	.05	.03	*.219*	.10	.03	.08	.01	*.213*

Table 2 Attribute weights and weighted performances of alternatives – 'sum' column (own construction)

CSR action	Contractors cost	Wages	Contractors cost	Perceived quality	Adaptability	Knowledge	Weighted performances		
	Weights								
DM1	**.24**	**.16**	**.025**	**.075**	**.4**	**.1**	**DM1**	**DM2**	**DM3**
DM2	**.18**	**.12**	**.0625**	**.1875**	**.3**	**.15**			
DM3	**.18**	**.12**	**.0375**	**.1125**	**.5**	**.05**			
A_1	1	5	1	5	2	5	*.178*	*.193*	*.176*
A_2	4	4	4	1	3	4	*.229*	*.205*	*.222*
A_3	3	3	3	4	2	4	*.183*	*.191*	*.180*
A_4	2	2	2	4	4	4	*.216*	*.213*	*.235*
A_5	5	1	5	3	2	4	*.193*	*.197*	*.187*

Table 3 New attributes and weights of the 3rd phase reconstruction; performance (values 1-5, similarly as in Table 1) and weighted performances of alternatives. (own construction)

One shared attribute was found and weighted differently. Cost were broken down to Contractors' cost (weight: 0.6) and Wages (weight: 0.4); Quality were broken down to Contractors' cost (weight: 0.25) and Perceived quality (weight: 0.75). Performance values referring to Perceived quality were supposed as the Quality values in the second phase. The results are summarized in *Table 3* and *Table 4*.

Experiment phases	DM1	DM2	DM3
Phase 1 (subjective ranking)	$A_2 \succ A_4 \succ A_5 \succ A_3 \succ A_1$	$A_2 \succ A_4 \succ A_5 \succ A_3 \succ A_1$	$A_4 \succ A_2 \succ A_5 \succ A_3 \succ A_1$
Phase 2 (AHP-type ranking)	$A_5 \succ A_2 \succ A_4 \succ A_3 \succ A_1$	$A_4 \succ A_5 \succ A_2 \succ A_3 \succ A_1$	$A_4 \succ A_2 \succ A_5 \succ A_3 \succ A_1$
Phase 3 (Ranking after attribute breakdown)	$A_2 \succ A_4 \succ A_5 \succ A_3 \succ A_1$	$A_4 \succ A_2 \succ A_5 \succ A_1 \succ A_3$	$A_4 \succ A_2 \succ A_5 \succ A_3 \succ A_1$

Table 4 Summary of orders (own construction)

It can be seen in *Table 4* that the properly constructed attribute structure resulted in a similar order than in the first case and the orders got in the second session were different. Although the construction of the new structure was part of a group work, and group work can result in a different outcome than individual ones, we did not consider that distortion, because the decision problem was simple.

5 Conclusions and limitations

The elaborated model is a simple one for supporting managerial decisions and our test results showed that it can be useful in case of simple problems. Technically it can be used in complex decisions too but the number of attributes decision-makers have to consider and evaluate is increasing with the number of interactions among attributes. Decision-makers tend to make their decisions intuitively if there are no exact numerical data available. If utility-based decisions are supported by the proposed model, the result is close to those of the intuitively made decisions but a preliminary condition in this case is that in the background of the intuitive decisions there have to be highly profound cognitive considerations.

We did not consider the well-known problem of rank reversal during elaboration of the model. The utility function was considered as a general one and we did not analyze the effect of the different independence conditions connecting to the form of utility functions. The logic of estimation by weighting was not validated on a representative sample. The elaborated model was not tested in case of an immensely complex decision problem.

Acknowledgement

"The described study was carried out as part of the EFOP-3.6.1-16-00011 "Younger and Renewing University – Innovative Knowledge City – institutional development of the University of Miskolc aiming at intelligent specialization" project implemented in the framework of the Szechenyi 2020 program. The realization of this project is supported by the European Union, co-financed by the European Social Fund."

References

Bouyssou, D. and Vincke, Ph. (eds) (1998). 'Preference modeling'. *Annals of Operations Research*, Baltzer Science Publishers.

Chen, M-F., Tzeng, G-H. and Ding, C. D. (2008). 'Combining fuzzy AHP with MDS in identifying the preference similarity of alternatives'. *Applied Soft Computing*, 8, pp. 110-117.

Demeny, A. and Musinszki, Z. (2016). 'Social Accounting – In the Wake of the Sustainability'. *Theory Methodology Practice*, 12 (2), pp. 26-40.

Doumpos, M. et al. (2016). 'Development of a robust multicriteria classification model for monitoring the postoperative behaviour of heart patients'. *Journal of Multi-Criteria Decision Analysis*, 23 (1-2), pp. 15-27.

Fishburn, P. (1970): *Utility theory and decision making*, New York: Wiley.

Forman, E. H. (1993). 'Facts and fictions about the Analytic Hierarchy Process'. *Mathematical and Computer Modelling*, 17 (4/5), pp. 19-26.

Gligor, D. C. and Muntenau, V. P. (2015). 'CSR benefits and costs in a strategic approach'. *Annals of University of Craiova - Economic Sciences Series*, 1 (43), pp. 96-105.

Gupta, M. and Mohanty, B. K. (2016). 'Attribute partitioning in multiple attribute decision making problems for a decision with a purpose – A fuzzy approach'. *Journal of Multi-Criteria Decision Analysis*, 23 (3-4), pp. 160-170.

Ishizaka, A. and Pereira, V. (2016). 'A fair and transparent employee performance management system based on multi-criteria decision analysis and visual techniques'. *International Journal of Manpower*, 37 (4), pp. 628-659.

Kaliszewski, I. (2016). 'On variant selection mechanisms in interactive MCDA - engineering versus reverse engineering'. *Journal of Multi-Criteria Decision Analysis*, 23 (1-2), pp. 40-48.

Koksalan, M. and Tuncer Sakar, C. (2016). 'An interactive approach to stochastic programming-based portfolio optimization'. *Annals of Operations Research*, 245, pp. 47-66.

Kunos, I. (2016). 'A coaching-related survey on personality differences'. *Theoretical, methodological and practical foundations of human resources management: Collective monograph*, ISMA University, pp. 59-79.

Lai, S-K. (1995). 'A preference-based interpretation of AHP'. *International Journal of Management Science*, 23 (4), pp. 453-462.

Leong, Y. T. et al. (2017). 'Multi-objective optimization for resource network synthesis in eco-industrial parks using an integrated analytic hierarchy process'. *Journal of Cleaner Production*, 143, pp. 1268-1283.

Musinszki, Z. (2016). 'Ipar 4.0 – költségrendszer 4.0?: Innovációk a költségrendszerekben (Industry 4.0 - cost system 4.0?: Innovations in cost systems)'. *Controller Info*, 4 (3), pp. 2-9.

Saaty, T. L. (1994). 'Highlights and critical points in the theory and application of the Analytic Hierarchy Process'. *European Journal of Operational Research*, 74, pp. 426-447.

Salabun, W., Ziemba, P. and Watrobski, J. (2016). 'The rank reversals paradox in management decisions: The comparison of the AHP and COMET methods'. *Intelligent Decision Technologies*, 181-191, Springer International Publishing, pp. 181-191.

Veres-Somosi, M. (2013): *Teljesítményalapú szervezetalakítás elmélete és módszertana (Theory and methodology of performance-based formation of organizations)*, University of Miskolc, Faculty of Economics, pp. 66-67.

Zanakis, S. H. et al. (1998). 'Multi-attribute decision making: A simulation comparison of select methods'. *European Journal of Operational Research*, 107, pp. 507-529.

Using the DEA-DA of ratios for classification units

Maryam Olfati[1]

Abstract. The aim of this research is developing a different method to allocate same weights to given inputs and outputs for all units and therefore make an optimum discrimination between efficient and inefficient according to per given by DEA and be able to rank them with the same scale. This method which is called discriminant data envelop analysis of ratios, provide an additional post optimally analysis of DEA fo r organizational units in case their multiple inputs and out- puts are available. The ratio between composite output and input has been constructed in case which the common weight of them are computed by non-linear optimization of goodness of separation between the groups. One of DR/DEA applications is to utilize the common weights for ranking the units by a unified scale. A different use of two-group discriminant criteria which is presented in this study for ratios and the traditional discriminant analysis is used for linear function. Also to verify the consistency between classification from DEA a post-classification achieved from DR/DEA non-parametric statistical tests have been used.

Keywords: Data Envelopment Analysis, Discriminant Analysis, Classification, Ranking.

JEL Classification: C44, C67

1 Introduction

The purpose of this study is the ranking all of organizational units within the same scale of DEA contents. This purpose is a settled approach for analyzing the units which is corresponded to management and social science. Units in DEA model are classified into two groups of efficient and inefficient. These units are not fully ranked on one scale by DEA model. Though there is a need to completely rank the units however DEA classifies the units into only two groups. To assess the highway maintenance of units in context of DEA, Cook (1990) and Roll (1991) argued the common weights approach first. A DEA structure based subjective ordinal preference ranking was given by Cook and Kress. They proposed a method to determine common weights by reduction the gap between upper and lower limits. Cooper and Tones had the ranking based on scalar measures of inefficiency in DEA related to the slack variables.

Some approaches for ranking of the units in the context of DEA were introduced by Sinuany et al (1994) which there was a two-stage linear discriminant analysis among them. First stage was about the distinguish between efficient and inefficient units. The second stage allows the discriminant analysis to affords a function of scoring based on linear combination of variables (inputs and outputs) for given two sets and rank the variables. However, the DA does not make any distinction between inputs and output and also it does not consider the ratio between weighted variables.

This study develops a different non-linear DA model for groups both. The ratio between composite input and outputs which is given in primary classification of units efficiency criteria

[1] VŠB-Technical University of Ostrava/Faculty of Economics, Department of Systems Engineering, 17. listopadu 15/2172, 708 33 Ostrava, maryam.olfati@vsb.cz.

in DEA makes the discriminant score. Therefore this new model weights all units similarly according to the best separation of units in efficiency criteria of DEA. These common weights will be used for rank scaling of units in a unified scale. In fact, the gap between Pareto optimum approach (which is as to the used extreme points in operations study) and multivariate statistical approach of average tendencies in classical econometrics (Madalla, 1977) will be closed as much as it is possible. Although The efficient units in the DEA ideal case should be ranked with highest value in the DR/DEA model however because of great variation of inputs and outputs weights from unit to unit in DEA model there might be inconsistency between these approaches (because DR/DEA model ranks the units with common weights). This method, which is presented has been developed by Zilla Sinuany Stern and Lea Friedman. Statistical tests are used to confirm the fit between two approaches. Higher fit results in higher reliability of the ranking. DEA model has been described versus the statistical analysis in section2. The development of two-group discriminant analysis has been presented. After that, the DR/DEA has been introduced and an example is given. Section 5 includes conclusions and potential uses of DR/DEA for future researchers.

2 DEA model versus statistical analyses

DEA as a non-parametric approach is needless of any assumption of functional form of production function Charnes, Cooper, & Rhodes (1978). Too many articles have been presented in the content of DEA that provide developments and examples for this model. A unit with single input and output in which the ratio of output to input defines the efficiency is the simplest one. Units that have multiple inputs and outputs are the main purpose DEA application. These inputs and outputs could be used along with an efficiency measure. It could be defined as the ratio of the sum of weighted outputs to the weighted inputs. Therefore a factor weights set which are solved through DEA model is required. This solution is as follows:

$$\begin{aligned} & max \quad & h_{kk} = \textstyle\sum_{r=1}^{k} u_{rk} y_{rk} / \sum_{i=1}^{m} v_{ik} x_{ik} \\ & st: \quad & h_{kj} = \textstyle\sum_{r=1}^{k} u_{rk} y_{rj} / \sum_{i=1}^{m} v_{ik} x_{ij} \le 1, j = 1, \dots, n \\ & & u_{rk} / \textstyle\sum_{i=1}^{m} v_{ik} x_{ik} \le \varepsilon \, , v_{ik} / \sum_{i=1}^{m} v_{ik} x_{ik} \le \varepsilon, r = 1, \dots, s \end{aligned} \tag{1}$$

While there are s outputs, m inputs and n units assume that in unit j, y_{rj} is the level r-th output and x_{ij} is the given level of i-th input. Positive numbers are allocated to all y_{rj} andx_{ij}. Best weights of u_{rk} and v_{ik}, which maximize the ratio between weighted outputs and inputs of unit k will be find for each unit k as the E.q (1).

Variable weights which should be determined by the solution of kth problem are u_{rk} and v_{ik} and a non-archimedian infinitesimal is defined as $\varepsilon > 0$, Banker, Charnes and Cooper (1984). Considering the limitations which allow to choose the optimal weights for inputs and outputs from the available data, the highest possible efficiency will be allocated to each unit k. According to DEA $0 < h_{kk} < 1$, since $h_{kk} = 1$ makes unit k efficient relative to others considered in problem k. The efficiency frontier restricts the measurement of units efficiency relative to other units and determines that units lie on or below this frontier. $h_{kk} < 1$ means that unit k is efficient because of the given freedom to this unit to receive the most the most desirable weight for the achievement of the maximal ratio h_{kk}. However presence of another unit (or units) that possesses the higher ratio for the equal weights with unit k, prevents the unit k to achieve the score of 1. The flexibility of weight selection specifies the DEA model as mentioned above. Pareto optimum solution like the efficient frontier is gained by this variety of weights. DEA methodology aims the frontiers more than central tendencies. DEA does not fits the regression through the center of the data; instead it floats a piecewise linear platform as the frontier which takes place at the summit of observations. The similarity of DEA and regression is the use of all pertinent information, but the difference is that DEA focuses on units separately while regression and canonical correlation use the means. Regression approach and canonical correlation adopt a unique function based on the average behavior for which prespicification of functional form is required (Freedman and Sinuany stern 1977). DEA-discriminates the efficiency of units in the sense of Pareto optimality. The relative inefficiencies that are missed by the average regression approach could be located by DEA.

Weights value in DEA could differ from unit to unit and this characteristic of flexibility in weight choosing specifies the DEA approach. Since the "efficiency scores" are gained from different groups of comparison for different units there for these scores could not be used for ranking. For this reason in practical applications, a principle of ranking would be required. The aim of this study is development of a new method in which all given inputs and outputs are provided with common weights and these common weights optimally discriminate between efficient and inefficient units according to the pregiven values by DEA to use a unified scale for ranking all units.

To find a score function that ranks the units to two sets of efficient and inefficient, Sinuany et al (1994) applied the traditional discriminant analysis. In their study, a one-dimensional linear function has been constructed by using the classical discriminant analysis of the two groups in the context of DEA.

"Assuming $D_j < D_c$ reclassifies the unit j to efficient group, otherwise to the inefficient group. In this equation D_c is a critical value that is obtained in the basis of the discriminant function values of both groups average" (Morrison, 1976, p. 232). Using this formulation the inputs and output are not distinguishable. These variables belong the same set of $(m + s)$ variables in a linear relation. However the inputs received negative sign, final weigh that is expected to be positive could remain negative. All the weak of these models have been overcame by the new method of this paper.

3 Two-group discriminant analysis of ratios

The two groups discriminant analysis of ratios there is no difference between input and output variables in classical discriminant analysis of two groups, therefore in this study, a new direction has been proceeded to make such discrimination. In this research, a ratio function between the linear combination of inputs and similar combination output has been constructed rather than consideration of a linear combination between inputs and outputs in one equation.
While this ratio function and DEA efficiency have similarities in several aspects, the weight provided for inputs and outputs in DEA model might vary for different units but the weights for all units in the method of the discriminant analysis of ratio are the same. Literally, the

weights in discriminant analysis of ratio are determined so that the two group of given observations could be discriminated optimally. Instead of the linear discriminant score, ratio has been used in this study as follows:

$$T_j = \sum_{r=1}^{k} u_{rk} y_{rj} / \sum_{i=1}^{m} v_{ik} x_{ij} \ , \quad j = 1, \dots, n \tag{2}$$

For efficient and inefficient groups the arithmetic average of the ratio score is defined as

$$\begin{aligned} \bar{T}_1 &= \sum_{j=1}^{n_1} T_j / n_1 \\ \bar{T}_2 &= \sum_{j=n_1+1}^{n_2} T_j / n_2 \end{aligned} \tag{3}$$

The number of efficient and inefficient units are respectively n_1 and n_2 in the DEA model. $\hat{T} = (n_1 T_1 + n_2 T_2)/n$ indicates the weighted average of all $n(n = n_1 + n_2)$ units.

The problem is to determine $v_i (i = 1, \dots, n)$ and $u_r (r = 1, \dots, s)$ common weights to ratio variance of T, $(SS_B(T))$ between two groups and variance of T, $(SS_W(T))$ within group will namely be maximum

$$\begin{aligned} max\lambda_{u_r v_i} &= \max_{u_r v_i} SS_B(T)/SS_W(T), \\ SS_B(T) &= n_1(\bar{T}_1 - \hat{T})^2 + n_2(\bar{T}_1 - \hat{T})^2 = \frac{n_1 n_2}{n_1 + n_2} (\bar{T}_1 - \bar{T}_2)^2, \\ SS_W(T) &= \sum_{j=1}^{n_1} (T_j - \bar{T}_1)^2 + \sum_{j=n_1+1}^{n_2} (T_j - \bar{T}_2)^2 \end{aligned} \tag{4}$$

Well-known criterion of discrimination is the objective function $SS_B/SSS_B(T)S_W$ and D in classical discriminant analysis indicates the linear combination of variables. In this case the two sets of linear combinations ratio is *D*.

In the next step S non- parametric statistic η that is equivalent to the ratio of Pearson's correlation will be defined as

$$\eta^2 = \frac{SS_B(T)}{SS_B(T) + SS_B(T)} \tag{5}$$

The weights u_r and v_i that maximize this equation are the equivalent to the criterion of maximizing the discriminant on λ in classical discriminant analysis that results in the maximum separation between two average groups. The squared of η have the value between *0* and *1* because it's a coefficient of correlation. The deviation of η^2 from 1 as the theoretical upper limit of bound can result the measure of goodness of separation between two groups. DR/DEA has perfectly classified the efficiency from the DEA when $\eta^2 = 1$. The Fisher F statistic could be conducted to test the statistical significance of η^2. Guttman(1988) has shown that simple transformation of η^2 is F, specially when the two group discriminant analysis of ratios,

$$F = (n-2)\eta^2/(1-\eta^2). \tag{6}$$

Conjugate gradient was used to solve the η^2 as $(m + s)$variables real function (Luenberger, 1973). An initial guess of $(m + s)$ coefficients is required but local maxima is the main drawback. Solving the eta squared for several initial different search points is necessary for increasing the chance of chance finding the global optimum. To find the optimal weights u_r and v_i DR/DEA requires an algorithmic procedure however, to this end a closed form solution is afforded in the traditional discriminant analysis. This difference originates from that there is a consideration of a linear function of inputs and outputs classical discriminant analysis but in DR/DEA there is an assumption of weighted inputs and outputs. To achieve the same scale for weights, each input or output could be divided to its standard deviation. The ratio scale does not vary. The achieved standard weights could be compared.

In the functional relation between inputs and output $u_r$and v_i which are weights, cannot be negative in order to be consistent with ordinary usage. To guarantee the positivity of the weights constraint should be introduced. Misclassification of inputs and outputs or improper raw data may lead in negative weights. In worse cases negative weighted variables removal is allowed.

4. New DR/DEA method

The overall process of the new method is a multi-stage procedure. In the first step, DEA is utilizes to discriminate between efficient units and inefficient ones. Next, two-group discriminant analysis related to ratio of the composite input and output is applied on two aforementioned classes of units. A new efficiency metric for each unit j is presented as follows based on resulting weights from previous step.

$$T_j = \sum_{r=1}^{k} u_{rk} y_{rj} / \sum_{i=1}^{m} v_{ik} x_{ij} \ , \quad j = 1, \dots, n \tag{7}$$

Hence, the scale of the units is ranked in a manner which rank 1 is assigned to the highest score.

$R_{T_1} = 1$ and the rank n is given to the lowest score, i.e. $R_{T_n} = n$. In an optimal situation, the first ranks should be allocated to the DEA efficient units. However, in practical circumstances, some errors may be occurred in the ranking process. In this paper, various non-parametric tests are performed in order to verify statistical significance of the results. It is worth to mention that unlike the DEA, upper bond of the efficiency ratio in DR/DEA is T_j. Since the statistical tests depend on the ratio score ranking not on the absolute values, this difference will not cause any problem.

The Mann-Whitney Rank-Sum test and the Fisher Exact Probability test are utilized to investigate matching between efficient and inefficient group categorizing using DEA and rank scaling using DR/DEA. The Mann-Whitney test is used to investigate the rank proper assignment, while the Fisher test is used to detect wrong classification using ratio scale parameter.

In the Mann-Whitney Rank-Sum test a statistic which defines as follows plays a critical role.

$$U = n_1 n_2 + \frac{n_1(n_1+1)}{2} - R_1 \ , \tag{8}$$

where R_1 denotes sum of the efficient ranks in DEA. If n_1 and $n_2 \geq 10$, then the statistic U can be approximated using normal distribution which its mean and standard deviation are $\eta_U = (n_1 n_2),/2$, $\sigma_U^2 = ((n_1 n_2(n_1 + n_2 + 1))/12$, respectively. In this test, null hypothesis is define as a situation that there is no matching between DEA and DR/DEA and one came to conclusion that ranks are not assigned properly. If the following condition met (which means both two groups have same efficiency scores), the null hypothesis is rejected.

$$(U - \mu_U)/\sigma_U > Z_\alpha \tag{9}$$

Where Z_α denotes upper α percentile of the standard normal distribution. In case of significant relationship between DEA classification and DR/DEA score ranking, the null hypothesis is rejected.

Brockett and Golany (1996) formerly used Mann-Whitney test along with DEA. However, their main purpose was to compare the ranks of two different educational programs. One of the most considerable result of their research is that because of a large number of units which is required in the parametric tests, the non-parametric test are more useful tools for this end rather than parametric ones.

For fisher test, a new type of efficient unit called DR/DEA efficient is proposed. The units with score greater than certain threshold are defined as DR/DEA efficient. The average analysis of DR/DEA matches DEA Pareto optimum analysis if DR/DEA scales have similar results to DEA discriminant. To this end, a proper threshold value should be determined for efficient units. Raveh (1989) utilized a non-parametric method to optimally determine the threshold value and minimize the classification errors. According to approach, a straightforward routine is proposed to determine the threshold value as follows:

All then units are ranked in a descending manner based on the resulting ratios in DR/DEA for the certain n_1 efficient units, if all the marked efficient units take place in DEA efficient units, then the threshold value is decreased.

For the certain n_1 efficient units, if all the marked efficient units does not take place in DEA efficient units, then the new threshold value is determined.

The final value of the threshold value is determined based on the minimum relevant classification error (M).

The classification errors consist of two subclasses which is called type I and type II. Type I corresponds to labeling *DEA inefficient* as *DR/DEA efficient*, while type II corresponds to labeling "*DEA efficient*" as "*DR/DEA inefficient*".

Considering M1 and M2 as type I and type II classification errors, respectively ($M = M_1 + M_2$) the null hypothesis for fisher test is the situation that there is no matching between DEA and DR/DEA. The Fisher exact probability for $M_1 < M_2$ is calculated as following:

$$\Pr = \sum_{i=0}^{M_1} \frac{\binom{n_1}{i}\binom{n_2}{N_1-i}}{\binom{n}{N_1}} \tag{10}$$

For the pr $< \alpha$, the null hypothesis is rejected and statistical significant relationship between DEA and DR/DEA is approved. Since the Mann-Whitney Rank-Sum test is based on rank summation, the Fisher Exact Probability test is dichotomic.

Since the Mann-Whitney test is a higher level test, in case of any matching according to this results, the Fisher Exact Probability test will approve the same results.

However, the threshold value in DR/DEA defines classification performance by itself, i.e. the units beyond the threshold are labeled as inefficient units previously, take place inefficient units group. So, this new merit potentially can predict the unit efficiency without DEA recursive procedure. For the certain data, the DR/DEA is valid if DR/DER is consistent with DEA.

4 Conclusions

Compared with other methods, DR/DEA has more than three advantages. Full ranking of the efficient and inefficient units in a same scale can be achieved on basis of the ratio between composite outputs and inputs when a non-linear optimization of goodness of separation has computed the common weights of these variables. DEA give this discrimination into two groups of efficient and inefficient. Another advantage is that the model, unlike the classical discriminant analysis, discriminates the output and inputs. The third advantage is that result of DR/DEA ranking is consistent with DEA result and non-parametric statistical tests can confirm it.

Safe ranges can be constructed around common weights. So, the common weights can be used to develop a production function of multiple outputs and inputs. Goal programming-discriminant function approach, which is a non-statistical parametric technique has been employed for the estimation of empirical production function from the results of DEA (Golany and Yu, 1990). The main objective of this research to adopt this method in classification of the Czech banks.

Acknowledgements

This paper was supported by SGS Project No. SP2017/141, VŠB-Technical University of Ostrava, Faculty of Economics "Diskriminační analýza versus analýza datových obalů".

References

Anderson, P. and Peterson, N.C. (1993). 'A procedure for ranking efficient units in data envelopment analysis'. *Management Science*, 39 (10), pp. 1261-1264.

Brockett, P.L. and Golany, B. (1996). 'Using rank statistics for determining programmatic efficiency difference in DEA'. *Management Science*, 42, pp. 466-472.

Charnes, A., Cooper, W.W. and Rhodes, E. (1978). 'Measuring the efficiency of decision making units'. *European Journal of Operational Research*, 2, pp. 429-444.

Charnes, A. and Cooper, W.W. (1984). 'The non-arcimedean CCR ratio for efficiency analysis: A rejoinder to Boyd and Fare'. *European Journal of Operational Research*, 15, pp. 333-334.

Cook, W.D. and Kress, M. (1990). 'Data envelopment model for aggregating preference ranking'. *Management Science*, 36 (11), pp.1302-1310.

Cook, W., Roll, Y. and Kazakov, A. (1990). 'A DEA model for measuring the relative efficiencies of highway maintenance patrols'. *INFOR*, 28 (2), pp. 113-124.

Cook, W.D. and Kress, M. (1991). 'A multiple criteria decision model with ordinal preference data'. *European Journal of Operational Research*, 54, pp. 191-198.

Cook, W., Kress, M. and Seiford, L. (1992). 'Prioritization models for frontier decision making units in DEA'. *European Journal of Operational Research*, 59, pp. 319-323.

Cooper, W.W. and Tone, K. (1997). 'Measures of inefficiency in data envelopment analysis and stochastic frontier estimation'. *European Journal of Operational Research*, 99 (1), pp.72-88.

Friedman, L. and Sinuany-Stern, Z. (1997). 'Scaling Units via the Canonical Correlation Analysis in the DEA Context'. *European Journal of Operational Research*, 100 (2), pp. 629-637.

Golany, B. and Yu, G. (1995). 'A goal programming-discriminant function approach to the estimation of an empirical production function based on DEA results'. *Journal of Productivity Analysis*, 6 (2), pp. 171-186.

Madalla, G.S. (1977). *Econometrics*. New York: McGraw-Hill.

Morrison, D.F. (1976). *Multivariate Statistical Methods*. 2nd ed. New York: McGraw-Hill.

Modeling production processes in dairy industry as the Hybrid Flow Shop Problem

Jan Pelikán, Michal Černý, Miroslav Rada[1]

Abstract. We present a mixed integer linear programming model of a form of the hybrid flow shop problem motivated by a real-world case study from dairy industry. We consider two formulations: in the first one, the total processing time is to be minimized. In the second formulation, we consider the case of dairy products with fast deterioration. Here, finish times for jobs are assumed to be restricted to (usually narrow) time windows because the dairy products are sensitive to long waiting times and just-in-time delivery is a standard for supply chains with fresh products. We also consider the case when the processing times are technology-dependent and the selection of technology is subject to optimization.

Keywords: Hybrid flow shop, mixed integer linear programming, management of dairy industry, just-in-time delivery.

JEL classification: C61, C44

1 Introduction

We study a form of the *Hybrid Flow Shop Problem* as a tool for modeling and optimization of production processes in dairy industry. Although we will illustrate its practical usefulness by a case study, where a family of dairy products is manufactured by a single production line, we would like to point out that the model can be understood more generally. Namely, it can serve as a tool for modeling a supply chain of a special structure, where each product has to pass through a fixed sequence of actions (called here as "a sequence of processors") and every action can be assigned to a one of identical subcontractors ("units" or "machines").

The paper is structured as follows. In Section 2 we formalize the problem in detail. We give a brief overview of related work on similar topics and put our work in a broader context. We also put it into the frame of Błażewicz classification of flow-shop type problems. This is done in Section 3. The most important sections are Section 4, where we present a mixed integer linear programming (MILP) model for our formalization of the problem, and Section 5 with the dairy-industry case study illustrating the practical usefulness of our model. Here we also discuss various formulations, taking into account either the requirement to minimize the overall production time, or to fit the finish times of jobs into user-specified time windows (which is essential namely in case of production of fresh or fast deteriorating dairy products). We also incorporate a selection of technology affecting processing times and production costs into the model. Section 6 concludes the paper.

[1]All authors: Department of econometrics, University of Economics, Prague, Winston Churchill Square 4, CZ13067 Prague, Czech Republic. E-mail: pelikan@vse.cz (corresponding author), cernym@vse.cz, miroslav.rada@vse.cz.

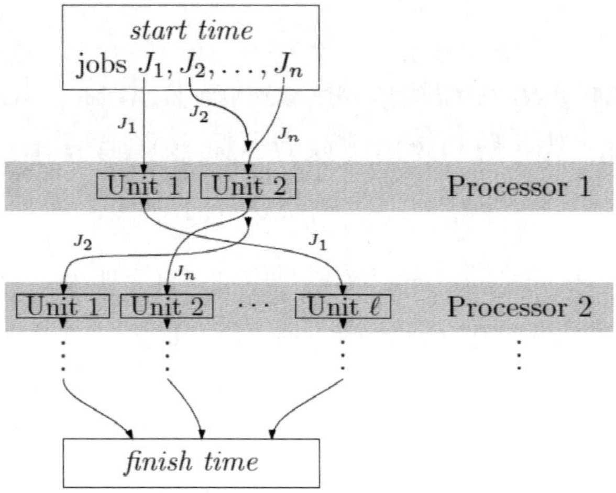

Figure 1 The processors with identical parallel units and a flow of jobs through the system

2 Problem formulation

Assume that we are given

- a family of jobs $J_1, J_2, \ldots, J_n$ and
- a family of processors $P_1, P_2, \ldots, P_K$,

where a job must proceed sequentially through the entire sequence of processors $P_1, \ldots, P_K$. The nontrivial point is that a processor has a number of identical parallel units ("sub-processors" or "machines"), where a job can be processed. To formalize this, let d_i^k stand for the processing time when job J_i is processed on a unit of processor P_k. The goal of the optimization is to determine *through which units of processors* $P_1, \ldots, P_K$ *a job* J_i *should flow.* All jobs are assumed to be available at the beginning of the time horizon (at the time zero), no pre-emption is allowed and no interruptions are allowed. The situation is depicted in Fig. 1.

Let us summarize the conditions more formally; these conditions will lead us to the main MILP model.

- In every moment, a unit of a processor is assigned to at most one job;
- each job is processed by at most one unit of a processor;
- all units within a processor are equivalent (meaning that the processing time of a job by a unit of a processor P_k does not depend on which unit was chosen);
- there is no pre-emption;
- no interruptions are allowed;
- a job flows sequentially through all processors $P_1, P_2, \ldots, P_K$;
- no waiting time is allowed: when the processing of a job by (a unit of) P_k is done, the job must immediately continue to (a unit of) P_{k+1}. In other words, no queuing *inside* the flow of a job through $P_1, \ldots, P_n$ is allowed, except for waiting on the starting line;
- ready times for all jobs are zero;
- a "hard" deadline for each job is given (meaning that it is not allowed to finish the job after the deadline).

Related work. Hybrid flow shops and their modeling remain a hot topic in Operations Research even several decades after the initial formulation of the problem. There are several recent works that may serve as an overview of flow shop problems and scheduling in general, see for example Ribas et al. (2010) and Ruiz and Vázquez-Rodríguez (2010) with hundreds of references. It is also worth mentioning some less recent but comprehensive works on scheduling and planning by Błażewicz et al. (1996), Leung (2004) or Pruhs et al. (2004).

To be more concrete, our paper follows up and generalizes the work of Pelikán (2011), where only two stages of processing were considered (with further restrictions). Related problems have also been addressed by Wang et al. (2015); Jiang et al. (2015); Feng et al. (2016); Elmi and Topaloglu (2013).

3 Błażewicz classification

The classification of scheduling problems, called "$(\alpha|\beta|\gamma)$", was proposed by Graham et al. (1979). It was later extended by Błażewicz et al. (1983) and others. Here we use the comprehensive scheme from the well-known reference book (Błażewicz et al., 1996) and its later editions.

In fact, there are several classificators hidden under each of the letters α, β and γ. The full form of the classification reads $(\alpha_1, \alpha_2|\beta_1, \beta_2, \beta_3, \beta_4, \beta_5, \beta_6, \beta_7, \beta_8|\gamma)$. The α-classificators determine the type and size of the system being scheduled and the β's determine the constraints imposed on the system. The γ-variable stands for the objective of the problem, i.e. what is actually being optimized.

Our problem can be classified as $\alpha_1 = F$ ("flow shop"), $\alpha_2 = \circ$ (variable number of processors), $\beta_1 = \circ$ (no pre-emption), $\beta_2 = \circ$ (no additional resources exist), $\beta_3 = \circ$ (no precedence), $\beta_4 = \circ$ (all ready times are zero), $\beta_5 = \circ$ (arbitrary processing times), $\beta_6 = d$ (deadlines are imposed on performance of all jobs), $\beta_7 = \circ$ (the problem is not the Job Shop), $\beta_8 =$ no-wait. The variable γ representing the objective function is discussed in the upcoming sections.

4 Mathematical model of hybrid flow shop

Now we introduce the MILP model of the hybrid flow shop problem described above. First we consider a version where the goal is to minimize the overall processing time (i.e. the goal is to minimize the finish time of the latest job). Then, in Section 5, we will consider a version with time windows and variable processing times depending on the choice of technology.

Given a number $a \in \mathbb{N}$, the symbol $[a]$ denotes the set of the first a naturals, i.e. $[a] := \{1, 2, \ldots, a\}$.

Parameters of the model. To define an instance of the problem, we need the following parameters (input data):

- n is the number of jobs;
- K is the number of processors (stages);
- m^k is the number of processing units of the processor P_k, $k \in [K]$;
- $d_i^k > 0$ is the processing time of the job J_i on the processor P_k (or, in other words, "in the k-th stage"), where $k \in [K]$ and $i \in [n]$;
- $M \gg 0$ is a sufficiently large number. See the remark below how to determine M from the input data.

Variables of the model. In the MILP formulation, we use the following variables:

- T is the makespan — the time when all jobs are finished;

- $\{y_{i\ell}^k \in \{0,1\} \mid i \in [n],\ k \in [K],\ \ell \in [m^k]\}$ is a system of binary variables satisfying

$$y_{i\ell}^k = \begin{cases} 1, & \text{if job } J_i \text{ is processed on the } \ell\text{-th unit of the processor } P_k, \\ 0 & \text{otherwise;} \end{cases}$$

- $\{t_i^k \mid i \in [n],\ k \in [K]\}$ is a system of nonnegative real variables with the following meaning: t_i^k is the time moment at which the processing of i-th job starts on the processor P_k;
- $\{x_{ij}^k \in \{0,1\} \mid i \in [n],\ j \in [n],\ i \neq j,\ k \in [K]\}$ is a system of binary variables determining the order of jobs on processors. These auxiliary variables are used to express the requirement that two jobs cannot be processed by the same unit (machine) simultaneously. In particular, given a processor P_k, if $y_{i\ell}^k = y_{j\ell}^k = 1$, the following holds:
  - $x_{ij}^k = 1$ if $t_i^k < t_j^k$,
  - $x_{ji}^k = 1$ if $t_j^k < t_i^k$.

  Otherwise, x_{ij}^k can be arbitrary.

The model. The resulting mathematical model can be formulated as follows:

$$\min T \quad \text{subject to} \tag{1}$$

$$x_{ij}^k + x_{ji}^k = 1, \quad i,j \in [n], i < j, k \in [K], \tag{2}$$

$$t_j^k \geq t_i^k + d_i^k - M(3 - x_{ij}^k - y_{i\ell}^k - y_{j\ell}^k), \quad i,j \in [n],\ k \in [K],\ \ell \in [m^k], \tag{3}$$

$$t_i^{k+1} = t_i^k + d_i^k, \quad i \in [n],\ k \in [K-1], \tag{4}$$

$$\sum_{\ell=1}^{m^k} y_{i\ell}^k = 1, \quad i \in [n],\ k \in [K], \tag{5}$$

$$t_i^K + d_i^K \leq T, \quad i \in [n], \tag{6}$$

$$t_i^1 \geq 0,\ y_{i\ell}^k \in \{0,1\},\ x_{ij}^k \in \{0,1\}, \quad i,j \in [n],\ k \in [K],\ \ell \in [m^k]. \tag{7}$$

Equation (2) formalizes the precedence of jobs: for every processor P_k, either J_i precedes J_j, or vice versa. Note that this is necessary *only if* both jobs are processed on the same unit of P_k. Otherwise, the x-variables do not impose any restrictions.

The core of the model lies in the set of inequalities (3). For example, the constraint (3) with i, j, k, ℓ ensures that the processing of J_j on P_k cannot start until the processing of J_i on P_k is finished. However, this restriction is imposed *only if* the following conditions are satisfied simultaneously:

- the job J_i precedes the job J_j on P_k,
- both jobs J_i, J_j are to be processed on the same unit ℓ of P_k.

This is ensured by subtraction of the term $M(3 - x_{ij}^k - y_{i\ell}^k - y_{j\ell}^k)$ on the right-hand side of (3), which decreases the right-hand side sufficiently if one of the conditions is not met.

The remaining constraints are quite obvious. Equation (4) captures that no waiting (queuing) is allowed. If processor P_k consists of multiple units, equation (5) assures the choice of a single unit per job. Inequalities (6) define the makespan variable T, which—jointly with (1)— is equal to the finish time of the latest job. Finally, the inequalities (7) set a starting point for processing.

Determining the number M. Note that the number M can be set to an upper bound of the makespan. For example, an upper bound can be determined by assuming one processing unit at every stage and relaxing the assumption on hard deadlines on individual units, i.e. $m^k = 1$ for every $k \in [K]$. In that case, the makespan is clearly $\sum_{i\in[n]} \sum_{k\in[K]} d_i^k$.

5 A case study in dairy industry

The model of Section 4 was used in a production line processing a family of batches of dairy products, such as yoghurts. Such a batch is a job in our terminology. There are six processors in the production line:

P_1: two preparative tanks,
P_2: one Pasteur equipment,
P_3: seven ripening tanks,
P_4: one cooler,
P_5: seven storage tanks,
P_6: six packing lines.

A modification of the basic model. For each batch it is necessary to choose a dairy microorganism culture for ripening. The times of ripening (= times d_i^3) depend on the chosen culture. Moreover, the costs of ripening are affected by the chosen culture, too. No other type of costs is considered.

We are also given time windows and each batch has to be finished within the respective time window. Now, the objective is to minimize the ripening costs.

We will use the model (1)–(7) with a pair of straightforward modifications reflecting the additional conditions described above.

a) The completion time $t_i^K + d_i^K$ of a job J_i has to be in a given interval $[T_i^{\min}, T_i^{\max}]$.
b) The choices of the microorganism cultures for each of the seven ripening tanks has to be added to the model, too, together with the associated costs in the objective function. The choice of the culture also affects the time of ripening.
   Actually, in this case study there are 6 different cultures available. The usage of a culture $s \in [6]$ for ripening of a batch is associated with costs c_s (which are assumed to depend only on the culture s, but are independent of the unit and batch).
   For a given job $i \in [n]$ and a given culture $s \in [6]$, the ripening process will take the time $\widetilde{d}_i^s$.
c) Under the assumptions of a) and b), we are minimizing costs (recall that the makespan is restricted by the time windows $[T_i^{\min}, T_i^{\max}]$).

Modifying the model to reflect the change a) is rather straightforward. We can replace the original constraints (6) by

$$T_i^{\max} \le t_i^K + d_i^K \le T_i^{\max}, \quad i \in [n]. \tag{8}$$

The change b) can be introduced in the model at a cost of a pair of additional binary variables. For $i \in [n]$ and $s \in [6]$ we define $f_i^s \in \{0, 1\}$ as follows:

$$f_i^s = \begin{cases} 1, & \text{if a culture } s \text{ is used for ripening of the batch } J_i, \\ 0 & \text{otherwise.} \end{cases}$$

Now we can add constraints

$$\sum_{s=1}^{6} f_i^s = 1, \quad i \in [n] \tag{9}$$

and

$$d_i^3 = \sum_{s=1}^{6} f_i^s \widetilde{d}_i^s, \quad i \in [n] \tag{10}$$

to ensure that a batch will be ripening with exactly one culture and that the processing time of a batch being processed by P_3 is correct.

The objective function, as described in c), can be also easily modeled:

$$\min \sum_{i=1}^{n} \sum_{s=1}^{6} f_i^s c_s. \tag{11}$$

Practical experience. Our model (2)–(5), (7)–(11) was run with a real dataset with $n = 12$ batches on a usual PC with IntelCore2Quad at 2.83 GHz. The resulting computation time of CPLEX 12.0 was 69 seconds. As the number n in the particular dairy company is always at most 20, it is possible to solve the model in a sufficiently short time exactly. Thus we conclude that the proposed approach is useful for real-world scheduling and production planning.

6 Conclusions

We proposed an MILP model of a hybrid flow shop, which is a production line where jobs (batches) are consecutively processed by a given chain of processors. The model was applied to a case study in dairy industry: we modeled a production process of dairy products.

The model provides a decision-maker with two kinds of information. First, it selects the optimal scheduling of jobs among the units of processors. Second, it is also able to select the optimal combination of processors to perform each particular job (in our case study, this corresponds to selection of technology).

The case study also demonstrates the power of the model: the solution can be restricted with respect to prescribed time intervals for batches. This is particularly important in the dairy industry since long waiting times might result in deterioration of fresh products. Moreover, the restrictions of finish times of batches are necessary if just-in-time delivery management is used, which is frequent case of dairy supply chains.

The computational time needed for solving the case study showed up to be reasonably small and justifies the practical usefulness of the formulation. The formulation itself might become a useful tool in the dairy industry.

Acknowledgements

The work was supported by the Czech Science Foundation under Grant 16-00408S.

References

Błażewicz, J., Ecker, K. H., Pesch, E., Schmidt, G. and Weglarz, J. (1996). *Scheduling Computer and Manafacturing Processes*. Berlin: Springer.

Błażewicz, J., Lenstra, J. and Kan, A. (1983). 'Scheduling subject to resource constraints: Classification and complexity'. *Discrete Applied Mathematics*, 5 (1), pp. 11–24.

Elmi, A. and Topaloglu, S. (2013). 'A scheduling problem in blocking hybrid flow shop robotic cells with multiple robots'. *Computers & Operations Research*, 40 (10), pp. 2543–2555.

Feng, X., Zheng, F. and Xu, Y. (2016). 'Robust scheduling of a two-stage hybrid flow shop with uncertain interval processing times'. *International Journal of Production Research*, 54 (12), pp. 3706–3717.

Graham, R. L., Lawler, E. L., Lenstra, J. K. and Kan, A. H. G. R. (1979). 'Optimization and Approximation in Deterministic Sequencing and Scheduling: A Survey'. In P.L. Hammer, E. L. J. and Korte, B. H., eds., *Annals of Discrete Mathematics*, 5, pp. 287–326. Elsevier.

Jiang, S., Liu, M., Hao, J. and Qian, W. (2015). 'A bi-layer optimization approach for a hybrid flow shop scheduling problem involving controllable processing times in the steelmaking industry'. *Computers & Industrial Engineering*, 87, pp. 518–531.

Leung, J. Y. (2004). *Handbook of Scheduling: Algorithms, Models, and Performance Analysis*. CRC Press.

Pelikán, J. (2011). 'Hybrid flow-shop with adjustment'. *Kybernetika*, 47 (1), pp. 50–59.

Pruhs, K., Sgall, J. and Torng, E. (2004). *Online Scheduling*. In: J. Y.-T. Leung (ed.), *Handbook of Scheduling: Algorithms, Models, and Performance Analysis*, chapter 15, pp. 15-1–41. CRC Press.

Ribas, I., Leisten, R. and Framiñan, J. M. (2010). 'Review and classification of hybrid flow shop scheduling problems from a production system and a solutions procedure perspective'. *Computers & Operations Research*, 37 (8), pp. 1439–1454.

Ruiz, R. and Vázquez-Rodríguez, J. A. (2010). 'The hybrid flow shop scheduling problem'. *European Journal of Operational Research*, 205 (1), pp. 1–18.

Wang, S., Liu, M. and Chu, C. (2015). 'A branch-and-bound algorithm for two-stage no-wait hybrid flow-shop scheduling'. *International Journal of Production Research*, 53 (4), pp. 1143–1167.

Evaluation of information technology projects using data envelopment analysis and balanced scorecard approach

Petr Řeháček, Jitka Baňařová, Lucie Chytilová [1]

Abstract. Information technology (IT) is important element for enterprises. IT helps to achieve a competitive advantage and organizational innovation. A general problem for IT management is to decide which IT project to select. There exist many methods how to evaluate the project. There are usually many quantitative and qualitative factors to be considered in evaluation process. This paper combines two well-established managerial methodologies - balanced scorecard (BSC) and data envelopment analysis (DEA). BSC approach is used as a comprehensive framework for defining IT projects evaluation criteria. DEA is used as a non-parametric technique for ranking IT projects. This special approach is used for the evaluation of polish IT projects. The results are showing that the I-DEA-BSC generally gives higher values of efficiency.

Keywords: Data Envelopment Analysis, Balanced Scorecard, imprecise data, project evaluation.

JEL classification: C67, O22

1 Introduction

The development of information technology (IT) is helping to all shareholders in the business. Moreover, the cross-function collaborations become feasible in the product development, marketing, distribution, customer service and so on. IT became complex support for efficient business operations and decision making, collaborations and also for the competition. Nowadays business could not exist without IT. Some authors even write that IT is a tool which is crucial for the enterprises to achieve a competitive advantage and organizational innovation (Tseng, 2008).

As it is written above, if enterprises want to be efficient, it is important for IT managers to chose a proper IT and IT project which they will support for their enterprise. They have a big responsibility and their decision may influence all kinds of parts of enterprise (data centers, servers, information systems etc.) even the strategic direction of the organization (Holtsnider and Jaffe, 2007). To select the right and proper project is a critical business activity and it does not depend on a field of study. The optimal selection process was analyzed and studied in many researchers. For example, Chen and Cheng (2008) selected the most suitable project by a significant resource allocation decision that can enhance the operational competitive advantage of a business. This approach is generally good and useful. The disadvantage is that in the analysis there should not be involved too many quantitative and qualitative factors. So, this is not approach for IT projects. On the other hand, the methods as analytic hierarchy process (AHP) (Schniederjans and Wilson, 1991), analytic network process (ANP) (Lee and Kim, 2001), data envelopment analysis (DEA) (Sowlati et al., 2005), DEA with balanced scorecard approach (BSC) (Asosheh et al. 2010) may be used to achieve more appropriate results.

[1] VŠB-TU Ostrava, Faculty of Economics, Department of Systems Engineering, Sokolská tř. 33, 702 00 Ostrava 1, Czech Republic, petr.rehacek@vsb.cz, jitka.banarova@vsb.cz, lucie.chytilova@vsb.cz.

The last mentioned method, combination of DEA and BSC, was found as one of the most complex. The BSC is used as a comprehensive framework for evaluation of criteria for IT projects. BSC is good for identification and monitoring the metrics as well as for judging the corporate performance. DEA is widely used for evaluation of efficiencies of decision making units (DMUs) in many kinds of applications. In this paper, we use the idea of this approach for DEA with imprecise data.

The rest of this paper is organized as follows: In Section 2, the literature overview of previous related works are reviewed. Section 3 describes the BSC and its fundamentals. Section 4 proposes DEA method which ranks DMUs in presence of imprecise data. Section 5, briefly describes the used data. In section 6 all mentioned methods are applied. Finally paper is closed with some concluding remarks in Section 7.

2 Literature overview

During last years, numerous methodologies have been developed for project selection. In this part of paper, we would like to look mainly at the application to a project with informatics system (IS).

Schniederjans and Wilson (1991) used a hybrid approach of analysis hierarchical process (AHP) and goal programming for IS project selection. They demonstrated that hybrid approaches have advantages from using these techniques separately. Santhanam and Kyparisis (1995) presented a multi-criteria decision model for IS project selection. The proposed model, explicitly consider interrelationships among candidate projects. DEA was used, for example, by Shafer and Byrd (2000). They have developed a framework for measuring efficiency of organization investment in IT and applied it on 200 large organizations. Also, Wen, Lim, and Huang (2003) have used DEA. They have proposed a model for evaluating e-commerce efficiency. This model has included financial and operational measures and e-commerce specific measures. They have illustrated that DEA model cannot only effectively reflect the relative efficiency of e-commerce firms, but also identify their potential efficiency problems. Sowlati et al. (2005) proposed a DEA model for prioritizing IS projects. Using the proposed model, each real project is compared to the set of defined projects and receives a score and the prioritization is based on this score. They believed that this is a significant advantage, because assessing the priority of a new added project would not affect the priority of already assessed ones.

Investigation of previous studies shows that the DEA model which is able to find most efficient IT projects by considering both cardinal and ordinal data should be good choice for the analysis. Furthermore, this paper uses BSC to define selection criteria.

3 Balanced scorecard approach

The balanced scorecard (BSC) is a strategic planning and management system that is used extensively in all kinds of businesses and organizations worldwide. BSC is used to align business activities to the vision and strategy organization, improve internal and external communications or to monitor organization performance (strategic goals). Originally, BSC was introduced by Kaplan and Norton (1992). Since then BSC has undergone great development. It has evolved, from the performance measurement tool to a tool for implementing strategies (Kaplan and Norton, 1996) and a framework for determining the alignment of an organizations human, information and organization capital with its strategy (Kaplan and Norton, 2004).

Nowadays, BSC is used a lot in businesses and all kinds of organizations by the top managers. They do not longer focus just on monetary success indicators in the financial area. They mainly use BSC which is designed to complement financial measures of past performance with their measures of the drivers of future performance (Bhagwat and Sharma, 2007). The increasing use of BSC framework is also seen in increasing number of researches, for example: R&D project (Eilat et al., 2006), and e-business (Bremser & Chung, 2005) and so on.

The bigest advantage of BSC is that it does not just include the financial measures. BSC is designed to improve managers decision making by guiding their attention to a broader vision of the companys operations (holistic performance measurement system). More precisely, BSC provides causal links connecting the multiple classes of non-financial measures. It can also be used as a strategic management system (Kaplan & Norton, 1996, 2004). The original BSC design identified the following four perspectives:

- *Financial perspective*: it links the company to its shareholders with main attention to the question: "How do we look to our shareholders and those with a financial interest in the organization?" Financial goals are to achieving profitability, maintaining liquidity and solvency both short term as well as long-term, growth in sales turnover and maximizing wealth of shareholders (Bhagwat &Sharma, 2007).
- *Customer perspective*: it is external oriented perspective to the organizations customers, who are the crucial factor for financial success generating revenue by buying products and services. The question is: "How do our customers perceive us in term of products, services, relationships and value-added?"
- *Internal-business-process perspective*: it focus on the internal processes that will have the greatest impact on customer satisfaction and achieving an organizations financial objectives. Organizations should decide what processes and competencies they must excel at and specify measures for each of them.
- *Learning and growth perspective*: it identifies the infrastructure that the organization must build to create longterm growth and improvement. Intense global competition requires that organizations continually improve their capabilities for delivering value to customers and shareholders. Thus the question remains: "To achieve our future vision, how will we continue to improve and create future value for our stakeholders?"

4 Data envelopment analysis

Data envelopment analysis (DEA) is non-parametric approach. It measurs the relative efficiency of decision making units (DMUs) when the data for multiple inputs and outputs are known exactly. Suppose, there is a set of T peer DMUs, (DMUk for $k = 1, \ldots, T$), with multiple inputs x_{ik} $(i = 1, \ldots, R)$ and multiple outputs y_{jk} $(j = 1, \ldots, S)$, respectively. Also, u_i $(i = 1, \ldots, R)$ and v_j $(j = 1, \ldots, S)$ be the weight of ith input and j^{th} output, respectively. Mathematically, the relative efficiency score of DMUk can be define as:

$$e_k = \frac{\sum_{j=1}^{S} v_j y_{jk}}{\sum_{i=1}^{R} u_i x_{ik}}, \text{ for } k = 1, 2, \ldots, T. \tag{1}$$

for $k = 1, \ldots, T$.

Charnes et al. (1978) proposed the very first DEA model CCR ratio model for measuring the efficiency score of under evaluation unit, DMU_Q where $Q \in \{1, \ldots, T\}$:

$$\begin{aligned} \max\ & e_Q = \frac{\sum_{j=1}^{S} v_j y_{jQ}}{\sum_{i=1}^{R} u_i x_{iQ}}, & \\ \text{s.t.}\ & \frac{\sum_{j=1}^{S} v_j y_{jk}}{\sum_{i=1}^{R} u_i x_{ik}} \leq 0, & k = 1, 2, \ldots, T, \\ & u_i \geq 0, & i = 1, 2, \ldots, R, \\ & v_j \geq 0, & j = 1, 2, \ldots, S. \end{aligned} \tag{2}$$

This model (2) can be transform into the following CCR multiplier problem:

$$\begin{aligned} \max\ & e_Q = \sum_{j=1}^{S} v_j y_{jQ}, & \\ \text{s.t.}\ & \sum_{i=1}^{R} u_i x_{iQ} = 1, & \\ & \sum_{j=1}^{S} v_j y_{jk} - \sum_{i=1}^{R} u_i x_{ik} \leq 0, & k = 1, 2, \ldots, T, \\ & u_i \geq 0, & i = 1, 2, \ldots, R, \\ & v_j \geq 0, & j = 1, 2, \ldots, S. \end{aligned} \tag{3}$$

When x_{ik} (for any i) and y_{jk} (for any j) are imprecise and unknown decision variables as bounded and ordinal data, see Cook et al (1993, 1996), model (3) becomes a non-linear and non-convex program, and it is called imprecise DEA (IDEA), see e.g. Zhu (2002). The bounded data can be expressed as:

$$\underline{y_{jk}} \leq y_{jk} \leq \overline{y_{jk}} \text{ and } \underline{x_{ik}} \leq x_{ik} \leq \overline{x_{ik}}, \tag{4}$$

for $j \in BO$ and $i \in BI$, where y_{jk} and x_{ik} are the lower bounds, and y_{jk} and x_{ik} are the upper bounds. BO and BI are the associated sets. These sets contain bounded outputs and inputs, respectively.

The weak ordinal data can be expressed as:

$$y_{jk} \leq y_{jl} \text{ and } x_{ik} \leq x_{il} \ \ \forall k \neq l \tag{5}$$

for $j \in$ DO and $i \in$ DI, or to simplify the presentation,

$$y_{j1} \leq y_{j2} \leq \ldots \leq y_{jl} \leq \ldots \leq y_{jn} \ \ (j \in DO), \tag{6}$$

$$x_{i1} \leq x_{i2} \leq \ldots \leq x_{il} \leq \ldots \leq x_{in} \ \ (i \in DI),$$

where DO and DI represent the associated sets containing weak ordinal outputs and inputs, respectively.

The strong ordinal data can be expressed as:

$$y_{j1} < y_{j2} < \ldots < y_{jl} < \ldots < y_{jn} \ \ (j \in SO), \tag{7}$$

$$x_{i1} < x_{i2} < \ldots < x_{il} < \ldots < x_{in} \ \ (i \in SI),$$

where SO and SI represent the associated sets containing strong ordinal outputs and inputs, respectively.

Model (3) involving (4) (7) then changes into the following model:

$$\begin{aligned}
&\max e_Q = \textstyle\sum_{j=1}^{S} v_j y_{jQ}, && \\
\text{s.t. } &\textstyle\sum_{i=1}^{R} u_i x_{iQ} = 1, && \\
&\textstyle\sum_{j=1}^{S} v_j y_{jk} - \sum_{i=1}^{R} u_i x_{ik} \leq 0, && k = 1, 2, \ldots, T, \\
&(x_{ik}) \in \theta_i^-, && i = 1, 2, \ldots, R, \\
&(y_{jk}) \in \theta_j^+, && j = 1, 2, \ldots, S, \\
&u_i \geq 0, v_j \geq 0, &&
\end{aligned} \tag{8}$$

where $(x_{ik}) \in \theta_i^-$ and $(yjk) \in \theta_j^+$ represents any of or all of (4) (7). The model (8) with the (4) (6) can be solved by the standard linear DEA models via concerning the bounded and ordinal data into exact data, Zhu (2002).

The model (8) when θ_i^- and θ_j^+ are in forms of (6) and obtain a set of optimal solutions y_{jk}^* and x_{ik}^* with the optimal e_Q^* is the following:

$$\begin{aligned}
&e_Q^* = \max \textstyle\sum_{j\in DO} v_j y_{jQ} + \sum_{j\notin DO} v_j y_{jQ}, \\
\text{s.t. } &\textstyle\sum_{i\in DI} u_i x_{iQ} + \sum_{i\notin DI} u_i x_{iQ} = 1, \\
&\textstyle\sum_{j\in DO} v_j y_{jk} + \sum_{j\notin DO} v_j y_{jk} - \sum_{i\in DI} u_i x_{ik} \\
&-\textstyle\sum_{i\notin DI} u_i x_{ik} \leq 0, \\
&k = 1, 2, \ldots, T, \\
&u_i \geq 0, v_j \geq 0, \quad i = 1, 2, \ldots, R, j = 1, 2, \ldots, S, \\
\text{where } &0 \leq y_{j1}^* \leq y_{j2}^* \leq \ldots \leq y_{jl}^* \leq \ldots \leq y_{jn}^* \leq M \ \ (j \in DO), \\
&0 \leq x_{i1}^* \leq x_{i2}^* \leq \ldots \leq x_{il}^* \leq \ldots \leq x_{in}^* \leq M \ \ (i \in DI).
\end{aligned} \tag{9}$$

Where M is sufficiently large, more accurate information are at articles by Zhu (2002). Note that in this case, model is no longer a non-linear program, but a linear CCR model.

5 Data

In this paper we use data from the Institute of Informatics of Wroclaw University of Technology. They have gathered data for the time period between 10 April and 15 June 2010 for IT projects in the Poland and they have asked such organizations as the Polish Informatics Society and the Project Management Society Poland Chapter to cooperate on the project. They gave questions to project managers both on IT company side as well as on the end-user side (i.e. the customer side) to get most useful data. They have received 381 responses, 14% of which came from the public sector and 86% from the private sector. The respondents from the private sector were less willing to give information about their projects. In the sample, there were three categories of project - development of a new system (28% of the project in the sample, projects realized from the stage of requirements gathering to final implementation), development of an existing system (36%, projects where systems implemented earlier in the organization were further developed) and implementation of an IT solution (36% implementations of systems known and existing on the market).

The provided database have got 80 IT projects. Unfortunately, for our research we had to adopt some criteria, so some missing data have been found and our final database was established by 73 IT projects.

The following Table 1 and Table 2 are showing used variables (inputs and outputs) with the description of use and its purpose. The first Table 1 is showing data for I-DEA model. These variables had been used just according to the analysis and discussion with experts.

DEA	Criteria	Max	Min	Average
Input				
	overrun on budget	2.500	0.833	1.238
	overrun on schedule	0.500	2.667	1.435
Output				
	percentage of scope realized	1.000	0.850	0.961
	customer satisfaction	2.000	4.000	3.091

Table 1 Input and output variables with description

Overrun on budget is in PLN and overrun on budget schedule is in months. Both these variables should be as small as possible, so that is why are both inputs. Percentage of scope realized and customer satisfaction (from 0 to 4, where 0 no satisfaction) are outputs as we would like to have highest values.

The Table 2 is showing the data which have been used according to the BSC.

DEA	BSC perspectives	Criteria	Max	Min	Average
Input	Financial perspective	planned budget	8000000	9500	1013656.25
Input		actual budget	6500000	12000	980217.64
Input	Customer perspective	planned duration	60	1	10.23
Input		actual duration	160	2	13.99
Output	Internal-business-process perspective	risk documentation	2	1	1.69
Output	Learning and growth perspective	experience of manager	23	1	4.78
Input		number of people	80	2	13.25

Table 2 Input and output variables with description

Planned and actual budget is in PLN and costumer would like to have this smaller as this could be (inputs). Planned and actual duration is in months and the idea is same for this variables as before. Risk documentation is ordinal - 1 if there is no documentation and 2 if the is documentation. Experience of manager with leading the projects is in years and we would like to have really experienced manager. The number of people is saying how many people are working and how much we should spent on them, so we would like as small as the expenditures should be.

6 Analysis and remarks

The mathematical model was implemented through a GAMS software. In Table 3 is showing the results for both models. The first model is called the I-DEA. This model uses all input and outputs from Table 1 and as the customer satisfaction is special variable, the model with imprecise date has to be used. The second model is called I-DEA-BSC and is based on variables from Table 2. It means, that the inputs and outputs are based on the BSC. In the bottom, there are overall descriptive statistics. The results are showing that the I-DEA-BSC gives always higher values of efficiency for all IT projects. Just in case of IT project 24, 39, 43 and 49 the values are same. These IT projects are efficient in both cases. These results show that BSC analysis for input and output variables is important and can provide more information to management. For example, from closer analysis we may see that the general problem is the actual duration of the project and also the amount of the spent money.

#IT	I-DEA	I-DEA-IBSC	#IT	I-DEA	I-DEA-BSC	#IT	I-DEA	I-DEA-BSC	#IT	I-DEA	I-DEA-BSC
1	0.525	0.618	21	0.817	0.875	41	0.933	1.000	61	0.938	1.000
2	0.413	0.443	22	0.924	1.000	42	0.870	0.969	62	0.724	0.800
3	0.870	0.969	23	0.635	0.680	43	1.000	1.000	63	0.594	0.694
4	0.697	0.776	24	1.000	1.000	44	0.875	0.976	64	0.700	0.833
5	0.640	0.686	25	0.857	0.920	45	0.732	0.789	65	0.917	1.000
6	0.493	0.533	26	0.571	0.634	46	0.910	1.000	66	0.917	1.000
7	0.847	0.917	27	0.938	1.000	47	0.691	0.778	67	0.888	0.990
8	0.762	0.818	28	0.589	0.636	48	0.917	1.000	68	0.917	1.000
9	0.756	0.848	29	0.700	0.824	49	1.000	1.000	69	0.840	1.000
10	0.824	0.980	30	0.680	0.740	50	0.772	0.829	70	0.873	0.910
11	0.712	0.761	31	0.720	0.833	51	0.883	0.990	71	0.818	0.875
12	0.917	1.000	32	0.708	0.791	52	0.745	0.830	72	0.844	0.870
13	0.864	0.932	33	0.815	0.914	53	0.709	0.836	73	0.923	1.000
14	0.576	0.641	34	0.721	0.824	54	0.568	0.622			
15	0.924	1.000	35	0.917	1.000	55	0.889	1.000			
16	0.655	0.707	36	0.917	1.000	56	0.870	0.969			
17	0.855	0.942	37	0.429	0.474	57	0.662	0.742	max	1.000	1.000
18	0.726	0.830	38	0.934	1.000	58	0.672	0.783	min	0.413	0.442
19	0.566	0.611	39	1.000	1.000	59	0.677	0.750	st.dev.	0.142	0.151
20	0.767	0.825	40	0.923	1.000	60	0.917	1.000	average	0.793	0.864

Table 3 Results for both models

7 Conclusion

The results in the previous chapter are based on the BSC and DEA model with imprecise data. If we compare results of both models, it may be seen, that there small difference between models. If we do the statistical test, it may be seen that model based on BSC is little bit better than the first model with categorical variables. So from there analysis we can conclude that it would be probably better to use DEA method with BSC. It provides more input and output variables and it may give more information to managers. So far we found that the biggest problem of the analysis are actual budget and duration. This was actually the problem in case of the first model as well, where the overrun of budget and duration were define as input variables. The output variable - risk documentation should be also more analyzed or more detailed info could be given.

In future, we would like to increase the database of variables and improve the model to use another type of variables which will help the managers to improve the situation of picking the best IT project.

Acknowledgements

This paper was supported by SGS project No. SP2017/144.

References

Asosheh, A., Nalchigar, S. and Jamporazmey. M. (2010). 'Expert Systems with Applications'. *Expert Systems with Applications*, 37, pp. 5931-5938.

Bhagwat, R. and Sharma, M. K. (2007). 'Performance measurement of supply chain management: A balanced scorecard approach'. *Computers and Industrial Engineering*, 53, pp. 43-62.

Bremser, W. and Chung, Q. B. (2005). 'A framework for performance measurement in the e-business environment'. *Electronic Commerce Research and Applications*, 4, pp. 395-412.

Charnes, A., Cooper, W.W. and Rhodes, E. (1978). 'Measuring the efficiency of decision making units'. *European Journal of Operational Research*, 2 (6), pp. 429-444.

Chen, C. T. and Cheng, H. L. (2008). 'A comprehensive model for selecting information system project under fuzzy environment'. *International Journal of Project Management*, 27 (4), pp. 389-399.

Cook, W.D., Kress, M. and Seiford, L.M. (1993). 'On the use of the ordinal data in Data Envelopment Analysis'. *Journal of the Operational Research Society*, 44 (2), pp. 133-140.

Cook, W.D., Kress, M. and Seiford, L.M. (1996). 'Data envelopment analysis in the presence of both quantitative and qualitative factors'. *Journal of the Operational Research Society*, 47, pp. 945-953.

Eilat, H., Golany, B. and Shtub, A. (2006). 'R&D project evaluation: An integrated DEA and balanced scorecard approach'. *Omega*, 36, pp. 895-912.

Kaplan, R. S. and Norton, D. P. (1992). *The balanced scorecard: Measures that drive performance*. Boston: Harvard Business Review, pp. 71-79.

Kaplan, R. S. and Norton, D. (1996). *The balanced scorecard - translating strategy into action*. Boston: Harvard Business School Press.

Kaplan, R. S. and Norton, D. P. (2004). *Organizational capital: Leadership, alignment, and teamwork*. Balanced Scorecard Report.

Santhanam, R. and Kyparisis, J. (1995). 'A multiple criteria decision model for information system project selection'. *Computers and Operations Research*, 22, pp. 807-816.

Schniederjans, M. J. and Wilson, R. L. (1991). 'Using the analytic hierarchy process and goal programming for information system project selection'. *Information and Management*, 20, pp. 333-342.

Shafer, S. M. and Byrd, T. A. (2000). 'A framework for measuring the efficiency of organizational investments in information technology using data envelopment analysis'. *Omega*, 28, pp. 125-141.

Sowlati, T., Paradi, J. C. and Suld, C. (2005). 'Information systems project prioritization using data envelopment analysis'. *Mathematical and Computer Modeling*, 41, pp. 1279-1298.

Tseng, S. M. (2008). 'The effects of information technology on knowledge management systems'. *Expert Systems with Applications*, 35, pp. 150-160.

Wen, H. J., Lim, B. and Huang, H. L. (2003). 'Measuring e-commerce efficiency: A data envelopment analysis (DEA) approach'. *Industrial Management and Data Systems*, 103 (9), pp. 703-710.

Zhu, J. (2002). 'Imprecise data envelopment analysis (IDEA): A review and improvement with an application'. *European Journal of Operational Research*, 144 (3), pp. 513-529.

On Testing the Weak Form of Efficiency of Stock Markets

Petr Seďa[1], María de los Baños García-Moreno García [2], José Ángel Roldán Casas[3]

Abstract. The efficient market hypothesis represents an analytical approach aimed to explain movements in prices of financial assets. This hypothesis is based on the insight that prices for such assets are determined by rational behavior of agents interacting in the market. In financial literature, the have been defined some patterns of behavior of efficient time series that are usually associated with random walk models. In financial econometrics, there have been proposed various linear and non-linear statistical methods to verify random walk models. This paper deals with reformulation of traditionally used approach of testing. New scheme of testing the weak form of efficiency will be designed. In addition, there will be proposed a simple approach how to measure the degree of efficiency or inefficiency. Our findings will be practically demonstrated on data from Spanish stock market.

Keywords: efficiency, information, random walk, stock index.

JEL Classification: C5, G1

1 Introduction

The idea of the efficient financial market was firstly seriously described by Samuelson (1965) and followed by Roberts (1967) who investigated efficiency from information point of view. His findings led to three level rating of efficiency according to rising availability of information for rational investors. The weak form of efficiency denotes that information available for market agents is limited to historical price series only. The semi-strong form of efficient market denotes that investors have all public information and the strong form of efficiency means that information set includes also inside information (Hančlová and Rublíková, 2006).

The weak form of information efficiency is usually associated with random walk models (Fama, 1991). According to financial theory, the random walk model 1 (RW1) has the most restrictive conditions, while the random walk model 2 (RW2) is the less restrictive, and the random walk model 3 (RW3) is the most realistic. Empirical testing the hypothesis of efficiency in a given stock market is important for both, investors and regulatory institutions. It provides information whether market participants are subjected to "fair game" where expectations of profit and loss are equivalent. In recent literature, there have been applied numerous statistical test and procedures to test the weak form of efficiency in financial markets in relation to random walk models. Nevertheless, practically all of them consider only one condition of the model that should be fulfilled. For instance, when applying linear tests or methods investigating linear dependency in data sample we get results that are necessary for all three types of random walk

[1] VSB-Technical University of Ostrava, Faculty of Economics, Department of Mathematical Methods in Economics, Sokolská třída 33, 701 21 Ostrava 1, Czech Republic, petr.seda@vsb.cz.

[2] University of Córdoba, Faculty of Law and Business and Economic Sciences, Department of Statistics, Econometrics, Operations Research, Business Organization and Applied Economics, Puerta Nueva S/N, 14071 Córdoba, Spain, d52gagam@uco.es.

3 University of Córdoba, Faculty of Law and Business and Economic Sciences, Department of Statistics, Econometrics, Operations Research, Business Organization and Applied Economics, Plaza Nueva S/N, 14001 Córdoba, Spain, ma2rocaj@uco.es.

models. Contrary to that, non-linear methods consider also possible presence of nonlinearities in financial assets returns. In general, when applying a statistical test that fulfill necessary but not sufficient condition it can lead to wrong or incorrect conclusion in any type of random walk model.

The aim of this paper is to design a scheme for testing the weak form of the efficiency using linear and non-linear statistical methods and to propose a simple statistical framework for testing the degree of the weak form of information efficiency. The novelty of this paper consists just in those aspects.

Our paper is organized as follows. In the Introduction section, the importance of topic is emphasized, and the added value of this paper is stressed. Second chapter delivers a summary of properties of different types of random walk models followed by the review of traditional statistical tests that are usually applied. This chapter is finished by a brief description of possible scheme for testing the weak form of efficiency using linear and non-linear statistical methods. Third chapter is devoted to description of data sample used. Moreover, a simple statistical framework how to measure the degree of the weak form of efficiency related to different forms of random walk models will be proposed. Conclusion summarizes this paper and opens possible extensions of investigated topic.

2 Theoretical Background

If we want to investigate the weak form of efficiency in a given financial market, it is usually necessary to verify whether time series follows some type of random walk model. In other words, there must be verified the degree of restrictions set for particular type of random walk model.

2.1 Random Walk Models

In general, there exist three basic types of random walk models. The RW1 expects increments that are independently and identically distributed. Contrary to that, the RW2 assumes just increments that are independent while RW3 expects uncorrelated increments only (Campbell, Lo and Mackinlay, 1997). When assuming the RW1, price P_t can be described as follows:

$$P_t = \mu + P_{t-1} + \varepsilon_t,\ \varepsilon_t \sim IID\left(0,\sigma^2\right), \tag{1}$$

where μ denotes the price change and $IID\left(0,\sigma^2\right)$ means that residual term ε_t have independent and identical distributions having zero mean value and constant σ^2. The property of independence of errors ε_t means that random walk model is also "fair game". The fact that errors are not correlated, but also that any nonlinear functions of errors are not correlated, is also important. Assuming the initial value of price P_0, the conditional mean and variance at time t can be written in the following way:

$$E\left[P_t \mid P_0\right] = P_0 + \mu t, \tag{2}$$

$$Var\left[P_t \mid P_0\right] = \sigma^2 t. \tag{3}$$

Equations (2) and (3) indicates that RW1 is a nonstationary process. Moreover, the conditional mean and variance have linear form. The same assumption holds also for RW2 and RW3 models. When consider the RW2, the assumptions that are hold for the RW1 can be naturally reduced or simplified. If time series follows the RW2, it is expected that this process assumes independent but not identically distributed errors.

2.2 Methods for Testing the Weak Form of Efficiency

Properties of financial time series can be verified with a help of either linear or non-linear statistical tests (Seďa and Jimber del Río, 2016). However, linear methods cannot detect any non-linear dependencies generated by returns. That is why; the validity of the weak form efficiency hypothesis should be tested not only by linear methods, but also by nonlinear approaches. Hinich, Mendes and Stone (2005) say: "Economic and other social systems are nonlinear, and linear approximation is possible only if the existence of weak nonlinearities in these systems. Testing the behavior of returns by nonlinear methods, it is actually validating the results of testing by linear methods".

Runs test is one of the easiest tests that can be utilized when detecting dependency in time series (Siegel and Castellan, 1988). This test belongs to the group of nonparametric tests that are independent on the distribution of financial time series. Runs test examines the randomness of returns. It is usually applied when testing the RW1. Ljung-Box test (Ljung and Box, 1978) and variance ratio test (Campbell, Lo and Mackinlay, 1997) represent other linear methods. Ljung-Box test examines whether all the autocorrelation coefficients of particular time series are significantly different from zero. Variance ratio test verified the predictability of time series by comparing variances of differences of the returns calculated over different time intervals.

When testing using nonlinear methods we examine whether it is possible to express the rate of return R_t as follows:

$$R_t = g_t(r_1) + \varepsilon_t h_t(r_2), \tag{4}$$

where ε_t is a random noise that has a specified distribution F, thus $\varepsilon_t \sim F(0,1)$, g_t and h_t are nonlinear functions containing historical information, r_1 and r_2 are vectors of independent variables. It is obvious that:

$$E_{t-1}(R_t) = g_t(r_1), \tag{5}$$

$$E_{t-1}(R_t - E_{t-1}(R_t))^2 = h_t^2(r_2). \tag{6}$$

If we find a g_t or h_t, or both functions simultaneously, we say that returns are nonlinear in the first moment, or are nonlinear in the second moment, or are nonlinear in both the first and second moments. It is also possible to test the presence of nonlinearities in higher moments. There exists a wide range of tests to detect nonlinearities in returns. Engle´s ARCH test (Engle, 1982) and BDS test (Brock et al, 1987) are examples of tests able to detect non-linearity in time series.

The proposed scheme of testing the weak form of efficiency is shown in Figure 1. This scheme is based on existing and traditionally used statistical tests for testing the efficiency.

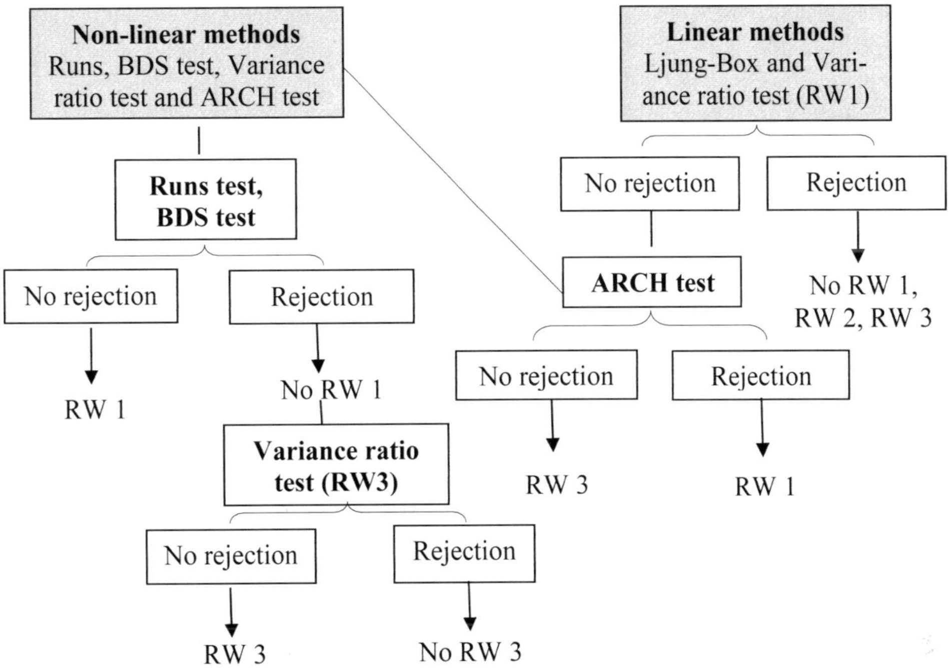

Figure 1 Proposed scheme of testing the weak form of efficiency related to RW1 and RW3 models [García-Moreno, 2015]

It is clear that proposed testing procedure can lead to different conclusions that depend on statistical test that we start to apply. These findings bring a logical question how to calculate the degree of compliance with the weak efficiency hypothesis in each testing period or sub-periods respectively.

3 Empirical Findings

In this chapter an empirical testing the weak form of efficiency of Spanish stock index IBEX35 within investigated periods using linear and nonlinear methods as defined in Section 2 will be performed.

3.1 Data Sample

Empirical investigation will be carried out using daily returns of the most valuable Spanish stock index IBEX35 in the period from January 2003 to July 2015. This basic data sample includes 4 592 trading days in total. We have more than 12 years long time series of the closing rates of IBEX35 index. This period was chosen intentionally to investigate changes of the weak form of market efficiency.

The basic testing period was divided into sub-periods in order to compare the degree of efficiency. Therefore, a potential influence of the global financial crisis and transitory nature of that efficiency can be demonstrated in easy way. In addition to this, when investigating sub-periods, it is possible to detect patterns that could remain hidden in longer periods. To sum up, the basic testing period was divided into five sub-periods in order to compare the degree of efficiency or inefficiency:

1) 01.01.2003 – 31.12.2004 (pre-crisis period I.),
2) 01.01.2005 – 31.12.2007 (pre-crisis period II.),
3) 01.01.2008 – 31.12.2009 (crisis period),
4) 01.01.2010 – 31.12.2012 (post-crisis period I.),
5) 01.01.2013 – 28.07.2015 (post-crisis period II.).

One can observe that there were defined two pre-crisis and two post-crisis periods. The sub-periods that immediately preceded (pre-crisis 2) or followed (post-crisis 1) the crisis period contain data from 3 previous or subsequent years. Our aim is to quantify possible effects of the global financial crisis in more detail.

3.2 Results of Testing the Weak Form of Efficiency

The results of applied methodology to determine whether the series of IBEX returns follow some type of random walk model or not are shown Table 1. For the purpose of this paper, just RW1 and RW3 models were considered. The contrast between RW1 or RW3 models and non-RW behavior is clearly described for the entire testing period and all 5 sub-periods as well.

IBEX35		Ljung-Box + ARCH test		Variance-Ratio (RW1) + ARCH test		Runs test		BDS test	
Entire period		Correlation + ARCH → No RW		Uncorr. + ARCH → RW3		No randomness + uncorr. but dependent → No RW		No IID + uncorr. but dependent → RW3	
Pre-crisis	I.	Uncorr. + ARCH → RW3	Uncorr. + ARCH → RW3	Un-corr. + ARCH → RW3	Uncorr. + ARCH → RW3	Random-ness → RW1	Random-ness → RW1	No IID + uncorr. but de-pendent → RW3	No IID + uncorr. but dependent → RW3
	II.		Uncorr. + ARCH → RW3		Uncorr. + ARCH → RW3		Random-ness → RW1		Inconclu-sive + uncorr. but dependent → RW3
Crisis period		Correlation + ARCH → No RW		Uncorr.+ ARCH → RW3		No randomness + uncorr. but dependent → RW3		IID → RW1	
Post-crisis	I.	Correla-tion + ARCH → No RW	Correla-tion + ARCH → No RW	Un-corr. + ARCH → RW3	Uncorr. + ARCH → RW3	No ran-domness + uncorr. but de-pendent → RW3	No ran-domness + uncorr. but dependent → RW3	Inconclu-sive + uncorr. but dependent → RW3	IID → RW1
	II.		Uncorr. + no ARCH → RW1		Uncorr. + no ARCH → RW1		No ran-domness + uncorr. but dependent → RW3		IID → RW1

Table 1 Results of testing the weak form of efficient market hypotheses: RW1 and RW3 versus non RW model [García-Moreno, 2015]

Regarding the entire period, the null hypothesis of the weak form of efficiency can be rejected in general. However, according to the variance test and the BDS test, the RW3 cannot be eliminated. Contrary to that, it can be concluded that the efficiency of the Spanish market in the pre-crisis period and both related pre-crisis sub-periods cannot be rejected in the form of the RW3, or even the RW1 when using the runs test. During the post-crisis period, the efficiency of the Spanish market cannot be rejected when utilizing any of mentioned statistical methods, except of the Ljung-Box test that leads to the conclusion of inefficiency in post-crisis period and in first pre-crisis sub-period. For the rest of the cases, the weak form of efficiency cannot be eliminated in the form of the RW3 when using variance-ratio and runs tests, except the second post-crisis sub-period. When focusing on the BDS test in both post-crisis sub-periods, achieved results showed that the hypothesis of efficiency cannot be rejected even in the form of the RW1.

3.3 Possible Approach of Testing the Degree of the Weak Form of Efficiency

This subchapter will describe the authors' contribution to the problem field. In other words, an improvement of known method as described in subchapter 2.2 will be proposed. Different statistical tests verify different type of dependency in data sample as shown in Table 1. That is why, when using just one type of test, it is impossible to decide what kind of random walk model investigated time series may follow. For this reason, it would be useful to propose some framework that allow us to calculate the degree of efficiency of stock index returns.

This feature may be based on the sum of the values that are assigned to conclusions of each statistical test. If the null hypothesis of efficiency is rejected, it connotes the value of 0. Contrary to that, the value of 1 can be assigned if the efficiency is accepted in the form of the RW3 model, and the value of 3 if the null hypothesis of efficiency is accepted in the strictest form of the RW1 model. It is obvious that the value of 2 would correspond to the RW2 model. When given statistical test cannot deliver a clear decision because its result is inconclusive the value of 0.5 is assigned. The idea is to analyze both numerically and visually, whether the degree of compliance with the efficient market hypothesis is decreasing or increasing. The results of the methodology proposed in this paper are shown in Table 2.

Results presented in Table 2 are also expressed graphically in Figure 2. This chart visualizes clearly the development of IBEX35 values and the degree of compliance with the weak form of efficiency in related periods and sub-periods respectively. First, it can be seen that the degree of efficiency is lower when investigating the entire period than when the data sample is divided into periods and sub-periods. It can concluded that the highest degree of efficiency can be observed in the pre-crisis period, decreasing slightly in the time of the global financial crisis and even more in the post-crisis period. The division of the pre-crisis period into sub-periods did not affect the degree of efficiency within that period. On the other hand, the degree of efficiency in the post-crisis period increases considerably when considering two sub-periods with higher degree of compliance with the hypothesis of efficiency in the second sub-period. This fact clearly coincides with the recovery of IBEX35 index.

IBEX	Entire period	Pre-crisis	Pre-crisis I.	Pre-crisis II.	Crisis	Post-crisis	Post-crisis I.	Post-crisis II.
Ljung-Box + ARCH	0	1	1	1	0	0	0	3
Variance-Ratio + ARCH	1	1	1	1	1	1	1	3
Runs + Variance-Ratio (RW3)	0	3	3	3	1	1	1	1
BDS + Variance-Ratio (RW3)	1	1	1	1	3	1	3	3
Total	2	6	6	6	5	3	5	10

Table 2 Degree of compliance with the weak form of efficiency in the form of RW1 or RW3 models [García-Moreno, 2015]

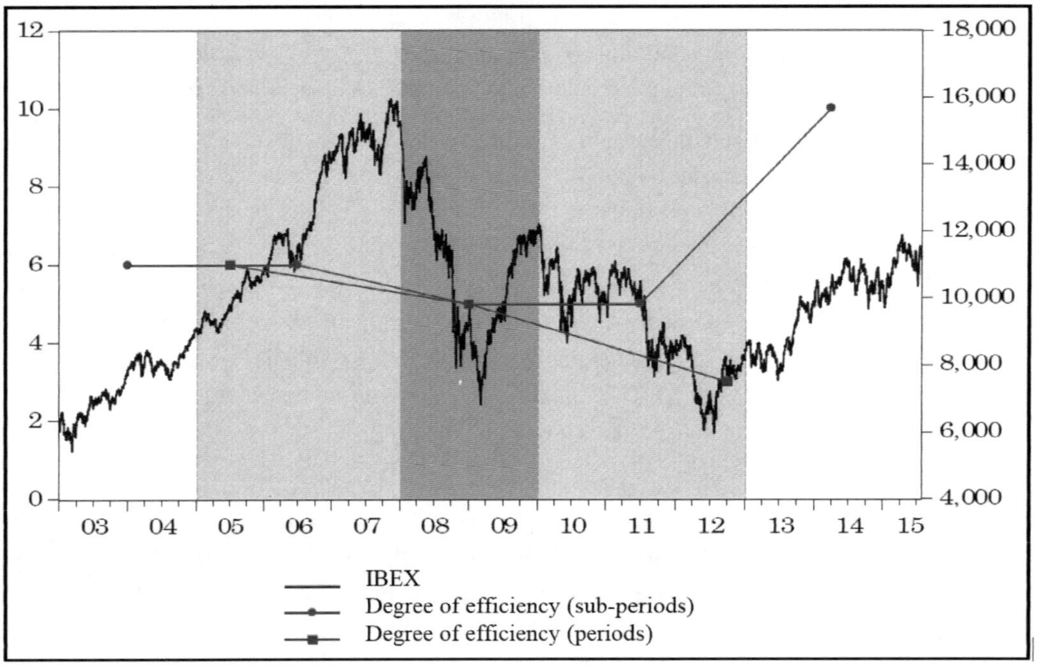

Figure 2 Evolution of the degree of compliance with the weak form of efficiency in the form of RW1 or RW3 models [García-Moreno, 2015]

4 Conclusions

Traditional statistical methods of testing the information efficiency have some shortcomings. Those methods allow for testing just necessary condition of particular random walk model. However, in practice, it is not enough to accept just some version of random walk model. That is why, when combining linear and non-linear methods of testing the weak form of efficiency of financial markets we developed a simple statistical approach in order to detect whether time series of financial returns follows some version of random walk model or not. Moreover, simple statistical framework how to compute the degree of efficiency was proposed as well. To sum up, our findings evoked some ways for future research. The testing system proposed in this paper can be improved by assessing the potency of applied statistical tests. The potency could be analyzed for instance using Monte Carlo simulation. Calculation of power of utilized statistical tests represents another approach that can be theoretically applied. Moreover, if we want to compare the power of statistical tests applied on different data sample, the value of likelihood function and consequent information criteria constitutes another way of future investigation.

Acknowledgements

This paper was supported by the Czech Science Foundation within project No. 13-13142S and Operational Programme Education for Competitiveness – project No. CZ.1.07/2.3.00/20.0296.

References

Brock, W. A., Dechert, W. D., Scheinkman, J. A. and LeBaron, B. (1996). 'A Test for Independence Based on the correlation Dimension'. *Econometric Reviews*, 15 (3), pp. 197-235.

Campbell, J. Y., Lo, A. and Mackinlay, A. C. (1997). *The Econometrics of Financial Markets*, 2nd ed. New York: Princeton University Press.

Engle, R. (1982). 'Autoregressive conditional heteroskedasticity with estimates of the variance of United Kingdom inflation'. *Econometrica*, 50 (4), pp. 987-1007.

Fama, E. F. (1991). 'Efficient capital markets: II'. *Journal of Finance*, 46 (5), pp. 1575-1617.

García-Moreno, M.B. (2015). *Modelos de optimización en redes de distribución*. Unpublished thesis.

Hančlová, J. and Rublíková, E. (2006). 'Testing the Weak Form of Efficiency on Czech and Slovak Stock Market'. *Operations Research and Decisions*, 16 (1), pp. 21-38.

Hinich, M. J., Mendes, E. M. and Stone, L. (2005). *A comparison between standard bootstrap and Theiler´s surrogate methods*. Austin: University of Texas in Austin.

Ljung, G. M. and Box, E. P. (1978). 'On a measure of lack of fit in time series models'. *Biometrika*, 65 (2), pp. 297-303.

Roberts, H. V. (1967). *Statistical versus clinical prediction of the stock market*. Unpublished manuscript.

Samuelson, P. A. (1965). 'Proof that properly anticipated prices fluctuate randomly'. *Industrial management review*, 6 (2), pp. 41-49.

Seďa, P. and Jimber del Río, J. A. (2016). 'Testing the Weak Form of Efficiency on Chinese Stock Market'. *Proceedings of 13th International Scientific Conference European Financial Systems 2016*, Brno, Czech Republic, pp. 669-677.

Siegel, S. and Castellan, N.J. (1988). *Nonparametric Statistics for the Behavioral Sciences*, 2nd ed., New York: McGraw-Hill.

A selecting model under constant returns to scale in data envelopment analysis

Mehdi Toloo[1], Maryam Allahyar[2]

Abstract. Data envelopment analysis (DEA) is a data-oriented mathematical programming approach that evaluates a set of peer decision making units (DMUs) dealing directly with the observed inputs and outputs (performance measures). Empirically, in order to have a logical assessment, there should be a balance between the number of performance measures and the number of DMUs. Accordingly, applying an appropriate method so that one can select some performance measures is very crucial for successful applications. In this paper, we suggest the envelopment form of selecting model under constant returns to scale (CRS) from both individual and aggregate points of view. We also show that applying these selecting models leads to the maximum discrimination between efficient units.

Keywords: Data envelopment analysis, Efficiency, The rule of thumb, Selective measures.

JEL Classification: C61, C67

1 Introduction

Data envelopment analysis (DEA) as a non-parametric technique pioneered by Farrell (1957) and later developed by Charnes, Cooper& Rhodes (1978) has proved to be an effective technique for evaluating a Decision Making Unit (DMU) in a set of similar DMUs which use multiple inputs to produce multiple outputs. The CCR (Charnes et al, 1978) and BCC (Banker et al, 1984) models are the two original DEA models which are extended under constant returns to scale (CRS) and the variable returns to scale (VRS) assumptions, respectively.

Let us consider evaluating a set of n DMUs, which use m inputs to produce s outputs. Practically, as mentioned in Cooper et al (2007), if the number of DMUs (n) is less than the total number of inputs and outputs $(m + n)$, then due to an inadequate number of degrees of freedom, a large portion of the DMUs will be identified as efficient. According to these facts, Cooper et al (2007) stated that a rough rule of thumb in the envelopment model is to choose $n \geq \max\{3(m + s), m \times s\}$. However, in real applications we may face cases in which the rule of thumb is violated. To have an acceptable result in such cases, it is needed to select some measures with the aim of keeping the rule of thumb. To deal with this issue, some attempts have been explored in DEA literature. Readers can refer to Jenkins and Anderson (2003), Morita and Avkiran (2009), Nataraja and Johnson (2011), Toloo and Babaee (2015), and Keshavarz and Toloo (2016). Toloo et al (2015) and Toloo and Tichý (2015) introduced the concept of *selective measures* and proposed a selecting approach which enables DMUs to

[1] Technical University of Ostrava, Department of Systems Engineering, Sokolska tř. 33, 701 21 Ostrava 1, Ostrava, Czech Republic, e-mail: mehdi.toloo@vsb.cz

[2] Technical University of Ostrava, Department of Systems Engineering, Sokolska tř. 33, 701 21 Ostrava 1, Ostrava, Czech Republic, e-mail: allahyar_maryam@yahoo.com

select measures optimally in the presence of large number of inputs and outputs under CRS and VRS assumptions, respectively. Specifically, Toloo et al (2015) presented the multiplier form of selecting model under CRS. In this paper, we extend the traditional envelopment CCR model and develop the envelopment form of selecting model under CRS. In addition, we compare the envelopment and multiplier forms of selecting model and drive a relation between them.

The outline of the paper is organized as follows: Section 2 gives a brief review on the selecting method proposed by Toloo et al (2015). The new selecting method is explained in Section 3. The penultimate section illustrates the applicability of our new method and makes a comparison between two alternative selecting models. Finally, we have come to conclusion in Section 5.

2 The multiplier form of selecting model under CRS

Consider a set of n DMUs, DMU_j ; $j \in \{1, \dots, n\}$, with m semi-positive inputs $\boldsymbol{x}_j = (x_{1j}, \dots, x_{mj})$ and s semi-positive outputs $\boldsymbol{y}_j = (y_{1j}, \dots, y_{sj})$. The input-efficiency of DMU_o($o \in \{1, \dots, n\}$), the unit being evaluated, can be obtained by solving any of the following two forms of CCR model, multiplier and envelopment:

multiplier form of CCR

$$
\begin{aligned}
&\max z_1 = \textstyle\sum_{r=1}^{s} u_r y_{ro} \\
&\text{s.t.} \\
&\textstyle\sum_{i=1}^{m} v_i x_{io} = 1 \\
&\textstyle\sum_{r=1}^{s} u_r y_{rj} - \sum_{i=1}^{m} v_i x_{ij} \le 0 && \forall j \\
&v_i \ge \varepsilon && \forall i \\
&u_r \ge \varepsilon && \forall r
\end{aligned}
\qquad (1)
$$

envelopment form of CCR

$$
\begin{aligned}
&\min z_2 = \theta - \varepsilon\left(\textstyle\sum_{i=1}^{m} s_i^x + \sum_{r=1}^{s} s_r^y\right) \\
&\text{s.t.} \\
&\textstyle\sum_{j=1}^{n} \lambda_j x_{ij} + s_i^x = \theta x_{io} && \forall i \\
&\textstyle\sum_{j=1}^{n} \lambda_j y_{rj} - s_r^y = y_{ro} && \forall r \\
&s_i^x, s_r^y \ge 0 && \forall i, \forall r \\
&\lambda_j \ge 0 && \forall j
\end{aligned}
\qquad (2)
$$

where

ε: The non-Archimedean infinitesimal,

λ_j: The intensity variable corresponding to DMU_j,

s_i^x: The ith input slack,

s_r^y: The r^{th}output slack,

v_i: The ith input weight,

u_r: The r^{th}output weight.

It is well known that models (1) and (2) are mutually dual and have the same objective function on optimality. Suppose that, model (1) is solved and the optimal solution $(\boldsymbol{v}^*, \boldsymbol{u}^*) \in \mathbb{R}^{m+s}$ is at hand. DMU_o is identified as an efficient unit if $z_1^* = 1$, otherwise it is inefficient.

As it is mentioned in the previous section, if the number of performance measures and DMUs will not meet the rule of thumb, the results are not reliable. In other words, if $n < \max\{3(m+s), m \times s\}$, then most DMUs are classified as efficient which is not acceptable. In some cases, the manager believes that some performance measures are more important than others so may fix them and ignore the others, otherwise, in the case that there is no priority in choosing measures, one approach must be adopted to select measures optimally and have a sharper discrimination among DMUs.

To handle this issue, Toloo et al (2015) proposed a selecting approach aim at choosing some inputs and outputs among selective measures in a way that produces acceptable results. In particular, the authors extended model (1) and presented the following individual selecting mixed integer programing (MIP) model:

$$
\begin{aligned}
&\max z_3 = \textstyle\sum_{r=1}^{s} u_r y_{ro} \\
&\text{s.t.} \\
&\textstyle\sum_{i=1}^{m} v_i x_{io} = 1 \\
&\textstyle\sum_{r=1}^{s} u_r y_{rj} - \sum_{i=1}^{m} v_i x_{ij} \leq 0 && \forall j \\
&\textstyle\sum_{r=1}^{s} b_r^y + \sum_{i=1}^{m} b_i^x \leq \min\left\{\left[\frac{n}{3}\right], 2\sqrt{n}\right\} \\
&\varepsilon b_i^x \leq v_i \leq M b_i^x && \forall i \\
&\varepsilon b_r^y \leq u_r \leq M b_r^y && \forall r \\
&b_i^x, b_r^y \in \{0,1\} && \forall i, \forall r
\end{aligned}
\qquad (3)
$$

where M is a large positive number and auxiliary binary variables b_i^x and b_r^y are introduced for each selective input and output measure, respectively. The ith selective input (r^{th} selective output) is selected if $b_i^x = 1(b_r^y = 1)$, otherwise, i.e. $b_i^x = 0\,(b_r^y = 0)$, the ith selective input (r^{th} selective output) will not selected. It should be noted that model (3) formulated with the assumption that all inputs and outputs are selective measures.

Toloo et al (2015) also proved that model (3) holds the rule of thumb on optimality due to the constraint $\sum_{r=1}^{s} b_r^y + \sum_{i=1}^{m} b_i^x \leq min\left\{\left[\frac{n}{3}\right], 2\sqrt{n}\right\}$ in the model formulation. Actually, the selecting model (3) decreases the number of performance measures in a way that the efficiency scores of unit under evaluation increases as much as possible.

The selecting model (3) should be solved for each individual DMU (i.e. n times). The final selected measures can be identified based on the majority choice among all DMUs. Afterward, the acceptable efficiencies, taking the selected measures into consideration, are calculated by applying the conventional CCR model. However, using such individual selecting models may fail when ties are encountered in the process of selecting. To handle such situation, Toloo et al (2015) also proposed the following aggregate model with the aim of choosing selective measures specific to collection of all DMUs:

$$
\begin{aligned}
&\max\ z_4 = \textstyle\sum_{r=1}^{s} u_r \left(\sum_{j=1}^{n} y_{rj}\right) \\
&\text{s.t.} \\
&\textstyle\sum_{i=1}^{m} v_i \left(\sum_{j=1}^{n} x_{ij}\right) = 1 \\
&\textstyle\sum_{r=1}^{s} u_r y_{rj} - \sum_{i=1}^{m} v_i x_{ij} \leq 0 && \forall j \\
&\textstyle\sum_{r=1}^{s} b_r^y + \sum_{i=1}^{m} b_i^x \leq \min\left\{\left[\frac{n}{3}\right], 2\sqrt{n}\right\} \\
&\varepsilon b_i^x \leq v_i \leq M b_i^x && \forall i \\
&\varepsilon b_r^y \leq u_r \leq M b_r^y && \forall r \\
&\textstyle\sum_{r=1}^{s} b_r^y \geq 1 \\
&b_i^x, b_r^y \in \{0,1\} && \forall i, \forall r \\
&v_i, u_r \geq \varepsilon && \forall i, \forall r
\end{aligned}
\qquad (4)
$$

Applying model (4) one can select measures by solving just one MIP model. Since traditional DEA models are formulated in two forms, multiplier and development, in the next section we extend the envelopment form of selecting model under CRS.

3 The proposed envelopment form of selecting model

To formulate the following selecting envelopment model under CRS, analogously, we adopt the auxiliary binary variables d_i^x and d_r^y corresponding to the ith selective input and r^{th} selective output, respectively, in model (2):

$$\begin{aligned}
&\min z_5 = \theta - \varepsilon\left(\textstyle\sum_{i=1}^{m} d_i^x s_i^x + \sum_{r=1}^{s} d_r^y s_r^y\right) && \\
&\text{s.t.} && \\
&\textstyle\sum_{j=1}^{n} \lambda_j x_{ij} + s_i^x = \theta x_{io} + M(1-d_i^x) && \forall i \\
&\textstyle\sum_{j=1}^{n} \lambda_j y_{rj} - s_r^y = y_{ro} - M\left(1-d_r^y\right) && \forall r \\
&\textstyle\sum_{r=1}^{s} d_r^y + \sum_{i=1}^{m} d_i^x \le \min\left\{\left[\frac{n}{3}\right], 2\sqrt{n}\right\} && \\
&d_i^x, d_r^y \in \{0,1\} && \forall i, \forall r \\
&s_i^x, s_r^y \ge 0 && \forall i, \forall r \\
&\lambda_j \ge 0 && \forall j
\end{aligned} \qquad (5)$$

As it can be seen, model (5) is a mixed integer nonlinear programming (MINP) due to the nonlinear terms $d_i^x s_i^x$ and $d_r^y s_r^y$ in its objective function. To linearize this model, we let $t_i^x = d_i^x s_i^x$ and impose the following restrictions to the model to have $t_i^x = 0$ when $d_i^x = 0$ and otherwise, i.e. $d_i^x = 1$, $t_i^x = s_i^x$:

$$0 \le t_i^x \le M d_i^x$$
$$s_i^x - M(1-d_i^x) \le t_i^x \le s_i^x.$$

If $d_i^x = 0$ then the constraint $s_i^x - M(1-d_i^x) \le t_i^x \le s_i^x$ is redundant and from $0 \le t_i^x \le M d_i^x$ we have $t_i^x = 0$. Otherwise, i.e. $d_i^x = 1$, the constraint $0 \le t_i^x \le M d_i^x$ would be redundant and on the other hand the constraint $s_i^x - M(1-d_i^x) \le t_i^x \le s_i^x$ convers to $s_i^x \le t_i^x \le s_i^x$ and hence $t_i^x = s_i^x$. Analogously, we $t_r^x = d_r^y s_r^y$ and impose the following constraints to the model:

$$0 \le t_r^y \le M d_r^y$$
$$s_r^y - M\left(1-d_r^y\right) \le t_r^y \le s_r^y.$$

As a result, the envelopment form of selecting model is formulated as the following MIP model:

$$\begin{aligned}
&\min z_6 = \theta - \varepsilon\left(\textstyle\sum_{i=1}^{m} t_i^x + \sum_{r=1}^{s} t_r^y\right) && \\
&\text{s.t.} && \\
&\textstyle\sum_{j=1}^{n} \lambda_j x_{ij} + s_i^x = \theta x_{io} + M(1-d_i^x) && \forall i \\
&\textstyle\sum_{j=1}^{n} \lambda_j y_{rj} - s_r^y = y_{ro} - M\left(1-d_r^y\right) && \forall r \\
&\textstyle\sum_{r=1}^{s} d_r^y + \sum_{i=1}^{m} d_i^x \le \min\left\{\left[\frac{n}{3}\right], 2\sqrt{n}\right\} && \\
&0 \le t_i^x \le M d_i^x && \forall i \\
&s_i^x - M(1-d_i^x) \le t_i^x \le s_i^x && \forall i \\
&0 \le t_r^y \le M d_r^y && \forall r \\
&s_r^y - M\left(1-d_r^y\right) \le t_r^y \le s_r^y && \forall r \\
&d_i^x, d_r^y \in \{0,1\} && \forall i, \forall r \\
&t_i^x, t_r^y \ge 0 && \forall i, \forall r \\
&s_i^x, s_r^y \ge 0 && \forall i, \forall r \\
&\lambda_j \ge 0 && \forall j
\end{aligned} \qquad (6)$$

Indeed, selecting multiplier and envelopment models (3) and (6) are two alternative approaches for selecting performance measures under CRS. One should note that since the selecting models (3) and (6) are MIP, unlike the multiplier and envelopment forms of CCR, their optimal objective function values are not necessarily equal.

The following theorem reveals the relation between the optimal values of these two selecting models.

Theorem 1. $0 < z_6^* \leq z_3^* \leq 1$

Proof. Suppose $(\boldsymbol{u}^*, \boldsymbol{v}^*, \boldsymbol{b}^{x^*}, \boldsymbol{b}^{y^*}) \in \mathbb{R}^{2(m+s)}$ and $(\theta^*, \boldsymbol{\lambda}^*, \boldsymbol{s}^{x^*}, \boldsymbol{s}^{y^*}, \boldsymbol{t}^{x^*}, \boldsymbol{t}^{y^*}, \boldsymbol{d}^{x^*}, \boldsymbol{d}^{y^*}) \in \mathbb{R}^{n+3(m+s)+1}$ are the optimal solution of models (3) and (6), respectively. Let $\bar{m} = \{i | d_i^{x^*} = 1\}$ and $\bar{s} = \{r | d_r^{y^*} = 1\}$. A trivial verification shows that $(\theta^*, \boldsymbol{\lambda}^*, \boldsymbol{s}^{x^*}, \boldsymbol{s}^{y^*})$ is the optimal solution of the following model:

$$\begin{array}{ll}
\min z_7 = \theta - \varepsilon\left(\sum_{i\in\bar{m}} s_i^x + \sum_{r\in\bar{s}} s_r^y\right) & \\
\text{s.t.} & \\
\sum_{j=1}^{n} \lambda_j x_{ij} + s_i^x = \theta x_{io} & i \in \bar{m} \\
\sum_{j=1}^{n} \lambda_j y_{rj} - s_r^y = y_{ro} & r \in \bar{s} \\
s_i^x, s_r^y \geq 0 & i \in \bar{m},\ r \in \bar{s} \\
\lambda_j \geq 0 & \forall j
\end{array} \tag{7}$$

Now, consider the dual of model (7) as follows:

$$\begin{array}{ll}
\max z_8 = \sum_{r\in\bar{s}} u_r y_{ro} & \\
\text{s.t.} & \\
\sum_{i\in\bar{m}} v_i x_{io} = 1 & \\
\sum_{r\in\bar{s}} u_r y_{rj} - \sum_{i\in\bar{m}} v_i x_{ij} \leq 0 & \forall j \\
v_i \geq \varepsilon & i \in \bar{m} \\
u_r \geq \varepsilon & r \in \bar{s}
\end{array} \tag{8}$$

Since the optimal objective value of CCR models are positive and less than or equal to 1and under the primal-dual relation in linear programing we have $0 < z_7^* = z_8^* \leq 1$. Let $(\tilde{\boldsymbol{v}}^*, \tilde{\boldsymbol{u}}^*)$ be the optimal solution of model (8). It is easy to verify that $(\tilde{\boldsymbol{u}}^*, \tilde{\boldsymbol{v}}^*, \tilde{\boldsymbol{b}}^x, \tilde{\boldsymbol{b}}^y)$ where

$$\tilde{b}_i^x = \begin{cases} 1 & i \in \bar{m} \\ 0 & i \notin \bar{m} \end{cases}, \quad \tilde{b}_r^y = \begin{cases} 1 & r \in \bar{s} \\ 0 & r \notin \bar{s} \end{cases}$$

is a feasible solution of model (3) with objective function z_8^*. Hence, we have $z_6^* \leq z_7^* = z_8^* \leq z_3^*$ and the proof is completed.■

Reference to Theorem 1 shows that the multiplier and envelopment forms of selecting model are actually formulated under optimistic and pessimistic perspective, respectively. In other words, since $z_6^* \leq z_3^*$ and as will illustrated in the next section, the proposed selecting model (6) can decrease the number of efficient DMUs even more than model (3) and subsequently results in the maximum discrimination between efficient units.

Similarly, we suggest the following MIP model as the aggregate version of the selecting envelopment form to select measures in favore of the collection of all DMUs:

$$\begin{aligned}
&\min z_9 = \theta - \varepsilon\left(\textstyle\sum_{i=1}^{m} t_i^x + \sum_{r=1}^{s} t_r^y\right) \\
&\text{s.t.} \\
&\textstyle\sum_{j=1}^{n} \lambda_j x_{ij} + s_i^x = \theta \sum_{j=1}^{n} x_{ij} + M(1 - d_i^x) && \forall i \\
&\textstyle\sum_{j=1}^{n} \lambda_j y_{rj} - s_r^y = \sum_{j=1}^{n} y_{rj} - M(1 - d_r^y) && \forall r \\
&\textstyle\sum_{r=1}^{s} d_r^y + \sum_{i=1}^{m} d_i^x \leq \min\left\{\left[\frac{n}{3}\right], 2\sqrt{n}\right\} \\
&t_i^x \leq M d_i^x && \forall i \\
&s_i^x - M(1 - d_i^x) \leq t_i^x \leq s_i^x && \forall i \\
&t_r^y \leq M d_r^y && \forall r \\
&s_r^y - M(1 - d_r^y) \leq t_r^y \leq s_r^y && \forall r \\
&d_i^x, d_r^y \in \{0,1\} && \forall i,\ \forall r \\
&t_i^x, t_r^y, s_i^x, s_r^y \geq 0 && \forall i,\ \forall r \\
&\lambda_j \geq 0 && \forall j
\end{aligned} \qquad (9)$$

The next section provides an application to illustrate the suggested method and make comparison between the obtained results from multiplier and envelopment forms of selecting model.

4 Application

In order to apply the selecting models to a real data set, we here use the data of the largest private bank in Iran extracted from Toloo et al (2015). This application includes twenty DMUs (bank branches) with six inputs and six outputs measures, which are defined as follows:

Inputs: Employees (x_1), Number of accounts (x_2), Assets (x_3), Space (x_4), Costs (x_5), and Expenses (x_6),

Outputs: Number of transactions (y_1), Deposits (y_2), Loans (y_3), Check card (y_4), Credit card (y_5), and OTP (y_6).

According to the calculated efficiency scores reported in Toloo et al (2015), 80% of all branches are efficient, which this result is questionable and is due to the large number of inputs and outputs measures in comparison to the number of DMUs . To decrease the number of efficient DMUs we apply both aggregate models (4) and (9) to the data set. Tables 1 summarizes all selected data through solving models (4), as well as the acceptable efficiency score which is obtained by the CCR model.

Banks	x_1	x_3	x_5	y_1	y_2	y_3	**Accepted Efficiency**
1	11	1753	10020	5214	72149	57537	0.86
2	17	2604	11440	5343	89781	51114	0.70
3	7	1155	8427	5145	42654	52485	1
4	12	1899	11816	3249	97812	67298	0.85
5	14	2215	12426	6706	77031	43487	0.64
6	14	2357	9907	6259	75923	41442	0.754
7	9	1370	10365	3652	47763	43262	0.65
8	5	829	5283	3913	45732	14237	1
9	6	985	11061	3566	55222	41062	0.88
10	6	1023	5856	4559	53323	37418	1
11	8	1311	8745	4441	69734	57883	0.99
12	9	1536	7326	5031	49153	47139	0.98
13	8	1367	8326	5053	92365	55543	1

14	7	1193	6525	4762	64235	22347	0.89
15	9	1359	8158	6876	89104	45717	1
16	7	1111	11135	4307	42012	73925	1
17	7	1182	6920	5331	69360	27246	0.99
18	7	1069	5864	4004	51438	26531	0.81
19	6	992	5039	2342	39948	20223	0.66
20	7	1180	8378	4238	154284	43928	1

Table 1 Selected measures through model (4) and the accepted efficiency scores

Analogously, the selected measures via model (9) along with acceptable efficiencies are displayed in Toloo, Barat, and Masoumzadeh (2015).

Banks	x_1	x_2	x_4	x_6	y_2	y_3	**Accepted Efficiency**
1	11	1250	97	3137	72149	57537	0.87
2	17	5019	150	4406	89781	51114	0.7
3	7	3217	61	2180	42654	52485	0.94
4	12	1061	105	6477	97812	67298	0.89
5	14	5219	123	3325	77031	43487	0.8
6	14	1389	123	3757	75923	41442	0.68
7	9	7166	79	2714	47763	43262	0.64
8	5	1475	44	2887	45732	14237	0.69
9	6	1800	52	2852	55222	41062	0.77
10	6	1689	52	2606	53323	37418	0.96
11	8	1780	70	4442	69734	57883	0.99
12	9	2669	79	1989	49153	47139	0.99
13	8	7175	70	3727	92365	55543	1
14	7	2120	61	3473	64235	22347	0.63
15	9	30618	79	3824	89104	45717	1
16	7	1464	61	1524	42012	73925	1
17	7	8924	68	3573	69360	27246	0.68
18	7	2388	61	2523	51438	26531	0.71
19	6	4714	52	2398	39948	20223	0.69
20	7	1866	62	3165	154284	43928	1

Table 2 Selected measures through model (9) and the accepted efficiency scores

As can be extracted from the last column of these two tables, the multiplier model and the proposed envelopment model are succeeded in decreasing the percentage of efficient DMUs from 93% to 36% and 20%, respectively. On the other hand, the multiplier aggregate model (4) selects three inputs and three outputs, meanwhile four inputs and two outputs are selected by the envelopment aggregate model (9). Actually, more efficient units introduced by multiplier model compared to envelopment model reveals the optimistic and pessimistic viewpoint of these models. In other words, the envelopment form of selecting model possesses higher discrimination than the multiplier form. These two extreme viewpoints can be considered as a tool for decision maker.

5 Conclusion

In this paper, we extended the traditional envelopment CCR model and developed a selecting approach to deal with the selective measures under CRS assumption. The proposed selecting model are formulated from both individual and aggregate points of view. We also compared the obtained results from the new selecting model with those obtained from the multiplier form of selecting model presented by Toloo et al (2015). The findings reveal that the maximum efficiency scores are achieved by applying the multiplier model of Toloo et al (2015) while the proposed envelopment form leads to maximum discrimination between efficient units.

Acknowledgement

The research was supported by the Czech Science Foundation through project No. 16-17810S and SGS project 2017/141 "Diskriminační analýza versus analýza datových obalů".

References

Banker, R. D., Charnes, A. and Cooper, W. W. (1984). 'Some Models for Estimating Technical and Scale Inefficiencies in Data Envelopment Analysis'. *Management Science*, 30 (9), pp. 1078–1092.

Charnes, A., Cooper, W. W. and Rhodes, E. (1978). 'Measuring the efficiency of decision making units'. *European Journal of Operational Research*, 2 (6), pp. 429–444.

Cooper, W. W., Seiford, L. M. and Tone, K. (2007). *Data envelopment analysis: A comprehensive text with models, applications, references and DEA-solver software*, 2nd ed. Springer US.

Farrell, M. J. (1957). The Measurement of Productive Efficiency. *Journal of the Royal Statistical Society. Series A (General)*, 120 (3), p. 253.

Jenkins, L. and Anderson, M. (2003). 'A multivariate statistical approach to reducing the number of variables in data envelopment analysis'. *European Journal of Operational Research*, 147, pp. 51–61.

Keshavarz, E. and Toloo, M. (2016). 'A single-stage approach for selecting inputs / outputs in DEA'. *34th International Conference Mathematical Methods in Economics MME 2016, Liberec, Czech Republic.*

Morita, H. and Avkiran, N. K. (2009). 'Selecting inputs and outputs in data envelopment analysis by designing statistical experiments'. *Journal of the Operations Research Society of Japan*, 52 (2), pp. 163–173.

Nataraja, N. R. and Johnson, A. L. (2011). 'Guidelines for using variable selection techniques in data envelopment analysis'. *European Journal of Operational Research*, 215 (3), pp. 662–669.

Toloo, M. and Babaee, S. (2015). 'On variable reductions in data envelopment analysis with an illustrative application to a gas company'. *Applied Mathematics and Computation*, 270, pp. 527–533.

Toloo, M., Barat, M. and Masoumzadeh, A. (2015). 'Selective measures in data envelopment analysis'. *Annals of Operations Research*, 226 (1), pp. 623–642.

Toloo, M. and Tichý, T. (2015). 'Two alternative approaches for selecting performance measures in data envelopment analysis'. *Measurement*, 65 (December), pp. 29–40.

Environmental Evaluation of V4 Steel Industries under Uncertainty

František Zapletal [1]

Abstract. The purpose of the paper is to evaluate the steel sectors of the Viszegrad Four countries. This evaluation is done with respect to the environmental performance of the sector. In particular, amount of different types of emissions released to the atmosphere is taken into consideration. Moreover, the influence of the emissions trading system of the EU is also involved as a criterion for evaluation (in the form of balance of the emissions allowances). In order to involve more periods during which input data are changing, PROMETHEE method for multi-criteria decision making with possible uncertain inputs is used. The result of the analysis is the ranking of national steel sectors based on the time period between 2013 and 2015.

Keywords: steel industry, benchmarking, EU ETS, MCDM, PROMETHEE, uncertainty.

JEL classification: C44, O13

1 Introduction

Policy makers, as well as managers of companies often require an assessment of units on which they can/must decide. It helps to improve resource allocation, rewarding/penalization of units and, also, it helps to understand the system and its structure. This fact holds also for steel sectors and their evaluation which is the goal of this paper. European iron and steel companies are still under the pressure made by (especially) Asian competitors on the market. So, the emphasis put on efficiency in this sector is reasonable. The more so, the countries of V4 (Czech Republic, Slovakia, Poland and Hungary) keep the long tradition of iron and steel production. Furthermore, focus on environmental impact is natural. European authorities still come up with steps targeting protection of environment and sustainability.

Many studies have been devoted to efficiency evaluation of steel sector, see e.g. Zhang et al. (2009), or particular steel companies, see e.g. Zapletal (2014). This paper is focused in more details on the environmental assessment of national steel sectors. While, this is also the topic researched often in the past, but approaches and criteria differ a lot there (especially because of different goals of those studies). For example, Kim and Worrell (2002) focusing on CO_2 trends in steel industry in selected American and Asian countries, Wei, Liao and Fan (2007) studying energetic efficiency of the Chinese steel sector or Zapletal and Chytilová (2016) with their study on economic-environmental efficiency of European national steel sector must be pointed out.

This paper is different from those mentioned above because it assesses the steel sector performance according to the burden in the form of emissions. Moreover, the impact of the main tool of environmental policy of the EU - emissions trading system with CO_2 allowances (EU ETS) is also taken into consideration in evaluation similarly to Zapletal and Chytilová (2016). Above that, uncertainty of input data caused by their development in time is considered here.

[1]VSB - Technical university of Ostrava, Faculty of Economics, Dpt. of Systems Engineering, frantisek.zapletal@vsb.cz

There are many possibilities which multi-criteria decision making (MCDM) method can be chosen for evaluation. Due to the fact that the performance of alternatives (i.e. national steel sectors) must be compared, any of methods using pair-wise comparison seems to be the reasonable choice. Another criteria for the method's selection is possibility to work with imprecise data. In particular, PROMETHEE method is used in this study.

The paper is organized as follows. After the introduction part, methodology of the PROMETHEE method with both deterministic and imprecise data is presented. The third section is devoted to the structure of the model for evaluation and description of data. The core of the paper lies in the fourth section where the evaluation of the V4 national steel sectors is done. The results of the study are discussed and some ideas for further research are concluded in the final section of the paper.

2 PROMETHEE method under uncertainty

As it was mentioned in the introduction, some of MCDM methods had to be selected for evaluation. There are more methods which are based on pair-wise comparing of alternatives. But not all of them has been already extended for using uncertain input data. Extensions of Analytic Hierarchy Process (see i.a. interval AHP by Entani (2009) or Fuzzy-AHP by Mikhailov (2000)) and extended PROMETHEE method are the ones which are often used for evaluation under uncertainty. An advantage of the AHP is a clear structuring of problem's hierarchy which is not necessary in this paper. On the other hand, results of the PROMETHEE are easy to interpret and also sensitivity analyses can be done easily.

A group of PROMETHEE (Preference Ranking Organization Method for Enrichment Evaluation) methods belongs to so called *outranking methods* of decision making, i.e. they are based on *outranking relations* which evaluate differences in performance of pairs of alternatives. In the sake of clarity, first the original (deterministic) version introduced by Brans et al. (1984) will be described.

Let us have a decision making problem consisting of n criteria (set of criteria $\mathcal{N}$) and k alternatives (set of alternatives $\mathcal{K}$). Then, let p_i be a preference function for the i-th criterion which assigns a preference level P_i to difference in performance of two alternatives regarding the i-th criterion (e.g. $P_i(a,b)$ stands for the preference degree corresponding to difference in performances alternatives a and b at criterion i). Preference degree can be understood as a strength of preference relation (how much important is the difference in values). Unfortunately, no precise 'recipe' which shape of preference function is the best to choose exists. The only one natural requirement for them is that they should be non-decreasing with function values ranging from 0 to 1 (and positive values of preference level can be assigned only to positive values of differences). The most common shapes of preference functions are summarized e.g. by Brans et al. (1984).

The algorithm of PROMETHEE can be described in 4 steps:

- computation of preference degrees $P_i(a,b)$ for $\forall i \in \mathcal{N}$ and $\forall$ pairs $(a,b); a,b \in \mathcal{K}, a \neq b$;
- aggregation and weighting of preference levels to preference indices $\pi(a,b)$ using Eq. (1);

$$\pi(a,b) = \sum_{i \in \mathcal{N}} w_i \cdot P_i(a,b), \text{ for } \forall a,b \in \mathcal{K} \tag{1}$$

- aggregation of preference indices to partial flows (positive ϕ^+ and negative ϕ^-) using Eq. (2) and Eq. (3), respectively;

$$\phi^(a) = \frac{1}{k-1} \cdot \sum_{a \neq b} \pi(a,b), \text{ for } \forall a \in \mathcal{K} \tag{2}$$

$$\phi^-(a) = \frac{1}{k-1} \cdot \sum_{a \neq b} \pi(b,a), \text{ for } \forall a \in \mathcal{K} \tag{3}$$

- aggregation of partial flows into net flows using Eq (4).

$$\phi(a) = \phi^+(a) - \phi^-(a), \text{ for } \forall a \in \mathcal{K} \tag{4}$$

Partial flows are used in PROMETHEE I (partial) ranking (see Eq. 5,6 and 7) and net flows in PROMETHEE II (complete) ranking (see Eq. 8 and 9), see Brans et al. (1984).

$$a \succ^I b \Leftrightarrow (\phi^-(a) \leq \phi^-(b)) \wedge (\phi^+(a) \geq \phi^+(b)) \tag{5}$$

where one of inequalities must be strict.

$$a =^I b \Leftrightarrow (\phi^-(a) = phi^-(b)) \wedge (\phi^+(a) = \phi^+(b)) \tag{6}$$

$$a \ominus^I b \Leftrightarrow \text{when none of (5) or (6) is satisfied} \tag{7}$$

Relations $\succ^I, =^I, \ominus^I$ stand for preference, equivalence and incomparability relations of partial ranking (PROMETHEE I).

$$a \succ^{II} b \Leftrightarrow \phi(a) > \phi(b) \tag{8}$$

$$a =^{II} b \Leftrightarrow \phi(a) = \phi(b) \tag{9}$$

Relations $\succ^{II}, =^{II}$ stand for preference and equivalence relations of complete ranking (PROMETHEE II).

It worth emphasizing that the PROMETHEE I (unlike PROMETHEE II) allows for incomparability of alternatives.

Before a description of a particular algorithm of PROMETHEE with inexact data can be given, it is desirable to explain that more ways and methods for such extension exist. Almost all studies devoted to PROMETHEE with uncertain data work with fuzzy inputs, see e.g. Goumas and Lygerou (2000) or Adali, Tus and Kundakci (2016). But, because of the fact that it would be meaningless to use fuzzy inputs in this study, the very first version of the PROMETHEE with uncertain data by Le Teno and Mareschal (1998) is chosen here. That version requires interval input data.

First, basic binary operations of addition and subtraction on intervals must be provided. Let $[\underline{a}, \overline{a}]$ and $[\underline{b}, \overline{b}]$ be intervals on $\mathbb{R}$. Then $[\underline{a}, \overline{a}] + [\underline{b}, \overline{b}] = [\underline{a} + \underline{b}, \overline{a} + \overline{b}]$ and $[\underline{a}, \overline{a}] - [\underline{b}, \overline{b}] = [\underline{a} - \overline{b}, \overline{a} + \underline{b}]$. The last necessary extension for this study is multiplication of intervals by a positive real number: $k \cdot [\underline{a}, \overline{a}] = [k \cdot \underline{a}, k \cdot \overline{a}], k \in \mathbb{R}^+$.

Le Teno and Mareschal (1998) proposed to use the same equations like in the deterministic case, but they suppose differences in values of alternatives to be intervals. Thus all operations of addition, subtraction and multiplication must be replaced by the interval extensions of operations above. Modified equations are below.

$$[\underline{\pi(a,b)}, \overline{\pi(a,b)}] = [\sum_{i\in\mathcal{N}} w_i \cdot \underline{P_i(a,b)}; \sum_{i\in\mathcal{N}} w_i \cdot \overline{P_i(a,b)}] \tag{10}$$

$$[\underline{\phi^+(a)}, \overline{\phi^+(a)}] = [\frac{1}{k-1} \cdot \sum_{a\neq b} \underline{\pi(a,b)}, \frac{1}{k-1} \cdot \sum_{a\neq b} \overline{\pi(a,b)}] \tag{11}$$

$$[\underline{\phi^-(a)}, \overline{\phi^-(a)}] = [\frac{1}{k-1} \cdot \sum_{a\neq b} \underline{\pi(b,a)}, \frac{1}{k-1} \cdot \sum_{a\neq b} \overline{\pi(b,a)}] \tag{12}$$

$$[\underline{\phi(a)}, \overline{\phi(a)}] = [\underline{\phi^+(a)}, \overline{\phi^+(a)}] - [\underline{\phi^-(a)}, \overline{\phi^-(a)}] \tag{13}$$

Le Teno and Mareschal (1998) proposed to design trapezoidal fuzzy intervals to put higher emphasis on values near to centers of intervals. For this paper, with respect to the input data described in Section 3.3, fuzzification is not used.

3 The model for evaluation

In this section, the model of multi-criteria decision making which will be used to evaluate the performance of the steel industries is established.

3.1 Set of criteria

A crucial task when building the decision-making model is selection of criteria. Naturally, there are no fixed set of criteria which should be considered for evaluation of environmental performance of units. The choice depends on many aspects like e.g. purpose of the analysis, complexity of analysis and, last but not least, availability of data.

Kim and Worrell (2002) focused, in particular, on CO_2 emissions, Zapletal and Chytilová (2016) involved both economic and environmental aspects. The purpose of this paper is to take environmental burden of steel industry more comprehensively. That is why several different undesirable products (wastes) are involved. Because not companies but the whole steel sectors are compared, there is no need to search for (very often sensitive) data of companies. On the other hand, a resulting disadvantage is that not all the data are collected (and thus available) for the national sectors as a whole.

The fact, which is good to take into consideration before a set of criteria is chosen, is that additional information about preferences/importance among criteria will be needed after that. Despite a decision-making (almost) always requires some subjective inputs of a decision-maker, a degree of subjectivity can be restricted to some extent. Let us have an example of two criteria - amount of production and amount of emissions (both of them are surely relevant when the overal performance of steel company is done). The problem occurs when setting weights of those criteria. Who is competent enough to decide on importance between importance of production and importance of environmental burden? And, how can/should it be done? Would the problem be really bi-criterial (perhaps managers would follow the production only and some other stakeholders like conservationists would prefer absolutely the emissions). Anyway, this problem will be really hard to solve. For this reason, only environmental criteria (or rather criteria related directly with environment) are considered.

Because of a lack of data on solid and liquid wastes in sectors, only air pollution is taken into account. In particular, the set of criteria consists of following elements:

- amount of CO_2 [tons per 1 ton of production];
- amount of SO_2 [tons per 1 ton of production];
- amount of NO_X [tons per 1 ton of production];
- amount of TSP (Total Suspended Particulate matter of size $< 10\mu m$) [tons per 1 ton of production];
- balance of emission permits [pcs of allowances].

The first four criteria belong to the biggest (and most important) air pollutants produced by steel industry. The last one (balance of emission permits) comes from the emissions trading system. In the line with Directive 2003/87/EC (2003), each heavy industrial company in the EU obtains some particular amount of emission allowances (1 emissions permit authorizes its owner to release 1 ton of CO_2) for free. If that amount is sufficient then the surplus can be sold on the market (it brings a profit) and, conversely, in the case of lack of allowances, it implies necessity to buy them and increase costs. It should be mentioned that the amount of permits granted to companies depends on CO_2 emissions in previous periods (i.e. positive balance of permits indicates capability to decrease CO_2 emissions supposing stable level of production).

In order to avoid discrimination of the national sectors with higher production, all criteria mentioned above are expressed per 1 ton of production. The author of this paper is aware of the fact that different manufacturing processes in steel industry produce different number of emissions. But, because whole sectors (not seperate companies) are compared, this simplification should not lead to significant distortions of results.

3.2 Weights for criteria

As it was mentioned in the section 3.1, the author of this paper wants to suppress unnecessary subjectivity as much as possible. And numerical expression of criteria's importance belongs to those parts of the model where it is possible to some extent. In particular, there are two possible different views how to compare noxiousness of different pollutants. The first one considers impact on companies in the sector (fees for emissions) and the second one considers the impact on environment/society. Due to the fact that values of fees for emissions are set also with respect to toxicity for environment, the former possibility is chosen here. In the line with Czech Law No. 201/2012 (2012), following prices for 1 ton of emissions are set for Czech companies (precise values of fees differ country by country, but here, the values are used only for obtaining the weights): 4200 CZK/t TSP, 1350 CZK/t SO_2, 1100 CZK/t NO_X. When maintaining the ratios, the weights can be computed easily: $w'_{\text{TSP}} = 0.63, w'_{\text{SO}_2} = 0.20, w'_{\text{NO}_X} = 0.17$.

Similarly to the non-carbon emissions, CO_2 and the balance of emission allowances can be also expressed in cash. One ton of CO_2 corresponds to 1 emission allowance with a market price. But, when considering the fact that 1 allowance costs between 4 and 7 EUR (between 2013 and 2015) and that amount of CO_2 per 1 ton of final product is approx 500-2000 times higher in comparison with the other investigated gases, the weights of both criteria related with CO_2 together would be very close to 1, and thus the importance of the other pollutants would drop almost to zero. However, such values would be undesirable (e.g. impact of TSP on human's health is substantially higher in comparison with CO2 etc.). For this reason, an artificial distribution of weights between non-CO2 and CO_2 criteria has to be set. Because, the EU ETS system is so supported by policy-makers, CO_2 criteria will get 50% of preferences together (25% for amount of CO_2 and 25% for balance of allowances) and remaining 50% will belong to non-CO_2 ones. After normalization, the final weights are obtained: $w_{\text{CO}_2} = 0.25, w_{\text{TSP}} = 0.32, w_{\text{SO}_2} = 0.10, w_{\text{NO}_X} = 0.08, w_{\text{BoA}} = 0.25$.

3.3 Input data

If the evaluation is done based on data of only one period (year), a situation would be easier and usual deterministic MCDM methods could be used. But, when the dynamics of performance is to be taken into consideration, a decision maker faces the uncertainty. Here, the uncertainty is not caused by ambiguity or vagueness of values of the criteria, but it comes from the volatility of values in time. So, in the analysis, values from 2013 to 2015 are used (it worth mentioning that no evident trend in data development can be discovered). More recent data are not available yet, on the other hand it would not make sense to go further to the past because of "balance of allowances" criterion - the EU ETS system has been driven by different rules and the results could be affected by this fact.

Here is the review of the data used in this paper:

- data on non-CO_2 emissions and amount of production (derived from Eurostat database [1]; originally by countries)
- data on CO_2 emissions and the balance of allowances (derived from the CarbonMarketData database[2]; originally by companies and then aggregated by countries).

There are more ways how to express uncertain data, e.g. random variables with given probability distribution (useless in this case because of a lack of data), fuzzy sets (but there is no natural way how to design their shape) or intervals (those seem to be the best choice for this paper). So, values of alternatives are taken as intervals with lower bounds given by minimum value and upper bounds by maximum value of the considered time period.

The last remaining remark on input data is devoted to the selection of preference functions. For the sake of simplicity (and because there is not any reason why not to do so), linear shape given by the function (14).

$$P_i(a,b) = \begin{cases} 0, & f_i(a) - f_i(b) \leq 0 \\ \frac{f_i(a)-f_i(b)}{f_i^{\max}}, & 0 \geq f_i(a) - f_i(b) \geq f_i^{\max} \\ 1, & f_i(a) - f_i(b) > f_i^{\max} \end{cases} \tag{14}$$

where i is a max-type criterion ($i \in \mathcal{N}$), $f_i(a), f_i(b)$ stands for performance of alternatives a, b with respect to the i-th criterion, $f_i^{\max}$ is the maximum value of difference between any pair of alternatives in $\mathcal{K}$ with respect to the i-th criterion.

The presented shape of preference functions guarantees that for each P_i there is exactly one pair of alternatives for which the corresponding P_i value reaches 0 and exactly one pair with P_i

[1] http://ec.europa.eu/eurostat/data/database
[2] www.carbonmarketdata.com

value of 1 (under the assumption that there are not two alternatives with an identical value of performance). This helps to avoid similar performances in overal ranking if possible.

Deterministic versions of the model will be solved using Visual PROMETHEE software which allows for useful graphical representation of results.

4 Evaluation of the V4 steel sectors

In this section, ranking of the national steel sectors of V4 countries is presented. Except of the model with interval data, final ranking of the sectors using deterministic data is provided here. In particular, scenario with (a): the best values of alternatives (i.e. the best performance of each alternative with respect to each criterion in the whole time period), (b): the worst values of alternatives (i.e. the worst performance of each alternative with respect to each criterion in the whole time period) are added into comparison to the model with interval input data.

Phi values of the alternatives are listed in Tab. 1.

Sector	ϕ
CZE	[0.0992, 0.4364]
SVK	[-0.3662, 0.0796]
POL	[-0.3157, 0.0391]
HUN	[-0.2752, 0.3028]

Table 1 Results of the model with interval data

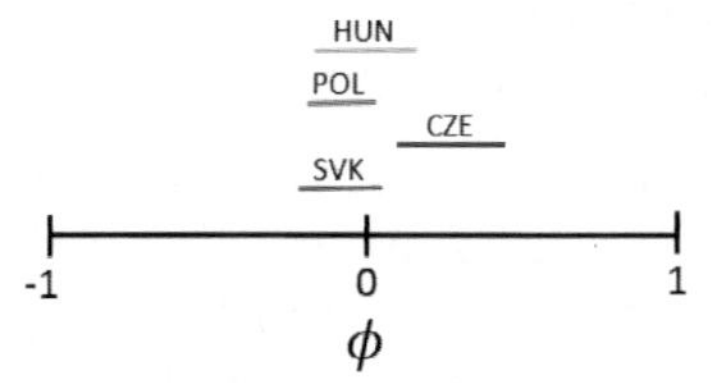

Figure 1 Results of the model with interval data

The results (Tab. 1 and Fig. 1) show that it is not possible to give the precise ranking of any alternative (there is no interval which does not intersect with any other). In particular, following facts can be regarded:

- Czech Republic can be either the first or the second one,
- Hungary can achieve all possible rankings (1st,2nd,3rd,4th)
- Slovakia and Poland can be at all positions except of the first one.

If all possible deterministic rankings should be summarized, they would be as follows:

- CZE$\succ$HUN$\succ$SVK$\succ$POL;
- CZE$\succ$HUN$\succ$POL$\succ$SVK;
- CZE$\succ$SVK$\succ$HUN$\succ$POL;
- CZE$\succ$SVK$\succ$POL$\succ$HUN;
- CZE$\succ$POL$\succ$HUN$\succ$SVK;
- CZE$\succ$POL$\succ$SVK$\succ$HUN;
- HUN$\succ$CZE$\succ$SVK$\succ$POL;
- HUN$\succ$CZE$\succ$POL$\succ$SVK.

In 75% of cases, the Czech Republic achieves the best overal values at given criteria and it is the most environmental friendly in production within steel industry. An interpretation of the remaining order depends on, to some extent, decision-maker's risk aversion. But, in the opinion of the author, it is very beneficial and reasonable to have more information about uncertainty in results.

Now, let us look at the results of deterministic scenarios (a) and (b). It is obvious that the ϕ values of both scenarios lie in the middles of the intervals obtained for the 'interval' version of the model. The results of the PROMETHEE I complete ranking are shown in Fig. 2. It may bee seen that the rankings differ for both scenarios, i.e. different possible deterministic rankings from the list identified by the analysis of the interval results. In particular, Slovakia and Poland are switched at the last two positions. Fig. 3 displays the tree of relations among alternatives. If a link between pair of alternatives exists, it means that they are comparable (by PROMETHEE I partial ranking). The incomparability of Poland and Slovakia as well as the first position of the Czech Republic are in the line with the results of the model with uncertainty. However, especially for the scenario (a), the rank of Hungary seems to be more unambiguous in comparison to the first model.

In order to get better idea about the influence of single criteria on the resulting ϕ value, the PROMETHEE rainbow is provided in Fig. 4. Except of final ϕ values, their structure with respect to comparisons of alternatives according to individual criteria is also displayed there. Criteria below the axis represent weaknesses of the alternative (source of greater ϕ^- value) and criteria above the axis represent strengths of the alternative (source of greater ϕ^+ value). Moreover, the greater distance from the axis, the greater 'power' of the weakness/strength.

Let's try to summarize some interesting facts which are tractable from the rainbow. The steel industry in the Czech Republic reached the best rank in both scenarios. Its position is not given by excellent performance at one or two particular citeria, but rather by the balanced profile without almost any weakness (no negative flow for the (a) scenario and very small one for the (b) scenario). The fact which can be considered to be interesting is that the greatest strength for (a) is the balance of allowances, meanwhile in (b), is the same criterion evaluated as the biggest (and the only one) weakness. This situation probably occurs because of high volatility of balances of allowances (and also because of closeness of performances at criteria). The two largest steel sectors (CZE, POL) have in common that performance at amount of CO2 is substantially better than performance at allowances, despite the fact that both these criteria are related with the same gas. The possible reasoning may be that CO_2 burden is lower for larger sectors with bigger companies (it is easier to achieve economies of scale for them). On the other hand, not so good results in ballance of allowances mean that the progress in CO_2 production is slower when comparing with smaller sectors of Hungary and Slovakia (increase in balance of allowances is mostly caused by decrease in CO_2 emissions, e.g. by implementing some cleaner technology in production). But, it has to be emphasized that allowances' balance mirrors changes in performance regardless how good/bad was the initial state.

5 Conclusions

In this paper, the multi-criteria decision making model evaluating environmental performance of the national steel sectors of the Czech Republic, Poland, Slovakia and Hungary was established. In order to involve the dynamics of perfomances, interval data have been taken as inputs. An environmental burden caused by the different types of emissions and impact of the emissions

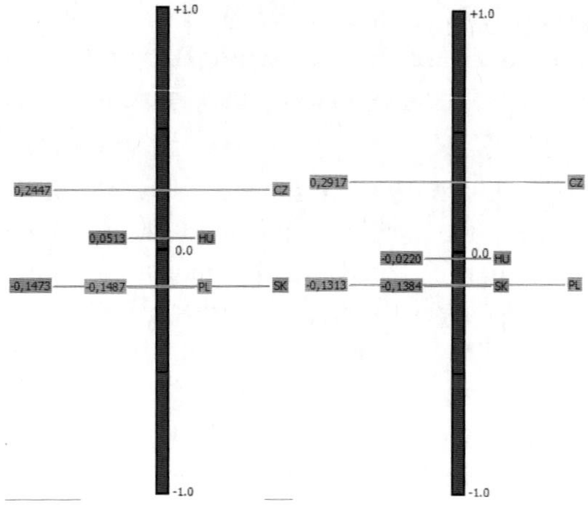

(a) scenario (b) scenario

Figure 2 Results of deterministic scenarios - complete ranking

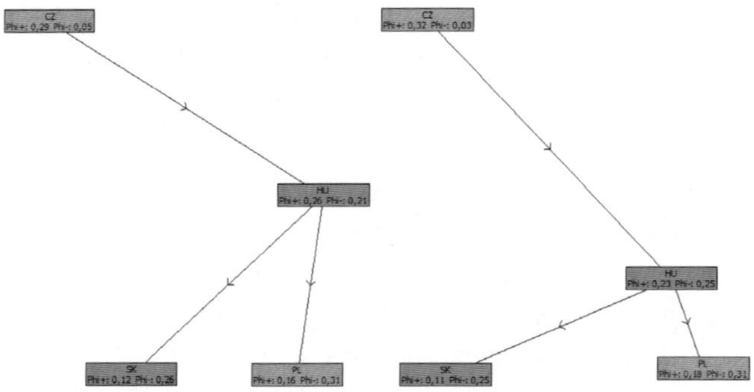

(a) scenario (b) scenario

Figure 3 Results of deterministic scenarios - relations

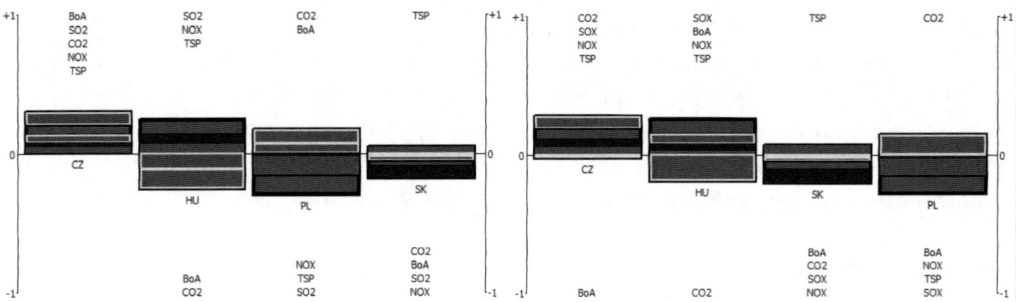

(a) scenario (b) scenario

Figure 4 Results of deterministic scenarios - performance by criteria

trading in the EU were considered as the criteria for evaluation. Using the original version of the PROMETHEE method and its extension for uncertain input data, the ranking of sectors has been found. The best performance within the considered time period has the Czech steel sector. Other positions are not so unambiguous because of the uncertainty. The interesting fact is that larger sectors (Czech Republic and Poland) overcome the others in CO_2 production (they produce less CO_2 per unit of production), meanwhile, their balance of emission allowances is worse compared to them.

Besides the final ranking of sectors, strengths and weaknesses of all the countries have been pointed out. Also, the benefit of using uncertain data has been confirmed. Different deterministic scenarios brought different order of the sectors and different profiles of strengths and weaknesses.

Acknowledgements

This paper was supported by grant No. GA 16-01298S of the Czech Science Foundation, SGS project No. SP2017/125 and the Operational Programme Education for Competitiveness Project CZ.1.07/2.3.00/20.0296. The support is greatly acknowledged.

References

Adali, E. A., Isik, A. T. and Kundakci, N. (2016). 'An Alterantive Approach Based on Fuzzy PROMETHEE Method for the Supplier Selection Problem'. *Uncertain Supply Chain Management*, 4.

Brans, J. P., Mareschal, B. and Vincke, P. (1984). 'PROMETHEE: A New family of outranking methods in multicriteria analysis'. *In proceedings of the Conference on Operational Research*, Washington.

Chytilová, L. and Zapletal, F. (2016). 'The Comparison of DEA and PROMETHEE Method to Evaluate the Environmental Efficiency of National Steel Sectors in Europe'. *In proceedings of Mathematical Methods in Economics conference*, Liberec, pp. 319-324.

EU Parliament. (2003). Directive 2003/87/EC of the European Parliament and of the Council of 13 October 2003 establishing a scheme for greenhouse gas emission allowance trading within the Community and amending Council Directive 96/61/EC.

Goumas, M. and Lygerou, V. (2000). 'An Extension of the PROMETHEE Method for Decision Making in Fuzzy Environment: Ranking of Alternative Energy Explitation Projects'. *European Journal of Operational Research*, 123.

Kim, Y. and Worrell, E. (2002). 'International comparison of CO2emission trends in the iron and steel industry'. *Energy Policy*, 30(10), pp. 827-838.

Law No. 201/2012. (2012) O ochraně ovzduší.

Le Téno, J. F. and Mareschal, B. (1998). 'An Interval Version of PROMETHEE for the Comparison of Building Products' design with Ill-defined Data on Environmental Quality'. *European Journal of Operational Research*, 109.

Mikhailov, M. (2000). 'A fuzzy programming method for deriving priorities in the analytic hierarchy process'. *Journal of Operational Research Society*, 51, pp. 341349.

Wei, Y. M., Liao, H. and Fan, Y. (2007). 'An empirical analysis of energy efficiency in China's iron and steel sector'. *Energy*, 32(12), pp. 2262-2270.

Zapletal, F. (2015). 'Fuzzy Optimiztion of Industrial Companies' Profit under Environmnetal Factors'. *In proceedings of Strategic Management and its Support by Information Systems*, Uherské Hradiště, pp. 318-328.

Zhang, X., Jiang, W., Deng, S. and Peng, K. (2009). 'Emergy evaluation of the sustainability of Chinese steel production during 19982004'. *Journal of Cleaner Production*, 17(11), pp. 1030-1038.

Elliptical Probability Distribution with VaR Objective Function for Portfolio Selection

Katerina Zelinkova[1]

Abstract. The least complex and most natural way to represent the problem of optimal portfolio selection is a constrained optimization problem. The main aim of this paper is to compare three models of elliptical distribution: normal, Student and Laplace, where objective function is Value at Risk, which is considered the risk measurement. It is assumed, that the least appropriate model will be the one assuming a normal distribution, since, we know that equity returns have generally a fat tail which means that equity returns are not normally distributed.

Keywords: Value at Risk, Laplace distribution, portfolio selection, risk.

JEL Classification: C16, G22

1 Introduction

Portfolio selection is one of the most significant problems in investment management. The first paper in the field dates back to the "Portfolio Selection" of Markowitz (1952), which became the pioneer work of modern portfolio theory. The main idea of the theoretical framework is to maximize the expected return for a given amount of risk or to minimize the risk when giving a specified level of return by choosing the weight of various assets. The Markowitz model is the type of the mean variance model, for which it is allowed to invest only to risk assets while short selling of the assets is not feasible.

Developments in portfolio optimization are stimulated by two basic requirements: (1) adequate modeling of utility functions, risks, and constraints; (2) efficiency, i.e., ability to hold large numbers of instruments and scenarios. Current regulations for finance businesses formulate some of the risk management requirements in terms of percentiles of loss distributions. An upper percentile of the loss distribution is called Value at Risk (*VaR*). For instance, 95%-*VaR* is an upper estimation of losses, which is exceeded with 5% probability. The popularity of *VaR* is mostly related to a simple and easy to understand representation of high losses. *VaR* can be quite efficiently estimated and managed when underlying risk factors are normally (log-normally) distributed.

The Value at Risk (*VaR*) is a risk measure representing a value of loss, which will not be exceeded over given risk horizon at some significance level. There is also a possibility to refer to *VaR* as managing risk methodology that is applied widely to modeling credit, operational, market and insurance risk. A good introduction to *VaR* methodology is provided by the technical document from Morgan (1996) or by many follow-up books such as Hull (2007), Alexander (2008b) and Jorion (2007).

The aim this paper is the comparison of three models of elliptical distribution: normal, Student and Laplace. Structure of the paper is following. Firstly, methodology, which is used in

[1] VŠB – Technical University of Ostrava, Faculty of Economics, Department of Management, Sokolská třída 33, Ostrava, Czech Republic, katerina.zelinkova@vsb.cz

empirical part, is described, namely selection portfolio and risk measure. Subsequently portfolios are optimized for different type of distribution.

2 Portfolio Model under Elliptical Distribution

In this chapter methodology used in this paper will be described. Firstly, we describe the individual distribution and *VaR* by assuming elliptical distribution.

VaR is defined as the smallest loss for the predicted level of probability for a given time interval. It is a function of two parameters, i.e. the risk horizon and the confidence level. We can also characterize the *VaR* as a one-sided confidence interval of potential loss of portfolio value for a given holding period, which can be written as

$$F(x) = P(X \leq -VaR_{\alpha,\Delta t}(x)) = \alpha, \tag{1}$$

$F(x)$ is cumulative distribution function, α is significance level and Δt is holding period or risk horizon.

2.1 Portfolio model by assuming normal distribution

For continuous random variables where $-\infty \leq x \leq \infty$, the probability density function of the normal distribution is following

$$\varphi(X) = \frac{1}{\sqrt{2\pi\sigma^2}} exp\left[-\frac{(x-\mu)}{2\sigma^2}\right], \tag{2}$$

where μ is the mean, σ^2 is variance. The formulas for each characteristic of the normal distribution are:

- mean = μ ,
- standard deviation = σ ,
- skewness = 0,
- kurtosis = 3.

If $\mu = 0$ and $\sigma = 1$, the distribution is called the standard normal distribution or the unit normal distribution. Portfolio model by assuming normal distribution is following

Task 1 The optimization portfolio normal distribution

Objective function: $VaR = \Phi^{-1}(\alpha) \cdot \sigma_p - \mu_p \rightarrow \min$

(C1) $\sum x_i = 1$,

(C2) $x_i \geq 0$, $for\ i = 1,2,\ldots,N,$

where $\sigma_p = \sqrt{\sigma^2(\mu_i)}$ and $\mu_p = \sum_{i=1}^{N} x_i \cdot \mu_i$.

The objective function is the minimal *VaR* of the portfolio by assuming Normal distribution that we are looking for. The Constraint (C1) states the sum of relative shares x_i. The sum of shares x_i is equal to one. The constraints (C2) exclude negativity, since short selling is not allowed there.

2.2 Portfolio model by assuming Student distribution

In probability and statistics, Student's *t*-distribution (or simply the *t*-distribution) is a family of continuous probability distributions. The Student distribution is closely related to the normal distribution; it is a symmetric curve that converges to the standard normal density as the degrees of freedom (v) increase. If $v \geq 30$ so we consider it as normal distribution. The degrees of freedom are the only parameter in the Student *t*-distribution and the lower the degrees of freedom the lower the peak of the distribution and the longer the tails. For continuous random variable where $-\infty \leq x \leq \infty$, the density function for the Student *t*-distribution with v degrees of freedom is (Alexander, 2008a),

$$f_v(t) = (v\pi)^{\frac{-1}{2}} \Gamma\left(\frac{v}{2}\right)^{-1} \Gamma\left(\frac{v+1}{2}\right)\left(1+\frac{t^2}{v}\right)^{-\left(\frac{v+1}{2}\right)}, \tag{3}$$

where Gamma function Γ is an extension of the factorial function $n!$ to non-integer values. The distribution has zero expectation and zero skewness and for $v > 2$, the variance of a Student *t*-distributed variable is $\sigma^2 = v(v-2)^{-1}$.

Task 2 The optimization portfolio Student *t*-distribution

Objective function: $VaR = \sqrt{v^{-1}(v-2)}t^{-1}(\alpha)\sigma - \mu \rightarrow \min$

(C1) $\sum x_i = 1,$

(C2) $x_i \geq 0, for\ i = 1,2,\ldots,N.$

2.3 Portfolio model by assuming Laplace distribution

The Laplace distribution is a continuous probability distribution named after Pierre-Simon Laplace. It is also sometimes called the *double exponential distribution*, because it can be thought of as two exponential distributions (with an additional location parameter) spliced together back-to-back, although the term 'double exponential distribution' is also used to refer to the Gumbel distribution. The difference between two independent identically distributed exponential random variables are governed by a Laplace distribution, as is a Brownian motion evaluated at an exponentially distributed random time. Increments of Laplace motion or a variance gamma process evaluated over the time scale have also a Laplace distribution. Density function for the Laplace probability distribution is given by (Zhuo et al. 2015),

$$f(x) = \frac{1}{2\sigma}\exp\left(-\frac{|x-\mu|}{\sigma}\right), \tag{4}$$

Laplace distribution often appears in the literature (Hendl, 2004), (Lewis, 2003) and (Beirlant et al. 2004) in a form of general distribution recommended for describing the behavior of financial time series.

Task 3 The optimization portfolio Laplace distribution

Objective function: $VaR = -\frac{1}{\sqrt{2}} \cdot ln(2\alpha)\sigma \rightarrow \min$

(C1) $\sum x_i = 1,$

(C2) $x_i \geq 0, for\ i = 1,2,\ldots,N.$

3 Optimization Portfolio for Elliptical Distribution

We will apply *VaR* for ten stocks from NASDAQ market. We will estimate *VaR* for 95 % confidence level over one day risk horizon. The period sample, which has been tested is between January 2013 and December 2016 and we are considering the daily log returns for the stocks over the whole period, i.e. 1/2013 – 12/2016. The basic numerical characteristics of individual stock returns, especially the mean, standard deviation, kurtosis, skewness are shown in the following table.

	Mean (%)	Standard deviation (%)	Skewness	Kurtosis
A1	0.10	1.54	-0.2377	11.8437
A2	0.00	1.47	-0.5981	5.9334
A3	0.01	3.89	0.2881	7.8339
A4	0.01	2.80	**-19.4983**	**38.6029**
A5	0.04	3.17	**-14.4493**	**35.0006**
A6	-0.13	4.21	**-19.4234**	**44.1306**
A7	-0.02	2.57	-1.1644	8.7510
A8	0.11	2.38	1.1529	22.6579
A9	0.17	1.81	1.7696	12.6174
A10	0.04	1.44	-0.2361	1.5935

Table 1 The basic characteristic

The skewness can be positive or negative depending on which side the deviations from the mean are bigger. If the probability density curve is symmetrical with respect to the mean value, the coefficient is zero. Measures of skewness indicate asymmetric distribution of revenues, and are placed more on the left, where values are negative. We can see that assets do not fit normal distribution because this parameter is not equal to zero, namely A4, A5 and A6.

The kurtosis characterizes the distribution of financial instrument and compares the distribution of normal probability distribution. The kurtosis for normal probability distribution should equal to three. We can see that results are greater than three, the deviations; so, kurtosis of stock returns is considerably higher than it is typical for a normal distribution (the value should be three). The coefficients' values do not correspond to the normal distribution and therefore it is not appropriate to use this distribution for portfolio optimization.

The next input data for portfolio optimization are correlation and covariance. The estimated correlation matrix of stocks is shown in Table 2. Information from correlation is important for portfolio manager. The more is invested to various stocks/shares with a low mutual dependence the bigger is the possibility of partial balance of favorable and unfavorable factors.

	A1	A2	A3	A4	A5	A6	A7	A8	A9	A10
A1	1									
A2	0.311	1.000								
A3	0.079	0.133	1.000							
A4	0.181	0.168	0.026	1.000						
A5	0.146	0.167	0.034	0.114	1.000					
A6	0.110	0.051	0.027	0.043	0.025	1.000				
A7	0.108	0.166	**0.005**	0.077	0.074	0.025	1.000			
A8	0.232	0.245	0.006	0.145	0.187	-0.011	0.154	1.000		
A9	0.290	0.257	0.107	0.172	0.164	0.056	0.155	0.146	1.000	
A10	**0.345**	**0.368**	0.094	0.113	0.161	0.143	0.244	0.222	0.300	1

Table 2 Correlation

The greatest dependency is between the assets A2 and A10, coefficient of correlation is equal to 36.8 %. Conversely, the lowest correlation is between stocks A3 and A7, which is equal to 0.5 %. Now the portfolio can be optimized. We will use significance levels $\alpha = 0.5\%$ and time horizon of one day. The share of stocks in portfolio and values of *VaR* and return of portfolio are shown in the following Table 3.

	Normal (%)	Student (%)	Laplace (%)
A1	3.60	2.51	4.41
A2	10.80	3.07	6.30
A3	2.58	16.47	17.30
A4	1.20	13.34	16.30
A5	16.00	8.64	11.55
A6	1.00	15.17	14.30
A7	4.30	7.83	5.28
A8	58.92	11.42	12.83
A9	0.60	4.02	3.15
A10	1.00	17.53	15.58
VaR	3.65	8.06	7.53
μ_p	1.20	3.32	2.36

Table 3 The portfolio optimization

If we optimize portfolio by assuming Student distribution, we need to know the degree of freedom. The degree of freedom is the specific parameter only used for Student distribution. We assume that the degree of freedom is equal to 4.

We can see values of *VaR* for different type of distribution. *VaR* represents risk measure. The highest risk is in Student model, and the lowest risk is by assuming normal model. Shares of stock in portfolio are different. The extreme values are found under the assumption of normal distribution. These values lead to instability of the portfolio. For the better overview, the results are shown in the following figure.

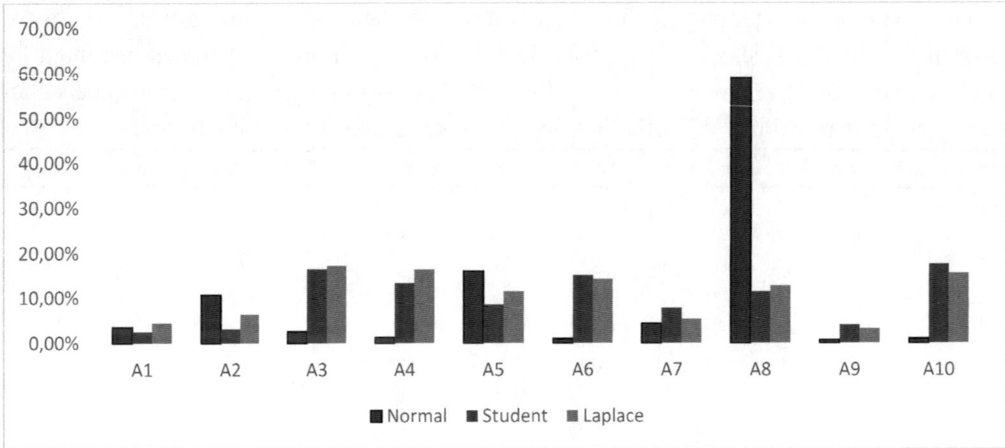

Figure 1 Share of individual assets

From the figure 1, it is evident that the portfolio optimization, under the assumption of normal distribution, leads to extreme values, especially with the assets A8 and A10. This means that the portfolio is not diversified optimally and can lead to destabilization of the whole portfolio. Due to this, it is appropriate to use different types of probability distribution other than normal distribution. The results of assets' proportion under the assumption of Student and Laplace distribution are merely the same. In order to state, which of these models is appropriate, it is necessary to analyze individual assets regarding the probability distribution in detail.

4 Conclusion

The aim of paper was comparison of three models of elliptical distribution: normal, Student and Laplace. It has been proven that the revenues do not have normal distribution because they have heavier tails of the distribution. Due to this fact, it is not appropriate to use normal distribution of probability. More suitable distribution is the Student and Laplace distribution of probability. In order to state, which of these models is appropriate, it is necessary to analyze individual assets regarding the probability distribution in detail. Therefore, if the manager is going to propose a portfolio for a client then it is suitable first to find out the correct type of probability distribution of a given portfolio.

Acknowledgements

This paper is supported by the Student Grant Competition of the Faculty of Economics, VSB-Technical University of Ostrava, project registration number SP2017/125 Application of outranking methods with uncertainty in business economics and management. All support is greatly acknowledged and appreciated.

References

Alexander, C. (2008a). *Quantitave Methods in Finance*. Chichester: Wiley.

Alexander, C. (2008b). *Value at Risk models*. Chichester: Wiley.

Beirlant, J., Y. Goegebeur, Segers, J. and Teugels, J. (2004). *Statistics of Extremes: Theory and Applications.* Chichester: Wiley.

Hendl, J. (2004). *Přehled statistických metod.* Praha: Portal s.r.o.

Hull, J. (2007). *Risk Management and Financial Institutions*. New Jersey: Pearson Education.

Jorion, P. (2007). *Value at Risk: The New Benchmark for Managing Financial Risk*. 2nd ed. New York: McGraw-Hill.

Lewis, N. C. (2003). *Market Risk Modelling*. London: Risk Books.

Markowitz, H. (1952). 'Portfolio selection'. *The Journal of Finance*, 7 (1), pp. 77-91.

McNeil, A., Fredy, J., R. and Embrechts, P. (2005). *Quantitative Risk Management: Concepts, Techniques and Tools.* Princeton: Princeton University Press.

Morgan, J.P. (1996). *RiskMeasuresTM Technical Document,* [Online]. Available at: www.yats.free.fr/papers/td4e.pdf [cited 2017-02-01].

Zhuo, S., Lu, Q., Han, L., Liu, Y. and Hu, F. (2015). 'A mean-CVaR-skewness portfolio optimization model based on asymmetric Laplace distribution'. *Annals of Operations Research,* 226 (1), pp. 727-739.

SECTION D

Advances in information systems design and implementation methods

SYNC-CALL operation of P/T Petri Process Multinets

Martin Čechák[1], Ivo Martiník[2]

Abstract. Property-preserving Petri net process algebras (PPPA) were originally designed for the specification and verification of manufacturing systems. PPPA does not need to verify composition of Petri process nets because all their algebraic operators preserve the specified set of the properties. We will generalize the class of P/T Petri process nets and their SYNC-PROC (*SYNChronous-PROCedure*) PPPA binary operator with the new special class of the P/T Petri process multinets (PPMN) and their SYNC-CALL operation and prove its base characteristic of the properly termination property in this article. This new class of PPMN with the support of SYNC-CALL operation can be then successfully used in the area of design, simulation and verification of programming systems executed in distributed or parallel environment. This fact is then demonstrated on the simple example of the distributed programming system based on the client-server architecture.

Keywords: P/T Petri process multinets, SYNC-CALL operation, property preservation, parallel systems modeling.

JEL Classification: C63, C88

1 Introduction

Petri nets (Diaz, 2009), (Reisig and Rozenberg, 1998) is one of mathematical modeling languages for the description of all the kind of parallel systems and they represent a popular formalism connecting advantages of the graphic representation of a modeled system with the possibilities of its simulation and the formal analyzability. *Property-preserving Petri net process algebras* (PPPA) (Huang et al, 2012) were originally designed for the specification and verification of manufacturing systems. PPPA also follows many ideas that can be originally seen in the class of the *workflow nets* (van der Alst and van Hee, 2002). The elements of PPPA are the *Petri process nets*, an ordinary connected Petri nets with a unique entry place, a unique exit place and a set of places for handling resource sharing with their initial marking allowed. Among other features, PPPA does not need to verify composite components because all of their operators preserve many properties.

We will generalize the class of the bi-relational P/T Petri nets (Martiník, 2011) and the class of the P/T Petri process nets (Martiník, 2016) and their SYNC-PROC (*SYNChronous-PROCedure*) PPPA binary operator (Martiník, 2015) in this article. We will define the new special class of the *P/T Petri process multinets* (PPMN) and their SYNC-CALL operation and prove its base characteristic of the properly termination property. This new class of PPMN with the support of SYNC-CALL operation can be then successfully used in the area of design, simulation and verification of programming systems executed in distributed or parallel environment (Žáček and Huňka, 2011). This fact is then demonstrated on the simple example of the distributed programming system based on the client-server architecture.

[1] VSB-Technical University of Ostrava, Faculty of Economics, Sokolská třída 33, Ostrava, Czech Republic, martin.cechak.st1@vsb.cz.
[2] VSB-Technical University of Ostrava, Faculty of Economics, Department of Applied Informatics, Sokolská třída 33, Ostrava, Czech Republic, ivo.martinik@vsb.cz.

The article is arranged into the following sections: in the section 2 the P/T Petri process multinets and their main properties are described; section 3 explains the SYNC-CALL operation of PPMNs and its selected properties are proved; section 4 gives an example of SYNC-CALL operation application at the modeling of chosen distributed programming system and the section 5 then gives the conclusions of the research to conclude the article.

2 P/T Petri process multinets and their properties

Let $\boldsymbol{N}$ denotes the set of all natural numbers, $\boldsymbol{N} := \{1, 2, \ldots\}$, $\boldsymbol{N}_0$ the set of all non-negative integer numbers, $\boldsymbol{N}_0 := \{0, 1, 2, \ldots\}$, $\varnothing$ the empty set, $|A|$ the cardinality of the given set A, where $|\boldsymbol{N}| = \aleph_0$, $\neg$ the logical negation operator, ***IDENT*** the set of all the identifiers. If $f: A \rightarrow B$ is a function, then the set A will be denoted by $\boldsymbol{dom}(f)$ and the set B by $\boldsymbol{cod}(f)$. *Multiset M* over a non-empty set S is a function $M: S \rightarrow \boldsymbol{N}_0$. The non-negative number $M(a) \in \boldsymbol{N}_0$, where $a \in S$, denotes the number of occurrences of the element a in the multiset M. The multiset M over a non-empty set S will be represented by the notation $M := [a^{M(a)}, b^{M(b)}, c^{M(c)}, \ldots]$, where $S := \{a, b, c, \ldots\}$. Notation S_{MS} then denotes the class of all the multisets over the set S.

Let ***PSNET*** denotes the class of all the P/T process nets (see below). *P/T process multinet* (PMN) *PMN* is an ordered tuple $PMN := (MN, NN)$, where MN is the *multinet*, i.e., the finite non-empty multiset over the set ***PSNET***, $MN \subset \boldsymbol{PSNET}_{\mathrm{MS}}$; NN is the injective *net number function*, $NN: MN \rightarrow \boldsymbol{N}$.

Let $PMN := (MN, NN)$ is a PMN. *P/T process net* (PN) *PN* within the PMN *PMN*, $PN \in MN$, is an ordered 13-tuple $PN := (NB, P, T, A, MA, AF, MAF, MAN, TP, RP, IP, OP, RM_s)$, where:

- NB is a *net number*, $NB \in \boldsymbol{cod}(NN)$;
- P is a finite non-empty set of *places*;
- T is a finite set of *transitions*, $P \cap T = \varnothing$;
- A is a finite set of *arcs*, $A \subseteq (P \times T) \cup (T \times P)$;
- MA is a finite set of *multiarcs*, $MA \subseteq A$;
- AF is an *arc function*, $AF: A \rightarrow \boldsymbol{N}$;
- MAF is a *multiarc function*, $MAF: MA \rightarrow \boldsymbol{N}$;
- MAN is a *multiarc net function*, $MAN: MA \rightarrow \boldsymbol{cod}(NN)$;
- TP is a *transition priority* function, $TP: T \rightarrow \boldsymbol{N}$;
- RP is a finite set of the *resource places*, $RP \subset P$;
- IP is the *input place*, $IP \in (P \setminus RP)$, it is the only one place such that $\bullet IP = \varnothing$;
- OP is the *output place*, $OP \in (P \setminus RP)$, it is the only one place such that $OP\bullet = \varnothing$;
- RM_s is the set of all *allowed resource places static markings*, $RM_s \subseteq \mathbf{M_s}$, where $\mathbf{M_s}$ is the set of all the static markings M_s of the PN (see below);
- (P, T, A) is a *connected net.*

The given PN is then described with a bipartite graph containing a finite non-empty set P of places used for expressing of the conditions of a modeled process (we usually use circles for their representation); a finite set T of transitions describing the changes in the modeled process (we usually draw them in the form of rectangles); a finite set A of arcs being principally oriented while connecting the place with the transition or the transition with the place and we usually draw them as lines with arrows; a finite set *MA* of newly introduced type of arc in PNs called *multiarcs* that is a subset of the set *A* of the arcs (they are represented in layouts of the net with oriented arrows drawn with dash line); the arc function *AF* assigning each arc (including each multiarc) with a natural number (such number has the default value of 1, if not explicitly indicated in the PN diagram) expressing the number of removed or added tokens from or to the place associated with that arc when firing a particular transition; the multiarc function *MAF* assigning the given multiarc with the natural number expressing the quantity of removed or added tokens from output place *OP* or input place *IP* of the selected PN being the value of *multiarc net function MAN* of the particular multiarc (if the value of the multiarc function *MAF* of a given multiarc is number 1, again we will not explicitly display that value in the net layout); transition priority function *TP* assigns with each transition the natural number value expressing its priority (with the default value of 1); the finite set *RP* of resource places is used for expressing conditions of a modeled process containing some initial resources and we use circles with the double line for their representation; the input place *IP* is the only one non-resource place of PN *PN* with no input arc(s) and the output place *OP* is the only one non-resource place of PN *PN* with no output arc(s); RM_s is the set of all the allowed resource places static markings that is subset of the set $\mathbf{M_s}$ of all the static markings M_s of the PN *PN* (the term static marking M_s of PN *PN* will be explained below); the net (*P*, *T*, *A*) must be connected.

Some commonly used notations for PNs are $\bullet y = \{x \mid (x, y) \in A\}$ for the *preset* and $y\bullet = \{x \mid (y, x) \in A\}$ for the *postset* of a PN element *y* (i.e., place or transition).

Let *PMN* := (*MN*, *NN*) is a PMN, $PN \in MN$ is a PN, $PN := (NB, P, T, A, MA, AF, MAF, MAN, TP, RP, IP, OP, RM_s)$. *Marking* ${}^{PN}M$ of the PN *PN* is a mapping ${}^{PN}M: P \to \mathbf{N}_0$. Marking ${}^{PN}M$ then expresses the current status of a modeled process. Marking ${}^{PN}M$ can be written as a $|P|$-vector ${}^{PN}M := ({}^{PN}M(IP), {}^{PN}M(P_1), {}^{PN}M(P_2), \ldots, {}^{PN}M(P_k), {}^{PN}M(R_1), {}^{PN}M(R_2), \ldots, {}^{PN}M(R_m), {}^{PN}M(OP))$, where $P := (IP, P_1, P_2, \ldots, P_n, R_1, R_2, \ldots, R_m, OP)$, $RP := \{R_1, R_2, \ldots, R_m\}$, $n \in \mathbf{N}_0$, $m \in \mathbf{N}_0$. *Marking M* of the PMN *PMN* is the union of all the markings ${}^{PN}M$ of all the PNs *PN* contained in the PMN *PMN*, i.e., $M := \cup_{PN \in MN} {}^{PN}M$. We will denote by the symbol ***AllPlaces*** the set of all the places contained in all the PNs *PN* of the PMN *PMN* := (*MN*, *NN*), i.e., ***AllPlaces*** $:= \{p \mid (p \in P \in PN) \wedge (PN \in MN)\}$, and similarly ***AllTransitions*** $:= \{t \mid (t \in T \in PN) \wedge (PN \in MN)\}$.

Figure 1, illustrates the PMN *PROC* := (*MN*, *NN*), where *MN* := {*Main*, *Sub*}, *NN* := {(*Main*, 1), (*Sub*, 3)}. PN *Main* := ($NB, P, T, A, MA, AF, MAF, MAN, TP, RP, IP, OP, RM_s$), where *NB* := 1, *P* := {IP, P1, P2, R1, OP}, *T* := {T1, T2, T3, T4}, *A* := {(IP, T1), (IP, T2), (T1, P1), (T2, P2), (R1, T1), (P1, T3), (T3, R1), (P2, T4), (T3, OP), (T4, OP)}, *MA* := {(T2, P2), (P2, T4)}, *AF* := {((IP, T1), 1), ((IP, T2), 1), ((T1, P1), 1), ((T2, P2), 1), ((R1, T1), 1), ((P1, T3), 1), ((T3, R1), 1), ((P2, T4), 1), ((T3, OP), 1), ((T4, OP), 1)}, *MAF* := {((T2, P2), 1), ((P2, T4), 1)}, *MAN* := {((T2, P2), 3), ((P2, T4), 3)}, *TP* := {(T1, 1), (T2, 1), (T3, 1), (T4, 1)}, *RP* := {R1}, *IP* := IP, *OP* := OP, $RM_s := \{(0, 0, 0, n, 0) \mid n \in \mathbf{N}\}$. PN *Sub* := ($NB, P, T, A, MA, AF, MAF, MAN, TP, RP, IP, OP, RM_s$), where *NB* := 3, *P* := {IP, OP}, *T* := {T1}, *A* := {(IP, T1), (T1, OP)}, *MA* := ∅, *AF* := {((IP, T1), 1), ((T1, OP), 1)}, *MAF* := ∅, *MAN* := ∅, *TP* := {(T1, 1)}, *RP* := ∅, *IP* := IP, *OP* := OP, RM_s := ∅. Marking of the PN *Main* is ${}^{Main}M := ({}^{Main}M(IP),$

$^{Main}M(P_1)$, $^{Main}M(P_2)$, $^{Main}M(R_1)$, $^{Main}M(OP)) = (3, 0, 0, 1, 0)$, marking of the PN *Sub* is $^{Sub}M :=$ $(^{Sub}M(IP)$, $^{Sub}M(OP)) = (0, 0)$. The notation $RM_s := \{(0, 0, 0, n, 0) \mid n \in \boldsymbol{N}\}$ means that in any allowed resource static marking RM_s the resource place R1 must contain at least one token.

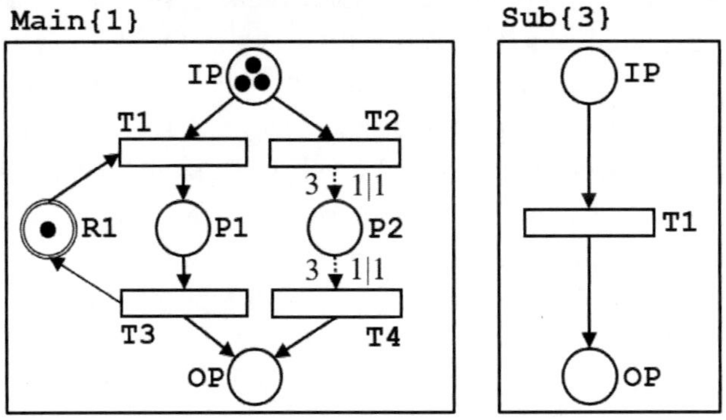

Figure 1 Process multinet *PROC*

Each place and transition with the unique identifier *elem_id* in the frame of the given PN can be also uniquely identified within the whole *PMN* := (*MN*, *NN*) by the unique identification in the form of *net_number.elem_id*, where *net_number* ∈ *NN*, or *net_name.elem_id*, where *net_name* is the unique identifier of PN *PN* within the PMN *PMN*. For instance the input place IP of the PN *Main* from Figure 1 can be uniquely identified within the PMN *PROC* by the identification 1.IP (where *NN*(*Main*) = 1) or *Main*.IP.

The transition $t \in$ ***AllTransitions*** is *enabled* in the marking *M* of the PMN *PMN* := (*MN*, *NN*) if the following conditions are simultaneously true:

- $\forall p \in \bullet t$: $((p, t) \in A \in PN \in MN) \Rightarrow (M(p) \geq AF(p, t))$;
- $\forall p \in \bullet t$: $((p, t) \in MA \in PN \in MN) \Rightarrow (M(MAN(p, t).OP) \geq MAF(p, t))$.

If the transition $t \in$ ***AllTransitions*** is enabled in the marking *M* of the PMN *PMN* we denote that fact in the form of *t* **en** *M*. *Firing of the transition* $t \in$ ***AllTransitions*** results in changing the marking *M* of the PMN *PMN* into its marking *M'* that is denoted by $M\,[t\rangle\, M'$, where:

- $M'(p) = M(p) - AF(p, t)$, where $p \in \bullet t$;
- $M'(p) = M(p) + AF(t, p)$, where $p \in t\bullet$;
- $M'(p) = M(p) - AF(p, t) + AF(t, p)$, where $p \in \bullet t \cup t\bullet$;
- $M'(p) = M(p) - MAF(q, t)$, where $q \in \bullet t$, $(q, t) \in MA$, $p = MAN(q, t).OP$;
- $M'(p) = M(p) + MAF(t, q)$, where $q \in t\bullet$, $(t, q) \in MA$, $p = MAN(t, q).IP$;
- $M'(p) = M(p)$ otherwise.

We say that the marking *M''* of PMN *PMN* is reachable from its marking *M* iff there exists a finite sequence $\sigma := t_1\, t_2\, ...\, t_n$, $n \in \boldsymbol{N}$, of the transitions $t_1, t_2, ..., t_n$, such that $M\,[t_1\, t_2\, ...\, t_n\rangle\, M''$. The set of all the *PMN*'s markings reachable from its given marking *M* will be denoted by the symbol $[M\rangle$, the set of all the transition sequences $\sigma := t_1\, t_2\, ...\, t_n$, $n \in \boldsymbol{N}$, of the transitions that are fireable from the marking *M* will be denoted by the symbol $[M\rangle\rangle$, i.e., $[M\rangle\rangle := \{t_1\, t_2\, ...\, t_n \mid \exists M'' \in [M\rangle: M\,[t_1\, t_2\, ...\, t_n\rangle\, M'', n \in \boldsymbol{N}\}$.

When enabling individual transitions of the given PMN so called *conflicts* can originate in its certain markings (or *conflict transitions*). At the enabling of the transitions t_1 and t_2 of the given PMN in its marking M the conflict occurs, if both transitions t_1 and t_2 have at least one input place, each of the transitions t_1 and t_2 is individually enabled in the marking M, but the transitions t_1 and t_2 are not in the marking M enabled in parallel and enabling of one of them will prevent enabling the other (i.e., $(\bullet t_1 \cap \bullet t_2 \neq \emptyset) \wedge (t_1 \textbf{ en } M) \wedge (t_2 \textbf{ en } M) \wedge \neg(\{t_1, t_2\} \textbf{ en } M)$). The term of conflict transitions can be obviously easily generalized for the case of a finite set $t_1, t_2, \ldots, t_n$, $n \in N$, of the transitions of a given PMN. A typical example of the conflict transitions in the particular marking of the PN *Confl* is shown in Figure 2, where the transitions *Confl*.T1 and *Confl*.T2 have the common input place *Confl*.IP, both are enabled, but they are not enabled in parallel. When solving such transitions conflict we will therefore follow the rule which determines, informally said, that from the set of conflict transitions the one will be enabled, whose value of the transition priority function *TP* is the highest. If such transition from the set of conflict transitions does not exist, the given conflict would have to be solved by other means. The transition *Confl*.T2 is then enabled on the basis of that rule in our studied example (because *TP*(*Confl*.T1) = 1 and *TP*(*Confl*.T2) = 2).

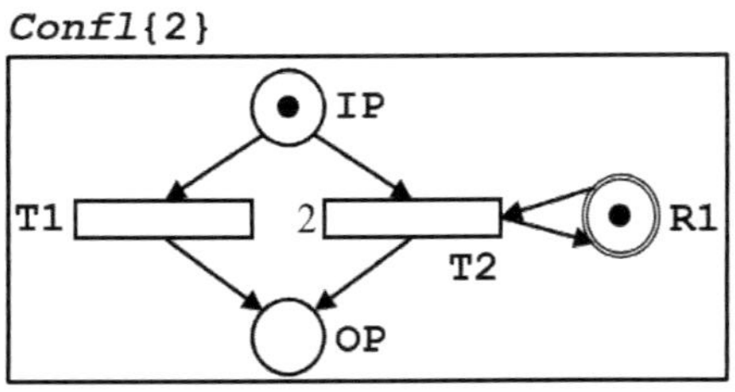

Figure 2 Conflict transitions in PMN

Let $k \in N$. The following special markings of the PN $PN := (NB, P, T, A, MA, AF, MAF, MAN, TP, RP, IP, OP, RM_s)$ are defined:

- *static marking* ${}^{PN}M_s$: $\forall p \in RP$: ${}^{PN}M_s(p) \geq 0$; $\forall p \in (P \setminus RP)$: ${}^{PN}M_s(p) = 0$; $\forall t \in T$: $\neg(t \textbf{ en } {}^{PN}M_s)$; ${}^{PN}M_s \in RM_s$;
- *entry marking* ${}^{PN}M_e$: ${}^{PN}M_e(IP) = k$; $\exists {}^{PN}M_s \in RM_s\ \forall p \in (P \setminus \{IP\})$: ${}^{PN}M_e(p) = {}^{PN}M_s(p)$;
- *exit marking* ${}^{PN}M_x$: ${}^{PN}M_x(OP) = {}^{PN}M_e(IP) = k$; $\exists {}^{PN}M_s \in RM_s\ \forall p \in (P \setminus \{OP\})$: ${}^{PN}M_x(p) = {}^{PN}M_s(p)$; $\forall t \in T$: $\neg(t \textbf{ en } {}^{PN}M_x)$.

The following special markings of the PMN $PMN := (MN, NN)$ are defined:

- *static marking* $M_s := \cup_{PN \in MN}\ {}^{PN}M_s$;
- *entry marking* $M_e := {}^{SN}M_e \cup (\cup_{PN \in MN \setminus \{SN\}}\ {}^{PN}M_s)$, where $SN \in MN$;
- *exit marking* $M_x := {}^{SN}M_x \cup (\cup_{PN \in MN \setminus \{SN\}}\ {}^{PN}M_s)$, where $SN \in MN$.

For the given PMN *PMN* we will denote the set of all its static markings M_s by the symbol $\mathbf{M_s}$, the set of all its entry markings M_e by the symbol $\mathbf{M_e}$ and the set of all its exit markings M_x by the symbol $\mathbf{M_x}$.

PN *Main* in Figure 1 is in its entry marking ${}^{Main}M_e := (3, 0, 0, 1, 0)$, PN *Sub* is in its static marking ${}^{Sub}M_s := (0, 0)$) and so the whole PMN *PROC* is in its entry marking M_e. The transitions *Main*.T1 and *Main*.T2 are enabled in parallel in this entry marking M_e (the transition *Main*.T2 is enabled because $\bullet Main.\text{T2} = \{Main.\text{IP}\}$, $((Main.\text{IP}, Main.\text{T2}) \in A) \Rightarrow (M_e(Main.\text{IP}) = 3 \geq 1 = AF(Main.\text{IP}, Main.\text{T2}))$. Firing of the transition *Main*.T2 changes the entry marking M_e of the PMN *PROC* into its marking *M'* that can be shown in Figure 3, where:

- $M'(Main.\text{IP}) = M_e(Main.\text{IP}) - AF(Main.\text{IP}, Main.\text{T2}) = 3 - 1 = 2$, where $Main.\text{IP} \in \bullet Main.\text{T2}$;
- $M'(Main.\text{P2}) = M_e(Main.\text{P2}) + AF(Main.\text{T2}, Main.\text{P2}) = 0 + 1 = 1$, where $Main.\text{P2} \in Main.\text{T2}\bullet$;
- $M'(Sub.\text{IP}) = M_e(Sub.\text{IP}) + MAF(Main.\text{T2}, Main.\text{P2}) = 0 + 1 = 1$, where $Main.\text{P2} \in Main.\text{T2}\bullet$, $(Main.\text{T2}, Main.\text{P2}) \in MA$, $Sub.\text{IP} = MAN(Main.\text{T2}, Main.\text{P2}).IP = 3.\text{IP}$;
- $M'(p) = M_e(p)$ otherwise, where $p \in \boldsymbol{AllPlaces} \setminus \{Main.\text{IP}, Main.\text{P2}, Sub.\text{IP}\}$.

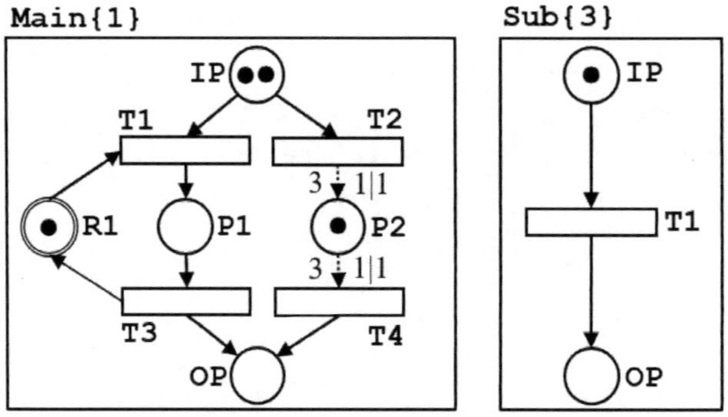

Figure 3 Firing of transition *Main*.T2 in PMN *PROC*

Multiarcs functionalities in the process of the transitions firing of the given PMN can be then simply demonstrated by *symbolic* substitution of every of its multiarc with the pair of standard net arcs (see Figure 4). In our example of PMN *PROC* from Figure 1, it is possible to make *symbolic* substitution of the multiarc (*Main*.T2, *Main*.P2) by the pair of arcs:

- (*Main*.T2, *Main*.P2) with the value of the arc function *AF* equals to 1;
- (*Main*.T2, *Sub*.IP) with the value of the arc function *AF* equals to 1, that is the original value of the multiarcs function *MAF* of the multiarc (*Main*.T2, *Main*.P2);

and similarly it is possible to *symbolically* substitute the multiarc (*Main*.P2, *Main*.T4) by the pair of arcs (*Main*.P2, *Main*.T4) and (*Sub*.OP, *Main*.T4) assigned with the corresponding values of the arc function *AF*.

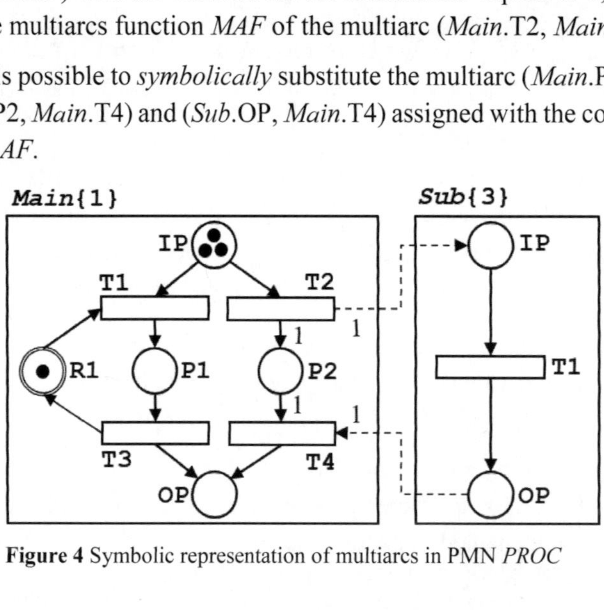

Figure 4 Symbolic representation of multiarcs in PMN *PROC*

A *P/T Petri process multinet* (PPMN) is an ordered couple $PPMN = (PMN, M_e)$, where PMN is a PMN and M_e is an entry marking of the PMN PMN. We will then denote a PPMNs by an ordered 3-tuple $PPMN := (MN, NN, M_e)$.

Definition 1. Let $PMN := (MN, NN)$ be a PMN, $PN \in MN$ be a PN, $PN := (NB, P, T, A, MA, AF, MAF, MAN, TP, RP, IP, OP, RM_s)$. Then:

- PN is said to be *safe* iff $\forall^{PN}M_e \in {}^{PN}\mathbf{M}_e\ \forall p \in P\ \forall\ {}^{PN}M \in [{}^{PN}M_e\rangle\text{: } {}^{PN}M(p) \leq 1$;
- PMN is said to be *safe* iff $\forall M_e \in \mathbf{M}_e\ \forall p \in \boldsymbol{AllPlaces}\ \forall M \in [M_e\rangle\text{: } M(p) \leq 1$;
- PN is said to be *k-bounded* iff
  $\exists k \in \boldsymbol{N}\ \forall^{PN}M_e \in {}^{PN}\mathbf{M}_e\ \forall p \in P\ \forall^{PN}M \in [{}^{PN}M_e\rangle\text{: } {}^{PN}M(p) \leq k$;
- PMN is said to be *k-bounded* iff
  $\exists k \in \boldsymbol{N}\ \forall M_e \in \mathbf{M}_e\ \forall p \in \boldsymbol{AllPlaces}\ \forall M \in [M_e\rangle\text{: } M(p) \leq k$;
- PN is said to *terminate properly* iff
  $\forall^{PN}M_e \in {}^{PN}\mathbf{M}_e\ ((\forall^{PN}M \in [{}^{PN}M_e\rangle\ \exists^{PN}M_x \in {}^{PN}\mathbf{M}_x\text{: } {}^{PN}M_x \in [{}^{PN}M\rangle) \wedge (|[{}^{PN}M_e\rangle\rangle| \neq \aleph_0))$;
- PMN is said to *terminate properly* iff
  $\forall M_e \in \mathbf{M}_e\ ((\forall M \in [M_e\rangle\ \exists M_x \in \mathbf{M}_x\text{: } M_x \in [M\rangle) \wedge (|[M_e\rangle\rangle| \neq \aleph_0))$. □

Example 1. Figure 5, shows two simple PMNs $N1 := (\{Net1\}, \{(Net1, 1)\})$ and $N2 := (\{Net2\}, \{(Net2, 1)\})$ in their entry markings M_e, where:

- PMN $N1$ does not terminate properly, because there exists the infinite sequence of its reachable markings $M_e\ [Net1.\text{T1}\rangle\ M_1\ [Net1.\text{T2}\rangle\ M_2\ [Net1.\text{T2}\rangle \ldots$;
- PMN $N2$ terminates properly for every of its entry markings M_e. □

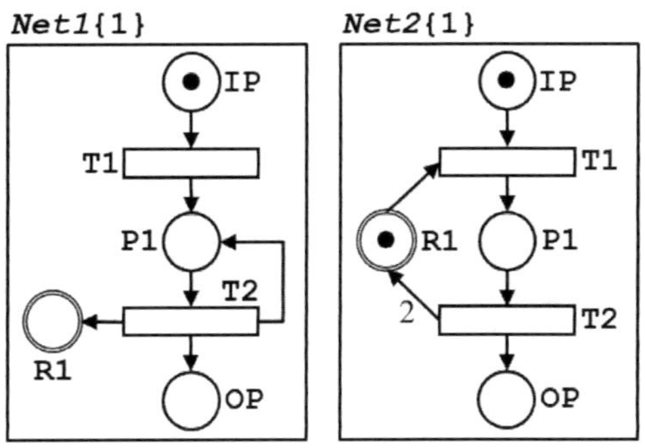

Figure 5 PMNs $N1$ and $N2$ in their entry markings M_e

Lemma 1. Let $PMN := (MN, NN)$ be a PMN. Then
(PMN terminates properly) $\Rightarrow$ ($\exists k \in N$: PMN is k-bounded).

Proof. Clear. (PMN terminates properly) $\Rightarrow (\forall M_e \in \mathbf{M}_e\text{: } ((\forall M \in [M_e\rangle\ \exists M_x \in \mathbf{M}_x\text{: } M_x \in [M\rangle) \wedge (|[M_e\rangle\rangle| \neq \aleph_0))) \Rightarrow (\forall M_e \in \mathbf{M}_e\text{: } ((|[M_e\rangle\rangle|$ is finite$) \wedge (\forall M \in [M_e\rangle\text{: } M$ is finite marking of $PMN))) \Rightarrow (\forall M_e \in \mathbf{M}_e\ \exists k \in N\text{: } PMN$ is k-bounded$)$. □

3 SYNC-CALL operation of PPMNs and its properties

The SYNC-CALL operation of PPMNs models synchronous calling of the chosen method represented by the PN $PN2 := (NB_2, P_2, T_2, A_2, MA_2, AF_2, MAF_2, MAN_2, TP_2, RP_2, IP_2, OP_2, RM_{s2})$ of a given generally parallel distributed programming system from the body of another method of the same programming system represented by a PN $PN1 := (NB_1, P_1, T_1, A_1, MA_1, AF_1, MAF_1, MAN_1, TP_1, RP_1, IP_1, OP_1, RM_{s1})$.

Definition 2. Let $PMN := (MN, NN)$ be a PMN, $PN1 := (NB_1, P_1, T_1, A_1, MA_1, AF_1, MAF_1, MAN_1, TP_1, RP_1, IP_1, OP_1, RM_{s1})$ and $PN2 := (NB_2, P_2, T_2, A_2, MA_2, AF_2, MAF_2, MAN_2, TP_2, RP_2, IP_2, OP_2, RM_{s2})$ be two PNs, $PN1 \cap PN2 = \varnothing$. Let $p \in P_1 \setminus RP_1$ is the place of the PN $PN1$, $ts \in T_1$, $te \in T_1$ are the transitions of the PN $PN1$, $ts \neq te$, such that:

- $(\bullet p = \{ts\}) \wedge (p\bullet = \{te\}) \wedge (\bullet te = \{p\})$;
- $((ts, p) \in MA_1) \wedge ((p, te) \in MA_1) \wedge (MAF_1(ts, p) = MAF_1(p, te)) \wedge (MAN_1(ts, p) = MAN_1(p, te) = NB_2)$.

Then we say there is the *synchronous calling* SYNC-CALL operation of the PN $PN2$ from the PN $PN1$ and we denote this fact by the formal statement $PN1.te =] PN2$.

□

Example 2. There is the SYNC-CALL operation *Main*.T4 =] *Sub* of the PN *Sub* from the PN *Main* in the PMN *PROC* in Figure 1, because

- $(\bullet Main.\text{P2} = \{Main.\text{T2}\}) \wedge (Main.\text{P2}\bullet = \{Main.\text{T4}\}) \wedge (\bullet Main.\text{T4} = \{Main.\text{P2}\})$;
- $((Main.\text{T2}, Main.\text{P2}) \in MA_{Main}) \wedge ((Main.\text{P2}, Main.\text{T4}) \in MA_{Main}) \wedge (MAF_{Main}(Main.\text{T2}, Main.\text{P2}) = MAF_{Main}(Main.\text{P2}, Main.\text{T4})) \wedge (MAN_{Main}(Main.\text{T2}, Main.\text{P2}) = MAN_{Main}(Main.\text{P2}, Main.\text{T4}) = 3 = NB_{Sub})$. □

Definition 3. Let $PMN := (MN, NN)$ be a PMN. We will say there is a *direct recursion* in PMN PMN iff $\exists PN \in MN\ \exists t \in T \in PN$: $PN.t =] PN$. We will say there is an *indirect recursion* in PMN PMN iff $\exists PN, PN1, PN2, \ldots, PNm \in MN\ \exists t \in T \in PN\ \exists t1 \in T1 \in PN1 \ldots \exists tm \in Tm \in PNm$: $(PN.t =] PN1) \wedge (PN1.t1 =] PN2) \wedge \ldots \wedge (PNm.tm =] PN)$, where $m \in \mathbf{N}$. We will say that the *PMN* is the PMN *without recursion* iff there is no direct or indirect recursion in the PMN *PMN*. □

Example 3. There is the indirect recursion in the PPMN $Rec := (MN, NN, M_e)$ in Figure 6, where $MN := \{R1, R2\}$, because $(R1.\text{T2} =] R2) \wedge (R2.\text{T2} =] R1)$.

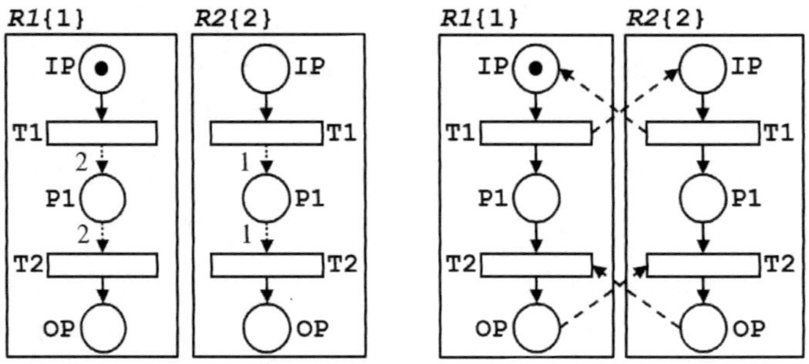

Figure 6 Indirect recursion in PPMN *Rec*

Definition 4. Let $PMN := (MN, NN)$ be a PMN, $PN \in MN$ be a PN, $PN := (NB, P, T, A, MA, AF, MAF, MAN, TP, RP, IP, OP, RM_s)$. We will say that PN is a *base* PN iff $MA = \varnothing$. PN $\underline{PN}$ associated with the PN PN is the base PN $\underline{PN} := (NB, P, T, A, \varnothing, AF, \varnothing, \varnothing, TP, RP, IP, OP, RM_s)$. □

Lemma 2. Let $PMN := (MN, NN)$ be a PMN, $MN := \{PN1, PN2\}$, $PN1 := (NB_1, P_1, T_1, A_1, MA_1, AF_1, MAF_1, MAN_1, TP_1, RP_1, IP_1, OP_1, RM_{s1})$ and $PN2 := (NB_2, P_2, T_2, A_2, MA_2, AF_2, MAF_2, MAN_2, TP_2, RP_2, IP_2, OP_2, RM_{s2})$, $PN1 \cap PN2 = \emptyset$. Let $\underline{PN1}$ terminates properly, $PN2$ is a base PN that terminates properly, $MAF_1 := \{(ts, p), (p, te)\}$, where $p \in P_1 \setminus RP_1$, $ts \in T_1$, $te \in T_1$, and let $PN1.te =] PN2$. Then PMN PMN terminates properly.

Proof. Clear. There exists (according the preconditions of the *Lemma 2*) the place $p \in P_1 \setminus RP_1$ and the transitions $ts \in T_1$, $te \in T_1$ in the PN $PN1$, $ts \neq te$, such that $(\bullet p = \{ts\}) \wedge (p\bullet = \{te\}) \wedge (\bullet te = \{p\}) \wedge ((ts, p) \in MA_1) \wedge ((p, te) \in MA_1) \wedge (MAF_1(ts, p) = MAF_1(p, te)) \wedge (MAN_1(ts, p) = MAN_1(p, te) = NB_2)$. If the transition ts will not be fired during the PN $PN1$ execution, then $PN1$ and $PN2$ must terminate properly (because $\underline{PN1}$ terminates properly and $PN2$ is a base PN that terminates properly) and also PMN PMN must terminate properly. If the transition ts will be fired during the PN $PN1$ execution, then the transition te must be enabled after the finite number of the transition firings because the $PN2$ is a base PN that terminates properly, so the PN $PN1$ must terminate properly according to the precondition of the *Lemma 2* and the whole PMN PMN must also terminate properly. □

Example 4. There is the SYNC-CALL operation *Main*.T4 =] *Sub* of the PN *Sub* from the PN *Main* in the PMN *PROC* in Figure 1, and it can be easily shown that PN $\underline{Main}$ (shown in Figure 4) terminates properly and PN *Sub* is the base PN (without any multiarcs) that terminates properly, so the whole PMN *PROC* according to the *Lemma 2* also terminates properly. □

Lemma 2 can be then generalized into the form of *Lemma 3* and proved by induction.

Lemma 3. Let $PPMN := (MN, NN, M_e)$ be a PPMN without recursion, $PN1 \in MN$, $PN1 := (NB_1, P_1, T_1, A_1, MA_1, AF_1, MAF_1, MAN_1, TP_1, RP_1, IP_1, OP_1, RM_{s1})$ and $PN2 \in MN$, $PN2 := (NB_2, P_2, T_2, A_2, MA_2, AF_2, MAF_2, MAN_2, TP_2, RP_2, IP_2, OP_2, RM_{s2})$, $PN1 \cap PN2 = \emptyset$, $M_e := {}^{PN1}M_e \cup (\cup_{PN \in MN \setminus \{PN1\}} {}^{PN}M_s)$. Let $\underline{PN1}$ terminates properly, $PN2$ is the PN that terminates properly, $MAF_1 = \{(ts, p), (p, te)\}$, where $p \in P_1 \setminus RP_1$, $ts \in T_1$, $te \in T_1$, and let $PN1.te =] PN2$. Then PPMN $PPMN$ terminates properly.

4 An example of SYNC-CALL operation at the modeling of distributed programming system

In the following simple example we will develop a design of a PPMN $ClientSrv := (MN, NN, M_e)$, where MN := {*Client*, *Srv*, *Db*}, modeling the distributed programming system operating on the client and application server side and realizing reading and writing procedures from the given database system on the basis of a client requests. Individual client requests are then executed via a finite set of programming threads on the server side (in our model of that programming system we assume availability of totally three server side programming threads) stored in the created pool of threads. At the moment of accepting the user request is for the needs of its responding a free thread randomly selected in pool which realizes such request, i.e., it will ensure execution of reading or writing data into the database system. In so doing it is required that in the case of realization of the request for the writing of the database no other thread can access the database environment and in the case of the request for the reading any finite number of threads realizing reading of the data can access the database.

Figure 7, shows the PN *Client* in its entry marking $^{Client}M_e$ (where $^{Client}M_e(Client.\mathrm{R1}) = 4$) that represents the client side of the whole distributed programming system. Client side will perform PARALLEL FOR cycles with the two programming threads (the tokens in the input place *Client*.IP) requesting the read and write server side database operations (firing of the transition *Client*.T2). Server side database service is represented by the place *Client*.P3 and will be requested by synchronous manner.

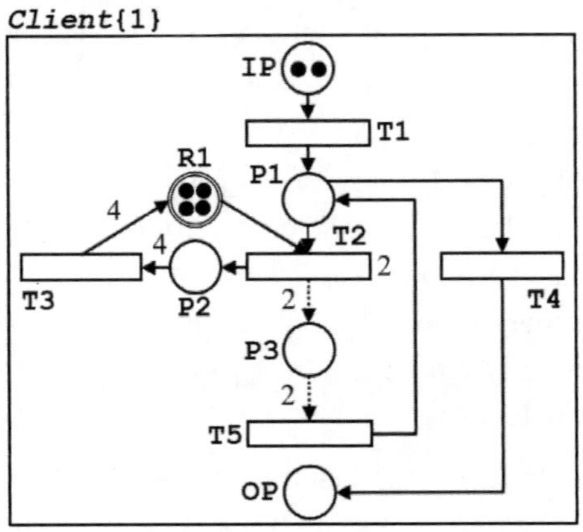

Figure 7 Process net *Client*

Figure 8, shows the PN *Srv* determined for the calling of the method represented by the PN *Db* that will realize the execution of user requirements on reading or writing into the database while using three accessible programming threads located in the common programming pool (see the resource place *Srv*.R1). The respective threads realize either reading (firing of the transition *Db*.T2, resp. *Db*.T1) or writing (firing of the transition *Db*.T5) of the data from or to the database via the mechanisms of PN *Db* (see Figure 9) that models the access into the database environment with the support of multiple-readers/single-writer lock. Following realization of the relevant event the programming thread will be returned back into the common pool of the threads represented by the resource place *Srv*.R1 and it will be ready for the execution of the next user request.

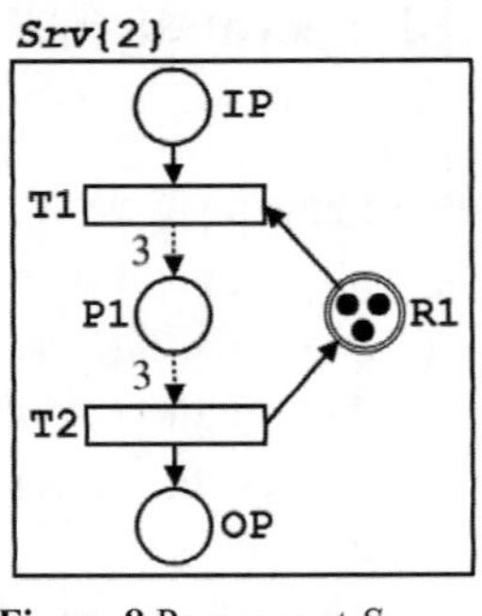

Figure 8 Process net *Srv*

The respective threads realize either reading (firing of the transition *Db*.T2, resp. *Db*.T1) or writing (firing of the transition *Db*.T5) of the data from or to the database via the mechanisms of PN *Db* that models the access into the database environment with the support of multiple-readers/single-writer lock. The token in the resource place *Db*.R1 represents single lock determined for obtaining the multiple-readers (represented by the tokens in the place *Db*.P2)/single-writer (represented by the single token in the place *Db*.P3) access of the database environment.

There are the SYNC-CALL operations *Client*.T5 =] *Srv* and *Srv*.T2 =] *Db* and so PPMN *ClientSrv* is the PPMN without recursion. It can be shown that PN *Client* and PN *Srv* terminates properly and *Db* is the base PN that also terminates properly. According to the *Lemma 3* then the whole PPMN *ClientSrv* also terminates properly.

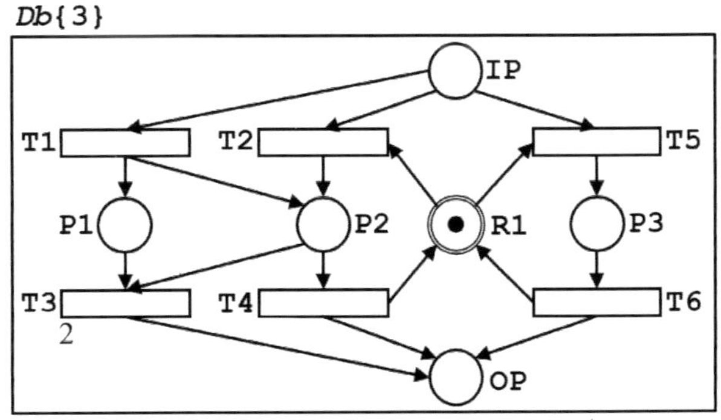

Figure 9 Process net *Db*

5 Conclusion

There is an opportunity to define additional operations for the class of PPMN and to generalize it (for instance the ASYNC-CALL operator that models asynchronous method processing). The principles introduced in the PPMNs are further generalized and implemented in the definition of the class of high-level Petri nets called the sequential object Petri nets (Martiník, 2012) which differ from PPMNs mainly by mutually differentiable tokens. The tokens alone are formed by non-empty sequences over the set of all the integer numbers (this is also where the name of this Petri nets class came from). Sequential object Petri nets are then specially determined for the design, modeling and verification of distributed multithreading programming systems based on the object oriented and functional paradigmas.

We have been also developing the MPNP programming system designed for modeling, verification and simulation of PNs and PPMNs that will entirely run in the mobile devices environment. It has been developing in the Java Gluon programming environment and it is fully portable among mobile devices with iOS, Android or MS Windows operating system installed.

Acknowledgements

This paper was supported by SGS project No. SP2017/144 and also within Operational Programme Education for Competitiveness - Project No. CZ.1.07/2.3.00/20.0296.

References

van der Alst, W. and van Hee, K. (2002). *Workflow Management: Models, Methods and Systems*. Massachusetts: The MIT Press.

Diaz, M. (2009). *Petri Nets: Fundamental Models, Verification and Applications*. London: Willey.

Huang, H., Jiao, L., Cheung, T. and Mak, W. M. (2012). *Property-Preserving Petri Net Process Algebra In Software Engineering*. Singapore: World Scientific Publishing Co. Pte. Ltd.

Martiník, I. (2011). 'Bi-relational P/T Petri Nets and the Modeling of Multithreading Object-oriented Programming Systems'. *Communications in Computer and Information Science,* 188 CCIS (Part 1), pp. 222-236.

Martiník, I. (2012). 'Sequential Object Petri Nets and the Modeling of Multithreading Object-Oriented Programming Systems'. *Petri Nets - Manufacturing and Computer Science*. InTech, Rijeka, Croatia, pp. 195-224.

Martiník, I. (2015). 'SYNC-PROC Composition Operator of P/T Petri Process Nets'. *Proceedings of the 11th International Conference on Strategic Management and its Support by Information Systems 2015, Uherské Hradiště, Czech Republic*. pp. 400-410.

Martiník, I. (2016). 'PLACE_SUBST Transformation of P/T Petri Process Nets and Its Properties'. *Computer Information Systems and Industrial Management. Lecture Notes in Computer Science,* 9842, pp. 504-515.

Reisig, W. and Rozenberg, G. (1998). *Lectures on Petri Nets I: Basic Models.* Heidelberg: Springer.

Žáček, J. and Huňka, F. (2011). 'Object Model Synchronization Base on Petri Nets'. *17th International Conference on Soft Computing, MENDEL 2011*. Brno, Czech Republic, pp. 523-527.

Strategic use of social media in health communication

Éva Görgényi Hegyes[1], Mária Fekete Farkas[2]

Abstract. Nowadays use of social media applications has become one of the most important factors in the daily life of both individuals and organizations. Due to the rapid diffusion of the Internet, organizations needed to change their communication strategy and focus on exploiting the opportunities offered by the Internet especially different web 2.0 applications. The study is intended to provide a clear understanding of the role of social media in health awareness communication through the theoretical background. Moreover, the study critically analyses different health awareness campaigns performed in social media applications via SWOT analysis.

Keywords: social media, health awareness, consumer behavior, marketing strategy, communication.

JEL Classification: D83, I12

1 Introduction

As stated in Internet World Stats data (2017), the number of internet users is continuously increasing globally year by year – nowadays more than the half of total population (more than 3.6 billion people) uses Internet in the world. The tendency represents a significant and impressive growth (918 %) between 2000 and 2016. While the world's biggest social networking site, Facebook has got over 1.6 billion users globally (1.23 billion daily active users on average), on the most famous microblogging site Twitter, there are 313 million active users (who log in at least once a month) and 500 million tweets per day. At the same time on the video sharing site YouTube, more than 6 billion hours of video are watched every month, and there are over 1 billion monthly active users. (Socialbakers, 2017)

Due to the rapid expansion of social media, health 2.0 is now commonly used terminology. According to the Council for Public Health and Health Care (2010), health 2.0 means that patients and healthcare providers work actively together, thus increasing the effectiveness and quality of health services. Last few years brought the social media usage to the mainstream of health communication, information generation and dissemination. Both healthcare staff and patients received a new information source – although doctors and health professionals continue to remain the first information source for most people with their health concern, patients have been becoming to information generators and sharers from the simple consumers of Internet content and use social media to search information or give feedbacks to others. (Lapointe, Ramaprasad and Vedel, 2014; Brodalski et al, 2011)

Public health organizations and practitioners have been trying to emphasize the health awareness through the social media for decades – the first health communication campaign that incorporates social marketing concepts was in the 1960's. Since then, social media campaigns in health awareness have been used in prevention of many public health issues, such as cancer,

[1] Szent István University, Faculty of Economics and Social Sciences, Doctoral School of Management and Business Administration, Hungary H-2100 Gödöllő, Páter K. u. 1., eva.hegyesne.gorgenyi@phd.uni-szie.hu.
[2] Szent István University, Faculty of Economics and Social Sciences, Institute of Economics, Law and Methodology, Hungary H-2100 Gödöllő, Páter K. u. 1., farkasne.fekete.maria@gtk.szie.hu.

diabetes, heart attack, stroke and asthma. The aim of these campaigns is always the prevention by influencing the knowledge and awareness in order to help to change many health-related behaviors. (Robinson et al, 2014).

The current paper is intended to summarize the most important literature in terms of social media and health awareness. Furthermore, the study aims to analyze the effective and strategic use of social media in certain health awareness campaigns via detailed SWOT analysis.

2 Social media definition and classification

Nowadays, social media plays a crucial role in online communication, especially in life of the Generation Y's or Digital Natives (born after 1981) (Bolton et al., 2013). To understand the definition of social media it is essential to distinguish this term from the term of web 2.0, which is a platform, spanning all connected devices. The term of social media was firstly used in 2004 to describe the new way of utilizing the World Wide Web by the software developers and end-users (Kaplan and Haenlein, 2010). The most comprehensive definition was written by O'Reilly in 2005: a platform delivering software as a continually-updated service that enables more people to use it better, consuming and remixing data from multiple sources, allows remixing by others and creating network effects through an architecture of participation (O'Reilly, 2005; Evans, 2014, Boulos and Wheelert, 2007). Kaplan and Haenlein (2010) define social media as the group of different online applications "that build on the ideological and technological foundations of Web 2.0 and that allow the creation and exchange of User Generated Content".

Despite of the diverse available definitions and literature, it is still complicated to exactly and generally define social media and its elements – there are numerous types of social media applications. Table 1 shows the classification of social media, summarizes the different social media channels, their short description and provides example platforms of these channels.

Social media channels	Short description	Examples
Blogs	Sites that contains regularly updated, date-stamped entries, displayed in reverse chronological order.	ReutersBlog (WordPress)
Collaborative projects	Online forums or discussion sites that allow certain groups of people to collaborate, work together in order to create online content.	Google Groups Business Forums
Media sharing sites	Contact channel that enables people to share different media content (photos, videos, clips etc.) with others.	YouTube Flickr
Microblogging	Allow users to share small amounts of digital content – such as short sentences, video links or images. The main difference in compared with blogs is the smaller content size.	Twitter Tumblr WeiBo
Podcasts	Series of digital media content (audio or video) distributed in websites.	Podomatic

Reviews and rating sites	Websites that enable the users to share their own opinions, feedbacks related to other people, products, services etc.	FourSquare Tripadvisor.com Amazon.com
Social networking sites	Online communities for information sharing, social connection and other interactions.	Facebook LinkedIn MySpace
Virtual game and social worlds	The group of platforms that simulate a three-dimensional world in which users can interact with others in this environment (similar to real life).	World of Warcraft Second Life
Wikis	Websites that enable users to edit and publish easily documents (interlinking pages) using a simple language and a web browser.	Ekopedia Familypedia Wikipedia
Widgets/badges/gadgets/buttons	Small applications that can be easily shared or embedded in other sites.	GALE Health & Wellness Resource Center

Table 1 Classification of social media channels (Kaplan and Haenlein, 2010; Ryan, 2014)

3 Importance of social media in marketing strategy

In the last few decades, communication needs and habits have been drastically changed – the rapid expansion of the Internet has shifted the focus from the use of traditional media tools (such as TV, radio, newspapers etc.) to the exploiting of the opportunities offered by the online world (especially social media) in case of health communication also. In this paper traditional communication methods mean the typical ATL and BTL tools – such as television, radio, newspapers, PR, DM, POS, newsletters and traditional online communication (web 1.0) – while social media or web 2.0 applications will be categorized as the new way for marketing communication. Table 2 represents the main differences between traditional media and social media:

Communication form	Traditional media	Social media
Interactivity	▪ One-way (one-to-many) communication / monologue; ▪ Connectivity – only informing the users; ▪ Less opportunity for misinformation; ▪ Static; ▪ Only search and browse.	▪ Many-way (many-to-many) communication / dialogue; ▪ Interactivity – engaging the audience; ▪ More dangerous - opportunity for misinformation; ▪ Dynamic; ▪ Also publish and subscribe.
Information sharing	▪ Fix deadlines (e.g. press, TV) and schedules; ▪ Structured information sharing; ▪ Centralized process for information; ▪ Users may have the control on the flow of information – they can also write and edit, not only read the content.	▪ Flexible and quick information sharing; ▪ Unstructured information sharing; ▪ Decentralized process for information distribution; ▪ Organization has control on the flow of information, users can only read the content.

Table 2 Differences between traditional media and social media (Mangold and Faulds, 2009)

To establish a presence in social media, each organization first has to understand the nature of its building components in order to be able to merge them with the current corporate strategy. According to Kietzmann et al. (2011) social media is built by seven blocks (as building components): identity, presence, relationships, reputation, groups, conversations and sharing.

Because of the above-mentioned characteristics as advantages of the social media, it has become more and more important in marketing communication. Although Kot, Ferencová and Kakalejcík (2016) state that the mostly used medium to find information about a product and the execution of purchase is the search engine and social networks do not have a significant effect to the customers' purchasing decisions, different web 2.0 applications can be effectively used in case of awareness campaigns. The emergence of costumer-to-costumer communication has made it possible for one user (individual or organization) to share information with hundreds or thousands of other people. (Mangold and Faulds, 2009). Hence, the appearance and spread of social media has made it necessary to rethink the original marketing promotional mix. Mangold and Faulds (2009) created a new paradigm presents the power and impact of discussions and consumer using social media – showed by Figure 1:

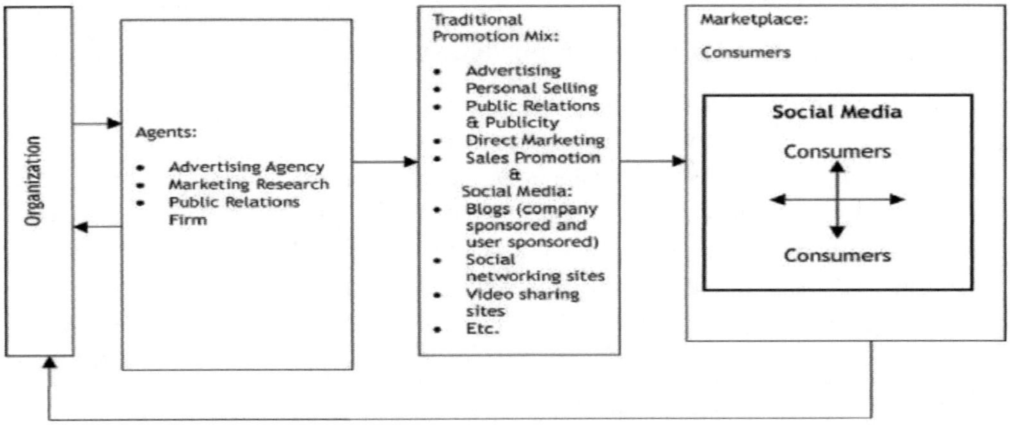

Figure 1 New communications paradigm (Mangold and Faulds, 2009)

Nowadays, there are some relevant trends that are representing in this new paradigm:

- The Internet has become a mass media opportunity – consumers use Internet for searching and sharing information, reviewing the feedback of other people, contacting with each other etc;
- Consumers changed their media usage habits – they turned away from traditional advertising methods, and also they have more control over their media consumption;
- Use of social media has become to influence the people' decision making – the social media can enable the organizations to change the consumers' behaviors;
- Social media has become more and more credible source of information.

The study performed by Social Media Examiner (2016) also confirms that social media marketing has become an important pillar for businesses. Major findings are listed below:

- Video has become essential – a significant 60 % of marketers use video in their marketing activity and 73 % plan on increasing their video use. Moreover, live video is a hot topic – a significant 50 % of marketers plan on using live video services such as Facebook Live and Periscope, and 50 % want to learn more about live video;

- Snapchat is on a growth trajectory – although only 5 % of marketers are using Snapchat, 16 % plan on increasing their Snapchat activities and 28 % of marketers want to learn more about Snapchat;
- The domination of Facebook is continuous – it is the most important social network for marketers. When asked to select their most important platform, 55 % of marketers chose Facebook, followed by LinkedIn at 18 %. Plus, 67 % of marketers plan on increasing their Facebook marketing activities;
- Facebook and YouTube hold the top platforms for future plans – at least 63 % of marketers plan on increasing their use of these particular social media sites;
- Many marketers are unsure about their Facebook marketing – a significant 40 % of marketers don't know if Facebook traffic has declined in the last 12 months and 35 % aren't sure if their Facebook marketing is effective;
- Facebook ads dominate – 86 % of social marketers regularly use Facebook ads;
- Tactics and engagement are top areas marketers want to master – at least 90 % of marketers want to know the most effective social tactics and the best ways to engage their audience with social media.

4 Relationship between social media and health awareness

To understand the role that the different social media applications can play in health awareness and health communication it is essential to know what the health and health awareness means. The most integrated, accepted and commonly used definition of health was defined by the World Health Organization (WHO) in 1948. According to the Preamble to the Constitution of the WHO: "Health is a state of complete physical, mental and social well-being and not merely the absence of disease or infirmity." (WHO, 2006) It is increasingly recognized fact that health can be maintained and improved not only through the health science and different healthcare services, but also through the smart lifestyle and health-conscious behavior of the individuals or society. Health awareness or health–conscious behavior is all of the individual attitudes, behaviors and activities in order to live longer and remain healthier. (WHO, 2016)

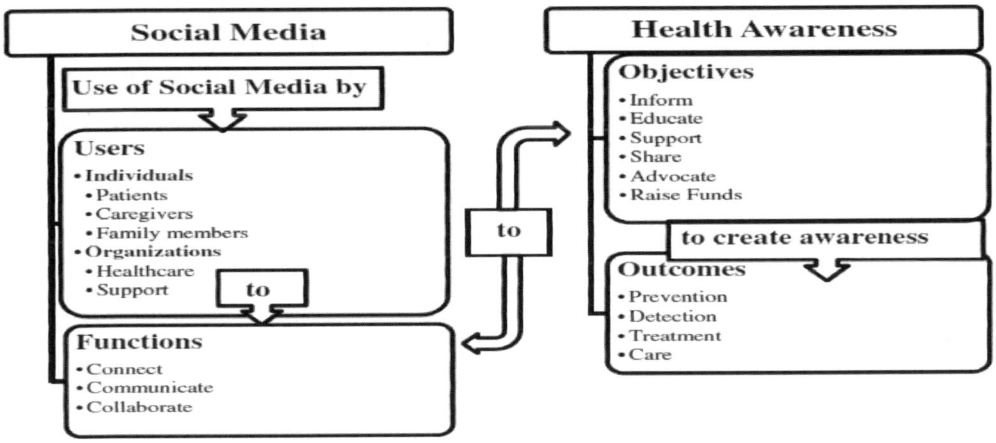

Figure 2 Link between social media and health awareness (Lapointe, Ramaprasad and Vedel, 2014)

In health communication, the information dissemination is the key element of building health awareness and thus, a crucial factor in the primary, secondary and tertiary prevention and early detection of chronic diseases. Lapointe, Ramaprasad and Vedel (2014) provide a comprehensive overview of the role of social media-enabled collaboration and its impact on creating health awareness through Figure 2. The strategic use of social media applications in health communication is a huge opportunity for organizations and individuals, as:

- Social media can increase the timely dissemination and potential impact of health and safety information;
- More diverse target audience can be reached;
- These types of communities can facilitate the information sharing;
- It is easily possible to personalize and force certain health messages that can be easily targeted to particular target audience;
- Social media also facilitate interactivity, online connection and public engagement thus health awareness can be created or increased;
- Empower the consumers to make healthier and safer decisions during their daily life.

5 Key findings of case study

Improving the understanding of impacts and operation of social media applications in health communication, a detailed SWOT analysis was performed by Authors in 2015. The motivation derives from the contribution of the Authors in a research in UK health sector, hence, the analysis is based on campaigns in UK and US. Based on the literature review, some inclusion criteria were identified for selecting high relevant organizations and health awareness campaigns.

The inclusion criteria for high relevant campaigns are the following:

- Campaigns related to public health and health awareness AND;
- Campaigns that had used social media platforms for delivers AND;
- Campaigns were organized from 2010 to 2015 AND;
- Campaigns are related to TOP10 diseases or risk factors.

Searching method:

- Databases used for searching: Google Scholar and ProQuest;
- Keywords:
  - "social media" AND "health¬*";
  - "social media" AND "health" AND "awareness" OR "campaign".

In general, the most important strengths, weaknesses opportunities and threats were determined in Figure 3 what help us to make the deep, detailed SWOT only for high relevant cases.

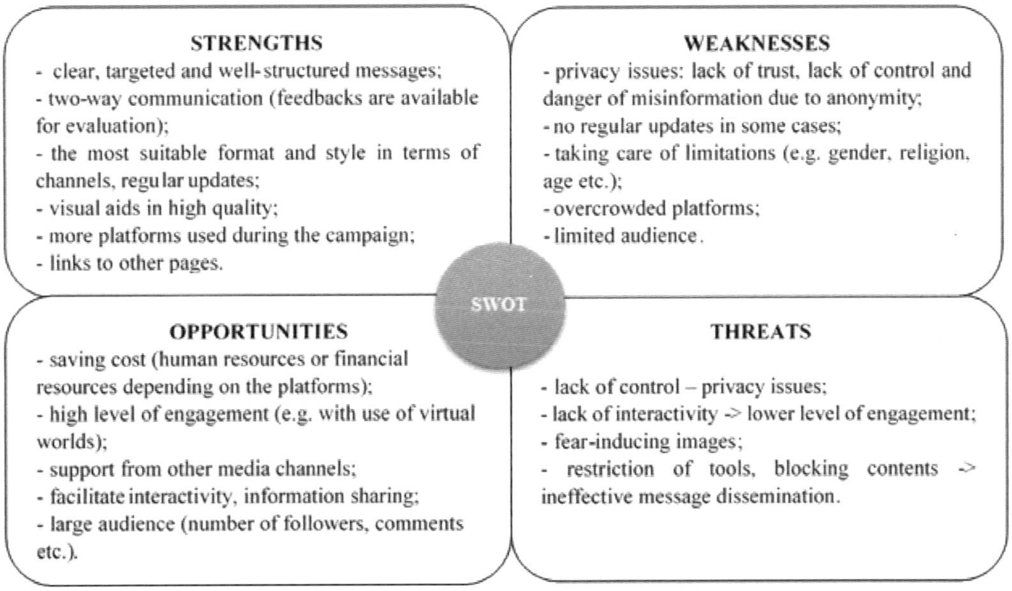

Figure 3 Criteria used for detailed SWOT analysis (own edition)

According to the applied searching method, 24 different health awareness campaigns (organized by various health organizations such as governmental institutions, research centers, charities etc.) were identified and signed as low, moderate or high relevant. Finally, 6 high relevant cases were included into detailed SWOT analysis where strengths, weaknesses, opportunities and threats of selected campaigns/programs were observed. Main results are listed below:

- Facebook and Twitter are the most popular platforms in health communication. However, Twitter and microblogs are more popular in the US than in Europe – it is very important to take care of special characteristics and limitations of target audience;
- Health organizations are aware of use of the most popular social media applications, however some platforms are overcrowded – most important features: good use of hyperlinks, pass short, clear and targeted messages, well-defined target audience, regular (daily) updates, good use of supporting campaign elements (independent website, use of traditional media etc.) However, they hardly use other options that can increase the level of engagement – such as virtual games, different apps or widgets embedded into popular SM sites. Use of specialized tools, games and apps are missing from campaign and programs – it is very likely that the higher resource needs mean the main barrier to use such tools, however, health organizations could increase the engagement level of consumers with use of them. Videos and images are in high number and high quality;
- In some cases the regular monitoring of comments and responses are missing. Due to this lack of interactivity, potential target groups can be lost;
- Messages are short, clear and usually follow similar structure.

Conclusion

Despite the many threats and various weaknesses it possesses, there is no doubt, that social media usage is growing rapidly and it is gradually influencing our life and decisions. As health sector has several specialties, the use of social media is a relatively new challenge in this field and it can be endangering and vulnerable in some cases. There are no sophisticated and fully-developed methods in this special area, however, based on the continuously increasing literature it is obvious that different actors are looking for new opportunities and ways to create awareness and health-conscious behavior. These facts demonstrate the need to use social media in health communication – this IT tool is the most effective way for knowledge transfer in all sectors in the 21st century. Moreover, one of the most important area of knowledge transfer in terms of sustainability is the social welfare. This study is intended to contribute to the application and necessity of social media in the special area of health sector and also the development of research methodology. According to SWOT analysis it is obvious that health institutions try to use the new opportunities offered by social media, however, their communication is not effective enough yet – the use of different applications is not based on a well-structured, knowledge-based strategy, but they have taken the initial steps. In order to increase health awareness through their communication organizations should achieve more interactivity from customers, follow STP (segmentation, targeting, positioning) marketing as a strategic approach and update regularly (continuous content management). Therefore, social media is a necessary channel, however, it should possess only an awareness-raising function instead of real healing function. Results and implications of analysis need further empirical confirmation, hence a representative research is planned in future work, which examines the health-conscious consumer behavior.

References

Bolton, R.N., Parasuraman, A., Hoefnagels, A., Kabadayi, S., Gruber, T., Loureiro, Y.K., Migchels, N. and Solnet, D. (2013). 'Understanding Gen Y and their use of social media: a review and research agenda'. *Journal of Service Management*, 24 (3), pp. 245-267.

Boulos M.N.K. and Wheelert, S., (2007). 'Blackwell Publishing Ltd The emerging Web 2.0 social software: an enabling suite of sociable technologies in health and health care education'. *Health Information and Libraries Journal*, 24, pp. 2-23.

Brodalski, D., Brink, H., Curtis, J., Diaz, S., Schindelar, J., Shannon, C. and Wolfson, C. (2011). *The Health Communicator's Social Media Toolkit*, Atlanta, USA.

Council for Public Health and Health Care (2010). *Health 2.0 – It's up to you.* The Hague: Koninklijke Broese & Peereboom.

Evans, R., (2014). 'The use of web 2.0 technologies in business'. *Lecture note*, Cranfield University.

Hegyesné Görgényi, É. (2015). 'Managing the health awareness knowledge via the advanced use of social media applications'. *Unpublished dissertation.*

Internet World Stats (2017). 'Usage and Population Statistics', [Online]. Available at: http://www.internetworldstats.com/ [cited 2017-01-27].

Kaplan, A. M. and Haenlein, M. (2010). 'Users of the world, unite! The challenges and opportunities of Social Media'. *Business Horizons*, 53 (1), pp. 59-68.

Kietzmann, J.H., Hermkens, K., McCarthy, I.P. and Silvestre, B.S. (2011). 'Social media? Get serious! Understanding the functional building blocks of social media'. *Business Horizons*, 54 (3), pp. 241-251.

Kot, S., Ferencová, M. and Kakalejcík, L. (2016). 'Using of Selected Social Media in Slovakia and Poland – Comparative Study'. *Mediterranean Journal of Social Sciences*, 7 (3), pp. 113-120.

Lapointe, L., Ramaprasad, J and Vedel, I. (2014). 'Creating health awareness: a social media enabled collaboration'. *Health and Technology*, 4 (1), pp. 43-57.

Mangold, W.G. and Faulds, D.J. (2009). 'Social media: The new hybrid element of the promotion mix'. *Business Horizons*, 52 (4), pp. 357-365.

O'Reilly, T. (2005). What is web 2.0, [Online]. Available at: http://www.oreilly.com/pub/a/web2/archive/what-is-web-20.html [cited 2015-06-20].

Robinson, M.N., Tansil, K.A., Elder, R.W., Soler, R.E., Labre, M.P., Mercer, S.L., Eroglu, D., Baur, C., Lyon-Daniel, K., Fridinger, F., Sokler, L.A., Green, L.W., Miller, T., Dearing, J.W., Evans, W.D., Snyder, L.B., Viswanath, K.K., Beistle, D.M., Chervin, D.D., Bernhardt, J.M., Rimer, B.K. and the Community Preventive Services Task Forces (2014). 'Mass Media Health Communication Campaigns Combined with Health-Related Product Distribution'. *American Journal of Preventive Medicine*, 47 (3), pp. 360-371.

Socialbakers (2017). Free Social Media Statistics, [Online]. Available at: https://www.socialbakers.com/statistics/ [cited 2017-01-27].

Social Media Examiner (2016). 2016 Social Media Marketing Industry Report, [Online]. Available at: https://www.socialmediaexaminer.com/wp-content/uploads/2016/05/SocialMediaMarketingIndustryReport2016.pdf [cited 2017-01-27].

WHO (2006). Basic Documents, Forty-fifth edition, Supplement, Contribution of the World Health Organization, [Online]. Available at: http://www.who.int/governance/eb/who_constitution_en.pdf [cited 2016-10-05].

WHO (2016). Health Impact Assessment, [Online]. Available at: http://www.who.int/hia/evidence/doh/en/ [cited 2016-10-05].

Components of Big Data Analytics for Strategic Management of Enterprise Architecture

Martin Lněnička[1], Renáta Máchová, Jitka Komárková, Ivana Čermáková [2]

Abstract. The concept of strategic management is currently being under pressure to adopt big data analytics as a tool for improving efficiency of decision-making and monitoring processes in organizations. This paper aims to provide a systematic approach to map the benefits driven by big data analytics in terms of enterprise architecture focusing on the importance for strategic management. The key components are identified and discussed in the context of TOGAF. The findings can be used as a guide to help developers and designers in reframing their enterprise architecture efforts.

Keywords: big data analytics, strategic management, enterprise architecture, design science research.

JEL Classification: L21, M15

1 Introduction

The global big data analytics market has seen a tremendous growth in the recent years that is helping businesses uncover more insights and making sense of their data in new ways. At the same time, they are exposed to continuously changing environments fueled by advancements in technologies, standards, regulations, and changing market requirements, which supposed to be solved at the level of Enterprise Architecture (EA). As recent contributions to EA theory suggest that Information Technology (IT) architecture should be agile enough to manage the large amounts of data, there is still a lack of research on components by which big data analytics supports the whole EA.

A key requirement to today's changing environment is the ability of organizations to adapt dynamically in an effective and efficient manner. Information and Communication Technologies (ICT) play an important role in addressing such adaptation requirements. However, as complexity of organization and modern IT systems increases, the role of EA relates to evolving business trends and technology advancements (Ahlemann et al, 2012; Romero and Vernadat, 2016; Shah and El Kourdi, 2007). For example, Zimmermann et al (2014) reported that the technological and business architectural impact of new mobility solutions, social networks, case-based business process management and services computing with big data in cloud settings has multiple aspects, which directly affect EA. Since Lagerström et al (2011) confirmed that there are significant correlations between organizations' success with IT and Enterprise Architecture Management (EAM) activities, the alignment of big data analytics with EA is solved in the context of strategic management. In that regard, EAM is no longer viewed as an IT department job but a strategic function that approaches enterprise related changes in a holistic and consistent way. It supports enterprise transformation in response to

[1] martin.lnenicka@gmail.com
[2] University of Pardubice, Faculty of Economics and Administration, Studentska 95, 53210 Pardubice, {renata.machova, jitka.komarkova, ivana.cermakova}@upce.cz

the increasingly dynamic enterprise environment (Ahlemann et al, 2012). Further, architecture is meaningful only in relation to other parts that together constitute the whole ecosystem (Tiwana, 2014). The main assumption that guides this paper is the need to map the benefits driven by big data analytics for stakeholders in terms of EA focusing on the importance for strategic management.

2 Research Methodology

We address this gap in the literature by exploring the relationship between big data analytics and EAM at the level of the individual components in the EA. These components were developed by: first, reviewing literature on big data analytics, EA and its management, and a set of EA frameworks to form a theoretical foundation; second, using the theoretical foundation to adapt requirements of big data analytics for strategic EAM; and third, consolidating these requirements into the existing EA framework in which benefits are highlighted. For this purpose, these basic architecture domains (layers) of The Open Group Architecture Framework (TOGAF) were used: business, data, application, and technology. TOGAF presents both the Architecture Development Method (ADM) and information model for architectural description. The cyclic ADM is designed as reference method for performing an architecture project, which in the sense of TOGAF is the way of performing EAM (The Open Group, 2009).

This paper employs a research method that follows the guidelines for Design Science Research (DSR) approach as described by Hevner et al (2004). DSR is a widely applied research approach and is concerned with developing useful artefacts. It is a problem-solving paradigm in which the boundaries of organizational capabilities to create new and innovative artefacts are extended together with the knowledge and understanding of a problem domain through the building and application of the design artefact (Hevner et al, 2004). In the context of EAM, it was previously applied by Aier, Gleichauf and Winter (2011). Aiming to provide a detailed overview to the issue of big data analytics for strategic management of EA, this paper is focused only on the first four steps of the DSR process while other steps will be described thoroughly in future research. In this regard, the objectives of this paper are: 1) discuss the preparedness of EA for big data analytics; 2) provide strategic alignment of big data analytics in the business ecosystem; 3) map these requirements on EA layers of TOGAF; and 4) propose a model containing components of big data analytics for strategic management of EA.

3 Theoretical Background

3.1 Importance of Enterprise Architecture and its Management

Architectures are largely technical decisions with enormous strategic consequences (Tiwana, 2014). EA frameworks identify the architecture's scope and decompose its elements and relationships into structured layers and architectural dimensions. These are useful for defining and developing the detailed description of the architecture, the principles governing its development and the standards applied during the architecture's development (Ahlemann et al, 2012; Shah and El Kourdi, 2007). While a wide range of these frameworks exists, a theme they have in common is layering. Layers comprise the basic structure of an EA model, representing distinct conceptual domains, which group together related elements (Simon et al, 2013). In this regard, Tiwana (2014) defined architecture as "*a conceptual blueprint that describes how the ecosystem is partitioned into a relatively stable platform and a complementary set of applications that are encouraged to vary, and the design rules binding on both*." The architecture of a platform or an application is a high-level description of its building blocks and how they are related to each other, not a working implementation (Tiwana, 2014). According to TOGAF, apart from the holistic nature of EA, it can be represented with specific focus and is suitable as a framework for reflecting new requirements on architecture (The Open Group, 2009).

EAM is expected to provide business value by guiding the continuous development and transformation in an increasingly turbulent business environment (Ahlemann et al, 2012; Aier, Gleichauf and Winter, 2011). The EAM function has taken on a strategic role and presents a coherent set of guidelines, architecture principles and governance regimes that provide direction and practical help in the design and development of enterprise strategies and visions (Ahlemann et al, 2012). Both practitioners and researchers put forward EAM as a mean for achieving success with IT and a considerable amount of literature describes the components of successful EAM (Lagerström et al, 2011). The empirical analysis of Aier, Gleichauf and Winter (2011) revealed eight determining design factors of EAM, a delineation of three different types of EAM design in the form of clusters as well as insight about the successfulness of the different types.

Buckl et al (2010) presented building blocks for EAM solutions, which can be selected and configured based on the specificities of the organization, i.e. the organizational context and the goals pursued. These building blocks form the solution models to be combined to an organization-specific EAM function. Aier, Gleichauf and Winter (2011) identified these factors: IT operations support, enterprise focus and management, EAM governance, IT strategy and IT governance support, information supply, integrative role, design impact, and business strategy support. Zimmermann et al (2014) investigated mechanisms for adaptable EA that will support the development of service-oriented ecosystems with integrated technologies like semantic technologies, web services, cloud computing, and big data management.

3.2 Towards Requirements of Big Data Analytics in an Enterprise

Big data analytics has many perspectives. Arguably, the three most discussed are the business perspective, i.e. value and business outcomes, the technology perspective, i.e. computing resources and IT infrastructure management, and the social perspective, i.e. stakeholders and their knowledge, skills and abilities (Lake and Drake, 2014). These perspectives are usually comprised of components, which represent both functional and non-functional requirements (Pääkkönen and Pakkala, 2015). Big data impacts both the strategy development process and the actual strategies developed in a number of ways, often called the 6V's (Demchenko, De Laat and Membrey, 2014; Lake and Drake, 2014). This concept is shown in Fig. 1. Variety allows greater visibility of business relationships and the business environment previously outside the scope of traditional management information systems. Volume allows more detailed analysis of strategic position, greater optimization of the supply chain and customer relationships. Velocity allows faster, more timely, feedback on experimental strategic initiatives, faster interactions with customers, suppliers, employees and other stakeholders. Other requirements have to be solved according to defined policies and procedures of an enterprise.

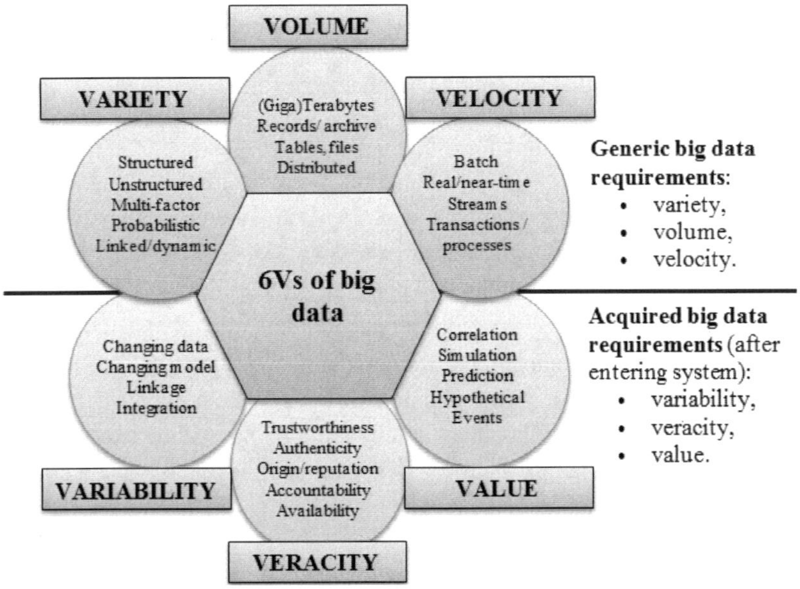

Figure 1 6Vs of big data [Demchenko, De Laat and Membrey, 2014]

Fig. 2 visualizes the importance of big data analytics for EA in the boundaries of the existing (as-is) architecture that provides the bases for planning the target (to-be) architecture. EAM includes the management tasks of planning and controlling business change from an architectural perspective. Among others, big data analytics should provide efficient resource allocation and use, efficient operating cost structure leading to savings, faster strategic change and delivery of results, support of decision-making on strategic level, etc.

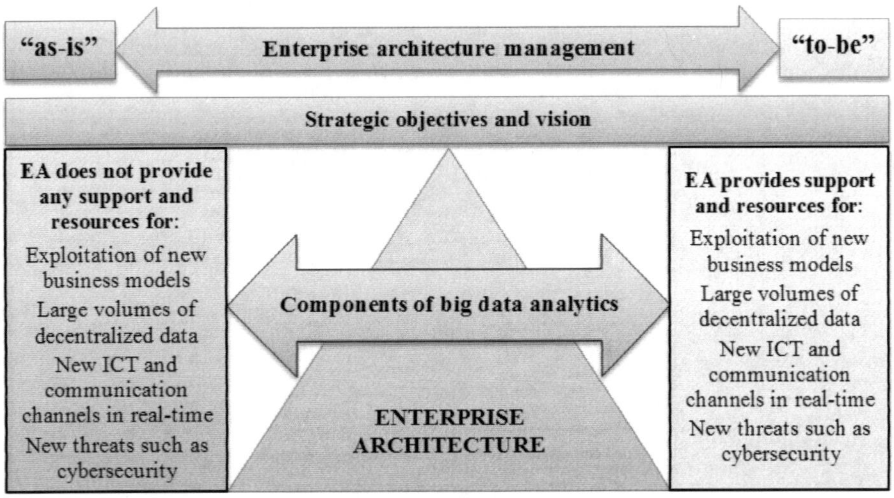

Figure 2 Importance of big data analytics in the context of EA [authors]

4 Identifying Components of Big Data Analytics in Business Ecosystem

As defined by Hevner et al (2004), the first two steps in the DSR process require the creation of an innovative, purposeful artefact (Guideline 1) for a specified problem domain (Guideline 2). The artefact can be presented in the form of a construct, a model, a method, or an instantiation. Here, the components are formalized in the model for a specified domain of big data analytics in business ecosystem. Since thorough evaluation of the artefact is crucial (Guideline 3), the components were verified for relevance through semi-structured interviews with four interviewees consisting of practitioners and researchers. Finally, research contributions (Guideline 4) are discussed as follows.

Efficient collaboration between architects and EA stakeholders is one of the main critical success factors for EA. Van Der Raadt, Schouten and Van Vliet (2008) reported that the basis for efficient collaboration between architects and EA stakeholders is mutual understanding. As big data analytics requires specific skills of stakeholders, any change of EA has to begin with identification of these stakeholders. Among EA stakeholders that are described e.g. in Ahlemann et al (2012), big data analytics should involve service provider who establishes and maintains a computing framework in which certain applications will be executed, and application provider who is responsible for the big data analytics lifecycle management and the execution of related activities using platforms, tools and services. This stakeholder is important because of the big data analytics complexity and the required level of technical skills to work with these data. Strategic planning is an important component since it motivates EA choices (Lake and Drake, 2014; Romero and Vernadat, 2016). This process was explored by many practitioners and researchers who suggest that it should be constantly monitored and evaluated to ensure the agility and adaptability of EA. Big data analytics is always solved in the context of project management. There are also various roadmap alternatives that address the differences between implementation of selected components. The basic layers of EA defined by TOGAF are highlighted in Fig. 3. Furthermore, some interviewees were skeptical about the cost model. Especially the lack of knowledge and skills of employees and the need to recruit new employees may cause problems. On the other hand, the use of computing resources in the cloud is recognized as a way to store large amounts of data and decrease cost for a data center.

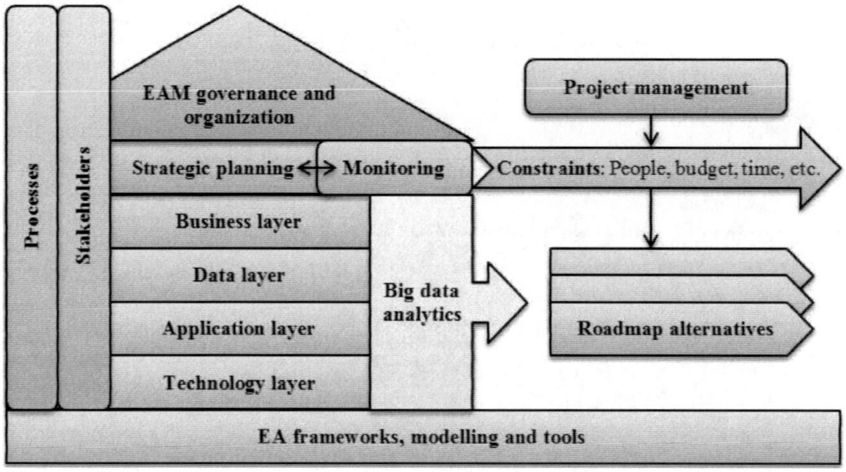

Figure 3 Strategic alignment and relationships of big data analytics in business ecosystem [authors]

Fig. 4 shows the requirements of big data analytics for EA layers. The change in EA represented by big data analytics affects all the layers defined by TOGAF. For business architecture it means that the principles of agility and adaptability should be followed by EA. Since every organization has to face competition and a changing digital development landscape, these principles can ensure that the benefits of new ICT will be recognized. The data architecture requires new components that fulfil the characteristics of 6Vs. The application architecture needs to be prepared for specific platforms, tools and services, such as those listed in Lněnička and Komárková (2015) or Pääkkönen and Pakkala (2015). Technology architecture offers computing resources for both data and application architecture. It is recommended to use distributed and cloud computing resources (Lake and Drake, 2014). Infrastructure has to be managed and monitored with related tools. Interfaces and modules ensure that every module works the same way and data are accurately collected, transmitted and stored.

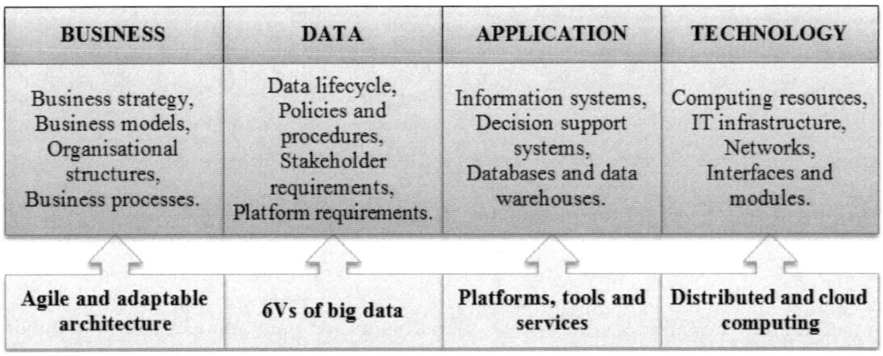

Figure 4 Mapping requirements of big data analytics on EA layers of TOGAF [authors]

The identified components of big data analytics for strategic management of EA are shown in Fig. 5. Both strategic management of EA and big data analytics try to deliver value through the efficient work with business data. Components of business architecture are framed within the goals and skills of stakeholders, which result in a strategy. Big data business models then shape the requirements for other architectures. Big data analytics requires specific data lifecycle phases and activities. The basic of them are presented in this paper, while the others can be found in Demchenko, De Laat and Membrey (2014) or Lněnička and Komárková (2015). The most widely used batch processing framework is an open-source Apache Hadoop, which is based on MapReduce by Google. For real-time or stream processing, there is Apache Storm. Because of large amounts of data, new databases such as NoSQL or NewSQL, and distributed file systems have to be implemented. Their functions then affect the processes. Finally, technology architecture has to be secure, scalable, reliable and available to provide resources for applications and data. It should also help to eliminate possible threats such as cyberattacks.

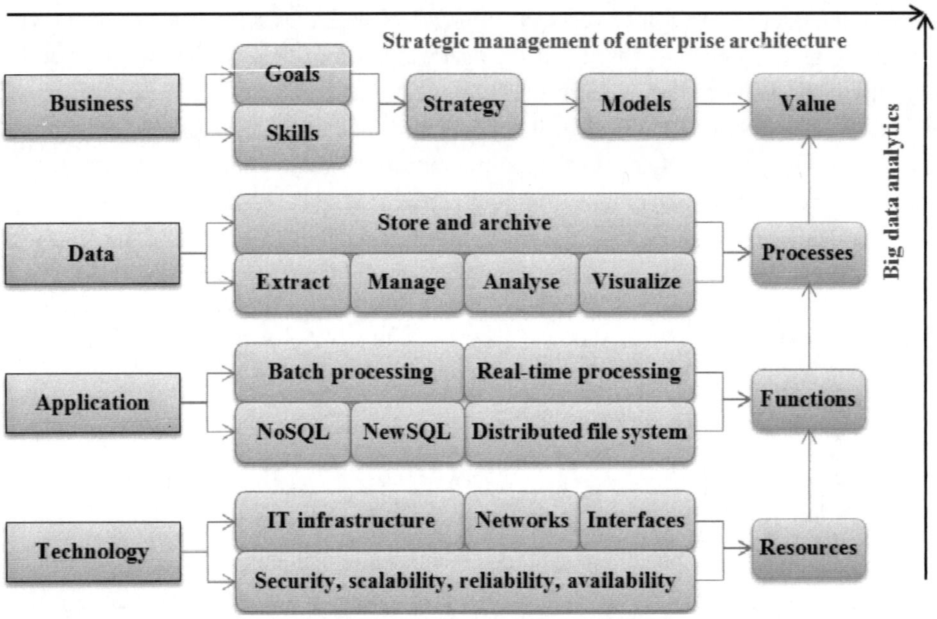

Figure 5 Model containing components of big data analytics for strategic management of EA [authors]

5 Discussion and Limitations

Apart from big data analytics, there are also other technologies that may initiate the change of EA. Romero and Vernadat (2016) discussed the Internet-of-Things and its role in terms of creating new or extending the abilities of existing devices or business model innovations by enabling new forms of creating and capturing value. Integration of business data with open data is another emerging field of value creation (Lněnička and Komárková, 2015). In this regard, the importance of EA's agility and adaptability has to be emphasized again. Further, when it comes to the manufacturing industry, the combination of industrial and digital technologies and business model innovations have created the Industry 4.0 vision, of a distributed global and virtual manufacturing factory of the future (Romero and Vernadat, 2016). On the other hand, not all organizations are prepared for the use of big data analytics as the maturity of their EA is low. Therefore, Lagerström et al (2011) provided a set of items (questions) to assess the maturity level of EA activities.

There are also some limitations in our work. First, the design components are most probably not stable over time but will change, either over the time of application within one organization or in dependency of some other aspect (Aier, Gleichauf and Winter, 2011). Moreover, it needs to be noted that the set of big data analytics components cannot be explained fully by our results. There is no information about how these components interact with each other in a specific business environment. This issue will be investigated in future research, according to the last three steps defined by Hevner et al (2004). Finally, since different EA stakeholder groups pursue different goals related to their specific role within the organization, it may be difficult to satisfy all stakeholders (Van Der Raadt, Schouten and Van Vliet, 2008).

6 Conclusion

Our principal contribution is a systematic approach dealing with the composition of architecture layers, components and relationships within agile and adaptable EA for big data analytics, by means of strategic management. In our paper, we applied the DSR approach to gain better understanding of EA's strategic management through analysis of existing literature to build more agile and adaptable EA and identify components that capture the requirements of big data analytics. The novelty in our paper comprises new aspects for mapping benefits of big data analytics in the context of architecture layers of the existing EA framework TOGAF.

The results of this study showed that it is important for executive decision-makers as well as developers and designers to understand how the requirements of big data analytics influence the strategic management of EA. A subsequent deeper evaluation and extension of our approach is planned as future work.

Acknowledgements

This research is supported by University of Pardubice, SGS_2017_17 project.

References

Ahlemann, F., Stettiner, E., Messerschmidt, M. and Legner, C. (2012). *Strategic Enterprise Architecture Management: Challenges, Best Practices, and Future Developments*. Berlin Heidelberg: Springer-Verlag.

Aier, S., Gleichauf, B. and Winter, R. (2011). 'Understanding Enterprise Architecture Management Design – An Empirical Analysis'. *Proceedings of the 10th International Conference on Wirtschaftsinformatik*, Zurich, Switzerland, pp. 645-654.

Buckl, S., Dierl, T., Matthes, F. and Schweda, C. M. (2010). 'Building Blocks for Enterprise Architecture Management Solutions'. *Proceedings of Second Working Conference, PRET 2010*, Delft, The Netherlands, pp. 17-46.

Demchenko, Y., De Laat, C. and Membrey, P. (2014). 'Defining architecture components of the Big Data Ecosystem'. *Proceedings of 2014 International Conference on Collaboration Technologies and Systems (CTS)*, Minneapolis, USA, pp. 104-112.

Hevner, A. R., March, S. T., Park, J. and Ram, S. (2004). 'Design science in information systems research'. *MIS quarterly*, 28 (1), pp. 75-105.

Lagerström, R., Sommestad, T., Buschle, M. and Ekstedt, M. (2011). 'Enterprise Architecture Management's Impact on Information Technology Success'. *Proceedings of the 44th Hawaii International Conference on System Sciences*, Koloa, Hawaii, pp. 1-10.

Lake, P. and Drake, R. (2014). *Information Systems Management in the Big Data Era*. Cham: Springer International Publishing.

Lněnička, M. and Komárková, J. (2015). 'The Impact of Cloud Computing and Open (Big) Data on the Enterprise Architecture Framework'. *Proceedings of the 26th International Business Information Management Association Conference*, Madrid, Spain, pp. 1679-1683.

Pääkkönen, P. and Pakkala, D. (2015). 'Reference Architecture and Classification of Technologies, Products and Services for Big Data Systems'. *Big Data Research*, 2 (4), pp. 166-186.

Romero, D. and Vernadat, F. (2016). 'Enterprise information systems state of the art: Past, present and future trends'. *Computers in Industry*, 79, pp. 3-13.

Shah, H. and El Kourdi, M. (2007). 'Frameworks for Enterprise Architecture'. *IT Professional*, 9 (5), pp. 36-41.

Tiwana, A. (2014). *Platform Ecosystems: Aligning Architecture, Governance, and Strategy*. Waltham: Morgan Kaufmann.

The Open Group (2009). *TOGAF Version 9: The Open Group Architecture Framework (TOGAF)*. The Open Group.

Van Der Raadt, B., Schouten, S. and Van Vliet, H. (2008). 'Stakeholder Perception of Enterprise Architecture'. *Proceedings of Second European Conference, ECSA 2008,* Paphos, Cyprus, pp. 19-34.

Zimmermann, A., et al. (2014). 'Adaptable Enterprise Architectures for Software Evolution of Smart-Life Ecosystems'. *Proceedings of the 2014 IEEE 18th International Enterprise Distributed Object Computing Conference Workshops and Demonstrations*, Ulm, Germany, pp. 316-323.

The Current State of Big Data Platform Implementation in Slovak and Czech Companies

Eva Menčlová[1], Lukáš Falát[2], Dušan Marček[3]

Abstract. In this paper we analyze the current situation regarding Big Data technologies in Slovak and Czech companies. The first part of the paper deals with the theoretical background of big data as well as with the motivation, i.e. why it is useful to implement Big Data technologies in a company. To analyze the current situation about Big Data we apply interrogatory method. We apply this interrogatory to multiple working areas. We perform the analysis of answers to find out that even though Big Data is relatively known term for respondents, very little subjects have these technologies implemented in their companies. These statements are confirmed by hypothesis testing. Finally, we present the use of this information for the future.

Keywords: big data, interrogatory, data, business intelligence, survey, Slovak, Czech.

JEL Classification: D80, C12

1 Introduction

In the past few years, the Internet of Things (IoT) has entered the public consciousness (Delgado, 2016). The concept of IoT aims to take a wide range of "things" and turn them into smart objects — anything from watches to fridges, cars and train tracks. Products that normally wouldn't be connected to the Internet and able to obtain and process data, are equipped with sensors and computer chips for data gathering. However, these chips are used mostly for gathering data that indicates customer usage patterns and product performance. Organizations are grabbing hold of the data around them, and the IoT is acting as a major source for that data. The IoT is essentially the means that collects and sends data. Information from IoT devices resides in big data and is measured against it. Very soon IoT will likely touch every aspect of our lives (Delgado, 2016).

Big data and the IoT basically go hand in hand and are almost made for each other. It's not just that big data and the IoT help each other, they also greatly impact each other. By the year 2020, the Internet of Things will generate a stunning 4.4 trillion GB of data in the world. It is no surprise as by 2020, tens of billions of devices and sensors will have some type of connection to the internet. All of these devices will be gathering, analyzing, sharing, and transmitting data, all in real time. Without that data, IoT devices would simply not have the same functions and capabilities that have caused them to gain so much worldwide attention. The more the Internet of Things grows, the more demands are placed on businesses' big data capabilities. (Kushmaro, 2016)

[1] Eva Menčlová, Department of Applied Informatics, VŠB-Technical University of Ostrava, Sokolská 33, 701 21 0strava, Czech Republic, e-mail: Dusan.Marcek@vsb.cz

[2] Lukáš Falát, Department of Macro and Microeconomy, Faculty of Management Science and Informatics, University of Žilina, Univerzitná 8215/1, 010 26 Žilina.

[3] Dušan Marček, Department of Applied Informatics, VŠB-Technical University of Ostrava, Sokolská 33, 701 21 0strava, Czech Republic, e-mail: Dusan.Marcek@vsb.cz

The drive to incorporate more big data within organizations is very powerful one. The use of big data analytics has grown tremendously in just the past few years. (Delgado, 2016). The amount of electronically stored data is increasing and this trend is supposed to continue in the future. According to study from 2011 performed by IDC (Chakraborty et al., 2013) the digital world produced 1.8 zettabytes of data in 2011; moreover, till 2020 the amount of data is supposed to grow by more than fifty times.

With the increased amount of data, the need to work and analyze these data is necessary. The analysis of big data is applied in many areas, e.g. monitoring social networks, telecommunication, banking industry, healthcare, information technology (IT) etc. In telecommunication big data can be used in determining the level of damages due to migration of client to a competitor. In banking industry, it is good to determine the most profitable product or the appropriate product for a specified client, or for modeling risk. In healthcare, there is the need for analyzing data sent from sensors as well as the need for analyzing historical patients' claims. The analysis of big data is also important in the area of information technologies, where these data are used for example for controlling the system (Zikopoulos and Deroos, 2013). On base of stated examples, we can state that the need for working with high amount and high volume of data, i.e. with data which are created very fast and in various ways. Overall, this area is called by the term Big Data. Following from the above, the big data problematics is becoming quite "hot" area today.

2 Theoretical Background of Big Data

Data are defined as facts retrieved by reading, observing, measuring, calculating, weighting, animating etc. Data are understood as the expression of knowledge and facts in a form which is appropriate for another processing, expressing ideas and facts in defined form so that it would be possible to transfer and process objectively processing reality on selected medium. In other words, the term data can be understood as the professional term for numbers, text, audio, video as well as other sensible perceptions (Pozar, 2010).

Information is data to which the receiver attributes sense. This sense is attributed according to his knowledge, experiences and wisdoms. Moreover, information decreases the level of entropy regarding his necessities and demands (Vymetal et al., 2005). Following from that, every information is data, however, whatever stored data is not information. The relation between these two terms can be expressed according to the relationship of set and subset (Pozar, 2010).

The use of relevant information in practical activity is defined as knowledge. Whereas information is the result of data interpretation on base of individual abilities, values and wisdoms, knowledge, on the other hand, is the result of active learning.

For successful companies it is important to get data and to transform them into information and knowledge (Pozar, 2010). For this purpose, plenty of methodologies and technologies are used. In IT this problematic is often connected with term such as Business Intelligence and Big Data.

Business Intelligence is defined as processes, technologies and tools, which are needed for transforming data into information, information into knowledge and knowledge into plans enabling the realization of an action which supports the accomplishment of primary goals of the organization (Arnost, 2007).

In this definition, data are understood as the unprocessed set which is used for another calculation and processing. Data can be collected, saved and processed, however, they cannot be given into context from which another sense can be derived. The term information denotes the result of processing and organization of data which then creates relations between data entries and provides their sense and context. Understanding the sense of information on base of sense and pattern recognition is called the knowledge.

Gartner company, which was founded in 1979, focuses on consulting services and for the realization of surveys in the area of information technologies. According to current definition defined by this company, Big Data are information assets characterized by big volume, big velocity and big variety, which need efficient an innovative forms of information processing for better understanding and decision-making process (Gartner, 2015).

The issue of Big Data was firstly defined in 2001 in the paper called "3-D Data Management: Controlling Data Volume, Velocity and Variety", by Doug Laney from META Group, Inc. In this paper (Laney, 2001). Big Data are characterized by 3V characteristics, i.e. Volume, Velocity and Variety. Today, there is also an extended definition of Big Data, e.g. IBM extends this basic concept by fourth V called veracity (Zikopoulos and Deroos, 2013).

Volume – today, big amount of data is being processed. Also, the beat of their creation is always increasing. Currently, it is not sufficient to measure volumes of data in terabyte; the measurement is starting to be defined in petabytes. Whereas in 2005 there was circa 1.3 billion of RFID (Radio Frequency Identification) chipsets in the World, in 2011 their amount was increased to 30 billion. With the increased number of RFID chipsets, the amount of data is increasing as well.

The reason for variety of Big Data is due to the effort to catch all data which can be helpful in decision-making process. The need for analyzing unstructured data (e.g. comments on Facebook) is growing. This analysis does not have to be connected only with texted data. For example, TerraEchos developed the system for classification of audios.

Velocity is, in context of Big Data, understood as the time which was needed for getting data into company where data are processed. Fast data analysis is important in many areas, e.g. in healthcare in analyzing the patient hood, in finance in analyzing messages from markets; according to some studies (Zikopoulos and Deroos, 2013) it is possible to analyze five million of messages from financial markets in one second.

3 Research

As we stated in Introduction, the reason for implementing Big Data platform in a company is due to transforming data into knowledge which could be used for more effective decision-making process. However, in order to suggest methodology for implementation Big Data platform into Slovak and Czech companies, we need to know the current state. Therefore, the analysis of the current state was performed. This analysis focused on finding the current level of knowledge regarding Big Data, the use of Big Data and the implementation of Big Data platform in selected Slovak and Czech companies.

The analysis was performed by the method of interrogatory. The focus is on finding if the term Big Data is known in Slovak and Czech companies and whether the Slovak and Czech Companies work with Big Data, which area was solved using these techniques and whether users experienced some problems in implementation Big Data platform. In order to get results and insights from the interrogatory we used the hypothesis testing.

3.1 Interrogatory Method

As for interrogatory method we sent 1323 demands regarding the filling of interrogatories on the Big Data topics. Categories of companies, to which these interrogatories were addressed, as well as formulated hypothesis and questions were set on base of literature regarding Big Data (Zikopoulos and Deroos, 2013) and on base of similar interrogatory surveys.

The interrogatory was created in a way so that the receiver would not be able to answer questions which are not relevant to them. For example, if the responder answered that they did not meet with the term Big Data, other questions regarding Big Data were skipped. So they did not answer questions what they thought about the term Big Data or whether they use Big Data technologies in their company. The interrogatory was created with Google Docs, where the dynamic customization of questions was possible. Thanks to this, questions to which respondent was not to express their opinion, were not shown to them.

3.2 Methodology

The research was realized during April, 2014 and May 2014. The request regarding the filling of questionnaire was sent to 1323 respondents, at which 735 were from the Czech Republic and 588 were from Slovakia. We used email and web formularies to collect our answers.

Our demand was to request at least 50 companies from every area (manufacturing organizations, sales organizations, telecommunication, IT, transport and logistics, education institutions, administrative or government, healthcare, finance sector, utilities) in the Czech Republic as well as in Slovakia. Contacts were searched using internet pages such as http://www.firmy.cz/, http://www.zlatestranky.cz/, http://seznamnemocnic.blogspot.com/, http://www.banky.cz/, http://firmy.sk/, http://greenpages.spectator.sme.sk/sk.html, http://www.itnews.sk/katalog-it-firiem, http://ministerstva.urad-online.sk/, http://katastralny.urad-online.sk/. The request for filling out the formulary was sent to searched companies. The formulary was available on the following link: https://docs.google.com/forms/d/1s1k9lJ_JwaFP9s-E2nuukGvG_AD-FaO821p8UpHUZkXw/viewform.

We sent our request using either email or using contact formulary which was present on their webpages. It is probable that we were not able to address all 1323 respondents; the message could be categorized as spam and the receiver was not able to read it. Also, some email addresses could be dead or questions from some contact formularies might not be checked. However, we were not able to check if our request was really delivered correctly.

3.3 Hypotheses Definition

Before the interrogatory itself, hypotheses were formulated. These hypotheses were then verified on base of results from interrogatories. We defined two hypotheses.

Regarding the fact that according to survey performed by EMC 64 % of answering subjects accepted with the fact that Big Data result in better business decision-making, we can assume that our answering subjects know the term Big Data. Therefore, the first hypothesis is:

1st hypothesis: More than 60 % of respondents understand the term Big Data

In survey performed by Gartner it was found out that less than 8 % of respondents use Big Data technologies in practice. Therefore, we can suppose that in Slovakia and in the Czech Republic these technologies are used by less than 10 % of respondents.

2nd hypothesis: Tools for Big Data are used by less than 10 % of respondents

4 Findings and Results

78 respondents answered the interrogatory. 40 out of them (i.e. 51 % of respondents who answered the interrogatory) use some tools of Business Intelligence, 34 (i.e. 44 % of respondents who answered the interrogatory) do not use any of them and 4 respondents did not know if there were any tools of Business Intelligence in their company.

The term Big Data was known to 45 respondents (58 % of respondents who answered the interrogatory), 33 respondents do not even know this term (i.e. 42 % of respondents who answered the interrogatory). Answering the question "What do you think about Big Data?" 19 respondents answered that the work with Big Data would certainly become the significant trend in the future, 12 respondents were of the opinion that the work with Big Data could become significant trend, however, it is soon to evaluate this claim. 6 respondents believed that the work with Big Data will become the necessary condition to be successful in an area. Only 4 respondents believed that Big Data is only a marketing term without practical sense.

Respondents were also asked for whether some technologies for working with Big Data are used in their companies. 8 subjects answered this question in a positive way (4 respondents use tools from IBM company, 3 of them use tools from Microsoft, three others from Oracle, 2 subjects from SAP, one respondent uses tools from SAS Institute, another one from T-System, another one from Teradata, another one from Cloudera, another one from HP).

As for the area where subjects use Big Data tools, four respondents use Big Data tools in marketing, three respondents use them in controlling, three other use them in research and development, three in sales, two in human resources and one respondent uses the Big Data tools in Fraud management.

As for contributions due to Big Data usage in the company, five respondents stated the higher efficiency of processes and decrease of costs, better decision-making was stated three times, better understanding of customers' needs as well as better targeting of marketing campaign and better risk detection were stated two times, higher sales numbers and better use of available information were stated once. These respondents worked in following areas: five of them worked in IT, two in telecommunication and one in education institution. As for the company headquarters, five respondents had the headquarters in the Czech Republic, two in Slovakia and one respondent stated it was the multinational company.

Regarding the fact that Big Data are defined by 3V attributes (Volume, Velocity, Variety) respondents were also questioned which of these areas they solved. The need for analyzing various data was stated five times (sometimes even unstructured), fast analysis was stated three times and the ability to work with high-volume data was stated two times.

In the section "Problems with implementation" technical problems and high costs were stated three time, non-appropriate area of use for Big Data was stated two times, deficiency of external experts and non-adequate analytical knowledge of the company was stated once; two respondents did not exhibit any problems regarding Big Data implementation.

Respondents also expressed their opinion to the question if the Big Data implementation met their expectations. One respondent answered that the implementation fulfilled their expectation to the fullest, four respondents stated that this implementation met their expectations overall and three subjects answered that the implementation met their expectation only partially.

As for respondents who use Big Data, three respondents think about another expansion of these Big Data tools and were in the phase of implementation. Three respondents were planning the expansion in one year, one respondent in five years. One respondents did not think about Big Data expansion.

Respondents, who were not using Big Data at that time, were asked if they thought about implementation of Big Data tools into the company. One respondent stated they were in the phase of implementation, two others planned to implement these technologies in one year, four respondents in 2 years, three in five years. 27 respondents did not even consider the Big Data implementation.

Respondents planned to use Big Data tools in following areas: seven time in controlling, three time for marketing purposes, two times in human resources, one time for logistics. Respondent stated they needed to solve these problems with Big Data tools: Eight times they stated analysis of various data, five times they stated the need for fast data analysis, the necessity to work with high-volume data was stated three times.

As for reasons why some respondents did not use the Big Data technologies: Twenty of them stated there were not appropriate areas where Big Data technologies could be used, twelve subjects stated there were other problems to solve in that time, non-adequate technical knowledge in the company was stated six times, non-adequate analytical knowledge and high costs were stated three times and deficiency of external experts was stated once

As for the structure of respondents according to particular working areas, the areas of government (19 respondents) and IT (15 respondents) were the most frequent areas. Healthcare was represented by 8 respondents, logistics by six, manufacturing by five as well as telecommunications, sales, finance, utility and education were represented by four respondents each, three respondents were from other areas.

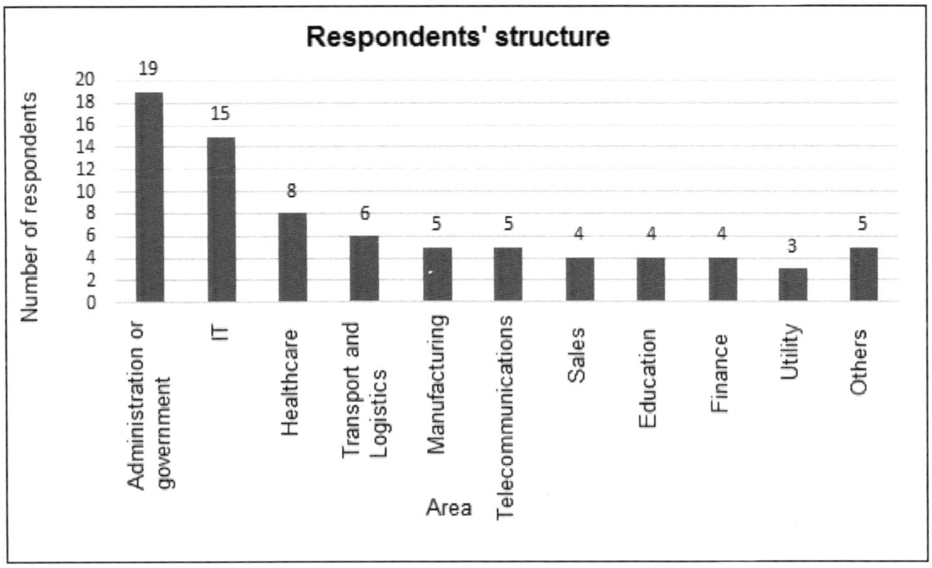

Figure 1 Respondents' structure

The structure of respondents regarding the headquarters of the company was as follows: 56 respondents (72 %) stated the headquarters was in Czechia, twenty respondents stated their headquarters was in Slovakia, two other stated "other".

4.1 Hypotheses Evaluation

Any assumption about parameters or shape of distribution of investigated character is called statistical hypothesis. To decide about correctness or incorrectness of hypothesis would be possible based on investigation of the whole population. However, such investigation would be not very economical (or technically impossible), therefore the investigation is realized only on a small size of the whole population known as sample. This sample is then used to decide whether the hypothesis is correct. The process of verification of correctness or incorrectness of hypothesis using results which were realized by random sample is called as hypothesis testing. The assumption regarding any characteristics which was defined is called as null hypothesis and is denoted as H_0. The alternative hypothesis is the opposite of the null hypothesis, is denoted as H_1 and it denies the formulation defined by null hypothesis.

In hypothesis testing the following procedure is used:

1) hypothesis formulation – we define the null hypothesis and alternative hypothesis.
2) the selection of testing criteria – testing criteria is the statistics (function of selection)
3) the construction of critical set – the set of values the testing criteria can have is called the sample space. The sample space can be divided into two subspaces. The subspace which contains values that is in account of H_0 is called as the set of acceptance. The subspace which contains values that are in account of H_1 is called as the critical definition set. Critical values separate these two subspaces.
4) Calculation of the value of testing criteria
5) Formulation of summaries

Two possible outcomes from hypothesis testing are:

a) the value of testing criteria lies within the critical definition set, the alternative hypothesis H1 is approved by test,
b) the value of testing criteria lies within the acceptance set, the alternative hypothesis H1 is not accepted by the test.

In our research, hypotheses were evaluated using relative frequency hypothesis test (Hindls et al., 2007). The basic assumption of following test is the Normal distribution of the sample. Within this test we tested that relative frequency of the characteristics π equaled to specified number π_0 . The null hypothesis was defined as follows:

$$H_0: \pi = \pi_0 \tag{1}$$

Testing criteria U was defined as

$$U = \frac{p-\pi_0}{\sqrt{\frac{\pi_0(1-\pi_0)}{n}}}, \tag{2}$$

where p was sampled relative frequency of given characteristics and n was the range of the sample.

For particular alternative hypothesis H_1 on 95 % significance level critic borders were as follows:

$$H_1: \pi < \pi_0, U \leq -1.645 \tag{3}$$

$$H_1: \pi > \pi_0, U \geq 1.645 \tag{4}$$

For testing the first hypothesis (Big Data term is understood by more than 60 % of respondents) following calculation is applied:

$$H_0: \pi = 0,6 \text{ (according to 1)}$$

$$H_1: \pi < 0,6 \text{ (according to 3)}$$

To question „Have you ever met the term Big data?" answered positively 45 respondents out of 78. Therefore, in this test, the calculation was

$$n = 78, p = \frac{45}{78}, p = 0,577 \tag{5}$$

Testing criteria U is then calculated as

$$U = \frac{0,577 - 0,6}{\sqrt{\frac{0,6 \cdot 0,4}{78}}}, \; U = -0.415 \tag{6}$$

Regarding the fact that the value -0.415 was larger than -1.645, we could conclude that this value did not fall into the critic part and hence, we did not deny the null hypothesis on 95 % significance level. We could not deny the claim that Big Data term was understood by more than 60 % of respondents.

Test of the second hypothesis

For testing the second hypothesis ("The tools for Big Data are used by less than 10 % of respondents), the following calculation was applied:

$$H_0 : \pi = 0{,}1 \tag{7}$$

$$H_1 : \pi > 0.1 \tag{8}$$

Eight respondents answer „yes" to the question: "Do you already use Big Data technologies in your company?", i.e.

$$n = 78,\ p = \frac{8}{78},\ p = 0.103 \tag{9}$$

Testing criteria U was then calculated as

$$U = \frac{0{,}103 - 0{,}1}{\sqrt{\frac{0{,}1 \cdot 0{,}9}{78}}},\ U = 0.088 \tag{10}$$

With regard to the fact that the value 0.088 was less than 1.645, we could state that it did not belong to the critic scope. On 95 % significance level we therefore did not deny the null hypothesis claiming that the Big Data tools were used by less than 10 % of respondents.

Discussion

Following from the interrogatory, it is obvious that the term Big Data is not an unknown term among the respondents; to 58 % of subjects this term was known. Moreover, we can observe the correlation between the reality whether users use tools of Business Intelligence and their knowledge of Big Data term. The interrogatory method confirmed that users from Big Data areas need to work with various data. Another interesting fact is that the respondents who use technologies for working with Big Data see the main contribution in decreasing costs and increased effectivity of processes. Also, we found out that the large part of respondents state the Big Data technologies are inappropriate to set in their company is the reason for not using these technologies. Moreover, another reason for not using Big Data platform is that the company had other, more important problems to solve. However, these reasons are very disputable. One reason for these statements could be that the users are not familiar with all possibilities where Big Data could be helpful in a company.

5 Conclusion

To conclude the most important facts coming out from our survey are as follows:

- 48 % of respondents who answered the interrogatory think Big Data will very probably become a trend in the future
- 15 % of respondents who answered the interrogatory think Big Data will become a necessary thing to be successful in business
- Today, for implementing Big Data companies use mainly products of IBM, Microsoft and Oracle.
- Big Data is used today mainly in marketing, controlling and human resources (HR).
- The main reasons why companies use Big Data are higher effectivity, lower costs, better decision-making and better understanding of customer needs

- The main problems in implementing Big Data are technical problems and deficiency of external experts
- 55 % of companies which do not use Big Data today, do not even see an appropriate use of these technologies in their company
- 73 % of companies which do not use Big Data today, do not even plan to implement these technologies into their companies in the future
- Almost 33 % of companies which do not use Big Data today, have to solve many operational problems and do not have sources to implement Big Data technologies
- Only 12 % of subjects who have Big Data implemented in their company, do not plan to extend the application of these technologies in the future; i.e. more than 87 % of companies with implemented Big Data plan to extends these technologies in the future

Even though findings from the interrogatory are interesting and helpful, it is necessary to say that the results of these surveys are always influenced by plenty of factors, e.g. the selection of respondents and willingness of respondents to fill out the interrogatory. For example, according to the findings of our survey it is obvious that the term Big Data is quite known as 58 % of people answered they had already met with it. However, we can suppose that mainly people keen on this topic were interested to fill out this survey. Despite the facts stated above we are of the opinion that this survey can be used for another work in this area. On base of this interrogatory method we can state two pieces of knowledge which are important for working with Big Data. The first one is the need to work with various types of data. The second one is the fact that quite lots of people stated there was not any areas in the company where Big Data could be used. However, we believe that opinions of these respondents could be influenced by not deep knowledge of Big Data; users do not know exactly what offer Big Data technologies.

In next paper we would like to focus on application of Big Data. We would like to suggest the solution how to work with Big Data technologies and how to use them in a specific company. We would like to demonstrate that the Big Data area can be helpful even for companies which are not persuaded about appropriateness of using Big Data in their companies.

Acknowledgements

This paper was supported within Operational Programme Education for Competitiveness – Project No. CZ.1.07/2.3.00/20.0296.

References

Arnošt, D. et al. (2007). *Business Intelligence*. Praha: Tate International.

Chakraborty, G., Pagolu, M. and Garla, S. (2013). *Text Mining and Analysis: Practical Methods, Examples, and Case Studies Using SAS*. SAS Institute.

Delgado, R. (2016). Big Data and The Internet of Things: A Match Made in Heaven, KD Nuggets, [Online]. Available at: www.kdnuggets.com/2016/09/big-data-iot-match-made-heaven.html.

Gartner, Inc. (2015). What Is Big Data - Gartner IT Glossary, [Online]. Available at: http://www.gartner.com/it-glossary/big-data [cited 2015-05-12].

Hindls, R. et al (2007). *Statistika pro ekonomy*. Praha: Professional Publishing.

Kushmaro, P. (2016). The IoT and Big Data: Making The Connection, Huffington Post, [Online]. Available at: www.huffingtonpost.com/philip-kushmaro/the-iot-and-big-data-maki_b_12116608.html.

Laney, D. (2001). 3-D Data Management: Controlling Data Volume, Velocity and Variety, [Online]. Available at:

http://blogs.gartner.com/doug-laney/files/2012/01/ad949-3D-Data-Management-Controlling-Data-Volume-Velocity-and-Variety.pdf [cited 2017-04-19].

Požár, J. (2010). *Manažerská informatika.* Plzeň: Vydavatelství a nakladatelství Aleš Čeněk, s.r.o.

Vymětal, J., Diačiková, A. and Váchová, M. (2005). *Informační a znalostní management v praxi.* LexisNexis CZ s.r.o.

Zikopoulos, P. and Deroos, D. (2013). *Harness the Power of Big Data - The IBM Big Data Platform.* New York: McGraw-Hill.

Process Support of Information Security according to COBIT®5

Jan Ministr[1], Tomas Pitner[2]

Abstract. Today Information security forms the basic property information system. The methodological framework COBIT®5 provides comprehensive support for implementing information security lifecycle of IT in organizations. COBIT®5 is very comprehensive method and for untrained users quite confusing. The article is therefore initially focused on explaining the basic structure of the methodological framework, which is built on five pillars and related enablers. Furthermore, the article describes the process structure of the methodology and its support for information security. The conclusion discusses the question of applicability of the approach to ensure information security in different types of organizations.

Keywords: Information security, Information security management system, methodology, framework, stakeholder, life cycle.

JEL Classification: M15

1 Introduction

The significance of information and related technologies is increasing in every aspect of business and public life, the need to reduce information risk, which includes protecting information and related IT assets from ever-changing threats, is constantly intensifying (Hunka, Belunek, 2015). Increasing regulation within the business landscape adds to the awareness of the board of directors of the criticality of information security for information and IT-related assets (Pochyla, 2015).

ISACA defines the information security as "Ensures that within the enterprise, information is protected against disclosure to unauthorized users (confidentiality), improper modification (integrity) and non-access when required (availability)." This definition covers the confidentiality, integrity and availability and forms the CIA concept where (ISACA, 2012a):

- *Confidentiality* means preserving authorized restrictions on access and disclosure, including means for protecting privacy and proprietary information.
- *Integrity* means guarding against improper information modification or destruction, and includes ensuring information non-repudiation and authenticity.
- *Availability* means ensuring timely and reliable access to and use of information.

Ensuring the security of information systems is nowadays one of the main tasks of designers and operators of information technology. This aspect of the information system is necessary to catch throughout the frame of project life cycle of information system. One of the methodological frameworks that comprehensively covers the entire life cycle of information systems development including information security is COBIT®5 (ISACA. 2012b)

[1] VSB – Technical University of Ostrava / Faculty of Economics, Department of Applied Informatics, Sokolská třída 33, 702 00, Ostrava 1, Czech Republic, jan.ministr@vsb.cz

[2] Masaryk University / Faculty of Informatics, Department of Computer Systems and Communications, Botanická 554/68a, 604 00 Brno, tomp@fi.muni.cz

Implementation of information security principles according COBIT®5 brings to stakeholders next capabilities (ISACA, 2010):

- *Up-to-date view* on information security governance and management thought alignment with standards of IT governance initiatives (ISO - International Organization for Standardization, IEC – International Electrotechnical Commission 38500, ISF - Information Security Forum and others).
- *Clear distinction between governance and management* on base of identification and clarify of the roles of governance and management in processes.
- *End-to-end view* through the entire process model of information security that integrates both business and IT functional responsibilities. It provides to separate the information security governance from management practices of information security in clear way.
- *Holistic guidance* that gives emphasis not only on processes but also to all enablers, including information, structures culture, policies and their interdependence.

The implementation of the above capabilities into live cycle of information system forms the basis for the creation and operation of information system, including of its information security (ISACA, 2011).

2 Information security background in COBIT®5

Information security according COBIT®5 is based on the same 5 principles as the COBIT®5 framework (ISACA, 2010), which are:

1) *Meeting the stakeholder needs where information security is one of major need, which converted into the related goals of information security of enterprise (Danel et al., 2012).*
2) *Covering the enterprise end-to end, i.e. all stakeholders, functions and processes within the enterprise that are relevant for information security (Hunka, 2015).*
3) *Applying a single, integrated framework that covers the complete enterprise. It provides a base for integrate other frameworks, standards and used practices by effectively way which allows the enterprise to use it as overarching governance and management framework (Kučera and Pitner, 2013).*
4) *Enabling a holistic approach that takes into account several interacting components by help of set enablers to support the implementation of information security as shows the figure 1. Enablers are factors, which have influence (individually or collectively) on information security governance and they are driven by the goals cascade, i.e. higher level of IT-related goals define what the different enablers should achieve (Kozel and Chuchrová, 2015). Enterprise enablers have the following meaning:*
   a) *Principles, processes and frameworks are the vehicles to translate the desired behavior into practical guidance for day-to-day management.*
   b) *Processes describe an organized set of practices and activities to achieve certain objectives and produce a set of outputs in support of achieving overall IT-related goals.*
   c) *Organizational structures are the key decision-making entities in an enterprise.*
   d) *Culture, ethic and behavior relate to individuals and the enterprise and are often underestimated as a success factor in governance and management activities.*

e) *Information deals with all information produced and used by the enterprise.*
f) *Services, infrastructure and applications that provide the enterprise with IT processing and services (ISACA, 2013b).*
g) *People, skills and competencies are linked to people required for successful completion of all activities for making correct decisions and taking corrective actions.*

5) *Separating governance from management makes a clear difference between governance and management where (Vitouš, 2013):*
   a) *Governance ensures that needs of stakeholders, conditions and options are evaluated to determine balanced and agreed enterprise objectives which to be achieved through prioritization, decision making, monitoring performance and compliance with agreed direction of objectives (ISACA, 2013a).*
   b) *Management plans, builds, runs and monitors activities in alignment with the direction set by the governance body to achieve the enterprise objectives.*

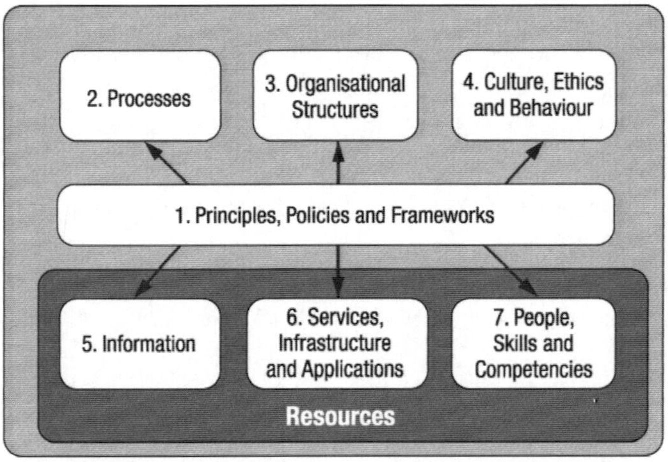

Figure 1 COBIT®5 Enterprise enablers [Bernard, 2012]

The enablers in COBIT®5 have four dimensions, which are:

1) *Stakeholders when each enabler has stakeholders which can be internal or external to the enterprise, all having their own (something conflicting) interests and needs.*
2) *Goals where each enabler has a number of goals (expected outcomes) which are divided into different categories which are:*
   - *Intrinsic quality that defines the extent to which enablers provide accurate, objective and reputable results (ISACA, 2011).*
   - *Contextual quality that defines the extent outcomes of the enablers are fit for purpose given the context in which they operate (ISACA, 2012c).*
   - *Access and security that defines the extent of enablers and how they are available (if needed) and how they are secured (Továrňák et al., 2014).*
3) *Life cycle from the beginning of the creation through an operational life until disposal. The phases of life cycle are: plan, design, build/acquire/create/implement, use/operate, evaluate/monitor and update/dispose (ISACA, 2012d).*
4) *Good practices that supports the achievement of the enabler goals. It require all policies to be part of an overall policy framework, providing a hierarchical structure.*

The enablers can be applied in practical situations and can be used to implement effective and efficient information security governance and management in the enterprise (Pitner and Ministr, 2015).

3 Support of information security processes

Governance processes and management processes in COBIT®5 are visible in process reference model that divides 37 processes into 5 categories of domains, which are:

1) *EDM - Evaluate , Direct and Monitor which contains following 5 processes:*
   - *EDM01 Ensure governance framework setting and performance,*
   - *EDM02 Ensure benefits delivery,*
   - *EDM03 Ensure risk optimisation,*
   - *EDM04 Ensure resource optimisation,*
   - *EDM05 Ensure stakeholder transparency.*
2) *APO - Align, Plan and Organise which contains following 13 processes:*
   - *APO01 Manage IT management framework,*
   - *APO02 Manage strategy,*
   - *APO03 Manage enterprise architecture,*
   - *APO04 Manage innovation,*
   - *APO05 Manage portfolio,*
   - *APO06 Manage budget and costs,*
   - *APO07 Manage human resources,*
   - *APO08 Manage relationships,*
   - *APO09 Manage service agreements,*
   - *APO10 Manage suppliers,*
   - *APO11 Manage Quality,*
   - *APO12 Manage risk,*
   - *APO13 Manage security.*
3) *BAI - Build, Acquire and Implement which contains following 10 processes:*
   - *BAI01 Manage programmes and projects,*
   - *BAI02 Manage requirements definition,*
   - *BAI03 Manage solutions identification and build,*
   - *BAI04 Manage availability and capacity,*
   - *BAI05 Manage organizational change enablement,*
   - *BAI06 Manage changes,*
   - *BAI07 Manage change acceptance and transitioning,*
   - *BAI08 Manage knowledge,*
   - *BAI09 Manage assets,*
   - *BAI10 manage configuration.*
4) *DSS - Deliver, Service and Support which contains following 6 processes:*
   - *DSS01 Manage operations,*
   - *DSS02 Manage service request and incidents,*
   - *DSS03 Manage problems,*
   - *DSS04 Manage continuity,*

- *DSS05 Manage security services,*
- *DSS06 Manage business process controls.*

5) *MEA – Monitor, Evaluate and Asses which contains following 3 processes:*
   - *MEA01 Monitor, evaluate and assess performance and conformance,*
   - *MEA02 Monitor, evaluate and assess the system of internal control,*
   - *MEA03 Monitor, evaluate and assess compliance with external requirements.*

Each process is described by attributes that are clearly positioned in two tables for each process as shows the table 2. First table describes Security-specific process goals and metrics and second table describes Security-specific process practices an, input/output and activities.

APO013 Manage security	**Area: Management** **Domain: Align, Plan and Organise**

COBIT®5 Process description
Define, operate and monitor a system for information security

COBIT®5 Process Purpose Statement
Keep the impact and occurrence of information security incidents within the enterprise's appetite levels.

APO13 Security-specific process Goals and metrics

Security-specific process Goals	**Related Metrics**
1. A system is in place that considers and effectively addresses enterprise information security requirements.	▪ Number of key security roles clearly defined ▪ Number of security related incidents
2. A security plan has been established, accepted and communicated throughout the enterprise.	▪ Level of stakeholder satisfaction with the security plan throughout the enterprise ▪ Number of security solutions deviating from the plan ▪ Number of security solutions deviating from the enterprise architecture
3. Information security solutions are implement and operated consistently throughout the enterprise	▪ Number of service with confirmed alignment to the security plan ▪ Number of security incidents caused by non-adherence to the security plan ▪ Number of solutions developed with confirmed alignment to the security plan

Table 1 APO13 – Manage security process – Security-specific goals and metrics [ISACA, 2012]

3.1 Recommended rules of process information security implementation

COBIT®5 is a methodological framework which covers the entire processes of information system life cycle. Therefore, it is necessary to take into account, that it is not enough to introduce only the processes that are directly related to information security (as subprocesses APO13, DSS02, DSS05 etc.). The successful implementation and operation of the ISMS requires to take into account all the principles and enabler of COBIT®5 which are associated with the type of information system and stakeholder requirements on information security. In short, when it is concrete security subprocess implemented, it is also necessary to use common sense and not to implement each information security sub-process into the life cycle, which is unnecessary and inefficient.

APO013 Security-specific Process Practices, Inputs/Outputs and Activities

Management Practice	Security-specific Inputs		Security-specific Outputs	
	From	**Description**	**Description**	**To**
APO13.01 Establish and maintain an information security management system (ISMS) Establish and maintain an ISMS that provides a standard, formal and continuous approach to security management for information, enabling secure technology and business that are aligned with business requirements security management.	Outside COBIT 5 for Information Security	Enterprise security approach	ISMS scope statement ISMS policy	APO01.02 DSS06.03 Internal

Security-specific Activities (in Addition to COBIT®5 Activities)

1. Define the scope and boundaries of the ISMS in terms of characteristics of the enterprise, the organization, its location, assets and technology. Include details of, and justification for, any exclusions from the scope.
2. Define an ISMS in accordance with enterprise policy and aligned with the enterprise, the organization its location, assets and technology
3. Align the ISMS with the overall enterprise approach to the management of security.
4. Obtain management authorization to implement and operate changes the ISMS.
5. Prepare and maintain a statement of applicability that describes the scope of ISMS.
6. Define and communicate information security roles and responsibilities.
7. Communicate the ISMS approach.

Table 2 APO13 – Manage security process – Security-specific Process Practices, Input/Outputs and Activities [ISACA, 2012]

4 Conclusion

Information security is becoming a critical property of information systems in all organizations, including households. COBIT5 provides a very comprehensive manual how to ensure information security.

It is often possible to meet with the opinion that COBIT5 is only suitable for management information systems of large organizations. Authors of the paper, however, believe that it is possible to implement the processes in all organizations regardless of their size. For larger companies, the successful implementation of information security processes depends on the appropriate fulfillment of all principles and skills that COBIT5 provides.

Acknowledgements

This work was supported by Grant "The Research Team for the Modelling of Economics and Financial Processes at VSB-Technical University of Ostrava" with reference number CZ.1.07/2.3.00/20.0296.

References

Bernard, P. (2012). *COBIT®5: A Management Guide.* Rolling Meadows: ISACA® Framework.

Danel, R. et al. (2012). 'Best practices in design of database of brownfield revitalization project'. *Proceedings of the 12th International mutltidisciplinary scientific geoconference (SGEM).* Albena, Bulgaria, pp. 49-56.

Hunka, F. (2015). 'Object role modeling perspective applied to business process modeling'. *Proceedings of the 11th International Conference on Strategic Management and its Support by Information Systems 2015.* Uherské Hradiště, Czech Republic, pp. 366-371.

Hunka, F. and Belunek, R. (2015). 'Transaction based business process modeling'. *Proceedings of the 2015 Federated Conference on Computer Science and Information Systems, FedCSIS 2015.* Lodz, Poland, pp. 1397-1402.

Kozel, R. and Chuchrová, K. (2015). 'Creation of System Support for Decision-Making Processes of Managers'. *Proceedings of IDIMT-2015: Information Technology and Society - Interaction and Interdependence: 23rd Interdisciplinary Information Management Talks*, Poděbrady, Czech Republic, pp. 163-170.

ISACA. (2010). *The business model for information security (BMIS).* Rolling Meadows: ISACA® Framework.

ISACA. (2011). COBIT® 5: Process Reference Guide Exposure Draft. Rolling Meadows: ISACA.

ISACA. (2012a). *COBIT®5 for Information Security,* Rolling Meadows: ISACA® Framework.

ISACA. (2012b). *Cobit 5 Enambing Processes*, Roling Meadovs: ISACA.

ISACA. (2012c). *Cobit 5 Implementation*. Roling Meadovs: ISACA.

ISACA. (2012d). *Cobit 5 Bussines Framework for the Governance and Management of Enterprise IT*. Roling Meadovs: ISACA.

ISACA. (2013a). *Cobit 5 Enabling information*. Roling Meadovs: ISACA.

ISACA. (2013b). *Process Assessment model (PAM) Using COBIT® 5*. Roling Meadovs: ISACA.

Kučera, A. and Pitner, T. (2013). 'Intelligent Facility Management for Sustainability and Risk Management'. *Environmental Software Systems. Fostering Information Sharing*. Berlin, Germany, pp. 608-617.

Pitner, T. and Ministr, J. (2015). 'Security aspects of Paas Cloud Model'. *Proceedings of the 11th International Conference on Strategic Management and its Support by Information Systems 2015*, Uherské Hradiště, Czech Republic, pp. 463-469.

Pochyla, M. (2015). 'Internet of Things: Big Challenge for Enterprises'. *Proceedings of the 11th International Conference on Strategic Management and its Support by Information Systems 2015*, Uherské Hradiště, Czech Republic, pp. 470-477.

Tovarňák, D., Nguyen, F. and Pitner, T. (2014). 'Distributed Event-Driven Model for Intelligent Monitoring of Cloud Datacenters'. *Intelligent Distributed Computing VII*. Cham, Switzerland, pp. 87-92.

Vitouš, M. (2013). 'COBIT 5 v malých a středních firmách'. *IT Systems,* 13 (10), pp. 21-23.

Application of the Cyber Security Act in Havířovská teplárenská společnost, a.s.

Ladislav Moravec[1], Roman Danel[2], Jakub Chlopecký[3]

Abstract. The paper summarizes the process and basic knowledge of information security analysis and design of implementation of the requirements under the Cyber Security Act (CSA) in Havířovská teplárenská společnost, a.s. (HTS, a.s.). The paper focuses primarily on the definition of weaknesses in two areas, namely: the area of organization and area of technical safety of information and communication technologies (ICT). HTS, a.s. meets the statutory criteria for inclusion in the Critical Information Infrastructure, and therefore the CSA is binding for the company. The authors of the article deal with these issues so that the imple-mentation part results from the specific findings in relation to the relevant legislative require-ments.

Keywords: Cyber Security Act, IT/ICT audit, Critical Information Infrastructure, remedy the deficiencies.

JEL Classification: D8, F5

1 Introduction

HTS, a.s. is a company whose primary goal is the quality and reliable supply of heat for central heating and delivery of hot water in the locality of Havířov, under licence for distribution of thermal energy no. 320100298 and also the concession deed for heat generation and distri-bution of thermal energy not subject to a licence, realized from heat sources with the installed power of one source over 50 kW, ref. no. 6520/2002/ŽÚ/Kuť. The emphasis is on the supply of thermal energy to all customers with minimal environmental impact. Investments are pri-marily focused on an increase in reliability and quality of supply of thermal energy and on the reduction of losses during supply to residents and other customers. Supply is covered by a central source of heat in Karviná, owned by Veolia Energie ČR, a.s. It is part of the Veolia multinational group, the global leader in providing environmental services and technological solutions in the areas of management of water services, waste management and energy ser-vices. Veolia Energie ČR, a.s. produces heat in the source for HTS, a.s. by combustion of coal; in the future, however, the construction of a fluidized bed boiler operating on the principle of combustion of fuel in a fluidized bed, developed for the combustion of a wide range of fuel, is under consideration.

The centralized heat supply system in Havířov is based on the hot water distribution system with the design parameters of the hot water supply of 160° C/60° C at the source,

[1] Havířovská teplárenská společnost, a.s., Konzumní 298/6a, Šumbark, 736 01 Havířov, Czech Republic, moravec@htsas.cz.
[2] VŠB-Technical University of Ostrava, Faculty of Mining and Geology, Institute of Economics and Control Systems, 17. listopadu 15/2172, 708 33 Ostrava Poruba, Czech Republic, roman.danel@vsb.cz.
[3] VŠB-Technical University of Ostrava, Faculty of Mining and Geology, Institute of Economics and Control Systems, 17. listopadu 15/2172, 708 33 Ostrava Poruba, Czech Republic, jakub.chlopecky@vsb.cz.

which respects the geographical situation of the town and the character of the consumption with the prevailing residential development. This system delivers heat energy using water-water ex-change stations connected to extensive secondary distribution systems with central tempera-ture regulation. Thermal energy is then delivered through 75 exchange stations, 192 pressure-independent residential stations and about 39 km of ducts of secondary heat networks to more than 20,000 households and 335,000 square metres of commercial space in the town. Besides the heat distribution, HTS also manufactures and supplies thermal energy from 9 local gas boilers with an installed capacity of 0.798 MWt. The consumption of thermal energy is measured by 1,029 ultrasonic heat meters, predominantly equipped with electronic transmission of the collected data. HTS, a. s. has a central dispatch centre for the continuous monitoring and control of the thermal energy distribution network. The system is built mainly on SCADA technologies from Siemens, Landis + Gyr and Johnson Controls (Moravec, 2015).

2 The Cyber Security Act

Act no.181/2014 Coll. On Cyber Security and amendments to related laws (Cyber Security Act, CSA) valid from 29. 8. 2014 and effective from 1. 1. 2015 regulates the rights and duties of persons, and also scope and powers of public authorities in the field of cyber security. The CSA identifies relevant entities as obliged persons and not only the state, but also private organizations have to obey it. This law does not apply to information or communications systems that handle classified information.

The basic aim of the CSA and closely related implementing regulations (Decree no. 316/2014 Coll., Decree no. 317/2014 Coll., Government Regulation No. 315/2014 Coll., amending Government Regulation No. 432/2010 Coll.) is to increase the security of cyberspace and, in particular, the effort to protect part of the infrastructure essential for the functioning of the state and whose disruption would lead to damage or threat to the interests of the Czech Republic. The aim of the legislative base is not solving all the risks in cyberspace such as copyright violations, leaks of electronic data or spreading of malicious e-content etc.

The primary objective of the CSA is to increase the security of critical national infrastructure and of important information systems managing personal data of a large number of people. In many cases, this is related to the need to implement extensive organizational and technical measures, including, in particular, the introduction of a system of information security and risk management, access control to the critical information infrastructure or significant information system (Pitner and Ministr, 2015).

3 Problem definition

It can be stated that critical infrastructure are productive and non-productive systems or services whose malfunction would have a serious impact on national security, the economy, public administration and providing basic living needs of the population. A typical example is the management information system of a specific heating plant or communication systems of air traffic management systems etc (Chlopecký et al, 2015).

The very definition of personnel covered by the Act is quite complicated; the law does not divide the obliged persons directly into different groups, but the inclusion is left purely in the hands of these subjects, but mentions the existence of two major groups - major information systems (MIS, here are typically public administration systems, where, according to the law, these systems can be managed only by a public authority) and critical information infrastructure (CII, classification based on compliance with cross-cutting and sectoral criteria according to Government Decree no. 432/2010 Coll., as amended by Amendment no. 315/2014 Coll.)

HTS, a.s. falls into the category of critical information infrastructure, as any violation of information security (confidentiality, availability or integrity) of its information and communication system can result in at least one of the cross-cutting criteria specified in § 1 of Government Decree no. 432/2010 Coll., as amended by Amendment no. 315/2014 Coll., which are:

a) Victims with a margin of more than 250 deaths or more than 2,500 people staying in hospital for longer than 24 hours;
b) Economic impact with the margin of national economic losses of more than 0.5% of GDP;
c) Impact on the public with a limit of extensive restrictions of provision of essential services or other serious intervention into everyday life involving more than 125,000 persons;
d) Meeting at least one of the sector criteria listed in Annex - industry VI., Part G of Government Decree no. 432/2010 Coll., as amended by Amendment no. 315/2014 Coll., which are:
    a) an information system which significantly or completely affects the activity of a designated critical infrastructure element, and which can be replaced only at disproportionate cost or within a time period exceeding eight hours;
    b) a communication system which significantly or completely affects the activity of a designated critical infrastructure element, and which can be replaced only at disproportionate cost or within a time period exceeding eight hours;
    c) an information system managed by a public authority containing personal data of more than 300,000 persons;
    d) a communication system providing a connection or interconnection of a critical infrastructure element with guaranteed data transfer capacity of at least 1 Gbit/s;
    e) sector criteria for identifying a critical infrastructure element referred to in points A to F in Annex - industry VI. will apply mutatis mutandis to cyber security if the protection of an element fulfilling the criteria is necessary to ensure cyber security.

HTS, a.s. is an obliged subject that must fulfil the obligations arising from the CSA since the scope for the supply of thermal energy to more than 20,000 households undoubtedly meets sectional criterion a) and especially the part defining more than 2,500 people at risk of hospitalization for more than 24 hours in the event of an extended power outage heat supply during adverse weather conditions.

4 Used method

An audit of the current state and subsequently the differential analysis focused separately on "Organizational measures" and separately on "Technical measures" and the state determined by the audit is specified in relation to the respective legislation. Analysis methodology:

- Firstly, the preparatory stage was carried out by analysing the architecture of the network and application environment from documents;
- The second stage consisted of managed interviews to refine the technical and organizational solutions of information security. Additional documentation was requested;
- In the third stage the additional (requested) documentation was analysed, and additional interviews with relevant employees to clarify details were conducted;
- In the fourth and final stage the existing measures were assessed and the final analysis completed. The differential analysis (GAP analysis) was subsequently reviewed (Janssen, 2011), (Perks, 2003) and its wording and conclusions agreed upon by all involved (verification).

For the purposes of comparative analysis with the requirements of the CSA the CII is defined as a system in HTS a.s. composed of the following parts:

a) Physical objects and spaces - headquarters (especially the Dispatch and server rooms), individual exchange stations;
b) Operating equipment - set of resources to ensure the management itself, monitoring, distribution and transmission of heat and hot water;
c) Communication system - set of resources to ensure data transfers between the Operating equipment and Information System of Dispatch;
d) Information System of Dispatch - set of hardware and software for processing and storing data from operating equipment, and operating the Dispatch (i.e. primary the Dispatch servers, workstations, operating systems, Dispatch applications);
e) Dispatch applications (SW Johnson ADX and Siemens ALFA);
f) Workplace readings - set of hardware and software for processing and storing data from operating equipment used for reading consumption data.

5 Audit IT/ICT in relation to the CSA and the detected deficiencies

The audit of IT/ICT in HTS, a.s. was aimed at assessing the current state of the entire ICT environment of the company in terms of information security. Profound disagreements with the recommended industry practice for information security were found. These disagreements have the character of absence or inadequate provision of both technical and organizational (procedural) measures. The fundamental shortcomings identified in the company are:

1) Network perimeter protection;
2) Addressing of the internal network not separated;
3) No segmentation of the internal network;
4) User accounts on terminals;
5) Absence of central management of accounts on terminals;
6) No strong password policy in place;
7) The users of operating applications have accounts with administrative privileges;

8) Event logging in business applications not defined;
9) Wi-Fi access points in the internal network protected only by a password without user authentication;
10) Operational needs for the time of restoration of individual systems and their data not specified;
11) Recoverability of the current backup system not regularly tested;
12) The configurations of network devices such as switches, firewalls not backed up;
13) Dispatch systems are freely accessible to persons with physical access to this workplace;
14) External backup array is located without increased physical protection in the IT office, which is freely accessible during working hours;
15) Internal documentation requirements cannot be systematically enforced through technical means and there is no ability to detect violations of these requirements.

5.1 Network perimeter protection

The existing firewall on the network perimeter is managed by HTS, a.s. There is no regular review of the set rules and configuration. Information flows from the internal network to the Internet (and vice versa) are not monitored, reported or evaluated for the detection of malicious or unwanted traffic. What is therefore missing is control and adequate security of the functionality of the device, which can result in penetration of malicious or unwanted traffic from the Internet to the internal network, theft of internal information, assault on internal systems and their use for illegal activities, inability to detect the listed events etc.

5.2 Addressing of the internal network

Addressing of the internal network of HTS, a.s is not separated. The entire internal LAN uses public IPv4 addresses. This makes any device with a public IP address potentially directly accessible from the Internet; access is not controlled, malicious/unwanted traffic is not filtered. The internal ICT systems of HTS, a.s. not being adequately separated from the public Internet significantly increases the likelihood of successful attacks (theft of inside information, assault and controlling of internal systems up to putting them out of service).

5.3 Segmentation of the internal network

The entire internal LAN has a flat architecture without any separation of systems, applications and users. This prevents access control on the network level between the various systems and users, which, in the case of a security incident, can result in uncontrolled and diffuse spread of contamination to all systems. Furthermore, it is not possible to separate the networks and control access between systems and users with respect to sensitive information.

5.4 User terminal accounts and strong password policy

All users have operating system accounts with administrative privileges. This poses a fundamental security risk because any successful attacker directly gains the highest possible privileges with full control over the whole station. Employees represent another risk because this gives them the ability to install any software (unlicensed, illegal, harmful), which is not necessary to perform their job duties. They can also change the system configuration at will. There is no strong password policy in place (minimum password length, special characters, frequency of changes, etc.). Weak and regularly unchanged passwords present a risk, because, given the current computational capabilities, they can be quickly "guessed", thus gaining permanent administrator system access.

5.5 Central management of terminal accounts

A central management of terminal accounts is not in place. All terminals are administrated locally (local accounts) and each one separately, which, given their number (50), is a problem with ensuring immutability of settings and permissions.

5.6 Logging in business applications

Event logging in business applications and operating systems is not defined. There are no defined types of logged events, their collection and assessment. This poses a risk of inability to demonstrate responsibility for carrying out certain actions in a business application or system by a specific user.

5.7 Wireless network access

The internal network has two Wi-Fi access points with LAN interconnection. Access is not controlled by authentication of individual users, but only by a password. The potential risk is the possibility of obtaining unauthorized access to the internal network, especially if the password is not strong enough and is not changed regularly.

5.8 Backup and recovery of systems

Operational needs for the time of restoration of individual systems and their data are not exactly specified. It is therefore possible that there is a mismatch between the expectations of accessibility, acceptable time of recovery and acceptable data loss, and the real possibilities of their existing technical support. The ability of recovery of the existing backup system is not regularly tested. The hardware equipment for testing data recovery of these systems is not available. It is therefore possible that in the case of a critical event data and system recovery will not be functional, representing an irreversible loss of data.

5.9 Backup of configurations of network devices

The configurations of network devices such as switches and firewalls are not backed up. When a device needs to be replaced there is no backup of the last configuration, thus restoring the functionality is much more time consuming.

5.10 Physical security

The Dispatch systems are freely accessible to persons with physical access to this workplace. The external backup array is located without increased physical protection in the IT office, which is freely accessible during working hours.

5.11 Internal directives

Requirements of the internal documentation cannot be systematically enforced by technical means and there is no ability to detect violations of these requirements. For example, users are prohibited from installing and using software and web applications not related to their professional activities. In reality, however, each terminal user has administrator permissions that allow installation of software and there is no monitoring of user traffic type at the network perimeter that violates this directive.

6 Results of the audit and recommendations to remedy the deficiencies

Before implementing specific measures to ensure compliance with the requirements of the Cyber Security Act, it is advisable that the management first pays attention to the findings described in the previous chapter, because they represent a baseline security setting of the entire IT/ICT environment.

Recommendations to remedy the deficiencies:

- Strict separation of the internal and external network environment - ensure addressing of the internal network using private IP ranges, implement IP address translation on the network perimeter for systems that need access to the Internet (or be accessible from the Internet);
- Ensure access control and filtering of inappropriate traffic between the internal (LAN) and external network (Internet);
- Determine the effectiveness of existing firewall rules, for example by logging of application of individual rules;
- Review the existing firewall rules. Examine whether only necessary traffic is explicitly allowed and whether the default setting blocks any other traffic;
- Rules update. Based on previous findings define new rules that forbid all traffic by default, and allow only explicitly permitted traffic; consider this set of rules a basic configuration with respect to further monitoring and assessment of changes;
- Define the process for approving new rules (change requests). If the need for new rules occurs, have the procedure defined for their approval and, if necessary, for their limited period of validity;
- Reports and traffic monitoring. Define the need and possibilities for reporting of traffic information (e.g. connection utilization, traffic types, equipment utilization, etc.), define the regularity of processing and assessment of such reports;
- Detection of security incidents. Define the events that trigger alarm conditions in order to determine the ability of detection and reaction to security incidents;
- Consider deploying the DHCP protocol for dynamic assigning of IP addresses in order to save the manual configuration interventions;
- Filtering of inappropriate outbound user traffic, for example, blocking or detection of visits of inappropriate web pages or services;
- Introduce the detection of application threats: Today's firewalls allow the detection and blocking of advanced threats on the application layer;
- Segmentation of the internal LAN - use an appropriate method to separate individual systems (e.g. using DMZ, VLAN or physically separate networks) in the network (or

groups of systems) with respect to their sensitivity and criticality. Recommended are, for example, separate segments for the user terminals, operation servers, voice VoIP system etc.;

- Architecture using firewall (DMZ). Openings between the segments checked and filtered by the firewall rules with only explicitly permitted traffic;
- Separation of Dispatch applications from LAN. Consider the possibility of strict, physical separation of the Dispatch systems from other systems on the internal network. If there is a real operational need for opening between LAN and Dispatch, then control it strictly, block and restrict by default to only a minimum of services and a minimum number of users;
- Eliminate the use of administrator privileges for terminal users;
- Administrator privileges to be used purely for the administration of systems - for normal operation of the administrator use the normal account;
- Define a strong password policy and enforce it at the terminals through technical means. Policy parameters are defined in §18 of Decree no. 316/2014 Coll.;
- Deployment of central management of user accounts and privileges. Given that it is a Windows environment with approx. 50 terminals, establishment of an Active Directory domain for central administration suggests itself;
- Define user groups (roles) and the needs of their privileges to individual business applications;
- Use technical means to control access and authorization (authentication and authorization) into various business applications;
- Use technical means to collect defined events – logging;
- Segment the network to enable access from Wi-Fi only to the Internet rather than to the internal network, e.g. by using firewall on the network perimeter;
- At the organizational level, analyse the impact of the malfunctioning ICT systems on the operations of HTS, a.s. and based on that, define maximum tolerated downtimes, recovery times and data loss;
- According to the output of impact analysis, determine/specify the backup plan, business continuity plan and possible demands on the backup technologies, redundant systems design and method of recovery;
- According to the output of impact analysis, examine or modify activities and SLA in supplier relations in relation to the replacement of non-functional HW or SW, service calls;
- Regularly test the ability to recover systems and data from existing backups;
- Add backup of network devices such as switches, firewalls etc.;
- For the Dispatch systems, consider their location in the company server room, which would ensure increased physical protection and better operating conditions. An alternative could be the placement of systems in a lockable rack in the Dispatch;
- It is not appropriate to put the external backup array in the server room because its role is to preserve data in the case of any critical events occurring in the server room itself. It is therefore advisable to use physical spaces with strictly limited access - for example a fire-proof safe or another room with limited access. Consider deploying

encryption of backups, especially of those stored outside the organization headquarters;
- Review and/or update the permitted activities of employees in relation to the IT/ICT resources;
- Provide technical enforcement of prohibited activities - limiting the options, violation detection: e.g. blocking and detection of visiting inappropriate web pages and services, inability to install software on workstations by permission constraints etc (Smejkal, 2015).

The specification of requirements arising from individual provisions of the Act and their binding to audit findings is conducted by the differential analysis; publication of the whole differential analysis by sections of the Act is beyond the scope of this article.

7 Conclusion

The above-mentioned results of the audit of IT/ICT in relation to the implementation of the Cyber Security Act define the measures that HTS must implement to fulfil the essence of the Act. The estimated time for implementation of measures to eliminate the identified deficiencies is three years; the preliminary cost estimate more then CZK million.

References

Chlopecký, J., Rolčíková, M. and Kratochvíl, M. (2015). 'Decision making influence of some macroeconomic factors concerning prospective sales of fine silicon carbide'. *Proceedings of 15th International Multidisciplinary Scientific GeoConference SGEM*, Albena, Bulgaria, pp. 171-178.

Janssen, M., Schol, H. and Tan, Y. (2011). *Electronic Government: 10th International Conference.* New York: Springer.

Pitner, T. and Ministr, J. (2015). 'Security Aspect of Paas Cloud Model'. *Proceedings of 11th International Conference on Strategic Management and its Support by Information Systems,* Uherské Hradiště, Czech Republic, pp. 463-469.

Moravec, L. (2015). Geografický informační systém ve společnosti HTS, a.s. [In Czech: Geographic Information System in Company HTS]. *Bachelor thesis*, supervisor: Michal Řepka, VŠB – Technical University of Ostrava, Czech Republic.

Perks, C. and Beveridge, T. (2003). *Guide to enterprise IT architecture.* New York: Springer.

Sbírka zákonů - Česká republika. Praha: Tiskárna Ministerstva vnitra.

Smejkal, V. and Rais, K. (2003). *Řízení rizik.* Praha: Grada Publishing.

Smejkal, V. (2015). *Kybernetická kriminalita.* Plzeň: Vydavatelství a nakladatelství Aleš Čeněk.

Stanovy společnosti: Havířovská teplárenská společnost a.s. Havířov (2016). [In Czech: Statutes of the company: HTS a.s.].

Výroční zpráva za rok 2015: Havířovská teplárenská společnost a.s. Havířov, 2016. [In Czech: HTS a.s. Annual Report].

On the determination of query execution patterns of the application of the Anchor Data modeling method using machine-learning methods

Radek Němec [1] , František Zapletal [2]

Abstract. The Anchor Data Modeling (ADM) is a relational data modeling method that supports the phenomenon of agile data modeling in which evolutionary aspects of data management are addressed. In this paper, we focus on the determination of possible patterns that could help to understand potential benefits for the query execution performance, when a database schema is implemented using the ADM method. Patterns should imply specific query structure that may be linked to positive impacts on the querying performance, if a data mart is designed using the ADM method.

The results show, however, that the set of variables we used provides a not very satisfactory evidence, when cluster analysis methods is used for the patterns determination.

Keywords: Anchor Data Modeling, agile data modeling, query execution performance, cluster analysis.

1 Introduction

Despite the growing popularity of other than relational data storages, e.g., Hadoop distributed data management system and NoSQL databases, these classical solutions are not yet obsolete. Relational databases still represent an important group of decision-making data sources hosting rather smaller datasets for highly specialized uses (e.g. dedicated data marts for business reporting etc.), see Poleto, de Carvalho and Costa (2015). The size of the data being processed is distinctively smaller in comparison with the processing and analysis of the Big Data, which usually originate in high velocities, large variety, and in vast amounts (Jina et al., 2015).

The changes in the business environment, however, influence usage of all data sources available for the modern decision-making. The evolution of requirements influences management of database schemas of traditional data sources as well as applications designed to process data from Big Data sources for a certain purpose. We can argue about the relevance of data modeling methods to support the agile-oriented data management in the first place, i.e. which can provide means for a simple database or eventually application code evolution.

In this work, we focus on the Anchor Data Modeling (ADM) method (Regardt et al., 2009) as one of the agile-oriented relational data modeling methods. The methods authors indicate that the ADM is as a tool that directly supports the agile-orientated design of data models. Next to the ADM method, there is the Data Vault relational data modeling method, which was proposed by Dan Linstedt and presented in Linstedt and Olschimke (2015). Both methods are intended for the use in the traditional data warehouse database design process and both were

[1]VSB - Technical university of Ostrava, Dpt. of Systems Engineering, Sokolská 33, Ostrava, Czech Republic, radek.nemec@vsb.cz.
[2]VSB - Technical university of Ostrava, Dpt. of Systems Engineering, Sokolská 33, Ostrava, Czech Republic, frantisek.zapletal@vsb.cz.

practically assessed through a successful usage in multiple real situations (according to statements on websites of methods authors). A sounder rather scientific evidence discussing a more general usability of both methods, as well as benefits that stem from the query performance aspects, is missing.

In this paper, we try to apply a fuzzy cluster analysis method to indicate patterns in the data containing selected query structure-related parameters and results of the actual query execution. We executed the queries in the environment of a relational database system and we applied principles of the ADM method. The effort may be helpful for the understanding of actual reasons why certain queries execute much faster and some much slower when the ADM based database schema is used (as determined in our previous works). In the end, such arguments may be eventually used in a possible proposal of the enhancement of query execution optimization procedures.

In the next chapter, we describe the methodological aspects of our paper and data used. Then we present cluster analysis results with a discussion, and finish with a conclusion of findings.

2 Relational data modeling and the agile orientation of data management

In the data analysis field, the traditional relational databases slowly lose their dominant place, mainly due to inherent limits in context of processing complex data that originate. The SQL language, however, stays as a still popular language for the data access and manipulation, even if we need to work with the unstructured content during the data analysis. Several modules and solutions were created to work with the more modern Big Data processing environments (i.e. Hadoop and NoSQL) that use the widely known SQL language for querying data in it (e.g. SparkSQL, HAWQ, Splice Machine or HiveQL). The reason for the non-decreasing popularity of the SQL language is simply because most business users and analysts are accustomed with the SQL for data manipulation and access because of its relative simplicity and semantic expressiveness. Having this in mind, certain project risks can be lowered appropriately, which is an essential aspect for the management of project not only in the IT (Řeháček, 2011).

As was stated by Poleto, de Carvalho and Costa (2015), the knowledge of the traditional relational data modeling is not obsolete. It is still quite important because data marts database schemas need changes from time to time. Although the traditional data marts are mostly not efficient at supporting modern advanced decision-making support tasks, e.g. data mining tasks over a large-scale datasets of unstructured content (text etc.), their use in the Business Intelligence field and small dataset analysis in not negligible. In addition, not every company requires extensive Big Data processing initiative for the decision-making support and simple business reporting is enough for them.

2.1 Brief overview of the ADM method

The ADM is based on the usage of several distinctive conceptual constructors. These are convertible into logical objects and physical relational tables at the end of the data modeling process. Each attribute of any entity is defined separately and represented as a single relation (the *Attribute*) with only 2 attributes (a composite key attribute and an actual value of the entity property). Attributes in the anchor data model are connected with the *Anchor relation*, which is a source of business keys for related *Attributes*. *Anchors* are then connected together using *Tie relations*, which represent m-*to*-n *relationships* between entities by default.

The overall structure of the resulting database schema must be normalized in the 5th normal form (i.e. relations cannot be further decomposed without losing certain information about the entity). The database schema can be normalized also into the 6th normal form (Date, Darwen and Lorentzos, 2003) in which the primary key of at least one relation includes additional attributes indicating validity of values in time. The database schema representing a multidimensional data model, which was used in this paper, was designed and constructed using hybrid ADM approach, described in Němec and Zapletal (2014a).

The aspect of high degree of normalization itself is the one that is linked with the query execution performance benefits in the original paper by Regardt et al. (2009). The paper, however, provides a small amount of evidence that justifies query execution benefits over the traditional data warehouse database schema normalized in the 3rd normal form. On the contrary, the paper by Golov and Rönnbäck (2015) brings evidence that the ADM method can be applied also in case of a Big Data processing task, with superior query execution results obtained in favor of the ADM method usage. There is, however, no work discussing actual differences between these two methods in comparison with the traditional data modeling approach (or their use in specialized cases, like OLAP-oriented data modeling etc.). We, therefore, try to create certain amount of arguments and evidence for further assessment in our ongoing work.

We studied the query-execution-performance benefits in Němec and Zapletal (2014ab), focusing on the business-reporting field and the environment of a sample data mart so far. In addition, similar results were obtained when the ADM method based database schema was used in connection with environments of certain selected Business Intelligence software (Němec, 2015), again with query processing results favoring the ADM based schema in most of the tools used in the test.

We, therefore, believe that the method has certain potential in multiple fields and we currently focus on finding relevant factors that indicate what specific query structure parameters are related with better query execution results when the ADM-method based database schema is used[1].

3 Methodology of selected clustering methods

Clustering methods are used for a classification of objects which are grouped to clusters based on similarity. For the analysis in this paper, non-hierarchical clustering is used because no structure tree of units can be identified here. The most common method for non-hierarchical clustering is the k-means algorithm. This method classifies objects into a predetermined number of clusters. A potential problem is that the method is deterministic, i.e. a relation of object's belonging to the cluster is given by values $\{0, 1\}$ (either the object belongs to the cluster or not and nothing in between). But, crisp boundaries among clusters are not always desirable. For instance, it is impossible to require the crisp boundaries when the input data are uncertain (e.g. given by intervals, random variables or fuzzy sets).

[1]These factors should relate with the execution of certain physical processing operations performed by the database systems query execution engine.

Despite the fact that all input data used in this paper are deterministic, the authors decide to consider clusters to be the non-deterministic sets. The reason is that a performance of the objects is very similar for most of attributes and thus it is reasonable to suppose that the crisp boundaries would bring some potential distortion of the results. That is why the fuzzy c-means method (an extension of the crisp k-means) is also used (beside the k-means).

Many researchers have focused on comparison of the k-means and the fuzzy c-means (established by Bezdek (1981)), see e.g. Singh and Mahajan (2013) or Ghosh and Dubey (2013). That researches agree that the main advantage of the k-means is a higher computational efficiency; the fuzzy c-means is slower. But, with respect to the size of the problem solved in this paper, an execution time is not a relevant problem. On the other hand, the mentioned sources confirm the usefulness of including uncertainty.

Now, a brief description of the both clustering algorithms will be given. The idea is the same - the aim is to partition n observations into k clusters in which each observation belongs to the cluster with the nearest mean.

3.1 k-means algorithm

Inputs for the k-means method is as follows:

- values of observations on n objects with m attributes,
- number of clusters k,
- distance measure,
- initial means (centroids) of the clusters (can by chosen randomly).

The clustering is done so that the criterion (1) is met:

$$\arg\min_{\mathcal{C}} \sum_{j=1}^{k} \sum_{\mathbf{x} \in c_j} (\mathcal{D}(x_i, u_j))^2 \tag{1}$$

where

- $\mathcal{C} = \{c_1, c_2, \ldots, c_k\}$: set of clusters;
- $\mathcal{X} = \{x_1, x_2, \ldots, x_n \in \mathbb{R}^m\}$: set of objects where each object is described by m-dimensional vector of attributes;
- $\mathcal{D}$: distance measure (in this paper, we use the Euclidean one);
- $u_j \in \mathbb{R}^m$: mean (centroid) of the j-th cluster.

For more details about the algorithm see e.g. Wu (2012).

3.2 Fuzzy c-means algorithm

Inputs for this algorithm is identical with those for the k-means. The only differences arise from the distinction of membership degrees for objects. Let μ_{ij} be the membership degree to which the i-th object belongs to the j-th cluster. Then, the criterion for clustering is given by (2).

$$\arg\min_{\mathcal{C}} \sum_{j=1}^{k} \sum_{\mathbf{x} \in c_j} \mu_{ij} (\mathcal{D}(x_i, u_j))^2 \tag{2}$$

The variable μ_{ij} is defined by (3).

$$\mu_{ij} = \frac{1}{\sum_{l=1}^{k} \left(\frac{\mathcal{D}(x_i, u_j)}{\mathcal{D}(x_i, u_l)} \right)}^{\frac{2}{s-1}} \tag{3}$$

where s is a parameter which defines the level of fuzziness ($s \in [1, \infty[$). It is worth noting that for s tending to 1, the fuzzy c-means is increasingly similar to the k-means. Due to the fact that s parameter is artificial, the choice of its value is not easy. In order to avoid that selection, the special case of the fuzzy c-means model by Dunn (1974) in which $s = 2$ will be used (the same choice was made by Hathaway and Bezdek, 2001).

The centroid of each cluster is computed as the mean of all objects, weighted by their membership degree of belonging to the cluster for each iteration, see (4).

$$c_j = \frac{\sum_{x_i \in c_j} \mu_{ij} x_i}{\sum_{x_i \in c_j} \mu_{ij}} \tag{4}$$

For further details on the fuzzy c-means, see e.g. Miyamoto, Ichihashi and Honda (2008).

Either in the k-means or in the fuzzy c-means, a number of clusters is an input of the method and its choice must be reasoned. In this paper, the gap statistics for the k-means is used to set the number of clusters, for more see Tibsihirani, Walther and Hastie (2000).

4 Clustering analysis

This section is devided into two subsections. In the first of them, the input data used for analysis are described and the clustering model is established. Results of the analysis are discussed in the second subsection.

4.1 Dataset and data querying results

The complete dataset contains a set of variables describing details of the execution of 290 SQL queries executed for 2 database schema variants (the ADM method based schema was marked as 'ADM' and the opposite one built using traditional data modeling principles was marked as 'STAR'). Both schema variants were constructed based on a banking data mart data model presented in Kimball and Ross (2013), depicted in the figure 1 and the ADM based one is depicted in the figure A1 in the Appendix. In both database schemas, where one of them was constructed based on the ADM method guidelines, facts represent bank account balance data with a monthly level of granularity. There are 50,000,000 fact records generated and 2 of the 6 dimensions contain more than 200,000 dimension members (i.e. rows).

During the recording of the data querying process, two aspects were used to divide the actual query execution time (QET) results in milliseconds. The first one represents the situation when the query is run for the first time and the query execution plan is not created yet to be used for optimal repeated execution of the query - the query is executed in a cold query execution environment (CQEE). The second one represents a situation when the query execution plan is already prepared and used for optimal query execution - the query is run in a hot query execution

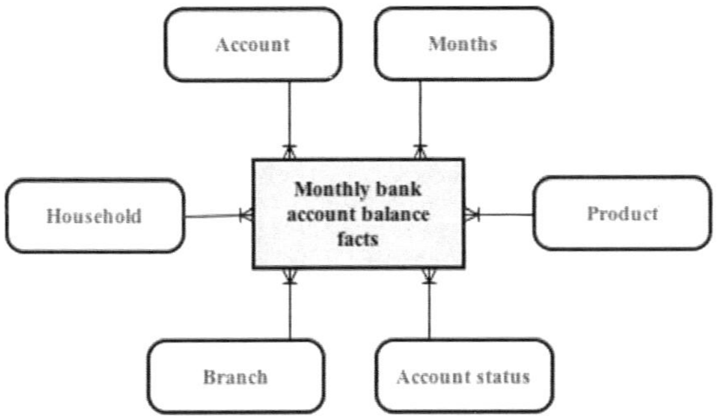

Figure 1 Multidimensional data model of the sample banking data mart

environment (HQEE). The testing was conducted on a 64-bit SQL Server 2012 Standard Edition database server, with following hardware configuration: Intel Xeon Quad-core 2.66 GHz CPU, 4 GB RAM.

Each query in the sample of 290 queries was executed 101 times and the first execution represents the CQEE aspect, and the other 100 represent the HQEE aspect (a mean value was calculated, according to the equation (5)).

$$\overline{QET\_HQEE}_q = \frac{1}{N}\sum_{i=2}^{101} QET_{i,q}, \tag{5}$$

where q is a number of a respective query used in the performance testing process, i is a number of the q-th query execution and $N = 100$. A QET difference for both aspects (CQEE, HQEE) was calculated to indicate whether the querying process performed better using the ADM of STAR schema variant, so: $QET\_CQEE_{diff} = QET\_CQEE_{STAR} - QET\_CQEE_{ADM}$ and $QET\_HQEE_{diff} = \overline{QET\_HQEE}_{STAR} - \overline{QET\_HQEE}_{ADM}$.

For the analysis in this paper, we used 7 out of total 11 variables (i.e. including actual QET_CQEE for each schema variant as well as mean QET_HQEE values) as follow:

- FP_LD - number of filtering predicates in the query from large dimensions (i.e. with 200,000 or 220,000 records),
- FP_SD - number of filtering predicates in the query from small dimensions (i.e. up to 1000 records),
- NF_LD - number of non-filtered attributes in the query from the same large dimension (i.e. there is at least one other but filtered attribute from the same dimension; existence of such attribute increases joining and scanning operations demands),
- NF_SD - number of non-filtered attributes in the query from the same large dimension (i.e. there is at least one other filtered attribute from the same dimension),
- $Output\_bytes$ - query output size (i.e. rows count $\times$ row size in bytes),
- QET_CQEE_{diff},
- QET_HQEE_{diff}.

It remains to add that the analysis in this paper has been done in R as well as all the outputs

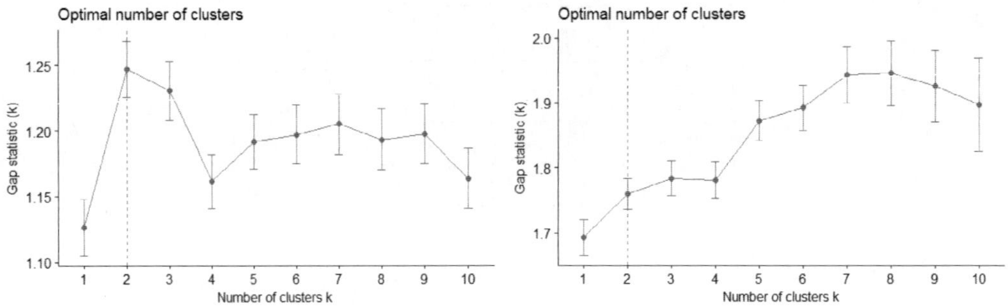

Figure 2 Determination of optimal k number of clusters by the CQEE (a) and HQEE aspect (b)

have been created by R studio.

4.2 Results and discussion

First, we determined optimal number of clusters for the k-means method. The figure 2 shows that for both the CQEE and HQEE aspect, it is 2.

Then we applied the fuzzy c-means method to determine assignment of query cases into certain clusters, and to determine memberships degree and, with that, potential overlap of clusters.

As seen in figures 3 and 4, there is a large overlap of both clusters for both query execution aspects. Figure 4.2 shows the distribution of frequency of CQEE-aspect related results and HQEE-aspect related results. In the figure, it is evident that the clusters for the HQEE aspect overlap mostly for query cases within the range of $QET\_HQEE_{diff} \sim \pm 500$ ms whereas the CQEE aspects clusters overlap mostly for query cases within a larger range of $QET\_CQEE_{diff} \sim \pm 1,000$ ms. For the CQEE aspect, it is due to several query cases with very large QET difference (either positive or negative).

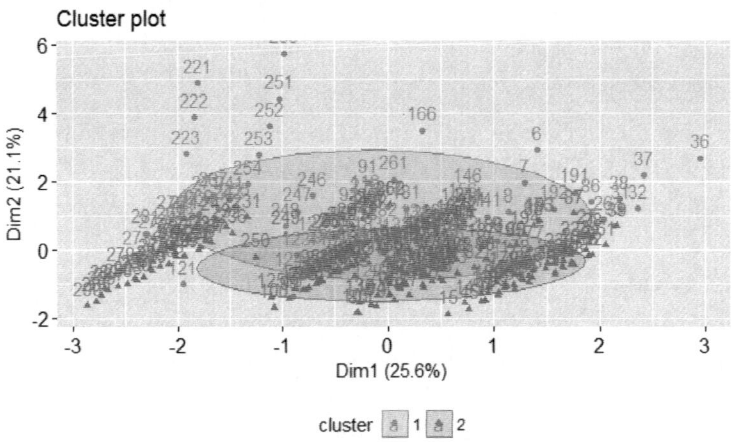

Figure 3 Fuzzy clusters related with the CQEE aspect

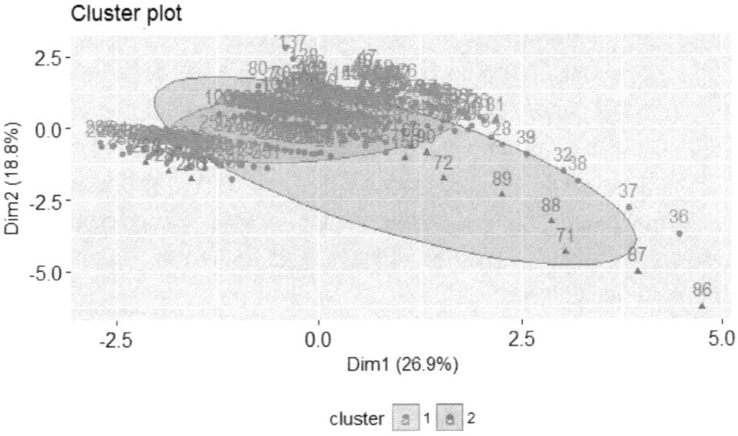

Figure 4 Fuzzy clusters related with the HQEE aspect

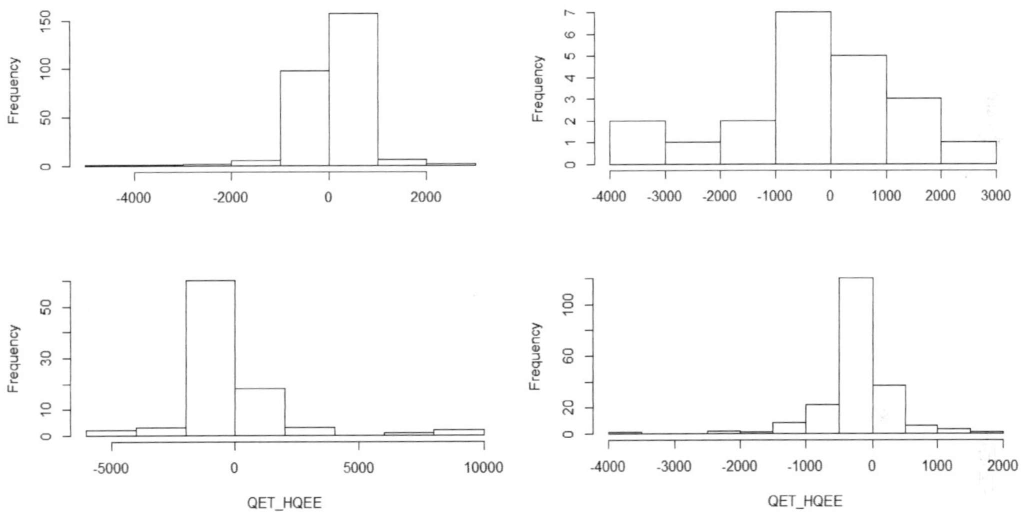

Figure 5 Frequency of QET_CQEE_{diff} values in cluster 1 (a) and cluster 2 (b) and QET_HQEE_{diff} values in clusters 1 (c) and cluster 2 (d)

Class	Aspect	FP_LD + FP_SD		NF_LD + NF_SD		Total output size	
		mean	st.dev.	mean	st.dev.	mean	st.dev.
1	CQEE	7.833	2.409	1.611	0.487	3,857,764	7,084,117
	HQEE	8.100	2.663	1.550	0.497		
2	CQEE	6.723	3.413	0.946	0.747	583,691	2,654,371
	HQEE	6.631	3.405	0.930	0.746		
3	CQEE	7.167	4.180	1.167	0.373	4,375,204	6,231,919
	HQEE	7.500	3.619	1.192	0.621		

Figure 6 The results in classes

We assigned a synthetic class number for each part of the range, i.e. class = 1 for $QET\_CQEE_{diff} < -1,000$, class = 2 for $-1,000 \leq QET\_CQEE_{diff} \leq 1,000$, and class = 3 for $QET\_CQEE_{diff} > 1,000$ (similar classes are assigned in case of the HQEE aspect but with the 500 ms range threshold). In the figure 6, we show mean amount of filtering predicates $(FP\_LD + FP\_SD)$ and mean amount of non-filtered attributes from the same dimension $(FP\_LD + FP\_SD)$ for each aspect and class. As the values in the figure 6 show, there are, however, no distinctive differences in both mean amount of filtering predicates and mean amount of non-filtered attributes. The only difference is in the total output size - this fact can be accounted for in our next work.

The query performance prediction using only query-text features was conducted also by Ganapathi et al. (2009). The authors stated that their initial results showed a weak prediction precision when such variables were used. They used measures of physical query processing instead (and machine-learning methods as well), with much more satisfactory results. Akdere et al. (2012) used similar approach, i.e. similar query performance measures and other machine learning methods.

In our case, we have the same problem as Ganapathi et al. (2009) had to solve, although our goal is not QET prediction in the first place. Our focus is to determine eventual parameters that can be used to determine query-structure related details that lead to a positive impact on the query execution performance when using the ADM based database schema. Therefore, we believe that in our future work, we should learn from results of approaches used by Ganapathi et al. (2009) and Akdere et al. (2012), i.e. we need to modify the variable set used for the pattern determination as the first step.

5 Conclusion

In the paper, we focused on the determination of patterns using query-text related measures and we tried to link them with differences in the query execution performance using selected clustering methods. Our set of variables was not proved very useful because no distinctive differences were discovered in terms of patterns determination that could indicate specific query structure parameters that lead to positive impact on the query execution performance when the ADM based database schema is used.

In our further work, we should consider more complex relationships between physical processing operators, query structure parameters and query execution performance results.

Acknowledgements

This paper was supported by grant No. GA 16-01298S of the Czech Science Foundation, SGS project No. SP2017/125 and the Operational Programme Education for Competitiveness Project CZ.1.07/2.3.00/20.0296. The support is greatly acknowledged.

References

Akdere, M. et al. (2012). 'Learning-based Query Performance Modeling and Prediction'. *IEEE 28th International Conference on Data Engineering (ICDE) 2012*. Washington, D.C.: IEEE, pp. 390-401.

Bezdek, J. C. (1981). *Pattern Recognition with Fuzzy Objective Function Algorithms*, New York: Plenum Press.

Date, C. J., Darwen, H. and Lorentzos, N. A. (2003). *Temporal Data and the Relational Model: A Detailed Investigation into the Application of Interval and Relation Theory to the Problem of Temporal Database Management*. Oxford: Elsevier.

Dunn, J. C. (1974). 'A Fuzzy Relative of the ISODATA Process and Its Use in Detecting Compact Well-Separated Clusters'. *Journal of Cybernetics*, 3.

Ganapathi, A. et al. (2009). 'Predicting Multiple Metrics for Queries: Better Decisions Enabled by Machine Learning'. *IEEE 25th International Conference on Data Engineering*. Shanghai: IEEE, pp. 592-603.

Golov, N. and Rönnbäck, L. (2015). 'Big Data Normalization for Massively Parallel Processing Databases'. *Advances in Conceptual Modeling, Lecture Notes in Computer Science*, 9382, pp. 154-163.

Ghosh, S. and Dubey, S. K. (2013). 'Comparative Analysis of K-means and Fuzzy C-means Algorithms', International *Journal of Advanced Computer Science and Applications*, 4 (4).

Hathaway, R. J. and Bezdek, J. C. (2001). 'Fuzzy C-means clustering of incomplete data', *IEEE Transactions on Cybernetics*, 31 (5).

Jina, X, Waha, B. W., Chenga, X. and Wanga, Y. (2015). 'Significance and Challenges of Big Data Research'. Big Data Research, 2 (2), pp. 5964.

Kim, Y. and Worrell, E. (2002). 'International comparison of CO2emission trends in the iron and steel industry'. *Energy Policy*, 30 (10), pp. 827-838.

Kimball, R. and Ross, M. (2013). *The Data Warehouse Toolkit: The Definitive Guide to Dimensional Modeling*. 3rd Ed., New York: Wiley.

Linstedt, D. and Olschimke, M. (2015). *Building a Scalable Data Warehouse with Data Vault 2.0*, Burlington: Morgan Kaufmann.

Miyamoto, S., Ichihashi, H. and Honda, K. (2008) *Algorithms for Fuzzy Clustering*, Berlin: Springer.

Němec, R. (2015). 'Assessment of query execution performance using selected Business Intelligence tools and experimental agile oriented data modeling approach'. *Proceedings of the 2015 Federated Conference on Computer Science and Information Systems*, Warsaw, Poland, pp. 1327-1333.

Němec, R. and Zapletal, F. (2014a). 'The Design of Multidimensional Data Model Using Principles of the Anchor Data Modeling: An Assessment of Experimental Approach Based on Query Execution Performance. *WSEAS Transactions on Computers*, 13, pp. 177-194.

Němec, R. and Zapletal, F. (2014b). 'Analysis of Query Execution Performance Factors in the Anchor Multidimensional Database Schema Environment'. *Selected Paper of the MEKON 2014 Conference*, Ostrava, pp. 481-491.

Němec, R. and Zapletal, F. (2015). 'Application of selected classification and clustering methods on the database query categorization'. *Proceedings of the 11th international conference Strategic Management and its Support by Information Systems 2015*, Ostrava, pp. 439-446.

Poleto, T., de Carvalho, V. D. H. and Costa, A. P. C. S. (2015). 'The Roles of Big Data in the Decision-Support Process: An Empirical Investigation'. *Proceedings of the 1st International Conference ICDSST 2015 (Lecture Notes in Business Information Processing 216)*. Belgrade, Serbia, pp. 10-21.

Řeháček, P. (2011). 'Risk management and FMEA. Risk management and FMEA'. *In proceedings of the Strategic Management and its Support by Information Systems international conference 2011*, Ostrava, pp. 154-158.

Regardt, O. et al. (2009). 'Anchor Modeling: An Agile Modeling Technique Using the Sixth Normal Form for Structurally and Temporally Evolving Data'. *Proceedings of ER 2009*, Rio Grande do Sul, pp. 234-250.

Singh, A. and Mahajan, P. (2013). 'Comparison of K-means and Fuzzy C-means Algorithms', *International Journal of Engineering Research & Technology*. 2 (5).

Tibsihirani, R., Walther, G. and Hastie, T. (2001). 'Estimating the number of clusters in a data set via the gap statistics'. *Journal of Royal Statistics Society: Series B*. 63. Wu, J. (2012). *Advances in K-means Clustering: A Data Mining Thinking*, Berlin: Springer.

Appendix

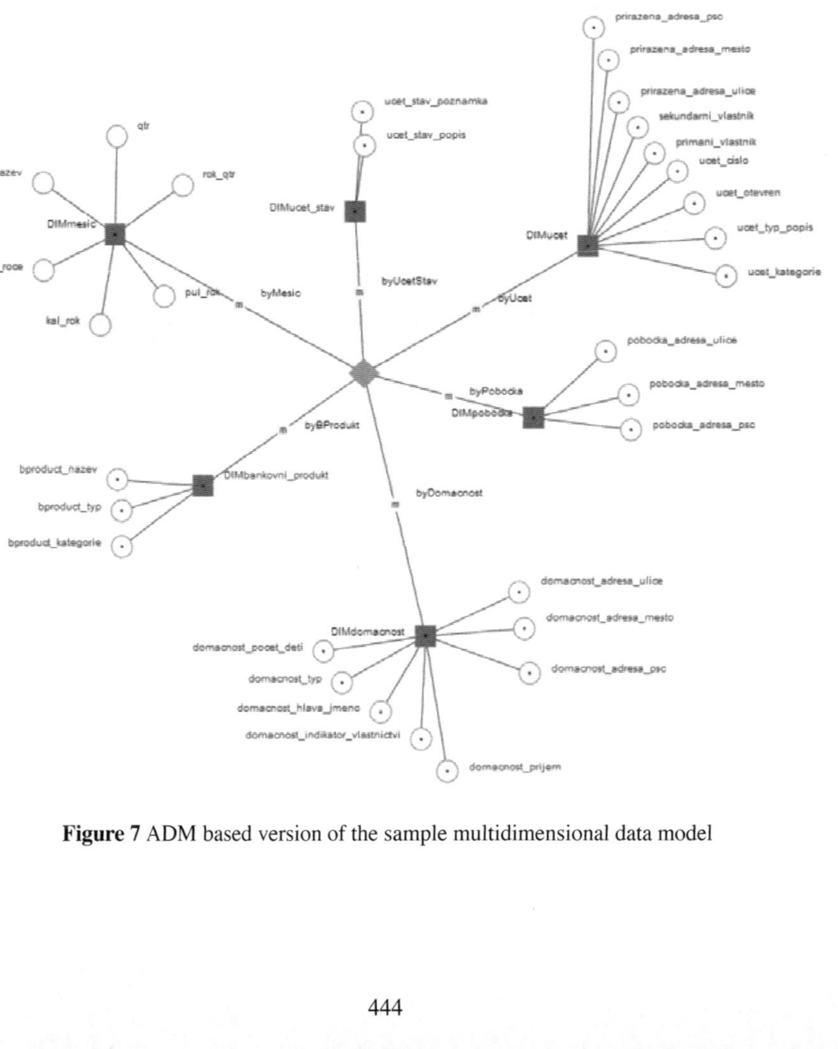

Figure 7 ADM based version of the sample multidimensional data model

Practical Aspects of Building Business Intelligence Solutions using Microsoft Office Tools

Vítězslav Novák[1]

Abstract. With the increasing usage of information technologies, the amount of data, which are stored in enterprise information systems, is also increasing and this invites to their further using for obtaining knowledge about the business, competition, customers etc. Business intelligence is becoming a common part of the decision-making processes in companies and should also become a common part of every economist's knowledge. Nowadays it is not necessary to use special sophisticated tools for data mining, but these tools are becoming a part of mainstream office software. This article has two goals. First, it should demonstrate which Microsoft Office applications can be used in which part of the Business Intelligence solution, an expanding goal is to show how these applications can be used to demonstrate a given part of BI solution e.g. for Business Intelligence teaching.

Keywords: business intelligence, dimensional modeling, Microsoft Office, Excel, PowerPivot, Access, Power BI.

JEL Classification: A23, M15

1 Introduction

With the increasing usage of information technologies, the amount of data, which are stored in enterprise information systems, is also increasing and this invites for their further using for obtaining knowledge about the business, competition, customers etc. An increasing IT area called Internet of Things is also becoming new generator of large amounts of data nowadays, as Pochyla (2015) writes. Business intelligence should therefore become a common part of the decision-making processes in companies and should become a common part of every economist knowledge as well. As Němec and Hančlová (2014) write, SMEs represent majority of enterprises in the EU but information system of a SME often lacks Business Intelligence capabilities. Fortunately, nowadays there is no need to use in all cases special sophisticated tools for data mining. These tools are becoming a part of mainstream office software where for many years Microsoft Office is the standard.

With the development of information technologies also Microsoft Office has been developing. Not only functionality of traditional applications such as Word or Excel has been extended, but also new applications responsive to the current needs of their users are constantly created and many of them are also available online as a part of Microsoft Office 365. Especially following Microsoft Office applications are presented themselves for Business Intelligence purpose:

- Excel (offline and online),
- PowerPivot (only offline; it is a part of Excel, but due to its different properties compared to Excel it will be mentioned separately),
- Access (only offline),

[1] VŠB - Technical university of Ostrava/Faculty of Economics, Department of Applied Informatics, Sokolská třída 33, 701 21 Ostrava 1, vitezslav.novak@vsb.cz.

- Power BI (it is a part of Microsoft Office 365, but not Microsoft Office 2016; offline version of Power BI can be downloaded for free for the desktop, the mobile phones or as an add-in to Excel).

This article has two goals. First, it should demonstrate which Microsoft Office applications can be used in which part of the Business Intelligence solution. An expanding goal is to show how these applications can be used to demonstrate a given part of BI solution e.g. for Business Intelligence teaching. For that purpose, a simplified BI system architecture solution will be described in the following chapters of this article and then Microsoft Office tools that can be used in various parts of the BI system architecture will be dealt with. The integrated BI solution built solely on Microsoft Office will be practically demonstrated at the conference SMSIS 2017.

2 The System Architecture of Business Intelligence Solutions

Business Intelligence (BI) is according to Laberge (2012) an overarching term that refers to the knowledge, processes, technologies and applications that make management decisions easier on the basis of business data processing, e.g. sale, production, finance and many other data sources.

The system architecture of BI solution according to Pour, Maryška and Novotný (2012) is not fixed. The specific arrangement of the components of BI can greatly vary depending on the situation and the needs of the given company. However, a simplified system architecture of BI solutions can be described in the figure below:

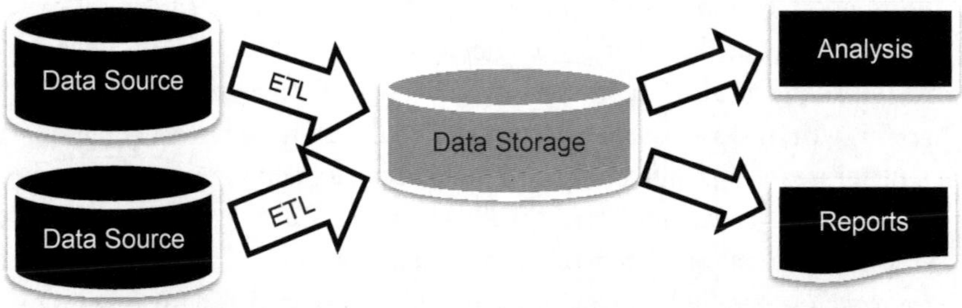

Figure 1 The simplified system architecture of BI solutions. Source: own.

Transactional databases that are used by different enterprise ERP, CRM and other systems are a typical data source for BI tools. These data are extracted using ETL tools (Extract), transformed to the desired form (Transform) and then loaded (Load) to specific data structures of the data warehouse. Consequently, these data can be analyzed and the analysis results can then be provided in the form of reports for decision-making of company managements.

3 Possible Microsoft Office Tools' Use in Different Parts of the Business Intelligence System Architecture

The following chapters will describe the possible use of individual Microsoft Office tools in different parts of the BI system architecture mentioned above. First, the use of Microsoft Office tools as a data source will be analyzed, and then their use as a data warehouse, subsequently their use as an ETL tool and as a tool for the creation of analyzes and reports. At the end, the consideration of the possibilities to integrate all these individual components into a single integrated BI solution will be stated.

3.1 Microsoft Office as a Data Source

Data sources for BI tools can be managed by all Microsoft Office applications mentioned above. The following table summarizes the basic advantages and disadvantages of using these applications as data source managers.

Data source manager	Advantages	Disadvantages
Excel	**The relative simplicity** (it is widely known and used tool).	**Low maximum number of records in the tables** (sheet of the workbook contains only 1,048,576 rows).
	It is included in all versions and editions of Microsoft Office (offline and online)	**Limited possibilities of relationships** (relationships between tables can be created only within pivot tables).
PowerPivot	**Without limiting the number of records in tables** (although it is a part of Excel, Excel restrictions are not valid for it).	**It does not allow editing of data** (it allows only data import from various sources and their reading)
	It allows to create relationships	**Inconsistency with Excel terminology** (although it is part of Excel)
Access	**All advantages of relational databases** (relationships, SQL etc.)	**Significant limitations compared to the enterprise DBMS** (e.g. database size is max. 2 GB, the number of columns in the table is max. 255, differences between Access SQL and SQL standard etc.)
Power BI	**The widest possibilities of importing data** (more than 59 types of data sources)	**It does not allow editing of data** (it allows only data import from various sources and their reading)
	The widest possibilities of data presentation (it may not be relevant for the data source)	**It can be the direct data source again only for the Power BI**

Table 1 Advantages and disadvantages of possible data source managers. Source: own.

The formats of data sources cannot be chosen in enterprise practice, where it is necessary to work with what is available, so the table mentioned above is addressed rather to BI teaching. As a possible data source manager from the mentioned above Access is most practical, because even in the enterprise practice as a data source for BI needs, relational OLTP databases, which are the basis of other information systems, are used mainly. A large amount of useful data is also located in the Excel workbooks which is the most common tool used by economists.

If then an OLTP database with a structure and a needed number of records close to the classical enterprise database is needed for teaching BI and there is no such one available, there are two possibilities how to solve this problem:

- To use an existing best freely available database that has a structure typical for OLTP databases and that also contains a sustainable amount of data. Here it is possible to recommend a simpler Northwind.accdb database, which is installed with the installation of

Access to PC, or a more complex database AdventureWorks.accdb, see CodePlex (2017). Surely, it is possible to find on the web also other suitable databases.
- If no existing database is available, it is necessary to manually create a new one and fill it with data. For BI needs, a great amount of records is necessary, that is why it would be more suitable to generate this data in some way. The process described, e.g. in Novák and Rozehnal (2014) is possible to use for such purpose.

3.2 Microsoft Office as a Data Storage

Němec (2014) divides the typical BI data storage system into three basic groups:
- central data warehouse,
- data mart,
- data staging area (the main purpose is to offer storage space for transforming data extracted in the ETL process).

The central data warehouse is a centralized enterprise storage while the data mart is typically designed for a narrower range of users, e.g. a branch within an enterprise. Data warehouse and data mart are built on similar principles, both of them therefore have two basic possibilities of storing multidimensionally organized data:
- in the form of a relational database schema,
- in the form of a multidimensional (OLAP) database represented by a data cube.

None of the Microsoft Office applications support creating multidimensional OLAP databases, therefore it is necessary to use a relational database schema (ROLAP) to create a data warehouse, so within Microsoft Office the best is to use the Access DBMS. The advantage of storing multidimensionally arranged data in the form of a relational database schema is the possibility to effectively solve data storage at the highest level of detail, as well as lower consumption of storage space. On the other hand, there may be a disadvantage in the performance deficiencies with aggregation operations over large amounts of data in the fact table.

Nowadays it is also possible to create relationships between tables and also a data warehouse by Power BI or Excel applications. Nevertheless, significant performance and capacity limits must be taken in account. Even Access is not suitable for professional usage as a data warehouse manager because of low performance (see table 1), it is constructed rather as a data management system for personal use. However, it can easily be used for demonstration of principles for pedagogical reasons. From family of Microsoft applications the Microsoft SQL Server could be used as a professional data warehouse manager. It is available in the Express edition for free and it would definitely be sufficient for small enterprises, but it is not a part of Microsoft Office.

The ordinary ROLAP database consists, according to Kimball a Ross (2013) of the dimension and fact tables arranged in a star schema or snowflake schema or their combination. It should be left to the creators of a data warehouse, which variant to choose, because each of them has its own advantages and disadvantages. However, if the data warehouse is made up for teaching needs, it seems to be better to use the star schema because the differences between OLAP and OLTP database star schema are more apparent there. The students can practically see that in OLAP databases performance is preferred to complying the third normal form.

As the most appropriate tool for the data staging area from the Microsoft Office tools there seems to be Microsoft Excel. It is because it contains a high-quality tool for performing transformations (Query Editor) and also it has extensive importing and exporting capabilities, see the chapter 3.3. Query Editor is also available in Power BI tool. Nevertheless, Power BI does not allow further data export, therefore this tool is not suitable as a data staging area tool. But because it enables the creation of large amounts of data visualizations, it is particularly suitable as a tool for creating reports, see chapter 3.4.

3.3 Microsoft Office as an ETL Tool

According to Vercellis (2009), ETL refers to the software that are devoted to performing in an automatic way three main functions: extraction, transformation and loading of data into the data warehouse.

All phases of the ETL may be performed in Microsoft Office at least to some extent by using the above-mentioned applications. Individual ETL phases are not always separated from each other, but can also fade together. E.g. selecting data or their aggregating (Extract) or possibly also the transforming (Transform) may be performed at the same time during importing the data (Load). Therefore, this chapter will not describe applications suitable for individual phases of ETL, but it will focus on several ways how to deal with ETL process.

Using SQL Statements in Access

If Access database is the data source and also the data warehouse, it is possible to use for all three phases of ETL the INSERT statement with IN clause of the SQL language. The INSERT statement allows not only to choose required columns of the source and target databases and insert selected records, but it also allows partial data transformations using built-in functions of the SQL language, e.g. the division of a date for the required time dimensions using the DatePart() function.

Němec (2014) states that the data pumps can operate in two modes: batch mode or real time mode. Scripts serving and automating the data pump can be created in Access or Excel by combination of SQL and Visual Basic for Application programming languages.

Import of the data

If the data warehouse in Access is created, it is possible to import data as well. Access has not only the possibility of importing data from Excel and Access, but also from other data sources (e.g. text or XML files). The possibilities of importing data are similar also in Excel.

Nevertheless, exceptional options of importing data provide Power BI application, but rather than as a data warehouse, Power BI is usable as a data staging area or as a tool for analysis and reporting. According to Microsoft (2017), the Power BI can connect to and import data from more than 59 different data sources, including cloud services or social networks. Power BI also contains a powerful Query Editor tool for data extraction.

Data Transformation

As it has been mentioned above; the basic data transformations can be performed at the extract phase of ETL process. However, if the transformations are more demanding, Excel or Power BI can be used at the transform phase of ETL process and the desired transformations can be performed there. Except traditional basic tools such as transposing, replacing values, filling etc., also advanced tools that are part of the Query Editor are usable. Power BI and Excel share Query Editor from 2016 version.

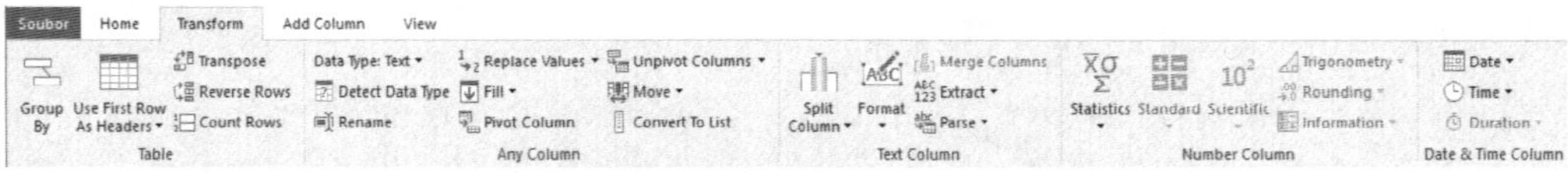

Figure 2 Transform tab of the Query Editor

3.4 Microsoft Office as a Tool for Analysis and Reports

For analyzes and reports, creating it is again possible to use all the above-mentioned Microsoft Office applications. Access seems to be the least suitable for this purpose. Although it is possible to create totals similar to Excel pivot tables by using the SELECT statement with PIVOT and TRANSFORM clauses of SQL language, which it is possible to visualize by using reports, but they do not by far reach the possibilities of Excel pivot tables. Access of previous versions allows direct creating pivot tables and charts, nevertheless, this functionality is not included in Access 2016 version.

Pivot tables and charts in Excel or PowerPivot are more suitable for creating basic analyzes and reports. Pivot tables and charts offer except basic data filtering also using of advanced slicers or timelines by which it is possible to unite filtering across multiple pivot tables or charts. And there are also completely new functions for data analyses in new versions of Excel or PowerPivot. The example can be Sheet Forecast, a very interesting new functionality of Excel, what is according to Microsoft (2017a) the possibility to create a forecast, if there historical time-based data are available. Next example could be the KPIs (Key Performance Indicator) tool, what is an interesting news of PowerPoint that allows you to view clearly the status of the specific task. It is, however impossible to create comprehensive dashboards in Excel or PowerPivot and to share those among multiple users.

The creation of analyzes, visualizations and subsequently dashboards from these visualization is possible within Microsoft Office applications by Power BI application. Power BI now offers more than 25 visualizations using all kinds of pivot tables, charts and maps, which can be pinned to the dashboard and shared among several users. The possibilities of data filtering are interesting as well because except usual options available, e.g. in Excel, Power BI allows you to ask questions also in natural human language, at this moment in English only. For greater availability of created dashboards, Power BI can also be installed on mobile phones as well as desktops, and that is true for all major platforms: Android, iOS and Windows Phone.

3.5 Possibilities of the Integration of Microsoft Office Tools into an Integrated BI Solution

One of the features of Microsoft Office applications is that they are very well integrated with each other. To create an integrated BI solution in the Microsoft Office it is essential that the stored data can be freely imported or exported among applications. However, there is no straightforward tool that would allow creating an integrated BI solution in the Microsoft Office. Therefore, it is necessary to reach for instruments, maybe not so straightforward, that allow creating an integrated BI solution. Such tools are the programming languages Visual Basic for Application and SQL.

Programing language Visual Basic for Application is an implementation of Microsoft's event-driven programming language Visual Basic 6 and is used in Microsoft Office applications (Walkenbach, 2013). VBA enables building macros, user-defined functions, graphical user interface, etc. It is essential for creating an integrated BI solution in the Microsoft Office that one Microsoft Office application can be programmatically controlled by another Microsoft Office application. It should not be a problem, for example, to perform data transformations using Excel tools from a data warehouse created in Access.

SQL is a computer language for working with sets of facts and the relationships between them. Relational database programs, such as Access, use SQL to work with data. Like many computer languages, SQL is an international standard that is recognized by standards bodies such as ISO and ANSI (Microsoft, 2017b). Unfortunately, the implementation of the SQL in Access differs from ISO or ANSI standards in some details. Nevertheless, by using SQL it is possible to create scripts, which allow extracting data from a relational data source type or uploading them to a data warehouse.

The graphical user interface of the resulting integrated BI solution can then be created in any of the Microsoft Office applications that enables the creation of such interface. In an integrated BI solution based on Microsoft Office that function can be performed by either Excel or Access. In both of these applications, you can create graphical user interfaces using VBA libraries. In Excel's VBA, it is specifically Microsoft Forms Object Library, Microsoft Access Object Library then in Access VBA.

4 Conclusion

The goal of this contribution was to show that using Business Intelligence is now possible without expensive, sophisticated tools, but it is also possible to use the universally available tools such as Microsoft Office. And when not on a professional level, so certainly for creating ad-hoc analyzes or reports or for educational purposes. Especially following Microsoft Office applications can be used in individual parts of the usual BI solutions: Excel and within the Excel PowerPivot tool, Access and relatively new Power BI tool available both as a cloud service within the Microsoft Office 365 and also as an offline application for desktop or mobile phone or Excel add-in. A serious problem appears to be only using Access as a data warehouse manager. On the other hand, Power BI seems to be very useful for creating analyzes and reports, and if it does not use the data from the data warehouse, it can be used for creating ad-hoc analyzes from many available data sources. Programming languages Visual Basic for Applications and SQL are then possible to use for creating an integrated BI solution. These programming languages are useful in most Microsoft Office applications and allow the creation of both functionalities of the integrated BI solution and its graphical user interface.

The Microsoft company seems to be very well aware of the growing importance of Business Intelligence for the successful management of companies, which can be proved by more and more new instruments added to everyday Microsoft Office applications. As an example of this, we can mention tools like Power BI or Query Editor available in Excel since version 2016. It will certainly be interesting to see what other tools for Business Intelligence solutions will appear in new versions of Microsoft Office applications.

References

CodePlex (2017). AdventreWorks in Access, [Online]. Available at: https://adventureworksaccess.codeplex.com/ [cited 2017-03-01].

Kimball, R. and Ross, M. (2013). *The Data Warehouse Toolkit: The Definitive Guide to Dimensional Modeling*, 3rd ed. New York: Wiley.

Laberge, R. (2011). *The Data Warehouse Mentor: Practical Data Warehouse and Business Insights*. New York: McGraw-Hill Education.

Microsoft (2017). Connect to Data Sources in Power BI Desktop, [Online]. Available at: https://powerbi.microsoft.com/en-us/guided-learning/powerbi-learning-1-2-connect-to-data-sources-in-power-bi-desktop/ [cited 2017-01-16].

Microsoft (2017a). Create a forecast in Excel 2016 for Windows, [Online]. Available at: https://support.office.com/en-us/article/Create-a-forecast-in-Excel-2016-for-Windows-22c500da-6da7-45e5-bfdc-60a7062329fd [cited 2017-01-19].

Microsoft (2017b). Introduction to Access SQL, [Online]. Available at: https://support.office.com/en-us/article/Introduction-to-Access-SQL-d5f21d10-cd73-4507-925e-bb26e377fe7e [cited 2017-03-06].

Němec, R. (2014). *Principy projektování a implementace systémů Business Intelligence*. Ostrava: VŠB-TU Ostrava.

Němec, R. and Hančlová, J. (2014). 'Enabling Business Intelligence for SMEs Information System'. *Proceedings of 22nd Interdisciplinary Information Management Talks (IDIMT) Conference*, Prague, Czech Republic, pp. 293-299.

Novák, V. and Rozehnal, P. (2014). 'Teaching Possibilities of Dimensional Modeling in Microsoft Excel'. *Proceedings of the IT for Practice 2014 17th International Conference*, Ostrava, Czech Republic, pp. 237-244.

Pochyla, M. (2015). 'Internet of Things: Big Challenge for Enterprises'. *11th International Conference on Strategic Management and its Support by Information Systems*, Uherské Hradiště, Czech Republic, pp. 470-477.

Pour, J., Maryška, M. and Novotný, O. (2012). *Business Intelligence v podnikové praxi*. Praha: Professional Publishing.

Vercellis, C. (2009). *Business Intelligence: Data Mining and Optimization for Decision Making*. New York: Wiley.

Walkenbach, J. (2013). *Excel 2013 Power Programming with VBA*. New York: Wiley.

Digital Inheritance on Social Networks – Young People's Perception

Antonín Pavlíček[1], Petr Doucek[2]

Abstract. The article discusses the perception of digital inheritance among youth. It defines the concept of digital inheritance and defines its content and scope. The research was focused on examining the views and perceptions of digital inheritance among 700 young people from both the Czech Republic and abroad. The results showed that young people do not care much about digital inheritance. Such attitude is widespread in both the Czech and foreign respondents, gender or other factors do not modify held view much. The preferred solution proposed in the case of death was to delete the profile, followed by letting the family to decide and edit the pro-file. The most widespread stance on this matter, however, is indifference.

Keywords: Facebook, social interactions, digital inheritance, youth survey.

JEL Classification: D83, L86

1 Introduction

Traditional physical media such as books, CDs or DVDs can be passed on to heirs without any legal complications, people can easily copy and pass on files that are stored on the computer hard drive, but current trend to store the data on remote servers opens new challenges. In contrast with physical assets, digital assets are quite ephemeral and subject to on-going change. When it comes to digital content or access rights (login credentials), the legal framework has failed to keep up pace with the rapid technological changes.

Intellectual property (copyright) and privacy (Sigmund, 2014) are additional factors. Transferring ownership can be more difficult if users' data (e.g. iTunes songs/videos, Amazon e-books, Facebook game achievements (Sudzina, 2013)), are digitally protected by content providers. Customers may be kept under the impression that they are "buying" songs, e-books and movies, however in reality many content sellers specify in their terms of service that they're merely offering a "license to use", or effectively "long-term rent", that isn't transferable.

And how to deal with the situation, when the content provider (cloud service company) goes bankrupt? Who owns the data[3]? It's not clear issue – Apple, Amazon, Facebook or Google have each different terms of use that just few customers bother to read. After all, any responsible company should take into consideration change of paradigm and plan accordingly in their innovation management schemes (Bazsova, 2016).

Issue of transference-upon-death is part of complex problem, which affects only few users so far – so the content providers have been slow to react so far. Digital inheritance may present

[1] University of Economics, Prague, Department of System Analysis, 4 W. Churchill sq. Prague, pavlant@vse.cz

[2] University of Economics, Prague, Department of System Analysis, 4 W. Churchill sq. Prague, doucek@vse.cz

[3] US cloud hosting companies historically observed the rule that the content does not belong to cloud hosting company, but to the customer only. However, this concept of mutual trust has been destroyed – not just for US citizens, but for all individuals and companies outside the United States – by court decision, which required Microsoft to provide US court access to the data stored in Ireland. Since than Germany does not regard US cloud hosting companies to be safe anymore.

a challenge for data heirs in its complexity and intricacy, especially when the average user is having in average 26 online accounts (25-34-year-olds have even more – over 40 online accounts, protected with only five different passwords) (Beach, 2014), digital inheritance has become a complex issue. To prevent estate issues, digital media owners should plan ahead – role of such responsible behavior lies also in a proper education (Hanclova and Doucek, 2011). Users can specify information - passwords and accounts to be passed on - in their will (Rosen, 2012).

Definition of digital inheritance:

"Digital inheritance is the process of handing over (personal) digital media, personal data and online assets and rights to (human) beneficiaries. The media in which a digital inheritance resides can be owned by or independent of the deceased. In the former category are personal computers, mobile phones and other devices, and in the latter category are the online corporations such as Google, Apple, Microsoft and Facebook. In between is a grey area of forums, blogs, personal websites and online banking." (Wikipedia, 2016)

1.1 Current situation with digital inheritance

The law hasn't caught up with technology. There has been some legislative progress for surviving family members. Some states in US (Idaho, Nebraska and Indiana) have enacted laws that allow next of kin to gain access to digital accounts, but Europe have not solved this problem so far. But the practice differs by the company:

Google has become the first of the large internet service providers to address inheritance problem and since 2013 users can leave behind their Google-run accounts (e.g. Gmail messages and Google+ profile) as a digital inheritance to their loved ones. Twitter in the event of the death works with a person authorized to act on the behalf of the estate or with a verified immediate family member of the deceased to have an account deactivated(Twitter.com, 2015). Yahoo states that its account is not transferable[4]. Same position holds Apple, but it allows heirs to circumvent this problem. If deceased person included his Apple ID and Password into a will, the new user (heir) can log-in and update name, change the email and password, and payment details making it – in effect – a new account with all of the old data in it. Without knowledge of log-in credentials Apple enables to completely close down an account, denying access to Apps and Music bought with that account (Hattersley, 2014).

1.2 Digital Inheritance in the environment of Facebook

Digital inheritance on Facebook is related to the provided data – both explicit and implicit. The elementary personal data are provided explicitly (consciously and clearly) during registration, for example name, email, gender and date of birth. In order to join social network service user must also pair his real-life friends and acquaintances with his Facebook profile. The set-up is completed by adding a profile picture and some more personal information such as employment, achieved education level, residence, accounts on other networks, marital status, important events and so on (Pavlicek and Pechar, 2012). Explicit data are supplemented by implicit data,

[4] But its stance was successfully challenged in 2005 lawsuit when a judge granted the father of a soldier who had died in Iraq access to his son's Yahoo e-mail account(Olsen, 2005).

which are expressed indirectly, and are available to be extracted by Facebook's sophisticated tools and procedures.

Above mentioned information stays within Facebook indefinitely and become the subject of digital inheritance. It should be noted here, that user must agree to the terms and conditions during the Facebook registration process.

In 2015 Facebook introduced a new legacy contact feature in the U.S., by which it allows its users to choose who would manage accounts once they've died. Facebook follows Google in providing this type of posthumous functionality, and we can expect other sites to follow suit. "When a person passes away, their account can become a memorial of their life, friendships and experiences."(Callison-Burch, 2015).

In Facebook's words, a legacy contact is "someone you choose to look after your account if it's memorialized." This person has the ability to manage friends list, add one last contribution, or adjust the profile picture and cover photo. But such person can not log into the account, change or remove the content which the deceased published, neither he can read personal messages (both send and received). Another problem is, that Facebook does not allow to delete the profile after user's death. The only way around it is to leave log-in credentials for a trusted person, who will maintain the Facebook account according to the last will.

2 Methodology

Research has been conducted at University of Economics, Faculty of Informatics and Statistics, thanks to the cooperation with students of the course New Media. Friends and acquaintances of students in have been surveyed. Invitations to study participation has been individually send by private message only to respondents eligible to undertake the survey. Thanks to that, high relevancy of the responses was guaranteed. The survey was carried out through Google Forms.

In the first part of questionnaire the scope of information that respondents consciously put on their Facebook profiles was analyzed. Thanks to that respondents were reminded of the digital footprint they left behind. In the second part were respondents asked about digital inheritance, its possible consequences and related open questions.

In total 697 responses were collected during November 2015. The answers were collected amongst Facebook users from the Czech Republic, Switzerland, and the USA, aiming primarily on user 18 - 30 years of age (91 % of respondents). Results were collected through eight separate questionnaires, where each one was targeted to one specific group of users. The questions, however, were identical (except for the fact that we used two language versions: Czech and English). The groups were as follows:

- family members of our students (Czech) – 23 respondents,
- friends of our students (Czechs) – 97 respondents,
- friends of our students (other nationalities but no Czech) – 39 respondents,
- members of FB group linked to University of Economics Prague – 253 respondents,
- members of FB group linked to Czech University of Life Sciences Prague – 95 respondents,
- members of FB group linked to Czech Technical University in Prague – 81 respondents,
- members of FB group linked to University of St. Gallen (Switzerland) – 31 respondents,

- members of FB group linked to New York University (USA) – 78 respondents.

Vast majority (69 %) of respondents were students (3 % at high school, 81 % bachelor level, 16 % master level), just 2 % retired and 2 % unemployed.

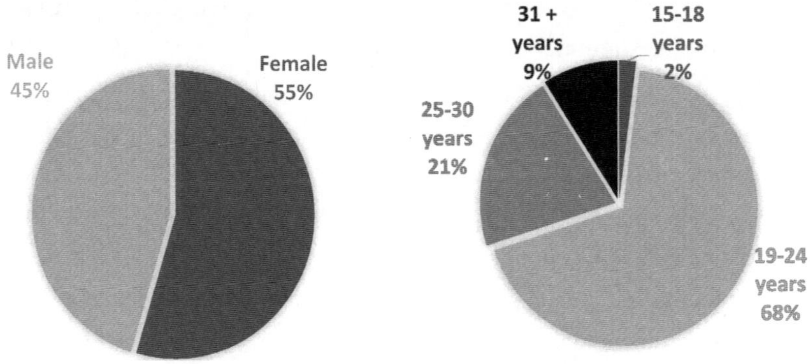

Figure 1. Gender and Age distribution of respondents

Regarding digital inheritance, there were 4 mayor question mapping the attitude towards. A quarter of the respondents had never thought about what happens to a Facebook account after user's death, and almost half of the users, even when this issue at least once crossed their minds, do not have a clue about what will happen with their Facebook profile.

Here is good to mention, that based on results, we could arguably state, that ¾ of respondents that are mainly young people, are approaching social networks with healthy curiosity in connection to idea, that they might actually leave something behind and they are curious what is going to happen with it. Especially when: 1) probably for each of those young respondents, will became digital inheritance an issue with which them or their relatives will be confronted sometime in the future, since the usage of social sites is still more and more common + users naturally age 2) although respondents were mainly young people with long life expectancy, they still realize, that information they will leave behind, are an issue, that should be handled with some degree of care.

Respondents did not differ much in relation to the age or cultural origin, however there was significant difference between genders: males were almost twice as much likely to know what exactly is going to happen in case of sudden death. For details see Table 1.

		Family	Friends	UEP	CULS	CTU	USG	NYU	ENG friends	SUM
Yes, **I know exactly** what happens in such case	F		1	9	6	1		4	1	**22**
	M		4	17	4	10	2	3	6	**46**
I **have an idea**, but I'm not sure where / how to Check it in settings of my account	F	1	12	33	14	3	1	14		**78**
	M	1	9	14	8	20	3	4	3	**62**
I **do not know**, but I've thought about it	F	2	20	70	37	11	1	26	3	**170**
	M	6	10	33	8	13	13	12	1	**96**
No, I **never thought** about it	F	6	15	49	14	6	1	8	1	**100**
	M	5	17	28	4	17	10	7	8	**96**

Table 1 Have you ever wondered what happens to a FB account after user's death?

Another issue which was surveyed was: What do you consider to be the best solution for Facebook accounts of deceased persons? – see Table 2. In this case we received most decisive answer – according to the majority of respondents (56 %) the family should be allowed to delete the profile (which is something Facebook does not support at the moment). 15 % expressed opinion, that family should edit the profile (which is currently supported by Facebook to some extent), nearly 20 % have not thought about it, but was interested in the problem. Men were twice as much inclined to allow family edit the profile than women, neither cultural origin, nor level of education played any role.

		Family	Friends	UEP	CULS	CTU	USG	NYU	ENG friends	SUM
Keep everything on the profile **as it is**	F	1	3	10	4	1		5		**24**
	M	3	6	6	1	6	2	2	1	**27**
Allow the **family** of the deceased to **edit** profile	F	2	4	10	6	5	2	9		**38**
	M	1	6	22	3	11	5	9	3	**60**
Allow the family of the deceased to **delete** the profile	F	2	36	108	49	11	1	21	5	**233**
	M	2	20	55	15	28	16	4	17	**157**
I **do not know** how to deal with this issue, but it sure is good to think about it	F	5	11	28	10	4		16	3	**77**
	M	3	5	2	4	10	3	11	7	**45**
I do **not** think it is actually **necessary to deal** with this topic	F	1	3	5	2			1	1	**13**
	M	3	3	7	1	5	2		2	**23**

Table 2 What do you consider to be the best solution for Facebook accounts of deceased persons?

44 % positive answers to the question "Would you choose someone as a caretaker of your profile in the event of your death?" is much higher percentage than expected. It is not majority, but gives us the justified right to say, that there is a strong desire, to have more control over users profile in terms of death related data management. See Table 3 for details.

		Family	Friends	UEP	CULS	CTU	USG	NYU	ENG friends	SUM
Yes	F	6	27	84	34	6	2	19	6	**184**
	M	4	16	43	11	23	8	12	8	**125**
No, I don't consider it to be important	F	5	29	77	37	15	1	33	3	**200**
	M	5	24	49	13	37	20	14	22	**184**

Table 3 Would you choose someone as a caretaker of your profile in the event of your death?

When dealing with topic of digital inheritance, especially in environment of social sites, it is important to point out sentimental side of the matter. In the past, personal correspondence, love letters, diaries, personal notes, medical records, and calendars were all in the paper form, as were the photos. These personal items were usually handed over (inherited) to the close living relatives (children, grandchildren), thus allowing them to get new glimpses of the other /hidden/ side of their close family relatives (grandmothers, grandfathers ...). Such approach is now being legally obstructed by privacy protection[5]

Attitude towards breaking the privacy laws in case of inheritance was tested by following question: “Would you like to be given access to profile of your grandmother her death?” – see Table 4.

		Family	Friends	UEP	CULS	CTU	USG	NYU	ENG friends	SUM
Yes, I would like to **know more** about her	F	1	2	8	7	1		11		**30**
	M	1	3	6	1	3	3	3	2	**22**
Yes, I would like to have her **friends' contacts**	F	5	12	22	9	4	1	13		**66**
	M	2	3	9	4	6	2	3		**29**
Yes, I would like to **edit** her profile	F		2	10	5	1		4	3	**25**
	M	1	2	9	1	1		4	4	**22**
Yes, I would like to **delete** her profile permanently	F	3	25	73	36	7	1	11	4	**160**
	M	3	11	35	10	23	9	4	11	**106**
No, I find it to be **pointless**	F	2	16	48	14	8	1	13	2	**104**
	M	5	21	33	8	27	14	12	13	**133**

Table 4 Would you like to be given access to profile of your mother / grandmother (or any other close family member) after his or her death?

There is significant part of users (66 %) that would want for some reason to have access to some extent to Facebook account of their close relatives in case of their death. But perhaps in order to have results more to the original point, the respondents in future surveys should be

[5] Facebook vs Stassen: Facebook refused on the grounds of privacy access to an account for parents who sought an explanation as to why their son committed suicide. Facebook even disobeyed Court Order, which released Facebook from their duty of client confidentiality. They upheld their policy of not allowing personal representatives access to accounts.

confronted with more thorough explanation of the above mentioned sentimental point of today digital vs. past classic inheritance.

3 Conclusion

It is possible to conclude, that the young users of social sites are widely ignorant in the terms of use and realities hidden behind the term "digital inheritance". Yet when confronted with the practicalities of it, the average respondent – young social network site user – shows a healthy curiosity and is willing or, to be more accurate, wants to gain a more substantial control over it.

Undoubtedly there is an ongoing need for deeper research of digital inheritance topic and urgent requirements to raise the self-awareness about it between users, since topics such as privacy and digital inheritance in the environment of social media are not part of a common discourse of society nowadays.

At the moment, the idea of inheriting a virtual material seems foreign to most of users but human mortality makes us predict, that the next generation will be dealing with this problem on daily basis.

The idea of digital inheritance does not come to mind to most of the people but an interesting conclusion can be drawn from the responses of our survey: the vast majority of young people, when confronted with the idea, find the topic of digital very important to think about and feel the responsibility to deal with it in the future. A correlation was found between all the surveyed groups, which means that Czech respondents have similar perception of the privacy and digital inheritance topics as the ones from Switzerland or the United States. Similar results have been also recorded, when compared from the point of view of age and educational level Some small differences have been observed between genders, but in general we can say, that the topic is universally perceived: about a half of young population does not care, the rest pays to the problem at least some attention, when asked. The preferred solution of digital heritage is to remove the data, followed by letting the family to decide and edit the profile. The most widespread stance on this matter, however, is indifference.

4 References

Bazsova, B. (2016). 'Influence of Innovation Management on Project Management in an Organization'. *Innovation Management and Education Excellence Vision 2020: From Regional Develop-Ment Sustainability to Global Economic Growth, Vols. I - VI.* Norristown: Int Business Information Management Assoc-IBIMA.

Beach, D. (2014). 5 Tips to Beat the Online Cyber-Criminals, [Online]. Available at: http://www.experian.co.uk/blogs/consumer-advice/beat-the-cyber-criminals-stay-safe-online/ [Accessed 2017-01-07].

Callison-Burch, V. (2015). Adding a Legacy Contact | Facebook Newsroom. *FB Newsroom*, [Online]. Available at: http://newsroom.fb.com/news/2015/02/adding-a-legacy-contact/ [Accessed 2017-01-07].

Hanclova, J. and Doucek, P. (2011). 'Education and ICT Sector in the EU (panel-National Application)'. *Efficiency and Responsibility in Education 2011*, Prague 6, Czech University Life Sciences Prague.

Hattersley, L. (2014). *How to Access iTunes Account, Music and Apps after Death - How to - Macworld UK*, [Online]. Available at: http://www.macworld.co.uk/how-to/apple/access-itunes-account-music-apps-after-death-3507255/ [Accessed 2016-05-20].

Olsen, S. (2005). *Yahoo Releases E-Mail of Deceased Marine,* [Online]. Available at: http://www.cnet.com/news/yahoo-releases-e-mail-of-deceased-marine/.

Pavlicek, A. and Pechar, Z. (2012). 'Availability of Users' Personal Data on Facebook'. *IDIMT 2012: ICT Support for Complex Systems,* 38, pp. 377–380.

Rosen, R.J. (2012). 'The Government Would Like You to Write a 'Social Media Will''. *The Atlantic*.

Sigmund, T. (2014). 'Privacy in the Information Society: How to Deal with Its Ambiguity?' *IDIMT-2014: Networking Societies - Cooperation and Conflict*, pp. 191–201.

Sudzina, F. (2013). 'Escapist Motives for Playing Facebook Games: Fine-Tuning Constructs'. *IDIMT-2013: Information Technology Human Values, Innovation and Economy*, pp. 151–158.

Twitter.com (2015). Contacting Twitter about a deceased user.

Wikipedia (2016). Digital Inheritance. *Wikipedia*.

Smart Contracts and Internet of Things Future

Martin Pochyla[1]

Abstract. The aims of this paper is to provide a conceptual context for new technologies around smart contracts and blockchain together with Internet of things. Blockchain, smart contracts and decentralized autonomous organizations have received significant attention recently. In the world of Internet of things, we can build very interesting concepts of use with these new technologies. This paper is focused on related issues for new complex solutions and implementation in enterprise world. In this regard, I first provide a brief overview of the core aspects of these technologies, as well as the smart contracts-based developments for Internet of things. I discuss key issues that must be considered in developing such as blockchain-based technologies in Internet of things context. The result of this effort is to show that future Internet of things application allows the contingency of future events to be more robustly orchestrated through smart contracts.

Keywords: Internet of Things, Blockchain, Smart Contracts, Decentralized Autonomous Organization, BlockchainDB.

JEL Classification: M13, O33

1 Introduction

Cryptocurrencies like Bitcoin represent much more than digital economic innovations. The true value of the underlying technology the blockchain has only just begun to be explored and potential applications to the Internet of Things and smart systems (houses, cities, environments, etc.) are vast.

Some of computing projects could include genome and microbiome research banks with billions of files, national property registries, searchable government records databases, astronomical data management, unified Electronic Medical Record systems, and Internet of Things connected sensor and device coordination. I suggest that blockchain technology could be one solution for creating a next-generation computational architecture to address these kinds of larger-scale computational projects that have been impossible before.

A 2016 Ericsson report predicted that IoT would result in 16 billion devices being connected to the Internet by 2021. By 2018, IoT will surpass mobile as the largest category of connected devices (Ericsson, 2016).

Blockchain technology is gaining steam among finance firms because of its potential to streamline processes and increase efficiency. The technology could cut costs by up to $20 billion annually by 2022, according to Santander (Liu, 2015).

According to Adams (2015a) combining the Internet of Things (IoT) and blockchain can develop mechanisms for both encouraging adoption of the IoT and protecting data rights.

The genius of the blockchain systems is threefold: it ensures privacy and security for the owner of the data; it allows the data owner to see when the data has been used. Main distributed

[1] VŠB-TU Ostrava, Faculty of Economics, Department of Applied Informatics, martin.pochyla@vsb.cz

ledger technology works as a transaction of the blockchain and gives the individual ownership of their own data, information or other assets. As Pitner and Ministr (2015) describes some of the security, directions could be similar to PaaS category of cloud computing.

2 Smart Contracts

In 1996, Nick Szabo described a smart contract as a "set of promises, specified in digital form, including protocols within which the parties perform on these promises." In its simplest form, a smart contract is a machine-readable program, written in code that will execute itself when a set of pre-determined terms are met. While the technology available to support smart contracts has evolved considerably since then, this definition continues to capture the essence of what a smart contract is and does. It is noteworthy that smart contracts do not need necessary Artificial Intelligence or Business Intelligence (Němec and Hančlová, 2014) to operate.

According to McConaghy (2016b) there's new opportunity for Artificial Intelligence (AI) with blockchains, which unlock the possibility for AI DAOs (Decentralized Autonomous Organizations). DAOs possibilities and models are more described further in the paper.

One interesting application of blockchain is the use of it together with smart contracts. An agreement between parties that is posted to the blockchain brings completely new opportunities and change paradigm of electronic formal contracts. These agreements can be established between peer-to-peer, person-to-organization or person-to-machine. The agreement could specify virtually anything. For example, it could state that once a particular condition is met (e.g. sales of commodity on exchange or fulfil leasing condition), some asset (e.g. digital currency, title to property, data) will be exchanged between the parties of the contract. The transaction would then be replicated and validated on the blockchain.

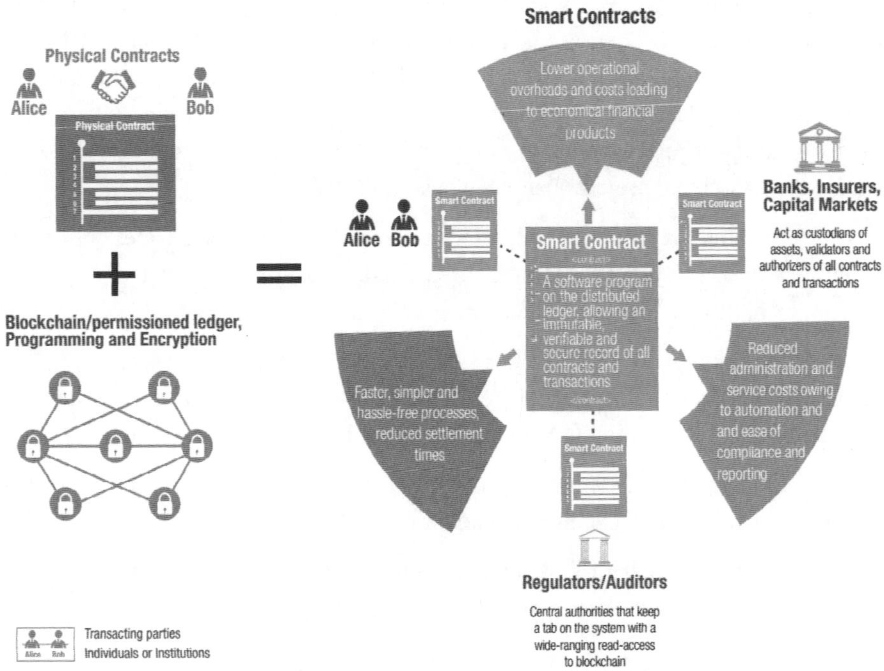

Figure 1 Smart contracts model in a blockchain system[Capgemini, 2016]

The main benefits of model displayed in Figure 1 can be extended to all major segments of the financial services industry or completely different environment. Smart contracts can drive significant value in three key areas: risk reduction, cost savings, and enhanced efficiencies.

Smart contracts allow us to exchange value without a third party being involved or knowing of the transfer. In effect, by minimizing the trust required for an exchange, they allow for the complete automation of contract fulfillment. In doing so, they by-pass the legal system and create a series of self-enforcing contractual mechanisms to create what has been called a "crypto-legal" contract (Morrison, 2017). This opens the potential for change of the entire legal system and creating a new form of virtual agreements. Companies like Ethereum are currently developing complex software to implement this vision.

The scripting language used today in smart contracts is based on Szabo's early efforts, but has taken a graphical tack with protocols such as Ethereum. The language of that protocol, called EtherScript, appears in modular, color-coded form to make it more human readable and intuitive. Simple script for loan management as shown in Figure 2. We can see four options for changing transforming visual model to Serpent, LLL or XML code. Serpent, LLL and Solidity all can be used to write smart contracts. Serpent used to be the flagship language together with LLL. Solidity is the flagship language now but it is still under development and may change in the future. All languages are compiled into bytecode before being deployed to the blockchain.

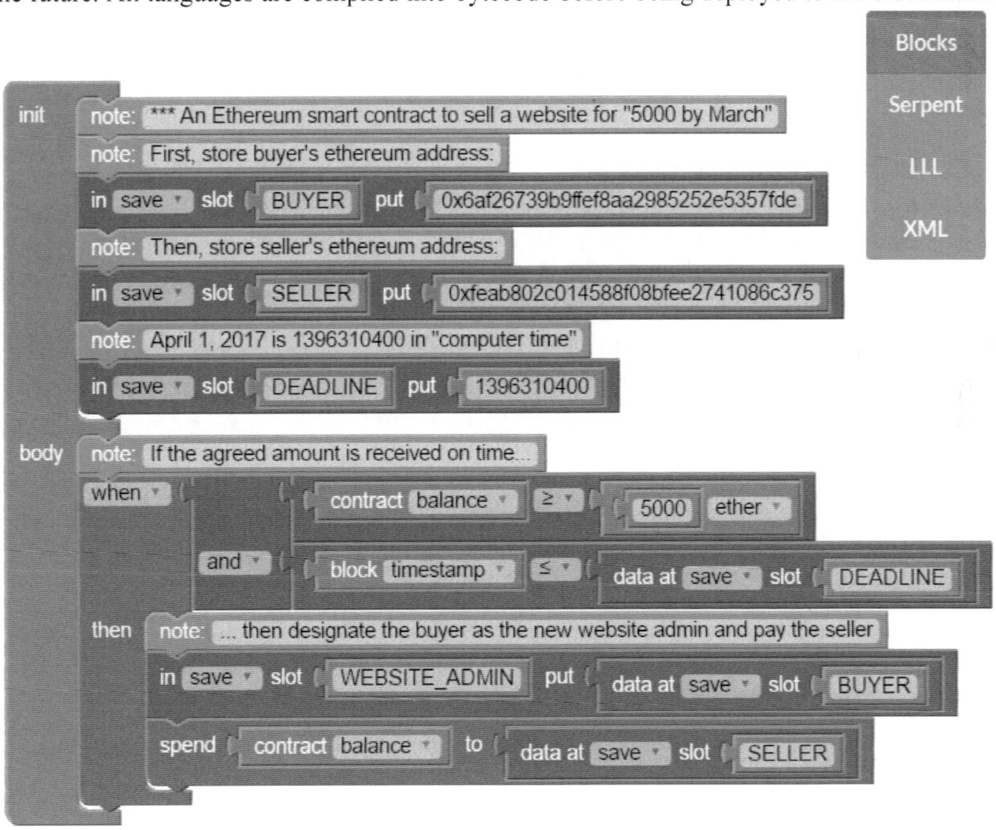

Figure 2 Graphical block version of the smart contract. [EtherScripter.com, 2017]

2.1 Smart Contracts from Legal Perspective

New technology and paradigms often outpaces regulatory frameworks and the current law (Rapier, 2016) (Perez, 2015). This current situation is very complex in the area of smart contracts as well. To make smart contracts interoperate with the existing legal system there must be work done on several problems from a legal standpoint:

Immutability – Smart contracts written as software programs on distributed ledgers would mean that the contracts, once agreed upon, could not be easily modified. This would cause practical problems in many real-world scenarios. One possible approach is what we often refer to as an 'escape hatch', a preprogrammed way of changing the terms of a smart contract. According to Eyal and Sirer (2016) an escape hatch is simply a mechanism to stop the operation of a smart contract, perhaps revert it to a lower-level safety mode, when something nefarious seems to be taking place.

Contractual secrecy – Normally, a copy of smart contracts executed on a blockchain or a permissioned ledger is shared with the chain's members. The anonymity of the parties can be secured, but the secrecy of contract execution is not necessarily secured. I believe that this is an area that is receiving huge attention and where progress will be made. MIT Enigma – encrypted cloud platform is a project that is trying to solve the problem of privacy preserving data sharing within organizations and between organizations, by use of advanced cryptographic structures. We can find a similarity in a concept known as "zero knowledge proofs" (Goldreich, 2002). In this concept is being to devise a way to separate the way of verifying a transaction from seeing the content of that transaction.

Legal enforceability and adjudication – The financial services industry is highly regulated, and specific licenses and approvals are issued to companies to participate in a distributed ledger-based market. For instance, the US Securities and Exchange Commission recently approved the internet retailer Overstock.com to issue company stock on a platform on top of the Bitcoin blockchain (Metz, 2016). However, the legality of financial smart contracts is yet to be established. Initial steps have been taken in the US, by the State of Vermont, to recognize distributed ledgers in the state courts (Higgins, 2016). Another case, the US State of Delaware recently launched a program to provide an enabling regulatory and legal environment for the development of blockchain technology (Prisco, 2016).

Accurate translation of legal terms and conditions into software logic is another key aspect to consider. Startups such as CommonAccord are working on a system that auto-translates legal documents into smart contracts (Reutzel, 2016), simplifying their interpretation by both lawyers and developers. Legislators, regulators and governments have begun to realize the potential for distributed ledgers in increasing transparency and ease of compliance and reporting. The push from these authorities will be instrumental in soon overcoming legal and administrative hurdles.

3 Decentralized Autonomous Organization.

For IoT world could be very interesting connection between smart contracts and devices used in network infrastructures. Ethereum founder Buterin (2014) has called entities, which are using smart contracts and blockchain structure Decentralized Autonomous Organizations (DAOs).

DAOs are using the power of blockchain together with smart contracts to create strong relationships between different entities to form organizations.

A DAO could exist in virtual space with smart contracts manage relationships between key actors. That is, the organization would have no central control and could be administered entirely on the web. Organization would have no reliance on conventional legal contracts. Autonomous machine agents would manage most activities and agreements would be self-enforcing via the blockchain.

Figure 3 - Main themes for DAO enabling [Mougayar, 2015]

Mougavar (2015) gives an interesting point of view for four main themes, which are cooperating in DAOs – Figure 3. All parts are necessary to allow DAOs to run without any human involvement under the control of an incorruptible set of business rules.

A DAO would not be entirely machine managed. Although machines and autonomous entities would play a key role, humans would still manage most of their interactions and be responsible for many main tasks. However, growing automation, even in formerly highly skilled occupations (e.g., programming, finance, data analysis), would increasingly be given over to machines (Jarche, 2016, Hančlová, 2016).

The advantages of DAOs are:

- **Efficiency**: DAOs would be extremely efficient as they would dispense with the overhead associated with oversight and routine management activities;
- **Transparent and Immune to Corruption**: All DAO actions could be tracked and audited and would be immune to manipulation by management or other actors;
- **Resistant to External Pressure**: A DAO could not be corrupted or influenced by external actors;
- **Highly Scalable**: A DAO could be easily scaled to encompass more participants and functions.

It is very important to point out, that the whole DAOs concept is very fragile in terms of privacy and security. The DAO network was compromised and 3.6 million ETH (approximate

$53 Million) were drained from the DAO. To put it into perspective, this was a third of its resources. According to Finley (2016) a $53 Million hack just showed that the DAO was all too human with all pros and cons. Stephan Tual, the COO of Slock.it, the company that built the DAO, says the thief probably never expected to be able to spend the currency ether. Each unit of ether is unique and traceable. If the hacker tries to sell any of the stolen ether in a cryptocurrency market, the system will flag it. On the other hand, it shows very strong transparency of the whole DAOs concept.

4 Blockchain Derivatives Applicable for Decentralized IoT

Current IoT ecosystems rely on centralized, brokered communication models, otherwise known as the server/client paradigm. All devices are identified, authenticated and connected through cloud servers that manage huge storage and processing capacities.

According to McConaghy (2016a) main major components that comprise the decentralized content registry are:

- **Licensing**: Coala IP is a blockchain-friendly, community driven protocol for attribution and licensing of IP. It reconciles existing formats and has flexibility for complex operations. Coala IP was just recently released – coalaip.org;
- **Database**: IPDB - Interplanetary Database Foundation is a global decentralized database to store attribution & licensing info. Specifically, IPDB is a global network with thoughtful governance that is running scalable decentralized database software (BigchainDB);
- **Storage data via Peer to Peer:** P2P file sharing services have left the central database for a decentralized parallel blockchain. We can imagine a large global cloud service in which customers' claims files as payments for their running digitally store and they do not need any substantial storage facilities. Huge and rapid development we can observe around projects like, Distributed Cloud Storage - storj.io or blockchain application - factom.com;
- **File system**: IPFS & FileCoin together are a global decentralized file system to store the content itself. Interplanetary File System – ipfs.io and FileCoin.io are working and testing very hard;
- **Identity management**: Digital identity formation, which eventually may be more important than the physical. Especially in the case of blockchain success, we will hear about project like Blockstack identity – onename.com.

All of these technologies and concepts have mostly open-source licenses. Other technologies can help further. For example, Ethereum project metioned above could be used for more complex licensing logic, or Mediachain an open, universal media library, could be used for richer attribution and connection between authors and media. Blockchain application frameworks such as Blockstack (Castillo, 2016), Monax Eris (Kuhlman, 2016), or BlockApps (Lilic, 2015) could further ease integration. Rozehnal and Novák (2016) pointed to the fact that the integration process is required to perform under specific framework and its rules.

For successfully promoting the implementation of blockchain, we could consider mainly these following areas:

1) The sales transaction as a virtual currency, but also to equities. The NASDAQ is experimenting on his private stock market with blockchain (Price, 2015);
2) Digital property - generally all kinds of digital goods and dematerialized claims, such as shares, stocks, items in different member clubs and programs or even ownership of objects of games. Examples can be projects like Coloredcoins - coloredcoins.org or Counterparty protocol – counterparty.io.

Blockchain certainly is not universally appropriate mechanism for sharing data between devices connected to IoT, but just the opposite. For specific applications of blockchain, there must be a principal justification for paying a high price for writing information into ledger. At this price, customers and companies buy the public credibility of certain events (time stamp), conclusive uncensored record. Companies or individuals must always ask themselves: "Do I need to make this record a globally public, 100 % accessible and completely bullet-proof?"

When we think of blockchain as a precious and limited resource, we get far more interesting use of specific cases, which are frequently based only on the hook into blockchain. The hook is really just a hash (40-character string) stored at a certain time in a blockchain and thus unquestionable. On it binds some information stored in a different data structure. That may no longer be a global public, may not be 100 % available, and may not even be unquestionable and perfectly distributed.

5 Conclusion

Chaotic growth of IoT environment introduce several challenges, including identifying, connecting, securing, and managing many different devices. As more and more devices create mass quantities of data and companies aim to leverage the IoT to create and employ those data, security and accountability will be major hurdles. The incorporation of blockchain rules and processes into IoT solutions could be one way to secure those data and ensure that devices are accurately registering and reporting correct and trustful information.

It will be very challenging for the current infrastructure and architecture underlying the Internet and online services to support huge IoT ecosystems of the future. This paper discuss how combining the IoT and blockchain can develop mechanisms for both encouraging adoption of the IoT and protecting data rights. Examples of running projects and new framework could help in orientation in this new blockchain paradigm. Organizations type as the DAO from institutions point of view mean the same thing as cryptocurrency in finance. Technologies are currently in the experimental stage, but perfectly fit into a trend that began with the mass expansion of the Internet. It is a trend of economically efficient decentralization.

However, it is important to mention that according to Smith and Anderson (2016) around half of Americans have heard of the alternate currency bitcoin – but just 1 % have actually used bitcoins themselves. The research cited by Fletcher (2014) observes that Bitcoin awareness is high among UK citizens, with 71 % of respondents heard about the digital currency. The study also found that Bitcoin has a reputation problem, as nearly one-quarter of respondents said the digital currency has a "fair" or "very bad" reputation and problem with lack of place to spend Bitcoin.

It is important to realize that blockchain is a very inefficient way of storing information. The fundamental fact is the presence of the mechanism of proof-of-work, which makes it impossible to falsify records in blockchain while making computationally very demanding records added. Together with bigger use of blockchain, we have to focus on economical part of equation. The main problem could be specifically, the large amounts of burned electricity (Deetman, 2016). Another problem, which was discussed above, is the size and the storage of data created by blockchain. We call it as data footprint and blockchain has already 100 Gigabytes (Blockchain info, 2017). If nowadays somebody want fully participate as a blockchain node, must calculate with such as amount of data to be downloaded.

I believe that a next-generation technology are enabling much larger-scale and more complex computing projects. Blockchain and smart contracts importance lies not in the fact that these are revolutionary technologies. More important it is in terms of a change in thinking and transform the functioning of human society.

References

Adams, T. (2015a). Let's Liquefy the World: Blockchain, Smart Contract, and the Internet-of-Things, [Online]. Available at: https://www.linkedin.com/pulse/lets-liquefy-world-blockchain-smart-contract-tori-adams?trk=mp-reader-card [cited 2017-01-28].

Adams, T. (2015b). Blockchain, Smart Contracts, and Health: Booz Allen Hamilton and the Blockchain Revolution, [Online]. Available at: https://www.linkedin.com/pulse/blockchain-smart-contracts-health-booz-allen-hamilton-tori-adams?trk=mp-reader-card [cited 2017-01-27].

Buterin, V. (2014). DAOs, DACs, DAs and More: An Incomplete Terminology Guide, [Online]. Available at: https://blog.ethereum.org/2014/05/06/daos-dacs-das-and-more-an-incomplete-terminology-guide/ [cited 2017-01-14].

Blockchain info (2017). Blockchain size, [Online]. Available at: https://blockchain.info/charts/blocks-size [cited 2017-01-14].

Capgemini (2016). Smart Contracts in Financial Services:Getting from Hype to Reality, [Online]. Available at: https://www.capgemini-consulting.com/resource-file-access/resource/pdf/smart-contracts.pdf [cited 2017-01-30].

Castillo, M. (2016). Bitcoin-Powered Internet Advances With $4 Million Blockstack Funding, [Online]. Available at: http://www.coindesk.com/blockstack-4-million-funding-series-a/ [cited 2017-01-30].

Deetman, S. (2016). Bitcoin Could Consume as Much Electricity as Denmark by 2020, [Online]. Available at: https://motherboard.vice.com/en_us/article/bitcoin-could-consume-as-much-electricity-as-denmark-by-2020 [cited 2017-01-28].

Ericsson (2016). Ericsson Mobility Report. On the pulse of the networked society, [Online]. Available at: https://www.ericsson.com/res/docs/2016/ericsson-mobility-report-2016.pdf [cited 2017-01-20].

Eyeal, I., Sirer E. G. (2016). A Decentralized Escape Hatch for DAOs, [Online]. Available at: http://hackingdistributed.com/2016/07/11/decentralized-escape-hatches-for-smart-contracts/ [cited 2017-01-28].

Finley, K. (2016). A $50 Million Hack Just Showed That the DAO Was All Too Human, [Online]. Available at: https://www.wired.com/2016/06/50-million-hack-just-showed-dao-human/ [cited 2017-01-20].

Fletcher, K. (2014). Bitcoin awareness high among respondents to UK 'Bitcoin Barometer', [Online]. Available at: https://coinreport.net/bitcoin-awareness-high-among-respondents-uk-bitcoin-barometer/ [cited 2017-01-28].

Goldreich, O. (2002). Zero-Knowledge: a tutorial by Oded Goldreich, [Online]. Available at: http://www.wisdom.weizmann.ac.il/~oded/zk-tut02.html [cited 2017-01-28].

Hančlová, J. (2016). 'A two-stage Data Envelopment Analysis Model with application to banking industry in the Visegrad Group'. *34th International Conference Mathematical Methods in Economics*: Sept 06-09, 2016, Liberec, Czech Republic, pp. 254-259. WOS:000385239500044.

Higgins, S. (2016). Vermont is Close to Passing a Law That Would Make Blockchain Records Admissible in Court, [Online]. Available at: http://www.coindesk.com/vermont-blockchain-timestamps-approval/ [cited 2017-01-28].

Jarche, H. (2016). Automate work, not people, [Online]. Available at: https://jarche.com/2016/04/automate-work-not-people/ [cited 2017-01-20].

Kuhlman, C (2016). What is Eris? 2016 Edition, [Online]. Available at: https://monax.io/2016/04/03/wtf-is-eris/ [cited 2017-01-20].

Lilic, J. (2015). Understanding BlockApps Strato; the full stack technology that allows enterprise to build smart contract enabled applications in five minutes, [Online]. Available at: https://www.linkedin.com/pulse/understanding-blockapps-strato-full-stack-technology-allows-lilic [cited 2017-01-20].

Liu, A. (2015). Santander: Distributed Ledger Tech Could Save Banks $20 Billion a Year, [Online]. Available at: https://ripple.com/insights/santander-distributed-ledger-tech-could-save-banks-20-billion-a-year/ [cited 2017-01-02].

McConaghy, T. (2016a). A Decentralized Content Registry for the Decentralized Web, [Online]. Available at: https://medium.com/ipdb-blog/a-decentralized-content-registry-for-the-decentralized-web-99cf1335291f#.auorv6bwg [cited 2017-01-28].

McConaghy, T. (2016b). Blockchains for Artificial Intelligence - From Decentralized Model Exchanges to Model Audit Trails, [Online]. Available at: https://blog.bigchaindb.com/blockchains-for-artificial-intelligence-ec63b0284984#.pjjzy9j1n [cited 2017-01-28].

Metz, C (2016). Overstock Begins Trading Its Shares Via the Bitcoin Blockchain, [Online]. Available at: (https://www.wired.com/2016/12/overstock-com-issues-stock-via-bitcoin-blockchain/ [cited 2017-01-28].

Morisson, A. (2017). The end game for public and private blockchains isn't just digital currency—it's digital business flows, [Online]. Available at: http://www.pwc.com/us/en/technology-forecast/blockchain/digital-business.html [cited 2017-01-10].

Mougayar, W. (2015). What Does it Take to Succeed as a Decentralized Autonomous Organization?, [Online]. Available at: http://www.coindesk.com/succeed-as-decentralized-autonomous-organization/ [cited 2017-01-25].

Němec, R. and Hančlová, J. (2014). 'Enabling Business Intelligence for SMEs Information System'. *IDIMT-2014: Networking Societies - Cooperation and Conflict: 22nd Interdisciplinary Information Management Talks*, Poděbrady, Czech Republic, pp. 293-299. WOS:000346148300032.

Perez, B. Y. (2015). UK Government Highlights Benefits of Blockchain Tech, [Online]. Available at: http://www.coindesk.com/uk-government-highlights-benefits-of-bitcoin-and-blockchain-tech/ [cited 2017-01-25].

Pitner, T. and Ministr, J. (2015). 'Security Aspect of PaaS Cloud Model'. *Proceedings of the 11th International Conference on Strategic Management and its Support by Information Systems*. Uherske Hradiste, Czech Republic, pp. 463-469. WOS: 000380497600046.

Price, R. (2015). Nasdaq is experimenting with the revolutionary technology behind bitcoin, [Online]. Available at: http://www.businessinsider.com/nasdaq-private-market-blockchain-bitcoin-experiment-currency-ledger-2015-5 [cited 2017-01-25].

Prisco, G. (2016). Delaware Blockchain Initiative to Streamline Record-Keeping for Private Companies, [Online]. Available at: https://bitcoinmagazine.com/articles/delaware-blockchain-initiative-to-streamline-record-keeping-for-private-companies-1462812187/ [cited 2017-01-28].

Rapier, G. (2016). Yellen Reportedly Urges Central Banks to Study Blockchain, Bitcoin, [Online]. Available at: https://www.americanbanker.com/news/yellen-reportedly-urges-central-banks-to-study-blockchain-bitcoin/ [cited 2017-01-28].

Reutzel, B. (2016). BNP Paribas Works With Blockchain Startup to Open Source Law, [Online]. Available at: http://www.coindesk.com/commonaccord-legal-smart-contracts-prove-beneficial-one-bank-veritcal/ [cited 2017-01-28].

Rozehnal, P. and Novák, V. (2016). 'The Approach to the Integration of the IT Governance Frameworks for SME'. *IDIMT-2016- INFORMATION TECHNOLOGY, SOCIETY AND ECONOMY STRATEGIC CROSS-INFLUENCES: 24th Interdisciplinary Information Management Talks*. Poděbrady, Czech Republic, pp. 367-374. WOS:000387756100041.

Smith, A. and Anderson, M. (2016). New modes of payment and the 'cashless economy', [Online]. Available at: http://www.pewinternet.org/2016/12/19/new-modes-of-payment-and-the-cashless-economy/ [cited 2017-01-10].

Szabo, N. (1996). Smart Contracts: Building Blocks for Digital Markets, [Online]. Available at: http://www.alamut.com/subj/economics/nick_szabo/smartContracts.html [cited 2017-01-10].

Business Relationship Management for IT Services

Robert Rankl[1], Roland Peplinski[2]

Abstract. The IT service strategy is starting point of every consideration in the IT service management. The Business Relationship Management (BRM) is the key factor to the external and internal customer for the success of the IT. The IT life cycle forms the bases. This reason turns into the system-oriented design of an integrated BRM in the draft on hand. The introduced solution is flexible and applicable for mid-sized and big enterprises.

Keywords: IT Infrastructure Library (ITIL®), IT Service Management (ITSM), Business Relationship Management (BRM), Strategic Management for IT Services, IT Marketing.

JEL Classification: D21, M21

1 Introduction

The ownership and own operation of assets or the internal execution of activities on the one hand are favorable, on the other hand the search for alternatives on the free market brings greater success to reduce the costs. The decision is caused by it in order to find the possibility with the highest profitability for the enterprise. This profitability thought or business orientation should develop organizations of the information technology within an enterprise. Because nowadays the IT divisions compete with the IT service offerings of great, commercial IT service providers. Efficiently managed and controlled IT organizations can proceed like a business within a business (for example as a profit center) and create values for the enterprise which surpass the services of external IT service providers. A possibility for this is the use of standard process standards, at this the "Information Technology Infrastructure Library" - abbreviated ITIL® - has gained acceptance as an approved procedure model. In the system design the customer-oriented IT services are thereupon developed up to the production handing over (see figure 1).

The IT Service Management (ITSM) based on the procedure model ITIL® is in core a digest of "best practices" which describes to findings, models and architectures gained the practice. These can be used for the systematic construction and for the operation of a professional IT service structure coordinated generally as a guideline. The ITSM concentrates on the issue, which tasks have to be finished in the individual processes, this, however, does not go into the concrete putting into action. Implementation instructions or form presentations, being not provided just like corresponding tools (Olbrich, 2008, p. 1). The practical putting into realization has consequently to be worked out and formed individually in every enterprise.

A component in the core process service strategy is the process Business Relationship Management (BRM) between the IT service provider and internal or external customers (see figure 2). The task of the BRM is the safeguarding of a uniform customer alignment of the IT organization. Among other things the BRM is responsible meet the anticipations of the individual

[1] Baden-Wuerttemberg Cooperative State University, Stuttgart/Faculty of Economics, Business administration and Service performance management, Paulinenstr. 50, 70178 Stuttgart, robert.rankl@t-online.de.
[2] Baden-Wuerttemberg Cooperative State University, Stuttgart/Faculty of Economics, Business administration and Service performance management, Paulinenstr. 50, 70178 Stuttgart, rolandpeplinski@aol.com.

lines of business portfolios of the enterprise to the IT organization of its own as a service provider.

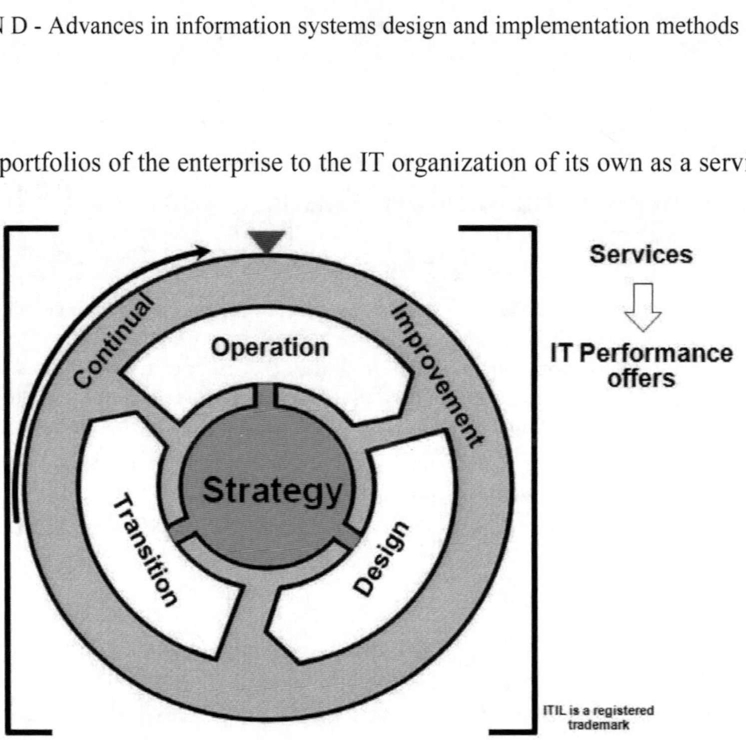

Figure 1 The Service-Lifecycle-Model of ITIL® [by analogy with Beims and Ziegenbein, 2015, p. 17]

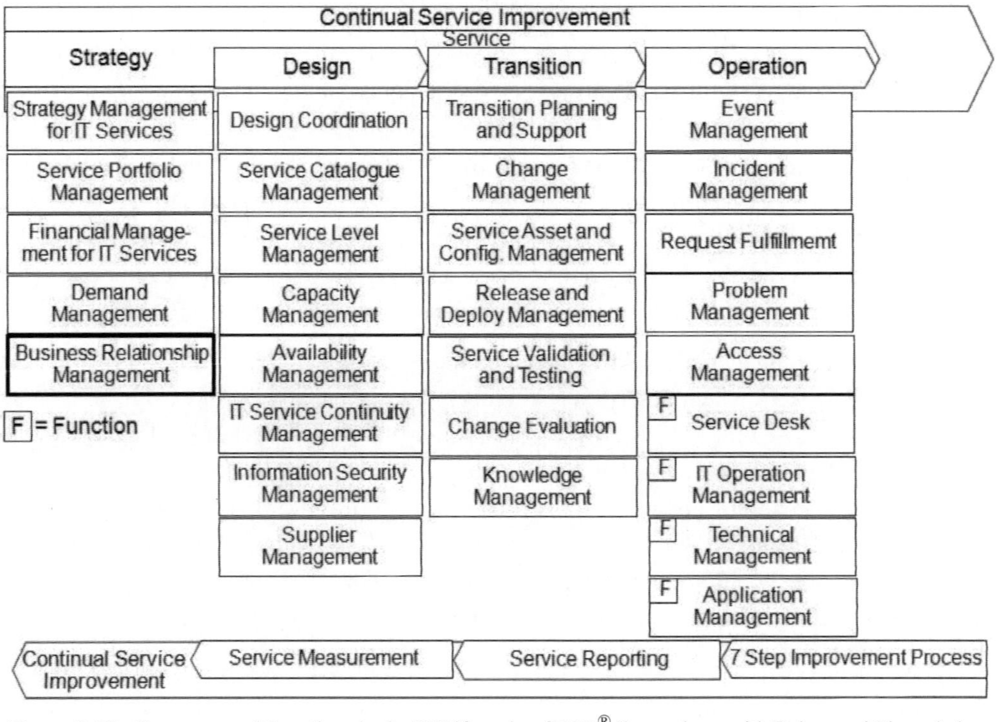

Figure 2 The Processes and Functions in the IT Lifecycle of ITIL® [by analogy with Beims and Ziegenbein, 2015, p. 16]

Action recommendations for a business relationship model in the context of the ITSMs exist only very insufficiently for the implementation until now. Those which exist are intended mainly for the use in large enterprises. The implementation of BRM would just produce substantial advantages among small and medium-sized enterprises. This strategic gap shall therefore be reduced at least.

1.1 Service Management

The service management consists of the business service management (BSM) and IT service management (ITSM). It deals with the coordination of all technical abilities within the enterprise and pursues the aim of implementing all processes in such a way so that services taking added value arise from available competences and resources (Olbrich, 2008, p. 1; Beims, 2010, p. 3]. An efficient service management therefore represents a substantial finishing-line of every IT. The IT operates as a safeguarding for the future of its own by the one and meets the challenge connected to that at the same time (Wischki, 2009, p. 171). This business centered focus applies both to IT organizations in the enterprise and to IT service providers (Augenstein and Rankl, 2015, p. 6).

Business processes are lined up flexibly for medium-sized enterprises since the corporate divisions are regarded as very easily comprehensible (Hamer, 1987, p. 28ff.). The organization building on it is consequently also organized very flexibly. Particularly if the IT does not belong to the core business but represents a support process, the IT contributes an integral proportion of the flexible practice of business processes. The importance of the IT and the strategic use of the IT differ widely, for example by data integration and its importance in the business decided by executives (Rudolph, 2009, p. 73). This behavior can be found at middle-class as well as at large-scale enterprises.

The IT organization as a strategic value driver contributes a high proportion for the attainment of the business objectives. It is exposed to a high pressure on costs, among other things what is seen with a not transparent profitability proof of the IT. The management of IT infrastructure takes a central importance because in the rule landscapes which are rather inefficient and intransparent find themselves to heterogeneous IT infrastructure over the years (Tiemayer, 2005, p. 82ff.). An internal IT marketing in the enterprise is necessary so that the units of the business also recognize the additional use which they can profit from the IT organization of their own. However, the cooperation between the IT organization and the business units becomes enterprise into much as described insufficiently (Rudolph, 2009, p. 75). The IT organization lacks the understanding about the contents and finishing-lines of the business units and often reversed. Reason for it is missing information exchange and a low communication under each other (Knöpp, Diercks and Altwasser, 2005, p. 6). This exchange between the two organizational units is, however, a prerequisite to render services and promote an IT integration into the core business processes. Core business processes can be modernized and arranged flexibly only in such a way.

In Summary, it can be noticed that IT organizations are between pressure on costs and increasing requirements on the IT. But only restricted resources are at this challenge's disposal (Rudolph, 2009, p. 76). It should be distinguished between two positions. On the one hand the relation between the IT organization which is taken on by a service provider. On the other hand the business units, which are internal customer and the IT control, which are still part of the enterprise of its own. In the two cases an adequate business relationship management is necessary, so that the requirements of the lines of business portfolios can be identified and are realized by the IT.

1.2 Business Service Management

In the annual business planning an interview and repositioning of the strategic alignment of all business activities is carried out. All modifications are included in "Business Case" considerations and taken into account as well in the medium-term planning period for the coming financial years. Already in this early phase of the different required or desired IT performance supplies, called also IT services, strategic decision need to be taken with regards to the corresponding business processes.

The leadership and their business activities need to be supported by IT. Therefore the business service management (BSM) needs to be established. The IT has to support the business processes purposefully, scalable and efficient to guarantee such a clear added value for the business activities (Augenstein and Rankl, 2015, p. 6).

A customer-oriented use of IT enables medium-sized enterprises consistently to develop additional business potentials. For IT service providers the best possible support of the respective external customers is the strategic finishing-line at the business activities.

1.3 IT Service Management

The IT performance management is determined by the business requirements. The IT service management (ITSM) manages all technical competencies of the organization.

Every enterprise must therefore develop a customized "IT service management" and implement it gradually overtime. Because of strict processes the required IT services can most likely be adapted to the customer´s various business processes as virtually reflected parallel IT processes.

As a framework for the IT process orientation the recommendations have been developed from the ITIL® core publications as a de-facto standard in the last decade. The success is lying in the generic solution approach. Every enterprise determines relevant "best practices" according to its individual needs with an internal project work. An important basis offers the common terminology which finds the same correspondence in the procedure model in all enterprises (Augenstein and Rankl, 2015, p. 7).

This common language basis makes an immediate intellectual interchange with different IT operating ranges possible. The same applies to an exchange of ideas between various enterprises and institutions. The IT processes generally describe the customer-oriented interplay of the processes with each other, the optimal design of new or changed IT services and their professional transition in the "production" to the support of the user customers. The last point is also responsible for the operative operational support.

Recognizing the ability to deliver an optimal ITSM based on the acute requirement of the IT service recipients, is the safety cushion of the individual units regarding their business handling.

This requirement can only be determined by an adequate communication and information exchange between the IT organization and the lines of business. This exchange works, however, in most companies insufficiently up to now (Tiemeyer, 2005, p. 98).

Three aspects are fundamentally and essentially responsible to generate added value:

(1) Customer orientation, (2) Competition orientation and (3) inter functional coordination. The latter describes initiatives a customer and competition-oriented perspective for the exercise of number one (Narver and Slater and Tietje, 1998, p. 21ff.). To survive the competition and to remain attractive for the internal as well as the external customers, the IT manager has to control the systematic structuring of the IT service offering and its alignment based on its IT (Rudolph, 2009, p. 78).

1.4 Business Relationship Management of IT Services

The BRM shall understand the requirements of existing and future customers and offers different opportunities of the "total" customer care. This differs from enterprise to enterprise. It is the task-of the BRM to recognize future developments early and to avoid risks by suitable behavior of the enterprise (Küng and Toscano-Ruffilli and Schillig, 2006, p. 20). The BRM offers action recommendations for the mediation in the context of the ITSM between the IT and the individual lines of business as customers.

1.5 Customer Orientation of Service Providers

BRM is a key discipline of a service provider to develop efficient operative structures and take strategic decisions. Being able to determine communication is necessary to build the construction of a strategic partnership, portfolio management, business transition management and an economic way of thinking (see figure 3).

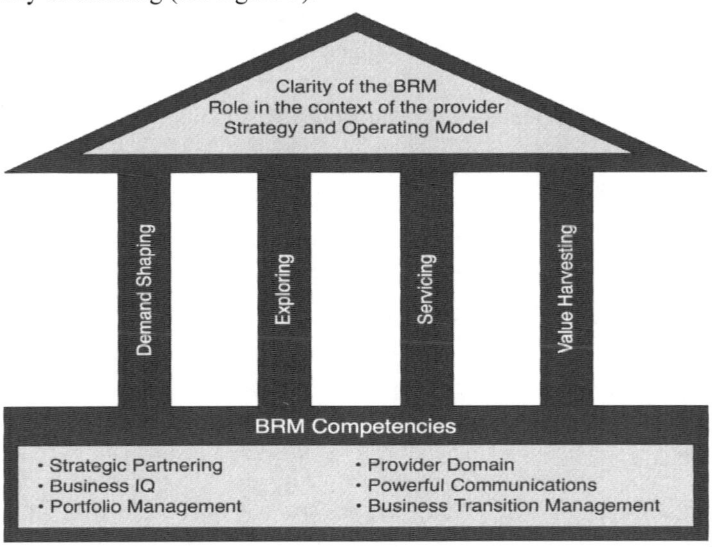

Figure 3 The Business relationship model for service provider [Business Relationship Management Institute, n.d.]

The main activities determine the finishing-lines of the BRMs. The four main activities can be described as follows (Business Relationship Management Institute, n.d.):

Demand management / "Demand Shaping"

The demand management indicates the cause of a demand for innovative IT services, products and capabilities at the lines of business. The individual business units shall use the capabilities for the IT organization to create competitive advantages. The portfolio is the basis to make business strategies possible for IT performance offers and the support with the suitable technologies.

Trend management / "Exploring"

The identification and the production of demand by the exploration of new ideas of business trends is a main task of BRM. This is an iterative process which evaluates new business ideas, industries and technologies easier to determine the potential for the business environment. The benefit of this task is the identification of new initiatives, especially services and products which become part of the portfolio of the service provider.

Maintenance and advertising / "Servicing"

Maintenance serves to coordinate resources interests of the different ones involved. The demand is realized in current demands on the deliveries. This contains for example roadmaps which define finishing-lines of business objectives and a special portfolio and program management.

Added value / "Harvesting"

The task of these activities is to control the business changes by new IT services. Important activities can be tracked and evaluated and the performance can be measured. This provides ways to increase the goodwill of the initiatives of the service provider and to catch up with feedback to cause a continuous improvement. This process offers stakeholders the possibility of recognizing and controlling the results of IT changes.

1.6 Business Relationship Management under IT Service Management

The BRM is an integral part of the service process in IT service management. It creates a connection between the internal and external customer and the service provider or an internal IT organization. The main task is customer care. The demands shall be proactively anticipated. This way, the expectations of the customer registered and controlled which enables a professional communication. Direct customer communication and related polls can be conducted in order to evaluate customer satisfaction. The optimization of the customer satisfaction is most important. The objective of this service process between the client and the service provider is a growth of customer satisfaction and the generation of additional sales turnover (Böttcher, 2013, p. 41ff.).

This can be achieved for example with the organization of workshops with professional experts. They present new technologies to improve customer processes and customer can directly intervene and help to optimize the model. The most important person in this concept is the Business Relationship Manager. He takes the role of a customer service person that is sales oriented. He will become the so called "face to the customer". This personality has to initiate and deepen the relationship to the customer in a way that a further development of the cooperation is seen as natural. The business activity of the customer needs to be understood so that the exact requirements can be captured by the IT service.

A proactive BRM can be influenced based on the expectation of the customer regarding new or modified IT services. This can be used for strategic discussions and decisions. The continuous cooperation in this relationship will develop a united perspective on the requirement specifications of the client and the portfolio of the IT service. The central role he is played by the Business Relationship Manager who represents the needs of the customer in the organization of the service provider. He fulfills the solicitations and manages all operative processes and activities of the customer.

In all phases of the life cycle of IT, the BRM is most relevant. To coordinate appropriate reactions on customer requests, the BRM will use the customer portfolio, which gathers all customer relationships and requests. An overview of all current projects is therefore absolutely necessary to be successful. The BRM bundles all relevant information of respective offers and provision of IT services. The following BRM process activities during the whole IT life cycle can be described (Rankl, 2009, p. 4):

Service Strategy

- Preparation of the customer organization and identification of contact names
- Information about potential and new IT services and clarification of the potential of business processes of the customer
- Intake and Validation of customer requirements
- Backup of the cooperation of the client regarding the service concept

Service Transition

- Coordination of the cooperation of the client during the process service transition phase
- Coordination of schedules, trainings and meetings

Service Operation

- Communication of severe service challenges
- Contact for escalations and claims

Continual Service Improvement

- Regular updates of completed service tasks and service quality
- Conduction and inquiry of customer satisfaction

The success of the BRM will be measured with key operating figures of customer satisfaction. A high number of customer satisfactions in connection with a decreasing amount of claims are key indicators of the functionality and the success of a BRM. Consequently, a low level of customer satisfaction and a high amount of claims demonstrate a need to improve, either by optimizing the service or service quality or by intensifying the customer relationship. To take corrective action of both factors with relevant activities is always the task of the BRM.

A central success factor for the successful implementation of an effective BRM is an overview of the existing roles between the IT organization and the business departments of the customer. On behalf of the customer, it is important to differentiate between the user and the contractee. The satisfaction of the customer as a contracting authority and the customer as a user might differ a lot. Nevertheless, the contractual service levels should always cover the user practicability.

1.7 Conclusion

A too developed BRM for IT services should if possible include both activities, a Service Provider and BSM in the ITSM Life Cycle. The most important factor is the practicability, especially for the acceptance and application in mid-sized enterprises.

The strategic direction of the respective enterprise, the take into account business processes and the distinct customer orders are crucial for the continuous development of IT services. Looking at and including both perspectives, a step by step model for an integrated BRM can be created:

Customer relationship

Of a BRM is to achieve a high customer satisfaction by fulfilling the expectations of the required specified demands of the customer. Therefore, a contention and controversy of the foundation of a high quality relationship followed by a high customer satisfaction is essential.
As a result, the area customer relationships need to add to the concept of BRM.

Service Level Management (SLM)

The SLM is next to the Service Desk the connection to the user in the ITSM (Wischki, 2009, p. 61). Hence, the SLM is the interface between the IT and the business itself, because their content is the basis for a contractual relationship, if necessary with penalties in case of damages or losses in the level of quality. On the one hand, it is mandatory to communicate with the customer and to understand the IT expectations; on the other hand, these expectations need to be transferred to IT in order to develop the service.

Innovation and Demand Management

To improve IT services is only possible with innovation management. Hence, the implementation of an effective innovation management is necessary in order to continue the development of innovative IT services. On top, it is a must to identify the demand of potential customers.

Communication Policy

A successful communication of existing service portfolios in the IT organization is in the interest of many external and internal customers. On the grounds of these facts should the communication in the sense of service marketing be a central part of an integral model. Innovation management and communication can herewith become precise instruments to analyze and explore trends from the perspective of the service provider. Therefore, they are as well part of a holistic Business Relationship Model.

The main difference between mid-sized and big enterprises is the shortage of resources due to the lower amount of employees. The existing tasks need to a greater degree be distributed to the existing man power and resources of the enterprise. The above described integrated approach and model is as a result indeed applicable for mid-sized enterprises because everything needs to be concentrated and focused on the essence of the BRM.

References

Augenstein, F., Rankl, R. (2015). *Das IT Service Management Tool.* Simmozheim: Conmethos.

Beims, M. and Ziegenbein, M. (2015). *IT-Service Management in der Praxis mit ITIL®.* München: Carl Hanser.

Beims, M. (2010). IT *Service Management in der Praxis mit ITIL®3. Zielfindung, Methoden, Realisierung*, 2nd ed. München: Carl Hanser.

Böttcher, R. (2013). *IT-Service-Management mit ITIL® 2011 Edition*, 3rd ed. Hannover: Heise.

Business Relationship Management Institute (2017), [Online]. Available at: http://brminstitute.org/about-business-relationship-management/ [cited 2017-01-31].

Hamer, E. (1987). *Das mittelständische Unternehmen: Eigenarten, Bedeutung, Risiken und Chancen.* Stuttgart: Poller.

Knöpp, M., Diercks, H.-J. and Altwasser, V. (2005). *ITIL® im Mittelstand einfach und erfolgreich umsetzen.* Kissing: WEKA.

Küng, P., Toscano-Ruffilli, R. and Schillig, B. (2006). *Key Account Management: Praxistipps, Beispiele, Werkzeuge.* St. Gallen/Zürich: Midas.

Narver, J. C., Slater, S. F. and Tietje, B. (1998). 'Creating a market orientation'. *Journal of Market-Focused Management*, 2, pp. 20-36.

Olbrich, A. (2008). *ITIL® kompakt und verständlich*, 4th ed. Wiesbaden:Vieweg&Sohn.

Rankl, R. (2009). 'Managerial informatics through ITIL'. *Strategic Management and its Support by Information Systems 2009*, Ostrava, Czech Republic, pp. 162-168.

Rudolph, S. (2009). *Servicebasierte Planung und Steuerung der IT-Infrastruktur im Mittelstand - ein Modellansatz zur Struktur der IT-Leistungserbringung.* Wiesbaden:Gabler.

Tiemeyer, E. (2005). *IT-Controlling kompakt.* München:Hanser.

Wischki, C. (2009). *ITIL® V2, ITIL® V3 und ISO/IEC 20000, Gegenüberstellung und Praxisleitfaden für die Einführung oder den Umstieg.* München:Hanser.

The Suggestion of Cobit Metamodel

Petr Rozehnal[1]

Abstract. Organizations want to increase the value from investments in information technology. Due to this fact, IT governance/management area is more and more attractive. Cobit is a worldwide known framework for IT governance. The paper proposes a metamodel for Cobit version 5. The metamodel is based on the main entities of the framework and describes it in a more structural way. The metamodel can be used as an interface for discussion about the framework concept as well as a way for integration efforts with other frameworks. The goal of the paper is to highlight some disputed issues of the Cobit metamodel.

Keywords: frameworks, Cobit, metamodel, governance, information technology.

JEL Classification: M15, O32

1 Introduction

As De Haes and Grembergen (2008) state, pervasive use of information technology (IT) and crucial role of IT in business calls for a focus on IT governance (ITG) area. Computers elevate the importance of information as one of the key assets in organization functioning. ITG respects the role of information in business. IT governance frameworks "help the management to ensure that organizations realize optimal value from IT business investments at an affordable cost with a known and acceptable level of risk." (Pajič, Pantelič and Stanojevič, 2014, p. 758). There are also other challenges, which should be taken into account: Internet of Things, infrastructure development, social networks (Pochyla, 2012). IT governance/management seems to be a still more attractive area also for academic researchers. Indeed, we can observe two interesting facts. Firstly, the most used ITG framework (Cobit) originally came from the area of audit and now plays an important role in IT. Generally, there is an overlap into other areas of interest. Secondly, the framework was established outside the academic environment mostly as the "best practice". Practitioners from business sphere put together their knowledge to define framework that could be valuable for better IT managing. Goeken and Alter (2009) state that due to this fact, such frameworks lack deeper theoretical basis. The theoretical analysis is suitable for further development. The goal of the paper is to support the efforts of Cobit framework concept description as a basis for exploring the possibilities of its integration with other frameworks (Neto and Neto, 2013) in the future (which is out of the scope of this paper).

In the following text, the paper focuses on Cobit framework. The reasons for Cobit are as follows. Cobit is a typical representative of the ITG area. ITIL is mentioned often as another one, but it rather represents the IT service management area. Goeken and Alter (2008) present other ITG frameworks.

[1] VŠB –TU Ostrava/Faculty of Economics, Department of Applied Informatics, Sokolská tř. 33, petr.rozehnal@vsb.cz

Chapter 2 discusses the reasons for metamodeling and the essence of metamodels. Hereafter, in chapter 3, the Cobit 5 metamodel is introduced and discussed. Some issues that should be examined are opened there.

2 The description of frameworks in metamodels and their usage

Best practice framework benefits have been verified first rather in practice than in theory, but due to the success of Cobit and similar approaches among the IT professional managers, a lot of articles from academic sphere have been published within the last ten years. It is possible to find some studies focused on different areas, e.g. the role of IT Governance (ITG) in the context of the general governance area (corporate governance) (Lunardi et al., 2009; Webb et al., 2006; Svatá, 2012) effects in organizations (Weil and Ross, 2004; Lingyu et al., 2010; de Haes and Grembergen, 2008); applying ITG in organizations/different area of organizations (Kulkarni, 2003; NCC, 2005) and last, but not least, the theoretical foundation of frameworks by designing them as conceptual metamodels (Goeken and Alter, 2009; Neto and Neto, 2013; Pereira and Silva, 2012).

Organizations have to be pragmatic in using the best practice frameworks. It is necessary to find the right way where and how to use it. We can follow many case studies which describe a framework deployment (e.g. www.isaca.org). Often, several frameworks are applied at the same time. Each one is utilized for the particular area management. An appropriate level and way of integration is necessary. The integration process can take many forms. We can mention at least two of them.

The first one of them is the mutual framework mapping as discussed in ITGI (2005; 2007a; 2008). ITGI (2007a, p. 5) stated several sources which deal with mutual framework mapping. Such a form of integration is based on the idea of defining the links between the content entities (between processes, between processes and phases).

In the literature, conceptual models which describe the main idea and linking between the core entities used in the framework are also applied. Pereira and da Silva (2012) introduce ITIL V3 and Cobit conceptual models. Links between the processes are described in these models, with the process as the core model entity. When the mutual mapping between these entities in different frameworks is used, we follow the approach stated above.

The second form how to discuss potential common issues as a platform for simultaneous use is to study its theoretical foundation. When the same methodology for the construction of metamodel is used, it is possible to compare the frameworks at a higher level of abstraction (Neto and Neto, 2013). In such a research, the models are used as a way of abstract from reality and real objects. As a matter of fact, it is necessary to work with metamodels, because the usage of the frameworks implies modeling a real world (organization) into the model while there is a need to compare the framework conception. The framework concept is described in a higher level of abstraction in metamodels. The comparison of metamodels can be used to define the basic entities used in modeling. Goeken and Alter (2009) talk about the building blocks (phenomenon), which are relevant in the world based on a principle or a viewpoint. Furthermore, they distinguish between linguistic and ontological metamodeling. While linguistic metamodel uses the definition of the language and relationships between its entities, ontological metamodeling approach works with the classification of entities according to their content (Goeken and Alter, 2009). These authors also proclaim the advantage of ontological metamodeling for the comparison of the framework concept purpose.

3 Cobit metamodel

The process of a metamodel creation should follow a guideline of modeling – the main principles (Goeken and Alter, 2009). The proposed principles are: (1) construction adequacy; (2) language adequacy; (3) economic efficiency; (4) clarity; (5) systematic design; (6) comparability.

3.1 Building the COBIT 5 Metamodel

The idea to create a metamodel of the Cobit framework is not new. It is possible to analyze and follow the metamodels that were already created. Gama, Silva and Francisco (2011) published a conceptual metamodel based on important approaches for organization modeling (include ITG, IT strategy). Goeken and Alter (2008; 2009) as well as Neto and Neto (2013) published their metamodel for Cobit 4.1 version. Due to the ontological nature of the description, it is possible to discuss some entities in metamodels. Both teams of authors differ in the description of the metamodel in some details. Moreover, Cobit version 5 has been introduced since then. Its new version brings some innovative issues which are not reflected in the above mentioned models, which do not fully fit the new version of the framework. Besides the academic resources, the official Cobit documentation is important to capture the essence of the new version of the framework (ISACA, 2012a; ISACA, 2012b; ISACA, 2012c; ISACA, 2013a; ISACA, 2016).

With regard to the above mentioned facts, the basic metamodel was created (Figure 1). It is worth emphasizing that the basic wording in terms of the design model must be further discussed and specified. There are many questions for discussion, see chapter 3.2. The proposed metamodel structure differs with (Neto and Neto, 2013, fig. 8) or (Goeken and Alter, 2009, fig. 2) in several entities due to the changes in the Cobit version. The main differences are summarized below. The modeling notation also differs from (Goeken and Alter, 2009), because it is valuable to have flexibility in the description of entity relationships. That is the way to fulfil the principles of language and construction adequacy (see above). Only the entities and their mutual links are modeled.

The Cobit framework is process-oriented. The central entity type is the **process**. There are 37 processes described in Cobit 5 that belong into **5 domains** (one for the governance area and four for the management). The process is characterized as follows: „a collection of practices influenced by the enterprise's policies and procedures that takes inputs from a number of sources (including other processes), manipulates the inputs and produces outputs (e.g. products, services)." (ISACA, 2012c, p. 92)

Cobit 5 processes description differs from the Cobit 4.1 process description structure. In Cobit 4.1., control objectives are defined for all 34 processes. The control objectives can be defined as follows: "generic action statements of the minimum management good practices to ensure that the process is kept under control." (ITGI, 2007b, p. 27). Besides the control objectives, activities are defined. The activities are not identical with the control objectives, although they are directly related with them. In Cobit 5, there is a corresponding description regarding the recommended process activities (high level requirements) identified as **Governance/Management Practice** (according to the domain). Practices are described in more details in **Activities**. The activities expand knowledge about the Practice (in broader context about the Process). ISACA (2012c, p. 20) presents the Activities as follows: "the main actions to operate the process". The activities are carried out by actors. They have a **role** in the organization. The RACI chart links the roles and level of responsibility (Responsible, Accountable, Consulted, Informed).

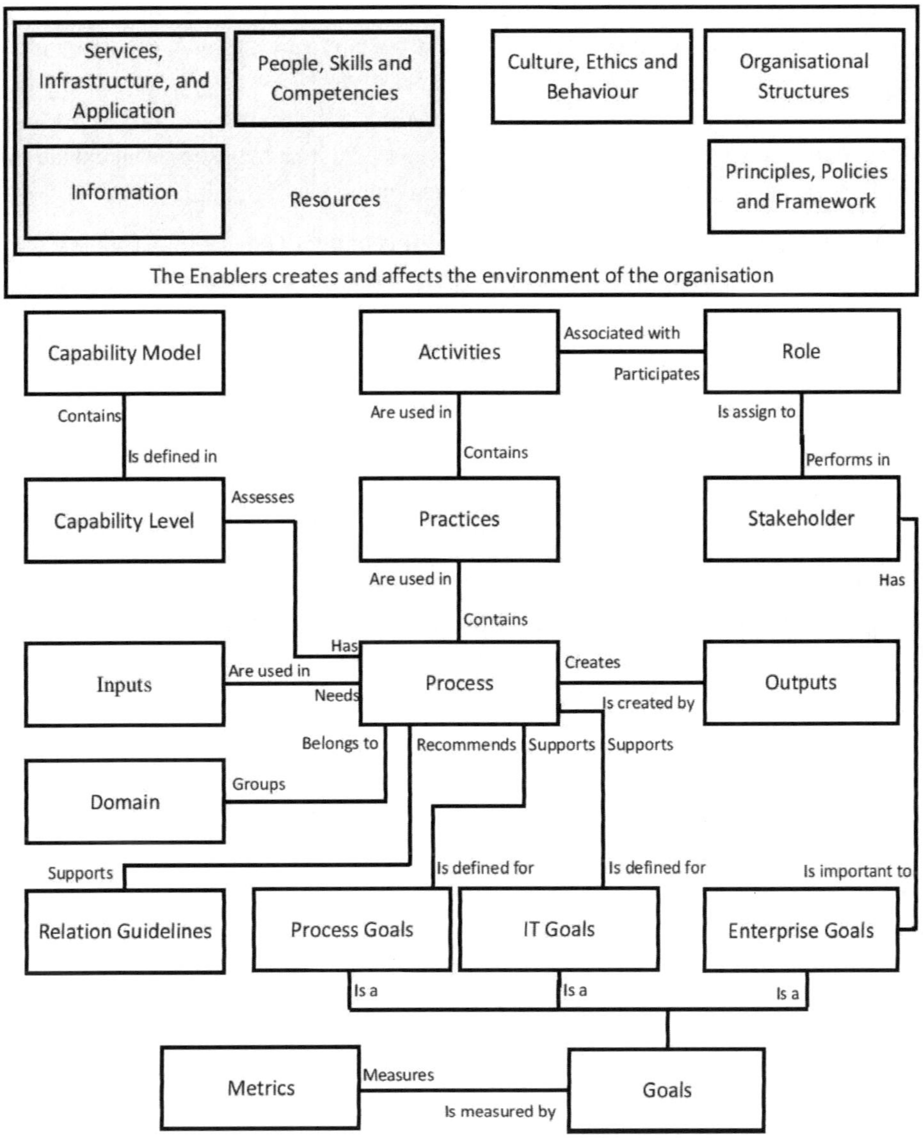

Figure 1 The Cobit 5 metamodel (Source: author)

Resources – Cobit 5 distinguishes between internal and external IT resources and in general defines the term Resources as follows: "any enterprise asset that can help the organization achieve its objective" (ISACA, 2012c, p. 92). The main resources mentioned in Cobit are: services, infrastructure and applications; people, skills and competencies; Information. These resources are the enablers at the same time. The resources are the entities which enables carrying out the processes.

Inputs and Outputs (1) are described in the Process reference guide and included in particular in the Practices that could be performed in the Process (ISACA, 2012a), (2) can be generally viewed as any inputs or outputs required in the processes. It is important to understand the input and output roles in the processes and within the Cobit framework. Besides the core inputs, which are defined in the practices (e.g. roadmap, results of analyses, risk factors, policies in short inputs/outputs of other process practices), there are many other different types of inputs/outputs needed for the process, e.g. other types of information related to the process and resources which may be included in the enablers. ISACA (2012c, p. 91) stated: "the illustrative Cobit 5 inputs and outputs should not be regarded as an exhaustive list". The role of inputs/outputs is also to express system approach of the framework.

The Cobit 5 framework includes a **process capability model** (ISACA, 2013b), which is based on the ISO/IEC 15 504 Software Engineering - Process Assessment Standard. The Cobit 4.1 operates with the maturity model. (ISACA, 2011). Both approaches differ in many issues. The most important differences can be summarized as follows: (1) names and meaning of capability levels; (2) differences in attributes defined in levels (ISACA, 2012c). The detailed description is beyond the scope of this paper.

IT Governance Focus Area – in contrast to Cobit 4.1, there are not any governance areas directly stated in Cobit 5. Cobit 5 puts emphasis on the separation of governance and management areas. Still, Cobit 5 operates with the general governance area. Officially, the governance objectives are realization of benefits, risk optimization and resource optimization. It does not mean that the strategic alignment and performance measurement (IT governance areas by ITGI (2003, p. 21) are not taken into account. In the author´s opinion, it is not necessary to model the focus area into the metamodel.

Stakeholders play an important role in the Cobit framework since they represent a human aspect of the organization (processes). ISACA (2012a, p. 19) stated literally that processes have stakeholders (internal or external) who have their roles with responsibility level documented in RACI chart. Moreover, stakeholders have an interest in the organization, and Cobit deals with their needs and enterprise (IT) goals.

3.2 Discussion of selected issues

Although Cobit 5 describes processes in a uniform manner, the whole framework uses many other artefacts that are not easy to assign. These questions should also be discussed because of the principles of systematic design and clarity (as discussed above).

Enablers are another artefact, which is not easy to classify. Cobit 5 introduced seven categories of enablers. One of them is the process itself. Some of them create the environment of the organizations, and in this way they can influence the processes (enabler – culture, ethics and behavior). Other (enabler – principles, policies and frameworks) serve as a practical guideline for management. How to model the relation of these issues? If the metamodel should work as an interface for better discussion, it is appropriate to cover all main aspects and ideas of the framework. A similar situation is in the TOGAF framework, where a relationship with all objects is also dealt with (Figure 2).

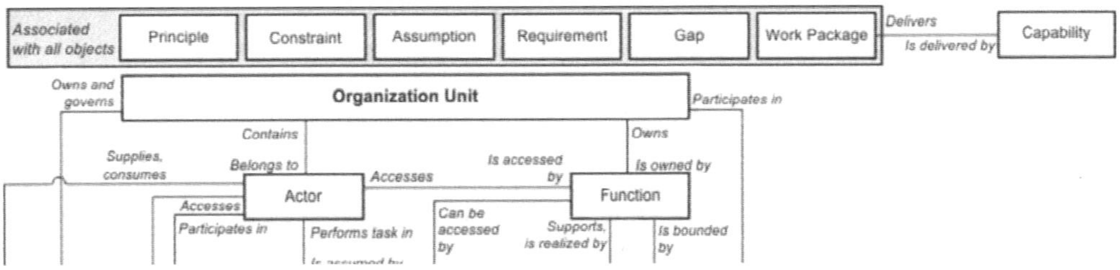

Figure 2 TOGAF description of association between objects (Open Group, 2011)

To better understand the difference between the source and the enablers as an artefact that creates an environment, it is worth following (AXELOS, 2011, p. 20), where the asset terms capabilities and resources are described. The resources are direct inputs for the production, while capabilities are experience, knowledge embedded within people, systems, processes and technologies. See the examples and comparison of capabilities versus resources in table 1 (AXELOS, 2011, p. 21).

Capabilities versus	**Resources**
Management	Financial capital
People (experience, skills and relationship)	People (number of employees)
Knowledge	Information

Table 1 Capabilities versus resources

In ISACA (2012c, p. 13), it is stated: "**Information** is a key resource for all enterprises". Information is understood as an enterprise asset – resource and at the same time as an enabler, which plays an important role, because adequate information is important to support business function. In the Cobit family books, information has an exceptional position. Its role is described in (ISACA, 2013a) in detail. This material is "reference guide for structured thinking about information and typical information governance and management issues" (ISACA, 2013a, p. 9). Due to these facts, the position of information is not linked directly with other entities in the metamodel.

Organizational structures is one of the enablers. It represents a general term for decision-making entities, which play a role in governance/management processes. ISACA (2012c, p. 92) names an example: Steering Committee. Such a group influences the processes, but it is not possible to link them directly.

Cobit uses **goals** in different areas. Thera are enterprise, IT goals and process goals as entities which are supported by the processes. Generally, the term goal is used as an enabler dimension. Each enabler has a number of goals, which can be defined as expected outcomes and application, or operation of the enabler itself (ISACA, 2012c). Although they are not strictly described as a goal in detail process description, some outputs of the activities can be considered as goals. In the paper, the metamodel includes goals as an expression of entities which are used in the Cobit approach for the required and defined future state.

4 Conclusion

The aim of the paper is to present a proposal of the Cobit 5 metamodel as a starting point for further research and discussion. The purpose of a metamodel is to describe the core entities and their position within other entities. One of the possible results stated above implies the possibility of an analysis with other frameworks. For the analysis, it is important to use the same entities with the same meaning, which is not quite possible. For example, a service can be an entity for further discussion. The service is defined in TOGAF (Open Group, 2011) in three meanings: for business, information systems and platforms. In general, it is meant as an element that provides functionality in response to a request. Cobit understands the service especially as an IT asset, but does not discuss its position as an autonomous entity. If the metamodel is a basis for the analysis and subsequent comparison with other approaches, a discussion about the core entities is necessary. Additional core entities can be: organization unit (TOGAF), organization (ITIL), function (TOGAF, ITIL). All these issues should be the topics of further research.

The metamodel describes the mutual relationships between entities. The model does not capture dynamic features of the framework (e.g. enterprise goal mapping to IT goals and further to processes or flows between the processes (input - process - output - process) like in (Pereira and Silva, 2012) or implementation life cycle). Due to this fact, it is quite important to take into account that the metamodel does not cover all the ideas of the Cobit framework concept. Moreover, the Cobit family books cover also specialized topic areas (Information Security, Risk Management etc.).

The best practice frameworks are rarely implemented completely. An individual implementation needs various kinds of adjustments based on a specific situation of the organization Ministr, J., Fiala, J and Stevko, M. (2009) or in case studies of ISACA (2016). There are also modifications for smaller organizations. For Cobit, see (ITGI, 2007c). The metamodels can be appropriate not only for comparison and integration of frameworks, but can also serve as a platform for general discussion.

References

AXELOS. (2011). *ITIL® Service Strategy*. Norwich: TSO.

De Haes, S. and Grembengen, W. (2008). 'Analysing the Relationship Between IT Governance and Business/IT Alignment Maturity'. *Proceedings of the 41st Hawaii International Conference on System Sciences – 2008*, Hawaii, USA.

Gama, N., Silva, M. M. and Francisco, E. A. (2011). 'A Conceptual Framework for Structuring an IT.

Organization'. *UK Academy for Information Systems Conference Proceedings 2011.*

Goeken, M. and Alter, S. (2008). 'IT Governance Frameworks as Methods'. *Proceedings of the 10th International Conference on Enterprise Information Systems (ICEIS 2008)*. Barcelona, Spain.

Goeken, M. and Alter, S. (2009). 'Towards Conceptual Metamodeling of IT Governance Frameworks Approach - Use – Benefits'. *Proceedings of the 42nd Hawaii International Conference on System Sciences – 2009,* Hawaii, USA.

ISACA. (2011). *COBIT Process Assessment Model (PAM): Using COBIT® 4.1* Rolling Meadows: ISACA.

ISACA. (2012a). *Cobit 5 Enabling Processes*. Rolling Meadows: ISACA.

ISACA. (2012b). *Cobit 5 Implementation*. Rolling Meadows: ISACA.

ISACA. (2012c). *Cobit 5 A Business Framework for the Governance and Management of Enterprise IT*. Rolling Meadows: ISACA.

ISACA. (2013a). *Cobit 5 Enabling Information*. Rolling Meadows: ISACA.

ISACA. (2013b). *Process Assessment Model (PAM): Using COBIT® 5*. Rolling Meadows: ISACA.

ISACA. (2016). Cobit 5. ISACA, [Online]. Retrieved from http://www.isaca.org/cobit/pages/default.aspx. [cited 2016-04-12].

ITGI. (2003). *Board Briefing on IT Governance, 2nd Edition*. Rolling Meadows: IT Governance Institute.

ITGI. (2005). Aligning Cobit®, ITIL® and ISO 17799 for Business Benefit: Management Summary.

ITGI. (2007a). TOGAF™ and COBIT® Mapping of TOGAF 8.1 with COBIT 4.0.

ITGI. (2007b). *Cobit 4.1*. Rolling Meadows: IT Governance Institute.

ITGI. (2007c). *COBIT® Quickstart, 2nd Edition*. Rolling Meadows: IT Governance Institute.

ITGI. (2008). Cobit Mapping, Mapping of ITIL v3 With COBIT® 4.1.

Kulkarni, M. (2003). 'Applying COBIT Framework in Change Management'. *Information Systems Control Journal*, 5.

Lingyu, H., Bingwu, L., Ruiping, Y. and Jianzhang, W. (2010). 'An IT Governance Framework of ERP System Implementation'. *Computing Control and Industrial Engineering*, CCIE, Wuhan, China. pp. 431-434.

Ministr, J., Fiala, J and Stevko, M. (2009). 'The IT Service continuity management principles implementation by method A2'. *Proceedings of 17th Interdisciplinary Information Management Talks, IDIMT 2009*. Jindrichuv Hradec, Czech Republic.

NCC. (2005). *IT Governance Developing a successful governance strategy*. Manchester: The National Computing Centre.

Neto, J. S. and Neto, A. N. F. (2013). 'Metamodel of the IT Governance Framework Cobit'. *Journal of Information Systems and Technology Management*, 10 (3), pp. 521-540.

Open Group. (2011). TOGAF Version 9.1., [Online]. Available at: http://pubs.opengroup.org/architecture/togaf9-doc/arch/ [cited 2017-01-24].

Pajič, A., Pantelič, O. and Stanojevič, B. (2014). 'Representing IT Performance Management as Metamodel'. *International Journal of Computers Communications & Control,* 9 (6), pp. 758-767

Pereira, R. and Silva, M. M. (2012). 'A Literature Review: Guidelines and Contingency Factors for IT Governance'. *European, Mediterranean & Middle Eastern Conference on Information Systems 2012*. Munich, Germany.

Pochyla, M. (2012). 'Future of Intranets and Social Networks in the Enterprise'. *Proceedings of 20th Interdisciplinary Information Management Talks, IDIMT 2012*. Jindrichuv Hradec, Czech Republic

Svatá, V. (2012). *Audit informačních systémů*. Praha: Professional Publishing.

Webb, P. et al. (2006). 'Attempting to Define IT Governance: Wisdom or Folly?'. *Proceedings of the 39th Hawaii International Conference on System Sciences – 2006*. Hawaii, USA.

Weil, P. and Ross, J. W. (2004). *IT Governance: How Top Performers Manage IT Decision Rights for Superior Result*, Boston, Massachusetts.

Towards a Common Logging and Monitoring Framework for Critical Infrastructures

Daniel Tovarňák[1], Adam Kučera[2], Tomáš Pitner[3], Filip Kšenzuliak[4], Jan Ministr[5]

Abstract. Modern complex computer systems such as clouds and critical infrastructures such as intelligent building require a reliable monitoring to ensure detection of failures or security breaches, allow fast recovery and serve for accounting and auditing purposes. The paper describes the requirements and conceptualization of computer system and intelligent building monitoring using a newly proposed Monitoring system reference framework.

Keywords: monitoring, computer system, intelligent building, cloud, security, monitoring system framework.

JEL Classification: M15

1 Introduction

Critical infrastructures such as electricity distribution networks, communication networks, computing facilities or physical building are gradually more dependent on reliable monitoring system relying on underlying computing and communication infrastructure to ensure secure and high-performance operation. The situation becomes tougher with growing complexity of computing infrastructures such as clouds, together with raising importance of security (NCC, 2016).

Primarily, we will define monitoring and shortly introduce different types of critical infrastructures with respect to different monitoring needs. Secondly, we focus at log collection and processing for analysis of the system operation, potential security threats, or malicious behavior of their users. Thirdly, we will present our attempts to design a common monitoring framework applicable to design and implement a monitoring system or to assess an existing one.

1.1 What is monitoring

Monitoring is a continuous and *systematic collection, analysis, and evaluation of data related to the state and behavior of monitored entity*. In the case of distributed computing environment (such as cloud or grid) its *state and behavior is determined by the state and behavior of its respective constituents*, see (Tovarňák et al, 2014).

State of monitored entity reflects its behavior at a discrete point in time and it is represented by a set of state *variables* contained within a *state vector*. Behavior is an *action* or an *internal state change* of the monitored entity represented by a corresponding *event*.

[1] Masaryk University, Faculty of Informatics, Botanická 68a, 602 00 Brno, danos@mail.muni.cz
[2] Masaryk University, Faculty of Informatics, Botanická 68a, 602 00 Brno, akucera@mail.muni.cz
[3] Masaryk University, Faculty of Informatics, Botanická 68a, 602 00 Brno, tomp@fi.muni.cz
[4] Masaryk University, Faculty of Informatics, Botanická 68a, 602 00 Brno, ksenzuliak@mail.muni.cz
[5] VŠB-Technical University, Faculty of Economics, Sokolská 33, 702 00 Ostrava, jan.ministr@vsb.cz

So, events are reflection of activities or changes in the system. Computer *logs* (system logs, console logs, or simply logs) are mechanisms to systematically *record events* (*log events*) as the primary source of information about the system behavior. Logs thus belong to the most important data for monitoring.

1.2 Purpose of monitoring

Monitoring data is used in a spectrum of mission critical tasks, such as:

- *Accounting* – in relation to clients to enable business models dependent on the usage of system resources by measuring their consumption – usually also checking SLA conformance;
- *Audit* tracking – to be able to prove correctness of the accounting data by internal processes or by a third party, including their non-repudiation;
- *Performance* and user experience – to measure performance, allow to optimize provisioning, scheduling, and scaling;
- *Reliability* – robustness and ability to quickly recover from incidents;
- *Security* purposes – security assurance incl. security incident handling;
- Help with *development* related tasks – debugging, diagnosis, fault detection, performance analysis, and profiling, particularly if the monitored system is heterogeneous or technologically complex, e.g. combining relational data and geodata (Danel, 2012).

In multi-tenant environments, such as clouds or even federation of clouds, many parties are involved in the operation and use of such a system with different or even opposite interests – infrastructure providers, application providers, and application users.

Monitoring systems must be able to help the above critical tasks while reflecting the (sometimes contradicting) needs of the system tenants. Moreover, there are also several non-functional requirements to be fulfilled.

1.3 Non-functional requirements for monitoring

A fully-fledged monitoring system should pose a range of characteristics ensuring its effective operation and to reach the desired impact. Software quality standard ISO 25010 (ISO/IEC 25010:2011, 2011) defines concepts used also for our purpose here.

- *Accuracy* – correspondence between the actual state of monitored system and state known and reflected to the monitoring system – high accuracy means the difference between the actual state of monitored entity and the state known to the monitoring system is as minimal as possible.
- *Elasticity* – is higher if a monitoring system can accommodate to changing and dynamic infrastructure to monitor resources dynamically created and destroyed.
- *Interoperability* – is higher if a monitoring system uses (standard) communication protocols and data formats well suited for further processing.
- *Intrusiveness* – the level how the monitoring system influences the system being monitored. For instance, resource consumption caused by the monitoring system can vary significantly and thus diminishing system performance when it crosses certain limit.
- *Latency* – time difference between the occurrence of a monitoring event and its detection, processing, or evaluation by the monitoring system.

- *Maintainability* – is higher if the monitoring system is extensible by adding new supported monitored resources and monitoring data types.
- *Network overhead* – extra load imposed on computer network by collection of monitoring data depending of its size and velocity.
- *Performance* of a monitoring system itself – whether it performs well in all phases of monitoring process (throughput, latency, and processing speed).
- *Reliability* – how a monitoring system or its component can perform its required functions under stated conditions for a specified period.
- *Scalability* – when a monitoring system can scale to reflect increasing volume, variety, and velocity of data; increasing number of sensors generating the data; growing number of producers (e.g. virtual machine instances), and in turn growing number of consumers.
- *Security* – whether a monitoring system can ensure data privacy and integrity and whether it can facilitate both preventive and reactive security controls including accountability and auditability.
- *Time behavior* – whether a monitoring system can synchronize time and ensure message ordering.

2 Monitoring domains

2.1 Large computer systems and clouds

Clouds as complex multi-tenant infrastructures mean a challenge for monitoring as it must be able to cope with a layered nature of such infrastructure due to manifold players – cloud infrastructure operators, application providers, and application users.

For this purpose, Spring (2011a, 2011b) presented a simple layered model partitioning cloud infrastructure into seven layers that must be monitored to facilitate overall cloud security. We extended the model with one additional layer (Virtualization). From the monitoring standpoint, we perceive the respective layers (ordered from bottom up) as follows:

- *Facility* can be simply described as the area (building) that physically contains the hardware and equipment of data center. Facility monitoring is generally related to the *environmental conditions* (e.g. temperature, humidity, and physical security) of the critical areas and the state of related *equipment* (e.g. power supply, air conditioning). Here we are see overlaps with building monitoring being part of *facility management*.
- *Network* (possibly virtualized) forms the distributed environment by interconnecting the computing resources both inside the data center as well as across multiple data centers. Network monitoring is concerned with the *performance, security* and *health* of the computer network using data collected from *firewalls, routers, switches* and other devices.
- *Hardware layer* represents the computing power in the form of physical computer system. Hardware monitoring per se relates to the state of the computer system *components* (e.g. CPU temperature, voltages, and fan speed).
- *Virtualization layer* is responsible for hardware virtualization to enable physical resource sharing. It is gateway for monitoring both physical and virtualized hardware (i.e. virtual machines). Monitoring of the virtualization layer itself generally differs little

from *operating system monitoring*. In contrast to monitoring of (virtualized) hardware resources,

- *operating system (OS) monitoring* is focused on the state and behavior of its components (e.g. I/O subsystem, process scheduler, and memory management).
- *Middleware* such as *application server,* or *message broker*, among others, is "a software layer between operating platform and application that enables the interaction of potentially distributed application components..." (Rackl, 2001). From the technological point of view, middleware monitoring works similarly as application monitoring.
- *Application monitoring* is focused on domain specific behavior and state of the targeted software application (e.g. web application deployed on application server, or SQL database). In contrast to OS monitoring, data can be potentially produced by many distributed producers (i.e. applications and services) spread across the computing nodes.
- *User* is represented by human or software agent from the outside of cloud environment (e.g. web browser). The monitoring is focused on the interactions realized by the users on lower layers.

With the advent of even more complex infrastructures than clouds, such as *federations of clouds*, new requirements on monitoring emerges. Typically, they are related to security aspects about the geolocation of the respective resource such as virtual machine or data storage being employed for a concrete user or application. Thus, *federated monitoring and auditing* which covers these issues must be introduced (Massonet et al, 2011).

2.2 Monitoring of intelligent buildings

We summarized in (Kučera et al, 2013) that modern buildings are often equipped with computer based system that integrates control and monitoring of various devices and systems that take part in building operation. We will refer to this system as *Building Management System (BMS)*. Typical systems that are integrated into BMS are BAS (*Building Automation System*) that controls HVAC (Heating, Ventilation, and Air conditioning) and lighting devices, access control systems, fire alarm systems, CCTV, elevator control or energy monitoring.

BMS ensures interconnection and collaboration of those systems and provides building operators with common user interface (web or desktop application) for all systems integrated under BMS that allows remote control and *monitoring of building operation*.

On the other hand, limited human resources increase risk of serious problems occurring in the situations when the BMS is not performing optimally. Some failures remain in the system unnoticed for many reasons; they failed to be delivered to responsible recipient due to nonexistent forwarding mechanism, *human operator mistake* because of *high workload* or *incompetence*, due to too sensitive rules or sending high priority alarms from *unimportant or unreliable sources*, and then missing the important events.

Auditing of operator's actions can become a complex task in environment where operators use their own workstations and logs are spread in multiple devices in distributed network.

2.3 Indirect monitoring

One way of fault detection in BMS relies on *indirect observation* of system operation. We can utilize other parts of BMS which provides different services than fault detection (application servers providing web user interface, archive server, application gateways) and examine their stored data and/or event logs for gathering information about devices operation. This method does not cause any additional communication in the system and allows us to study past behavior of the system (i.e. in the time when we were not aware of the fault) from historical records. Main disadvantage of this method is usually insufficient information about overall state of the system. Application log of archive server (text file placed in the file system of the application server) contains even more information than the database itself.

3 Logging

Monitoring relies in many aspects and levels on logging and log processing. Logs are a crucial source of monitoring information.

3.1 Log lifecycle

Log management performs several operations that facilitate storing, analyzing and deleting data. These operations do not modify the original log messages (Kšenzuliak, 2017):

- *Log parsing* is a technique for extracting data from logs recorded as strings. Extracted data is then used as input for further log processing.
- *Log filtering.* Due to the large amount of data, it is in some cases appropriate to reduce the number of logs by filtering that are likely to contain information important for us.
- *Grouping events* when similar records are merged into a common item containing the number of occurrences. For example, a number of entries on the common test may be merged into a single entry, which helps event correlation.
- *Storage and archiving* include several activities such as *compression*, data reduction or log record *integrity check.*
- *Analysis* looks for correlation and similarity between two or more logs. Correlation may also be performed based on statistical methods and visualization tools.
- *Deleting logs* that were created before a certain period and are no longer needed, are removed from the system in order not to overload (storage) resources.

3.2 Logging and SIEM systems

SIEM systems usually support a few dozen types of log sources and formats such as syslog or firewalls. SIEM typically understands the meaning of each specific log field. SIEM systems offer the possibility of centralized logging using log management functionality. Key features of these systems include the following functionality (Kšenzuliak, 2017):

- *Collecting logs and contextual data* – SIEM provides a centralized location to collect logs from multiple sources. This will offer an opportunity to identify vulnerabilities in the system and assess their severity.
- *Data archiving* – a centralized storage offers data archiving for a longer period to be a comparison of different periods.

- *Normalization* is a process which converts the original log into a universal format that facilitates the recognition of key data in the report.
- *Correlation* is a process of statistical or algorithmic derivation of information that can come from several possible sources. It can not only correlate log contents but also contextual information.
- *Notification* – the system generates warnings to potential risks, per previous analysis of logs.
- *Prioritizing events* helps us to distinguish critical events detected by the system and to distinguish them from less important.
- *Visualization* – large number of SIEM systems provide visualization in the form of information panels (dashboards) or charts that provide an overview of the system and can thus draw attention to anomalies which occur in the system.

4 Monitoring system reference framework

4.1 Need for a uniform view

Nowadays, monitoring of critical infrastructures evolves on one hand independently in the respective domain, e.g. computer systems, clouds, or intelligent buildings. On the other hand, we see many commonalities and trends for unification of the approaches and technology, mainly because of similarities and cost-saving efforts.

4.2 Framework dimensions

Therefore, to uniformly describe the aspects of existing or planned monitoring systems, we propose a common framework. The framework contains the following dimensions that are further split into subdimensions:

- *Subject (layer)* – *Physical* (Area, Facility); *Cyber-physical* (Network, Hardware); *Cybernetic* (*Software*) *layer* (Virtualization, Operating system, Middleware, Application); *Human* (Administrator, User)
- *Purpose* – *Performance* (bottleneck detection, performance optimization); *Reliability* (failure prevention, detection and mitigation); *Security* (SEM/SIEM system); *Accounting* (operator accounting, user/customer accounting); *Auditing* (internal or external/3rd party system/service auditing); *Testing* (during development)
- *Mandate* – *General* (law); *Internal* (organization policy, internal regulation); *Contractual* (business contracts, SLAs); *Other*
- *Management* - *Lifecycle* (characterizes initiation and evolution of monitoring system using *PDCA* (Plan, Do, Check, Act) which includes initial and continuous decision-making (Kozel & Chuchrová, 2015)); *Stakeholders*
- *Context* – *Organization* (structure, domain); Methodological *frameworks & standards* used (ISO 27k, COBIT®5)
- *Operation* – *Monitoring infrastructure* (monitoring devices such as HW probes, software modules, networks/communication infrastructure, data storage); *Processes* (monitoring data acquisition processes, preprocessing, validation, storing, data processing, correlation, reporting, human tasks, …) modeled e.g. an object-oriented way (Hunka,

2015); *Human actors* (managers, designers, implementers, administrators, operators, ...)

Relations between the components are depicted in Fig. 1.

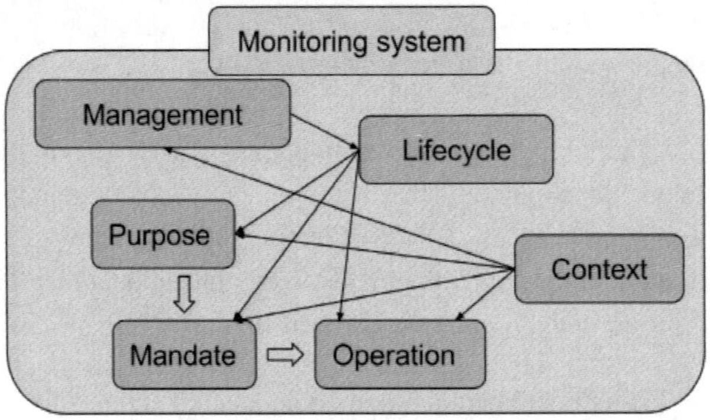

Figure 1 Monitoring system reference framework

5 Conclusion

The paper outlined the principles of monitoring of modern critical infrastructures such as clouds and intelligent buildings. Then it proposed a uniform reference framework for assessment of monitoring systems and for designing new ones.

We plan to validate the proposed framework was used for description of selected monitoring (sub)systems being in regular use for monitoring of different computer- and cyber-physical systems.

References

Danel, R. et al. (2012). 'Best practices in design of database of brownfield revitalization project'. *Proceedings of the 12th International multidisciplinary scientific geoconference (SGEM)*. Albena, Bulgaria, pp. 49-56.

Hunka, F. (2015). 'Object role modeling perspective applied to business process modeling'. *Proceedings of the 11th International Conference on Strategic Management and its Support by Information Systems 2015,* Uherské Hradiště, Czech Republic, pp. 366-371.

Kozel, R. and Chuchrová, K. (2015). 'Creation of System Support for Decision-Making Processes of Managers'. *Proceedings of IDIMT-2015: Information Technology and Society - Interaction and Interdependence: 23rd Interdisciplinary Information Management Talks.* Poděbrady, Czech Republic, pp. 163-170.

Kšenzuliak, F. (2017). 'Analytical environment for log management'. *Master Thesis*. Masaryk University.

Kučera, A., Glos, P. and Pitner, T. (2013). 'Fault detection in building management system networks'. *12th IFAC Conference on Programmable Devices and Embedded Systems, PDeS 2013*. Neuveden: International Federation of Automatic Control, pp. 416-421. doi:10.3182/20130925-3-CZ-3023.00027.

Massonet, P., Naqvi, S., Ponsard, C., Latanicki, J., Rochwerger, B. and Villari, M. (2011). 'A monitoring and audit logging architecture for data location compliance in federated cloud infrastructures'. *Parallel and Distributed Processing Workshops and Phd Forum (IPDPSW)*, IEEE International Symposium on, pp. 1510-1517.

Ministr, J. and Pitner, T. (2014). 'Modelling and Simulation of Public Administration Processes'. *FOKUS 2020 - Conference Proceedings of the 33rd International Conference on Organizational Science Development.* Maribor: University of Maribor, pp. 1-7.

Montes, J., Sánchez, A., Memishi, B., Pérez, M.S. and Antoniu, G. (2013). 'GMonE: A complete approach to cloud monitoring'. *Future Generation Computer Systems*, 29 (8), pp. 2026-2040. http://dx.doi.org/10.1016/j.future.2013.02.011.

National Center for Cybersecurity (2016). Aid to audit security measures according to the law on cyber security.

Nguyen, F. and Pitner, T. (2012). 'Information System Monitoring and Notifications Using Complex Event Processing'. *Fifth Balkan Conference in Informatics BCI 2012*, Novi Sad, Serbia, pp. 211-216. doi:10.1145/2371316.2371358.

Pitner, T. and Ministr, J. (2015). 'Security aspects of Paas cloud model'. *Proceedings of the 11th International Conference on Strategic Management and Its Support by Information Systems 2015*, Uherské Hradiště, Czech Republic, pp. 463-469.

Spring, J. (2011a, 2011b). 'Monitoring Cloud Computing by Layer, Part 1 and 2'. *Security & Privacy*, 9 (2 march-april 2011, may-june 2011).

Tovarňák, D., F. Nguyen and Pitner, T. (2014). 'Distributed Event-Driven Model for Intelligent Monitoring of Cloud Datacenters'. *Intelligent Distributed Computing VII*, Cham, Switzerland, pp. 87-92. doi:10.1007/978-3-319-01571-2_11.

VŠB - Technical University of Ostrava
17. Listopadu 15/2172
708 33 Ostrava - Poruba
Czech Republic

ISBN 978-1-5108-4091-1

CURRAN ASSOCIATES INC.
proceedings.com

4th International Symposium on Affective Science and Engineering and 29th Modern Artificial Intelligence and Cognitive Science Conference (ISASE-MAICS 2018)

Spokane, Washington, USA
31 May - 2 June 2018

JSKE